CONCORDANCE

TO

CHRISTIAN SCIENCE HYMNAL

AND

HYMNAL NOTES

THE CHRISTIAN SCIENCE PUBLISHING SOCIETY

Boston, Massachusetts, U.S.A.

CONTENTS

FOREWORD TO CONCORDANCE

IN the compilation of the Concordance to the Christian Science Hymnal, the aim has been to follow the plan of the Concordances to the writings of Mary Baker Eddy. The references include nouns, main verbs, except "to be," adjectives, important adverbs, and other distinctive words.

To facilitate the use of the Concordance, separate classifications have been made in instances where there are many items for one word; there are separate headings for capitalized and uncapitalized terms such as Love, love, Truth, truth, etc.; and two or more divisions appear in cases such as "light," which may be either a noun, adjective, or verb.

Words are indexed by hymn and stanza numbers, the first number referring to the hymn and the second designating the stanza. Two numbers in the second column connected by a dash indicate that the word is used in each of these stanzas and in any intervening. A phrase may be repeated in a hymn, but it is listed only once.

Endeavor has been made to select such words as will give the most appropriate context, in order that seekers in the Concordance may easily recall familiar passages and readily locate those desired.

The General Index has been brought from the Hymnal itself to this volume in order to make room for separate, less compendious indexes, easier of consultation by the average user. This transfer brings advantage to those who consult the Concordance; for, with this companion volume at hand, one may avoid the back-and-forth turning of pages in the same book. The General Index gives a conspectus of the entire Hymnal; thus, for instance, the available alternative tunes for any hymn may be known at a glance, and associations of author and composer with poem or tune may more speedily become definite and helpful.

The book is designed as an effective adjunct to our Hymnal; and it is our hope that it will prove anew to its readers the truth of our Leader's words on page 234 of "Science and Health with Key to the Scriptures," "Whatever inspires with wisdom, Truth, or Love—be it song, sermon, or Science—blesses the human family with crumbs of comfort from Christ's table, feeding the hungry and giving living waters to the thirsty."

THE PUBLISHERS

CONCORDANCE

TO THE

CHRISTIAN SCIENCE HYMNAL

A

abhorring
143:3 A· each evasive art,

abide
6:1 A· not in the realm
7:1 A· with me; fast breaks
1 unfailingly a· in Thee.
2 trustingly a· in Thee.
3 Thou dost a· with me.
8:1 A· with me; fast falls
1 Lord, with me a·.
1, 2 O a· with me.
3 if Thou a· with me.
99:1 and undisturbed a·;
100:1 secret place a·.
146:2 A· in heavenly light.
147:2 A· in heavenly light.
180:3 In Soul, not flesh, a·.
232:1 peace our thoughts a·;
406:1 peace our thoughts a·;
291:3 thus with Thee a·,
390:1 A· in me;
1 Master's word a· in

abides
172:2 but Truth a·;
174:1 whose home a· in peace.

abiding
7:3 Love divine, a· constantly,
148:1 In heavenly Love a·,
154:2 safe a· From every
155:2 safe a· From every
156:2 safe a· From every
175:1 Thy Word a·,
313:2 God, in light a·,
350:2 when in Christ a·,

able
160:2 God a· is To raise
161:2 God a· is To raise
162:2 God a· is To raise

abode
21:1 hath love its true a·.
22:1 hath love its true a·.
44:3 In this divine a·,
71:1 His own a·:

abound
164:2 hope and joy a·.
165:2 hope and joy a·.
417:2 hope and joy a·.
224:2 all things and a·,
225:2 all things and a·,

about
96:2 him who went a·
148:1 God is round a· me,

above
4:1 fragrance from a·:
9:2 lift our thoughts a·,
12:1 A· all doctrine,
13:1 A· all doctrine,
18:2 God watches a· thee,
20:3 true to God a·,
416:3 true to God a·,
21:2 born from a·.
22:2 born from a·.
23:4 so far a· All mortal
24:4 so far a· All mortal
25:4 so far a· All mortal
26:4 so far a· All mortal
27:4 so far a· All mortal
28:4 so far a· All mortal
39:1 light and comfort from a·;

above
40:3 pure from a·;
53:1 beneath, around, a·;
65:2 shining from a·,
67:3 Hear, a· all, hear
68:3 Hear, a· all, hear
72:1 blessings from a·;
405:1 blessings from a·;
76:2 Hear His voice a·
79:2 and comfort from a·;
84:1 mists, around, a·;
108:4 glad feast a·,
121:2 guidance from a·.
122:2 guidance from a·.
126:2 Our wishes all a·,
127:2 Our wishes all a·,
403:2 Our wishes all a·,
134:2 bends serene a·,
141:4 a· the sod,
142:2 other names a·;
149:2 a· the shadows dim,
426:2 a· the shadows dim,
163:3 glorify our God a·.
172:2 a· earth's restless
181:3 good gifts from a·.
182:3 That blessing from a·;
185:3 on the mountain here a·,
201:4 With Christ in God a·.
404:4 With Christ in God a·.
204:2 Thy banner a· them;
214:1 around us, and a·,
222:1 A· thy deep and dreamless
223:1 A· thy deep and dreamless
232:3 a· the mists of wrong:
406:3 a· the mists of wrong:
236:4 all earth's treasures a·.
240:2 joy of things a·.
241:3 joy of things a·.

7

above
258:3 watch a· His own.
293:1 a· life's raging sea.
294:1 a· life's raging sea.
295:1 a· life's raging sea.
311:3 radiance from a·.
420:3 radiance from a·.
319:2 all life, below, a·,
342:1 perfect gifts are from a·,
349:2 on earth from heaven a·.
355:2 heart of heaven a·,
367:1 reigns in light a·.
374:2 Lord of all a·,
375:2 Lord of all a·,
414:1 unseen things a·,

abreast
258:2 keep a· of Truth,

abroad
45:2 Is shed a· o'er all
357:1 smile is on the world a·,
358:1 smile is on the world a·,
407:1 smile is on the world a·,
386:3 best proclaim a·,
387:3 best proclaim a·,

abundantly
6:3 Meets all thy need a·.
65:3 grace for grace a·

abuse
337:2 scoffers may a· Her,
338:2 scoffers may a· Her,

accents
54:3 no a· flow,
94:3 low, sweet a·
242:1 a· sweet and strong

accept
70:3 a· His wealth,
269:1 more than we a·;
270:1 more than we a·;

acclaim
378:3 Thy wondrous power a·,

accord
125:1 beautiful the sweet a·
153:1 all in glad a·!
266:4 all with one a·
318:3 with clear a·,
378:1 sing in sweet a·;

according
215:3 A· as her labors

accuser's
112:2 a· mocking voices

across
20:2 a· the ocean,

act
296:3 valor's a· supreme;
303:2 No a· falls fruitless;
354:3 power by which we a·,
386:1 In every a·,
387:1 In every a·,

action
4:1 Be every a· love.
126:3 every a· glow.
127:3 every a· glow.
403:3 every a· glow.

actions
88:1 a· bold and meek
89:1 a· bold and meek
88:2 with a· brotherly
89:2 with a· brotherly
273:3 by holy a· shown;
274:3 by holy a· shown;

active
356:2 lies our a· rest.

acts
281:1 mighty a· proclaim.

added
46:4 So shall a· years
47:4 So shall a· years

adoration
149:3 radiant light of a·,
426:3 radiant light of a·,
283:3 joyous and glad a·;
317:2 in breathless a·,
356:1 we bring our a·,

adore
177:2 Thy faithful saints a·.
196:1 One common Lord a·.
224:3 I triumph and a·;
225:3 I triumph and a·;
236:4 the Mind we a·;
246:2 declare Him and a· Him.
282:1 ye heavens, a· Him;

adored
362:2 Forevermore a·;

adores
261:2 unseen presence she a·,
262:2 unseen presence she a·,

adoring
109:1 hearts, unsealed, a·,
110:1 hearts, unsealed, a·,
112:1 hearts a· Yield

advances
177:1 Day a·, day a·,

advocates
2:2 a· of error Foresee

afar
172:2 to those who watch a·.
253:6 tired joy and grief a·,
254:6 tired joy and grief a·,
255:6 tired joy and grief a·,
256:6 tired joy and grief a·,
257:6 tired joy and grief a·,
335:1 tidings from a·,

affection
370:2 set our whole a·
381:1 thrilled with new a·,

affections
91:3 pure a· Thee define
422:3 pure a· Thee define

affiance
77:2 His truth be thine a·,
78:2 His truth be thine a·,

afflicted
347:2 O thou a·, tossed
348:2 O thou a·, tossed

affliction
388:1 he went a· fled,

afford
105:1 friendly aid a·,
106:1 friendly aid a·,
107:1 friendly aid a·,
137:1 Can peace a·.
334:1 and promise still a·

affright
57:3 Naught shall a· us,

afraid
80:1 make our heart a·?
339:1 none friendless, none a·,

afresh
108:2 taste a· the calm

after
108:4 Feast a· feast thus
216:2 a· His own counsel,
313:1 cheer us a· rain.
325:1 follow a· me.

aftersmile
207:5 heaven's a· earth's
208:5 heaven's a· earth's
209:5 heaven's a· earth's
210:5 heaven's a· earth's
211:5 heaven's a· earth's
212:5 heaven's a· earth's

again
34:1 Christ comes a·
3 A· each empty cup
51:3 brought the light a·

again
52:3 brought the light a.
56:1 turn unfilled to Thee a.
97:2 Look a, the fields
98:2 Look a, the fields
101:3 rise to Life a;
134:1 all is well a:
218:1 hither turn a.
219:1 hither turn a.
220:1 hither turn a.
271:4 songs be heard a
272:4 songs be heard a
310:1 come a to earth,
   1, 2 th' angelic song a:
313:1 comes to us a
315:2 win them back a.
316:2 win them back a.
372:3 we are whole a.
373:2 we are whole a.

against (see also 'gainst)
146:3 naught a Infinity
147:3 naught a Infinity
201:1 A the light of
404:1 A the light of
264:1 Leads a the foe;
347:3 formed a His own
348:3 formed a His own

age
37:1 every a and clime.
38:1 every a and clime.
71:3 fails from a to a?
226:3 lead forth this a
251:1 on from a to a.
252:1 on from a to a.
261:1 Through every a
262:1 Through every a
334:2 light to every a,
363:1 it hastens, every a

ages
93:2 unchanged while a run;
101:3 falsehood a taught
157:1 through all the a,
186:1 What are a in Thy
187:1 What are a in Thy
213:1, 4 our help in a past,
   3 thousand a in Thy
   4 our guard while a last,
236:1 a have blest,
264:4 through countless a
275:2 A have seen His might,
278:1 Heir of the a
279:1 Heir of the a
363:1 beams of a shine;
368:2 Traveler, a are its own;
369:2 Traveler, a are its own;
   (see also Rock of Ages)

ages'
391:4 a long lament;

agree
5:2 With God alone a.
86:1 men a to praise.
87:1 men a to praise.
173:4 Joining hand in hand a;

aid
80:1 our unfailing a;
105:1 friendly a afford,
106:1 friendly a afford,
107:1 friendly a afford,
123:2 still give thee a;
329:3 O, a me in suppression
396:2 his promised a,
397:2 his promised a,

aids
320:2 heavenly a impart.
321:2 heavenly a impart.
409:2 heavenly a impart.

aim
5:2 no other a than right;
322:3 with that a alone
323:3 with that a alone

aims
266:3 hopes and a the same,

air
4:1 A holy a is breathing
44:2 bright, celestial a
195:2 heaven's own healing a;
284:3 Christian's native a:
285:3 Christian's native a:
286:3 Christian's native a:
383:1 breath of summer a,

alarm
33:3 no tumult can a
216:1 when fears a,
364:1 lest foes a;

alarms
53:3 earth's fears and vain a

alien
326:3 the a armies flee:

alike
130:2 rests a on man
355:1 comes a to all

alive
381:2 A forevermore

All
56:3 Thee, A in all.

All
58:1 Thou art A;
   2 Thou our A.
160:4 And God is A.
161:4 And God is A.
162:4 And God is A.
181:4 God is A, and
267:2 Our God is A;
268:2 Our God is A;

all
3:4 loves and blesses a.
4:3 a his gracious word,
5:2 Then a of Truth
6:3 Meets a thy need
7:1 banishing a night;
   2 love in a around I see
9:1 A glory be to God
   1 Till a the world
   2 a winged with light
   3 Through a the world
   4 bids a discord cease,
10:1 A power is given
411:1 A power is given
10:3 life to a is giving;
411:3 life to a is giving;
10:3 In Him we a are living.
411:3 In Him we a are living.
11:1 Woke with music a
   2 Truth, for a mankind,
12:1 Above a doctrine,
13:1 Above a doctrine,
12:2 And prove to a
13:2 And prove to a
14:2 a thy God hath wrought;
   3 a things are thine.
15:3 radiance a divine.
17:1 A scowling shapes of
18:1 dare a and prevail.
19:1 stills a pain and strife.
23:4 A mortal strife,
24:4 A mortal strife,
25:4 A mortal strife,
26:4 A mortal strife,
27:4 A mortal strife,
28:4 A mortal strife,
23:5 With a thou art—
24:5 With a thou art—
25:5 With a thou art—
26:5 With a thou art—
27:5 With a thou art—
28:5 With a thou art—
29:2 meekness a divine,
34:2 are with us a;
   3 a the storms of earth
35:3 Scatter a my unbelief;
41:1 a around him waves
   2 that we a may share;

all
41:2 To $a\cdot$ the world
42:2 $a\cdot$ enjoy the blessing
  2 $a\cdot$, Thy love possessing,
43:2 $a\cdot$ ye heavy laden,
  2 come to end $a\cdot$ strife.
44:1 $a\cdot$ the sounds of weeping
45:1 Through $a\cdot$ the earth
  2 shed abroad o'er $a\cdot$
46:1 $A\cdot$ my sanguine hopes
47:1 $A\cdot$ my sanguine hopes
48:1 $A\cdot$ good and perfect gifts
  2 Nor errs at $a\cdot$
  3 Dominion over $a\cdot$.
49:1 Lord and Father of us $a\cdot$,
50:1 Lord and Father of us $a\cdot$,
49:4 $a\cdot$ our strivings cease;
50:4 $a\cdot$ our strivings cease;
53:3 keep us $a\cdot$ the way,
54:3 $A\cdot$ utterance faileth
56:1 $a\cdot$ the best that earth
  3 Thee, All in $a\cdot$.
59:1 with $a\cdot$ thy might,
60:1 with $a\cdot$ thy might,
61:1 with $a\cdot$ thy might,
59:3 $a\cdot$ in $a\cdot$ to thee.
60:3 $a\cdot$ in $a\cdot$ to thee.
61:3 $a\cdot$ in $a\cdot$ to thee.
62:1 From $a\cdot$ that dwell
63:1 From $a\cdot$ that dwell
64:1 dawn of $a\cdot$ things real
  2 Love is $a\cdot$ around.
66:3 we $a\cdot$ must prove,
421:3 we $a\cdot$ must prove,
67:2 $A\cdot$ with warning voice
68:2 $A\cdot$ with warning voice
67:3 Hear, above $a\cdot$,
68:3 Hear, above $a\cdot$,
69:2 quell $a\cdot$ selfish pride,
423:2 quell $a\cdot$ selfish pride,
70:1 giveth light to $a\cdot$
  3 $a\cdot$ His glory share.
71:1 smile at $a\cdot$ thy foes.
  3 $a\cdot$ fear of want
72:1 Bid $a\cdot$ strife and tumult
405:1 Bid $a\cdot$ strife and tumult
72:2 $A\cdot$ ye people, raise
405:2 $A\cdot$ ye people, raise
73:1 $a\cdot$ the power of nations,
  2 $a\cdot$ condemnation ending,
  2 for $a\cdot$ mankind.
74:2 Truth is there for $a\cdot$
76:1 Though $a\cdot$ earthly friends
79:1 $A\cdot$ the path in which
81:1 $A\cdot$ His way made plain
82:2 brotherhood of $a\cdot$ mankind,

all
83:1 $a\cdot$ His creatures free;
  3 $a\cdot$ our slavery cease,
  3 $A\cdot$ God's children dwell
85:1 $A\cdot$ Thy love we have
  1 $A\cdot$ Thy truth is ours
  3 $A\cdot$ the way that we
86:1 strange in $a\cdot$ its ways,
87:1 strange in $a\cdot$ its ways,
86:1 of $a\cdot$ things on earth,
87:1 of $a\cdot$ things on earth,
90:2 $a\cdot$ my journey through.
91:2 Blot out $a\cdot$ fear,
422:2 Blot out $a\cdot$ fear,
91:2 on $a\cdot$ our need.
422:2 on $a\cdot$ our need.
97:1 influence $a\cdot$ divine.
98:1 influence $a\cdot$ divine.
102:3 guide us $a\cdot$ the way,
103:3 guide us $a\cdot$ the way,
105:3 in $a\cdot$ things grow;
106:3 in $a\cdot$ things grow;
107:3 in $a\cdot$ things grow;
108:1 $a\cdot$ my weariness upon
111:3 we $a\cdot$ shall see
112:2 $a\cdot$ the world rejoices,
115:1 $A\cdot$ our paths were
116:1 $A\cdot$ our paths were
117:3 $A\cdot$ Thy works shall
118:3 Holy Spirit, $a\cdot$ divine,
119:1 $a\cdot$ Thy radiance
  1 $a\cdot$ burdens and $a\cdot$ sadness;
  3 Banish $a\cdot$ our fears
123:3 grace, $a\cdot$ sufficient,
126:2 Our wishes $a\cdot$ above,
127:2 Our wishes $a\cdot$ above,
403:2 Our wishes $a\cdot$ above,
128:3 teachings $a\cdot$ may come,
129:3 teachings $a\cdot$ may come,
130:1 dispels $a\cdot$ blindness.
  1 Thou holdest $a\cdot$ things
  2 wisdom past $a\cdot$ seeking;
133:3 $a\cdot$ tears, $a\cdot$ woes,
424:3 $a\cdot$ tears, $a\cdot$ woes,
134:1 $a\cdot$ is well again:
  2 turns $a\cdot$ to good.
  3 Thy hand in $a\cdot$ things
  3 $a\cdot$ things in Thy hand.
135:1 $a\cdot$ mankind and me:
  2 $A\cdot$ good, from Thee
136:1 bids $a\cdot$ fear to cease:
  2 $A\cdot$ unafraid I wait,
138:3 $a\cdot$ these blinding veils
139:2 truth is free to $a\cdot$,
427:2 truth is free to $a\cdot$,
139:2 $a\cdot$ may walk with Love
427:2 $a\cdot$ may walk with Love
140:1 hallow $a\cdot$ we find,

all
141:2 $A\cdot$ the branches
  4 $A\cdot$ the earth to
142:2 $A\cdot$ other names
  4 Spirit overbrooding $a\cdot$.
146:2 $a\cdot$ the paths of
147:2 $a\cdot$ the paths of
149:1 $a\cdot$ earth-born fear
426:1 $a\cdot$ earth-born fear
153:1 Sing $a\cdot$ in glad
157:1 for $a\cdot$ his brethren:
  1 through $a\cdot$ the ages,
  1 these alone But for $a\cdot$,
    that through $a\cdot$ time
  2 Life of $a\cdot$ things,
  2 Blesses $a\cdot$ and injures
  2 find $a\cdot$ being one.
  3 $a\cdot$ men and nations
  3 God's children $a\cdot$
158:3 $a\cdot$ the world send back
159:3 $a\cdot$ the world send back
163:2 $a\cdot$ wrong outweigh;
168:1 $a\cdot$ the earth with songs
  1 $A\cdot$ mindful of our
170:2 fills them $a\cdot$ with praise.
174:1 bids $a\cdot$ tumult cease;
  2 $a\cdot$ earthly loss is gain;
  3 stills $a\cdot$ our demanding,
175:1 $A\cdot$ the ills that
  2 $A\cdot$ true being one
176:1 Shining that $a\cdot$ may
  2 peace to $a\cdot$ it gave,
178:1 $a\cdot$ His ways are bright;
  2 $A\cdot$ compassion is and kind;
179:2 $A\cdot$ the law does
  3 Love bids $a\cdot$ discord cease.
180:1 $A\cdot$ laws fulfillment find.
  3 may we $a\cdot$ behold
181:3 $a\cdot$ awake to praise Thee
183:1 $a\cdot$ to Truth must come.
184:1 $a\cdot$ to Truth must come.
185:3 Through $a\cdot$ earth's
186:2 $A\cdot$ that being e'er shall
187:2 $A\cdot$ that being e'er shall
186:2 $A\cdot$ eternity can show,
187:2 $A\cdot$ eternity can show,
188:2 His Word to $a\cdot$ mankind,
  3 maketh $a\cdot$ men free.
189:2 Fulfilleth $a\cdot$ my need;
192:1, 5 $a\cdot$ my song shall be,
193:1, 5 $a\cdot$ my song shall be,
192:3 $A\cdot$ that Thou sendest
193:3 $A\cdot$ that Thou sendest
196:1 $a\cdot$ shall dwell together,
  2 $a\cdot$ that now divides us
  3 $a\cdot$ that now unites us
199:1 thank we $a\cdot$ our God
  2 God Through $a\cdot$ our life

10

all

201:3 *a·* who know its power;
404:3 *a·* who know its power;
201:3 *a·* who will may light
404:3 *a·* who will may light
202:1 *a·* dreams of error
412:1 *a·* dreams of error
202:1 bonds of *a·* captivity.
412:1 bonds of *a·* captivity.
202:2 wipe *a·* tears away;
412:1 wipe *a·* tears away;
202:3 confidence for *a·* thy fears.
412:2 confidence for *a·* thy fears.
203:2 know that *a·* is well
    2 *a·* Thy children dwell
204:1 rulest in *a·* Thy creation;
    3 Salvation to *a·* men
206:3 *a·* our ways reflecting
428:3 *a·* our ways reflecting
207:2 me, and mine, and *a·*.
208:2 me, and mine, and *a·*.
209:2 me, and mine, and *a·*.
210:2 me, and mine, and *a·*.
211:2 me, and mine, and *a·*.
212:2 me, and mine, and *a·*.
214:1 presence glows in *a·*,
    2 with *a·*, and *a·* with Thee.
215:2 *a·* their stores of gold.
    3 *a·* her paths are peace.
216:2 *A·* good for you His
218:1, 4 maketh *a·* things new,
219:1, 4 maketh *a·* things new,
220:1, 4 maketh *a·* things new,
221:1 may *a·* obey thee
222:1 fears of *a·* the years
223:1 fears of *a·* the years
224:1 *a·* material streams
225:1 *a·* material streams
224:2 *A·* good, where'er it
225:2 *A·* good, where'er it
224:2 must have *a·* things
225:2 must have *a·* things
224:3 here *a·* good provide;
225:3 here *a·* good provide;
226:2 hearts *a·* unafraid,
227:3 *a·* heaven before our
229:1 o'er the heads of *a·*.
    2 beyond *a·* law,
233:1 *a·* who walk the ways
419:1 *a·* who walk the ways
236:4 *a·* earth's treasures
237:3 *A·* made pure by
238:2 *a·* of good the past
239:2 *a·* of good the past
243:1 gift to *a·* His own:
244:1 gift to *a·* His own:
246:2 *A·* flesh shall see it
    and *a·* shall be healed;

all

246:2 *a·* is plain before Him.
251:2 O'er *a·* the lands
252:2 O'er *a·* the lands
258:1 be made by *a·* men
261:3 *a·* God's faithful sons,
262:3 *a·* God's faithful sons,
263:3 *a·* hearts in Him...blend.
    3 *a·* a sure release,
264:2 *A·* one body we,
266:1 Love, and *a·* His sons
    4 *a·* with one accord
267:4 crown Thee Lord of *a·*.
268:4 crown Thee Lord of *a·*.
269:1 fount is free to *a·*,
270:1 fount is free to *a·*,
271:2 *A·* people shall
272:2 *A·* people shall
271:3 *a·* the sons of want
272:3 *a·* the sons of want
276:2 *a·* Thy revelations,
277:2 *a·* Thy revelations,
278:3 So *a·* the merciful,
279:3 So *a·* the merciful,
280:2 from *a·* our foes.
281:1 *A·* His mighty acts
282:1 *a·* ye stars of light;
    2 earth, and *a·* creation,
287:3 *a·* creation hears anew
408:3 *a·* creation hears anew
288:2 know that God is *a·*;
289:2 know that God is *a·*;
291:1 *a·* that pleaseth Thee.
292:2 exalted as head over *a·*!
293:2 refuge from *a·* wrong,
294:2 refuge from *a·* wrong,
295:2 refuge from *a·* wrong,
297:4 fulfill *a·* prophecy.
298:2 your tears *a·* away,
299:2 your tears *a·* away,
300:2 your tears *a·* away,
301:2 your tears *a·* away,
302:2 your tears *a·* away,
298:3 *A·* thy sorrow and
299:3 *A·* thy sorrow and
300:3 *A·* thy sorrow and
301:3 *A·* thy sorrow and
302:3 *A·* thy sorrow and
298:4 Life of *a·* being divine:
299:4 Life of *a·* being divine:
300:4 Life of *a·* being divine:
301:4 Life of *a·* being divine:
302:4 Life of *a·* being divine:
303:4 *a·* that serve the right,
304:1 *A·* the rugged way.
305:1 *A·* the rugged way.
306:1 *A·* the rugged way.
307:1 *A·* the rugged way.

all

308:1 *A·* the rugged way.
309:1 *A·* the rugged way.
311:2 to *a·* who roam,
420:2 to *a·* who roam,
311:3 *a·* the gifts His hand
420:3 *a·* the gifts His hand
311:3 To us and *a·* mankind:
420:3 To us and *a·* mankind:
312:1 *a·* His strength endued,
    2 *a·* the powers of darkness
    2 having *a·* things done,
    2 *a·* your conflicts past,
319:2 Lord of *a·* life,
    3 *a·* Thy living altars
324:3 only, *a·* for Thee.
325:2 *a·* fear and danger brave;
326:1 In *a·* the armor
327:1 *a·* that they contain
328:1 *a·* that they contain
327:2 *a·* oppressed by wrong
328:2 *a·* oppressed by wrong
327:3 *A·* human need supplies.
328:3 *A·* human need supplies.
329:1 who made *a·* things;
    2 judgments *a·* are pure,
330:4 *a·* the length of days
332:1 *a·* the earth be still,
333:1 friend to *a·* who bowed
335:2 till *a·* the lowly
    2 till *a·* the holy
336:1 *a·* the glories of the sky,
337:1 dogmas *a·* may perish;
338:1 dogmas *a·* may perish;
337:3 *A·* their glories cease
338:3 *A·* their glories cease
339:3 *a·* things made new
340:3 lives would be *a·* sunshine
342:1 *A·* perfect gifts are
    1 *a·* our blessings show
    2 freely given to *a·*
345:2 finding *a·* our duty,
    3 *a·* shall see where Thine
    3 *a·* shall learn how God
346:2 now to *a·* mankind
401:2 now to *a·* mankind
347:4 *A·* tongues that rise
348:4 *A·* tongues that rise
349:2 truly *a·* Thou art
    2 *a·* the sunshine of Thy
350:1-3 *A·* will be well;
    1-3 *A·* must be well;
    1-3 *A·*, *a·* is well.
351:2 *a·* the path we tread:
354:1 strength is *a·* His own.
355:1 comes alike to *a·*
    1 let us *a·* unite,
    2 *a·* pervading Love,

all
360:1 $A \cdot$ its wealth is living
361:1 Trust $a \cdot$ to God,
   2 $a \cdot$ His doings ponder,
   3 $A \cdot$ glad in this confiding,
362:1 $a \cdot$ the hosts of heaven.
   3 $a \cdot$ his paths are peace.
364:2 $a \cdot$ our toil and labor,
   3 $a \cdot$ good is given
368:2 bursts o'er $a \cdot$ the earth.
369:2 bursts o'er $a \cdot$ the earth.
370:2 $A \cdot$ our thoughts into
371:1 reflect in $a \cdot$ our ways
   1 free us from $a \cdot$ fear;
     $A \cdot$ strife is stilled,
     $a \cdot$ grief consoled,
372:4 Lord and Master of us $a \cdot$,
373:2 Lord and Master of us $a \cdot$,
374:1 Father of us $a \cdot$,
375:1 Father of us $a \cdot$,
374:2 Lord of $a \cdot$ above,
375:2 Lord of $a \cdot$ above,
379:1 $a \cdot$ things losing,
380:1 $a \cdot$ things losing,
379:1 with $a \cdot$ true bliss
380:1 with $a \cdot$ true bliss
379:3 who, $a \cdot$ forsaking,
380:3 who, $a \cdot$ forsaking,
379:4 $a \cdot$ our fullness lies.
380:4 $a \cdot$ our fullness lies.
381:2 Mind, $a \cdot$ good supplying,
382:4 Dominion over $a \cdot$.
384:1 $a \cdot$ creation makes anew,
   3 through $a \cdot$ the earth
386:2 doctrine $a \cdot$ divine.
387:2 doctrine $a \cdot$ divine.
388:3 To $a \cdot$ with willing hands
389:1 my God and my $a \cdot$.
   2 my God, and my $a \cdot$.
391:3 $a \cdot$ that was and is
392:4 For God is $a \cdot$,
393:4 For God is $a \cdot$,
394:1 $A \cdot$ the world awakes
395:1 $A \cdot$ the world awakes
396:3 spite of $a \cdot$ His foes.
397:3 spite of $a \cdot$ His foes.
398:2 $a \cdot$ your lamps be bright,
418:2 clearly through them $a \cdot$,
   4 notes will $a \cdot$ be dumb,
425:2 wipe $a \cdot$ tears away,

Alleluia
66:1-4 $A \cdot$! $A \cdot$!
421:1-4 $A \cdot$! $A \cdot$!

all-gracious
158:1 heaven's $a \cdot$ King;
159:1 heaven's $a \cdot$ King;

all-harmonious
263:2 $A \cdot$, He doth move;

All-in-all
267:1 Our God is $A \cdot$,
268:1 Our God is $A \cdot$,

allots
  6:3 present hour $a \cdot$ thy task,

all-power
  81:2 His $a \cdot$ Helps
172:1 whose $a \cdot$ no tempest
297:4 fall through Love's $a \cdot$;

all-transforming
42:1 Come, Thou $a \cdot$ Spirit,

allured
376:2 $A \cdot$ by ways of error,
377:2 $A \cdot$ by ways of error,

almighty
  10:1 $A \cdot$ is His power;
411:1 $A \cdot$ is His power;
117:1, 3 Lord God $A \cdot$,
133:1 $A \cdot$ One, dost move;
424:1 $A \cdot$ One, dost move;
346:1 Thou whose $a \cdot$ Word
401:1 Thou whose $a \cdot$ Word
349:1 Thy will, $a \cdot$ Father,
351:3 the One $A \cdot$ Father

Almighty's
  33:1 Rest beneath th'$A \cdot$ shade;
  99:1 underneath th'$A \cdot$ shade
100:1 beneath th'$A \cdot$ shade;

alone
  5:2 With God $a \cdot$ agree.
  7:3 Thou $a \cdot$ art power;
  10:2 Our Lord is God $a \cdot$,
411:2 Our Lord is God $a \cdot$,
  21:1 In God $a \cdot$ hath love
  22:1 In God $a \cdot$ hath love
  30:5 Love $a \cdot$ is Life;
  31:5 Love $a \cdot$ is Life;
  32:5 Love $a \cdot$ is Life;
  58:2 Thou $a \cdot$ art good
  81:2 God $a \cdot$ can give
  83:3 Love $a \cdot$, is Lord.
  91:1 obey and love $a \cdot$;
422:1 obey and love $a \cdot$;
  92:3 shod for God $a \cdot$,
      And God $a \cdot$ obey.
115:1 live to Thee $a \cdot$;
116:1 live to Thee $a \cdot$;
117:2 Thou $a \cdot$ art holy,
125:2 In Thee $a \cdot$ will rest.
135:2 good, from Thee $a \cdot$.
142:2 love $a \cdot$ knows

alone
143:3 loving Thee $a \cdot$.
153:2 who $a \cdot$ art mighty
157:1 prayed he for these $a \cdot$
   2 live in God $a \cdot$;
179:3 Love $a \cdot$ is power.
195:1 $a \cdot$ can be my soul's
234:4 In peace that God $a \cdot$
235:4 In peace that God $a \cdot$
246:Ref. He $a \cdot$ is Lord.
258:3 Truth $a \cdot$ is strong;
269:3 words $a \cdot$ are vain,
270:3 words $a \cdot$ are vain,
276:1 th' eternal source $a \cdot$.
277:1 th' eternal source $a \cdot$.
291:3 take a step $a \cdot$,
312:2 through Christ $a \cdot$,
317:2 $A \cdot$ with Thee, amid the
   2 $A \cdot$ with Thee, in breath-
     less
322:3 with that aim $a \cdot$
323:3 with that aim $a \cdot$
339:2 ruled by Love $a \cdot$.
342:2 Not for such gifts $a \cdot$,
343:1 the Way: to thee $a \cdot$
344:1 the Way: to thee $a \cdot$
429:1 the Way: to thee $a \cdot$
343:2 the Truth: thy word $a \cdot$
344:2 the Truth: thy word $a \cdot$
429:2 the Truth: thy word $a \cdot$
349:1 Thine $a \cdot$ be ever done;
368:2 will its beams $a \cdot$
369:2 will its beams $a \cdot$
374:2 good $a \cdot$ is here.
375:2 good $a \cdot$ is here.

along
  55:3 rocks $a \cdot$ our way.
139:1-3 Love $a \cdot$ the way,
427:1-3 Love $a \cdot$ the way,
158:2 $a \cdot$ the climbing way
159:2 $a \cdot$ the climbing way
247:1 $a \cdot$ the road,
248:1 $a \cdot$ the road,

aloud
30:4 finger traced $a \cdot$
31:4 finger traced $a \cdot$
32:4 finger traced $a \cdot$

altar
196:1 Around one $a \cdot$ kneeling,

altars
319:3 living $a \cdot$ claim

although
86:2 $a \cdot$ He seems invisible.
87:2 $a \cdot$ He seems invisible.

alway
23:5 saint, Our stay, a.
24:5 saint, Our stay, a.
25:5 saint, Our stay, a.
26:5 saint, Our stay, a.
27:5 saint, Our stay, a.
28:5 saint, Our stay, a.
66:2 we live and sing a.
421:2 we live and sing a.
207:4 I am with you a,"—
208:4 I am with you a,"—
209:4 I am with you a,"—
210:4 I am with you a,"—
211:4 I am with you a,"—
212:4 I am with you a,"—

always
3:1 Where there is a room
45:3 would be a praising
133:1 cannot a trace
424:1 cannot a trace
133:1 I can a, a say
424:1 I can a, a say
138:3 has a guided me.
273:3 a works by love.
274:3 a works by love.
324:2 A, only, for my King.
357:3 pure in heart are a glad;
358:3 pure in heart are a glad;
407:3 pure in heart are a glad;

ambush
5:1 The foe in a

ambushed
67:1 A lies the evil one:
68:1 A lies the evil one:

Amen
271:4 repeat the long A.
272:4 repeat the long A.

amid (*see also* **mid**)
36:1 A the voices of this
2 a the words of earth,
2 A the hurrying crowds
3 A the restless eyes
96:1 A the suffering
169:1 a the encircling gloom,
204:2 light a shadows of fear,
317:2 a the changing shadows,
336:3 a dissolving spheres,

amiss
390:3 we ask a.

among
157:3 a all men and nations
197:3 made flesh a us:
198:3 made flesh a us:

ample
260:1 my a creed,

amplitude
342:1 a of God's dear love

anchors
297:2 where hope a fast,

ancient
242:1 forth the a word:
258:2 makes a creeds uncouth;
331:3 Thine a prophets teach,
345:1 repeats its a story
391:2 a prophets' lay,

Ancient of Days
150:1 Renewer, the A of D,

anew
108:2 drink a the royal wine
202:2 comes a, to humble
412:1 comes a, to humble
287:3 creation hears a
408:3 creation hears a
384:1 all creation makes a,

angel
33:2 charge His a legions
169:3 those a faces smile,
214:3 send its a to our
253:2 white-winged a throng
254:2 white-winged a throng
255:2 white-winged a throng
256:2 white-winged a throng
257:2 white-winged a throng
271:4 Let a songs be heard
272:4 Let a songs be heard
297:1 a with the flaming

angelic
310:1-2 Hear th' a song

angel's
74:2 From out the a hand;

angels
3:3 a of His presence
9:1 a sang, in days
2 God's a ever come
3 He knows the a
11:1 A at the Saviour's
2 tidings a bring
99:3 gives His a charge
100:3 gives His a charge
136:2 a bring release,
158:1 a, bending near
159:1 a, bending near
158:1,2 hear the a sing.
159:1,2 hear the a sing.
158:3 now the a sing.
159:3 now the a sing.
170:1 song the a sung,
181:1 a of Thy presence

angels
192:3 A to beckon me
193:3 A to beckon me
207:4 with the a sing:
208:4 with the a sing:
209:4 with the a sing:
210:4 with the a sing:
211:4 with the a sing:
212:4 with the a sing:
264:4 Men and a sing.
282:1 a, in the height;
310:1 Men and a, anthems

angels'
72:2 a glorious theme;
405:2 a glorious theme;

angel-song
9:4 hear the a

anger
376:1 tells us not of a,
377:1 tells us not of a,

angry
37:4 surge's a shock,
38:4 surge's a shock,
104:1 senses' a shock,
253:4 troubled, a sea
254:4 troubled, a sea
255:4 troubled, a sea
256:4 troubled, a sea
257:4 troubled, a sea

anguish
40:1 here tell your a;
374:3 thank Thee, when in a
375:3 thank Thee, when in a

another
179:1 Love one a,—

another's
126:1 one a peace
127:1 one a peace
403:1 one a peace

answer
54:3 a silent prayer.
341:3 a every prayer,

answered
76:2 prayer to Him is a,
149:1 prayer is fully a,
426:1 prayer is fully a,
168:3 through a prayer.
179:2 is our a prayer.

answers
139:2 a every call;
427:2 a every call;

13

anthems
310:1 Men and angels, $a\cdot$ raise;

anxious
93:3 From $a\cdot$ fear man finds
154:3 No $a\cdot$ thought,
155:3 No $a\cdot$ thought,
156:3 No $a\cdot$ thought,

any
19:1 from sin or $a\cdot$ stain,
34:4 $a\cdot$ shades of coming
    night;
182:2 at $a\cdot$ time we cease
205:1 $a\cdot$ earthly woe;
415:3 no sorrow, nor $a\cdot$ sighing,
   3 $a\cdot$ tears there, nor $a\cdot$
    dying:

apart
4:2 never drawn $a\cdot$,
349:2 know from Thee $a\cdot$,
382:2 In Christly paths $a\cdot$.

appall
389:1 no terrors $a\cdot$;

appear
35:1 in my heart $a\cdot$.
71:2 cloud and fire $a\cdot$
88:2 Thy life in mine $a\cdot$;
89:2 Thy life in mine $a\cdot$;
97:2 rising grain $a\cdot$;
98:2 rising grain $a\cdot$;
192:3 let the way $a\cdot$,
193:3 let the way $a\cdot$,
204:2 no foes that $a\cdot$
237:4 own image will $a\cdot$,
314:2 duly shall $a\cdot$

appearing
276:2 Thy bright $a\cdot$ cheer us,
277:2 Thy bright $a\cdot$ cheer us,
392:1 hail the new $a\cdot$;
393:1 hail the new $a\cdot$;

appears
186:2 before Thee now $a\cdot$.
187:2 before Thee now $a\cdot$.
261:1 church of God $a\cdot$
262:1 church of God $a\cdot$

applies
364:3 in faith to God $a\cdot$.

applying
350:3 His truth we are $a\cdot$,

approaching
196:1 is the time $a\cdot$,

approve
5:2 all of Truth you must $a\cdot$,
51:3 heaven and earth $a\cdot$.
52:3 heaven and earth $a\cdot$.
204:2 uphold and $a\cdot$ them.

approved
124:3 goodness stands $a\cdot$,
402:3 goodness stands $a\cdot$,

ardor
320:4 With growing $a\cdot$ onward
321:4 With growing $a\cdot$ onward
409:4 With growing $a\cdot$ onward

aright
149:1 turn to God $a\cdot$.
426:1 turn to God $a\cdot$.
329:3 Lay hold of Thee $a\cdot$.
357:2 To worship Thee $a\cdot$;
358:2 To worship Thee $a\cdot$;
407:2 To worship Thee $a\cdot$;

arise
5:1 voice of Truth, $a\cdot$,
12:1 $A\cdot$ ye people,
13:1 $A\cdot$ ye people,
14:1,4 $A\cdot$, $a\cdot$ and shine,
35:1 Sun of righteousness, $a\cdot$,
62:1 Creator's praise $a\cdot$;
63:1 Creator's praise $a\cdot$;
93:4 where no storms $a\cdot$,
160:3 sense, $a\cdot$, go hence!
161:3 sense, $a\cdot$, go hence!
162:3 sense, $a\cdot$, go hence!
172:1 O man, $a\cdot$ and shine,
200:1 $A\cdot$, for the night of
275:1 where the hills $a\cdot$,
   2 like the dawns $a\cdot$
312:1 Soldiers of Christ, $a\cdot$,
381:1 Lord in life $a\cdot$.
396:1 $A\cdot$, and follow where
397:1 $A\cdot$, and follow where

ark
297:3 $A\cdot$ where the dove

arm
41:3 No $a\cdot$ so weak
53:1 His the $a\cdot$ we lean
   2 With His $a\cdot$ to lean
76:1 His $a\cdot$ enfolds thee
115:1 Thine $a\cdot$ has been
116:1 Thine $a\cdot$ has been
115:2 rest upon Thine $a\cdot$,
116:2 rest upon Thine $a\cdot$,
200:2 $a\cdot$ that subdued them
207:2 His $a\cdot$ encircles me,
208:2 His $a\cdot$ encircles me,

arm
209:2 His $a\cdot$ encircles me,
210:2 His $a\cdot$ encircles me,
211:2 His $a\cdot$ encircles me,
212:2 His $a\cdot$ encircles me,
216:2 by His mighty $a\cdot$;
311:2 taketh in His $a\cdot$;
420:2 taketh in His $a\cdot$;
312:1 $a\cdot$ you for the fight,
343:3 thy conquering $a\cdot$;
344:3 thy conquering $a\cdot$;
429:3 thy conquering $a\cdot$;
364:1 God's protecting $a\cdot$.

armed
102:2 $A\cdot$ with faith, may we
103:2 $A\cdot$ with faith, may we
166:3 $A\cdot$ with faith and winged
167:3 $A\cdot$ with faith and winged

armies
326:3 the alien $a\cdot$ flee;

armor
5:1 Put $a\cdot$ on,
67:1 Gird thy heavenly $a\cdot$
68:1 Gird thy heavenly $a\cdot$
292:1 $a\cdot$ of pure consecration,
312:1 put your $a\cdot$ on,
326:1 all the $a\cdot$ of his God;

arms
53:1 Everlasting $a\cdot$ of Love
   3 Safe in His encircling $a\cdot$,
59:3 His $a\cdot$ are near;
60:3 His $a\cdot$ are near;
61:3 His $a\cdot$ are near;
304:3 Take them in Thine $a\cdot$;
305:3 Take them in Thine $a\cdot$;
306:3 Take them in Thine $a\cdot$;
307:3 Take them in Thine $a\cdot$;
308:3 Take them in Thine $a\cdot$;
309:3 Take them in Thine $a\cdot$;

army
37:1 one $a\cdot$ strong,
38:1 one $a\cdot$ strong,
264:2 Like a mighty $a\cdot$,

around
7:2 in all $a\cdot$ I see
41:1 all $a\cdot$ him waves
53:1 beneath, $a\cdot$, above;
64:2 Love is all $a\cdot$.
77:1 hosts encamp $a\cdot$ me,
78:1 hosts encamp $a\cdot$ me,
84:1 mists, $a\cdot$, above;
115:1 arm has been $a\cdot$ us,
116:1 arm has been $a\cdot$ us,

around
134:2 $A\cdot$ me flows Thy
140:3 $A\cdot$ us hover
196:1 $A\cdot$ one altar kneeling,
214:1 $a\cdot$ us, and above,

arrayed
146:3 Can ever be $a\cdot$.
147:3 Can ever be $a\cdot$.
342:3 robes of joy $a\cdot$,

arrow
30:1 $a\cdot$ that doth wound
31:1 $a\cdot$ that doth wound
32:1 $a\cdot$ that doth wound

art
143:3 each evasive $a\cdot$,
291:1 free from $a\cdot$;

ascend
54:3 no words $a\cdot$;
75:3 daily vows, $a\cdot$;

ascends
287:1 waking thought $a\cdot$,
408:1 waking thought $a\cdot$,
368:2 that star $a\cdot$;
369:2 that star $a\cdot$;

ashes
202:3 Beauty for $a\cdot$ of
412:2 Beauty for $a\cdot$ of
361:3 gives, for $a\cdot$, beauty,

aside
108:2 lay $a\cdot$ each earthly
376:2 Nor ever turn $a\cdot$,
377:2 Nor ever turn $a\cdot$,

ask
6:3 strength and patience $a\cdot$;
55:2 Do we $a\cdot$ our way
70:1 Who $a\cdot$ with prayer
92:2 nor question $a\cdot$
121:2 $a\cdot$ no more Than guidance
122:2 $a\cdot$ no more Than guidance
169:1 I do not $a\cdot$ to see
247:2 His blessing $a\cdot$
248:2 His blessing $a\cdot$
269:1 can we $a\cdot$ for more?
270:1 can we $a\cdot$ for more?
269:1 $A\cdot$ not the Lord
270:1 $A\cdot$ not the Lord
269:2 $a\cdot$ Him to change
270:2 $a\cdot$ Him to change
278:2 $a\cdot$ of thy Lord,
279:2 $a\cdot$ of thy Lord,
319:2 $a\cdot$ no lustre of our own.
374:1 before we $a\cdot$ Thee

ask
375:1 before we $a\cdot$ Thee
390:2, 3 $A\cdot$ what thou wilt,
3 $a\cdot$ and have not
when we $a\cdot$ amiss.
3 what we $a\cdot$ we

asleep
130:2 when we lie $a\cdot$,

assail
10:1 Whatever may $a\cdot$;
411:1 Whatever may $a\cdot$;
172:1 storms of life $a\cdot$;

assailing
176:1 mid the tempest's $a\cdot$,

assigned
190:2 through every task $a\cdot$,
191:2 through every task $a\cdot$,

assuage
71:3 shall their thirst $a\cdot$,—

assurance
390:2 blest $a\cdot$ from our

assured
93:1 $A\cdot$ God's goodness
354:2 $A\cdot$ that we shall reach
381:4 $A\cdot$ and safe in Love's

astray
245:2 far $a\cdot$ we roam,

atmosphere
144:1 $a\cdot$ of Love divine,
145:1 $a\cdot$ of Love divine,

atonement
263:3 find the true $a\cdot$,

at-one-ment
263:3 Love is our $a\cdot$,

attend
396:1 peace $a\cdot$ your way.
397:1 peace $a\cdot$ your way.

attends
62:2 $a\cdot$ Thy word;
63:2 $a\cdot$ Thy word;

attested
197:2 word and deed $a\cdot$.
198:2 word and deed $a\cdot$.

attuned
206:2 thought $a\cdot$ to praise,
428:2 thought $a\cdot$ to praise,

aught
368:1 $A\cdot$ of hope or joy
369:1 $A\cdot$ of hope or joy

author
102:1 $A\cdot$ of celestial
103:1 $A\cdot$ of celestial
374:2 Love is not the $a\cdot$
375:2 Love is not the $a\cdot$

awake
5:2 $a\cdot$ to love:
94:2 each worthier thought $a\cdot$,
142:3 $a\cdot$ and blow The mists
181:3 all $a\cdot$ to praise Thee
200:1 $a\cdot$ from thy sadness;
$A\cdot$, for thy foes

awakening
149:2 grandeur of a heart's $a\cdot$,
426:2 grandeur of a heart's $a\cdot$,

awakes
394:1 world $a\cdot$ to light.
395:1 world $a\cdot$ to light.

awaking
317:3 When hearts $a\cdot$ see

away
30:1 chased the clouds $a\cdot$?
31:1 chased the clouds $a\cdot$?
32:1 chased the clouds $a\cdot$?
41:3 $A\cdot$ with gloomy doubts
44:1 From shadows come $a\cdot$;
46:2 Cast foreboding fears $a\cdot$;
47:2 Cast foreboding fears $a\cdot$;
51:1 His works pass not $a\cdot$.
52:1 His works pass not $a\cdot$.
57:1 we turn $a\cdot$ from sorrow,
66:4 sweep $a\cdot$ the veil,
421:4 sweep $a\cdot$ the veil,
75:1 take $a\cdot$ transgression,
124:3 bear a song $a\cdot$.
402:3 bear a song $a\cdot$.
139:1 none can take $a\cdot$
427:1 none can take $a\cdot$
142:3 mists of earth $a\cdot$.
163:2 shall die $a\cdot$.
171:1 rolled the stone $a\cdot$.
413:1 rolled the stone $a\cdot$.
173:2 Prophecy will fade $a\cdot$,
183:3 Fling ease and self $a\cdot$;
184:3 Fling ease and self $a\cdot$;
196:2 Remove and pass $a\cdot$,
202:2 wipe all tears $a\cdot$;
412:1 wipe all tears $a\cdot$;
243:2 burdens fall $a\cdot$,
244:2 burdens fall $a\cdot$,
298:2 wipes your tears all $a\cdot$,

away
299:2 wipes your tears all $a\cdot$,
300:2 wipes your tears all $a\cdot$,
301:2 wipes your tears all $a\cdot$,
302:2 wipes your tears all $a\cdot$,
310:2 rolled the mists $a\cdot$;
336:3 and earth have past $a\cdot$.

away
363:4 the lingering mist $a\cdot$.
367:3 Thy darkness past $a\cdot$,
425:2 wipe all tears $a\cdot$,
  2 and sighing flee $a\cdot$,

awful
385:1 $a\cdot$ guide, in smoke

awhile
169:3 long since, and lost $a\cdot$.

ayont
160:4 $A\cdot$ hate's thrall:
161:4 $A\cdot$ hate's thrall:
162:4 $A\cdot$ hate's thrall:

B

babe
11:1 $b\cdot$ in meekness lay,
23:3 The Bethlehem $b\cdot$—
24:3 The Bethlehem $b\cdot$—
25:3 The Bethlehem $b\cdot$—
26:3 The Bethlehem $b\cdot$—
27:3 The Bethlehem $b\cdot$—
28:3 The Bethlehem $b\cdot$—

back
51:2 clouds of sense roll $b\cdot$,
52:2 clouds of sense roll $b\cdot$,
148:2 turn me $b\cdot$;
158:3 send $b\cdot$ the song
159:3 send $b\cdot$ the song
163:3 bring the wanderer $b\cdot$
303:3 call it $b\cdot$ to life;
315:2 win them $b\cdot$ again.
316:2 win them $b\cdot$ again.
390:1 heart shrink $b\cdot$ at

bade
94:2 $b\cdot$ each worthier thought

balm
49:3 Thy coolness and Thy $b\cdot$;
50:3 Thy coolness and Thy $b\cdot$;

band
29:2 united in one $b\cdot$.
37:2 One working $b\cdot$,
38:2 One working $b\cdot$,
351:1 goes the pilgrim $b\cdot$,

bands
69:3 Christly $b\cdot$ of Love
423:3 Christly $b\cdot$ of Love
83:1 ordained no other $b\cdot$
297:4 Loosener of prison $b\cdot$

banish
119:3 $B\cdot$ all our fears
202:2 $b\cdot$ pain, and wipe
412:1 $b\cdot$ pain, and wipe
359:2 wreaths of mist can $b\cdot$

banished
287:1 $b\cdot$ in the glow
408:1 $b\cdot$ in the glow

banishing
7:1 $b\cdot$ all night;

banner
71:2 deriving from their $b\cdot$,
82:3 the $b\cdot$ of Christ
204:2 Love is Thy $b\cdot$
296:1 lift your $b\cdot$ high;

banners
264:1 See, his $b\cdot$ go.

baptized
261:3 pure in heart her $b\cdot$
262:3 pure in heart her $b\cdot$
333:1 lips $b\cdot$ in humble

bar
201:1 do not $b\cdot$ your mind
404:1 do not $b\cdot$ your mind

barren
90:1 through this $b\cdot$ land:
304:2 Strangers on a $b\cdot$ shore,
305:2 Strangers on a $b\cdot$ shore,
306:2 Strangers on a $b\cdot$ shore,
307:2 Strangers on a $b\cdot$ shore,
308:2 Strangers on a $b\cdot$ shore,
309:2 Strangers on a $b\cdot$ shore,

base
359:2 mountains from their $b\cdot$

baseless
267:1 $b\cdot$ evil fall,
268:1 $b\cdot$ evil fall,

battle
204:3 $b\cdot$ the victory claim,—
264:1 Forward into $b\cdot$,

battling
290:1 $b\cdot$ for a brighter

beacon
48:1 mine to raise this $b\cdot$
172:2 $B\cdot$ of hope

beacons
176:3 page $b\cdot$ and brightens.

beam
2:1 $b\cdot$ of Truth displaces
23:4 gentle $b\cdot$ of living
24:4 gentle $b\cdot$ of living
25:4 gentle $b\cdot$ of living
26:4 gentle $b\cdot$ of living
27:4 gentle $b\cdot$ of living
28:4 gentle $b\cdot$ of living
226:2 Beneath Thy $b\cdot$ grow
229:1 whose constant $b\cdot$
287:2 Revealed in morning's $b\cdot$.
408:2 Revealed in morning's $b\cdot$.
304:3 Till the morning's $b\cdot$;
305:3 Till the morning's $b\cdot$;
306:3 Till the morning's $b\cdot$;
307:3 Till the morning's $b\cdot$;
308:3 Till the morning's $b\cdot$;
309:3 Till the morning's $b\cdot$;
336:2 a heavenly $b\cdot$ I see,
  2 $b\cdot$ conducts to Thee.

beams
11:2 radiant $b\cdot$ we find
35:2 mercy's $b\cdot$ I see;
334:3 $b\cdot$ of heavenly day.
363:1 $b\cdot$ of ages shine;
368:2 will its $b\cdot$ alone
369:2 will its $b\cdot$ alone

bear
41:2 joyful tidings $b\cdot$;
104:1 Lord, to $b\cdot$ the cross,
105:1 Each other's cross to $b\cdot$;
106:1 Each other's cross to $b\cdot$;
107:1 Each other's cross to $b\cdot$;
109:2 witness $b\cdot$ of Thee;
110:2 witness $b\cdot$ of Thee;
124:3 $b\cdot$ a song away.
402:3 $b\cdot$ a song away.
144:3 we His image $b\cdot$.
145:3 we His image $b\cdot$.
166:1 to do, or $b\cdot$.
167:1 to do, or $b\cdot$.
181:4 to $b\cdot$ the message
203:1 may we $b\cdot$ each hour
234:1 help me $b\cdot$ The strain
235:1 help me $b\cdot$ The strain

bear
242:3 $b\cdot$ our harvest home.
266:1 His image $b\cdot$, we know;
273:1 let us $b\cdot$ the strife,
274:1 let us $b\cdot$ the strife,
291:2 I the burden $b\cdot$?
333:3 piercing glance could $b\cdot$;
360:1 $b\cdot$ thy brother's burden,
   1 $b\cdot$ both it and thee.

bearing
88:3 Pressing on and $b\cdot$ up.
89:3 Pressing on and $b\cdot$ up.
97:1 $B\cdot$ still the precious
98:1 $B\cdot$ still the precious
346:3 $B\cdot$ the lamp of grace,
401:3 $B\cdot$ the lamp of grace,

bears
53:1 God it is who $b\cdot$ us
124:2 hand which $b\cdot$ creation
402:2 hand which $b\cdot$ creation
280:2 He gently $b\cdot$ us,
322:3 $b\cdot$ her to the King
323:3 $b\cdot$ her to the King

beauteous
120:1 $b\cdot$ on the mountains
352:1 how $b\cdot$, how divine,
353:1 how $b\cdot$, how divine,
368:1 does its $b\cdot$ ray
369:1 does its $b\cdot$ ray
370:2 $b\cdot$ things of Mind.

beautiful
125:1 $b\cdot$ the sweet accord
233:2 $b\cdot$ and swift to bless,
419:2 $b\cdot$ and swift to bless,
324:2 Swift and $b\cdot$ for Thee.

beauty
45:2 Such tender $b\cdot$, Lord,
   3 $b\cdot$ of Love's holiness,
49:4 $b\cdot$ of Thy peace.
50:4 $b\cdot$ of Thy peace.
51:1 His $b\cdot$, power and
52:1 His $b\cdot$, power and
109:2 unveil Thy $b\cdot$,
110:2 unveil Thy $b\cdot$,
113:2 In $b\cdot$ of holiness;
150:3 For $b\cdot$ and love
202:3 $B\cdot$ for ashes of the
412:2 $B\cdot$ for ashes of the
314:2 verdure, $b\cdot$, strength,
329:1 $b\cdot$, grandeur, order,
345:2 ineffable in $b\cdot$,
361:3 gives, for ashes, $b\cdot$,
378:1 would Thy $b\cdot$ see,

because
135:1 $B\cdot$ I live in Thee;
367:3 $B\cdot$ that light on thee
414:1 $B\cdot$ I know 'tis true,

beckon
192:3 Angels to $b\cdot$ me
193:3 Angels to $b\cdot$ me

become
18:1 brave $b\cdot$ bolder
283:3 $b\cdot$ our salvation.
378:3 is $b\cdot$ our song,

becomes
113:1 Holiness $b\cdot$ Thy house,
363:2 Gospel light $B\cdot$ effulgent

beds
372:3 by our $b\cdot$ of pain;
373:2 by our $b\cdot$ of pain;

befall
   3:4 Whatever else $b\cdot$,

before
10:3 $b\cdot$ Him fly,
411:3 $b\cdot$ Him fly,
11:2 Shines $b\cdot$ us
19:1 stand $b\cdot$ the throne
57:2 skies seem dark $b\cdot$ us,
59:2 Life ... $b\cdot$ us lies,
60:2 Life ... $b\cdot$ us lies,
61:2 Life ... $b\cdot$ us lies,
64:1 pathway lies $b\cdot$ me,
69:2 Bowing $b\cdot$ Thee,
423:2 Bowing $b\cdot$ Thee,
73:1 Come $b\cdot$ Him with
74:1 $B\cdot$ that still small
75:2 $B\cdot$ Him on the mountains
81:1 way made plain $b\cdot$ me,
91:1 a joy $b\cdot$ unknown.
422:1 a joy $b\cdot$ unknown.
148:3 pastures are $b\cdot$ me,
166:3 day $b\cdot$ thee;
167:3 day $b\cdot$ thee;
183:2 $b\cdot$ thine eyes.
184:2 $b\cdot$ thine eyes.
186:2 $b\cdot$ Thee now appears.
187:2 $b\cdot$ Thee now appears.
196:2 $B\cdot$ the blaze of day.
197:3 stone $b\cdot$ him melt,
198:3 stone $b\cdot$ him melt,
213:2 $B\cdot$ the hills in order
   3 $B\cdot$ the rising sun.
227:3 heaven $b\cdot$ our eyes.
246:2 all is plain $b\cdot$ Him.
264:1, Ref. Going on $b\cdot$.
269:1 'Twas infinite $b\cdot$.
270:1 'Twas infinite $b\cdot$.
282:1 rejoice $b\cdot$ Him,

before
319:2 $B\cdot$ Thy ever blazing
326:2 shield $b\cdot$ him spread.
342:2 hear $b\cdot$ we call,
351:1 Clear $b\cdot$ us through
352:3 the scoffs of men, $b\cdot$?
353:3 the scoffs of men, $b\cdot$?
354:1 paths $b\cdot$ unknown;
374:1 $b\cdot$ we ask Thee
375:1 $b\cdot$ we ask Thee
382:3 flee $b\cdot$ the light.
385:1 God $b\cdot$ her moved,
391:1 $B\cdot$ your feet Life's

began
238:1 since time $b\cdot$,
239:1 since time $b\cdot$,

begin
357:1 gladsome song $b\cdot$,
358:1 gladsome song $b\cdot$,
407:1 gladsome song $b\cdot$,

begirt
113:1 $b\cdot$ with majesty,

begun
351:3 the march in God $b\cdot$;

beheld
15:3 $B\cdot$ God's child
101:1 $b\cdot$ in light Man's

behest
356:2 ever follow Thy $b\cdot$:

behind
258:3 $b\cdot$ the dim unknown
273:2 forget the things $b\cdot$,
274:2 forget the things $b\cdot$,

behold
6:2 $B\cdot$, to-day hath need
19:1 $B\cdot$, they stand in robes
21:4 $b\cdot$ that God who loveth
22:4 $b\cdot$ that God who loveth
85:2 We $b\cdot$ reality,
99:3 $b\cdot$ His power
100:3 $b\cdot$ His power
120:2 $B\cdot$, O earth,
134:3 in all things I $b\cdot$,
138:2 $B\cdot$ Thy face
171:2 $b\cdot$ Life's purity,
413:2 $b\cdot$ Life's purity,
180:3 may we all $b\cdot$
206:2 to praise, $B\cdot$ reality.
428:2 to praise, $B\cdot$ reality.
207:2 Can I $b\cdot$ the snare,
208:2 Can I $b\cdot$ the snare,
209:2 Can I $b\cdot$ the snare,
210:2 Can I $b\cdot$ the snare,

behold
211:2 Can I b· the snare,
212:2 Can I b· the snare,
227:1 b· Thy mercy seat;
232:2 waiting hopes b·
406:2 waiting hopes b·
314:3 Lift up thine eyes, b·,
361:2 B· His works of
370:1 b· the perfect man;
384:3 the blind b·,

beholdeth
112:3 the light b·.

being
11:2 Star of b·, still
157:2 we find all b· one.
175:2 All true b· one
186:2 All that b· e'er shall
187:2 All that b· e'er shall
298:4 Life of all b· divine:
299:4 Life of all b· divine:
300:4 Life of all b· divine:
301:4 Life of all b· divine:
302:4 Life of all b· divine:

believe
12:1 they that b·
13:1 they that b·
121:3 Persuades, and they b·,—
122:3 Persuades, and they b·,—
283:3 unto them that b·
390:3 we only half b·

bells
418:1-4 clanging b· of time,

belong
23:2 tear, To thee b·.
24:2 tear, To thee b·.
25:2 tear, To thee b·.
26:2 tear, To thee b·.
27:2 tear, To thee b·.
28:2 tear, To thee b·.
72:2 thanks to God b·;
405:2 thanks to God b·;
73:1 Unto God the Lord b·;
275:1 power to Him b·,

beloved
21:1-4 B·, let us love:
22:1-4 B·, let us love:
23:3 B·, replete,
24:3 B·, replete,
25:3 B·, replete,
26:3 B·, replete,
27:3 B·, replete,
28:3 B·, replete,
149:3 man b· is in God's
426:3 man b· is in God's

beloved
221:2 God's own Son b·,
245:2 know, b· Shepherd,
278:1 b· and protected,
279:1 b· and protected,
382:1 For His b· son?
385:1 Israel, of the Lord b·,

below
62:1 dwell b· the skies
63:1 dwell b· the skies
104:2 Thy cup on earth b·,
105:3 spotless here b·.
106:3 spotless here b·.
107:3 spotless here b·.
240:3 vanity of things b·,
241:3 vanity of things b·,
319:2 all life, b·, above,

bend
30:1 on the same branch b·.
31:1 on the same branch b·.
32:1 on the same branch b·.

bended
259:1 lifted eye or b· knee.
331:1 lifted eye and b· knee

bending
30:2 b· reed wouldst break
31:2 b· reed wouldst break
32:2 b· reed wouldst break
158:1 b· near the earth,
159:1 b· near the earth,
158:2 forms are b· low,
159:2 forms are b· low,

bends
134:2 calmness b· serene

beneath (*see also* 'neath)
33:1 Rest b· th' Almighty's
53:1 Are b·, around,
100:1 dwell b· the Almighty's
124:2 B· His watchful eye
402:2 B· His watchful eye
138:3 dawn B· whose light
158:2 b· life's crushing
159:2 b· life's crushing
207:4 B· the shadow of His
208:4 B· the shadow of His
209:4 B· the shadow of His
210:4 B· the shadow of His
211:4 B· the shadow of His
212:4 B· the shadow of His
226:2 B· Thy beam grow
242:2 forth b· His sky.
243:3 B· its tender, healing
244:3 B· its tender, healing
261:2 B· the pine or palm,

beneath (*see also* 'neath)
262:2 B· the pine or palm,
297:3 pass b· His rod;
333:1 B· life's weary load,

benediction
43:1 They tell of b·,
104:3 Thy b· rare,

benedictions
29:2 Christlike in its b·,
171:3 Filled with b·
413:3 Filled with b·

benevolence
388:3 gifts of our b·.

benighted
2:3 hearts and homes b·

benign
141:2 by a power b·;

beside
49:2 B· the Syrian sea,
50:2 B· the Syrian sea,
117:2 there is none b· Thee,
148:2 Shepherd is b· me,
158:2 rest b· the weary
159:2 rest b· the weary
224:3 can I want b·?
225:3 can I want b·?

best
56:1 b· that earth imparts,
173:4 greatest . . . , And the b·,
224:1 b·, my ever Friend.
225:1 b·, my ever Friend.
386:3 b· proclaim abroad,
387:3 b· proclaim abroad,
414:3 who know it b·

bestow
367:1 His spirit only can b·
396:2 needful strength b·;
397:2 needful strength b·;

bestoweth
345:3 how God Himself b·

Bethel
192:4 B· I'll raise;
193:4 B· I'll raise;

Bethlehem
23:3 B· babe—Beloved,
24:3 B· babe—Beloved,
25:3 B· babe—Beloved,
26:3 B· babe—Beloved,
27:3 B· babe—Beloved,
28:3 B· babe—Beloved,
102:3 star of B· shining,

Bethlehem
103:3 star of B· shining,
222:1 little town of B·,
223:1 little town of B·,
236:1 B· star that ages

betide
53:2 Faithful is, whate'er b·;
160:1 peace is thine,Whate'er b·.
161:1 peace is thine,Whate'er b·.
162:1 peace is thine,Whate'er b·.
278:2 though trials b· thee,
279:2 though trials b· thee,
291:2 What to-morrow may b·

betides
392:2 endless joy b·
393:2 endless joy b·

betray
76:1 earthly friends b· thee,
259:3 b· Where'er the stream

better
69:1 choose the b· part
423:1 choose the b· part
102:1 be b· understood.
103:1 be b· understood.
315:1 b· far To rule by love
316:1 b· far To rule by love
329:2 b· far than gold.
376:1 keep the b· way.
377:1 keep the b· way.

between
135:2 B· my Lord and me:

beyond
66:2 b· Thy omnipresence
421:2 b· Thy omnipresence
190:4 Hope soars b· death,
191:4 Hope soars b· death,
229:2 Love b· all law,
291:3 a care b· its own,

Bible
114:1 Holy B·, book divine,

bid
10:1 b· our foes defiance.
411:1 b· our foes defiance.
72:1 B· all strife
405:1 B· all strife
75:1 b· the weak be strong;
118:3 B· my troubled thoughts
143:1 b· us search and try.
303:3 love b· sin depart
374:3 b· mankind to waken
375:3 b· mankind to waken

bids
9:4 b· all discord cease,
136:1 b· all fear to
174:1 b· all tumult cease;
179:3 b· all discord cease.
188:2 b· them find and keep
195:1 b· fear and doubt depart,
347:2 b· the storm to cease;
348:2 b· the storm to cease;
392:3 b· us freely enter,
393:3 b· us freely enter,

big
399:1 b· with mercy,
400:1 b· with mercy,

bind
69:3 bands of Love ... to b·.
423:3 bands of Love ... to b·.
214:2 b· its tender blessing
253:1 b· The power of pain,
254:1 b· The power of pain,
255:1 b· The power of pain,
256:1 b· The power of pain,
257:1 b· The power of pain,
304:2 b· the stubborn will,
305:2 b· the stubborn will,
306:2 b· the stubborn will,
307:2 b· the stubborn will,
308:2 b· the stubborn will,
309:2 b· the stubborn will,

binding
109:2 B· up the broken-hearted,
110:2 B· up the broken-hearted,

binds
126:4 golden chain that b·
127:4 golden chain that b·
403:4 golden chain that b·

bird
45:2 In b·, in sunbeam,
317:1 When the b· waketh,

birds
30:1 Like brother b·,
31:1 Like brother b·,
32:1 Like brother b·,

bird-voices
236:3 b· mingle in joyful

birth
2:1 springing into b·.
11:1 at the Saviour's b·
75:2 Spring in His path to b·.
222:2 Proclaim the holy b·,
223:2 Proclaim the holy b·,

birth
310:1 lowly Saviour's b·.
368:2 that gave them b·?
369:2 that gave them b·?

birthright
382:1 What is thy b·, man,

bitter
54:2 dried the b· tear.
399:2 have a b· taste,
400:2 have a b· taste,

bitterness
8:3 and tears no b·;

black
29:1 B· with error, doubt,

blade
314:2 tender b·, the stalk,

blameless
357:3 To b· hearts reveal.
358:3 To b· hearts reveal.
407:3 To b· hearts reveal.

blast
213:1 from the stormy b·,

blaze
196:2 Before the b· of day.

blazing
319:2 Thy ever b· throne

blemish
383:2 From every b· free,

blend
30:1 our spirits b·
31:1 our spirits b·
32:1 our spirits b·
178:2 hearts in friendship b·,
236:3 hues in harmony b·,
247:3 b· it with a song.
248:3 b· it with a song.
263:3 in Him may b·.
264:4 B· with ours your

blending
73:2 with Love's will b·;

bless
7:2 Thee at hand to b·,
8:3 Thee at hand to b·;
34:3 Christ is here to b·,
42:1 B· the sower and
58:3 children live to b·,
101:1-3 we b· Thee, Lord.
113:2 Be Thou near to b·.
137:Ref. O b· me now,

bless
153:1, 2 magnify and $b\cdot$ Thee,
202:2 $b\cdot$ thee on his wings of
412:1 $b\cdot$ thee on his wings of
203:1 $b\cdot$ a hungry world.
214:1 Thy Word we $b\cdot$,
217:1 God deigns to $b\cdot$,
229:1 $b\cdot$ us while we dream,
233:2 swift to $b\cdot$,
419:2 swift to $b\cdot$,
243:1 power to heal and $b\cdot$,
244:1 power to heal and $b\cdot$,
251:1 We $b\cdot$ Thee for
252:1 We $b\cdot$ Thee for
269:3 Forever waits to $b\cdot$.
270:3 Forever waits to $b\cdot$.
280:3 swift to $b\cdot$.
342:3 thank and $b\cdot$ the Lord.
363:4 to $b\cdot$ but not destroy;
364:2 God that labor $b\cdot$;
371:2 $b\cdot$ Thy mighty name
374:1, 2 thank Thee and we $b\cdot$
375:1, 2 thank Thee and we $b\cdot$
378:3 we $b\cdot$ Thy name,

blessed (*see also* **blest**)
2:1 shines the $b\cdot$ light;
3 shines the $b\cdot$ token
3 $b\cdot$ Truth is given,
41:4 $B\cdot$ are they who
57:3 Chastened and $b\cdot$ we
58:1 in Thy $b\cdot$ way.
93:1 with joy is $b\cdot$,
95:1 O $b\cdot$ thought,
131:1 Our $b\cdot$ Master said;
132:1 Our $b\cdot$ Master said;
199:1 $b\cdot$ us on our way
221:2 Is perfect, holy, $b\cdot$.
260:4 O $b\cdot$ thought of God.
276:2 In Thy $b\cdot$ freedom
277:2 In Thy $b\cdot$ freedom

blessedness
76:2 $B\cdot$ and joy are near
368:2 Traveler, $b\cdot$ and light,
369:2 Traveler, $b\cdot$ and light,

blesses
3:4 loves and $b\cdot$ all.
157:2 $B\cdot$ all and injures
275:2 $b\cdot$ opened eyes,

blessing
42:2 all enjoy the $b\cdot$
54:1 Faith grasps the $b\cdot$
65:2 fullness of His $b\cdot$
130:2 every $b\cdot$ shower;
182:3 That $b\cdot$ from above;
214:2 bind its tender $b\cdot$

blessing
238:4 God's love and $b\cdot$,
239:4 God's love and $b\cdot$,
247:2 His $b\cdot$ ask
248:2 His $b\cdot$ ask
249:1 leave unsung one $b\cdot$,
250:1 leave unsung one $b\cdot$,
278:3 the $b\cdot$ how kind;
279:3 the $b\cdot$ how kind;

blessings
9:2 $b\cdot$ from on high,
16:2 Whose $b\cdot$ never cease.
72:1 Send Thy $b\cdot$ from
405:1 Send Thy $b\cdot$ from
75:2 His $b\cdot$ come as
138:1 for $b\cdot$ sent
163:2 only $b\cdot$ know,
164:2 his $b\cdot$ flow,
165:2 his $b\cdot$ flow,
417:2 his $b\cdot$ flow,
222:3 $b\cdot$ of His heaven.
223:3 $b\cdot$ of His heaven.
249:2 trials bloom in $b\cdot$,
250:2 trials bloom in $b\cdot$,
260:2 unfolds His $b\cdot$ new,
271:2 $b\cdot$ on His name.
272:2 $b\cdot$ on His name.
271:3 $b\cdot$ flow where'er He
272:3 $b\cdot$ flow where'er He
314:3 God's $b\cdot$ manifold.
342:1 all our $b\cdot$ show
374:3 For $b\cdot$, light and grace
375:3 For $b\cdot$, light and grace
378:2 $B\cdot$ of peaceful hours,
399:1 In $b\cdot$ on your head.
400:1 In $b\cdot$ on your head.

blest (*see also* **blessed**)
23:1 $B\cdot$ Christmas morn,
24:1 $B\cdot$ Christmas morn,
25:1 $B\cdot$ Christmas morn,
26:1 $B\cdot$ Christmas morn,
27:1 $B\cdot$ Christmas morn,
28:1 $B\cdot$ Christmas morn,
34:1 the sinner $b\cdot$,
39:3 may be forever $b\cdot$.
56:2 $b\cdot$ when faith can hold
80:3 His unclouded presence $b\cdot$,
86:2 $b\cdot$ is he to whom
87:2 $b\cdot$ is he to whom
86:3 $b\cdot$ is he who can
87:3 $b\cdot$ is he who can
121:1 $b\cdot$ are they whose hearts
122:1 $b\cdot$ are they whose hearts
125:2 They are the truly $b\cdot$
128:3 love them, and be $b\cdot$.
129:3 love them, and be $b\cdot$.

blest (*see also* **blessed**)
143:2 With understanding $b\cdot$,
169:3 power hath $b\cdot$ me,
186:3 love Thee and be $b\cdot$.
187:3 love Thee and be $b\cdot$.
196:2 a $b\cdot$ land of love.
236:1 ages have $b\cdot$,
245:3 Our $b\cdot$, eternal home.
271:3 sons of want are $b\cdot$
272:3 sons of want are $b\cdot$.
297:1 perfect Son, $b\cdot$ unity;
319:1 $B\cdot$ star of hope,
335:2 $B\cdot$ river of salvation,
355:2 O Spirit $b\cdot$.
363:3 New regions $b\cdot$,
390:2 $b\cdot$ assurance from

blight
197:2 $b\cdot$ and mildew rested:
198:2 $b\cdot$ and mildew rested:
258:1 the bloom or $b\cdot$,
339:2 healeth sorrow's $b\cdot$,

blind
327:3 $b\cdot$ receive their sight,
328:3 $b\cdot$ receive their sight,
346:2 Sight to the inly $b\cdot$,
401:2 Sight to the inly $b\cdot$;
384:3 the $b\cdot$ behold,
399:3 $B\cdot$ unbelief is
400:3 $B\cdot$ unbelief is

blinded
34:1 lift our $b\cdot$ eyes
202:4 $b\cdot$ eyes to see;
412:2 $b\cdot$ eyes to see;

blindfold
86:3 mortals' $b\cdot$ eye.
87:3 mortals' $b\cdot$ eye.

blinding
138:3 all these $b\cdot$ veils

blindly
337:2 Worldlings $b\cdot$ may refuse
338:2 Worldlings $b\cdot$ may refuse

blindness
130:1 dispels all $b\cdot$.
178:1 Healing mind . . . of $b\cdot$;

bliss
79:1 $B\cdot$ He wakes
83:2 $b\cdot$ and glory find
108:4 bridal feast of $b\cdot$
121:4 Whose $b\cdot$ no human
122:4 Whose $b\cdot$ no human
133:3 all woes, to $b\cdot$,
424:3 all woes, to $b\cdot$,
205:3 e'en here the hallowed $b\cdot$

bliss
266:3 same immortal $b\cdot$,
379:1 with all true $b\cdot$
380:1 with all true $b\cdot$

bloom
  3:1 come to perfect $b\cdot$.
 95:2 Eden's bowers $b\cdot$,
249:2 trials $b\cdot$ in blessings,
250:2 trials $b\cdot$ in blessings,
258:1 the $b\cdot$ or blight,

blooming
218:1 $b\cdot$ earth, the thoughts
219:1 $b\cdot$ earth, the thoughts
220:1 $b\cdot$ earth, the thoughts

blossoms
236:3 As $b\cdot$ their hues

blot
 91:2 $B\cdot$ out all fear,
422:2 $B\cdot$ out all fear,

blow
142:3 $B\cdot$, winds of God,
  3 $b\cdot$ The mists of earth
170:1 lilies bud and $b\cdot$.

body
264:2 All one $b\cdot$ we,

bold
 88:1 actions $b\cdot$ and meek
 89:1 actions $b\cdot$ and meek
384:3 the fearful $b\cdot$,
392:4 meek and $b\cdot$ defender
393:4 meek and $b\cdot$ defender

bolder
 18:1 brave become $b\cdot$

bond
196:2 closer $b\cdot$ of union,

bondage
  5:2 End $b\cdot$, O be free.
 69:1 from sinful $b\cdot$ be set
423:1 from sinful $b\cdot$ be set
226:3 darkened $b\cdot$ free:
337:3 from $b\cdot$ sets them
338:3 from $b\cdot$ sets them
385:1 Out of the land of $b\cdot$

bonds
202:1 $b\cdot$ of all captivity.
412:1 $b\cdot$ of all captivity.
266:3 $b\cdot$ of love our hearts

book
 74:2 little open $b\cdot$
114:1 Bible, $b\cdot$ divine,
176:3 with $B\cdot$ unsealed,

border
329:1 earth's remotest $b\cdot$

bore
104:1 cross our Master $b\cdot$;
168:2 $b\cdot$ the light Of Gospel
352:3 so humbly $b\cdot$ Scorn
353:3 so humbly $b\cdot$ Scorn

born
 11:1 $B\cdot$ the gracious news to
 21:2 sons, $b\cdot$ from above.
 22:2 sons, $b\cdot$ from above.
 23:1 Thy light was $b\cdot$
 24:1 Thy light was $b\cdot$
 25:1 Thy light was $b\cdot$
 26:1 Thy light was $b\cdot$
 27:1 Thy light was $b\cdot$
 28:1 Thy light was $b\cdot$
170:1 holy child was $b\cdot$,
  2 the Lord Christ $b\cdot$.
266:2 truly $b\cdot$ of God
317:2 nature, newly $b\cdot$;
362:1 Child of Hope is $b\cdot$,

borne
112:1 $B\cdot$ on faith's triumphant

borrows
334:2 gives but $b\cdot$ none.

bosom
126:3 Through every $b\cdot$ flow;
127:3 Through every $b\cdot$ flow;
403:3 Through every $b\cdot$ flow;
126:4 $b\cdot$ glow with love.
127:4 $b\cdot$ glow with love.
403:4 $b\cdot$ glow with love.
298:2 "Come to my $b\cdot$,
299:2 "Come to my $b\cdot$,
300:2 "Come to my $b\cdot$,
301:2 "Come to my $b\cdot$,
302:2 "Come to my $b\cdot$,

both
 76:2 save $b\cdot$ thine and thee.
125:3 $b\cdot$ sun and shield,
327:1 $b\cdot$ heaven and earth
328:1 $b\cdot$ heaven and earth
360:1 bear $b\cdot$ it and thee.

bound
392:3 its $b\cdot$ and center.
393:3 its $b\cdot$ and center.

bounding
388:2 With $b\cdot$ steps the halt

boundless
 16:2 $b\cdot$ source of might,
138:2 Truth and $b\cdot$ Love?

boundless
379:2 God, whose $b\cdot$ love
380:2 God, whose $b\cdot$ love

bounds
229:1 Nor $b\cdot$, nor clime,

bountiful
236:4 God's $b\cdot$ peace,

bow
 30:4 A $b\cdot$ of promise
 31:4 A $b\cdot$ of promise
 32:4 A $b\cdot$ of promise

bowed
149:3 nor $b\cdot$ with tired
426:3 nor $b\cdot$ with tired
333:1 friend to all who $b\cdot$

bowers
 95:2 Eden's $b\cdot$ bloom,
104:4 Lead us to heaven's $b\cdot$:

bowing
 69:2 $B\cdot$ before Thee,
423:2 $B\cdot$ before Thee,

branch
 30:1 on the same $b\cdot$ bend.
 31:1 on the same $b\cdot$ bend.
 32:1 on the same $b\cdot$ bend.

branches
141:2 All the $b\cdot$ and

brave
 18:1 The $b\cdot$ become bolder
104:1 To $b\cdot$ the senses'
325:3 fear and danger $b\cdot$;

bread
 40:3 see the $B\cdot$ of Life,
 46:1 Lord, my daily $b\cdot$.
 47:1 Lord, my daily $b\cdot$.
 90:1 $B\cdot$ of heaven!
108:2 upon the $b\cdot$ of God;
  3 $b\cdot$ and wine remove,
151:1 $b\cdot$ and wine Thou art,
152:1 $b\cdot$ and wine Thou art,
298:4 the $b\cdot$, and the wine.
299:4 the $b\cdot$, and the wine.
300:4 the $b\cdot$, and the wine.
301:4 the $b\cdot$, and the wine.
302:4 the $b\cdot$, and the wine.

break
 11:1 at $b\cdot$ of day
 30:2 bending reed wouldst $b\cdot$
 31:2 bending reed wouldst $b\cdot$
 32:2 bending reed wouldst $b\cdot$
 66:4 $B\cdot$ earth-bound fetters,

break
421:4 $B\cdot$ earth-bound fetters,
74:1 rocks may seem to $b\cdot$,
75:1 comes to $b\cdot$ oppression,
111:1 truth shall $b\cdot$ through
120:2 $B\cdot$ forth in hymns
138:1 To $b\cdot$ the dream
160:5 The centuries $b\cdot$,
161:5 The centuries $b\cdot$,
162:5 The centuries $b\cdot$,
296:3 $b\cdot$ the earthly dream.
304:2 $B\cdot$ earth's stupid rest.
305:2 $B\cdot$ earth's stupid rest.
306:2 $B\cdot$ earth's stupid rest.
307:2 $B\cdot$ earth's stupid rest.
308:2 $B\cdot$ earth's stupid rest.
309:2 $B\cdot$ earth's stupid rest.
333:2 $b\cdot$ The fetters of
399:1 will $b\cdot$ In blessings
400:1 will $b\cdot$ In blessings
418:4 glorious morn shall $b\cdot$,

breaketh
317:1 when purple morning $b\cdot$,

breaking
29:1 $B\cdot$ through the clouds
64:1 dawn . . . is $b\cdot$ o'er me,
177:1 saints, the day is $b\cdot$,
197:1 day of Truth is $b\cdot$;
198:1 day of Truth is $b\cdot$;
202:1 dreams of error $b\cdot$,
412:1 dreams of error $b\cdot$,
238:3 A light is $b\cdot$,
239:3 A light is $b\cdot$,
335:1 morning light is $b\cdot$,

breaks
2:2 $b\cdot$ oppression's chain.
7:1 $b\cdot$ the morning light;
222:2 wakes, the glory $b\cdot$,
223:2 wakes, the glory $b\cdot$,
236:1 day of . . . promise $b\cdot$

breast
195:1 tumult of my troubled $b\cdot$.
207:5 upon the troubled $b\cdot$,
208:5 upon the troubled $b\cdot$,
209:5 upon the troubled $b\cdot$,
210:5 upon the troubled $b\cdot$,
211:5 upon the troubled $b\cdot$,
212:5 upon the troubled $b\cdot$,
214:3 calm upon the $b\cdot$;
236:1 hope in each $b\cdot$,
284:1 trembles in the $b\cdot$.
285:1 trembles in the $b\cdot$.
286:1 trembles in the $b\cdot$.
304:2 Wound the callous $b\cdot$,
305:2 Wound the callous $b\cdot$,

breast
306:2 Wound the callous $b\cdot$,
307:2 Wound the callous $b\cdot$,
308:2 Wound the callous $b\cdot$,
309:2 Wound the callous $b\cdot$,

breastplate
292:1 $b\cdot$ of righteousness
326:2 righteousness, a $b\cdot$

breath
218:4 the fuller $b\cdot$,
219:4 the fuller $b\cdot$,
220:4 the fuller $b\cdot$,
243:3 $b\cdot$ of opening flower.
244:3 $b\cdot$ of opening flower.
269:1 with $b\cdot$ of praise
270:1 with $b\cdot$ of praise
284:3 Christian's vital $b\cdot$,
285:3 Christian's vital $b\cdot$,
286:3 Christian's vital $b\cdot$,
383:1 $b\cdot$ of summer air,
418:1 hush our $b\cdot$ to hear,
3 thy $b\cdot$ doth wrap us

breathe
44:2 $B\cdot$ through the bright
49:3 $B\cdot$ through the pulses
50:3 $B\cdot$ through the pulses
144:1 live, and move, and $b\cdot$,
145:1 live, and move, and $b\cdot$;
195:2 I $b\cdot$ that love as

breathed
253:2 $b\cdot$ in raptured song,
254:2 $b\cdot$ in raptured song,
255:2 $b\cdot$ in raptured song,
256:2 $b\cdot$ in raptured song,
257:2 $b\cdot$ in raptured song,

breathes
334:1 spirit $b\cdot$ upon the Word

breathing
4:1 A holy air is $b\cdot$
390:2 $b\cdot$ from the Word.

breathless
317:2 with Thee, in $b\cdot$ adoration,

breeze
335:1 $b\cdot$ that sweeps the ocean

brethren
157:1 prayer for all his $b\cdot$:
236:2 may their $b\cdot$ uphold.

bridal
108:4 $b\cdot$ feast of bliss

bride
180:3 The Spirit and the $b\cdot$.

bridegroom
398:2 The $b\cdot$ draweth near.

bright
15:2 likeness clear and $b\cdot$,
37:3 towers, serene and $b\cdot$,
38:3 towers, serene and $b\cdot$,
44:2 $b\cdot$, celestial air
80:2 river pure and $b\cdot$,
119:1 Thy radiance $b\cdot$;
125:3 grace and glory $b\cdot$;
148:3 $B\cdot$ skies will soon
173:3 ever shine more $b\cdot$;
178:1 all His ways are $b\cdot$;
186:2 $B\cdot$ before Thee now
187:2 $B\cdot$ before Thee now
192:4 $b\cdot$ with Thy praise,
193:4 $b\cdot$ with Thy praise,
200:1 $b\cdot$ o'er thy hills dawns
205:2 shines more $b\cdot$ and clear
218:2 the $b\cdot$ hope glows,
219:2 the $b\cdot$ hope glows,
220:2 the $b\cdot$ hope glows,
226:2 Thy beam grow $b\cdot$;
233:3 of Truth divinely $b\cdot$,
419:3 of Truth divinely $b\cdot$,
253:3 A world more $b\cdot$.
254:3 A world more $b\cdot$.
255:3 A world more $b\cdot$.
256:3 A world more $b\cdot$.
257:3 A world more $b\cdot$.
276:2 With Thy $b\cdot$ appearing
277:2 With Thy $b\cdot$ appearing
317:3 in the $b\cdot$ morning,
334:3 such a $b\cdot$ display
350:3 expect a $b\cdot$ to-morrow,
352:2 so calm, so $b\cdot$,
353:2 so calm, so $b\cdot$,
357:2 mak'st our lives so $b\cdot$.
358:2 mak'st our lives so $b\cdot$.
407:2 mak'st our lives so $b\cdot$.
367:2 path, though thorny, $b\cdot$;
398:2 all your lamps be $b\cdot$,

brightening
97:2 scene of verdure $b\cdot$,
98:2 scene of verdure $b\cdot$,
351:2 $B\cdot$ all the path

brightens
79:1 His mercy $b\cdot$ All the
146:2 $b\cdot$ all the paths
147:2 $b\cdot$ all the paths
176:3 page beacons and $b\cdot$.
329:2 man's pathway $b\cdot$,

brighter
263:1 wait the b· morrow;
290:1 for a b· crown.
376:2 way will b· grow,
377:2 way will b· grow,

brightly
311:1 So b· burns Love's
420:1 So b· burns Love's
336:1 So b· as Thy sacred
385:2 b· shines the prosperous

brightness
79:2 His b· streameth;
320:4 With growing b· shine.
321:4 With growing b· shine.
409:4 With growing b· shine.
363:1 makes its b· more divine.
381:1 What b· dawned in

bring
9:2 b· us blessings from
11:2 tidings angels b·
40:1 b· your wounded hearts,
119:2 B· to us the richest
131:2 b· that quick'ning life
132:2 b· that quick'ning life
136:2 Thy angels b· release,
144:2 would b· to light
145:2 would b· to light
150:1 with glad hearts we b·.
163:3 b· the wanderer back
201:2 b· the light of liberty
404:2 b· the light of liberty
202:3 b· full compensation,
412:2 b· full compensation,
227:2 ever b· Thee where
   3 b· all heaven before
245:2 b· us safely home.
263:1,3 can b· us gladness,
271:4 creature rise, and b·
272:4 creature rise, and b·
280:1 thy tribute b·.
303:4 b· thy mite,
311:3 His hand doth b·
420:3 His hand doth b·
315:3 joy that it may b·,
316:3 joy that it may b·,
342:2 to b· Him praise
346:2 dost come to b·
401:2 dost come to b·
356:1 we b· our adoration,
372:1 b· the Lord Christ down;
373:1 b· the Lord Christ down;
418:1 do not b· us peace;

bringing
202:4 tidings of salvation b·.
412:2 tidings of salvation b·.

brings
9:4 b· us sweet release;
104:2 inspiration that it b·,
120:1 feet of him that b·,
153:2 help to Israel b·.
329:1 night its tribute b·.
334:1 b· the truth to sight;
335:1 B· tidings from afar,
368:1 it b· the day,
369:1 it b· the day,

brink
205:1 tremble on the b·

broad
37:1 City of God, how b·
38:1 City of God, how b·
131:2 indwelling, deep and b·,
132:2 indwelling, deep and b·,
260:1 deep it is and b·,
326:2 faith's b· shield
376:2 paths are b· and wide.
377:2 paths are b· and wide.

broadcast
314:1 B· it o'er the land.

broadening
234:4 future's b· way;
235:4 future's b· way;

broader
340:2 love of God is b·

broadly
182:1 they may b· run;

broke
128:2 gloomy night he b·,
129:2 gloomy night he b·,

broken
2:3 light has b· forth,
71:1 word cannot be b·,
217:1 heals the spirit b·,
282:1 never shall be b·

broken-hearted
109:2 Binding up the b·,
110:2 Binding up the b·,

brood
30:1 B· o'er us with Thy
31:1 B· o'er us with Thy
32:1 B· o'er us with Thy

brooding
197:3 peace is b· o'er us.
198:3 peace is b· o'er us.

brother
30:1 Like b· birds,
31:1 Like b· birds,
32:1 Like b· birds,
163:3 win our b· man,
217:2 b· man, fold to thy heart
    thy b·,
230:4 our b·, and our Lord,
231:4 our b·, and our Lord,
265:2 with rejoicing, b·:
351:1 B· clasps the hand of b·,

brotherhood
82:2 b· of all mankind,
179:3 Showing true b·,
221:1 Through love and b·.

brotherly
88:2 with actions b·
89:2 with actions b·

brother's
105:1 feel his b· care.
106:1 feel his b· care.
107:1 feel his b· care.
126:2 his b· failings hide,
127:2 his b· failings hide,
403:2 his b· failings hide,
126:2 show a b· love.
127:2 show a b· love.
403:2 show a b· love.
360:1 bear thy b· burden,

brothers
29:2 sisters and our b·
170:2 b· mine,
264:2 B·, we are treading

brought
4:3 nearer to each other b·,
51:3 b· the light again.
52:3 b· the light again.
115:1 b· us On through
116:1 b· us On through
330:3 home, rejoicing, b· me.

bud
170:1 lilies b· and blow.
399:2 b· may have a bitter
400:2 b· may have a bitter

build
105:2 b· each other up,
106:2 b· each other up,
107:2 b· each other up,
141:1 Lord b· not the house
    1 b· in vain;

builded
216:1 b· on the sand.

built
80:3 *B·* by the word of His

bulwarks
80:3 Firm as ... the *b·* stand;
364:1 Vain our *b·* and our

burden
124:3 drop my *b·* at His
402:3 drop my *b·* at His
291:2 I the *b·* bear?
360:1 Is thy *b·* hard
  1 bear thy brother's *b·*,

burdens
119:1 all *b·* and all sadness;
124:1 cast your *b·* on
402:1 cast your *b·* on

burdens
243:2 *b·* fall away,
244:2 *b·* fall away,
253:3 Life's *b·* light.
254:3 Life's *b·* light.
255:3 Life's *b·* light.
256:3 Life's *b·* light.
257:3 Life's *b·* light.

buries
288:1 That *b·* wrong
289:1 That *b·* wrong

burn
233:3 sacred shrine shall *b·*
419:3 sacred shrine shall *b·*
319:3 hearts that *b·* for Thee,
398:2 golden flame *b·* clear;

burned
94:1 heart within thee *b·*
333:2 heart that *b·* to break

burning
385:3 *b·* and a shining light.

burns
311:1 So brightly *b·* Love's
420:1 So brightly *b·* Love's
351:1 *b·* the guiding light;
392:2 heart ... *b·* and sings,
393:2 heart ... *b·* and sings,

bursts
368:2 *b·* o'er all the earth.
369:2 *b·* o'er all the earth.
392:4 the day *B·* forth
393:4 the day *B·* forth

C

call (noun)
5:1 *c·* to rise from earth;
  1 heed high heaven's *c·*.
6:1 hear the *c·* of God
17:3 sound the trumpet *c·*,
48:3 Thine every *c·*,
58:2 heed no other *c·*;
70:1 to hear that *c·*;
139:2 answers every *c·*;
427:2 answers every *c·*;
190:3 Thine is the *c·* and
191:3 Thine is the *c·* and
242:2 We hear the *c·*;
  3 O Thou whose *c·*
267:4 hear Thy loving *c·*,
268:4 hear Thy loving *c·*,
278:2 the *c·* of His word.
279:2 the *c·* of His word.
287:3 Truth's *c·*, Let there
408:3 Truth's *c·*, Let there
296:2 your Captain's *c·*,
318:3 Publish my *c·* with
372:4 we hear thy *c·*,
373:2 we hear thy *c·*,
374:1 Thy children's *c·*.
375:1 Thy children's *c·*.
390:1 back at duty's *c·*?

call (verb)
33:1 *C·* the Lord thy sure
56:3 those that on Thee *c·*;
202:4 *c·* the dumb to joyful
412:2 *c·* the dumb to joyful
204:1 *c·* and entreat every

call (verb)
214:1 Thy name we *c·*,
245:2 *c·* us, faithful
275:2 we *c·* His name;
281:1 *C·* upon His holy name;
292:2 for succor we *c·*;
303:3 *c·* it back to life;
337:2 and *c·* it night;
338:2 and *c·* it night;
342:2 hear before we *c·*,
355:1 Her name dare *c·*

calling
41:2 high *c·* that we all
49:2 gracious *c·* of the Lord,
50:2 gracious *c·* of the Lord,
84:1 O hear it *c·*.
374:3 may hear Thee *c·*:
375:3 may hear Thee *c·*:

callous
304:2 Wound the *c·* breast,
305:2 Wound the *c·* breast,
306:2 Wound the *c·* breast,
307:2 Wound the *c·* breast,
308:2 Wound the *c·* breast,
309:2 Wound the *c·* breast,

calls
298:2 Mourner, it *c·* you,—
299:2 Mourner, it *c·* you,—
300:2 Mourner, it *c·* you,—
301:2 Mourner, it *c·* you,—
302:2 Mourner, it *c·* you,—

calls
298:3 Sinner, it *c·* you,—
299:3 Sinner, it *c·* you,—
300:3 Sinner, it *c·* you,—
301:3 Sinner, it *c·* you,—
302:3 Sinner, it *c·* you,—

calm
3:3 *C·* watch by day or
36:2 Thy step how *c*
49:3 small voice of *c·*.
50:3 small voice of *c·*.
57:2 Comes with its *c·*
64:2 I feel the *c·*
85:3 perfect, *c·* reflection;
94:1 evening's *c·* and holy
95:2 By waters *c·*,
108:2 *c·* of sin forgiven.
118:2 to *c·* the tossing sea,
174:1 *c·*, that bids all tumult
214:3 *c·* upon the breast;
238:3 breaking, *c·* and clear.
239:3 breaking, *c·* and clear.
263:2 Heavenly *c·* and comfort
265:3 trustful, *c·* endeavor,
290:2 *c·* resolve to triumph
297:2 *C·* of Shekinah where
317:2 *c·* dew and freshness
322:1 peace and *c·* may we
323:1 peace and *c·* may we
352:2 so *c·*, so bright,
353:2 so *c·*, so bright,
379:2 *C·* and pure and faithful
380:2 *C·* and pure and faithful

calmly
186:3 C· in this thought we
187:3 C· in this thought we
291:2 C· to Thy wisdom
325:3 C· all fear and danger

calmness
134:2 Thy c· bends serene

came
 10:2 to error's thraldom c·,
411:2 to error's thraldom c·,
 19:1 out of tribulation c·,
114:1 tell me whence I c·;
128:2 From heaven he c·,
129:2 From heaven he c·,
142:2 knows whence it c·,
158:1 c· upon the midnight
159:1 c· upon the midnight
356:1 whom Jesus c· to prove.
385:1 land of bondage c·,
386:1 our great Master c·
387:1 our great Master c·
388:2 their great deliverer c·;

campeth
283:2 He c· about us,

Canaan's
281:1 C· promised land,

cannon
236:2 From c· and sword

Captain's
296:2 hear your C· call,

captive
 75:1 set the c· free,
202:1 O c·, rise and sing,
412:1 O c·, rise and sing,
202:4 O c·, rise, thy Saviour
412:4 O c·, rise, thy Saviour
327:2 sets the c· free.
328:2 sets the c· free.

captives
 82:3 set their c· free,

captivity
202:1 bonds of all c·.
412:1 bonds of all c·.

care
 10:2 His c· doth e'er
411:2 His c· doth e'er
 56:2 our c· we cast;
 99:2 love and watchful c·
100:2 love and watchful c·
105:1 feel his brother's c·.
106:1 feel his brother's c·.
107:1 feel his brother's c·.

care
124:1 His constant c·.
402:1 His constant c·.
140:2 every cross and c·.
149:3 is in God's c·,
426:3 is in God's c·,
154:3 no load of c·.
155:3 no load of c·.
156:3 no load of c·.
166:1 sin and fear and c·;
167:1 sin and fear and c·;
189:1 Whose c· is ever nigh.
190:3 and Thine the c·,
191:3 and Thine the c·,
199:2 His eternal c·
224:1 on Thy c· depend;
225:1 on Thy c· depend;
224:3 cast my c· on Thee;
225:3 cast my c· on Thee;
227:3 and sweeten c·;
234:1 the fret of c·.
235:1 the fret of c·.
291:2 that Thou wilt c·,
    3 c· beyond its own,
303:4 Nor c· how small
327:3 With constant c·,
328:3 With constant c·,
374:1 tender, constant c·,
375:1 tender, constant c·,
376:2 loving c· wilt show.
377:2 loving c· wilt show.

cared
278:1 C· for, watched over,
279:1 C· for, watched over,

cares
 57:2 vain c· that vex
 79:3 earthly c· entwineth
361:1 He c· for thee
389:1 No c· can o'erwhelm

caring
361:2 Thy c· and contriving,

caroling
 11:2 With their joyful c·,

case
365:2 the sorrows of thy c·
366:2 the sorrows of thy c·

cast
 12:1 C· out your idols
 13:1 C· out your idols
 46:2 C· foreboding fears
 47:2 C· foreboding fears
 56:2 our care we c·;
124:1 c· your burdens on
402:1 c· your burdens on

cast
221:1 c· out sin and pain.
224:3 I c· my care on
225:3 I c· my care on
288:2 be not c· down.
289:2 be not c· down.
391:1 Life's pearl is c·.

casting
 96:2 c· demons out.

casts
179:2 c· out every fear,

cause
  5:2 The c· requires
123:2 c· thee to stand,
240:2 C· us to run the
241:2 C· us to run the
258:1 A great c·, God's
    3 c· of evil prosper,
296:1 Servants of a mighty c·,
391:3 holds the Mind and C·;
396:3 The c· is God's
397:3 The c· is God's

cease
  9:1 song that ne'er shall c·,
    4 bids all discord c·,
 16:2 Whose blessings never c·.
 17:2 idle words must c·.
 43:1 love which cannot c·.
 44:1 sounds of weeping c·,
 49:4 all our strivings c·;
 50:4 all our strivings c·;
 72:1 strife and tumult c·.
405:1 strife and tumult c·.
 83:3 all our slavery c·,
 93:1 goodness ne'er will c·;
 94:3 heavenly echoes never c·.
136:1 all fear to c·:
    3 quest shall never c·,
157:3 Warfare shall forever c·,
174:1 bids all tumult c·;
179:3 bids all discord c·.
182:2 at any time we c·
    3 They c· to have who c·
           to give:
263:1 divine shall never c·.
320:3 youthful vigor c·;
321:3 youthful vigor c·;
409:3 youthful vigor c·;
337:3 glories c· to be;
338:3 glories c· to be;
347:2 bids the storm to c·;
348:2 bids the storm to c·;
362:3 reign shall never c·;
368:3 let thy wanderings c·,
369:3 let thy wanderings c·,
418:1 they never c·;

ceaseless
146:4 threads of c joy;
147:4 threads of c joy;
324:1 flow in c praise.
360:2 but a c fountain
    2 its c longings still.

ceasing
361:3 without c prays.

celestial
44:2 bright, c air
54:1 Love, c Love,
102:1 Author of c good,
103:1 Author of c good,
104:3 Thy day, c, fair.
215:1 who c wisdom makes
330:2 With food c feedeth.
384:2 C streams shall

center
392:3 Love its bound and c.
393:3 Love its bound and c.

centuries
160:5 The c break,
161:5 The c break,
162:5 The c break,
363:3 as c roll,

chaff
200:2 fled like the c

chain
    2:2 breaks oppression's c.
126:4 golden c that binds
127:4 golden c that binds
403:4 golden c that binds

chains
10:2 from its c unbound us.
411:2 from its c unbound us.
168:3 Our c unbind,
271:3 leaps to loose his c,
272:3 leaps to loose his c,
297:4 self-forged c that fall

challenge
17:2 c, Who goes there?

change
44:3 C leaves no saddening
93:3 Love that cannot c,
148:1 No c my heart shall
166:4 c to glad fruition,
167:4 c to glad fruition,
269:2 ask Him to c
270:2 ask Him to c

changeless
75:3 His c name of Love.
79:2 His c goodness
281:1 c still shall stand.
350:1 c is His favor;

changes
148:1 nothing c here.
418:2 c rise and fall,

changeth
59:3 He c not,
60:3 He c not,
61:3 He c not,

changing
261:1 Unchanged by c place.
262:1 Unchanged by c place.
317:2 amid the c shadows,

channels
182:1 c for the streams of
    2 Such c to provide,

chaos
176:1 O'er night and c
310:2 c, fear and night;
346:1 C and darkness heard,
401:1 C and darkness heard,

charge
33:2 c His angel legions
99:3 gives His angels c
100:3 gives His angels c

chariots
200:2 their c of war.

charity
178:2 C the law fulfilleth,
222:2 c stands watching
223:2 c stands watching
264:2 One in c.

chart
230:3 miss with c of creeds.
231:3 miss with c of creeds.
251:2 is the c and compass
252:2 is the c and compass

chartered
37:1 thy c freemen are,
38:1 thy c freemen are,

chased
30:4 What c the clouds
31:4 What c the clouds
32:4 What c the clouds

chasing
351:2 C far the gloom

chastened
57:3 C and blessed we learn

chastens
30:3 c pride and earth-born
31:3 c pride and earth-born
32:3 c pride and earth-born

check
136:2 will and woe would c

cheer
43:2 come to c the night.
168:2 and c the heart.
199:2 strengthen us and c us;
276:2 bright appearing c us,
277:2 bright appearing c us,
313:1 c us after rain.

cheering
97:1 the c sun will shine;
98:1 the c sun will shine;
265:3 Guiding, c, like

cheerless
35:2 Dark and c is the morn

cheers
319:1 C the long watches

cherish
337:1 which thousands c,
338:1 which thousands c,

chide
114:2 c me when I rove,
280:3 Slow to c,

chiding
154:2 truth a perfect c,
155:2 truth a perfect c,
156:2 truth a perfect c,

child
15:2 God forever sees His c
    3 God's c forever pure
16:1 pure and happy c.
51:3 God's own c,
52:3 God's own c,
154:1 as God's own c;
155:1 as God's own c;
156:1 as God's own c;
166:1 Know, O c, thy full
167:1 Know, O c, thy full
166:2 C of heaven, can'st
167:2 C of heaven, can'st
170:1 holy c was born,

child
207:1 Keep Thou my $c\cdot$ on
208:1 Keep Thou my $c\cdot$ on
209:1 Keep Thou my $c\cdot$ on
210:1 Keep Thou my $c\cdot$ on
211:1 Keep Thou my $c\cdot$ on
212:1 Keep Thou my $c\cdot$ on
232:1 Man is the $c\cdot$ of God.
406:1 Man is the $c\cdot$ of God.
232:2 man is God's own $c\cdot$.
406:2 man is God's own $c\cdot$.
233:3 every weary $c\cdot$ shall
419:3 every weary $c\cdot$ shall
278:1 $c\cdot$ of the day.
279:1 $c\cdot$ of the day.
291:1 as a little $c\cdot$,
    2 as a $c\cdot$ receive,
    3 little $c\cdot$ relies
362:1 $C\cdot$ of Hope is born,
382:1 $C\cdot$ of the perfect One;
    2 art Truth's honest $c\cdot$,

child-heart
359:3 to thy $c\cdot$ shall come

childlike
139:3 $c\cdot$ trust be yours
427:3 $c\cdot$ trust be yours

children
58:1 we Thy loving $c\cdot$
    3 Thy $c\cdot$ live to bless,
    3 Thy $c\cdot$ know Thee,
66:1 these Thy $c\cdot$ gathered
421:1 these Thy $c\cdot$ gathered
76:1 mother leave her $c\cdot$?
83:3 God's $c\cdot$ dwell in peace,
119:1 O'er Thy $c\cdot$ shed
124:2 guard His $c\cdot$ well.
402:2 guard His $c\cdot$ well.
157:3 God's $c\cdot$ all shall
174:1 God comforteth His $c\cdot$;
181:1 Father, we Thy $c\cdot$
    4 Thy $c\cdot$ far and near:
203:2 all Thy $c\cdot$ dwell
236:3 God's loving $c\cdot$ in concord
253:6 where Thine own $c\cdot$ are,
254:6 where Thine own $c\cdot$ are,
255:6 where Thine own $c\cdot$ are,
256:6 where Thine own $c\cdot$ are,
257:6 where Thine own $c\cdot$ are,
267:1 His $c\cdot$ cannot fear;
268:1 His $c\cdot$ cannot fear;
310:1, Ref. Sing, ye joyous $c\cdot$,
318:1 Suffer the $c\cdot$ to come
339:3 we, God's $c\cdot$ true,
347:2 His $c\cdot$ shall be taught
348:2 His $c\cdot$ shall be taught

children
356:2 We are Thy $c\cdot$,
374:2 Thy $c\cdot$ know Thee
375:2 Thy $c\cdot$ know Thee

children's
374:1 hear'st Thy $c\cdot$ call.
375:1 hear'st Thy $c\cdot$ call.

chime
418:1 wearied with their $c\cdot$,

chimes
190:4 Heaven's music $c\cdot$ the
191:4 Heaven's music $c\cdot$ the

choice
36:1 Father's gracious $c\cdot$;
136:1 serve Thee is my $c\cdot$,
170:2 be the $c\cdot$ of days
215:1 His early, only $c\cdot$.
258:1 So can $c\cdot$ be made

choose
39:2 know and $c\cdot$ Thy way;
69:1 $c\cdot$ the better part
423:1 $c\cdot$ the better part
169:2 $c\cdot$ and see my path;
318:2 ready to $c\cdot$ my way,
324:3 way that Thou shalt $c\cdot$.

choosing
379:1 one thing needful $c\cdot$
380:1 one thing needful $c\cdot$

chord
281:1 joy tune every $c\cdot$,

chosen
281:1 He leads His $c\cdot$

Christ
11:2 $C\cdot$, the Truth,
14:1 and $C\cdot$ thy light,
23:2 Dear $C\cdot$, forever here
24:2 Dear $C\cdot$, forever here
25:2 Dear $C\cdot$, forever here
26:2 Dear $C\cdot$, forever here
27:2 Dear $C\cdot$, forever here
28:2 Dear $C\cdot$, forever here
34:1 $C\cdot$ comes again
    3 tender $C\cdot$ is here
35:1 $C\cdot$, whose glory fills
    1 $C\cdot$, the true, the perfect
39:3 Lead us, O $C\cdot$,
51:2 $C\cdot$ is the perfect
52:2 $C\cdot$ is the perfect
59:1 $C\cdot$ is thy strength,
    and $C\cdot$ thy right;

Christ
60:1 $C\cdot$ is thy strength,
    and $C\cdot$ thy right;
61:1 $C\cdot$ is thy strength,
    and $C\cdot$ thy right;
59:2 $C\cdot$ is the path, and
    $C\cdot$ the prize.
60:2 $C\cdot$ is the path, and
    $C\cdot$ the prize.
61:2 $C\cdot$ is the path, and
    $C\cdot$ the prize.
59:3 $C\cdot$ is all in all to thee.
60:3 $C\cdot$ is all in all to thee.
61:3 $C\cdot$ is all in all to thee.
82:3 banner of $C\cdot$ unfurled,
96:1 stood of old, the holy $C\cdot$,
104:1 the rock Of $C\cdot$,
112:2 $C\cdot$, our mighty Counsel,
121:4 $C\cdot$ the Lord prepare;
122:4 $C\cdot$ the Lord prepare;
170:2 the Lord $C\cdot$ born.
197:2 $C\cdot$ to-day to us
198:2 $C\cdot$ to-day to us
201:4 hid With $C\cdot$ in God
404:4 hid With $C\cdot$ in God
202:1 The $C\cdot$ is here, all
412:1 The $C\cdot$ is here, all
221:2 The $C\cdot$, eternal manhood,
222:3 dear $C\cdot$ enters in.
223:3 dear $C\cdot$ enters in.
224:3 While $C\cdot$ is rich,
225:3 While $C\cdot$ is rich,
251:2 $C\cdot$, the living Word.
252:2 $C\cdot$, the living Word.
253:4 I see $C\cdot$ walk,
254:4 I see $C\cdot$ walk,
255:4 I see $C\cdot$ walk,
256:4 I see $C\cdot$ walk,
257:4 I see $C\cdot$ walk,
264:1 $C\cdot$, the royal Master,
    4 Unto $C\cdot$ the King;
265:2 By the $C\cdot$ road,
275:3 Ours is the risen $C\cdot$,
283:3 $C\cdot$ is become our
293:3 $C\cdot$, the Truth, foundation
294:3 $C\cdot$, the Truth, foundation
295:3 $C\cdot$, the Truth, foundation
296:Ref. with $C\cdot$ to victory
298:4 Thou the $C\cdot$, and not
299:4 Thou the $C\cdot$, and not
300:4 Thou the $C\cdot$, and not
301:4 Thou the $C\cdot$, and not
302:4 Thou the $C\cdot$, and not
310:1, Ref. Glorious is the $C\cdot$,
312:1 Soldiers of $C\cdot$, arise,
    2 o'ercome through $C\cdot$
    alone,

Christ
326:3 Through $C\cdot$, who gives
346:2 $C\cdot$, thou dost come
401:2 $C\cdot$, thou dost come
350:2 when in $C\cdot$ abiding,
356:3 and $C\cdot$ is Thine,
370:1 hid with $C\cdot$ forever
  1, 2 hid with $C\cdot$ in God,
    2 the risen $C\cdot$ has lifted
372:1 bring the Lord $C\cdot$ down;
373:1 bring the Lord $C\cdot$ down;
381:2 $C\cdot$, undimmed by dying,
392:2 $C\cdot$ now guides us,
393:2 $C\cdot$ now guides us,
392:4 and $C\cdot$ the way;
393:4 and $C\cdot$ the way;
396:1 Ye messengers of $C\cdot$,
397:1 Ye messengers of $C\cdot$,

Christian
264:1, Ref. Onward, $C\cdot$ soldiers,
265:1 Onward, $C\cdot$, though
313:1 $C\cdot$ while he sings;
326:1 $C\cdot$ warrior, see him

Christian's
284:3 the $C\cdot$ vital breath,
    The $C\cdot$ native air:
285:3 the $C\cdot$ vital breath,
    The $C\cdot$ native air:
286:3 the $C\cdot$ vital breath,
    The $C\cdot$ native air:

Christians
266:4 how true $C\cdot$ love;

Christian Science
29:1 Comes the $C\cdot S\cdot$ gospel,

Christlike
29:2 $C\cdot$ in its benedictions,
337:3 $C\cdot$, crowns the humble,
338:3 $C\cdot$, crowns the humble,

Christly
69:3 $C\cdot$ bands of Love
423:3 $C\cdot$ bands of Love
382:2 In $C\cdot$ paths apart.

Christmas
23:1 Blest $C\cdot$ morn,
24:1 Blest $C\cdot$ morn,
25:1 Blest $C\cdot$ morn,
26:1 Blest $C\cdot$ morn,
27:1 Blest $C\cdot$ morn,
28:1 Blest $C\cdot$ morn,
170:1 The $C\cdot$ lilies bud
    2 your $C\cdot$ sign,
222:2 $C\cdot$ comes once more.
223:2 $C\cdot$ comes once more.

Christ's
12:1 $C\cdot$ promise stands:
13:1 $C\cdot$ promise stands:
88:1 $C\cdot$ own gracious spirit
89:1 $C\cdot$ own gracious spirit
88:2 Follow $C\cdot$ sincerity.
89:2 Follow $C\cdot$ sincerity.
221:1 $C\cdot$ precious Science
264:3 $C\cdot$ own promise,
297:4 $C\cdot$ morning meal
356:3 For we are $C\cdot$,

church
36:1 $C\cdot$ of the ever-living
37:2 One holy $c\cdot$,
38:2 One holy $c\cdot$,
113:3 Maintain Thy $c\cdot$
176:1 stood, O $c\cdot$ of God,
    3 $c\cdot$ of God, with Book
261:1 One holy $c\cdot$ of God
262:1 One holy $c\cdot$ of God
264:2 Moves the $C\cdot$ of God;
    3 But the $C\cdot$ of Jesus
    3 'Gainst that $C\cdot$ prevail;

cistern
138:1 my shallow $c\cdot$ spent,

city
37:1 $C\cdot$ of God, how broad
38:1 $C\cdot$ of God, how broad
37:4 heavenly $c\cdot$ stands.
38:4 heavenly $c\cdot$ stands.
71:1 Zion, $c\cdot$ of our God;
80:2 $c\cdot$ of our God remains.
415:3 $c\cdot$ to which I journey;

claim
41:2 $C\cdot$ the high calling
135:2 Dost $c\cdot$ me as Thine
204:3 battle the victory $c\cdot$,—
311:1 none can $c\cdot$ he doth not
420:1 none can $c\cdot$ he doth not
319:3 Thy living altars $c\cdot$
386:3 subdues the $c\cdot$ of sin.
387:3 subdues the $c\cdot$ of sin.

claims
5:1 foe in ambush $c\cdot$
6:2 From duty's $c\cdot$ no life

clanging
418:1-4 $c\cdot$ bells of time,

clasps
351:1 Brother $c\cdot$ the hand of

clay
51:1 thought th' eternal $c\cdot$:
52:1 thought th' eternal $c\cdot$:

clean
304:3 Shepherd, wash them $c\cdot$.
305:3 Shepherd, wash them $c\cdot$.
306:3 Shepherd, wash them $c\cdot$.
307:3 Shepherd, wash them $c\cdot$.
308:3 Shepherd, wash them $c\cdot$.
309:3 Shepherd, wash them $c\cdot$.

cleanse
118:1 $C\cdot$ my thought in Thy
298:3 $C\cdot$ the foul senses
299:3 $C\cdot$ the foul senses
300:3 $C\cdot$ the foul senses
301:3 $C\cdot$ the foul senses
302:3 $C\cdot$ the foul senses

cleansing
15:1 $c\cdot$ fires of Truth
141:4 $C\cdot$ men of fear
206:2 its pure and $c\cdot$ rays
428:2 its pure and $c\cdot$ rays
345:1 Thy $c\cdot$ fire repeats its

clear
6:1 with $c\cdot$ eye the present
14:2 Truth's $c\cdot$ light
15:2 likeness $c\cdot$ and bright,
17:1 morning star shines $c\cdot$.
29:1 radiance soft and $c\cdot$;
64:1 into Truth's $c\cdot$ day;
66:4 give us vision $c\cdot$,
421:4 give us vision $c\cdot$,
88:2 with wisdom kind and $c\cdot$
89:2 with wisdom kind and $c\cdot$
136:1 $c\cdot$ light of Truth
158:1 upon the midnight $c\cdot$,
159:1 upon the midnight $c\cdot$,
170:2 inward sight is $c\cdot$,
176:2 $C\cdot$ as the Word that
185:2 $c\cdot$ vision thou hast
205:2 shines more bright and $c\cdot$
230:2 dim or $c\cdot$, we own
231:2 dim or $c\cdot$, we own
234:2 some $c\cdot$ winning word
235:2 some $c\cdot$ winning word
238:3 breaking, calm and $c\cdot$.
239:3 breaking, calm and $c\cdot$.
313:1 season of $c\cdot$ shining,
318:3 with $c\cdot$ accord,
351:1 $C\cdot$ before us through
398:2 golden flame burn $c\cdot$;

clearer
19:2 an ever $c\cdot$ light,
64:3 to me grows $c\cdot$,

cleareth
263:2 the shadow $c\cdot$,

clearly
70:2 $C \cdot$ thy pathway thou
233:1 mysteries are so $c \cdot$ shown
419:1 mysteries are so $c \cdot$ shown
418:2 Sounding $c \cdot$ through them

cleaving
192:5 joyful wing $C \cdot$ the sky,
193:5 joyful wing $C \cdot$ the sky,

cleft
392:4 Has $c \cdot$ the night
393:4 Has $c \cdot$ the night

climb
136:3 I $c \cdot$, with joy,
372:1 We may not $c \cdot$
373:1 We may not $c \cdot$

climbing
158:2 along the $c \cdot$ way
159:2 along the $c \cdot$ way

clime
37:1 Of every age and $c \cdot$.
38:1 Of every age and $c \cdot$.
229:1 nor $c \cdot$, nor creed

close
297:3 $c \cdot$ her faltering wings,
337:2 $C \cdot$ their eyes and call
338:2 $C \cdot$ their eyes and call

closely
185:2 more $c \cdot$ to thine own.

closer
196:2 A $c \cdot$ bond of union,
234:3 In $c \cdot$, dearer company,
235:3 In $c \cdot$, dearer company,

clothe
113:3 $C \cdot$ us in the grace

clothed
318:3 $C \cdot$ in a glory kings

cloud
8:2 Thro'$c \cdot$ and sunshine,
30:4 bow of promise on the $c \cdot$.
31:4 bow of promise on the $c \cdot$.
32:4 bow of promise on the $c \cdot$.
71:2 $c \cdot$ and fire appear
111:1 break through every $c \cdot$
281:2 given the $c \cdot$ by day,

cloudless
336:3 shine in $c \cdot$ day,
363:4 the $c \cdot$ lamp of day
367:2 in $c \cdot$ light enshrined,
383:3 leads to $c \cdot$ day.

clouds
23:1 though murky $c \cdot$ Pursue
24:1 though murky $c \cdot$ Pursue
25:1 though murky $c \cdot$ Pursue
26:1 though murky $c \cdot$ Pursue
27:1 though murky $c \cdot$ Pursue
28:1 though murky $c \cdot$ Pursue
29:1 Breaking through the $c \cdot$
30:4 chased the $c \cdot$ away?
31:4 chased the $c \cdot$ away?
32:4 chased the $c \cdot$ away?
51:2 $c \cdot$ of sense roll back,
52:2 $c \cdot$ of sense roll back,
85:2 $c \cdot$ of sense are riven,
128:2 $c \cdot$ of gloomy night
129:2 $c \cdot$ of gloomy night
133:2 $c \cdot$ my darkened path,
424:2 $c \cdot$ my darkened path,
139:2 dispels the $c \cdot$ of gray
427:2 dispels the $c \cdot$ of gray
148:3 darkest $c \cdot$ have been.
230:1 through transfigured $c \cdot$
231:1 through transfigured $c \cdot$
238:3 Through $c \cdot$ of doubt
239:3 Through $c \cdot$ of doubt
337:1 Pass like $c \cdot$ that
338:1 Pass like $c \cdot$ that
359:2 the $c \cdot$ that vanish
399:1 $c \cdot$ ye so much dread
400:1 $c \cdot$ ye so much dread

cloudy
90:2 the fiery $c \cdot$ pillar
385:2 $c \cdot$ screen To temper

cold
304:3 day grows dark and $c \cdot$,
305:3 day grows dark and $c \cdot$,
306:3 day grows dark and $c \cdot$,
307:3 day grows dark and $c \cdot$,
308:3 day grows dark and $c \cdot$,
309:3 day grows dark and $c \cdot$,

come
3:1 $c \cdot$ to perfect bloom.
9:2 angels ever $c \cdot$ and
11:2 the dawn has $c \cdot$,
30:3 $C \cdot$ from that Love,
31:3 $C \cdot$ from that Love,
32:3 $C \cdot$ from that Love,
39:1 $C \cdot$, gracious Spirit,
40:1 $C \cdot$, ye disconsolate,
3 $C \cdot$ to the feast of love,
   $c \cdot$, ever knowing,
41:1-4 $C \cdot$, labor on:
42:1 $C \cdot$, Thou all-transforming
43:1,2 $C \cdot$ unto me,
1 $c \cdot$ to hearts oppressed.

come
43:2 $c \cdot$ to cheer the night.
2 $C \cdot$, all ye heavy laden,
2 $c \cdot$ to end all strife.
44:1 $C \cdot$ to the land of peace;
   From shadows $c \cdot$ away;
3 $C \cdot$, trusting heart, $c \cdot$ to
   thy God,
51:3 His kingdom $c \cdot$;
52:3 His kingdom $c \cdot$;
58:2 $C \cdot$ we daily then,
73:1 $C \cdot$ into His presence
1 $C \cdot$ before Him with
75:2 His blessings $c \cdot$ as
92:2 orders $c \cdot$ from heaven.
119:1 $C \cdot$ with all Thy
124:1 $C \cdot$, cast your burdens
402:1 $C \cdot$, cast your burdens
128:3 teachings all may $c \cdot$,
129:3 teachings all may $c \cdot$,
137:Ref. I $c \cdot$ to Thee.
139:3 $C \cdot$, walk with Love
427:3 $C \cdot$, walk with Love
151:1,2 Lord, I $c \cdot$ to Thee;
152:1,2 Lord, I $c \cdot$ to Thee;
158:2 $C \cdot$ swiftly on the
159:2 $C \cdot$ swiftly on the
158:3 $c \cdot$ the time foretold;
159:3 $c \cdot$ the time foretold;
164:1 the Lord is $c \cdot$,
165:1 the Lord is $c \cdot$,
417:1 the Lord is $c \cdot$,
183:1 all to Truth must $c \cdot$.
184:1 all to Truth must $c \cdot$.
188:3 O $c \cdot$ and find,
3 I am Life, $c \cdot$ unto Me.
204:1 Thy kingdom is $c \cdot$ upon
205:3 then, whate'er may $c \cdot$,
213:1,4 hope for time to $c \cdot$,
227:2 bring Thee where they $c \cdot$;
242:3 To do Thy will we $c \cdot$,
245:3 joy at length we $c \cdot$,
253:4 And $c \cdot$ to me,
254:4 And $c \cdot$ to me,
255:4 And $c \cdot$ to me,
256:4 And $c \cdot$ to me,
257:4 And $c \cdot$ to me,
276:2 Thy blessed freedom $c \cdot$.
   $C \cdot$ with all Thy
277:2 Thy blessed freedom $c \cdot$
   $C \cdot$ with all Thy
276:2 $C \cdot$ with Thy deep
277:2 $C \cdot$ with Thy deep
283:1 $C \cdot$ let us sing,
298:2 "$C \cdot$ to my bosom,
299:2 "$C \cdot$ to my bosom,
300:2 "$C \cdot$ to my bosom,
301:2 "$C \cdot$ to my bosom,

come
302:2 "C· to my bosom,
298:3 "C· to this fountain,
299:3 "C· to this fountain,
300:3 "C· to this fountain,
301:3 "C· to this fountain,
302:3 "C· to this fountain,
310:1 c· again to earth,
318:1 children to c· to me,
1-3 C· unto me.
335:2 Proclaim, The Lord is c·.
341:3 To thy Father c·,
342:2 c· to-day to bring
346:2 dost c· to bring
401:2 dost c· to bring
347:3 prosper nor c· near.
348:3 prosper nor c· near.
355:2 C·, all pervading Love,
359:3 c· strength in weakness,
368:3 Son of God is c·.
369:3 Son of God is c·.
391:3 was and is to c·
418:4 feel the silence c·;

comes
17:3 c·, God's messenger
29:1 C· the Christian Science
34:1 Christ c· again
57:2 C· with its calm
75:1 God c·, with succor
1 c· to break oppression,
108:4 c· and passes by;
131:1 to the Father c·,
132:1 to the Father c·,
164:2 Where'er he c·, his
165:2 Where'er he c·, his
417:2 Where'er he c·, his
202:2 c· to bless thee on
412:1 c· to bless thee on
202:2 c· anew, to humble
412:1 c· anew, to humble
202:3 c· to give thee joy
412:2 c· to give thee joy
202:4 c· to call the dumb
412:2 c· to call the dumb
202:4 thy Saviour c· to thee.
412:2 thy Saviour c· to thee.
222:2 Christmas c· once more.
223:2 Christmas c· once more.
258:1 C· the moment to decide,
263:2 C· the healing word
313:1 c· to us again
314:2 full corn c· at length.
355:1 Truth c· alike to all

cometh
57:1 joy c· with the morrow;
189:1 Help c· from on high;
311:2 c· He to all

cometh
420:2 c· He to all
398:2 The signal c·
425:1, 2, Ref. Joy c· in the
morning.

comfort
9:3 To c·, guard and
39:1 light and c· from above;
79:3 Hope and c· from above;
95:1 with heavenly c· fraught.
114:3 to c· in distress,
133:2 heart sweet c· hath,
424:2 heart sweet c· hath,
174:1 C· is calm, that bids
1 C· is hope and courage
3 C· of God, that seeks
228:1 We feel Thy c·,
263:2 Heavenly calm and c·
313:1 c· seems declining,
389:2 My c· and joy
390:2 precious c· breathing

comforted
378:2 c· in grief,

Comforter
40:2 Here speaks the C·,

comforteth
174:1 God c· His children;

comforts
8:1 helpers fail, and c· flee,

coming
34:4 shades of c· night;
189:2 My going and my c·
222:3 may hear his c·,
223:3 may hear his c·,

command
80:3 word of His c·,
92:4 waits but Thy c·,
176:1 wrought by God's c·,
177:1 Darkness flees at His c·.
180:1 this c· forever strong,
331:3 Love . . .: this great c·

commands
6:2 of thy Lord's c·:
58:2 Thy right c·.
84:2 God's c· forever heeding,
124:1 gentle God's c·,
402:1 gentle God's c·,

common
196:1 One c· Lord adore.
238:2 Our c·, daily life
239:2 Our c·, daily life

commotion
335:1 nations in c·,

commune
113:2 here c· with Thee,
194:3 God and man c·.
410:3 God and man c·.

communion
151:1 With Thee I hold c·;
152:1 With Thee I hold c·;
261:3 Love, her c· cup.
262:3 Love, her c· cup.
269:3 true c· gain.
270:3 true c· gain.
297:3 c· with the Lamb

companions
34:2 c· such as these.

company
234:3 closer, dearer c·,
235:3 closer, dearer c·,

compass
251:2 is the chart and c·
252:2 is the chart and c·

compassion
178:2 All c· is and kind;
278:3 teach thee c·,
279:3 teach thee c·,

compensation
202:3 bring full c·,
412:2 bring full c·,

complaint
249:2 C· is poverty,
250:2 C· is poverty,

complete
93:1 Each day, c·,
149:3 satisfied, c·, divinely
426:3 satisfied, c·, divinely
312:2 stand c· at last.
326:2 panoply of truth c·,

completeness
66:2 in Thy c· held,
421:2 in Thy c· held,

comprehend
54:3 God Himself doth c·

comprehendeth
142:2 And c· Love.

concern
224:3 my great c· shall be
225:3 my great c· shall be

concord
236:3 children in c· remain.

condemnation
73:2 all c· ending,
283:3 there is no c·;

condemning
347:4 tongues that rise c·
348:4 tongues that rise c·

conducts
336:2 every beam c· to Thee.

conferred
168:4 which health c·:

confess
49:4 our ordered lives c·
50:4 our ordered lives c·
142:2 lips c· the name

confide
99:1 in Him I will c·.
100:1 in Him I will c·
232:1 in this truth c·:
406:1 in this truth c·:
275:3 evermore in Love c·.
361:1 C· thou in none

confidence
146:3 With c· it hails
147:3 With c· it hails
202:3 c· for all thy fears.
412:2 c· for all thy fears.

confident
150:3 c· giving and giving's
190:2 c· and humble mind,
191:2 c· and humble mind,

confiding
76:2 c· in His will;
148:1 safe is such c·,
313:2 while in Him c·,
350:2 still, in God c·,
361:3 glad in this c·,

confined
227:2 within no walls c·,

confirm
12:2 let your works c·
13:2 let your works c·
105:2 c· our hope,
106:2 c· our hope,
107:2 c· our hope,

conflict
351:3 One the c·, one the

conflicts
312:2 all your c· past,

confound
77:1 What terror can c·
78:1 What terror can c·

congregation
119:3 Rest upon this c·,
276:1 Peace be to this c·;
277:1 Peace be to this c·;

congregations
73:1 ye joyous c·,

conquer
133:2 c· dread and doubts
424:2 c· dread and doubts
296:Ref. c· death and sin;

conquered
276:1 fruit of c· sin;
277:1 fruit of c· sin;
325:2 He c· sin, and death,

conquering
29:2 C· every subtle error,
102:2 C· every storm
103:2 C· every storm
179:3 C· hate, enthroning
343:3 Proclaims thy c· arm;
344:3 Proclaims thy c· arm;
429:3 Proclaims thy c· arm;

conqueror
326:3 more than c· proves,

conquers
290:3 c· sin and death;

conquest
296:3 long the c· waits
320:2 the c· to the meek,
321:2 the c· to the meek,
409:2 the c· to the meek,

consciousness
317:1 Dawns the sweet c·,

consecrated
324:1 C·, Lord, to Thee.

consecration
109:2 deeper c· Show Thee
110:2 deeper c· Show Thee
237:1 Seek with c· whole,
292:1 armor of pure c·,

consolations
276:2 with Thy deep c·,
277:2 with Thy deep c·,
333:1 His c· flowed.

consoled
371:1 all grief c·,

constancy
249:2 They test our c·.
250:2 They test our c·.

constant
17:2 c· challenge, Who
46:1 by c· mercy fed,
47:1 by c· mercy fed,
124:1 trust His c· care.
402:1 trust His c· care.
180:2 By c· purpose proves
229:1 Love divine, whose c·
264:3 C· will remain;
311:1 c· shines its light,
420:1 c· shines its light,
327:3 With c· care,
328:3 With c· care,
374:1 tender, c· care,
375:1 tender, c· care,

constantly
7:3 Love divine, abiding c·,
233:2 by reflection c·
419:2 by reflection c·

consume
123:3 Thy dross to c·

contain
327:1 all that they c·
328:1 all that they c·

contemplation
313:2 In holy c· We
329:3 In daily c· Of Thee,

contend
236:3 As stars . . . never c·,

content
180:2 Here we rest c·:
332:1 true c· to fill.

contented
322:3 C· with that aim
323:3 C· with that aim

contrite
69:2 meek and c· heart,
423:2 meek and c· heart,
331:2 humble, c· mind,

contriving
361:2 Thy caring and c·,

control
221:3 Love's sweet c·.

coolness
49:3 Thy $c\cdot$ and Thy balm;
50:3 Thy $c\cdot$ and Thy balm;

corn
314:2 full $c\cdot$ comes at length.

corner stone
141:1 Father, may our $c\cdot s\cdot$

correcting
376:1 For Thy $c\cdot$ rod,
377:1 For Thy $c\cdot$ rod,

counsel
112:2 Christ, our mighty $C\cdot$,
178:1 is God's $c\cdot$ gentle,
216:2 after His own $c\cdot$,
356:2 understand Thy holy $c\cdot$,

Counsellor
362:2 The Wonderful, the $C\cdot$,

count
379:1 doth $c\cdot$ as naught,
380:1 doth $c\cdot$ as naught,
383:1 $c\cdot$ it sin to thee.

counteth
246:1 on Thee he ever $c\cdot$,

countless
140:1 of $c\cdot$ price,
199:1 $c\cdot$ gifts of love
264:4 through $c\cdot$ ages
345:3 men, a $c\cdot$ host,

country
415:2 $c\cdot$ so dark and dreary,

courage
77:2 My heart, with $c\cdot$
78:2 My heart, with $c\cdot$
85:3 Patience, $c\cdot$, meekness
104:3 $c\cdot$ may sustain our
139:3 with $c\cdot$ go, Give
427:3 with $c\cdot$ go, Give
146:3 With $c\cdot$ undismayed,
147:3 With $c\cdot$ undismayed,
150:3 $c\cdot$ that rises undaunted
151:2 give me needed $c\cdot$
152:2 give me needed $c\cdot$
174:1 hope and $c\cdot$ for
278:1 Walk thou with $c\cdot$
279:1 Walk thou with $c\cdot$
320:2 $c\cdot$ in the evil hour
321:2 $c\cdot$ in the evil hour
409:2 $c\cdot$ in the evil hour
396:2 With sacred $c\cdot$ go.
397:2 With sacred $c\cdot$ go.
399:1 saints, fresh $c\cdot$ take,
400:1 saints, fresh $c\cdot$ take,

courageously
55:1 Live our lives $c\cdot$.

course
140:1 on our daily $c\cdot$,
368:2 truth its $c\cdot$ portends;
369:2 truth its $c\cdot$ portends;

courses
236:3 stars in their $c\cdot$

covenant
75:3 His $c\cdot$ remove;
347:1 His $c\cdot$ be proved.
348:1 His $c\cdot$ be proved.

cover
82:1-3 waters $c\cdot$ the sea.
99:2 $c\cdot$ thy unguarded head.
100:2 $c\cdot$ thy unguarded head,

covering
71:2 a glory and a $c\cdot$,

cowards
18:1 though $c\cdot$ may fail;

cradle
23:2 No $c\cdot$ song, No natal
24:2 No $c\cdot$ song, No natal
25:2 No $c\cdot$ song, No natal
26:2 No $c\cdot$ song, No natal
27:2 No $c\cdot$ song, No natal
28:2 No $c\cdot$ song, No natal

crag
169:3 o'er $c\cdot$ and torrent,

created
143:2 $C\cdot$ to be free,

creation
58:3 Seeing only Thy $c\cdot$,
124:2 which bears $c\cdot$ up
402:2 which bears $c\cdot$ up
130:2 $c\cdot$ owns Thy power.
204:1 rulest in all Thy $c\cdot$;
282:2 earth, and all $c\cdot$,
287:3 $c\cdot$ hears anew
408:3 $c\cdot$ hears anew
384:1 all $c\cdot$ makes anew,

creation's
30:4 swelled $c\cdot$ lay:
31:4 swelled $c\cdot$ lay:
32:4 swelled $c\cdot$ lay:
292:2 $c\cdot$ wondrous story,

creative
267:3 We see $c\cdot$ Mind,
268:3 We see $c\cdot$ Mind,
275:1 Praise now $c\cdot$ Mind,
381:2 $C\cdot$ Mind, all good

Creator
246:Ref. $C\cdot$ is of heaven and

Creator's
62:1 $C\cdot$ praise arise;
63:1 $C\cdot$ praise arise;

creature
170:1 Let every $c\cdot$ hail
271:4 every $c\cdot$ rise, and bring
272:4 every $c\cdot$ rise, and bring

creatures
83:1 all His $c\cdot$ free;

credit
224:2 $c\cdot$ what my Saviour saith,
225:2 $c\cdot$ what my Saviour saith,

creed
12:1 doctrine, form or $c\cdot$
13:1 doctrine, form or $c\cdot$
23:5 Or cruel $c\cdot$, or
24:5 Or cruel $c\cdot$, or
25:5 Or cruel $c\cdot$, or
26:5 Or cruel $c\cdot$, or
27:5 Or cruel $c\cdot$, or
28:5 Or cruel $c\cdot$, or
229:1 nor $c\cdot$ Thou know'st,
260:1 my ample $c\cdot$, So deep
298:4 Christ, and not the $c\cdot$;
299:4 Christ, and not the $c\cdot$;
300:4 Christ, and not the $c\cdot$;
301:4 Christ, and not the $c\cdot$;
302:4 Christ, and not the $c\cdot$;
333:3 no lifeless $c\cdot$,

creeds
131:2 too large for $c\cdot$;
132:2 too large for $c\cdot$;
230:3 miss with chart of $c\cdot$.
231:3 miss with chart of $c\cdot$.
238:3 doubt and $c\cdot$ of fear
239:3 doubt and $c\cdot$ of fear
258:2 makes ancient $c\cdot$ uncouth;
337:1 $C\cdot$ and dogmas all may
338:1 $C\cdot$ and dogmas all may

creeps
267:2 No subtle error $c\cdot$;
268:2 No subtle error $c\cdot$;

cringing
296:2 $c\cdot$ host of fear

cross
18:2 remember the $c\cdot$.
104:1 to bear the $c\cdot$,
1 $c\cdot$ our Master bore;
4 The $c\cdot$ laid down;
105:1 Each other's $c\cdot$

cross
106:1 Each other's c
107:1 Each other's c
136:2 discord c my path
140:2 every c and care.
192:1 though it be a c
193:1 though it be a c
253:3 I kiss the c,
254:3 I kiss the c,
255:3 I kiss the c,
256:3 I kiss the c,
257:3 I kiss the c,
264:1, Ref. With the c of Jesus
288:2 No c, no crown;
289:2 No c, no crown;
296:1 soldiers of the c,
325:1-3 Take up thy c,
    2 for thee the c endured,
381:2 triumphed over c

crowds
36:2 Amid the hurrying c

crown
59:1 Thy joy and c
60:1 Thy joy and c
61:1 Thy joy and c
104:4 The c forever ours.
139:3 c your joy-filled
427:3 c your joy-filled
178:1 life's true c and
267:4 c Thee Lord of all.

crown
268:4 c Thee Lord of all.
273:2 c of righteousness.
274:2 c of righteousness.
288:2 No cross, no c;
289:2 No cross, no c;
290:1 for a brighter c.
326:4 an immortal c.

crowned
171:1 C with light that
413:1 C with light that
398:3 be with honor c.

crowneth
189:2 c with His grace.

crowns
65:2 C every dawning day;
264:3 C and thrones may
337:3 c the humble,
338:3 c the humble,

cruel
23:5 Or c creed, or
24:5 Or c creed, or
25:5 Or c creed, or
26:5 Or c creed, or
27:5 Or c creed, or
28:5 Or c creed, or
139:1 I suffer c fear,
427:1 I suffer c fear,

crumble
337:3 totter, empires c,
338:3 totter, empires c,

crushing
158:2 life's c load
159:2 life's c load

crystal
90:2 Open is the c fountain,

cup
34:3 empty c is filled;
104:2 to drink Thy c
259:1 c of healing oil
261:3 her communion c.
262:3 her communion c.

cure
40:2 that Love cannot c.
293:3 C is there for every
294:3 C is there for every
295:3 C is there for every
298:3 c All thy sorrow
299:3 c All thy sorrow
300:3 c All thy sorrow
301:3 c All thy sorrow
302:3 c All thy sorrow

cured
168:4 Which c disease,

D

daily
46:1 my d bread.
47:1 my d bread.
46:2 D strength for d needs:
47:2 D strength for d needs:
46:4 my d task shalt give;
47:4 my d task shalt give;
58:2 Come we d then,
75:3 d vows, ascend;
140:1 on our d course,
238:2 d life divine,
239:2 d life divine,
247:2 to your d task
248:2 to your d task
253:7 some d good to do
254:7 some d good to do
255:7 some d good to do
256:7 some d good to do
257:7 some d good to do
275:3 D we keep our tryst,
280:2 our d needs He knows;
283:2 D He campeth

daily
329:3 In d contemplation
332:2 fill our d lives

danger
205:2 in d knows no fear,
325:3 all fear and d brave;
389:2 refuge in sorrow and d;

dangers
115:1 through d oft unknown.
116:1 through d oft unknown.

dare
18:1 d all and prevail.
190:3 deemed impossible I d,
191:3 deemed impossible I d,
355:1 on Her name d call

dares
41:1 Who d stand idle
86:3 d to side with what
87:3 d to side with what

daring
204:3 Thy truth is their d,

dark
2:1 d and hidden places
35:2 D and cheerless is
57:1 D though the night,
    2 skies seem d before us,
128:2 D clouds of gloomy
129:2 D clouds of gloomy
149:1 Fade as the d when
426:1 Fade as the d when
169:1 The night is d,
172:3 Pierce thou the d
181:1 in fear's d night
222:1 thy d streets shineth
223:1 thy d streets shineth
222:2 The d night wakes,
223:2 The d night wakes,
245:1 d and heavy shadows
251:1 earth's d sky,

dark
252:1 earth's $d\cdot$ sky,
304:3 day grows $d\cdot$ and cold,
305:3 day grows $d\cdot$ and cold,
306:3 day grows $d\cdot$ and cold,
307:3 day grows $d\cdot$ and cold,
308:3 day grows $d\cdot$ and cold,
309:3 day grows $d\cdot$ and cold,
383:3 How $d\cdot$ soever it
415:2 country so $d\cdot$ and dreary,

darkened
133:2 clouds my $d\cdot$ path,
424:2 clouds my $d\cdot$ path,
226:3 From $d\cdot$ bondage
371:3 find through $d\cdot$ days

darkens
111:1 veils and $d\cdot$ Thy designs.

darker
18:1 the $d\cdot$ the night.

darkest
79:2 hour that $d\cdot$ seemeth,
148:3 $d\cdot$ clouds have been.
168:2 truth o'er $d\cdot$ night,
346:3 in earth's $d\cdot$ place
401:3 in earth's $d\cdot$ place

darkling
160:3 $d\cdot$ sense, arise,
161:3 $d\cdot$ sense, arise,
162:3 $d\cdot$ sense, arise,
226:2 let the $d\cdot$ past

darkness
2:1 $d\cdot$ of the night.
8:1 The $d\cdot$ deepens;
17:1 shapes of $d\cdot$ flee;
29:1 through the clouds of $d\cdot$,
70:3 No death nor $d\cdot$
77:1 $d\cdot$ and temptation,
78:1 $d\cdot$ and temptation,
84:1 $d\cdot$, world-enthralling,
102:3 depths of error's $d\cdot$
103:3 depths of error's $d\cdot$
104:3 Out of the $d\cdot$
117:2 $d\cdot$ cannot hide Thee,
177:1 $D\cdot$ flees at His command.
192:2 $D\cdot$ be over me,
193:2 $D\cdot$ be over me,
205:2 In $d\cdot$ feels no doubt;
229:2 saw the $d\cdot$ overflowed
245:2 ever out of $d\cdot$,
258:1 Twixt the $d\cdot$ and the
281:2 From the $d\cdot$ into light.
287:1 $D\cdot$ is banished

darkness
408:1 $D\cdot$ is banished
288:1 turns the $d\cdot$ into light,
289:1 turns the $d\cdot$ into light,
311:2 $d\cdot$ they did stray
420:2 $d\cdot$ they did stray
312:2 powers of $d\cdot$ down,
334:3 world of $d\cdot$ shine
335:1 The $d\cdot$ disappears;
346:1 Chaos and $d\cdot$ heard,
401:1 Chaos and $d\cdot$ heard,
351:1 through the $d\cdot$ Gleams
367:2 In whom no $d\cdot$ is.
3 Thy $d\cdot$ past away,
368:3 $d\cdot$ takes its flight,
369:3 $d\cdot$ takes its flight,
392:1 $d\cdot$ and the dream,
393:1 $d\cdot$ and the dream,

darts
30:1 $D\cdot$ not from those
31:1 $D\cdot$ not from those
32:1 $D\cdot$ not from those

daughter
200:1 $d\cdot$ of Zion, awake
3 $d\cdot$ of Zion, the power

daughters
71:3 supply thy sons and $d\cdot$,

dawn
11:2 the $d\cdot$ has come,
23:1 Nor $d\cdot$ nor day!
24:1 Nor $d\cdot$ nor day!
25:1 Nor $d\cdot$ nor day!
26:1 Nor $d\cdot$ nor day!
27:1 Nor $d\cdot$ nor day!
28:1 Nor $d\cdot$ nor day!
64:1 The $d\cdot$ of all things
138:3 gives promise of a $d\cdot$
140:2 $d\cdot$ on every cross
149:1 $d\cdot$ pours forth her
426:1 $d\cdot$ pours forth her
243:1 tender as the $d\cdot$,
244:1 tender as the $d\cdot$,
263:2 $d\cdot$ the shadow cleareth,
281:2 Light of $d\cdot$ leads
368:3 morning seems to $d\cdot$;
369:3 morning seems to $d\cdot$;

dawned
14:1 hath $d\cdot$ the day;
381:1 $d\cdot$ in resurrection

dawning
2:1 glorious day is $d\cdot$,
37:3 meet the $d\cdot$ day.

dawning
38:3 meet the $d\cdot$ day.
65:2 Crowns every $d\cdot$ day;
179:3 $d\cdot$ over every nation;
317:3 fairer than the $d\cdot$,

dawns
200:1 $d\cdot$ the day-star
275:2 like the $d\cdot$ arise
287:2 widening vision $d\cdot$
408:2 widening vision $d\cdot$
310:2 $D\cdot$ on earth
317:1 $D\cdot$ the sweet conscious-ness,
382:3 Truth $d\cdot$ on the sight;

day
2:1 glorious $d\cdot$ is dawning,
3:3 watch by $d\cdot$ or night.
11:1 at break of $d\cdot$
14:1 hath dawned the $d\cdot$;
17:1 God's $d\cdot$ of rest
23:1 Nor dawn nor $d\cdot$!
24:1 Nor dawn nor $d\cdot$!
25:1 Nor dawn nor $d\cdot$!
26:1 Nor dawn nor $d\cdot$!
27:1 Nor dawn nor $d\cdot$!
28:1 Nor dawn nor $d\cdot$!
35:3 to the perfect $d\cdot$.
37:3 meet the dawning $d\cdot$.
38:3 meet the dawning $d\cdot$.
46:1 $D\cdot$ by $d\cdot$ the manna
47:1 $D\cdot$ by $d\cdot$ the manna
46:2 $D\cdot$ by $d\cdot$ the promise
47:2 $D\cdot$ by $d\cdot$ the promise
46:4 $D\cdot$ by $d\cdot$ to Thee I
47:4 $D\cdot$ by $d\cdot$ to Thee I
64:1 Truth's clear $d\cdot$;
65:2 every dawning $d\cdot$;
67:1 Wear it ever night and $d\cdot$;
68:1 Wear it ever night and $d\cdot$;
71:2 and shade by $d\cdot$,
77:2 Thy $d\cdot$ shall mercy
78:2 Thy $d\cdot$ shall mercy
86:4 right the $d\cdot$ must win;
87:4 right the $d\cdot$ must win;
93:1 Each $d\cdot$, complete,
102:3 Truth's eternal $d\cdot$.
103:3 Truth's eternal $d\cdot$.
104:3 darkness into $d\cdot$,
Thy $d\cdot$, celestial,
124:3 Unchanged from $d\cdot$ to $d\cdot$:
402:3 Unchanged from $d\cdot$ to $d\cdot$:
128:2 Love's immortal $d\cdot$.
129:2 Love's immortal $d\cdot$.
139:1 it is a holy $d\cdot$;

day
427:1 it is a holy $d\cdot$;
139:3 your joy-filled $d\cdot$.
427:3 your joy-filled $d\cdot$.
140:3 each returning $d\cdot$,
157:3 $D\cdot$ by $d\cdot$ the understanding
166:3 Heaven's eternal $d\cdot$
167:3 Heaven's eternal $d\cdot$
169:2 loved the garish $d\cdot$,
171:1 rejoices every $d\cdot$,
413:1 rejoices every $d\cdot$,
171:3 Every $d\cdot$ will be
413:3 Every $d\cdot$ will be
172:3 shines to the perfect $d\cdot$.
173:2 in the light of $d\cdot$;
177:1 saints, the $d\cdot$ is breaking,
  1 $D\cdot$ advances, $d\cdot$ advances,
196:2 Before the blaze of $d\cdot$.
197:1 $d\cdot$ of Truth is breaking;
198:1 $d\cdot$ of Truth is breaking;
203:1 gladly $d\cdot$ by $d\cdot$
226:1 Unto Thy perfect $d\cdot$.
228:3 triumph $d\cdot$ by $d\cdot$.
229:2 tides of everlasting $d\cdot$.
236:1 $d\cdot$ of fresh promise
238:3 noises of our $d\cdot$,
239:3 noises of our $d\cdot$,
260:4 my strength by $d\cdot$,
278:1 child of the $d\cdot$.
279:1 child of the $d\cdot$.
281:2 given the cloud by $d\cdot$,
288:1 to that eternal $d\cdot$,
289:1 to that eternal $d\cdot$,
298:2 of one endless $d\cdot$."
299:2 of one endless $d\cdot$."
300:2 of one endless $d\cdot$."
301:2 of one endless $d\cdot$."
302:2 of one endless $d\cdot$."
304:3 when $d\cdot$ grows dark
305:3 when $d\cdot$ grows dark
306:3 when $d\cdot$ grows dark
307:3 when $d\cdot$ grows dark
308:3 when $d\cdot$ grows dark
309:3 when $d\cdot$ grows dark
310:2 on earth harmonious $d\cdot$.
312:2 the well-fought $d\cdot$.
319:1 the glow of $d\cdot$;
329:1 Each $d\cdot$ repeats
334:3 beams of heavenly $d\cdot$.
336:3 shine in cloudless $d\cdot$,
342:1, 3 $d\cdot$ the Lord hath made,
354:2 Secure in endless $d\cdot$.
363:4 cloudless lamp of $d\cdot$
367:3 In which is perfect $d\cdot$.
368:1 the $d\cdot$, Promised $d\cdot$
369:1 the $d\cdot$, Promised $d\cdot$
383:3 leads to cloudless $d\cdot$.

day
385:2 shines the prosperous $d\cdot$,
392:4 $d\cdot$ Bursts forth
393:4 $d\cdot$ Bursts forth
418:1 Night and $d\cdot$ they never

daylight
317:1 lovelier than the $d\cdot$,
359:1 joys of $d\cdot$ seem

day's
35:2 Joyless is the $d\cdot$ return,

days
9:1 in $d\cdot$ of yore,
57:2 cares that vex our $d\cdot$
158:3 $d\cdot$ are hastening on,
159:3 $d\cdot$ are hastening on,
170:2 the choice of $d\cdot$
190:4 chimes the glad $d\cdot$ in,
191:4 chimes the glad $d\cdot$ in,
199:1 from the $d\cdot$ of yore
324:1 moments and my $d\cdot$,
330:4 all the length of $d\cdot$
350:3 through $d\cdot$ of sorrow,
356:3 through endless $d\cdot$.
365:1-3 As thy $d\cdot$ thy strength
366:1-3 As thy $d\cdot$ thy strength
371:3 through darkened $d\cdot$

dayspring
35:1 $D\cdot$ from on high,
281:2 $d\cdot$ from on high.

day-star
7:1 Our $d\cdot$ rises,
35:1 $D\cdot$, in my heart
200:1 $d\cdot$ of gladness;
359:1 $d\cdot$ yet shall gleam.

dazzling
384:1 $d\cdot$ glories view?

dead
388:2 and raised the $d\cdot$.

deaf
202:4 The $d\cdot$ to hear;
412:2 The $d\cdot$ to hear;
384:3 The $d\cdot$ shall hear,

dear
3:4 $d\cdot$ Father-Mother, God,
23:2 $D\cdot$ Christ, forever here
24:2 $D\cdot$ Christ, forever here
25:2 $D\cdot$ Christ, forever here
26:2 $D\cdot$ Christ, forever here
27:2 $D\cdot$ Christ, forever here
28:2 $D\cdot$ Christ, forever here
45:1 $D\cdot$ God, how glorious
48:1 $D\cdot$ Father-Mother, Thou

dear
49:1 $D\cdot$ Lord and Father
50:1 $D\cdot$ Lord and Father
58:1 Come we . . ., $d\cdot$ Father,
59:3 and thou art $d\cdot$;
60:3 and thou art $d\cdot$;
61:3 and thou art $d\cdot$;
126:3 $d\cdot$ esteem In every
127:3 $d\cdot$ esteem In every
403:3 $d\cdot$ esteem In every
134:3 deep in Thy $d\cdot$ love,
150:3 $D\cdot$ Father and Saviour,
151:1, 2 $D\cdot$ Lord, I come
152:1, 2 $D\cdot$ Lord, I come
221:1 Jesus, our $d\cdot$ Master,
222:3 $d\cdot$ Christ enters in.
223:3 $d\cdot$ Christ enters in.
243:1 God's $d\cdot$ gift to all
244:1 God's $d\cdot$ gift to all
245:3 the way, $d\cdot$ Shepherd,
288:1 Press on, $d\cdot$ traveler,
289:1 Press on, $d\cdot$ traveler,
322:1 revealed by His $d\cdot$ love.
323:1 revealed by His $d\cdot$ love.
342:1 God's $d\cdot$ love

dearer
234:3 closer, $d\cdot$ company,
235:3 closer, $d\cdot$ company,

death
10:3 The hosts of $d\cdot$
411:3 The hosts of $d\cdot$
34:4 no pain or $d\cdot$
48:2 He knows not $d\cdot$
70:3 No $d\cdot$ nor darkness
114:3 triumph over $d\cdot$.
135:1 I know no $d\cdot$,
  1 frees us From $d\cdot$
173:1 than $d\cdot$ itself more
188:3 with dreams of $d\cdot$.
190:4 beyond $d\cdot$, pain and sin,
191:4 beyond $d\cdot$, pain and sin,
218:4 Life that knows no $d\cdot$,—
219:4 Life that knows no $d\cdot$,—
220:4 Life that knows no $d\cdot$,—
229:2 o'ercoming $d\cdot$ and sin,
275:3 Saviour from $d\cdot$
282:2 $d\cdot$ shall not prevail.
284:3 overcoming $d\cdot$:
285:3 overcoming $d\cdot$:
286:3 overcoming $d\cdot$:
290:3 conquers sin and $d\cdot$;
296:Ref. conquer $d\cdot$ and sin;
325:2 sin, and $d\cdot$, and hell.
326:4 Sin, $d\cdot$ and hell
343:1 sin and $d\cdot$ we flee ;
344:1 sin and $d\cdot$ we flee ;

death
429:1 sin and $d\cdot$ we flee;
343:3 $d\cdot$ nor hell shall harm.
344:3 $d\cdot$ nor hell shall harm.
429:3 $d\cdot$ nor hell shall harm.

deathless
23:4 Love, And $d\cdot$ Life!
24:4 Love, And $d\cdot$ Life!
25:4 Love, And $d\cdot$ Life!
26:4 Love, And $d\cdot$ Life!
27:4 Love, And $d\cdot$ Life!
28:4 Love, And $d\cdot$ Life!
172:2 splendor of her $d\cdot$ star.
391:2 $d\cdot$ as His spirit free,

death's
8:3 Where is $d\cdot$ sting?
287:3 $D\cdot$ drear and gloomy
408:3 $D\cdot$ drear and gloomy

debt
178:2 Love, our $d\cdot$ to God

deceitful
385:2 temper the $d\cdot$ ray.

deceive
144:1 sense that would $d\cdot$.
145:1 sense that would $d\cdot$.

decide
258:1 the moment to $d\cdot$,

declare
121:4 No human voice $d\cdot$.
122:4 No human voice $d\cdot$.
246:2 word and deed $d\cdot$ Him
329:1 heavens $d\cdot$ the glory

declared
176:2 the Word that $d\cdot$ it;
188:1 nor tongue $d\cdot$,

declaring
204:3 to all men $d\cdot$.

declining
313:1 comfort seems $d\cdot$,

decree
327:2 saved by His $d\cdot$;
328:2 saved by His $d\cdot$;

deed
160:2 in thought and $d\cdot$—
161:2 in thought and $d\cdot$—
162:2 in thought and $d\cdot$—
189:2 faithful word and $d\cdot$.
197:2 word and $d\cdot$ attested.
198:2 word and $d\cdot$ attested.

deed
217:2 each kindly $d\cdot$ a prayer.
226:3 word and $d\cdot$ Thy truths
246:2 word and $d\cdot$ declare Him
298:4 Truth in thought and $d\cdot$;
299:4 Truth in thought and $d\cdot$;
300:4 Truth in thought and $d\cdot$;
301:4 Truth in thought and $d\cdot$;
302:4 Truth in thought and $d\cdot$;
303:1 slightest word or $d\cdot$,

deeds
48:2 Upon his thoughts or $d\cdot$?
230:3 words are less than $d\cdot$;
231:3 words are less than $d\cdot$;
259:3 $d\cdot$ of peace and love
269:3 may our $d\cdot$ our pure
270:3 may our $d\cdot$ our pure
296:3 rest not, do the $d\cdot$

deem
303:1 Nor $d\cdot$ it void

deemed
190:3 Things $d\cdot$ impossible I
191:3 Things $d\cdot$ impossible I

deep
111:2 are a mighty $d\cdot$.
130:2 are a mighty $d\cdot$,
131:2 indwelling, $d\cdot$ and broad,
132:2 indwelling, $d\cdot$ and broad,
134:3 Embosomed $d\cdot$ in Thy
188:2 whose Spirit searcheth $d\cdot$
222:1 $d\cdot$ and dreamless sleep
223:1 $d\cdot$ and dreamless sleep
260:1 $d\cdot$ it is and broad,
276:2 with Thy $d\cdot$ consolations,
277:2 with Thy $d\cdot$ consolations,
315:3 the heart's $d\cdot$ well;
316:3 the heart's $d\cdot$ well;
332:1 earnest $d\cdot$ desire

deepens
8:1 The darkness $d\cdot$;

deeper
49:1 In $d\cdot$ reverence, praise.
50:1 In $d\cdot$ reverence, praise.
57:3 learn life's $d\cdot$ meaning,
109:2 may $d\cdot$ consecration
110:2 may $d\cdot$ consecration
342:2 the higher, $d\cdot$ ways

deepest
95:2 scenes of $d\cdot$ gloom,

deeply
356:3 our $d\cdot$ grateful praise;

deeps
372:1 search the lowest $d\cdot$,
373:1 search the lowest $d\cdot$,

defender
389:1 my help and $d\cdot$,
392:4 meek and bold $d\cdot$
393:4 meek and bold $d\cdot$

defense
80:1 our refuge and $d\cdot$,
99:2 be thy strong $d\cdot$.
100:2 be thy strong $d\cdot$.
361:1 He is thy sole $d\cdot$;

deferred
207:3 hope $d\cdot$, ingratitude,
208:3 hope $d\cdot$, ingratitude,
209:3 hope $d\cdot$, ingratitude,
210:3 hope $d\cdot$, ingratitude,
211:3 hope $d\cdot$, ingratitude,
212:3 hope $d\cdot$, ingratitude,

defiance
10:1 bid our foes $d\cdot$.
411:1 bid our foes $d\cdot$.

define
91:3 Thee $d\cdot$ In tender
422:3 Thee $d\cdot$ In tender
206:1 eyes undimmed $d\cdot$
428:1 eyes undimmed $d\cdot$

deigns
217:1 which God $d\cdot$ to bless,

delay
17:2 $D\cdot$ the Prince of Peace?

delays
361:3 naught His hand $d\cdot$;

delight
126:1 one another's peace $d\cdot$,
127:1 one another's peace $d\cdot$,
403:1 one another's peace $d\cdot$,
224:1 I would $d\cdot$ in Thee,
225:1 I would $d\cdot$ in Thee,
329:3 Thee, I take $d\cdot$;

delightful
126:3 in one $d\cdot$ stream,
127:3 in one $d\cdot$ stream,
403:3 in one $d\cdot$ stream,

delighting
240:2 $D\cdot$ in Thy will.
241:2 $D\cdot$ in Thy will.

deliver
265:3 hearts thou shalt $d\cdot$;

delivered
216:1 *D·* by His mighty

deliverer
90:2 Strong *D·*! Strong *D·*!
298:4 Strongest *d·*, friend
299:4 Strongest *d·*, friend
300:4 Strongest *d·*, friend
301:4 Strongest *d·*, friend
302:4 Strongest *d·*, friend
388:2 hail their great *d·*

demanding
174:3 stills all our *d·*,

demons
96:2 casting *d·* out.

deny
325:1 Thyself *d·*,

depart
5:2 *D·* from sin, awake
39:2 from Thee may ne'er *d·*.
94:2 dream of earth *d·*.
195:1 bids fear and doubt *d·*,
303:3 love bid sin *d·*
304:3 White ..., ere they *d·*,
305:3 White ..., ere they *d·*,
306:3 White ..., ere they *d·*,
307:3 White ..., ere they *d·*,
308:3 White ..., ere they *d·*,
309:3 White ..., ere they *d·*,
347:1 mountains may *d·* from
348:1 mountains may *d·* from

depend
224:1 on Thy care *d·*;
225:1 on Thy care *d·*;

depending
396:2 *D·* on his promised
397:2 *D·* on his promised

depends
246:1 who *d·* on Thee,

depths
94:1 its inmost *d·* discerned
102:3 *d·* of error's darkness
103:3 *d·* of error's darkness
372:1 no *d·* can drown:
373:1 no *d·* can drown:

deriving
71:2 *d·* from their banner,

descend
119:2 quickening showers *d·*;

desert (adj.)
33:2 in *d·* wilds thou sleep.

desert (verb)
18:1 *d·* not the right;

design
123:3 *d·* Thy dross to consume
258:2 to God's supreme *d·*.
269:2 change His infinite *d·*?
270:2 change His infinite *d·*?
311:1 for us His wise *d·*.
420:1 for us His wise *d·*.

designs
111:1 darkens Thy *d·*.

desire
49:3 the pulses of *d·*
50:3 the pulses of *d·*
73:2 Every true *d·*
118:1 every high *d·*;
237:3 to Him the heart's *d·*,
269:2 In such *d·* sends up
270:2 In such *d·* sends up
269:3 pure *d·* For growth
270:3 pure *d·* For growth
284:1 heart's sincere *d·*,
285:1 heart's sincere *d·*,
286:1 heart's sincere *d·*,
332:1 deep *d·* for grace,

desires
54:1 the blessing she *d·*,
227:3 faint *d·* to rise,

desolate
40:2 Joy of the *d·*,
77:2 When faint and *d·*:
78:2 When faint and *d·*:

desolation
202:3 give thee joy for *d·*,
412:2 give thee joy for *d·*,

despair
303:4 Work and *d·* not;

despite
228:3 meet the low *d·*

despoil
236:2 man's spirit *d·*,

destroy
144:2 sense we must *d·*,
145:2 sense we must *d·*,
363:4 to bless but not *d·*;

destroyed
200:3 foe is *d·* that enslaved
342:3 For sin *d·*, for sorrow

detain
415:1 Do not *d·* me,

dew
141:2 by a heavenly *d·*
218:1 wet with Thy *d·*,
219:1 wet with Thy *d·*,
220:1 wet with Thy *d·*,
317:2 calm *d·* and freshness
322:2 dwell as heavenly *d·*,
323:2 dwell as heavenly *d·*,

dews
49:4 Drop Thy still *d·*
50:4 Drop Thy still *d·*

did
166:2 Think what Jesus *d·*
167:2 Think what Jesus *d·*

die
163:2 sin shall *d·* away.
337:1 Truth ... can never *d·*.
338:1 Truth ... can never *d·*.

dies
183:2 thing that never *d·*,
184:2 thing that never *d·*,

differing
230:2 *d·* phrase we pray;
231:2 *d·* phrase we pray;

dim
20:2 dispels the shadows *d·*.
416:2 dispels the shadows *d·*.
148:2 sight is never *d·*;
149:2 above the shadows *d·*,
426:2 above the shadows *d·*,
230:2 *d·* or clear, we own
231:2 *d·* or clear, we own
258:3 behind the *d·* unknown
332:2 understanding never *d·*,

dimly
230:2 we *d·* see,
231:2 we *d·* see,

dims
370:2 *D·* the radiant peace
383:1 *d·* thy sense of truth

dire
236:2 No more let *d·* hate

directing
115:2 Follow wholly Thy *d·*,
116:2 Follow wholly Thy *d·*,

direction
85:3 take at Thy *d·*,

disappear
108:3 the symbols $d\cdot$;
170:2 outward symbols $d\cdot$
243:3 and harshness $d\cdot$
244:3 and harshness $d\cdot$
382:3 Vain dreams shall $d\cdot$

disappears
335:1 The darkness $d\cdot$;

discerned
94:1 its inmost depths $d\cdot$

disciple
325:1 thou wouldst my $d\cdot$ be ;

disconsolate
40:1 Come, ye $d\cdot$, where'er

discord
9:4 bids all $d\cdot$ cease,
136:2 $d\cdot$ cross my path
179:3 Love bids all $d\cdot$ cease.
267:3 But never $d\cdot$, strife.
268:3 But never $d\cdot$, strife.
374:2 not the author Of $d\cdot$,
375:2 not the author Of $d\cdot$,

disdain
207:3 ingratitude, $d\cdot$!
208:3 ingratitude, $d\cdot$!
209:3 ingratitude, $d\cdot$!
210:3 ingratitude, $d\cdot$!
211:3 ingratitude, $d\cdot$!
212:3 ingratitude, $d\cdot$!

disease
168:4 Which cured $d\cdot$,

disloyalty
86:4 doubt would be $d\cdot$,
87:4 doubt would be $d\cdot$,

dismayed
33:1 nor ever be $d\cdot$.
123:2 O be not $d\cdot$, For I
148:1 can I be $d\cdot$?

dispel
240:1 $D\cdot$ the gloomy shades
241:1 $D\cdot$ the gloomy shades

dispels
20:2 Truth $d\cdot$ the shadows
416:2 Truth $d\cdot$ the shadows
130:1 Word $d\cdot$ all blindness.
139:2 He $d\cdot$ the clouds
427:2 He $d\cdot$ the clouds

dispense
388:3 with willing hands $d\cdot$

displaces
2:1 beam of Truth $d\cdot$

display
35:3 more thyself $d\cdot$,
39:2 Truth to us $d\cdot$,
240:2 to our eyes $d\cdot$
241:2 to our eyes $d\cdot$
334:2 such a bright $d\cdot$

displayed
1:1 be on earth $d\cdot$,

dissolved
278:3 His love hath $d\cdot$ it,
279:3 His love hath $d\cdot$ it,

dissolving
336:3 amid $d\cdot$ spheres,

distant
169:1 see The $d\cdot$ scene ;
196:1 many a $d\cdot$ shore,

distress
114:3 to comfort in $d\cdot$,
280:3 our fathers in $d\cdot$;

distrust
291:1 From $d\cdot$ and envy free,

divided
135:1 know no life $d\cdot$,
264:2 We are not $d\cdot$,

divides
196:2 all that now $d\cdot$ us

Divine
267:4 O, Perfect and $D\cdot$,
268:4 O, Perfect and $D\cdot$,

divine
4:2 In sympathy $d\cdot$,
7:3 O Love $d\cdot$, abiding
12:2 Word ... is power $d\cdot$.
13:2 Word ... is power $d\cdot$.
14:3 Obscure the light $d\cdot$,
15:3 radiance all $d\cdot$.
29:2 meekness all $d\cdot$,
30:5 Fed by Thy love $d\cdot$
31:5 Fed by Thy love $d\cdot$
32:5 Fed by Thy love $d\cdot$
35:3 Fill me, radiancy $d\cdot$,
44:3 In this $d\cdot$ abode,
51:1 that fashions is $d\cdot$,
52:1 that fashions is $d\cdot$,
86:3 blest is he who can $d\cdot$
87:3 blest is he who can $d\cdot$
91:1 O Love $d\cdot$,
422:1 O Love $d\cdot$,

divine
91:2, 3 Thou Love $d\cdot$,
422:2, 3 Thou Love $d\cdot$,
97:1 an influence all $d\cdot$.
98:1 an influence all $d\cdot$.
104:4 our Spirit, Mind $d\cdot$,
114:1 Holy Bible, book $d\cdot$,
118:1 Holy Spirit, Light $d\cdot$,
2 Holy Spirit, Peace $d\cdot$,
3 Holy Spirit, all $d\cdot$,
142:3 Shine out, O light $d\cdot$,
144:1 atmosphere of Love $d\cdot$,
145:1 atmosphere of Love $d\cdot$,
149:1 In Love $d\cdot$ all
426:1 In Love $d\cdot$ all
163:1 O what power $d\cdot$
172:1 that great Light $d\cdot$,
175:1 Truth $d\cdot$, that overcometh
2 Love $d\cdot$, ... faileth never,
2 Life $d\cdot$, Thy Word
206:1 in Thy radiancy $d\cdot$
428:1 in Thy radiancy $d\cdot$
207:1 O Life $d\cdot$, that owns
208:1 O Life $d\cdot$, that owns
209:1 O Life $d\cdot$, that owns
210:1 O Life $d\cdot$, that owns
211:1 O Life $d\cdot$, that owns
212:1 O Life $d\cdot$, that owns
228:1 Love $d\cdot$, that dwells
229:1 Love $d\cdot$, whose constant
237:2 Love $d\cdot$ its promise
238:2 common, daily life $d\cdot$,
239:2 common, daily life $d\cdot$,
243:3 grace of Love $d\cdot$
244:3 grace of Love $d\cdot$
247:3 task $d\cdot$ ye still shall
248:3 task $d\cdot$ ye still shall
251:2 art the gift $d\cdot$,
252:2 art the gift $d\cdot$,
263:1 Joy $d\cdot$ shall never
269:2 Mind, Intelligence $d\cdot$;
270:2 Mind, Intelligence $d\cdot$;
269:3 know how Love $d\cdot$
270:3 know how Love $d\cdot$
293:1-3 Rock of Ages, Truth $d\cdot$,
294:1-3 Rock of Ages, Truth $d\cdot$,
295:1-3 Rock of Ages, Truth $d\cdot$,
297:3 Love's law $d\cdot$
298:4 Life of all being $d\cdot$:
299:4 Life of all being $d\cdot$:
300:4 Life of all being $d\cdot$:
301:4 Life of all being $d\cdot$:
302:4 Life of all being $d\cdot$:
311:1 lit by Love $d\cdot$
420:1 lit by Love $d\cdot$
320:4 path of life $d\cdot$;
321:4 path of life $d\cdot$;
409:4 path of life $d\cdot$;

divine
336:2 truth $d \cdot$ and precepts
352:1 how beauteous, how $d \cdot$,
353:1 how beauteous, how $d \cdot$,
356:1 To Love $d \cdot$, in whom
363:1 its brightness more $d \cdot$.
374:2 Love $d \cdot$, we thank Thee
375:2 Love $d \cdot$, we thank Thee
376:1 Love $d \cdot$, that helps us
377:1 Love $d \cdot$, that helps us
386:2 doctrine all $d \cdot$.
387:2 doctrine all $d \cdot$.
391:4 "one far-off $d \cdot$ event"

divinely
30:3 that Love, $d \cdot$ near,
31:3 that Love, $d \cdot$ near,
32:3 that Love, $d \cdot$ near,
51:2 The form $d \cdot$ fair.
52:2 The form $d \cdot$ fair.
149:3 complete, $d \cdot$ fair.
426:3 complete, $d \cdot$ fair.
233:3 of Truth $d \cdot$ bright,
419:3 of Truth $d \cdot$ bright,
253:4 and tenderly, $D \cdot$ talk.
254:4 and tenderly, $D \cdot$ talk.
255:4 and tenderly, $D \cdot$ talk.
256:4 and tenderly, $D \cdot$ talk.
257:4 and tenderly, $D \cdot$ talk.

do
12:1 His works shall $d \cdot$,
13:1 His works shall $d \cdot$,
19:2 They $d \cdot$ His will,
41:3 may $d \cdot$ service here;
82:2 What can we $d \cdot$
95:1 Whate'er I $d \cdot$,
151:2 To $d \cdot$ Thy will is
152:2 To $d \cdot$ Thy will is
166:1 Something still to $d \cdot$,
167:1 Something still to $d \cdot$,
183:1 haste, O man, to $d \cdot$
184:1 haste, O man, to $d \cdot$
230:3 To $d \cdot$ Thy will is
231:3 To $d \cdot$ Thy will is
242:3 $d \cdot$ Thy will we come,
253:7 some daily good to $d \cdot$
254:7 some daily good to $d \cdot$
255:7 some daily good to $d \cdot$
256:7 some daily good to $d \cdot$
257:7 some daily good to $d \cdot$
269:3 seek Thy will to $d \cdot$,
270:3 seek Thy will to $d \cdot$,
296:3 rest not, $d \cdot$ the deeds
315:1 good we may $d \cdot$ here.
316:1 good we may $d \cdot$ here.
332:1 wait to $d \cdot$ His will.
354:3 works in us to $d \cdot$;

do
394:2 work they have to $d \cdot$.
395:2 work they have to $d \cdot$.
414:1 nothing else can $d \cdot$.

doctrine
12:1 Above all $d \cdot$, form or
13:1 Above all $d \cdot$, form or
264:2 One in hope and $d \cdot$,
386:2 prove the $d \cdot$ all divine.
387:2 prove the $d \cdot$ all divine.

dogmas
337:1 Creeds and $d \cdot$ all may
338:1 Creeds and $d \cdot$ all may

doing
18:1 Then up and be $d \cdot$,
96:2 $d \cdot$ good And casting
217:3 holy work was $d \cdot$ good;

doings
361:2 all His $d \cdot$ ponder,

dominion
12:3 given $d \cdot$ unto man,
13:3 given $d \cdot$ unto man,
48:3 have $D \cdot$ over all.
66:3 Joy and $d \cdot$, love
421:3 Joy and $d \cdot$, love
112:1 Yield ... to Love's $d \cdot$.
181:4 have no more $d \cdot$.
370:1 Of $d \cdot$ over evil:
382:4 $D \cdot$ over all.

done
51:3 God's will is $d \cdot$;
52:3 God's will is $d \cdot$;
65:3 things He hath $d \cdot$,
101:2 dream of sorrow $d \cdot$;
153:2 $d \cdot$ to me great things,
157:1 God's will be $d \cdot$.
183:1 Whatever must be $d \cdot$;
184:1 Whatever must be $d \cdot$;
190:1-3 Thy will be $d \cdot$.
191:1-3 Thy will be $d \cdot$.
190:4 Thy will is $d \cdot$.
191:4 Thy will is $d \cdot$.
199:1 wondrous things hath $d \cdot$,
216:2 His will is $d \cdot$ and
246:2 God's will is $d \cdot$, and
290:3 His word, Well $d \cdot$!
312:2 having all things $d \cdot$,
349:1 Thine alone be ever $d \cdot$;
390:2 shall be $d \cdot$ for thee.

doomed
236:1 Gaunt warfare is $d \cdot$,

door
64:2 reach Mind's open $d \cdot$,
222:2 holds wide the $d \cdot$,
223:2 holds wide the $d \cdot$,
304:2 enter by the $d \cdot$,
305:2 enter by the $d \cdot$,
306:2 enter by the $d \cdot$,
307:2 enter by the $d \cdot$,
308:2 enter by the $d \cdot$,
309:2 enter by the $d \cdot$,
392:3 $d \cdot$ of Life unseals
393:3 $d \cdot$ of Life unseals

doors
345:1 the sunless prison $d \cdot$;

doth
160:5 Who $d \cdot$ His will—
161:5 Who $d \cdot$ His will—
162:5 Who $d \cdot$ His will—

doubt
9:4 sorrow, $d \cdot$ and fear,
29:1 Black with error, $d \cdot$,
86:4 $d \cdot$ would be disloyalty,
87:4 $d \cdot$ would be disloyalty,
121:3 faith unmixed with $d \cdot$
122:3 faith unmixed with $d \cdot$
195:1 fear and $d \cdot$ depart,
205:2 In darkness feels no $d \cdot$;
232:1 turn from $d \cdot$ and fear !
406:1 turn from $d \cdot$ and fear !
238:3 Through clouds of $d \cdot$
239:3 Through clouds of $d \cdot$
314:1 To $d \cdot$ and fear give
347:2 tossed with $d \cdot$,
348:2 tossed with $d \cdot$,
351:1 night of $d \cdot$ and sorrow
368:3 $D \cdot$ and terror are with-
      drawn;
369:3 $D \cdot$ and terror are with-
      drawn;

doubted
115:1 $d \cdot$, sent us light;
116:1 $d \cdot$, sent us light;

doubts
41:3 Away with gloomy $d \cdot$
133:2 dread and $d \cdot$ reprove;
424:2 dread and $d \cdot$ reprove;
138:2 and $d \cdot$ remove;

dove
30:1 that doth wound the $d \cdot$
31:1 that doth wound the $d \cdot$
32:1 that doth wound the $d \cdot$
44:2 The spirit of the $d \cdot$.
297:3 $d \cdot$ may close her faltering
346:3 Life-giving, holy $d \cdot$,
401:3 Life-giving, holy $d \cdot$,

down
104:4 The cross laid $d\cdot$;
157:1 $d\cdot$ through all the
192:2 the sun gone $d\cdot$,
193:2 the sun gone $d\cdot$,
197:1 sweeping $d\cdot$ the years
198:1 sweeping $d\cdot$ the years
207:5 No night drops $d\cdot$
208:5 No night drops $d\cdot$
209:5 No night drops $d\cdot$
210:5 No night drops $d\cdot$
211:5 No night drops $d\cdot$
212:5 No night drops $d\cdot$
234:4 Far $d\cdot$ the future's
235:4 Far $d\cdot$ the future's
258:2 serenely $d\cdot$ the future
288:2 be not cast $d\cdot$.
289:2 be not cast $d\cdot$.
290:1 each temptation $d\cdot$,
312:2 powers of darkness $d\cdot$,
326:4 and hell he tramples $d\cdot$,
372:1 the Lord Christ $d\cdot$;
373:1 the Lord Christ $d\cdot$;

drag
360:1 thy steps $d\cdot$ wearily ?

draweth
398:2 The bridegroom $d\cdot$ near.

drawing
82:1 the time is $d\cdot$ near ;
418:1 thy shores are $d\cdot$ near,

drawn
4:2 we be never $d\cdot$ apart,
138:3 blinding veils are $d\cdot$,

draws
41:2 Harvest $d\cdot$ nigh.
64:3 its goal $d\cdot$ nearer,
82:1 nearer $d\cdot$ the time,

dread
33:3 $d\cdot$ no hidden snare ;
133:2 conquer $d\cdot$ and doubts
424:2 conquer $d\cdot$ and doubts
388:2 grave could hold no $d\cdot$,
399:1 clouds ye so much $d\cdot$
400:1 clouds ye so much $d\cdot$

dreads
143:1 $d\cdot$ the piercing eye ;

dream
94:2 every $d\cdot$ of earth
101:2 $d\cdot$ of sorrow done ;
138:1 To break the $d\cdot$
229:1 bless us while we $d\cdot$,
296:3 break the earthly $d\cdot$.

dream
359:1 seem so like a $d\cdot$;
392:1 darkness and the $d\cdot$,
393:1 darkness and the $d\cdot$,

dreamer
202:1 O $d\cdot$, leave thy dreams
412:1 O $d\cdot$, leave thy dreams

dreamless
222:1 thy deep and $d\cdot$ sleep
223:1 thy deep and $d\cdot$ sleep

dreams
6:1 not in the realm of $d\cdot$,
188:3 sad with $d\cdot$ of death.
192:2 Yet in my $d\cdot$ I'd be
193:2 Yet in my $d\cdot$ I'd be
202:1 leave thy $d\cdot$ for joyful
412:1 leave thy $d\cdot$ for joyful
202:1 all $d\cdot$ of error breaking,
412:1 all $d\cdot$ of error breaking,
242:2 no more in $d\cdot$
382:3 Vain $d\cdot$ shall disappear

drear
154:1 earth-clouds $d\cdot$ and wild.
155:1 earth-clouds $d\cdot$ and wild.
156:1 earth-clouds $d\cdot$ and wild.
265:1 seem $d\cdot$ and lone ;
287:3 $d\cdot$ and gloomy night ;
408:3 $d\cdot$ and gloomy night ;

dreary
97:2 prospect seem most $d\cdot$,
98:2 prospect seem most $d\cdot$,
394:1 from its $d\cdot$ night
395:1 from its $d\cdot$ night
415:2 country so dark and $d\cdot$,

dress
372:3 healing of the seamless $d\cdot$
373:2 healing of the seamless $d\cdot$

dried
54:2 $d\cdot$ the bitter tear.
182:2 seem parched and $d\cdot$.
224:1 material streams are $d\cdot$,
225:1 material streams are $d\cdot$,

drifting
37:4 vain the $d\cdot$ sands ;
38:4 vain the $d\cdot$ sands ;

drink
104:2 strength to $d\cdot$ Thy cup
108:2 $d\cdot$ anew the royal wine

drop
49:4 $D\cdot$ Thy still dews
50:4 $D\cdot$ Thy still dews

drop
124:3 I $d\cdot$ my burden
402:3 I $d\cdot$ my burden

dropped
315:3 $D\cdot$ in the heart's deep
316:3 $D\cdot$ in the heart's deep

drops
207:5 No night $d\cdot$ down
208:5 No night $d\cdot$ down
209:5 No night $d\cdot$ down
210:5 No night $d\cdot$ down
211:5 No night $d\cdot$ down
212:5 No night $d\cdot$ down

dross
123:3 Thy $d\cdot$ to consume

drown
372:1 him no depths can $d\cdot$:
373:1 him no depths can $d\cdot$:

due
113:3 praise to Thee is $d\cdot$;
171:3 God the honor $d\cdot$,
413:3 God the honor $d\cdot$,

duly
314:2 It $d\cdot$ shall appear

dumb
49:3 Let sense be $d\cdot$,
50:3 Let sense be $d\cdot$,
202:4 the $d\cdot$ to joyful singing ;
412:2 the $d\cdot$ to joyful singing ;
384:3 the $d\cdot$ shall sing,
418:4 notes will all be $d\cdot$,

during
204:3 And $d\cdot$ the battle

duties
258:2 occasions teach new $d\cdot$,

duty
18:1 Thy $d\cdot$ pursuing,
345:2 finding all our $d\cdot$,
361:3 lights the way of $d\cdot$,

duty's
6:2 From $d\cdot$ claims
390:1 back at $d\cdot$ call ?

dwell
33:1 secret habitation $D\cdot$,
62:1 $d\cdot$ below the skies
63:1 $d\cdot$ below the skies
83:3 children $d\cdot$ in peace,
88:1 Gracious Spirit, $d\cdot$ with
89:1 Gracious Spirit, $d\cdot$ with

dwell
88:2 Truthful Spirit, $d\cdot$ with
89:2 Truthful Spirit, $d\cdot$ with
88:3 Mighty Spirit, $d\cdot$ with
89:3 Mighty Spirit, $d\cdot$ with
100:1 $d\cdot$ beneath th'Almighty's
113:1 dost $d\cdot$ in light;
118:3 $D\cdot$ within this heart
124:2 saints securely $d\cdot$;
402:2 saints securely $d\cdot$;
157:3 $d\cdot$ in joy and peace.
196:1 all shall $d\cdot$ together,
203:2 all Thy children $d\cdot$
226:3 light, within us $d\cdot$,
228:2 in Thee we $d\cdot$,
271:2 $D\cdot$ on His love
272:2 $D\cdot$ on His love

dwell
303:2 $d\cdot$ Within it silently.
322:2 $d\cdot$ as heavenly dew,
323:2 $d\cdot$ as heavenly dew,
367:4 by grace shall $d\cdot$
384:1 with men to $d\cdot$,

dwellest
227:2 $D\cdot$ with them of humble

dwelleth
21:3 loveth not $d\cdot$ in night.
22:3 loveth not $d\cdot$ in night.

dwelling
44:2 Fear hath no $d\cdot$ here;
58:3 In Thy house securely $d\cdot$,
93:3 $D\cdot$ in Love that

dwelling
99:3 $D\cdot$ within His secret
100:3 $D\cdot$ within His secret

dwellings
125:1 lovely are Thy $d\cdot$, Lord,

dwells
34:2 Who $d\cdot$ with Love
166:2 spirit $d\cdot$ within thee;
167:2 spirit $d\cdot$ within thee;
217:2 where love $d\cdot$, the peace
228:1 divine, that $d\cdot$ serene,
367:2 Who $d\cdot$ in cloudless

dying
381:2 Christ, undimmed by $d\cdot$,
415:3 there, nor any $d\cdot$:

E

each
29:1 $e\cdot$ somber shadow,
34:3 $e\cdot$ empty cup is filled;
41:1 to $e\cdot$ servant does
42:1 $e\cdot$ heart Thy grace
67:2 mark $e\cdot$ warrior's way;
68:2 mark $e\cdot$ warrior's way;
69:3 $e\cdot$ wound and smart
423:3 $e\cdot$ wound and smart
71:2 Round $e\cdot$ habitation
93:1 $E\cdot$ day, complete,
94:2 $e\cdot$ worthier thought
105:1 $e\cdot$ his friendly aid
106:1 $e\cdot$ his friendly aid
107:1 $e\cdot$ his friendly aid
108:2 $e\cdot$ earthly load,
126:2 $E\cdot$ can his brother's
127:2 $E\cdot$ can his brother's
403:2 $E\cdot$ can his brother's
140:2 heaven in $e\cdot$ we see;
   3 $e\cdot$ returning day,
143:3 $e\cdot$ evasive art,
146:3 hails $e\cdot$ task,
147:3 hails $e\cdot$ task,
176:3 $e\cdot$ in his place,
203:1 may we bear $e\cdot$ hour
207:1 owns $e\cdot$ waiting hour,
208:1 owns $e\cdot$ waiting hour,
209:1 owns $e\cdot$ waiting hour,
210:1 owns $e\cdot$ waiting hour,
211:1 owns $e\cdot$ waiting hour,
212:1 owns $e\cdot$ waiting hour,
214:2 Round $e\cdot$ with all,
217:2 $E\cdot$ smile a hymn, $e\cdot$
   kindly deed a prayer.

each
217:3 $E\cdot$ loving life a psalm
221:2 Within $e\cdot$ heart is
236:1 hope in $e\cdot$ breast,
247:3 $E\cdot$ task divine ye still
248:3 $E\cdot$ task divine ye still
258:1 Shows to $e\cdot$ the bloom
260:2 $E\cdot$ morn unfolds His
278:1 $e\cdot$ step of the way.
279:1 $e\cdot$ step of the way.
290:1 treading $e\cdot$ temptation
303:1 $e\cdot$ wind-wafted seed
329:1 $E\cdot$ day repeats
   1 $E\cdot$ night its tribute
335:1 $E\cdot$ breeze that sweeps
336:2 In $e\cdot$ a heavenly beam
398:1 $E\cdot$ in his office wait,
414:2 $e\cdot$ time I tell

each other
   4:3 nearer to $e\cdot$ $o\cdot$
105:1 help $e\cdot$ $o\cdot$, Lord,
106:1 help $e\cdot$ $o\cdot$, Lord,
107:1 help $e\cdot$ $o\cdot$, Lord,
105:2 to build $e\cdot$ $o\cdot$ up,
106:2 to build $e\cdot$ $o\cdot$ up,
107:2 to build $e\cdot$ $o\cdot$ up,
217:2 is to love $e\cdot$ $o\cdot$;
266:2 to love $e\cdot$ $o\cdot$, Lord,

each other's
105:1 $E\cdot$ $o\cdot$ cross to bear,
106:1 $E\cdot$ $o\cdot$ cross to bear,
107:1 $E\cdot$ $o\cdot$ cross to bear,

eager
58:2 $E\cdot$ ears, expectant,

eagles
246:1 On wings of $e\cdot$ he,

ear
54:2 Unheard by human $e\cdot$,
175:1 every listening $e\cdot$.
222:3 No $e\cdot$ may hear
223:3 No $e\cdot$ may hear
314:2 the stalk, the $e\cdot$;

early
117:1 $E\cdot$ in the morning
215:1 His $e\cdot$, only choice.
271:2 $e\cdot$ blessings on His
272:2 $e\cdot$ blessings on His

earnest
276:1 the $e\cdot$ of salvation;
277:1 the $e\cdot$ of salvation;
332:1 An $e\cdot$ deep desire
351:2 $e\cdot$ looking forward,

ears
58:2 Eager $e\cdot$, expectant,

earth
1:1 be on $e\cdot$ displayed,
2:1 o'er the waking $e\cdot$
   3 Upon the startled $e\cdot$.
5:1 call to rise from $e\cdot$;
9:1 on the $e\cdot$ be peace,
11:1 With music all the $e\cdot$,
34:3 storms of $e\cdot$
36:1 voices of this $e\cdot$
   2 the words of $e\cdot$,
   3 restless eyes of $e\cdot$

earth
40:1-3 $E\cdot$ has no sorrow
45:1 Through all the $e\cdot$
2 abroad o'er all the $e\cdot$;
51:3 heaven and $e\cdot$ approve.
52:3 heaven and $e\cdot$ approve.
56:1 best that $e\cdot$ imparts,
66:4 new heaven and $e\cdot$
421:4 new heaven and $e\cdot$
72:1 Peace on $e\cdot$ to man
405:1 Peace on $e\cdot$ to man
74:1 $e\cdot$ to open wide;
75:2 Upon the thirsty $e\cdot$;
82:1, 2 $e\cdot$ shall be filled
3 $e\cdot$ may be filled
83:3 newborn $e\cdot$ record
86:1 of all things on $e\cdot$,
87:1 of all things on $e\cdot$,
94:2 every dream of $e\cdot$
104:2 Thy cup on $e\cdot$
117:3 $e\cdot$, and sky and sea;
120:2 Behold, O $e\cdot$,
141:4 All the $e\cdot$ to worship
142:3 mists of $e\cdot$ away.
146:2 all the paths of $e\cdot$,
147:2 all the paths of $e\cdot$,
158:1 bending near the $e\cdot$,
159:1 bending near the $e\cdot$,
158:1 peace on $e\cdot$, good will
159:1 peace on $e\cdot$, good will
158:3 heaven and $e\cdot$ shall own
159:3 heaven and $e\cdot$ shall own
163:1 transform our $e\cdot$ to
heaven.
164:1 $e\cdot$ receive her King;
165:1 $e\cdot$ receive her King;
417:1 $e\cdot$ receive her King;
168:1 $e\cdot$ with songs rejoice;
171:2 turn from $e\cdot$ to Spirit,
413:2 turn from $e\cdot$ to Spirit,
176:3 wide $e\cdot$ enlightens.
204:1 is come upon $e\cdot$,
213:2 $e\cdot$ received her frame,
217:3 the wide $e\cdot$ seem
218:1 blooming $e\cdot$, the thoughts
219:1 blooming $e\cdot$, the thoughts
220:1 blooming $e\cdot$, the thoughts
222:2 peace to men on $e\cdot$;
223:2 peace to men on $e\cdot$;
246:Ref. of heaven and $e\cdot$,
271:4 $e\cdot$ repeat the long Amen.
272:4 $e\cdot$ repeat the long Amen.
275:1 Maker of $e\cdot$ and heaven;
278:1 Pilgrim on $e\cdot$,
279:1 Pilgrim on $e\cdot$,
282:2 Heaven and $e\cdot$, and
310:1 come again to $e\cdot$,
1, 2 Peace on $e\cdot$, good will

earth
310:2 Dawns on $e\cdot$
327:1 both heaven and $e\cdot$
328:1 both heaven and $e\cdot$
332:1 all the $e\cdot$ be still,
335:1 sons of $e\cdot$ are waking
336:3 heaven and $e\cdot$ have past
349:2 peace on $e\cdot$ from heaven
362:1 tribes of $e\cdot$ obey,
368:2 bursts o'er all the $e\cdot$.
369:2 bursts o'er all the $e\cdot$.
384:3 through all the $e\cdot$

earth-born
23:5 cruel creed, or $e\cdot$ taint:
24:5 cruel creed, or $e\cdot$ taint:
25:5 cruel creed, or $e\cdot$ taint:
26:5 cruel creed, or $e\cdot$ taint:
27:5 cruel creed, or $e\cdot$ taint:
28:5 cruel creed, or $e\cdot$ taint:
30:3 pride and $e\cdot$ fear,
31:3 pride and $e\cdot$ fear,
32:3 pride and $e\cdot$ fear,
149:1 $e\cdot$ fear and sorrow
426:1 $e\cdot$ fear and sorrow

earth-bound
66:4 Break $e\cdot$ fetters,
421:4 Break $e\cdot$ fetters,
160:5 the $e\cdot$ wake, God's
161:5 the $e\cdot$ wake, God's
162:5 the $e\cdot$ wake, God's
265:3 $E\cdot$ hearts thou shalt

earth-clouds
154:1 lose the $e\cdot$ drear
155:1 lose the $e\cdot$ drear
156:1 lose the $e\cdot$ drear

earthly
76:1 all $e\cdot$ friends betray
79:3 He with $e\cdot$ cares
108:2 aside each $e\cdot$ load,
151:2 $e\cdot$ thought released,
152:2 $e\cdot$ thought released,
174:2 all $e\cdot$ loss is gain;
205:1 Of any $e\cdot$ woe;
237:3 find our $e\cdot$ longings
267:4 seek no $e\cdot$ shrine
268:4 seek no $e\cdot$ shrine
296:3 break the $e\cdot$ dream.

earthquake
49:3 Speak through the $e\cdot$,
50:3 Speak through the $e\cdot$,

earth's
53:3 From $e\cdot$ fears
172:2 $e\cdot$ restless tides,
185:3 Through all $e\cdot$ valleys

earth's
203:2 through $e\cdot$ shade,
207:5 $e\cdot$ tear-drops gain,
208:5 $e\cdot$ tear-drops gain,
209:5 $e\cdot$ tear-drops gain,
210:5 $e\cdot$ tear-drops gain,
211:5 $e\cdot$ tear-drops gain,
212:5 $e\cdot$ tear-drops gain,
236:4 $e\cdot$ treasures above.
251:1 light of $e\cdot$ dark sky,
252:1 light of $e\cdot$ dark sky,
253:4 $e\cdot$ troubled, angry sea
254:4 $e\cdot$ troubled, angry sea
255:4 $e\cdot$ troubled, angry sea
256:4 $e\cdot$ troubled, angry sea
257:4 $e\cdot$ troubled, angry sea
304:2 Break $e\cdot$ stupid rest.
305:2 Break $e\cdot$ stupid rest.
306:2 Break $e\cdot$ stupid rest.
307:2 Break $e\cdot$ stupid rest.
308:2 Break $e\cdot$ stupid rest.
309:2 Break $e\cdot$ stupid rest.
329:1 To $e\cdot$ remotest border
346:3 in $e\cdot$ darkest place
401:3 in $e\cdot$ darkest place
379:4 $e\cdot$ tempting vanities,
380:4 $e\cdot$ tempting vanities,

ease
34:2 with Love hath perfect $e\cdot$,
55:1 Not for $e\cdot$ that prayer
183:3 $e\cdot$ and self away;
184:3 $e\cdot$ and self away;
242:2 selfish $e\cdot$ we lie,

east
215:2 $e\cdot$ or west unfold;

Easter
171:1 sing of $E\cdot$ gladness
413:1 sing of $E\cdot$ gladness
171:1 glory of an $E\cdot$
413:1 glory of an $E\cdot$
171:3 will be an $E\cdot$
413:3 will be an $E\cdot$

eastern
11:1 in the $e\cdot$ sky Saw

Eastertide
171:3 Of his wondrous $E\cdot$;
413:3 Of his wondrous $E\cdot$;

ebbing
142:1 A never $e\cdot$ sea,—

echoes
94:3 heavenly $e\cdot$ never cease.
157:1 $E\cdot$ down through all

eclipse
228:1 life has no e,

Eden's
95:2 where E bowers bloom,

e'en
79:2 E the hour that
192:1 E though it be a cross
193:1 E though it be a cross
203:2 E though we wander
205:3 We taste e here
283:2 E while we sleep
345:2 radiance e to us
374:1 e before we ask Thee
375:1 e before we ask Thee
379:1 E himself doth count
380:1 E himself doth count

e'er
10:2 doth e surround us.
411:2 doth e surround us.
16:2 praise must e increase,
186:2 being e shall know,
187:2 being e shall know,
189:2 love doth e uphold
204:2 e from their loyalty

effulgence
221:1 Reveal their full e
345:3 where Thine e gloweth,

effulgent
363:2 e more and more.

eloquence
54:1 The e of praise.

else
3:4 Whatever e befall,
361:2 E is thy toil in
414:1 As nothing e can do.

emblem
84:1 E of eternal Love;

embosomed
134:3 E deep in Thy

embound
23:3 replete, by flesh e—
24:3 replete, by flesh e—
25:3 replete, by flesh e—
26:3 replete, by flesh e—
27:3 replete, by flesh e—
28:3 replete, by flesh e—

empire
72:2 Power no e can
405:2 Power no e can

empires
337:3 totter, e crumble,
338:3 totter, e crumble,

employ
97:2 thy thoughts e;
98:2 thy thoughts e;
381:4 love their hands e.

empty
34:3 e cup is filled;
360:2 a well left e?

encamp
77:1 hosts e around me,
78:1 hosts e around me,

encircles
207:2 His arm e me,
208:2 His arm e me,
209:2 His arm e me,
210:2 His arm e me,
211:2 His arm e me,
212:2 His arm e me,

encircling
53:3 Safe in His e arms,
169:1 amid the e gloom,

encompassed
199:2 E by His grace,

encompasseth
65:2 blessing E our way;

end
5:2 E bondage, O be free.
41:4 to the e endure;
43:2 come to e all strife.
75:3 kingdom without e.
263:1 that e in sadness,
275:2 mourning and sorrow e,

endeavor
174:1 hope and courage for e,
265:3 thy trustful, calm e,
283:1 joyous and loving e;

ending
43:1 joy that hath no e,
73:2 all condemnation e,

endless
72:2 E thanks to God
405:2 E thanks to God
83:2 that e happy whole,
213:2 To e years the same.
298:2 glories of one e day."
299:2 glories of one e day."
300:2 glories of one e day."
301:2 glories of one e day."

endless
302:2 glories of one e day."
354:2 Secure in e day.
356:3 through e days.
392:2 e joy betides us.
393:2 e joy betides us.

ends
213:3 watch that e the night

endued
96:2 be with power e
312:2 all His strength e,

endure
41:4 who to the end e;
174:2 Joy must e, Love's
329:2 And ever shall e.
355:1 right, Which shall e.
425: Ref. may e for a night,

endured
325:2 for thee the cross e,

endureth
283:1 His mercy e forever.

energy
320:3 human e shall faint,
321:3 human e shall faint,
409:3 human e shall faint,

enfold
232:2 our lives Thou dost e,
406:2 our lives Thou dost e,
245:3 Thou gently dost e.
371:1 thoughts our lives e,

enfolded
199:2 E in His love.
303:2 e dwell Within it

enfolds
76:1 His arm e thee

engrafted
121:3 Th'e word receive,
122:3 Th'e word receive,

engrounds
253:5 e me on the rock,
254:5 e me on the rock,
255:5 e me on the rock,
256:5 e me on the rock,
257:5 e me on the rock,

enhavened
93:4 E where no storms

enjoy
42:2 all e the blessing

enlightens
176:3 the wide earth *e·*.
329:2 Word the thought *e·*,

enmity
266:2 Can live in *e·*.

enough
169:1 one step *e·* for me.
291:2 *e·* that Thou wilt

enraptured
64:3 Thought soars *e·*,

enshrined
201:2 Where it shall be *e·*.
404:2 Where it shall be *e·*.
367:2 in cloudless light *e·*,

enshroud
245:1 *E·* the way with

enshrouds
23:1 where storm *e·*
24:1 where storm *e·*
25:1 where storm *e·*
26:1 where storm *e·*
27:1 where storm *e·*
28:1 where storm *e·*

enslaved
200:3 foe is destroyed that *e·*
201:2 Your long *e·* mind,
404:2 Your long *e·* mind,

enslaves
112:2 fear no more *e·*

enter
304:2 *e·* by the door,
305:2 *e·* by the door,
306:2 *e·* by the door,
307:2 *e·* by the door,
308:2 *e·* by the door,
309:2 *e·* by the door,
318:2 in this wise *e·* heaven;
392:3 bids us freely *e·*,
393:3 bids us freely *e·*,

entered
188:1 *e·* heart of man,

enters
222:3 dear Christ *e·* in.
223:3 dear Christ *e·* in.
284:3 *e·* heaven with prayer.
285:3 *e·* heaven with prayer.
286:3 *e·* heaven with prayer.

enthrall
5:1 let not fear *e·*.

enthroning
179:3 Conquering hate, *e·* peace,

entreat
204:1 call and *e·* every nation,

entwineth
79:3 with earthly cares *e·*

envy
126:2 free from *e·*, scorn,
127:2 free from *e·*, scorn,
403:2 free from *e·*, scorn,
291:1 distrust and *e·* free,

equal
260:1 *e·* to my every need,—

equity
75:1 And rule in *e·*.

ere
304:3 *e·* they depart,
305:3 *e·* they depart,
306:3 *e·* they depart,
307:3 *e·* they depart,
308:3 *e·* they depart,
309:3 *e·* they depart,

err
399:3 unbelief is sure to *e·*,
400:3 unbelief is sure to *e·*,

erring
315:2 Speak gently to the *e·*
316:2 Speak gently to the *e·*

error
2:2 The advocates of *e·*
29:1 Black with *e·*, doubt,
2 every subtle *e·*,
102:2 every storm of *e·*
103:2 every storm of *e·*
120:1 From *e·* gives release
201:2 will from *e·* free
404:2 will from *e·* free
202:1 dreams of *e·* breaking,
412:1 dreams of *e·* breaking,
267:2 No subtle *e·* creeps;
268:2 No subtle *e·* creeps;
322:2 weeds of *e·* grew.
323:2 weeds of *e·* grew.
376:2 Allured by ways of *e·*,
377:2 Allured by ways of *e·*,

error's
10:2 to *e·* thraldom came,
411:2 to *e·* thraldom came,
74:1 *e·* tempest and its fire
102:3 depths of *e·* darkness
103:3 depths of *e·* darkness
179:1 frees from *e·* thrall,—
382:4 art not *e·* thrall;

errs
48:2 Nor *e·* at all

escaping
195:2 *e·* every snare.

established
347:3 *E·* in His righteousness,
348:3 *E·* in His righteousness,

esteem
126:3 union sweet, and dear *e·*
127:3 union sweet, and dear *e·*
403:3 union sweet, and dear *e·*

eternal
33:3 *e·* safeguard there.
37:4 upon th'*e·* Rock,
38:4 upon th'*e·* Rock,
48:3 *E·* Life and Truth
51:1 *E·* Mind the Potter
52:1 *E·* Mind the Potter
51:1 thought th'*e·* clay:
52:1 thought th'*e·* clay:
62:2 *E·* are Thy mercies,
63:2 *E·* are Thy mercies,
62:2 *E·* truth attends Thy
63:2 *E·* truth attends Thy
71:3 Springing from *e·* Love,
72:2 Goodness one *e·* stream.
405:2 Goodness one *e·* stream.
76:1 God, the true, *e·* good;
84:1 God's *e·* Word
1 Of *e·* might the token,
1 Emblem of *e·* Love;
2 O Word *e·*,
85:1 *e·* good, Lift our
93:2 *E·* Love His holiest
102:3 Into Truth's *e·* day.
103:3 Into Truth's *e·* day.
108:1 Here grasp ... th'*e·* grace,
111:1 *e·* God, Thy goodness
112:3 lives in Life *e·*
113:2 *E·* God, Be Thou
134:1 Thy touch, *e·* Love,
142:4 *E·* Love, remains.
144:2 wonders of *e·* Mind,
145:2 wonders of *e·* Mind,
166:3 Heaven's *e·* day
167:3 Heaven's *e·* day
199:2 From His *e·* care
205:3 Of our *e·* home.
213:1, 4 And our *e·* home.
221:2 Christ, *e·* manhood,
238:1 present wrong, th' *e·*
right;
239:1 present wrong, th' *e·*
right;

44

eternal
245:3 Our blest, e· home.
271:3 weary find e· rest,
272:3 weary find e· rest,
276:1 From th' e· source
277:1 From th' e· source
288:1 to that e· day,
289:1 to that e· day,
312:1 Through His e· Son.
331:3 on e· pillars stand;
340:2 heart of the E·
343:4 Whose joys e· flow.
344:4 Whose joys e· flow.
429:4 Whose joys e· flow.
349:1 The great, e·, Holy
351:3 the far e· shore
355:2 shall see E· rest.
359:1 Trust the E· when the
    2 Trust the E·, for the
    3 Trust the E·, and repent
370:1 this pure e· union
391:3 God lives in e· laws,

eternally
16:2 Love is Life e·,
59:1 joy and crown e·.
60:1 joy and crown e·.
61:1 joy and crown e·.
135:2 frees us From death e·.

eternity
64:3 touch the fringes of e·.
80:2 in e· of light,
175:2 Now and through e·.
186:2 All e· can show,
187:2 All e· can show,
315:3 E· shall tell.
316:3 E· shall tell.
418:1-4 E·! E·!

evasive
143:3 Abhorring each e· art,

eve
34:1 on that e· in Galilee.
314:1 At e· hold not

even (see also e'en)
372:2 sweet, tender, e· yet
373:1 sweet, tender, e· yet

evening
213:3 like an e· gone,

evening's
94:1 e· calm and holy hour,

event
391:4 "one far-off divine e·"
    4 that e· is Love.

eventide
8:1 fast falls the e·;
34:4 e· it shall be light.

ever (see also e'er)
9:2 e· come and go,
10:3 Our King is e· near;
411:3 Our King is e· near;
12:3 e· through our work
13:3 e· through our work
16:3 Thine is e· mine,
19:2 an e· clearer light,
33:1 nor e· be dismayed.
40:3 come, e· knowing,
55:1 e· Live our lives
56:2 E· our longings turn
    3 unchanged hath e· stood;
58:1 keep us E· in Thy
67:1 e· night and day;
68:1 e· night and day;
70:1 Truth is e· near.
71:3 E· shall their thirst
88:3 E· by triumphant hope
89:3 E· by triumphant hope
99:3 salvation e· nigh.
100:3 salvation e· nigh.
108:3 Nearer than e·,
115:2 e· at Thy side.
116:2 e· at Thy side.
136:3 Thy presence e· goes
146:3 Can e· be arrayed.
147:3 Can e· be arrayed.
148:2 His wisdom e· waketh,
163:2 e· flow A love
169:2 was not e· thus,
171:3 Looking e· to the
413:3 Looking e· to the
173:2 Love will e· with us
    3 Love will e· shine
189:1 Whose care is e· nigh.
224:1 best, my e· Friend.
225:1 best, my e· Friend.
226:1 grace that e· grows,
227:2 e· bring Thee where
232:1 our Mother, e· near,
406:1 our Mother, e· near,
232:2 e· one with Thee.
406:2 e· one with Thee.
232:3 joy that e· will remain
406:3 joy that e· will remain
245:2 e· out of darkness,
246:1 on Thee he e· counteth,
278:2 E· one thing do thou
279:2 E· one thing do thou
283:2 E· new mercies
313:2 find it e· new.
317:3 So shall it e· be
319:2 Thy e· blazing throne
324:3 E·, only, all for Thee.

ever (see also e'er)
329:2 And e· shall endure.
349:1 Thine alone be e· done;
    3 e· point the path
352:2 like thee did e· go
353:2 like thee did e· go
352:4 e· on the road
353:4 e· on the road
356:2 we would e· follow
362:3 justice e· guards
376:2 Nor e· turn aside,
377:2 Nor e· turn aside,
415:1 fountains are e· flowing:
    2 glory is e· shining;

ever-circling
158:3 with the e· years
159:3 with the e· years

everlasting
53:1 E· arms of Love
213:2 From e· Thou art God,
222:1 The e· Light;
223:1 The e· Light;
229:2 tides of e· day.
246:Ref. e· God Creator is
247:1 Wait on the e· God,
248:1 Wait on the e· God,
249:2 An e· gold,
250:2 An e· gold,
280:1 Praise the e· King.
334:3 e· thanks be Thine
336:3 fixed for e· years,
374:2 know Thee As e· Love.
375:2 know Thee As e· Love.

ever-living
36:1 Church of the e· God,

evermore
90:1 Feed me now and e·.
96:1 e· the same.
112:3 E· the light beholdeth.
117:1, 3 art, and e· shalt be.
226:3 And praise Thee e·.
275:3 e· in Love confide.

ever-presence
157:2 One the Love whose e·
221:2 e· Within each heart

ever-present
53:2 He our e· guide

every
3:1 e· lovely, Godlike
4:1 Be e· thought from
    1 Be e· action love.
7:3 Thy presence e· passing
8:2 Thy presence e· passing
29:1 Filling e· heart with
    2 Conquering e· subtle

every
29:2 known in $e^{.}$ land,
37:1 Of $e^{.}$ age and clime.
38:1 Of $e^{.}$ age and clime.
39:1 $e^{.}$ thought and step
   2 joy in $e^{.}$ heart,
48:3 obey Thine $e^{.}$ call,
51:3 ring from $e^{.}$ tongue,
52:3 ring from $e^{.}$ tongue,
62:1 $e^{.}$ land, by $e^{.}$ tongue.
63:1 $e^{.}$ land, by $e^{.}$ tongue.
65:2 Crowns $e^{.}$ dawning day;
73:2 $E^{.}$ heart may understand
   2 $E^{.}$ true desire
76:2 $E^{.}$ prayer to Him
92:2 Rising to $e^{.}$ task,
94:2 $e^{.}$ dream of earth
99:2 $e^{.}$ harm and pestilence.
102:2 $e^{.}$ storm of error
103:2 $e^{.}$ storm of error
104:2 lighten $e^{.}$ woe.
111:1 break through $e^{.}$ cloud
118:1 Kindle $e^{.}$ high desire;
120:1 $e^{.}$ tribe and nation:
121:3 $e^{.}$ sign of heavenly
122:3 $e^{.}$ sign of heavenly
126:3 Through $e^{.}$ bosom flow;
127:3 Through $e^{.}$ bosom flow;
403:3 Through $e^{.}$ bosom flow;
126:3 In $e^{.}$ action glow.
127:3 In $e^{.}$ action glow.
403:3 In $e^{.}$ action glow.
130:2 $e^{.}$ blessing shower;
133:3 $e^{.}$ gloomy thought
424:3 $e^{.}$ gloomy thought
134:1 to Thee in $e^{.}$ need,
137:1-3 need Thee $e^{.}$ hour,
   Ref. $E^{.}$ hour I need
139:2 answers $e^{.}$ call;
427:2 answers $e^{.}$ call;
140:2 $e^{.}$ cross and care.
142:4 $e^{.}$ symbol wanes:
150:2 that meets $e^{.}$ need,
154:2 $e^{.}$ thought that giveth
155:2 $e^{.}$ thought that giveth
156:2 $e^{.}$ thought that giveth
164:1 Let $e^{.}$ heart prepare
165:1 Let $e^{.}$ heart prepare
417:1 Let $e^{.}$ heart prepare
166:1 find, in $e^{.}$ station,
167:1 find, in $e^{.}$ station,
168:1 $e^{.}$ man His praise
170:1 Let $e^{.}$ creature hail
   2 who $e^{.}$ morn Feels
171:1 rejoices $e^{.}$ day,
413:1 rejoices $e^{.}$ day,
171:3 $E^{.}$ day will be
413:3 $E^{.}$ day will be

every
175:1 $e^{.}$ listening ear.
   2 guide us $e^{.}$ hour.
177:1 His Word in $e^{.}$ land:
   2 shall $e^{.}$ idol perish,
179:2 casts out $e^{.}$ fear,
   2 heals our $e^{.}$ ill,
   3 dawning over $e^{.}$ nation;
180:3 They whose $e^{.}$ thought
182:1 fill them $e^{.}$ one.
190:2 $e^{.}$ task assigned,
191:2 $e^{.}$ task assigned,
195:2 God, on $e^{.}$ side,
   2 escaping $e^{.}$ snare.
202:3 $e^{.}$ tear to bring full
412:2 $e^{.}$ tear to bring full
204:1 call and entreat $e^{.}$ nation,
205:1 pressed by $e^{.}$ foe;
207:3 for $e^{.}$ scalding tear,
208:3 for $e^{.}$ scalding tear,
209:3 for $e^{.}$ scalding tear,
210:3 for $e^{.}$ scalding tear,
211:3 for $e^{.}$ scalding tear,
212:3 for $e^{.}$ scalding tear,
207:3 love more for $e^{.}$ hate,
208:3 love more for $e^{.}$ hate,
209:3 love more for $e^{.}$ hate,
210:3 love more for $e^{.}$ hate,
211:3 love more for $e^{.}$ hate,
212:3 love more for $e^{.}$ hate,
224:1 To Thee in $e^{.}$ trouble
225:1 To Thee in $e^{.}$ trouble
227:1 $e^{.}$ place is hallowed
233:3 $e^{.}$ sacred shrine
419:3 $e^{.}$ sacred shrine
233:3 $e^{.}$ weary child shall
419:3 $e^{.}$ weary child shall
238:2 $e^{.}$ land a Palestine.
239:2 $e^{.}$ land a Palestine.
249:1 Widespread in $e^{.}$ place
250:1 Widespread in $e^{.}$ place
258:1 to $e^{.}$ man and nation
259:2 $e^{.}$ outward grace;
260:1 to my $e^{.}$ need,—
261:1 $e^{.}$ age and race,
262:1 $e^{.}$ age and race,
271:4 Let $e^{.}$ creature rise,
272:4 Let $e^{.}$ creature rise,
276:1 Peace to $e^{.}$ heart
277:1 Peace to $e^{.}$ heart
281:1 joy tune $e^{.}$ chord,
290:2 Victorious over $e^{.}$ ill,
293:3 there for $e^{.}$ ill.
294:3 there for $e^{.}$ ill.
295:3 there for $e^{.}$ ill.
324:3 Take my $e^{.}$ thought,
334:2 light to $e^{.}$ age,
335:2 thou to $e^{.}$ nation,

every
336:2 $e^{.}$ beam conducts to Thee.
341:1 throne in $e^{.}$ place:
   3 heart, in $e^{.}$ strait,
   3 will answer $e^{.}$ prayer,
342:1 $e^{.}$ heart may know.
   2 And $e^{.}$ need supply;
350:3 $e^{.}$ need supplying,
355:2 $e^{.}$ heart shall see
363:1 as it hastens, $e^{.}$ age
364:2 $E^{.}$ talent we possess.
383:2 From $e^{.}$ blemish free,
384:2 spring on $e^{.}$ tree;
386:1 $e^{.}$ act, in $e^{.}$ thought,
387:1 $e^{.}$ act, in $e^{.}$ thought,
399:2 Unfolding $e^{.}$ hour;
400:2 Unfolding $e^{.}$ hour;

everywhere
79:3 $E^{.}$ His glory shineth;
144:3 Is with us $e^{.}$;
145:3 Is with us $e^{.}$;
154:3 love and truth are $e^{.}$.
155:3 love and truth are $e^{.}$.
156:3 love and truth are $e^{.}$.
194:1 seeks God $e^{.}$.
410:1 seeks God $e^{.}$.
238:4 now and here and $e^{.}$.
239:4 now and here and $e^{.}$.
341:1-3 God is present $e^{.}$.

evil
67:1 lies the $e^{.}$ one:
68:1 lies the $e^{.}$ one:
99:3 No $e^{.}$ therefore shalt
100:3 No $e^{.}$ therefore shalt
179:2 Love knows no $e^{.}$,
189:2 keepeth me from $e^{.}$,
258:1 the good or $e^{.}$ side.
   3 cause of $e^{.}$ prosper,
267:1 See baseless $e^{.}$ fall,
268:1 See baseless $e^{.}$ fall,
320:2 courage in the $e^{.}$ hour
321:2 courage in the $e^{.}$ hour
409:2 courage in the $e^{.}$ hour
370:1 Of dominion over $e^{.}$:
396:3 In vain shall $e^{.}$ strive,
397:3 In vain shall $e^{.}$ strive,

exalted
1:1 Be Thou, O God, $e^{.}$
292:2 $e^{.}$ as head over all!
371:2 In this $e^{.}$ hour,

exalts
298:3 $e^{.}$ thee, and will cure
299:3 $e^{.}$ thee, and will cure
300:3 $e^{.}$ thee, and will cure
301:3 $e^{.}$ thee, and will cure
302:3 $e^{.}$ thee, and will cure

example
217:3 Follow ... the great $e\cdot$

exceeding
170:1 God's $e\cdot$ grace,

excellent
123:1 in His $e\cdot$ Word.

exclaim
67:2 with warning voice $e\cdot$,
68:2 with warning voice $e\cdot$,

exiles
381:3 like $e\cdot$ yearning For

expect
350:3 $e\cdot$ a bright to-morrow,

expectant
58:2 Eager ears, $e\cdot$,

expectation
351:1 Singing songs of $e\cdot$,

express
269:3 growth in grace $e\cdot$,
270:3 growth in grace $e\cdot$,
386:2 lips and lives $e\cdot$
387:2 lips and lives $e\cdot$

expressed
221:2 Thy name we see $e\cdot$

extol
153:2 O Lord, will I $e\cdot$,
283:1 $e\cdot$ Him with joyous

extolled
200:3 $E\cdot$ with the harp

eye
  6:1 with clear $e\cdot$ the present
 36:3 steadfast is thine $e\cdot$,
 86:3 mortals' blindfold $e\cdot$.
 87:3 mortals' blindfold $e\cdot$.
124:2 His watchful $e\cdot$
402:2 His watchful $e\cdot$
143:1 dreads the piercing $e\cdot$;
188:1 No $e\cdot$ hath seen,
207:2 only with mine $e\cdot$
208:2 only with mine $e\cdot$
209:2 only with mine $e\cdot$
210:2 only with mine $e\cdot$
211:2 only with mine $e\cdot$
212:2 only with mine $e\cdot$
218:2 $e\cdot$ to $e\cdot$ the signals
219:2 $e\cdot$ to $e\cdot$ the signals
220:2 $e\cdot$ to $e\cdot$ the signals
259:1 lifted $e\cdot$ or bended knee.
331:1 lifted $e\cdot$ and bended knee
384:1 What $e\cdot$ the dazzling
391:2 an open $e\cdot$ to see.

eyes
 34:2 lift our blinded $e\cdot$
 35:2 Glad my $e\cdot$, and warm
 36:3 restless $e\cdot$ of earth
 59:2 Lift up thine $e\cdot$,
 60:2 Lift up thine $e\cdot$,
 61:2 Lift up thine $e\cdot$,
 85:2 Open now our $e\cdot$
117:2 $e\cdot$ of sinful men
144:1 mortal $e\cdot$ may see it not,
145:1 mortal $e\cdot$ may see it not,
168:2 glad the $e\cdot$ and cheer
183:2 Set these before thine $e\cdot$.
184:2 Set these before thine $e\cdot$.
189:1 Mine $e\cdot$ look toward
202:4 blinded $e\cdot$ to see;
412:2 blinded $e\cdot$ to see;
206:1 with $e\cdot$ undimmed define
428:1 with $e\cdot$ undimmed define
227:3 heaven before our $e\cdot$.
229:1 $e\cdot$ that will not see,
240:2 to our $e\cdot$ display
241:2 to our $e\cdot$ display
275:2 blesses opened $e\cdot$,
314:3 Lift up thine $e\cdot$,
337:2 Close their $e\cdot$ and call
338:2 Close their $e\cdot$ and call
381:1 Mary's wondering $e\cdot$!
391:1 look with tearful $e\cdot$
418:1 strain our $e\cdot$ to see
    4 $e\cdot$ the King will see,

F

face
 51:1 Reflected $f\cdot$ to $f\cdot$.
 52:1 Reflected $f\cdot$ to $f\cdot$.
 59:2 and seek His $f\cdot$;
 60:2 and seek His $f\cdot$;
 61:2 and seek His $f\cdot$;
108:1 I'd see Thee $f\cdot$ to $f\cdot$;
136:3 see Thee $f\cdot$ to $f\cdot$.
138:2 Behold Thy $f\cdot$
181:2 see Thee $f\cdot$ to $f\cdot$.
183:3 Up, $f\cdot$ the task
184:3 Up, $f\cdot$ the task
267:2 Truth's glowing $f\cdot$,
268:2 Truth's glowing $f\cdot$,
296:Ref. rouse ye, $f\cdot$ the foe,
346:3 on the waters' $f\cdot$,
401:3 on the waters' $f\cdot$,
359:2 loving from His $f\cdot$.
374:3 see Thee $f\cdot$ to $f\cdot$.
375:3 see Thee $f\cdot$ to $f\cdot$.

faces
169:3 angel $f\cdot$ smile,

fade
149:1 $F\cdot$ as the dark when
426:1 $F\cdot$ as the dark when
171:1 light that cannot $f\cdot$.
413:1 light that cannot $f\cdot$.
173:2 Prophecy will $f\cdot$ away,

fadeless
 40:2 $f\cdot$ and pure;

fail
  8:1 When other helpers $f\cdot$,
 18:1 though cowards may $f\cdot$;
 57:2 Should fond hopes $f\cdot$
 70:1 doth not $f\cdot$ to hear
 88:3 unaided man must $f\cdot$;
 89:3 unaided man must $f\cdot$;
224:2 word can never $f\cdot$.

fail
225:2 word can never $f\cdot$.
247:3 ye shall not $f\cdot$;
248:3 ye shall not $f\cdot$;
264:3 And that cannot $f\cdot$.
282:2 shall His promise $f\cdot$;

faileth
 54:3 All utterance $f\cdot$ there;
175:2 divine, that $f\cdot$ never,
330:1,4 goodness $f\cdot$ never;

failing
176:1 thy light, never $f\cdot$;

failings
126:2 brother's $f\cdot$ hide,
127:2 brother's $f\cdot$ hide,
403:2 brother's $f\cdot$ hide,

fails
 71:3 Never $f\cdot$ from
142:4 The letter $f\cdot$,

faint
58:1 neither f nor fall.
59:3 F not nor fear,
60:3 F not nor fear,
61:3 F not nor fear,
71:3 Who can f, while
77:2 When f and desolate:
78:2 When f and desolate:
227:3 teach our f desires
247:3 Ye shall not f,
248:3 Ye shall not f,
320:3 human energy shall f,
321:3 human energy shall f,
409:3 human energy shall f,

fainting
37:3 With never f ray;
38:3 With never f ray;
320:2 Supports the f heart;
321:2 Supports the f heart;
409:2 Supports the f heart;

faintly
230:2 We f hear,
231:2 We f hear,

fair
6:1 however f it seems;
51:2 form divinely f.
52:2 form divinely f.
104:3 day, celestial, f.
149:3 complete, divinely f.
426:3 complete, divinely f.
197:1 sweet and f the leaves
198:1 sweet and f the leaves
259:3 spring not rich and f,
318:3 how f they grow,

fairer
317:1 F than morning,
3 f than the dawning,

faith
30:3 f to kiss, and know;
31:3 f to kiss, and know;
32:3 f to kiss, and know;
34:2 F, hope, and joy
54:1 F grasps the blessing
56:2 blest when f can hold
57:3 in the heart f singeth
102:3 Armed with f, may we
103:2 Armed with f, may we
104:1 f secure upon the rock
105:2 Increase our f,
106:2 Increase our f,
107:2 Increase our f,
114:3 show, by living f,
121:3 f unmixed with doubt

faith
122:3 f unmixed with doubt
123:1 Is laid for your f
143:2 Our f, O God,
149:2 on wings of f we
426:2 on wings of f we
166:3 Armed with f and
167:3 Armed with f and
166:4 F to sight and
167:4 F to sight and
171:1 hope and f uplifted;
413:1 hope and f uplifted;
173:3 F will vanish into
4 F and hope and love
190:4 F sings in triumph,
191:4 F sings in triumph,
205:1 f that will not shrink,
2 f that shines more
3 such a f as this,
222:2 f holds wide the door,
223:2 f holds wide the door,
224:2 had a stronger f,
225:2 had a stronger f,
227:3 To strengthen f and
230:1 our f and sight
231:1 our f and sight
234:3 keeps f sweet and
235:3 keeps f sweet and
253:2 thoughts, illumed By f,
254:2 thoughts, illumed By f,
255:2 thoughts, illumed By f,
256:2 thoughts, illumed By f,
257:2 thoughts, illumed By f,
259:2 In true and inward f
273:3 In our lives our f
274:3 In our lives our f
273:3 F by holy actions
274:3 F by holy actions
273:3 F that mountains can
274:3 F that mountains can
273:3 F that always works
274:3 F that always works
290:3 still look in f
292:1 shield of true f,
296:2 f that walks with God.
332:2 perfect f in Him,
339:3 see by f all things
350:3 F can sing through
351:2 f which never tires,
364:3 in f to God applies.
371:2 in f proclaim Thy
372:2 f has yet its Olivet,
373:1 f has yet its Olivet,
381:3 With hope and f,
383:2 Redeemer's holy f
390:1 f in God's great love
3 If weak in f,

faithful
18:1 Be firm and be f;
53:2 F is, whate'er betide;
95:Ref. His f follower
101:3 Word, His f Word,
109:2 F witness bear
110:2 F witness bear
126:4 hearts that f prove;
127:4 hearts that f prove;
403:4 hearts that f prove;
130:1 f is Thy kindness.
153:1 f is His word.
1 f is Thy word.
160:2 To f His.
161:2 To f His.
162:2 To f His.
176:2 Ah, they were f,
177:2 Thy f saints adore.
189:2 f word and deed.
245:2 call us, f Shepherd,
261:3 all God's f sons,
262:3 all God's f sons,
263:1 F, heed the Father's
332:2 heed His f Word,
333:2 f witness to the truth,
365:3 F, positive, and sure:
366:3 F, positive, and sure:
379:2 Calm and pure and f
380:2 Calm and pure and f

faithfully
237:4 F to Him reflected,

faithfulness
280:3 Glorious in His f.

faithless
41:3 Away with … f fear.

faith-lighted
287:2 F peaks of Spirit
408:2 F peaks of Spirit

faith's
112:1 f triumphant pinion;
326:2 f broad shield

fall
58:1 neither faint nor f.
97:1 rain will f from heaven,
98:1 rain will f from heaven,
142:4 the systems f,
207:2 snare, the pit, the f:
208:2 snare, the pit, the f:
209:2 snare, the pit, the f:
210:2 snare, the pit, the f:
211:2 snare, the pit, the f:
212:2 snare, the pit, the f:
229:1 Thy favors f;

fall
243:2 burdens f away,
244:2 burdens f away,
267:1 baseless evil f,
268:1 baseless evil f,
297:4 f through Love's
322:2 upon the heart Now f
323:2 upon the heart Now f
389:2 my hope, should I f;
418:2 changes rise and f,

fallen
327:3 By Him the f rise;
328:3 By Him the f rise;

falling
189:2 keepeth me from f,

falls
8:1 fast f the eventide;
303:2 No act f fruitless;

false
160:3 F fears are foes—
161:3 F fears are foes—
162:3 F fears are foes—

falsehood
101:3 Reject the f ages
172:2 F and fear shall pass,
258:1 strife of Truth with f,

falter
86:4 To f would be sin.
87:4 To f would be sin.
203:1 not f by the way

faltering
134:2 nerve my f will:
207:1 nestling's f flight!
208:1 nestling's f flight!
209:1 nestling's f flight!
210:1 nestling's f flight!
211:1 nestling's f flight!
212:1 nestling's f flight!
297:3 close her f wings,

famishing
91:2 F hearts and hopes
422:2 F hearts and hopes

far (*see also* **far-off**)
2:3 F shines the blessed
23:4 so f above All mortal
24:4 so f above All mortal
25:4 so f above All mortal
26:4 so f above All mortal
27:4 so f above All mortal
28:4 so f above All mortal
37:1 how broad and f

far (*see also* **far-off**)
38:1 how broad and f
54:2 sweeter f the still
121:4 f greater things
122:4 f greater things
134:1 mightier f Than sin
142:3 wide and f we stray.
169:1 I am f from home,
181:4 children f and near:
200:2 arm ... was mightier f;
215:2 treasures greater f
234:4 F down the future's
235:4 F down the future's
237:1 F from sense and hid
245:2 f astray we roam,
315:1 better f To rule
316:1 better f To rule
329:2 sweeter f than honey,
2 better f than gold.
347:1 hills be f removed,
348:1 hills be f removed,
351:2 Chasing f the gloom
3 the f eternal shore
391:1 seek f off for
394:3 nations f and near
395:3 nations f and near

faring
204:3 Thy promise forth f,

far-off
391:4 "one f divine event"

farthest
186:2 through f years,
187:2 through f years,
261:2 on f shores,
262:2 on f shores,

fashions
51:1 The hand that f
52:1 The hand that f

fast
7:1 f breaks the morning
8:1 f falls the eventide;
56:2 can hold Thee f.
185:2 good to hold f
297:2 where hope anchors f,
399:2 purpose ripens f,
400:2 purpose ripens f,

Father
49:1 Dear Lord and F
50:1 Dear Lord and F
55:1 F, hear the prayer
56:1 F, Thou joy of loving

Father
57:1 F, to Thee we turn
58:1 F, we Thy loving
2 Come we ..., dear F,
3 We ... know Thee, F,
66:1 Thy praise, O F, shall
421:1 Thy praise, O F, shall
72:1 Gracious F, in Thy
405:1 Gracious F, in Thy
73:1 Unto God the F raise.
102:1 O gracious F, Author
103:1 O gracious F, Author
115:1 Holy F, Thou hast
116:1 Holy F, Thou hast
131:1 to the F comes,
132:1 to the F comes,
135:1 know no death, O F,
2 Thou, my God and F,
139:2 Our F answers every
427:2 Our F answers every
141:1 F, may our corner stone
148:3 My F has my treasure,
150:3 Dear F and Saviour,
157:1 F, that they may
181:1 Loving F, we Thy
3 learn, O gracious F,
190:1 My God, my F, make me
191:1 My God, my F, make me
203:1 F, may we bear each
204:1 F, Thy kingdom is come
251:2 Word of God the F,
252:2 Word of God the F,
253:6 F, where Thine own
254:6 F, where Thine own
255:6 F, where Thine own
256:6 F, where Thine own
257:6 F, where Thine own
263:2 Feels the F Love
269:3 loving F, well we know
270:3 loving F, well we know
275:2 F we call His name;
291:3 F, Friend, and Guide.
297:1 F and perfect Son,
341:3 To thy F come, and
343:1 would the F seek,
344:1 would the F seek,
429:1 would the F seek,
349:1 almighty F, Thine,
351:3 the One Almighty F
356:3 Christ is Thine, O F:
357:1 our loving F, God,
358:1 our loving F, God,
407:1 our loving F, God,
361:1 all to God, the F,
374:1 F of us all,
375:1 F of us all,
376:1 thank Thee, heavenly F,
377:1 thank Thee, heavenly F,

father
359:1 pities like a f;

fatherless
217:1 widow and the f.

father-like
280:2 F, He tends and spares

Father-Mother
3:4 dear F, God,
12:3 F God, whose plan
13:3 F God, whose plan
48:1 Dear F, Thou dost
203:2 O loving F, God.
206:1 God, our F, Love,
428:1 God, our F, Love,
206:2 God, our F, Truth,
428:2 God, our F, Truth,
206:3 God, our F, Life,
428:3 God, our F, Life,
221:2 O God, our F,
356:2 Thou our F,
371:3 O F Love,
374:1, 3 We thank Thee, F,
375:1, 3 We thank Thee, F,

Father-Motherhood
76:1 Trust His F.

Father's
20:3 fulfill our F plan;
416:3 fulfill our F plan;
36:1 F gracious choice;
46:4 my F will.
47:4 my F will.
128:3 from the F home,
129:3 from the F home,
166:2 F smiles are thine;
167:2 F smiles are thine;
217:3 seem our F temple,
242:2 for our F work,
263:1 heed the F voice.
266:4 glorify our F grace,
370:1 the F holy plan.
382:1 What is thy F plan
386:1 in his F name,
387:1 in his F name,

fathers
280:3 our f in distress;

fathers'
385:1 f God before her

favor
280:3 His grace and f
350:1 changeless is His f;
364:2 His grace and f,

favors
229:1 Thy f fall;

fear (noun)
5:1 let not f enthrall.
7:2 I know no f,
9:4 sorrow, doubt and f,
10:3 let us know no f,
411:3 let us know no f,
29:1 error, doubt, and f;
30:3 pride and earth-born f,
31:3 pride and earth-born f,
32:3 pride and earth-born f,
41:3 Away with . . . faithless f.
44:2 F hath no dwelling
58:3 can feel no f;
71:3 f of want remove.
91:2 Blot out all f,
422:2 Blot out all f,
93:3 From anxious f
97:2 Let not f thy
98:2 Let not f thy
112:2 f no more enslaves
136:1 bids all f to cease:
    3 time and space and f
139:1 suffer cruel f,
427:1 suffer cruel f,
141:4 Cleansing men of f
146:1 knows no f, no feud,
147:1 knows no f, no feud,
149:1 earth-born f and sorrow
426:1 earth-born f and sorrow
149:3 Not wrapt in f nor
426:3 Not wrapt in f nor
154:2 thought that giveth f;
155:2 thought that giveth f;
156:2 thought that giveth f;
166:1 sin and f and care;
167:1 sin and f and care;
171:3 Freed of f, of pain,
413:3 Freed of f, of pain,
172:2 Falsehood and f shall
179:2 casts out every f,
181:4 F shall have no more
195:1 f and doubt depart,
204:2 amid shadows of f,
205:2 in danger knows no f,
232:1 turn from doubt and f!
406:1 turn from doubt and f!
238:3 doubt and creeds of f
239:3 doubt and creeds of f
296:2 cringing host of f
310:2 chaos, f and night;
314:1 To doubt and f give
315:1 rule by love than f;
316:1 rule by love than f;
325:3 all f and danger
347:3 thee free from f;
348:3 thee free from f;
371:1 free us from all f;

fear (noun)
374:2 discord, pain and f;
375:2 discord, pain and f;
382:3 phantoms of thy f

fear (verb)
8:3 I f no foe,
59:3 Faint not nor f,
60:3 Faint not nor f,
61:3 Faint not nor f,
77:1 foe have I to f?
78:1 foe have I to f?
123:2 F not, I am with
135:2 f no tribulation,
148:1 my heart shall f;
195:2 And f no foe,
207:3 and f No ill,—
208:3 and f No ill,—
209:3 and f No ill,—
210:3 and f No ill,—
211:3 and f No ill,—
212:3 and f No ill,—
267:1 His children cannot f;
268:1 His children cannot f;
290:2 and f no foe,

fearful
384:3 the f bold,

fearless
99:1 F and undisturbed
175:2 Sinless, f, whole,
351:1 Stepping f through

fearlessly
203:2 Teach us to follow f

fear's
181:1 in f dark night

fears
46:2 Cast foreboding f
47:2 Cast foreboding f
53:3 f and vain alarms
119:3 Banish all our f
138:2 and f grow still;
140:3 Old f are past,
160:3 False f are foes—
161:3 False f are foes—
162:3 False f are foes—
169:2 and, spite of f,
202:3 confidence for all thy f.
412:2 confidence for all thy f.
216:1 when f alarm,
222:1 hopes and f of all
223:1 hopes and f of all
381:3 giveth rest from f.

feast
40:3 to the f of love,
108:3 The f, though not
    4 F after f thus comes
    4 the glad f above,
    4 bridal f of bliss

fed
30:5 F by Thy love divine
31:5 F by Thy love divine
32:5 F by Thy love divine
34:2 lonely heart is f.
46:1 by constant mercy f,
47:1 by constant mercy f,
388:1 healed, the hungry f.

feed
42:1 the hungry f;
71:2 f upon the manna,
90:1 F me now and evermore.
91:2 hearts and hopes to f;
422:2 hearts and hopes to f;
108:2 f upon the bread
203:1 f and bless a hungry
304:1 How to f Thy sheep;
305:1 How to f Thy sheep;
306:1 How to f Thy sheep;
307:1 How to f Thy sheep;
308:1 How to f Thy sheep;
309:1 How to f Thy sheep;
304:3 F the hungry, heal
305:3 F the hungry, heal
306:3 F the hungry, heal
307:3 F the hungry, heal
308:3 F the hungry, heal
309:3 F the hungry, heal

feedeth
330:2 With food celestial f.

feeds
217:1 f the widow and the

feel
58:3 can f no fear;
64:2 I f the calm
105:1 f his brother's care.
106:1 f his brother's care.
107:1 f his brother's care.
134:1 I f Thy touch,
139:1 f God's presence
427:1 f God's presence
181:2 we f the power
228:1 We f Thy comfort,
357:3 smile of God they f;
358:3 smile of God they f;
407:3 smile of God they f;
418:4 f the silence come;

feels
29:1 its holy power f,
170:2 F in his heart
205:2 darkness f no doubt;
263:2 F the Father Love

feet
81:1 pilgrim f be led.
92:3 His f are shod
120:1 f of him that brings,
124:3 burden at His f,
402:3 burden at His f,
169:1 Keep Thou my f;
218:1 Our pilgrim f,
219:1 Our pilgrim f,
220:1 Our pilgrim f,
234:2 wayward f to stay,
235:2 wayward f to stay,
280:1 To His f thy tribute
297:2 walk with unshod f;
324:2 Take my f, and let
    3 At Thy f its treasure
326:1 f are with the gospel
391:1 Before your f Life's

fell
46:1 the manna f:
47:1 the manna f:

fellow-man
20:3 To self, and to our f.
416:3 To self, and to our f.

fellowship
83:2 One in f of Mind,
367:1 That f of love

felt
197:3 presence we have f,
198:3 presence we have f,
298:1 F ye the power of
299:1 F ye the power of
300:1 F ye the power of
301:1 F ye the power of
302:1 F ye the power of

fen
169:3 O'er moor and f,

festal
108:4 foretaste of the f joy,

festival
36:4 Unending f we keep

fettered
226:3 the f page From

fetterless
64:3 soars . . . , f and free;

fetters
66:4 Break earth-bound f,
421:4 Break earth-bound f;
333:2 f of the world.

feud
146:1 no fear, no f,
147:1 no fear, no f,

few
394:2 reapers still are f,
395:2 reapers still are f,

field
86:2 God is on the f,
87:2 God is on the f,
150:2 the wide harvest f,

fields
97:2 f are whitening,
98:2 f are whitening,
242:1 white harvest f,
331:2 groves or Sharon's f.
394:2 ripening f we see,
395:2 ripening f we see,

fiery
90:2 f cloudy pillar
123:3 through f trials

fight
5:1 for the f go forth.
59:1 F the good f
60:1 F the good f
61:1 F the good f
77:1 Firm in the f
78:1 Firm in the f
82:3 F we the f with
290:1 in your holy f,
312:1 arm you for the f,
    2 wrestle, f, and pray;
326:4 Fights his good f

fights
326:4 F his good fight

fill
23:5 F us today With all
24:5 F us today With all
25:5 F us today With all
26:5 F us today With all
27:5 F us today With all
28:5 F us today With all
35:3 F me, radiancy divine,
118:3 peace my spirit f.
182:1 f them every one.
199:2 f our thoughts with
232:3 f with this glad song
406:3 f with this glad song
293:3 our life to f,

fill
294:3 our life to f,
295:3 our life to f,
332:1 true content to f.
   2 f our daily lives
360:1 f with gold the plain.
   2 its void can f ;

filled
  34:3 empty cup is f ;
  82:1, 2 earth shall be f
   3 earth may be f
  96:1 power that f the
128:1 reverence f the place.
129:1 reverence f the place.
171:3 F with benedictions
413:3 F with benedictions
324:2 F with messages

fillest
151:1 with love Thou f,
152:1 with love Thou f,

filling
  29:1 F every heart with

fills
   1:1 Thy glory f the sky,
  35:1 glory f the skies,
  36:3 f the morning sky.
  72:1 glory f the sky;
405:1 glory f the sky;
109:1 F with light their
110:1 F with light their
134:2 Thy presence f my
170:2 f them all with
195:3 f my soul with peace,
228:2 it f the heart;

find
   9:4 our hearts f peace.
  11:2 radiant beams we f
  16:3 f myself in Thee.
  49:1 Thy service f,
  50:1 Thy service f,
  56:3 them that f Thee,
  73:2 in Him we f Joy
  83:2 bliss and glory f
  85:3 F Thy perfect, calm
  91:1 F we a joy before
422:1 F we a joy before
  92:4 highest pleasure f
138:1 I f Thy font
140:1 hallow all we f,
146:1 f a precious gift
147:1 f a precious gift
154:1 f my life as God's
155:1 f my life as God's
156:1 f my life as God's

find
157:2 f all being one.
166:1 f, in every station,
167:1 f, in every station,
171:2 f in Love the refuge
413:2 f in Love the refuge
180:1 laws fulfillment f.
188:2 bids them f and keep
   3 f, the Spirit saith,
190:2 in service I would f,
191:2 in service I would f,
224:2 Its source doth f
225:2 Its source doth f
227:2 they f their home.
230:3 can f Thy ways
231:3 can f Thy ways
237:2 we shall f Him,
   3 f our earthly longings
245:3 we f, O Shepherd,
263:3 f the true atonement,
267:3 Soul and substance f,
268:3 Soul and substance f,
271:3 weary f eternal rest,
272:3 weary f eternal rest,
278:3 merciful, mercy shall f.
279:3 merciful, mercy shall f.
313:2 f it ever new.
325:3 f immortal Life
332:2 seek Him Life shall f,
341:1 F that throne in every
367:2 f Thy heart made
370:2 radiant peace we f,
371:2 f within Thy perfect law
   3 f through darkened days

finding
207:4 Seeking and f,
208:4 Seeking and f,
209:4 Seeking and f,
210:4 Seeking and f,
211:4 Seeking and f,
212:4 Seeking and f,
345:2 in reflection f all

finds
  93:3 man f release;
126:4 f His bosom glow
127:4 f His bosom glow
403:4 f His bosom glow
174:3 seeks and f His own.
207:5 mother f her home
208:5 mother f her home
209:5 mother f her home
210:5 mother f her home
211:5 mother f her home
212:5 mother f her home
238:3 prelude f its way;
239:3 prelude f its way;

finger
  30:4 Love whose f traced
  31:4 Love whose f traced
  32:4 Love whose f traced

fire
  15:1 gold by f is tested,
  49:3 earthquake, wind and f,
  50:3 earthquake, wind and f,
  71:2 cloud and f appear
  74:1 tempest and its f
118:1 Cleanse . . . in Thy pure f
237:3 by Love's pure f.
281:2 moving f by night;
284:1 of a hidden f,
285:1 of a hidden f,
286:1 of a hidden f,
345:1 cleansing f repeats

fires
  15:1 cleansing f of Truth

firm
  17:1 Be f, ye sentinels
  18:1 Be f and be faithful;
  77:1 F in the fight
  78:1 F in the fight
  80:3 F as His throne
111:2 f Thy justice stands,
123:1 How f a foundation,
281:1 F and changeless still

firmament
336:1 starry f on high,

firmer
108:1 grasp with f hand

firmness
143:3 May we with f own,

first
186:1 Mighty God, the F,
187:1 Mighty God, the F,

fit
  51:2 and Love must f.
  52:2 and Love must f.

fix
276:2 F within our hearts
277:2 F within our hearts

fixed
  36:3 F on the silent
336:3 f for everlasting years,

fixing
379:4 F them on Him
380:4 F them on Him

flag
203:1 f of hope and peace

flame
123:3 f shall not hurt
319:3 one heavenly f.
385:1 in smoke and f.
398:2 golden f burn clear;

flames
233:3 f of Truth divinely
419:3 f of Truth divinely

flaming
297:1 with the f sword,

fled
123:1 for your refuge have f:
200:2 f like the chaff
388:1 he went affliction f,

flee
8:1 fail, and comforts f,
17:1 shapes of darkness f;
224:1 in every trouble f,
225:1 in every trouble f,
293:2 from mortal sense I f,
294:2 from mortal sense I f,
295:2 from mortal sense I f,
317:1 and the shadows f,
3 see the shadows f,
326:3 the alien armies f;
343:1 sin and death we f;
344:1 sin and death we f;
429:1 sin and death we f;
365:1 To His ... promise f,
366:1 To His ... promise f,
382:3 f before the light.
418:2 our moments onward f,
425:2 and sighing f away,

flees
177:1 Darkness f at His

flesh
23:3 replete, by f embound—
24:3 replete, by f embound—
25:3 replete, by f embound—
26:3 replete, by f embound—
27:3 replete, by f embound—
28:3 replete, by f embound—
49:3 let f retire;
50:3 let f retire;
180:3 In Soul, not f,
197:3 Word made f among
198:3 Word made f among
228:2 Not in the f,
246:2 All f shall see it

flight
194:1 f of silent prayer,
410:1 f of silent prayer,
207:1 nestling's faltering f!
208:1 nestling's faltering f!
209:1 nestling's faltering f!
210:1 nestling's faltering f!
211:1 nestling's faltering f!
212:1 nestling's faltering f!
346:1 And took their f;
401:1 And took their f;
346:3 Speed forth thy f;
401:3 Speed forth thy f;
363:2 in loftier f,
368:3 darkness takes its f,
369:3 darkness takes its f,

fling
183:3 F ease and self away;
184:3 F ease and self away;
345:1 Lo, wide we f

floods
85:3 f of trouble flow
363:4 f of light and joy,

flow
30:3 joys supernal f,
31:3 joys supernal f,
32:3 joys supernal f,
54:3 No accents f, no words
65:3 from His fullness f.
66:1 Father, shall forever f.
421:1 Father, shall forever f.
75:2 righteousness shall f.
85:3 floods of trouble f
90:2 healing waters f;
126:3 Through every bosom f;
127:3 Through every bosom f;
403:3 Through every bosom f;
163:2 must ever f A love
164:2 his blessings f,
165:2 his blessings f,
417:2 his blessings f,
271:3 blessings f where'er He
272:3 blessings f where'er He
324:1 f in ceaseless praise.
330:2 living water f
335:2 F thou to every
343:4 joys eternal f.
344:4 joys eternal f.
429:4 joys eternal f.
363:4 Shall f to bless
384:2 streams shall gently f,

flowed
128:1 f the gospel sound
129:1 f the gospel sound
260:3 f From out their thought
333:1 His consolations f.

flower
45:2 sunbeam, light and f
130:2 alike on man and f:
197:2 f and fruitage now
198:2 f and fruitage now
243:3 breath of opening f.
244:3 breath of opening f.
399:2 sweet will be the f.
400:2 sweet will be the f.

flowers
75:2 joy and hope, like f,
322:2 And f of grace
323:2 And f of grace

floweth
276:1 f as a river
277:1 f as a river

flowing
40:3 see waters f Forth
142:1 Forever f free,
415:1 fountains are ever f:

flows
57:1 whence our healing f;
92:1 love and labor f,
134:2 f Thy quickening life
218:2 the greeting f,
219:2 the greeting f,
220:2 the greeting f,
249:1 how f the fountain
250:1 how f the fountain
280:2 as His mercy f.

fly
10:3 before Him f,
411:3 before Him f,
41:2 hours too swiftly f,
192:5 Upward I f,
193:5 Upward I f,

foe
5:1 f in ambush claims
8:3 I fear no f,
77:1 What f have I
78:1 What f have I
80:1 What f can make
195:2 And fear no f,
200:3 f is destroyed that
205:1 pressed by every f;
264:1 Leads against the f;
290:2 and fear no f,
296:Ref. rouse ye, face the f,

foes
10:1 bid our f defiance.
411:1 bid our f defiance.
71:1 smile at all thy f.

foes
120:2 Upon thy f has trod;
160:3 False fears are f —
161:3 False fears are f —
162:3 False fears are f —
200:1 Awake, for thy f
    2 O many thy f, but
204:2 no f that appear
280:2 from all our f.
364:1 watch, lest f alarm;
396:3 spite of all His f.
397:3 spite of all His f.

foil
  8:2 f the tempter's power?

fold
  6:2 not in sleep to f
196:1 One Shepherd and one f.
217:2 f to thy heart thy
297:3 F where the sheep
304:3 lambkins to the f,
305:3 lambkins to the f,
306:3 lambkins to the f,
307:3 lambkins to the f,
308:3 lambkins to the f,
309:3 lambkins to the f,

folded
57:2 f in Thy peace.

follow
49:2 Rise up and f thee.
50:2 Rise up and f thee.
84:2 F where His love
88:2 F Christ's sincerity.
89:2 F Christ's sincerity.
115:2 F wholly Thy
116:2 F wholly Thy
195:2 f still my guide,
203:2 Teach us to f
217:3 F with reverent steps
245:1 long to f thee,
    1 f where thou leadest,
273:2 F God, the only Mind,
274:2 F God, the only Mind,
296:2 f where he trod;
304:1 I will f and rejoice
305:1 I will f and rejoice
306:1 I will f and rejoice
307:1 I will f and rejoice
308:1 I will f and rejoice
309:1 I will f and rejoice
325:1 humbly f after me.
356:2 ever f Thy behest:
396:1 Arise, and f where
397:1 Arise, and f where

follower
95: Ref. His faithful f I

followers'
128:2 led his f way.
129:2 led his f way.

following
12:2 prove to all with f sign
13:2 prove to all with f sign
230:4 But simply f thee.
231:4 But simply f thee.

fond
57:2 Should f hopes fail

font
138:1 I find Thy f

food
201:1 Truth will be your f.
404:1 Truth will be your f.
327:2 hungry needful f
328:2 hungry needful f
330:2 f celestial feedeth.

foolish
49:1 Forgive our f ways;
50:1 Forgive our f ways;
325:2 thy f pride rebel;
330:3 Perverse and f oft

foot
189:1 f shall not be moved,

footsteps
202:2 f of the upward way.
412:1 f of the upward way.
251:1 lantern to our f,
252:1 lantern to our f,
283:2 our f still holdeth
304:1 Lest my f stray;
305:1 Lest my f stray;
306:1 Lest my f stray;
307:1 Lest my f stray;
308:1 Lest my f stray;
309:1 Lest my f stray;
352:4 To trace thy f, Son
353:4 To trace thy f, Son

forbear
249:1 F a psalm to raise,
250:1 F a psalm to raise,

foreboding
46:2 Cast f fears away;
47:2 Cast f fears away;

fore'er
11:2 God and man f at one.

foresee
2:2 F the glorious morn,

foretaste
108:4 f of the festal joy,

foretell
368:1 hope or joy f?
369:1 hope or joy f?

foretold
158:3 come the time f;
159:3 come the time f;
196:1 prophets long f,

forever (*see also* fore'er)
10:1-3 His kingdom is f.
411:1-3 His kingdom is f.
15:2 God f sees His child
    3 God's child f pure
19:2 they shall f shine;
23:2 Dear Christ, f here
24:2 Dear Christ, f here
25:2 Dear Christ, f here
26:2 Dear Christ, f here
27:2 Dear Christ, f here
28:2 Dear Christ, f here
39:3 we may be f blest.
42:2 And f, and f
55:2 Not f in green
    3 Not f by still
58:3 Love and Life f near.
66:1 shall f flow.
421:1 shall f flow.
75:3 name shall stand f:
84:2 God's commands f
     heeding,
94:3 voice of God, f near,
101:2 Truth, f one,
104:4 The crown f ours.
111:2 F firm Thy justice
142:1 Immortal Love, f full,
     F flowing free,
     F shared, f whole,
157:3 Warfare shall f cease,
174:2 Love's giving is f;
180:1 command f strong,
237:4 with Him f near.
269:3 F waits to bless.
270:3 F waits to bless.
275:3 goodness f guide;
280:3 still the same f,
283:1 His mercy endureth f.
293:1-3 Thy strength f mine.
294:1-3 Thy strength f mine.
295:1-3 Thy strength f mine.
311:3 F doth His gift
420:3 F doth His gift
330:1 He is mine f.
    4 Within Thy house f.
370:1 hid with Christ f

forever (*see also* **fore'er**)
379:4 Fixing them on Him f
380:4 Fixing them on Him f

forevermore
93:2 Life, f the same,
104:1 rock Of Christ, f.
153:1 Saviour, F the same,
177:2 Through the world f :
351:3 Reigns in love f.
362:2 F adored;
381:2 Alive f to save;

forget
76:1 unchanging Love f ?
154:2 Should I f that Thou
155:2 Should I f that Thou
156:2 Should I f that Thou
273:2 f the things behind,
274:2 f the things behind,

forgetful
6:2 F of thy Lord's

forgive
49:1 F our foolish ways;
50:1 F our foolish ways;
163:1 F, as ye would be

forgiven
108:2 calm of sin f.
140:3 old sins f,
163:1 as ye would be f ;
280:1 healed, restored, f,
318:2 peace of sin f,

forgiving
352:3 meek, f, Godlike,
353:3 meek, f, Godlike,

forgot
192:5 Sun, moon, and stars f,
193:5 Sun, moon, and stars f,

forlorn
415:2 wandered f and weary:

form
12:1 doctrine, f or creed
13:1 doctrine, f or creed
51:2 The f divinely fair.
52:2 The f divinely fair.
194:2 lips may never f
410:2 lips may never f
230:4 nor f, nor ritual
231:4 nor f, nor ritual
284:2 simplest f of speech
285:2 simplest f of speech
286:2 simplest f of speech

formed
71:1 F thee for His
347:3 f against His own
348:3 f against His own

forms
131:2 not hedged with f ;
132:2 not hedged with f ;
158:2 Whose f are bending
159:2 Whose f are bending

forsake
18:2 F those that love thee,
76:1 ne'er will He f thee,
189:1 never shall f me;
325:1 deny, the world f,

forsaken
76:2 I have not f thee;

forsaking
379:3 who, all f,
380:3 who, all f,

forspent
246:1 on Thee, ne'er is f,

forth
2:3 light has broken f,
5:1 for the fight go f.
12:2 Show f the Truth
13:2 Show f the Truth
14:4 living light show f
15:1 Its purity shown f,
40:3 F from the throne
74:1 Go f and stand
82:3 March we f in
97:1 goeth f with weeping,
98:1 goeth f with weeping,
109:2 Show Thee f in
110:2 Show Thee f in
113:2 Send Thou f Thy
120:2 Break f in hymns
149:1 pours f her light;
426:1 pours f her light;
176:3 the Word shines f,
178:2 Showeth f the perfect
203:1 mirror f Love's sacred
204:3 Thy promise f faring,
206:2 Send f Thy light
428:2 Send f Thy light
221:3 Shows f Love's sweet
226:2 Shine f, O Light,
2 Shine f, and let
2 Shine f, and touch
3 lead f this age
242:1 Sounds f the ancient
2 Go f beneath His
260:2 Shines f the thought

forth
346:3 Speed f thy flight;
401:3 Speed f thy flight;
350:1 the hand stretched f
392:4 the day Bursts f
393:4 the day Bursts f

fortress
3:2 A grateful heart a f
10:3 stay and f strong,
411:3 stay and f strong,
99:1 f, shield and stay,
100:1 f, shield and stay,
293:2 Truth, our f strong,
294:2 Truth, our f strong,
295:2 Truth, our f strong,

forward
12:2 Go f then, and
13:2 Go f then, and
264:1 F into battle,
278:2 Grace to go f,
279:2 Grace to go f,
351:2 earnest looking f,

foul
298:3 Cleanse the f senses
299:3 Cleanse the f senses
300:3 Cleanse the f senses
301:3 Cleanse the f senses
302:3 Cleanse the f senses

found
12:1 Is f the Truth that
13:1 Is f the Truth that
40:1 health and peace are f,
64:1 I have f the way.
115:1 Thou hast f us;
116:1 Thou hast f us;
149:2 unknown till f in
426:2 unknown till f in
224:2 where'er it may be f,
225:2 where'er it may be f,
227:1 seek Thee, Thou art f,
229:2 but f within,
259:3 stream has f its way;
298:1 was f by you and me
299:1 was f by you and me
300:1 was f by you and me
301:1 was f by you and me
302:1 was f by you and me
333:3 which sought him f
339:2 joy is f therein,
398:3 In watchful service f ;

foundation
123:1 How firm a f,
293:3 Truth, f sure,
294:3 Truth, f sure,
295:3 Truth, f sure,

foundations
111:2 mountains their f keep:

founded
71:1 On the Rock of Ages f,
176:1 F secure on timeless

fount
56:1 Thou F of life,
228:2 welling f, it fills
259:2 living f of joy
269:1 open f is free to all,
270:1 open f is free to all,

fountain
57:1 Thou art the f
90:2 Open is the crystal f,
111:3 like a f rich and
249:1 how flows the f
250:1 how flows the f
298:3 "Come to this f,
299:3 "Come to this f,
300:3 "Come to this f,
301:3 "Come to this f,
302:3 "Come to this f,
360:2 Nothing but a ceaseless f

fountains
55:3 smite the living f
75:2 hill to vale the f
120:1 streams from living f,
260:3 f of their patience
415:1 where the f are ever

founts
182:2 very f of love

foursquare
141:1 corner stone Stand f

fowler
207:5 No snare, no f,
208:5 No snare, no f,
209:5 No snare, no f,
210:5 No snare, no f,
211:5 No snare, no f,
212:5 No snare, no f,

fowler's
99:2 from the f snare,
100:2 from the f snare.

fragrance
4:1 A f from above:
109:1 f of Thy praise.
110:1 f of Thy praise.

frame
213:2 earth received her f,

fraught
95:1 with heavenly comfort f.
379:1 with all ... bliss is f.
380:1 with all ... bliss is f.

free
5:2 End bondage, O be f.
6:2 no life is f,
7:1 Truth that maketh f,
12:2 that makes men f.
13:2 that makes men f.
12:3 man ..., whole and f.
13:3 man ..., whole and f.
16:3 heart is joyous, f,
19:1 f from sin or any
30:5 F us from human strife.
31:5 F us from human strife.
32:5 F us from human strife.
64:3 fetterless and f;
69:1 bondage be set f.
423:1 bondage be set f.
75:1 set the captive f,
81:2 heals, and sets me f.
82:3 set their captives f,
83:1 all His creatures f;
99:2 Shall f thee from
100:2 Shall f thee from
105:3 made us f indeed,
106:3 made us f indeed,
107:3 made us f indeed,
111:3 fountain rich and f,
112:1 F from sin, our
121:1 their thoughts are f,
122:1 their thoughts are f,
125:1 noise and trouble f;
126:2 f from envy, scorn,
127:2 f from envy, scorn,
403:2 f from envy, scorn,
131:3 that makes men f,
132:3 that makes men f,
139:2 truth is f to all,
427:2 truth is f to all,
142:1 Forever flowing f,
143:2 Created to be f,
148:3 path in life is f;
175:1 know Thee and be f.
188:3 maketh all men f.
200:3 and Zion is f.
201:2 will from error f
404:2 will from error f
202:1 sing, for thou art f;
412:1 sing, for thou art f;
203:1 that makes men f
214:2 meek, and make us f;
221:3 Truth that makes us f.
226:3 darkened bondage f:
233:2 so pure, so f,
419:2 so pure, so f,

free
234:1 paths of service f;
235:1 paths of service f;
269:1 fount is f to all,
270:1 fount is f to all,
291:1 simple, f from art;
1 distrust and envy f,
298:1 Truth that made us f,
299:1 Truth that made us f,
300:1 Truth that made us f,
301:1 Truth that made us f,
302:1 Truth that made us f,
303:4 holy, true, and f.
319:3 to make us f,
327:2 sets the captive f.
328:2 sets the captive f.
337:3 bondage sets them f.
338:3 bondage sets them f.
339:2 setteth f from thought
347:3 holds thee f from fear;
348:3 holds thee f from fear;
350:1 F and changeless is His
365:3 Thy promise full and f,
366:3 Thy promise full and f,
371:1 f us from all fear;
383:2 From every blemish f,
391:2 deathless as His spirit f,

freed
171:3 F of fear, of pain,
413:3 F of fear, of pain,

freedom
65:1 What f we may know.
136:1 love Thy way of f,
218:3 f of the truth,
219:3 f of the truth,
220:3 f of the truth,
276:2 Thy blessed f come.
277:2 Thy blessed f come.
349:3 walk in f and in peace

freedom's
355:1 f star in sight,

freely
48:3 freemen are, and f have
58:3 joy and spend it f.
342:2 Good things are f
392:3 bids us f enter,
393:3 bids us f enter,

freemen
2:2 thousand f rally,
37:1 true thy chartered f
38:1 true thy chartered f
48:3 Thy f are, and freely

freer
218:4 f step, the fuller
219:4 f step, the fuller
220:4 f step, the fuller

frees
135:1 life it is that f us
179:1 f from error's thrall,—

frequent
385:3 storm the f night,

fresh
236:1 day of f promise
399:1 saints, f courage take,
400:1 saints, f courage take,

freshly
260:2 rising f to my view,

freshness
317:2 f of the morn.
322:2 grace in f start
323:2 grace in f start

fret
234:1 toil, the f of care.
235:1 toil, the f of care.

friend
96:2 Thy f and guide
178:2 Him, our heavenly F.
224:1 My best, my ever F.
225:1 My best, my ever F.
230:4 Our f, our brother,
231:4 Our f, our brother,
263:3 God the perfect F;
275:2 Him our God and F.
291:3 Father, F, and Guide.
298:4 f of the friendless,
299:4 f of the friendless,
300:4 f of the friendless,
301:4 f of the friendless,
302:4 f of the friendless,
333:1 loving f to all who

friendless
298:4 friend of the f,
299:4 friend of the f,
300:4 friend of the f,
301:4 friend of the f,
302:4 friend of the f,
339:1 There are none f,

friendly
105:1 his f aid afford,
106:1 his f aid afford,
107:1 his f aid afford,

friends
76:1 earthly f betray
140:2 Old f, old scenes,

friendship
178:2 hearts in f blend,

fringes
64:3 the f of eternity.

froward
291:1 my f heart,

frowns
359:3 pride which f and

fruit
97:1 plenteous f be given,
98:1 plenteous f be given,
150:2 We gather the f
276:1 f of conquered sin;
277:1 f of conquered sin;
303:1 f in each wind-wafted

fruitage
197:2 flower and f now are
198:2 flower and f now are

fruitful
141:3 F shall our tillage
350:2 F, when in Christ

fruition
166:4 change to glad f,
167:4 change to glad f,

fruitless
303:2 No act falls f;

fruits
97:2 reap the f of joy:
98:2 reap the f of joy:

fulfill
20:3 f our Father's plan;
416:3 f our Father's plan;
41:3 can our God f
46:4 shall added years f
47:4 shall added years f
126:1 so f His word;
127:1 so f His word;
403:1 so f His word;
137:3 promise, Lord, In me f.
166:4 f thy holy mission,
167:4 f thy holy mission,
179:2 law does love f.
297:4 dost f all prophecy.
349:3 holy purpose to f,

fulfilled
173:3 Hope shall be f in

fulfilleth
178:2 Charity the law f,
189:2 F all my need;

fulfillment
171:1 the promise and f,
413:1 the promise and f,
180:1 All laws f find.

full
41:4 How f their joy,
111:1 goodness in f glory
142:1 Love, forever f,
166:1 thy f salvation;
167:1 thy f salvation;
202:3 bring f compensation,
412:2 bring f compensation,
221:1 their f effulgence
278:3 F is the promise,
279:4 F is the promise,
314:2 The f corn comes at
350:2 such a f salvation,
365:3 promise f and free,
366:3 promise f and free,

fuller
218:4 the f breath,
219:4 the f breath,
220:4 the f breath,

fullest
121:2 f light of love;
122:2 f light of love;

fullness
65:2 f of His blessing
2 f of His promise
2 f of His glory
2 f of His love.
3 from His f flow.
224:1 Thy f is the same;
225:1 Thy f is the same;
379:4 all our f lies.
380:4 all our f lies.

fully
149:1 prayer is f answered,
426:1 prayer is f answered,

future
226:2 touch the f vast
258:2 serenely down the f
3 scaffold sways the f,
391:1 Why search the f

future's
234:4 f broadening way;
235:4 f broadening way;

G

gain
174:2 earthly loss is g ;
207:3 and loss is g.
208:3 and loss is g.
209:3 and loss is g.
210:3 and loss is g.
211:3 and loss is g.
212:3 and loss is g.
207:5 earth's tear-drops g,
208:5 earth's tear-drops g,
209:5 earth's tear-drops g,
210:5 earth's tear-drops g,
211:5 earth's tear-drops g,
212:5 earth's tear-drops g,
238:1 steady g of man.
239:1 steady g of man.
269:3 true communion g.
270:3 true communion g.

'gainst
172:1 'G whose all-power
253:5 'G which the winds
254:5 'G which the winds
255:5 'G which the winds
256:5 'G which the winds
257:5 'G which the winds
264:3 'G that Church prevail;

Galilee
34:1 that eve in G.
297:4 meal by joyous G:
372:2 And love its G.
373:1 And love its G.

garden
3:1 grateful heart a g is,

garish
169:2 loved the g day,

garment
150:1 the g of praise.
171:2 Truth's healing g
413:2 Truth's healing g

garment's
96:1 filled the g hem

garner
360:1 mildew in the g,

gate
398:1 watchful at His g.

gates
264:3 G of hell can never

gather
150:2 We g the fruit
304:1 How to g, how to sow,—
305:1 How to g, how to sow,—
306:1 How to g, how to sow,—
307:1 How to g, how to sow,—
308:1 How to g, how to sow,—
309:1 How to g, how to sow,—
359:1 when the shadows g,

gathered
66:1 these Thy children g
421:1 these Thy children g
128:1 thousands g round
129:1 thousands g round
141:3 g from the tree
363:1 g beams of ages

gaunt
236:1 G warfare is doomed,

gave
30:4 God, who g that word
31:4 God, who g that word
32:4 God, who g that word
176:2 peace to all it g,
368:2 that g them birth?
369:2 that g them birth?

gav'st
130:1 Thou g the treasure

gaze
54:1 points the upward g ;

Gennesaret
96:2 The Healer by G

Gentile
196:1 Jew and G, meeting

gentle
23:4 g beam of living Love,
24:4 g beam of living Love,
25:4 g beam of living Love,
26:4 g beam of living Love,
27:4 g beam of living Love,
28:4 g beam of living Love,
69:3 a g, loving heart,
423:3 a g, loving heart,
76:2 His g Peace, be still.
124:1 How g God's commands,
402:1 How g God's commands,
178:1 is God's counsel g,
203:2 way our g Master trod,
207:1 O g presence, peace
208:1 O g presence, peace

gentle
209:1 O g presence, peace
210:1 O g presence, peace
211:1 O g presence, peace
212:1 O g presence, peace
243:3 g grace of Love
244:3 g grace of Love
291:1 Make me g, pure,
318:1 G and loving, they

gentleness
128:1 lips of g and grace,
129:1 lips of g and grace,
243:1 happy grace of g.
244:1 happy grace of g.
243:2 with touch of g
244:2 with touch of g

gently
81:1 g o'er me Are His
185:2 g mold Our lives
245:3 Thou g dost enfold.
280:2 He g bears us,
315:1 Speak g, it is better
316:1 Speak g, it is better
315:1 Speak g, let no harsh
316:1 Speak g, let no harsh
315:2 Speak g to the erring
316:2 Speak g to the erring
315:3 Speak g, 'tis a little
316:3 Speak g, 'tis a little
330:3 on His shoulder g laid,
384:2 streams shall g flow,

gift
45:1 Thy g unspeakable,
96:1 healing g God gives
146:1 find a precious g
147:1 find a precious g
146:1 The g of gratitude.
147:1 The g of gratitude.
222:3 wondrous g is given;
223:3 wondrous g is given;
226:1 have shown Thy g
243:1 g to all His own:
244:1 g to all His own:
251:2 art the g divine,
252:2 art the g divine,
297:1 God's g, the glory
311:3 His g of love
420:3 His g of love
382:4 hast the g of God—

gifts
48:1 good and perfect g
181:3 good g from above.

58

gifts
199:1 countless g· of love
311:3 g· His hand doth bring
420:3 g· His hand doth bring
342:1 All perfect g· are
     2 Not for such g· alone,
345:3 priceless pearl of g·,
388:3 g· of our benevolence.
392:2 With g· of healing
393:2 With g· of healing

gild
368:2 G· the spot that gave
369:2 G· the spot that gave

gilds
334:2 glory g· the sacred

gird
  5:1 the sword now g·,
 67:1 G· thy heavenly armor
 68:1 G· thy heavenly armor
113:1 G· us with Truth,
292:1 righteousness valiantly g·,

girded
242:2 g· for our Father's

girds
  3:2 G· man with mighty

girt
195:2 G· with the love of God,

give
 10:3 g· thanks to God
411:3 g· thanks to God
 30:5 power our hope we g·,
 31:5 power our hope we g·,
 32:5 power our hope we g·,
 42:2 holy word doth g· ;
 43:1 I will g· you rest.
    2 I will g· you light.
    2 I will g· you life.
 46:1 G· me, Lord, my daily
 47:1 G· me, Lord, my daily
 46:4 daily task shalt g· ;
 47:4 daily task shalt g· ;
 66:4 g· us vision clear,
421:4 g· us vision clear,
 69:1-3 G· me, O Lord,
423:1-3 G· me, O Lord,
 77:2 will g· thee peace.
 78:2 will g· thee peace.
 81:2 God alone can g·
 92:4 G· us, O God, this mind,
104:3 G· us, O Truth,
114:2 g· a rich reward;
123:2 still g· thee aid;

give
136:1 I will g· thee peace.
  2, 3 dost g· me peace.
139:3 G· of your heart's
427:3 G· of your heart's
151:2 g· me needed courage
152:2 g· me needed courage
173:1-3 Therefore g· us love.
182:3 who cease to g· :
202:3 comes to g· thee joy
412:2 comes to g· thee joy
202:3 To g· thee confidence
412:2 To g· thee confidence
205:3 g· us such a faith
234:4 God alone can g·,
235:4 God alone can g·,
263:1, 3 can g· us peace.
314:1 g· thou no heed;
342:1, 3 g· thanks, rejoice.
352:4 And g· me ever
353:4 And g· me ever

given
  2:3 blessed Truth is g·,
 10:1 All power is g· unto
411:1 All power is g· unto
 12:3 Hath g· dominion
 13:3 Hath g· dominion
 14:3 g· thee His Son,
 30:3 wisdom's rod is g·
 31:3 wisdom's rod is g·
 32:3 wisdom's rod is g·
 72:1 Peace . . . to man is g·,
405:1 Peace . . . to man is g·,
 86:2 is g· The instinct
 87:2 is g· The instinct
 92:2 as the word is g·,
 97:1 plenteous fruit be g·,
 98:1 plenteous fruit be g·,
168:3 g· The key that shuts
192:3 In mercy g·;
193:3 In mercy g·;
222:3 wondrous gift is g· ;
223:3 wondrous gift is g· ;
281:2 g· the cloud by day,
        G· the moving fire
342:2 freely g· to all
362:1 a Son is g· ;
364:3 all good is g·
383:3 that grace be g· To

giver
 71:3 like the Lord, the g·,
276:1 speaks the heavenly G· ;
277:1 speaks the heavenly G· ;

gives
 71:2 g· them when they pray.
 96:1 healing gift God g·
 99:3 g· His angels charge

gives
100:3 g· His angels charge
120:1 From error g· release
125:3 G· grace and glory
138:3 That Truth g· promise
178:2 to God who g· it,
180:3 g· a joy untold:
320:2 He g· the conquest
321:2 He g· the conquest
409:2 He g· the conquest
326:3 g· him victory.
327:2 g· the hungry needful
328:2 g· the hungry needful
334:2 g· a light to every
    2 g· but borrows none.
361:3 g·, for ashes, beauty,

givest
150:1 Who g·, for mourning,

giveth
 70:1 God g· light to all
154:2 thought that g· fear;
155:2 thought that g· fear;
156:2 thought that g· fear;
174:2 g· joy for sorrow,—
325:3 Life G· thee victory
381:3 God Who g· rest

giving
 10:3 life to all is g· ;
411:3 life to all is g· ;
108:4 G· sweet foretaste
150:3 For confident g·
171:3 G· God the honor
413:3 G· God the honor
174:2 Love's g· is forever;
360:1 grows rich in g· ;

giving's
150:3 giving and g· reward,

glad
 35:2 G· my eyes, and warm
 80:2 Whose streams make g·
108:4 the g· feast above,
150:1 with g· hearts we bring.
153:1 all in g· accord !
158:2 g· and golden hours
159:2 g· and golden hours
166:4 change to g· fruition,
167:4 change to g· fruition,
168:2 g· the eyes and cheer
190:4 chimes the g· days in,
191:4 chimes the g· days in,
207:3 make me g· for every
208:3 make me g· for every
209:3 make me g· for every
210:3 make me g· for every

glad
211:3 make me g for every
212:3 make me g for every
232:3 with this g song
406:3 with this g song
238:2 make our own time g,
239:2 make our own time g,
243:2 light, rejoice, are g,
244:2 light, rejoice, are g,
283:3 joyous and g adoration;
298:1 Heard ye the g sound?
299:1 Heard ye the g sound?
300:1 Heard ye the g sound?
301:1 Heard ye the g sound?
302:1 Heard ye the g sound?
311:3 g and willing mind
420:3 g and willing mind
342:1, 3 Be g, give thanks,
357:3 pure ... are always g;
358:3 pure ... are always g;
407:3 pure ... are always g;
361:3 g in this confiding,

gladly
53:2 G then we journey
203:1 Obeying g day by day
278:2 G obeying the call
279:2 G obeying the call

gladness
29:1 every heart with g,
51:3 g ring from every
52:3 g ring from every
119:1 Spirit, source of g,
120:2 forth in hymns of g,
150:2 For g that ripens
153:2 Thee, Lord, with g,
171:1 sing of Easter g
413:1 sing of Easter g
179:2 lifts the heart to g.
200:1 the day-star of g;
218:1 In g hither turn
219:1 In g hither turn
220:1 In g hither turn
249:2 g is the treasure
250:2 g is the treasure
263:1, 3 can bring us g,
351:3 the g of rejoicing
357:2 Lord, our g leave,
358:2 Lord, our g leave,
407:2 Lord, our g leave,
370:2 in God, O g:
384:2 g spring on every

gladsome
357:1 A g song begin,
358:1 A g song begin,
407:1 A g song begin,

glance
333:3 piercing g could bear;

gleam
37:3 How g thy watch fires
38:3 How g thy watch fires
140:2 g of love and prayer
359:1 day-star yet shall g.

gleams
238:1 g upon our sight,
239:1 g upon our sight,
351:1 G and burns the guiding

gloom
35:3 g of sin and grief;
95:2 scenes of deepest g,
169:1 amid the encircling g,
181:2 g is lost in glory
245:1 the way with g,
298:2 lift the shade of g,
299:2 lift the shade of g,
300:2 lift the shade of g,
301:2 lift the shade of g,
302:2 lift the shade of g,
351:2 Chasing far the g

gloomy
41:3 Away with g doubts
128:2 clouds of g night
129:2 clouds of g night
133:3 g thought remove,
424:3 g thought remove,
240:1 g shades of night,
241:1 g shades of night,
287:3 drear and g night;
408:3 drear and g night;

glories
111:3 g promised in Thy
164:3 g of his righteousness
165:3 g of his righteousness
417:3 g of his righteousness
298:2 g of one endless day."
299:2 g of one endless day."
300:2 g of one endless day."
301:2 g of one endless day."
302:2 g of one endless day."
336:1 g of the sky,
337:3 their g cease to be;
338:3 their g cease to be;
384:1 dazzling g view?

glorified
160:5 wake, God's g!
161:5 wake, God's g!
162:5 wake, God's g!
171:3 of God was g,
413:3 of God was g,

glorify
163:3 g our God above.
266:4 g our Father's grace,

glorious
2:1 g day is dawning,
2 Foresee the g morn,
30:3 greetings g from high
31:3 greetings g from high
32:3 greetings g from high
45:1 how g is Thy name
71:1 G things of thee
72:2 angels' g theme;
405:2 angels' g theme;
82:3 g Gospel of truth
120:2 g Salvation of our God.
154:1 light of g splendor
155:1 light of g splendor
156:1 light of g splendor
158:1 That g song of old,
159:1 That g song of old,
177:2 God ... , high and g,
202:4 g tidings of salvation
412:2 g tidings of salvation
273:1 Partners of a g hope,
274:1 Partners of a g hope,
280:3 G in His faithfulness.
282:2 for He is g;
310:1, Ref. G is the Christ,
317:3 Rises the g thought,
346:1 Sheds not its g ray,
401:1 Sheds not its g ray,
352:3 So g in humility.
353:3 So g in humility.
355:2 Our g trinity,
363:3 More g still, as
418:4 g morn shall break,

glory
1:1 as Thy g fills
9:1 All g be to God
12:3 light whose g, Lord,
13:3 light whose g, Lord,
35:1 Christ, whose g fills
42:2 To Thy praise and g
65:1, 3 From g unto g,
2 fullness of His g,
70:3 all His g share.
71:2 g and a covering,
72:1 G be to God on high,
God whose g fills
405:1 G be to God on high,
God whose g fills
73:1 G, honor, praise
79:3 His g shineth;
81:1 His g round me

glory
82:1-3 with the g of God
83:2 bliss and g find
85:2 g of Thy heaven;
86:1 God's g is a wondrous
87:1 God's g is a wondrous
111:1 goodness in full g
117:2 Thy g cannot see.
121:1 shall His g see.
122:1 shall His g see.
125:3 grace and g bright;
166:3 on from grace to g,
167:3 on from grace to g,
171:1 in g of an Easter
413:1 in g of an Easter
178:1 true crown and g,
181:2 gloom is lost in g
194:2 That g into speech.
410:2 That g into speech.
222:2 wakes, the g breaks,
223:2 wakes, the g breaks,
224:1 g in Thy name.
225:1 g in Thy name.
246:2 g of God be revealed,
247:2 prove His g there.
248:2 prove His g there.
264:4 G, laud and honor
275:1 G and power to Him
290:2 to higher g still.
292:2 power and the g,
297:1 g of the risen Lord;
318:3 Clothed in a g
329:1 heavens declare the g
334:2 g gilds the sacred
345:1 light of pentecostal g,
    2 see the g shine from
354:3 His be the g too.
371:3 We g in Thy light,
389:2 My treasure, my g,
414:1 Jesus and his g,
    Ref. my theme in g
415:2 g is ever shining;

glory-beaming
368:1 See that g star;
369:1 See that g star;

glow
65:1 rising splendors g,
126:3 In every action g.
127:3 In every action g.
403:3 In every action g.
126:4 bosom g with love.
127:4 bosom g with love.
403:4 bosom g with love.
185:3 light's triumphant g
266:1 love to man will g.
287:1 banished in the g
408:1 banished in the g

glow
311:1 burns Love's holy g,
420:1 burns Love's holy g,
319:1 on our path the g

glowed
229:2 with light which g

gloweth
345:3 Thine effulgence g,
379:2 heart wherein it g
380:2 heart wherein it g

glowing
267:2 see Truth's g face,
268:2 see Truth's g face,

glows
146:1 g so still, serene
147:1 g so still, serene
214:1 presence g in all,
218:2 the bright hope g,
219:2 the bright hope g,
220:2 the bright hope g,

go
5:1 for the fight g forth.
9:2 ever come and g,
12:2 G forward then,
13:2 G forward then,
41:1 G work to-day.
65:3 to strength we g,
74:1 G forth and stand
    2 G, take the little
75:2 Peace, the herald, g;
85:3 way that we must g
136:1 shall g with thee
139:3 with courage g,
427:3 with courage g,
160:3 sense, arise, g hence!
161:3 sense, arise, g hence!
162:3 sense, arise, g hence!
204:3 g in Thy strength,
222:1 silent stars g by;
223:1 silent stars g by;
242:2 G forth beneath
264:1 See, his banners g.
278:1 Grace to g forward,
279:1 Grace to g forward,
290:2 resolve to triumph g;
296:Ref. to victory g,
304:1 show me how to g
305:1 show me how to g
306:1 show me how to g
307:1 show me how to g
308:1 show me how to g
309:1 show me how to g
312:2 to strength g on;
339:1 up to light they g.

go
352:2 like thee did ever g
353:2 like thee did ever g
352:4 be mine to g,
353:4 be mine to g,
396:2 With sacred courage g.
397:2 With sacred courage g.

goal
64:3 its g draws nearer,

God
1:1 Be Thou, O G, exalted
3:4 dear Father-Mother, G,
4:2 O G, unite us heart to
5:2 With G alone agree.
6:1 hear the call of G
9:1 All glory be to G
    2 whisper G is Love.
    3 hearts that wait on G
10:2 Our Lord is G alone,
411:2 Our Lord is G alone,
10:3 give thanks to G
411:3 give thanks to G
11:1 G with us, Immanuel.
    2 G and man fore'er
12:2 Word of G is power
13:2 Word of G is power
12:3 Father-Mother G, whose
13:3 Father-Mother G, whose
14:1 G is thy sun,
    2 thy G hath wrought;
    3 G hath given thee
    4 Man's unity with G.
15:2 G forever sees His
18:2 G watches above thee,
19:2 G saith, These are
20:2 G is the only perfect
416:2 G is the only perfect
20:3 True to our G whose
416:3 True to our G whose
20:3 true to G above,
416:3 true to G above,
21:1 for Love is G; In G
    alone hath love
22:1 for Love is G; In G
    alone hath love
21:4 G who loveth us.
22:4 G who loveth us.
30:4 G, who gave that word
31:4 G, who gave that word
32:4 G, who gave that word
34:4 promise of our G
36:1 of the ever-living G,
37:1 City of G, how broad
38:1 City of G, how broad
39:3 Lead us to G,
40:3 from the throne of G,
41:3 can our G fulfill

61

God
222:3 G imparts to human
223:3 G imparts to human
224:2 G is G to me.
225:2 G is G to me.
224:3 G, I cast my care
225:3 G, I cast my care
232:1 is the child of G.
406:1 is the child of G.
233:1 walk the ways of G,
419:1 walk the ways of G,
234:4 G alone can give,
235:4 G alone can give,
236:4 Our G is one Mind,
237:2 G is watching with
    2 G is Life that
245:2 on and up to G.
246:Ref. The everlasting G
    2 glory of G be revealed,
247:1 walk with G along
248:1 walk with G along
247:1 the everlasting G,
248:1 the everlasting G,
247:2 Without your G repair,
248:2 Without your G repair,
251:1 Word of G, most holy,
252:1 Word of G, most holy,
251:2 Word of G the Father,
252:2 Word of G the Father,
253:7 whereto G leadeth me.
254:7 whereto G leadeth me.
255:7 whereto G leadeth me.
256:7 whereto G leadeth me.
257:7 whereto G leadeth me.
258:3 Standeth G within
260:1 is the thought of G.
    2 forth the thought of G.
    3 their thought of G.
    4 blessed thought of G.
261:1 holy church of G
262:1 holy church of G
263:1,3 Only G can bring
    1,3 Only G can give
    3 G the perfect Friend;
264:2 Moves the Church of G;
265:1 G hath set a guardian
266:1 Our G is Love, and
    1 love to G inspired,
    2 truly born of G
267:1 G is All-in-all,
268:1 G is All-in-all,
267:1 know that G is here.
268:1 know that G is here.
267:2 G is All; in space
268:2 G is All; in space
269:1 G is Love, unchanging
270:1 G is Love, unchanging
269:2 G is Mind, the perfect

God
270:2 G is Mind, the perfect
271:1 Our G shall reign
272:1 Our G shall reign
273:2 G, the only Mind,
274:2 G, the only Mind,
275:2 our G and Friend.
276:2 O Thou G of peace,
277:2 O Thou G of peace,
276:2 Peace of G which
277:2 Peace of G which
282:2 G hath made His
    2 G of our salvation;
283:1 our G and our King,
287:1 Great G of light,
408:1 Great G of light,
288:2 know that G is all;
289:2 know that G is all;
288:2 way that leads to G.
289:2 way that leads to G.
296:Ref. side with G, and win!
    2 that walks with G.
297:2 G and men do meet,
303:4 G is with all that
311:3 To G then praises
420:3 To G then praises
312:1 strength which G supplies
    1 The panoply of G.
313:2 G, in light abiding,
326:1 armor of his G;
327:1 The G who made both
328:1 The G who made both
331:3 Love G and man:
332:1 know that He is G,
333:3 G and heaven were
340:2 love of G is broader
341:1-3 G is present
    2 to G in prayer,
345:3 G Himself bestoweth
347:2 G bids the storm
348:2 G bids the storm
350:1 love of G our
    2 still, in G confiding,
    3 G is every need supply-
      ing,
351:2 hope our G inspires;
    3 march in G begun:
352:1 love, O Son of G.
353:1 love, O Son of G.
352:3 footsteps, Son of G.
353:3 footsteps, Son of G.
354:1 G the Spirit leads
    3 G works in us to will,
356:1 To Thee, O G, we bring
357:1 our loving Father, G,
358:1 our loving Father, G,
407:1 our loving Father, G,
357:3 The smile of G they

God
358:3 The smile of G they
407:3 The smile of G they
359:1 G the unchanging pities
360:1 G will bear both
    2 None but G its void
361:1 Trust all to G,
    3 G lights the way
364:2 G that labor bless;
    3 in faith to G applies.
365:2 G has promised needful
366:2 G has promised needful
367:4 G by grace shall dwell
    4 G Himself is Light.
368:3 Son of G is come.
369:3 Son of G is come.
370:1,2 hid with Christ in G.
371:1 G of Life, to Thee,
    2 G of Truth, to Thee,
    3 G of Love, to Thee,
    3 That Thou art G.
376:1 leads us home to G.
377:1 leads us home to G.
378:1 Thou art G.
    3 G, we bless Thy name,
379:2 G, whose boundless love
380:2 G, whose boundless love
381:3 G Who giveth rest
382:4 hast the gift of G—
383:3 And pray of G, that
384:1 G is seen with men
385:1 fathers' G before her
386:3 of our Saviour, G,
387:3 of our Saviour, G,
389:1 While Thou, O my G,
    1 my G and my all.
    2 my G, and my all.
391:3 G lives in eternal
392:4 For G is all, and
393:4 For G is all, and
399:3 G is His own interpreter,
400:3 G is His own interpreter,
425:1 G in His own Word
    2 G shall wipe all tears

God-idea
23:3 G, Life-encrowned,
24:3 G, Life-encrowned,
25:3 G, Life-encrowned,
26:3 G, Life-encrowned,
27:3 G, Life-encrowned,
28:3 G, Life-encrowned,

Godlike
3:1 every lovely, G grace
29:2 G in its strength
352:3 So meek, forgiving, G,
353:3 So meek, forgiving, G,

God's
3:2 Where G omnipotence,
9:2 G angels ever come
15:3 Beheld G child
17:1 G day of rest is
3 G messenger of love,
19:2 G messengers of Love
20:2 seen as G own son,
416:2 seen as G own son,
51:3 G will is done;
52:3 G will is done;
51:3 as G own child,
52:3 as G own child,
59:2 through G good grace,
60:2 through G good grace,
61:2 through G good grace,
82:2 to work G work,
83:3 All G children dwell
84:1 G eternal Word
2 G commands forever
86:1 G glory is a wondrous
87:1 G glory is a wondrous
92:3 G will he makes his
93:1 Assured G goodness
95:1 G hand that leadeth
120:1 G reign of joy
124:1 gentle G commands,
402:1 gentle G commands,
139:1 G presence with me
427:1 G presence with me
139:2 G healing truth is
427:2 G healing truth is
146:4 man is G great heir.
147:4 man is G great heir.
149:2 Held by G love
426:2 Held by G love
149:3 is in G care,
426:3 is in G care,
154:1 as G own child;
155:1 as G own child;
156:1 as G own child;
157:1 G will be done.
3 G children all shall
160:5 wake, G glorified!
161:5 wake, G glorified!
162:5 wake, G glorified!
166:3 G own hand shall
167:3 G own hand shall
168:1 our G great name
170:1 G exceeding grace,
176:1 wrought by G command,
2 in G great Word,
178:1 Truly is G counsel
216:1 trusts in G protection
1 G law can understand,
221:2 G own Son beloved,
3 G idea, man, rejoices,
232:2 man is G own child.

God's
406:2 man is G own child.
236:1 G kingdom at hand!
2 G love be retold,
3 So G loving children
4 G bountiful peace,
237:4 G own image will
238:4 G love and blessing,
239:4 G love and blessing,
243:1 G dear gift to all
244:1 G dear gift to all
246:2 G will is done,
249:1 when we see G mercy
250:1 when we see G mercy
258:1 G new Messiah,
2 G supreme design.
261:3 all G faithful sons,
262:3 all G faithful sons,
269:1 G promises are kept.
270:1 G promises are kept.
292:1 is G mighty Word!
297:1 G gift, the glory
313:2 theme of G salvation,
314:3 G blessings manifold.
322:1 in G healing service
323:1 in G healing service
325:3 in G own strength,
339:3 we, G children true,
340:1 wideness in G mercy,
342:1 amplitude of G dear
351:2 of G own presence,
364:1 G protecting arm.
390:1 faith in G great love
396:3 cause is G and will
397:3 cause is G and will
414:2 G own holy word.

God-sent
221:3 Science, G message

goes
17:2 challenge, Who g there?
136:3 presence ever g with
351:1 g the pilgrim band,

goeth
97:1 g forth with weeping,
98:1 g forth with weeping,

going
189:2 My g and my coming
263:2 stars in order g,
264:1, Ref. G on before.
415:1 I am g To where

gold
15:1 g by fire is tested,
123:3 and thy g to refine.
215:2 their stores of g.

gold
249:2 An everlasting g,
250:2 An everlasting g,
329:2 better far than g.
360:1 fill with g the plain.

golden
41:1 waves the g grain,
126:4 g chain that binds
127:4 g chain that binds
403:4 g chain that binds
158:2 glad and g hours
159:2 glad and g hours
398:2 g flame burn clear;

Golden Rule
178:2 Love, the G R of

gone
29:2 g across the ocean,
108:2 is past and g;
169:3 till The night is g,
192:2 The sun g down,
193:2 The sun g down,
213:3 like an evening g,
310:2 G are chaos, fear

good
48:1 g and perfect gifts
51:3 The longing to be g
52:3 The longing to be g
56:3 seek Thee Thou art g;
58:2 Thou alone art g
59:1 Fight he g fight
60:1 Fight the g fight
61:1 Fight the g fight
59:2 through God's g grace,
60:2 through God's g grace,
61:2 through God's g grace,
76:1 the true, eternal g;
85:1 eternal g, Lift our
96:2 doing g And casting
102:1 Author of celestial g,
103:1 Author of celestial g,
120:1 G tidings of g things;
125:3 No g from him shall
134:2 turns all to g.
135:2 shall inherit All g,
150:2 the Sower's g seed.
160:3 Our God is g.
161:3 Our God is g.
162:3 Our God is g.
180:2 G from God is sent
2 neighbor's g his own.
181:3 g gifts from above.
185:1 'tis g to be here,
2 'tis g to hold fast
201:1 Against the light of g;
404:1 Against the light of g;

good
207:3 since God is g, and
208:3 since God is g, and
209:3 since God is g, and
210:3 since God is g, and
211:3 since God is g, and
212:3 since God is g, and
216:2 All g for you His
217:3 work was doing g;
224:2 All g, where'er it
225:2 All g, where'er it
224:3 here all g provide;
225:3 here all g provide;
238:2 all of g the past
239:2 all of g the past
253:7 some daily g to do
254:7 some daily g to do
255:7 some daily g to do
256:7 some daily g to do
257:7 some daily g to do
258:1 the g or evil side.
315:1 The g we may do here.
316:1 The g we may do here.
315:3 The g, the joy that
316:3 The g, the joy that
326:4 Fights his g fight
330:4 G Shepherd, may I
342:2 G things are freely
364:3 all g is given
374:2 g alone is here.
375:2 g alone is here.
381:2 Mind, all g supplying,

goodness
45:2 Thy grace and g
57:3 on Thy g leaning;
72:2 G one eternal stream.
405:2 G one eternal stream.
79:2 changeless g prove;
93:1 God's g ne'er will
111:1 Thy g in full glory
124:3 g stands approved,
402:3 g stands approved,
150:1 In mercy, in g, how
2 strong with Thy g
275:3 Mercy and g forever
330:1, 4 g faileth never;
374:1 praise Thee for Thy g
375:1 praise Thee for Thy g

good will
158:1 peace on earth, g w
159:1 peace on earth, g w
236:2 men of g w may their
310:1, 2 Peace on earth, g w

gospel
29:1 Christian Science g,
42:1 From the G, from the G

gospel
82:3 glorious G of truth
128:1 flowed the g sound
129:1 flowed the g sound
168:2 light Of G truth
177:2 the g be victorious
233:1 with the g shod;
419:1 with the g shod;
326:1 with the g shod:
363:2 the G light Becomes
386:2 holy g we profess;
387:2 holy g we profess;

Gospel-day
346:1 where the G Sheds not
401:1 where the G Sheds not

gospel's
363:1 the G sacred page

governed
141:2 G by a power

grace
3:1 lovely, Godlike g
8:2 Thy g can foil
42:1 heart Thy g inherit;
43:1 pardon, g, and peace,
45:2 Thy g and goodness
51:1 beauty, power and g,
52:1 beauty, power and g,
59:2 through God's good g,
60:2 through God's good g,
61:2 through God's good g,
65:3 g for g abundantly
71:3 G, which like the Lord,
91:1-3 G for to-day,
422:1-3 G for to-day,
91:3 love and perfect g.
422:3 love and perfect g.
99:3 His power and g,
100:3 His power and g;
108:1 grasp ... th'eternal g,
113:3 Clothe us in the g
123:3 My g, all sufficient,
125:3 Gives g and glory
128:1 lips of gentleness and g,
129:1 lips of gentleness and g,
164:3 world with truth and g,
165:3 world with truth and g,
417:3 world with truth and g,
166:3 on from g to glory,
167:3 on from g to glory,
170:1 God's exceeding g,
176:3 worthy such a g,
189:2 crowneth with His g.
199:2 Encompassed by His g,
226:1 g that ever grows,
240:1 Thy g is unconfined;

grace
241:1 Thy g is unconfined;
243:1 happy g of gentleness.
244:1 happy g of gentleness.
243:3 gentle g of Love
244:3 gentle g of Love
249:1 Of His unbounded g,
250:1 Of His unbounded g,
259:2 every outward g;
266:4 our Father's g,
4 that g to prove.
269:3 growth in g express,
270:3 growth in g express,
278:2 G to go forward,
279:2 G to go forward,
280:3 His g and favor
322:2 And flowers of g
323:2 And flowers of g
332:1 deep desire for g,
341:1 seek the throne of g,
346:3 the lamp of g,
401:3 the lamp of g,
350:1 g that sealed us,
354:2 Supported by His g,
364:2 His g and favor,
365:2 promised needful g:
366:2 promised needful g:
367:4 God by g shall dwell
374:3 blessings, light and g
375:3 blessings, light and g
383:3 pray of God, that g
386:3 g subdues the claim
387:3 g subdues the claim

gracious
4:3 all his g word,
11:1 the g news to tell,
36:1 Father's g choice;
39:1 g Spirit, heavenly
49:2 The g calling of
50:2 The g calling of
58:2 alone art good and g,
72:1 G Father, in Thy
405:1 G Father, in Thy
88:1 G Spirit, dwell
89:1 G Spirit, dwell
88:1 I myself would g be,
89:1 I myself would g be,
88:1 Christ's own g spirit
89:1 Christ's own g spirit
102:1 prayer, O g Father,
103:1 prayer, O g Father,
123:2 g, omnipotent hand;
137:1 Most g Lord;
181:3 learn, O g Father,
199:2 know our g God
201:3 this most g hour.
404:3 this most g hour.

gracious
281:1 great and g˙ Lord,
365:1 To His g˙ promise
366:1 To His g˙ promise

grain
41:1 waves the golden g˙,
97:2 rising g˙ appear;
98:2 rising g˙ appear;
360:1 wealth is living g˙;

grander
218:4 wide horizon's g˙ view;
219:4 wide horizon's g˙ view;
220:4 wide horizon's g˙ view;

grandeur
149:2 the g˙ of a heart's
426:2 the g˙ of a heart's
329:1 beauty, g˙, order,

grant
3:4 G˙ then, dear
48:1 dost g˙ All good
104:2 G˙ us, O Love,
319:3 G˙ us Thy truth
343:4 G˙ us that Way to
344:4 G˙ us that Way to
429:4 G˙ us that Way to

grants
281:2 He it is who g˙ us

grasp
108:1 g˙ with firmer hand

grasps
54:1 Faith g˙ the blessing

grateful
3:1 g˙ heart a garden is,
2 g˙ heart a fortress is,
3 g˙ heart a temple is,
4 largess of a g˙ heart
45:3 hearts in g˙ song
199:1 g˙ hearts and voices
249:2 g˙ hearts will hold.
250:2 g˙ hearts will hold.
259:1 thrice more g˙, Lord,
356:3 deeply g˙ praise;

gratitude
73:1 Psalms of g˙ and praise
146:1 The gift of g˙.
147:1 The gift of g˙.
146:2 g˙ doth steadfastly
147:2 g˙ doth steadfastly
146:4 In seamless g˙ I weave
147:4 In seamless g˙ I weave
217:3 life a psalm of g˙.
233:3 turn In g˙ toward

gratitude
419:3 turn In g˙ toward
249:2 Our g˙ is riches,
250:2 Our g˙ is riches,

grave
8:3 where, g˙, thy victory?
325:3 victory o'er the g˙.
381:2 over cross and g˙.
388:2 g˙ could hold no dread,

graven
76:2 thy name is g˙,

gray
139:2 dispels the clouds of g˙
427:2 dispels the clouds of g˙

great
34:2 G˙ are companions such
65:3 g˙ things He hath
90:1 O Thou g˙ Jehovah,
92:4 In Thy g˙ work to
96:2 The G˙ Physician
108:4 Lamb's g˙ bridal feast
113:1 with Thy g˙ might.
131:2 the heart's g˙ needs.
132:2 the heart's g˙ needs.
146:4 is God's g˙ heir.
147:4 is God's g˙ heir.
150:1 how g˙ is our King;
153:2 done to me g˙ things,
168:1 our God's g˙ name,
172:1 that g˙ Light divine,
176:2 in God's g˙ Word,
183:2 useful and the g˙,
184:2 useful and the g˙,
217:3 the g˙ example Of him
224:3 g˙ concern shall be
225:3 g˙ concern shall be
258:1 A g˙ cause, God's
281:1 g˙ and gracious Lord,
287:1 G˙ God of light,
408:1 G˙ God of light,
312:1 in His g˙ might,
331:3 this g˙ command Doth
347:2 g˙ shall be their peace.
348:2 g˙ shall be their peace.
349:1 The g˙, eternal, Holy
362:2 g˙ and mighty Lord,
378:3 our song, G˙ I AM.
381:4 G˙ peace have they,
386:1 Jesus our g˙ Master
387:1 Jesus our g˙ Master
388:2 their g˙ deliverer
390:1 in God's g˙ love
2 How g˙ the promise,
394:2 G˙ the work they have
395:2 G˙ the work they have

greater
121:4 g˙ things than these
122:4 g˙ things than these
151:2 is g˙ Than sacrifice
152:2 is g˙ Than sacrifice
215:2 has treasures g˙ far
390:2 could there g˙ be?

greatest
173:4 the g˙ of the three,

greatness
292:2 His is the g˙,

green
55:2 forever in g˙ pastures
148:3 G˙ pastures are before
245:3 Truth's g˙ pastures

greet
190:1 To g˙ them with this
191:1 To g˙ them with this
391:4 rise and g˙ the signs

greeting
218:2 hand the g˙ flows,
219:2 hand the g˙ flows,
220:2 hand the g˙ flows,

greetings
30:3 g˙ glorious from high
31:3 g˙ glorious from high
32:3 g˙ glorious from high

grew
322:2 weeds of error g˙.
323:2 weeds of error g˙.

grief
29:1 and g˙ it heals.
35:3 gloom of sin and g˙;
253:6 tired joy and g˙ afar,
254:6 tired joy and g˙ afar,
255:6 tired joy and g˙ afar,
256:6 tired joy and g˙ afar,
257:6 tired joy and g˙ afar,
371:1 all g˙ consoled,
378:2 comforted in g˙,

griefs
192:4 Out of my stony g˙
193:4 Out of my stony g˙

grieving
101:1 g˙ hearts were healed;

ground
64:2 I stand is holy g˙;
164:2 thorns infest the g˙;
165:2 thorns infest the g˙;
417:2 thorns infest the g˙;

ground
227:1 place is hallowed g.
384:2 On parched g shall

groves
331:2 Sheba's g or Sharon's

grow
57:2 Then we g quiet,
105:3 in all things g;
106:3 in all things g;
107:3 in all things g;
138:2 and fears g still;
164:2 sin and sorrow g,
165:2 sin and sorrow g,
417:2 sin and sorrow g,
226:2 Thy beam g bright;
243:2 How hearts g light,
244:2 How hearts g light,
318:3 how fair they g,
330:2 verdant pastures g,
360:2 serving love will g.
376:2 way will brighter g,
377:2 way will brighter g,
384:2 shall lilies g

growing
320:4 With g ardor onward
321:4 With g ardor onward
409:4 With g ardor onward
320:4 With g brightness
321:4 With g brightness
409:4 With g brightness

grows
64:3 to me g clearer,
226:1 grace that ever g,
304:3 when day g dark
305:3 when day g dark
306:3 when day g dark
307:3 when day g dark
308:3 when day g dark
309:3 when day g dark
360:1 g rich in giving;

growth
269:3 g in grace express,
270:3 g in grace express,

guard
9:3 comfort, g and guide.
114:2 to guide and g;
115:2 only g from harm.
116:2 only g from harm.
124:2 g His children well.
402:2 g His children well.
175:2 G and guide us every
213:4 g while ages last,

guardian
39:1 Be Thou our g,
99:1 God his g made,
100:1 God his g made
265:1 set a g legion

guards
207:1 that g the nestling's
208:1 that g the nestling's
209:1 that g the nestling's
210:1 that g the nestling's
211:1 that g the nestling's
212:1 that g the nestling's
362:3 ever g his throne,

guidance
70:2 Plain shall His g
81:2 my perfect g be,
121:2 ask no more Than g
122:2 ask no more Than g
282:1 For their g hath He

guide
8:2 my g and stay can be?
9:3 comfort, guard and g.
39:1 guardian, Thou our g,
53:2 our ever-present g
90:1 G me, O Thou great
96:2 friend and g to be;
102:3 Love will g us all
103:3 Love will g us all

guide
114:2 art to g and guard;
148:2 He may g me,
160:1 So Love doth g;
161:1 So Love doth g;
162:1 So Love doth g;
166:3 hand shall g thee
167:3 hand shall g thee
175:2 Guard and g us every
181:1 G us upward to
195:2 follow still my g,
214:3 know no other g,
234:2 g them in the homeward
235:2 g them in the homeward
245:1 Love will g us,
251:2 g us to our Lord;
252:2 g us to our Lord;
275:3 goodness forever g;
278:2 wherever He g thee,
279:2 wherever He g thee,
291:3 Father, Friend, and G.
385:1 awful g, in smoke and

guided
138:3 love has always g
185:1 G ... to joy-crowned

guides
281:2 G His Israel on
376:1 g us in our journey
377:1 g us in our journey
392:2 Christ now g us,
393:2 Christ now g us,

guiding
11:1 G them at break of
265:3 G, cheering, like
283:2 protecting and g;
350:2 the Spirit's g;
351:1 burns the g light;

guile
33:3 G nor violence shall
121:1 g their thoughts are
122:1 g their thoughts are

H

habitation
33:1 In His secret h
71:2 Round each h hovering,
207:2 His h high is here,
208:2 His h high is here,
209:2 His h high is here,
210:2 His h high is here,
211:2 His h high is here,
212:2 His h high is here,

had
224:2 h a stronger faith,
225:2 h a stronger faith,
238:2 good the past hath h
239:2 good the past hath h

hail
170:1 every creature h
247:3 ye still shall h,

hail
248:3 ye still shall h,
388:2 h their great deliverer
392:1 h the new appearing;
393:1 h the new appearing;

hails
146:3 With confidence it h
147:3 With confidence it h

half
384:1 h the wonders tell,
390:3 we only h believe

hallow
140:1 to h all we find,
345:1 To purge and h us,

hallowed
205:3 e'en here the h bliss
227:1 every place is h
251:1 from the h page,
252:1 from the h page,

halt
388:2 the h and lame

hand
7:2 Thee at h to bless,
8:3 Thee at h to bless;
46:3 times are in Thy h:
47:3 times are in Thy h:
51:1 The h that fashions
52:1 The h that fashions
72:2 wonders of His h:
405:2 wonders of His h:
73:1 In His h is all
74:2 out the angel's h;
76:2 In My h thy name
77:1 God at my right h?
78:1 God at my right h?
90:1 with Thy powerful h.
95:1 God's h that leadeth
Ref. By His own h He
Ref. For by His h He
2 His h that leadeth
108:1 grasp with firmer h
115:1 Thy h hath brought
116:1 Thy h hath brought
123:2 gracious, omnipotent h,
124:2 That h which bears
402:2 That h which bears
134:3 Thy h in all things
3 all things in Thy h.
138:2 I take Thy h
166:3 God's own h shall
167:3 God's own h shall
173:4 Joining h in h
174:3 Heaven is at h, when
177:1 are near at h;
218:2 h to h the greeting
219:2 h to h the greeting
220:2 h to h the greeting
228:1 lay our h upon
236:1 God's kingdom at h!
245:3 strong h doth uphold;
280:2 In His h He gently
311:3 gifts His h doth bring

hand
420:3 gifts His h doth bring
314:1 hold not thy h;
326:1 sword is in his h;
350:1 Strong the h
351:1 the h of brother,
361:3 naught His h delays;

handiwork
45:1 heavens, Thy h,
329:1 His h is shown.

handle
108:1 and h things unseen;

hands
6:2 sleep to fold thy h,
58:2 hearts and willing h,
83:1 united hearts and h.
111:2 wonders of Thy h;
320:1 working of His h?
321:1 working of His h?
409:1 working of His h?
324:1 Take my h, and let
381:4 love their h employ.
388:3 with willing h dispense

happiness
58:3 We can share Thy h,

happy
16:1 Thy pure and h child.
83:2 endless h whole,
92:1 H the man who knows
93:1 H the man whose heart
215:1 h is the man who
243:1 h grace of gentleness.
244:1 h grace of gentleness.
264:4 Join our h throng;
350:2 H still, in God
398:3 O, h servant he,

harbor
297:2 H of refuge till

hard
190:1 tasks of life seem h
191:1 tasks of life seem h
360:1 burden h and heavy?

hardness
278:3 Healed is thy h,
279:3 Healed is thy h,

harm
33:3 violence shall h thee
99:2 h and pestilence.
115:2 only guard from h.
116:2 only guard from h.
311:2 Unconscious of their h:

harm
420:2 Unconscious of their h:
343:3 nor hell shall h.
344:3 nor hell shall h.
429:3 nor hell shall h.

harmonies
94:3 Thy h to hear

harmonious
310:2 Dawns on earth h day.

harmony
236:3 hues in h blend,
371:3 to find ... Thy h.

harms
304:3 Tear or triumph h,
305:3 Tear or triumph h,
306:3 Tear or triumph h,
307:3 Tear or triumph h,
308:3 Tear or triumph h,
309:3 Tear or triumph h,

harp
200:3 Extolled with the h

harpstrings
253:1 waiting h of the mind
254:1 waiting h of the mind
255:1 waiting h of the mind
256:1 waiting h of the mind
257:1 waiting h of the mind

harsh
238:3 h noises of our day,
239:3 h noises of our day,
315:1 let no h word mar
316:1 let no h word mar

harshness
243:3 and h disappear
244:3 and h disappear

harvest
37:2 one h song,
38:2 one h song,
41:1 idle on the h plain?
2 H draws nigh.
97:2 H time is surely
98:2 H time is surely
150:2 the wide h field,
242:1 for white h fields,
3 bear our h home.
314:3 h now is white;
394:2 Mighty shall the h
395:2 Mighty shall the h
394:3 Lord of h, let
395:3 Lord of h, let

has
40:1-3 Earth h· no sorrow
85:3 that h· no turning,
148:3 Father h· my treasure,
228:1 life h· no eclipse,
361:1 who h· thy treasure,

hast
183:1 h· no time to lose
184:1 h· no time to lose
382:4 h· the gift of God—

haste
166:3 H· thee on from
167:3 H· thee on from
183:1 Make h·, O man,
184:1 Make h·, O man,

hasten
82:2 do to h· the time,

hastening
158:3 days are h· on,
159:3 days are h· on,

hastens
363:1 as it h·, every age

hate
48:2 what hold has h·
141:4 of fear and h·,
179:3 Conquering h·,
207:3 love more for every h·,
208:3 love more for every h·,
209:3 love more for every h·,
210:3 love more for every h·,
211:3 love more for every h·,
212:3 love more for every h·,
228:3 such as h· our Master's
232:3 sorrow, h·, and pain,
406:3 sorrow, h·, and pain,
236:3 No more let dire h·

hate's
160:4 Ayont h· thrall:
161:4 Ayont h· thrall:
162:4 Ayont h· thrall:

hath
6:2 to-day h· need of thee.
7:2 Sin h· no power
21:1 In God alone h· love
22:1 In God alone h· love
34:2 dwells with Love h·
43:1 that h· no ending,
44:2 Fear h· no dwelling
133:2 heart sweet comfort h·,
424:2 heart sweet comfort h·,
153:1 spirit h· rejoicing,

hatred
18:2 if h· and loss,

have
5:2 h· no other aim
8:3 Ills h· no weight,
44:1 no more h· sway.
48:3 h· Dominion over all.
85:1 Thy love we h· for
154:3 h· no pain or sorrow,
155:3 h· no pain or sorrow,
156:3 h· no pain or sorrow,
181:4 h· no more dominion.
182:3 They cease to h· who
224:2 must h· all things
225:2 must h· all things
260:1 One thought I h·,
263:3 H· we all a sure
264:3 h· Christ's own promise,
318:2 He shall h· peace
381:4 Great peace h· they,
390:3 ask and h· not
394:2 Great the work they h·
395:2 Great the work they h·
399:2 h· a bitter taste,
400:2 h· a bitter taste,

haven
392:1 h· of rest is nearing.
393:1 h· of rest is nearing.

head
99:2 cover thy unguarded h·.
100:2 cover thy unguarded h·,
105:3 Thee, our living H·,
106:3 Thee, our living H·,
107:3 Thee, our living H·,
292:2 as h· over all!
326:2 helmet on his h·,
399:1 blessings on your h·.
400:1 blessings on your h·.
425:1 pilgrim, lift your h·,

heads
19:1 joy upon their h·,
229:1 o'er the h· of all.

heal
5:2 mission is to h·.
88:1 words that help and h·
89:1 words that help and h·
175:2 to save and h· us,
243:1 power to h· and bless,
244:1 power to h· and bless,
304:3 h· the heart,
305:3 h· the heart,
306:3 h· the heart,
307:3 h· the heart,
308:3 h· the heart,
309:3 h· the heart,

healed
30:2 loved and h· mankind:
31:2 loved and h· mankind:
32:2 loved and h· mankind:
34:1 The sick are h·,
101:1 grieving hearts were h·;
150:2 when sorrow is h·;
175:1 His Word and h· them,
246:2 all shall be h·;
278:3 H· is thy hardness,
279:3 H· is thy hardness,
280:1 h·, restored, forgiven,
342:3 for sorrow h·,
350:1 the Love that h· us,
388:1 The sick were h·,

Healer
96:2 The H· by Gennesaret

healeth
151:1 Thy presence h· me.
152:1 Thy presence h· me.
339:2 h· sorrow's blight,

healing
12:2 love and h· ministry
13:2 love and h· ministry
17:3 h· in his wings
57:1 whence our h· flows;
69:3 with Thy h· touch,
423:3 with Thy h· touch,
85:2 seek Thy perfect h·
90:2 the h· waters flow;
96:1 h· gift God gives
109:1 God, Thy h· presence
110:1 God, Thy h· presence
139:2 God's h· truth is free
427:2 God's h· truth is free
141:3 the h· of mankind.
146:4 silent, h· prayer,
147:4 silent, h· prayer,
168:4 h· power once more
171:2 Truth's h· garment
413:2 Truth's h· garment
175:1 tender h· message
176:2 H· and peace to all
178:1 H· mind and heart
181:3 reflect Thy h· love.
195:2 heaven's own h· air;
202:2 on his wings of h·;
412:1 on his wings of h·;
221:1 h· power makes plain:
243:3 tender, h· power.
244:3 tender, h· power.
259:1 One cup of h· oil
263:2 h· word of Love.
313:1 h· in his wings.
322:1 in God's h· service
323:1 in God's h· service

healing
339:3 His h love make
346:2 bring ... H and sight,
401:2 bring ... H and sight,
371:2 proclaim Thy h power.
372:3 h of the seamless dress
373:2 h of the seamless dress
378:2 H and joy are ours,
392:2 of h in his wings
393:2 of h in his wings

healing's
109:2 forth in h sign,
110:2 forth in h sign,

heals
29:1 and grief it h.
81:2 h, and sets me free.
179:2 Love h our every
217:1 h the spirit broken,

health
7:2 H, hope and love
40:1 h and peace are found,
70:3 is thy light and h ;
73:2 Joy, h, hope, for all
168:4 which h conferred:
4 and h to us restore.
195:3 Thou art my h,
341:2 in our h,
342:3 h and peace restored;
346:2 H to the sick
401:2 H to the sick

hear
2:2 h in shrinking terror,
6:1 h the call of God
9:4 h the angel-song
55:1 Father, h the prayer
58:2 h no other voices,
67:2 H the victors who
68:2 H the victors who
67:3 H, ..., h thy Lord;
68:3 H, ..., h thy Lord;
70:1 to h that call;
76:2 H His gentle Peace,
2 H His voice above
84:1 O h it calling.
2 h thy living voice,
94:3 Thy harmonies to h
102:1 H our prayer, O
103:1 H our prayer, O
136:1 I h Thy promise
158:1,2 h the angels sing.
159:1,2 h the angels sing.
170:1 To h the song
202:4 The deaf to h ;
412:2 The deaf to h ;
222:3 may h his coming,

hear
223:3 may h his coming,
230:2 We faintly h,
231:2 We faintly h,
237:1 to h the message,
242:2 We h the call;
267:4 h Thy loving call,
268:4 h Thy loving call,
290:3 shall ye h His word,
296:2 h your Captain's
310:1, 2 H th' angelic song
332:2 So h and heed His
342:2 will h before we call,
346:1 H us, we humbly pray,
401:1 H us, we humbly pray,
372:4 we h thy call,
373:2 we h thy call,
374:3 may h Thee calling:
375:3 may h Thee calling:
384:3 The deaf shall h,
414:3 thirsting To h it
418:1 hush our breath to h,

heard
5:1 from heaven we have h,
49:2 like theirs who h,
50:2 like theirs who h,
176:2 faithful, they who h,
246:Ref. Have ye not h,
271:4 songs be h again
272:4 songs be h again
281:1 Word we have h
298:1 H ye the glad sound?
299:1 H ye the glad sound?
300:1 H ye the glad sound?
301:1 H ye the glad sound?
302:1 H ye the glad sound?
346:1 Chaos and darkness h,
401:1 Chaos and darkness h,
374:1 hast h our prayer.
375:1 hast h our prayer.
414:2 some have never h
418:2 voice that must be h,

heareth
263:2 word of wisdom h

hears
73:2 Man, ..., h His voice.
215:1 h Instruction's warning
287:3 all creation h anew
408:3 all creation h anew

hear'st
374:1 h Thy children's call.
375:1 h Thy children's call.

heart
3:1 grateful h a garden

heart
3:2 grateful h a fortress
3 grateful h a temple
4 largess of a grateful h
4:2 unite us h to h,
14:2 praise, O waking h,
16:3 My h is joyous,
29:1 Filling every h with
30:5 h to h Speaks kindly
31:5 h to h Speaks kindly
32:5 h to h Speaks kindly
34:2 lonely h is fed.
35:1 Day-star, in my h
2 and warm my h.
39:2 holy joy in every h,
42:1 Let each h Thy grace
44:3 Come, trusting h, come
54:2 made the h rejoice,
57:3 Low in the h faith
64:1 My h is singing:
67:3 Hide within thy h
68:3 Hide within thy h
69:1 an understanding h,
423:1 an understanding h,
69:2 a meek and contrite h,
423:2 a meek and contrite h,
69:3 a gentle, loving h,
423:3 a gentle, loving h,
73:2 h may understand His
77:2 My h, with courage
78:2 My h, with courage
77:2 His might thy h shall
78:2 His might thy h shall
80:1 make our h afraid?
81:2 h that peace inherit
91:3 Patient of h his way
422:3 Patient of h his way
93:1 whose h can rest,
94:1 h within thee burned
2 to thy silent h,
118:1 Shine upon this h
2 Still this restless h
3 Dwell within this h
121:4 no human h can reach,
122:4 no human h can reach,
133:2 h sweet comfort hath,
424:2 h sweet comfort hath,
148:1 No change my h shall
1 h may low be laid;
151:1 h with love Thou
152:1 h with love Thou
164:1 Let every h prepare
165:1 Let every h prepare
417:1 Let every h prepare
168:2 and cheer the h.
170:2 Feels in his h
178:1 Healing mind and h

70

heart
179:2 lifts the h to
180:1 h and soul and mind.
188:1 entered h of man,
201:4 open wide your h
404:4 open wide your h
217:2 fold to thy h thy
218:2 h to h the bright
219:2 h to h the bright
220:2 h to h the bright
221:2 Within each h is
228:2 it fills the h;
234:2 slow of h to move
235:2 slow of h to move
238:4 h shall sigh no more
239:4 h shall sigh no more
259:2 Within the pious h
261:3 The pure in h her
262:3 The pure in h her
266:1 h with love to God
269:2 The h that yearns for
270:2 The h that yearns for
276:1 Peace to every h
277:1 Peace to every h
291:1 my froward h,
303:3 may touch the h
304:3 heal the h,
305:3 heal the h,
306:3 heal the h,
307:3 heal the h,
308:3 heal the h,
309:3 heal the h,
320:2 Supports the fainting h;
321:2 Supports the fainting h;
409:2 Supports the fainting h;
322:2 Thy truth upon the h
323:2 Thy truth upon the h
331:1 The h a stranger to
333:2 from a h that burned
340:2 h of the Eternal
341:3 my h, in every strait,
342:1 every h may know
343:2 And purify the h.
344:2 And purify the h.
429:2 And purify the h.
345:2 shine from h to h.
351:3 as from the h of one;
355:2 Thou h of heaven
   2 every h shall see
357:3 pure in h are always
358:3 pure in h are always
407:3 pure in h are always
360:1 h grows rich in giving;
   2 h a well left empty?
   2 h a living power?
367:2 Thy h made truly His,
379:2 h wherein it gloweth
380:2 h wherein it gloweth

heart
381:1 Her h was thrilled
382:2 pure and sinless h;
390:1 h shrink back at
392:2 h that knows him
393:2 h that knows him
415:2 longing h, my longing h

heart-desire
194:1 Unceasing, voiceless, h
410:1 Unceasing, voiceless, h

heart's
131:2 the h great needs.
132:2 the h great needs.
139:3 h rich overflow,
427:3 h rich overflow,
149:2 of a h awakening,
426:2 of a h awakening,
194:2 h own longing lifts
410:2 h own longing lifts
218:3 h perennial youth,
219:3 h perennial youth,
220:3 h perennial youth,
237:3 Lift ... the h desire,
284:1 h sincere desire,
285:1 h sincere desire,
286:1 h sincere desire,
315:3 in the h deep well;
316:3 in the h deep well;
359:3 h pride which frowns

hearts
  2:3 h and homes benighted
  9:3 longing h that wait
  4 our h find peace.
 19:1 whose h are pure,
 40:1 bring your wounded h,
 43:1 come to h oppressed.
 45:3 We lift our h in
 56:1 joy of loving h,
 58:1 Lift our h in joy
  2 Open h and willing
  3 Loyal h can feel
 66:1 From h made whole,
421:1 From h made whole,
 72:2 H o'erflowing with His
405:2 H o'erflowing with His
 83:1 united h and hands.
 85:1 Lift our h to
 91:2 Famishing h and hopes
422:2 Famishing h and hopes
101:1 grieving h were healed;
109:1 h, unsealed, adoring,
110:1 h, unsealed, adoring,
112:1 our h adoring Yield
121:1 whose h are pure;
122:1 whose h are pure;
126:4 h that faithful prove;

hearts
127:4 h that faithful prove;
403:4 h that faithful prove;
150:1 with glad h we bring.
163:2 So from our h must
175:1 In our h Thy Word
178:2 Loving h in friendship
197:3 h of stone before him
198:3 h of stone before him
199:1 grateful h and voices
202:2 to humble h revealing
412:1 to humble h revealing
206:1 Purge Thou our h
428:1 Purge Thou our h
222:3 imparts to human h
223:3 imparts to human h
226:1 lift Our h in praise
  2 With h all unafraid,
232:1 h now in this truth
406:1 h now in this truth
232:3 h to fill with this
406:3 h to fill with this
242:3 our h hath stirred,
243:2 How h grow light,
244:2 How h grow light,
249:2 grateful h will hold.
250:2 grateful h will hold.
263:1 our h rejoice;
  3 h in Him may blend.
265:3 Earth-bound h thou
266:3 love our h unite,
273:1 Lift your h and
274:1 Lift your h and
276:2 Fix within our h
277:2 Fix within our h
317:3 When h awaking see
319:3 kindling h that burn
333:3 longing h which sought
357:1 joy our h within.
358:1 joy our h within.
407:1 joy our h within.
357:3 To blameless h reveal.
358:3 To blameless h reveal.
407:3 To blameless h reveal.
371:1-3 We lift our h in
378:2 Our h redeemed from
379:4 h might sever From
380:4 h might sever From
381:3 The h of men are

heaven
  2:3 Point upward unto h.
  5:1 A voice from h
 30:3 glorious from high h,
 31:3 glorious from high h,
 32:3 glorious from high h,
 51:3 h and earth approve.
 52:3 h and earth approve.

heaven
66:4 new $h\cdot$ and earth
421:4 new $h\cdot$ and earth
72:1 well-beloved of $h\cdot$.
405:1 well-beloved of $h\cdot$.
85:2 glory of Thy $h\cdot$;
90:1 Bread of $h\cdot$!
92:2 orders come from $h\cdot$.
97:1 rain will fall from $h\cdot$,
98:1 rain will fall from $h\cdot$,
108:2 royal wine of $h\cdot$;
112:1 High to $h\cdot$ let song
126:4 he's an heir of $h\cdot$
127:4 he's an heir of $h\cdot$
403:4 he's an heir of $h\cdot$
128:2 From $h\cdot$ he came, of $h\cdot$
     he spoke, To $h\cdot$ he led
129:2 From $h\cdot$ he came, of $h\cdot$
     he spoke, To $h\cdot$ he led
131:3 quick'ning life from $h\cdot$,
132:3 quick'ning life from $h\cdot$,
140:2 more of $h\cdot$ in each
    3 reveal our $h\cdot$.
158:3 the new $h\cdot$ and earth
159:3 the new $h\cdot$ and earth
163:1 our earth to $h\cdot$.
164:1 $h\cdot$ and nature sing.
165:1 $h\cdot$ and nature sing.
417:1 $h\cdot$ and nature sing.
166:2 Child of $h\cdot$, can'st
167:2 Child of $h\cdot$, can'st
168:1 $h\cdot$ return the joyful
    3 shuts and opens $h\cdot$,
174:3 $H\cdot$ is at hand, when
181:4 God is All, and $h\cdot$ is
192:3 appear Steps unto $h\cdot$;
193:3 appear Steps unto $h\cdot$;
222:3 blessings of His $h\cdot$.
223:3 blessings of His $h\cdot$.
224:3 made my $h\cdot$ secure,
225:3 made my $h\cdot$ secure,
227:3 $h\cdot$ before our eyes.
246:1 who spreadest the $h\cdot$
    Ref. Creator is of $h\cdot$ and
275:1 Maker of earth and $h\cdot$;
278:1 home and $h\cdot$ are within
279:1 home and $h\cdot$ are with$\cdot$
280:1 the King of $h\cdot$;
282:2 $H\cdot$ and earth, and all
284:3 enters $h\cdot$ with prayer.
285:3 enters $h\cdot$ with prayer.
286:3 enters $h\cdot$ with prayer.
318:2 in this wise enter $h\cdot$;
327:1 made both $h\cdot$ and earth
328:1 made both $h\cdot$ and earth
333:3 God and $h\cdot$ were there.
336:3 $h\cdot$ and earth have
349:2 on earth from $h\cdot$ above.

heaven
355:2 heart of $h\cdot$ above,
362:1 all the hosts of $h\cdot$.
364:3 still the hope of $h\cdot$
392:3 $h\cdot$ of heavens reveals
393:3 $h\cdot$ of heavens reveals

heaven-drawn
251:2 $h\cdot$ picture Of Christ,
252:2 $h\cdot$ picture Of Christ,

heavenly
30:2 holy thoughts and $h\cdot$
31:2 holy thoughts and $h\cdot$
32:2 holy thoughts and $h\cdot$
37:4 The $h\cdot$ city stands.
38:4 The $h\cdot$ city stands.
39:1 gracious Spirit, $h\cdot$ Love,
    3 God, our $h\cdot$ rest,
67:1 Gird thy $h\cdot$ armor on,
68:1 Gird thy $h\cdot$ armor on,
80:2 glad the $h\cdot$ plains;
94:3 $h\cdot$ echoes never cease.
95:1 with $h\cdot$ comfort fraught.
109:1 home to $h\cdot$ ways,
110:1 home to $h\cdot$ ways,
121:3 sign of $h\cdot$ power
122:3 sign of $h\cdot$ power
126:1 how $h\cdot$ is the sight,
127:1 how $h\cdot$ is the sight,
403:1 how $h\cdot$ is the sight,
141:2 Nourish by a $h\cdot$ dew
146:2 Abide in $h\cdot$ light.
147:2 Abide in $h\cdot$ light.
148:1 In $h\cdot$ Love abiding,
178:1 in $h\cdot$ wisdom taught
    2 in Him, our $h\cdot$ Friend.
207:5 her home and $h\cdot$ rest.
208:5 her home and $h\cdot$ rest.
209:5 her home and $h\cdot$ rest.
210:5 her home and $h\cdot$ rest.
211:5 her home and $h\cdot$ rest.
212:5 her home and $h\cdot$ rest.
240:2 to run the $h\cdot$ way,
241:2 to run the $h\cdot$ way,
263:2 $H\cdot$ calm and comfort
276:1 speaks the $h\cdot$ Giver;
277:1 speaks the $h\cdot$ Giver;
319:3 one $h\cdot$ flame.
320:2 His $h\cdot$ aids impart.
321:2 His $h\cdot$ aids impart.
409:2 His $h\cdot$ aids impart.
322:2 dwell as $h\cdot$ dew,
323:2 dwell as $h\cdot$ dew,
334:3 beams of $h\cdot$ day.
336:2 a $h\cdot$ beam I see,
372:1 climb the $h\cdot$ steeps
373:1 climb the $h\cdot$ steeps

heavenly
376:1 thank Thee, $h\cdot$ Father,
377:1 thank Thee, $h\cdot$ Father,
398:1 of His $h\cdot$ word,

heaven's
5:1 heed high $h\cdot$ call.
104:4 Lead us to $h\cdot$ bowers:
158:1 $h\cdot$ all-gracious King;
159:1 $h\cdot$ all-gracious King;
166:3 $H\cdot$ eternal day before
167:3 $H\cdot$ eternal day before
190:4 $H\cdot$ music chimes the
191:4 $H\cdot$ music chimes the
195:2 $h\cdot$ own healing air;
207:5 $h\cdot$ aftersmile earth's
208:5 $h\cdot$ aftersmile earth's
209:5 $h\cdot$ aftersmile earth's
210:5 $h\cdot$ aftersmile earth's
211:5 $h\cdot$ aftersmile earth's
212:5 $h\cdot$ aftersmile earth's

heavens
45:1 The wondrous $h\cdot$, Thy
111:1 High in the $h\cdot$,
282:1 ye $h\cdot$, adore Him;
329:1 $h\cdot$ declare the glory
392:3 heaven of $h\cdot$ reveals
393:3 heaven of $h\cdot$ reveals

heavy
43:2 all ye $h\cdot$ laden,
245:1 dark and $h\cdot$ shadows
360:1 burden hard and $h\cdot$?

hedged
131:2 is not $h\cdot$ with forms;
132:2 is not $h\cdot$ with forms;

heed
5:1 $h\cdot$ high heaven's call.
10:2 No other voice we $h\cdot$,
411:2 No other voice we $h\cdot$,
58:2 $h\cdot$ no other call;
263:1 $h\cdot$ the Father's voice.
314:1 give thou no $h\cdot$;
325:2 nor $h\cdot$ the shame;
329:2 To $h\cdot$ His testimony,
332:2 $h\cdot$ His faithful Word,

heeded
163:1 If $h\cdot$, O what power

heeding
84:2 commands forever $h\cdot$,

heeds
48:2 when Truth he $h\cdot$;

height
185:1 to joy-crowned h·
282:1 angels, in the h· ;
368:1 yon mountain's h·
369:1 yon mountain's h·

heights
136:3 the h· of Mind,

heir
51:2 Christ is the perfect h· ;
52:2 Christ is the perfect h· ;
126:4 he's an h· of heaven
127:4 he's an h· of heaven
403:4 he's an h· of heaven
146:4 is God's great h·.
147:4 is God's great h·.
278:1 H· of the ages
279:1 H· of the ages

heirs
266:3 H· of the same immortal

held
66:2 in Thy completeness h·,
421:2 in Thy completeness h·,
134:3 H· in Thy law, I
149:2 H· by God's love
426:2 H· by God's love

hell
264:3 Gates of h· can never
325:2 sin, and death, and h·.
326:4 Sin, death and h·
343:3 nor h· shall harm.
344:3 nor h· shall harm.
429:3 nor h· shall harm.
396:3 h· in vain oppose;
397:3 h· in vain oppose;

helmet
292:1 the h· of salvation—
326:2 Salvation's h· on his

help
8:1 H· of the helpless,
10:2 No other h· we need;
411:2 No other h· we need;
75:1 To h· the poor and
77:1 My light, my h· is
78:1 My light, my h· is
88:1 words that h· and heal
89:1 words that h· and heal
104:1 H· us, O Lord, to bear
105:1 H· us to h· each other,
106:1 H· us to h· each other,
107:1 H· us to h· each other,
105:2 H· us to build each
106:2 H· us to build each
107:2 H· us to build each

help
115:2 H· us turn to Thee
116:2 H· us turn to Thee
123:2 strengthen thee, h·
153:2 Sure h· to Israel
172:3 joy to h· and save,
189:1 H· cometh from on
203:2 H· us to know that
213:1, 4 h· in ages past,
234:1 h· me bear The strain
235:1 h· me bear The strain
234:2 H· me the slow of
235:2 H· me the slow of
356:2 H· us to understand
360:1 H· to bear thy brother's
372:2 A present h· is he;
373:1 A present h· is he;
389:1 my h· and defender,

helper
361:1 Thy h· is omnipotence.

helpers
8:1 When other h· fail,

helpless
8:1 Help of the h·,

helps
81:2 His all-power H· and
376:1 Love divine, that h· us
377:1 Love divine, that h· us

hem
96:1 filled the garment's h·

hence
160:3 sense, arise, go h· !
161:3 sense, arise, go h· !
162:3 sense, arise, go h· !

henceforth
206:3 h· we may live to
428:3 h· we may live to
224:3 H· my great concern
225:3 H· my great concern
238:4 H· my heart shall
239:4 H· my heart shall

herald
75:2 Shall Peace, the h·,

heralds
2:1 h· of the morning

here
1:1 h· and now obeyed.
23:2 Dear Christ, forever h·
24:2 Dear Christ, forever h·
25:2 Dear Christ, forever h·
26:2 Dear Christ, forever h·
27:2 Dear Christ, forever h·

here
28:2 Dear Christ, forever h·
34:3 Christ is h· to bless,
40:1 H· health and peace
1 H· bring your wounded
1 h· tell your anguish;
2 H· speaks the Comforter,
3 H· see the Bread of
41:3 may do service h· ;
44:2 hath no dwelling h· ;
48:1 raise this beacon h·,
97:2 Harvest . . . is surely h·.
98:2 Harvest . . . is surely h·.
105:3 And spotless h· below.
106:3 And spotless h· below.
107:3 And spotless h· below.
108:1 H· . . . I'd see Thee
1 H· would I touch and
1 H· grasp with firmer
2 H· would I feed upon
2 H· drink anew the royal
2 H· would I lay aside
2 H· taste afresh the calm
3 but Thou art h·,
109:1 H·, O God, Thy healing
110:1 H·, O God, Thy healing
109:1 H· Thy tender sweet
110:1 H· Thy tender sweet
113:2 h· commune with Thee,
139:1 presence with me h· ;
427:1 presence with me h· ;
148:1 For nothing changes h·.
175:1 Word of God is h·.
180:2 H· we rest content:
181:4 and heaven is h·.
185:1 'tis good to be h·,
3 mountain h· above,
188:1 God hath h· prepared
202:1 The Christ is h·,
412:1 The Christ is h·,
205:3 h· the hallowed bliss
207:2 habitation high is h·,
208:2 habitation high is h·,
209:2 habitation high is h·,
210:2 habitation high is h·,
211:2 habitation high is h·,
212:2 habitation high is h·,
224:3 h· all good provide;
225:3 h· all good provide;
227:3 H· we may prove
238:4 h· and everywhere.
239:4 h· and everywhere.
263:3 H· from prisoning pain
267:1 know that God is h·.
268:1 know that God is h·.
315:1 good we may do h·.
316:1 good we may do h·.
371:1 For Thou art h·.

here
374:2 good alone is h.
375:2 good alone is h.
388:1 lowly Jesus sojourned h,
391:3 And h to-day upholds
415:2 H in this country

heritage
101:1 Man's h revealed;
275:3 Life is our h;
347:4 This is thy precious h,
348:4 This is thy precious h,

hid
201:3 H treasures it reveals
404:3 H treasures it reveals
201:4 know your life is h
404:4 know your life is h
237:1 and h in Soul.
370:1 h with Christ forever
1, 2 h with Christ in God.

hidden
2:1 dark and h places
33:3 dread no h snare;
109:1 light their h places,
110:1 light their h places,
228:2 our h joy can tell,
284:1 motion of a h fire
285:1 motion of a h fire
286:1 motion of a h fire

hide
67:3 H within thy heart
68:3 H within thy heart
69:2 presence safely h.
423:2 presence safely h.
117:2 darkness cannot h Thee,
126:2 brother's failings h,
127:2 brother's failings h,
403:2 brother's failings h,
293:2 h myself in Thee.
294:2 h myself in Thee.
295:2 h myself in Thee.

hie
368:3 H thee to thy quiet
369:3 H thee to thy quiet

high
1:1 O God, exalted h,
5:1 h heaven's call.
9:1 to God most h,
2 blessings from on h,
10:3 thanks to God on h,
411:3 thanks to God on h,
20:1 unto thy h ideal,
416:1 unto thy h ideal,
30:3 glorious from h heaven,
31:3 glorious from h heaven,
32:3 glorious from h heaven,

high
35:1 Dayspring from on h,
36:4 praise we lift on h,
37:2 steadfast h intent,
38:2 steadfast h intent,
41:2 Claim the h calling
72:1 to God on h,
405:1 to God on h,
99:3 shall be God most h;
100:3 shall be God most h,
111:1 H in the heavens,
112:1 H to heaven let song
118:1 Kindle every h desire;
125:2 that reigns on h,
172:2 Hold h thy lamp
177:2 God . . . , h and glorious,
189:1 cometh from on h;
194:2 longing lifts it h
410:2 longing lifts it h
207:2 habitation h is here,
208:2 habitation h is here,
209:2 habitation h is here,
210:2 habitation h is here,
211:2 habitation h is here,
212:2 habitation h is here,
251:1 wisdom from on h,
252:1 wisdom from on h,
281:2 dayspring from on h.
282:2 Hosts on h, His power
284:2 The Majesty on h.
285:2 The Majesty on h.
286:2 The Majesty on h.
296:1 lift your banner on h;
336:1 firmament on h,
352:3 forgiving, Godlike, h,
353:3 forgiving, Godlike, h,

higher
66:3 That h selfhood which
421:3 That h selfhood which
290:2 to h glory still.
342:2 the h, deeper ways
368:2 H yet that star
369:2 H yet that star

highest
92:4 h pleasure find
131:3 Is h ministry.
132:3 Is h ministry.

hill
2:2 from h and valley,
75:2 From h to vale

hills
200:1 o'er thy h dawns
213:2 h in order stood,
275:1 where the h arise,
347:1 h be far removed,
348:1 h be far removed,

hillside
304:1 O'er the h steep,
305:1 O'er the h steep,
306:1 O'er the h steep,
307:1 O'er the h steep,
308:1 O'er the h steep,
309:1 O'er the h steep,

hillsides
96:2 The Syrian h

hither
218:1 In gladness h turn
219:1 In gladness h turn
220:1 In gladness h turn

hold
48:2 what h has hate
56:2 faith can h Thee
59:1 Lay h on Life,
60:1 Lay h on Life,
61:1 Lay h on Life,
90:1 H me with Thy
151:1 I h communion;
152:1 I h communion;
172:2 H high thy lamp
185:2 'tis good to h fast
249:2 grateful hearts will h.
250:2 grateful hearts will h.
314:1 h not thy hand;
329:2 Wisdom's way to h,
3 Lay h of Thee aright.
365:1 Laying h upon His
366:1 Laying h upon His
388:2 could h no dread,

holdest
130:1 Thou h all things

holdeth
283:2 still h from sliding;

holds
144:3 He h us perfect
145:3 He h us perfect
222:2 h wide the door,
223:2 h wide the door,
347:3 h thee free from
348:3 h thee free from
391:3 h the Mind and Cause

holier
217:1 That h worship, which
238:4 olden time and h shore:
239:4 olden time and h shore:

holiest
93:2 Love His h name.

holiness
45:3 beauty of Love's h,

holiness
113:1 H becomes Thy house,
   2 In beauty of h ;
273:1 Keep the h of life.
274:1 Keep the h of life.

hollow
333:3 No h rite, no

holy
  4:1 h air is breathing
 19:1 praise His h name.
 29:1 its h power feels,
 30:2 Seek h thoughts and
 31:2 Seek h thoughts and
 32:2 Seek h thoughts and
 34:1 again with h power,
 37:2 One h church, one
 38:2 One h church, one
 39:2 Plant h joy in every
 42:2 Thy h word doth give;
 44:3 Thy h resting-place.
 64:2 stand is h ground;
 73:2 h thought is sending;
 94:1 calm and h hour,
 96:1 of old, the h Christ,
101:1 Word, His h Word,
102:1 laws so pure and h
103:1 laws so pure and h
114:1 H Bible, book divine,
115:1 H Father, Thou hast
116:1 H Father, Thou hast
117:1,3 H , H , H , Lord God
  1,3 H , H , H , merciful
   2 H , H , H , darkness
   2 Thou alone art h ,
139:1 it is a h day;
427:1 it is a h day;
153:1 h is Thy name.
163:3 Mind's most h plan
166:4 fulfill thy h mission,
167:4 fulfill thy h mission,
170:1 h child was born,
174:3 O h presence, that
178:1 H works of love he
181:2 Thy h secret place,
214:2 its h influence pour
   3 Its h calm upon the
217:3 h work was doing good;
221:2 perfect, h , blessed.
222:2 Proclaim the h birth,
223:2 Proclaim the h birth,
251:1 Word of God, most h ,
252:1 Word of God, most h ,
261:1 One h church of God
262:1 One h church of God
266:3 praise His h name.
273:3 by h actions shown;
274:3 by h actions shown;

holy
281:1 upon His h name;
290:1 in your h fight,
303:4 h , true, and free.
311:1 burns Love's h glow,
420:1 burns Love's h glow,
313:2 In h contemplation
319:3 One h light, one
322:1 h , thoughtful prayer,
323:1 h , thoughtful prayer,
332:1 in His h place,
335:2 all the h Proclaim,
336:2 Thy h Word supplies,
346:3 Life-giving, h dove,
401:3 Life-giving, h dove,
349:1 great, eternal, H One.
   3 Thy h purpose to
350:2 H , through the Spirit's
356:2 Thy h counsel,
370:1 the Father's h plan.
383:2 Redeemer's h faith
386:2 h gospel we profess;
387:2 h gospel we profess;
414:2 God's own h word.

Holy Ghost
229:1 white wings of the H G .
345:3 of gifts, the H G .

Holy Spirit
118:1 H S , Light divine,
   2 H S , Peace divine,
   3 H S , all divine,
119:1 H S , source of

homage
331:1 Are but vain h ,

home
 80:3 our h , our hope,
109:1 h to heavenly ways,
110:1 h to heavenly ways,
128:3 from the Father's h ,
129:3 from the Father's h ,
169:1 I am far from h ,
174:1 h abides in peace.
203:2 safely h to Thee,
205:3 Of our eternal h .
207:5 mother finds her h
208:5 mother finds her h
209:5 mother finds her h
210:5 mother finds her h
211:5 mother finds her h
212:5 mother finds her h
213:1,4 And our eternal h .
227:2 they find their h .
242:3 bear our harvest h .
245:1 safely lead us h .
   2 bring us safely h .
   3 blest, eternal h .

home
276:2 our hearts Thy h ;
277:2 our hearts Thy h ;
278:1 h and heaven are within
279:1 h and heaven are within
311:2 safely, surely h .
420:2 safely, surely h .
330:3 h , rejoicing, brought
335:2 reach their h :
368:3 to thy quiet h .
369:3 to thy quiet h .
376:1 leads us h to God.
377:1 leads us h to God.

homelands
381:3 yearning For h

homeless
 93:3 h longings range,

homes
  2:3 hearts and h benighted

homeward
234:2 in the h way.
235:2 in the h way.
381:3 men are h turning

honest
170:2 With h zeal
382:2 Truth's h child,

honey
329:2 sweeter far than h ,

honor
 73:1 Glory, h , praise
171:3 Giving God the h
413:3 Giving God the h
264:4 Glory, laud and h
398:3 be with h crowned.

honors
271:4 h to our King;
272:4 h to our King;
288:1 and h right.
289:1 and h right.
386:3 h of our Saviour,
387:3 h of our Saviour,

hope
  7:2 Health, h and love
 10:3 our h , our song;
411:3 our h , our song;
 30:5 power our h we give,
 31:5 power our h we give,
 32:5 power our h we give,
 34:2 Faith, h , and joy
 40:2 H of the penitent,
 54:1 H points the upward
 73:2 Joy, health, h

hope
75:2 joy and $h\cdot$, like
79:3 $H\cdot$ and comfort from
80:3 our home, our $h\cdot$,
88:3 by triumphant $h\cdot$
89:3 by triumphant $h\cdot$
104:2 The $h\cdot$ serene that
105:2 faith, confirm our $h\cdot$,
106:2 faith, confirm our $h\cdot$,
107:2 faith, confirm our $h\cdot$,
141:4 Lifting $h\cdot$ above
148:3 $h\cdot$ I cannot measure;
164:2 $h\cdot$ and joy abound.
165:2 $h\cdot$ and joy abound.
417:2 $h\cdot$ and joy abound.
166:4 $H\cdot$ shall change to
167:4 $H\cdot$ shall change to
171:1 $h\cdot$ and faith uplifted;
413:1 $h\cdot$ and faith uplifted;
172:2 Beacon of $h\cdot$ to those
173:3 $H\cdot$ shall be fulfilled
  4 Faith and $h\cdot$ and love
174:1 Comfort is $h\cdot$ and
190:4 $H\cdot$ soars beyond
191:4 $H\cdot$ soars beyond
203:1 flag of $h\cdot$ and peace
207:3 $h\cdot$ deferred, ingratitude,
208:3 $h\cdot$ deferred, ingratitude,
209:3 $h\cdot$ deferred, ingratitude,
210:3 $h\cdot$ deferred, ingratitude,
211:3 $h\cdot$ deferred, ingratitude,
212:3 $h\cdot$ deferred, ingratitude,
213:1, 4 $h\cdot$ for time to come,
218:2 the bright $h\cdot$ glows,
219:2 the bright $h\cdot$ glows,
220:2 the bright $h\cdot$ glows,
234:4 In $h\cdot$ that sends
235:4 In $h\cdot$ that sends
236:1 $h\cdot$ in each breast,
264:2 One in $h\cdot$ and doctrine,
273:1 of a glorious $h\cdot$,
274:1 of a glorious $h\cdot$,
297:2 where $h\cdot$ anchors fast,
319:1 Blest star of $h\cdot$,
336:2 The $h\cdot$ Thy holy Word
351:2 $h\cdot$ our God inspires;
362:1 Child of $H\cdot$ is born,
364:3 the $h\cdot$ of heaven
368:1 Aught of $h\cdot$ or joy
369:1 Aught of $h\cdot$ or joy
381:3 With $h\cdot$ and faith,
389:1 my $h\cdot$ in my God
  2 $h\cdot$, should I fall;

hopes
46:3 All my sanguine $h\cdot$
47:3 All my sanguine $h\cdot$
57:2 Should fond $h\cdot$ fail

hopes
91:2 hearts and $h\cdot$ to feed;
422:2 hearts and $h\cdot$ to feed;
216:1 And $h\cdot$ in Him when
222:1 $h\cdot$ and fears of all
223:1 $h\cdot$ and fears of all
232:2 our waiting $h\cdot$ behold
406:2 our waiting $h\cdot$ behold
266:3 $h\cdot$ and aims the same,

Horeb
297:2 $H\cdot$ whereon we walk

horizon's
218:4 wide $h\cdot$ grander view;
219:4 wide $h\cdot$ grander view;
220:4 wide $h\cdot$ grander view;

host
296:2 cringing $h\cdot$ of fear
345:3 men, a countless $h\cdot$,

hostile
33:2 walk through $h\cdot$ regions,

hosts
10:3 The $h\cdot$ of death before
411:3 The $h\cdot$ of death before
77:1 $h\cdot$ encamp around me,
78:1 $h\cdot$ encamp around me,
101:3 $h\cdot$ who toil in vain
125:2 Lord God of $H\cdot$,
282:2 $H\cdot$ on high, His power
362:1 all the $h\cdot$ of heaven.

hour
6:3 The present $h\cdot$ allots
7:3 every passing $h\cdot$,
8:2 every passing $h\cdot$;
23:2 No natal $h\cdot$ and
24:2 No natal $h\cdot$ and
25:2 No natal $h\cdot$ and
26:2 No natal $h\cdot$ and
27:2 No natal $h\cdot$ and
28:2 No natal $h\cdot$ and
79:2 E'en the $h\cdot$ that
94:1 calm and holy $h\cdot$,
137:1-3 need Thee every $h\cdot$;
  Ref. Every $h\cdot$ I need
175:2 guide us every $h\cdot$.
194:3 that transcendent $h\cdot$
410:3 that transcendent $h\cdot$
201:3 this most gracious $h\cdot$.
404:3 this most gracious $h\cdot$.
203:1 may we bear each $h\cdot$
207:1 owns each waiting $h\cdot$,
208:1 owns each waiting $h\cdot$,
209:1 owns each waiting $h\cdot$,
210:1 owns each waiting $h\cdot$,
211:1 owns each waiting $h\cdot$,

hour
212:1 owns each waiting $h\cdot$,
297:4 at midnight $h\cdot$,
303:1 waits its natal $h\cdot$.
317:3 O, in that $h\cdot$,
320:2 courage in the evil $h\cdot$
321:2 courage in the evil $h\cdot$
409:2 courage in the evil $h\cdot$
322:1 Sweet $h\cdot$ of holy,
323:1 Sweet $h\cdot$ of holy,
371:2 In this exalted $h\cdot$,
399:2 Unfolding every $h\cdot$;
400:2 Unfolding every $h\cdot$;

hours
41:2 $h\cdot$ too swiftly fly,
158:2 glad and golden $h\cdot$
159:2 glad and golden $h\cdot$
364:1 night's weary $h\cdot$,
378:2 of peaceful $h\cdot$,

house
58:3 In Thy $h\cdot$ securely
113:1 becomes Thy $h\cdot$,
141:1 build not the $h\cdot$
330:4 Within Thy $h\cdot$ forever.

hover
140:3 Around us $h\cdot$ while

hovering
71:2 each habitation $h\cdot$,

however
6:1 $h\cdot$ fair it seems;

hues
236:3 $h\cdot$ in harmony blend,

human
30:5 Free us from $h\cdot$ strife.
31:5 Free us from $h\cdot$ strife.
32:5 Free us from $h\cdot$ strife.
54:2 Unheard by $h\cdot$ ear,
121:4 $h\cdot$ heart can reach,
  No $h\cdot$ voice declare.
122:4 $h\cdot$ heart can reach,
  No $h\cdot$ voice declare.
136:2 Though $h\cdot$ will and woe
138:1 dream of $h\cdot$ power;
194:2 $h\cdot$ lips may never form
410:2 $h\cdot$ lips may never form
222:3 imparts to $h\cdot$ hearts
223:3 imparts to $h\cdot$ hearts
320:3 $h\cdot$ energy shall faint,
321:3 $h\cdot$ energy shall faint,
409:3 $h\cdot$ energy shall faint,
327:3 $h\cdot$ need supplies.
328:3 $h\cdot$ need supplies.
340:2 seen by $h\cdot$ mind,
364:3 on $h\cdot$ strength relies;

humanity
221:3 message To tired $h\cdot$,

humble
190:2 confident and $h\cdot$ mind,
191:2 confident and $h\cdot$ mind,
202:2 to $h\cdot$ hearts revealing
412:1 to $h\cdot$ hearts revealing
227:2 with them of $h\cdot$ mind;
331:2 $h\cdot$, contrite mind,
333:1 baptized in $h\cdot$ prayer,
337:3 Christlike, crowns the $h\cdot$,
338:3 Christlike, crowns the $h\cdot$,

humbly
325:1 $h\cdot$ follow after me.
346:1 Hear us, we $h\cdot$ pray,
401:1 Hear us, we $h\cdot$ pray,
352:3 like thee so $h\cdot$ bore
353:3 like thee so $h\cdot$ bore

humility
151:1 Yea, with $h\cdot$.
152:1 Yea, with $h\cdot$.

humility
176:2 in $h\cdot$ shared it.
216:2 Be silent in $h\cdot$;
352:3 So glorious in $h\cdot$.
353:3 So glorious in $h\cdot$.

hungering
414:3 Seem $h\cdot$ and thirsting

hungry
42:1 weak, the $h\cdot$ feed;
203:1 bless a $h\cdot$ world.
304:3 Feed the $h\cdot$, heal
305:3 Feed the $h\cdot$, heal
306:3 Feed the $h\cdot$, heal
307:3 Feed the $h\cdot$, heal
308:3 Feed the $h\cdot$, heal
309:3 Feed the $h\cdot$, heal
327:2 $h\cdot$ needful food
328:2 $h\cdot$ needful food
388:1 healed, the $h\cdot$ fed.

hurled
333:2 just rebuke was $h\cdot$

hurrying
36:2 Amid the $h\cdot$ crowds

hurt
123:3 shall not $h\cdot$ thee;

hush
317:2 Solemn the $h\cdot$ of nature,
418:1 $h\cdot$ our breath to hear,

hushed
149:2 $H\cdot$ in the grandeur
426:2 $H\cdot$ in the grandeur

hymn
217:2 Each smile a $h\cdot$,
249:1 our $h\cdot$ of praise?
250:1 our $h\cdot$ of praise?

hymns
72:2 $h\cdot$ your voices raise.
405:2 $h\cdot$ your voices raise.
120:2 forth in $h\cdot$ of gladness,
310:1 $H\cdot$ of joy and shouts

I

I AM
378:3 Great $I\,A\cdot$.

idea
221:3 God's $i\cdot$, man,

ideal
20:1 unto thy high $i\cdot$,
416:1 unto thy high $i\cdot$,

idle
17:2 $i\cdot$ words must cease.
41:1 $i\cdot$ on the harvest plain?
329:3 $i\cdot$ thought or word;

idly
55:3 we $i\cdot$ quiet stay,

idol
177:2 shall every $i\cdot$ perish

idols
12:1 Cast out your $i\cdot$
13:1 Cast out your $i\cdot$

ill
179:2 heals our every $i\cdot$,
207:3 fear No $i\cdot$,—since
208:3 fear No $i\cdot$,—since
209:3 fear No $i\cdot$,—since
210:3 fear No $i\cdot$,—since
211:3 fear No $i\cdot$,—since

ill
212:3 fear No $i\cdot$,—since
290:2 Victorious over every $i\cdot$,
293:3 Cure . . . for every $i\cdot$.
294:3 Cure . . . for every $i\cdot$.
295:3 Cure . . . for every $i\cdot$.

ills
8:3 $I\cdot$ have no weight,
175:1 $i\cdot$ that seem to be,

illume
352:4 $i\cdot$ my way of woe
353:4 $i\cdot$ my way of woe

illumed
253:2 thoughts, $i\cdot$ By faith,
254:2 thoughts, $i\cdot$ By faith,
255:2 thoughts, $i\cdot$ By faith,
256:2 thoughts, $i\cdot$ By faith,
257:2 thoughts, $i\cdot$ By faith,
314:3 $I\cdot$ by Love's transforming

illumination
119:3 Send us Thine $i\cdot$;

illusive
359:2 $i\cdot$ wreaths of mist

image
12:3 In Thine own $i\cdot$
13:3 In Thine own $i\cdot$

image
51:3 The $i\cdot$ of His love.
52:3 The $i\cdot$ of His love.
73:2 Man, His $i\cdot$, hears
144:3 we His $i\cdot$ bear.
145:3 we His $i\cdot$ bear.
237:4 God's own $i\cdot$ will
266:1 His $i\cdot$ bear, we know;

Immanuel
11:1 God with us, $I\cdot$.

immortal
51:1 $I\cdot$; perfect as his Mind
52:1 $I\cdot$; perfect as his Mind
64:2 joy of things $i\cdot$,
128:2 Unveiling Love's $i\cdot$ day.
129:2 Unveiling Love's $i\cdot$ day.
142:1 $I\cdot$ Love, forever full,
144:3 For God, $i\cdot$ Principle,
145:3 For God, $i\cdot$ Principle,
172:1 $I\cdot$ ray of that great
197:1 Of Love's $i\cdot$ waking.
198:1 Of Love's $i\cdot$ waking.
266:3 the same $i\cdot$ bliss,
325:3 thou find $i\cdot$ Life
326:4 wins . . . , an $i\cdot$ crown.
339:2 $I\cdot$ joy is found
359:3 thine $i\cdot$ life shall be

impart
35:2 they inward light i,
143:3 truth Thou dost i
168:2 work that light i,
320:2 heavenly aids i.
321:2 heavenly aids i.
409:2 heavenly aids i.
343:2 True wisdom doth i;
344:2 True wisdom doth i;
429:2 True wisdom doth i;
345:2 radiance e'en to us i,

imparts
56:1 best that earth i,
222:3 God i to human
223:3 God i to human

imperfect
51:2 could not make i man
52:2 could not make i man

impossible
190:3 deemed i I dare,
191:3 deemed i I dare,

imposture
143:1 I shrinks from light,

improve
105:2 Our little stock i;
106:2 Our little stock i;
107:2 Our little stock i;
322:1 and calm may we i,
323:1 and calm may we i,

impulse
324:1 the i of Thy love.

incline
258:2 thought of men i

increase
16:2 praise must e'er i,
57:2 cares that vex . . . i,
77:2 His love thy joy i;
78:2 His love thy joy i;
82:2 i The brotherhood
105:2 I our faith, confirm
106:2 I our faith, confirm
107:2 I our faith, confirm
157:3 our oneness shall i,
215:3 So her rewards i;
269:1 prayer for Love's i
270:1 prayer for Love's i
320:3 strength shall still i.
321:3 strength shall still i.
409:3 strength shall still i.

increasing
75:3 His kingdom still i,
362:3 His power, i, still

indeed
105:3 made us free i,
106:3 made us free i,
107:3 made us free i,

indwelling
131:2 A life, i, deep and
132:2 A life, i, deep and

ineffable
236:4 I joy His love
345:2 Perfect and pure, i

infant
271:2 i voices shall proclaim
272:2 i voices shall proclaim
284:2 i lips can try;
285:2 i lips can try;
286:2 i lips can try;

infest
164:2 thorns i the ground;
165:2 thorns i the ground;
417:2 thorns i the ground;

infinite
23:4 Truth i,—so far above
24:4 Truth i,—so far above
25:4 Truth i,—so far above
26:4 Truth i,—so far above
27:4 Truth i,—so far above
28:4 Truth i,—so far above
51:2 man His model i;
52:2 man His model i;
64:3 vision i to me grows
269:1 'Twas i before.
270:1 'Twas i before.
269:2 change His i design?
270:2 change His i design?

Infinity
146:3 naught against I
147:3 naught against I

influence
97:1 an i all divine.
98:1 an i all divine.
214:2 Love its holy i pour

ingratitude
207:3 hope deferred, i, disdain!
208:3 hope deferred, i, disdain!
209:3 hope deferred, i, disdain!
210:3 hope deferred, i, disdain!
211:3 hope deferred, i, disdain!
212:3 hope deferred, i, disdain!

inherit
42:1 heart Thy grace i;
81:2 heart that peace i
135:2 I richly shall i All

injures
157:2 Blesses all and i none.

inly
346:2 Sight to the i blind;
401:2 Sight to the i blind;

inmost
94:1 i depths discerned

inspiration
104:2 i that it brings,

inspired
266:1 love to God i,

inspires
54:1 celestial Love, i
351:2 the hope our God i;

inspiring
66:4 Thou, Soul, i—
421:4 Thou, Soul, i—

instinct
86:2 i that can tell
87:2 i that can tell

instruction's
215:1 hears I warning voice;

Intelligence
269:2 Mind, I divine;
270:2 Mind, I divine;

intent
37:2 steadfast high i,
38:2 steadfast high i,

interpreter
399:3 God is His own i,
400:3 God is His own i,

invisible
86:2 although He seems i.
87:2 although He seems i.

invite
143:1 truths the test i,

inward
35:2 they i light impart,
170:2 i sight is clear,
259:2 true and i faith

Israel
153:2 help to I brings.
281:2 Guides His I on
368:1 Promised day of I.
369:1 Promised day of I.
385:1 I, of the Lord beloved,

J

Jacob
177:2 God of J, high and

Jehovah
90:1 O Thou great J,

Jerusalem
120:2 gladness, O waste J;

Jesus
4:3 life of J taught,
43:1 tender words of J,
2 loving words of J,
2 peaceful words of J,
163:1 J, what precept is
166:2 J did to win thee;
167:2 J did to win thee;
178:1 J knew the law of
217:1 he whom J loved
221:1 J, our dear Master,
264:1, Ref. the cross of J
3 But the Church of J
265:2 J trod it, press thou
356:1 whom J came to prove.
386:1 J our great Master
387:1 J our great Master
388:1 lowly J sojourned
3 Where J triumphed
414:1 J and his glory,
1, Ref. J and his love.

Jesus'
157:1 J prayer for all

Jew
196:1 J and Gentile, meeting

join
72:2 J the hymns your
405:2 J the hymns your
264:4 J our happy throng;

joining
173:4 J hand in hand

journey
53:2 Gladly then we j
90:2 all my j through.
351:2 object of our j,
376:1 guides us in our j
377:1 guides us in our j
376:2 throughout the j
377:2 throughout the j
415:3 city to which I j;

journeys
271:1 his successive j run;
272:1 his successive j run;

joy
19:1 j upon their heads,
1 j shall never wane.
34:2 Faith, hope, and j
39:2 j in every heart,
40:2 J of the desolate,
41:4 How full their j,
43:1 j that hath no ending,
56:1 j of loving hearts,
57:1 j cometh with the
58:1 Lift our hearts in j
3 Share Thy j and
59:1 Thy j and crown
60:1 Thy j and crown
61:1 Thy j and crown
64:2 feel the calm and j
66:3 J and dominion, love
421:3 J and dominion, love
73:2 J, health, hope
75:2 j and hope, like
76:2 Blessedness and j
77:2 His love thy j
78:2 His love thy j
91:1 a j before unknown.
422:1 a j before unknown.
93:1 with j is blessed,
4 j of perfect work
97:2 reap the fruits of j:
98:2 reap the fruits of j:
108:4 of the festal j,
112:3 Loveliness and j
120:1 reign of j and peace.
128:1 j and reverence
129:1 j and reverence
136:3 I climb, with j, the
139:1 j that none can take
427:1 j that none can take
146:4 of ceaseless j;
147:4 of ceaseless j;
149:2 Unfolds a j unknown
426:2 Unfolds a j unknown
157:3 in j and peace.
164:1 J to the world,
165:1 J to the world,
417:1 J to the world,
164:2 hope and j abound.
165:2 hope and j abound.
417:2 hope and j abound.
166:1 J to find, in every
167:1 J to find, in every
172:3 Send out its light of j
174:2 giveth j for sorrow,—
2 J must endure, Love's
180:3 gives a j untold:
190:2 My j in service I

joy
191:2 My j in service I
195:3 art my health, my j,
202:3 j for desolation,
412:2 j for desolation,
207:1 peace and j and power;
208:1 peace and j and power;
209:1 peace and j and power;
210:1 peace and j and power;
211:1 peace and j and power;
212:1 peace and j and power;
218:3 j of paths untrod,
219:3 j of paths untrod,
220:3 j of paths untrod,
221:1 With j may all obey
228:2 hidden j can tell,
232:3 j that ever will
406:3 j that ever will
236:4 Ineffable j His love
240:3 j of things above.
241:3 j of things above.
245:3 With j at length we
249:2 life from j is minted,
250:2 life from j is minted,
253:6 tired j and grief
254:6 tired j and grief
255:6 tired j and grief
256:6 tired j and grief
257:6 tired j and grief
259:2 fount of j and praise.
263:1 J divine shall never
275:1 J of the sun and
1 praise with j and song.
281:1 Strains of j tune
310:1 Hymns of j and
315:3 j that it may bring,
316:3 j that it may bring,
339:2 Immortal j is found
342:3 robes of j arrayed,
356:3 His j remains in us
357:1 j our hearts within.
358:1 j our hearts within.
407:1 j our hearts within.
357:3 the secret of His j
358:3 the secret of His j
407:3 the secret of His j
363:4 floods of light and j,
368:1 Aught of hope or j
369:1 Aught of hope or j
371:3 With j to find
378:2 Healing and j are
381:4 and unsought j;
384:3 j through all the
389:2 My comfort and j
392:1 love and peace and j

79

joy
393:1 love and peace and j
392:2 endless j betides us.
393:2 endless j betides us.
394:3 J and strength to
395:3 J and strength to
418:4 j and peace sublime,
425:1, 2, Ref. j cometh in the
    morning.

joy-crowned
185:1 Guided by thee to j

joy-filled
139:3 crown your j day.
427:3 crown your j day.

joyful
11:2 their j caroling,
41:2 the j tidings bear;
58:2 ears, expectant, j,
109:2 j self-surrender
110:2 j self-surrender
168:1 return the j voice;
177:1 J times are near
192:5 on j wing Cleaving
193:5 on j wing Cleaving
202:1 dreams for j waking,
412:1 dreams for j waking,
202:4 dumb to j singing;

joyful
412:2 dumb to j singing;
236:3 mingle in j refrain,
271:2 shall with j tongue
272:2 shall with j tongue
384:2 wilderness shall j be;

joyfully
42:2 J Thy truth receive;

joyfulness
357:2 j for praise receive,
358:2 j for praise receive,
407:2 j for praise receive,

joyless
35:2 J is the day's return,

joyous
16:3 heart is j, free,
65:1 this our j song;
73:1 ye j congregations,
283:1 j and loving endeavor;
   3 j and glad adoration;
297:4 meal by j Galilee:
310:1, Ref. Sing, ye j children,

joys
30:3 Whence j supernal
31:3 Whence j supernal

joys
32:3 Whence j supernal
263:1 J are vain that end
275:2 J like the dawns
343:4 Whose j eternal flow.
344:4 Whose j eternal flow.
429:4 Whose j eternal flow.
359:1 j of daylight seem

jubilee
120:2 Thy j proclaim;

Judah's
385:3 stoops on J path

judge
170:2 j not him who

judgments
111:2 Thy j are a mighty
130:2 Thy j are a mighty
329:2 His j all are pure,

just
125:3 ways are j and right.
333:2 j rebuke was hurled

justice
111:2 firm Thy j stands,
258:2 side of perfect j
340:1 kindness in His j,
362:3 j ever guards his

K

keep
3:3 k Calm watch by day
33:2 ward o'er thee to k,
36:4 festival we k
53:3 He will k us
58:1 Thou wilt k us
111:2 their foundations k:
115:2 K us from our own
116:2 K us from our own
115:2 K us ever at Thy
116:2 K us ever at Thy
169:1 K Thou my feet;
170:2 K while ye need it,
182:3 share, if we would k
188:2 bids them find and k
207:1 K Thou my child on
208:1 K Thou my child on
209:1 K Thou my child on
210:1 K Thou my child on
211:1 K Thou my child on
212:1 K Thou my child on
214:2 k us meek, and make

keep
258:2 k abreast of Truth,
273:1 K the holiness of
274:1 K the holiness of
275:3 we k our tryst,
283:2 doth He tenderly k;
329:3 k me from transgression,
364:1 K we watch, lest
376:1 k the better way.
377:1 k the better way.

keeper
189:1 My k is the Lord,

keepeth
93:1, 3 God k him in perfect
   2 God k him, and God
189:2 God k me from falling,
   2 He k me from evil,

keeping
130:2 trust us to Thy k.
258:3 K watch above His

keeps
234:3 k faith sweet and
235:3 k faith sweet and
237:2 its promise k;

kept
269:1 God's promises are k.
270:1 God's promises are k.

key
168:3 k that shuts and

kills
29:1 Sin it k and grief

kind
69:3 be more tender, k,
423:3 be more tender, k,
88:2 wisdom k and clear
89:2 wisdom k and clear
124:1 How k His precepts
402:1 How k His precepts
173:1 Love is k and suffers
178:2 compassion is and k;

kind
259:3 K deeds of peace
278:3 the blessing how k;
279:3 the blessing how k;
340:2 most wonderfully k.

kindle
118:1 K every high desire;

kindling
319:3 k hearts that burn

kindly
30:5 Speaks k when we meet
31:5 Speaks k when we meet
32:5 Speaks k when we meet
169:1 Lead, k Light, amid
217:2 each k deed a prayer.

kindness
73:2 In His k may rejoice.
130:1 faithful is Thy k.
178:1 knew the law of k,
340:1 a k in His justice,
347:1 His k shall remain
348:1 His k shall remain

King
10:3 Our K is ever near;
411:3 Our K is ever near;
36:4 presence of the K.
37:2 One K omnipotent.
38:2 One K omnipotent.
150:1 how great is our K;
158:1 heaven's all-gracious K;
159:1 heaven's all-gracious K;
158:3 Prince of Peace their K,
159:3 Prince of Peace their K,
164:1 earth receive her K;
165:1 earth receive her K;
417:1 earth receive her K;
222:2 sing to God the K,
223:2 sing to God the K,
264:4 Unto Christ the K;
271:4 honors to our K;
272:4 honors to our K;
280:1 the K of heaven;
1 the everlasting K.
283:1 our God and our K,
322:3 to the K of kings,
323:3 to the K of kings,
324:2 only, for my K.
330:1 The K of Love my
418:4 eyes the K will see,

king
310:1, Ref. Christ, our k.

kingdom
10:1-3 His k is forever.
411:1-3 His k is forever.

kingdom
51:3 His k come;
52:3 His k come;
75:3 His k still increasing,
     A k without end.
204:1 Thy k is come upon
221:3 Thy k, God, within
236:1 God's k at hand!
271:1 His k stretch from
272:1 His k stretch from

kingdoms
264:3 K rise and wane,

kings
297:3 makes us priests and k;
318:3 glory k ne'er know;
322:3 to the King of k,
323:3 to the King of k,

kiss
30:3 For faith to k;
31:3 For faith to k,
32:3 For faith to k,
253:3 I k the cross,
254:3 I k the cross,
255:3 I k the cross,
256:3 I k the cross,
257:3 I k the cross,

knee
259:1 lifted eye or bended k.
331:1 lifted eye and bended k

kneeling
196:1 Around one altar k,

knew
178:1 Jesus k the law of
381:2 k the Christ, undimmed

know
5:2 only k the real.
7:2 I k no fear, with Thee
3 I k Thy presence
3 I k Thy peace, for
10:3 let us k no fear,
411:3 let us k no fear,
30:3 faith to kiss, and k;
31:3 faith to kiss, and k;
32:3 faith to kiss, and k;
39:2 k and choose Thy way;
58:3 Thy children k Thee,
64:2 k that where I stand
65:1 freedom we may k.
2 to k The fullness
69:1 to k myself in Thee,
423:1 to k myself in Thee,
85:2 K the glory of Thy
101:2 men rejoice to k
135:1 k no life divided,
1 k no death, O Father,

know
136:3 I yet shall k as
149:3 k that man beloved
426:3 k that man beloved
163:2 only blessings k,
166:1 K, O child, thy full
167:1 K, O child, thy full
170:1 k, through God's
1 within myself to k
171:2 we k his promised
413:2 we k his promised
175:1 k Thee and be free.
185:3 k that the Truth
186:2 being e'er shall k,
187:2 being e'er shall k,
188:1 k what God hath
195:3 what I k of Thee,
199:2 k our gracious God
201:3 all who k its power;
404:3 all who k its power;
201:4 k your life is hid
404:4 k your life is hid
203:2 k that all is well
2 k that all Thy
206:3 And k reality.
428:3 And k reality.
214:3 k no other guide,
240:3 teachings make us k
241:3 teachings make us k
245:1 k that Love will
2 k, beloved Shepherd,
249:1 k how flows the fountain
250:1 k how flows the fountain
253:3 k A world more bright.
254:3 k A world more bright.
255:3 k A world more bright.
256:3 k A world more bright.
257:3 k A world more bright.
263:3 K in God the perfect
266:1 His image bear, we k;
267:1 k that God is here.
268:1 k that God is here.
269:3 k That words alone
270:3 k That words alone
269:3 k how Love divine
270:3 k how Love divine
288:2 k that God is all;
289:2 k that God is all;
311:1 claim he doth not k
420:1 claim he doth not k
318:3 glory kings ne'er k;
332:1 k that He is God,
339:1 saving Truth who k,
342:1 every heart may k.
343:4 that Way to k,
344:4 that Way to k,
429:4 that Way to k,
349:2 life we k from Thee

know
367:1 k That fellowship
370:1 k that sin can never
374:2 Thy children k Thee
375:2 Thy children k Thee
414:1 Because I k 'tis true,
　　3 those who k it best

knowest
229:1 nor creed Thou k,

knoweth
379:2 nothing k But his God,
380:2 nothing k But his God,

knowing
40:3 k, Earth has no sorrow
58:1 K well that Thou
102:2 K nothing but Thy
103:2 K nothing but Thy

knowledge
363:2 to year does k soar;

known
29:2 k in every land,
76:1 k in loving-kindness,
136:3 know as I am k
141:3 K the work of
174:3 needs but to be k !
233:1 perfect path is k
419:1 perfect path is k
246:Ref. have ye not k
273:3 our faith be k,
274:3 our faith be k,
329:1 mighty power is k ;
339:3 healing love make k,

knows
9:1 all the world k peace.
　　3 He k the angels
20:1 that k no sin,
416:1 that k no sin,
48:2 He k not death
92:1 Happy the man who k
119:2 that k no measure,
142:2 k whence it came,

knows
146:1 That k no fear,
147:1 That k no fear,
148:2 He k the way He
179:2 Love k no evil,
205:2 in danger k no fear,
218:4 Life that k no death,—
219:4 Life that k no death,—
220:4 Life that k no death,—
221:3 k the reign of Soul.
280:2 daily needs He k ;
392:2 heart that k him
393:2 heart that k him

know'st
304:2 Thou k Thine own;
305:2 Thou k Thine own;
306:2 Thou k Thine own;
307:2 Thou k Thine own;
308:2 Thou k Thine own;
309:2 Thou k Thine own;

L

labor
41:1-4 Come, l on:
92:1 life of love and l
141:1 l build in vain;
149:3 bowed with tired l,
426:3 bowed with tired l,
364:2 our toil and l,
　　2 God that l bless;

laborers
242:1 l for the Lord.

labors
215:3 as her l rise,

lab'ring
304:2 L long and lone,
305:2 L long and lone,
306:2 L long and lone,
307:2 L long and lone,
308:2 L long and lone,
309:2 L long and lone,

lack
148:2 nothing can I l.
330:1 nothing l, for I am His

laden
43:2 Come, all ye heavy l,

laid
104:4 The cross l down;

laid
123:1 l for your faith
148:1 heart may low be l ;
259:1 l on mercy's shrine,
330:3 on His shoulder ... l,

Lamb of God
297:3 with the L of G,

lambkins
304:3 Thy l to the fold,
305:3 Thy l to the fold,
306:3 Thy l to the fold,
307:3 Thy l to the fold,
308:3 Thy l to the fold,
309:3 Thy l to the fold,

Lamb's
108:4 L great bridal feast

lambs
311:2 The l who wander
420:2 The l who wander

lame
384:3 The l shall walk,
388:2 the halt and l

lament
391:4 the ages' long l ;

lamp
172:2 Hold high thy l
346:3 the l of grace,
401:3 the l of grace,
363:4 cloudless l of day

lamps
398:2 all your l be bright,

land
12:1 idols from the l,
13:1 idols from the l,
29:2 known in every l,
44:1 to the l of peace;
62:1 Through every l,
63:1 Through every l,
90:1 through this barren l:
177:1 Word in every l:
196:2 blest l of love.
236:1 breaks over the l,
238:2 every l a Palestine.
239:2 every l a Palestine.
281:1 Canaan's promised l,
314:1 Broadcast it o'er the l.
351:1 to the promised l.
385:1 Out of the l of bondage
389:2 l of the stranger;

lands
251:2 O'er all the l
252:2 O'er all the l

languish
40:1 where'er ye l,

lantern
251:1 l to our footsteps,
252:1 l to our footsteps,

lapse
261:1 by the l of years,
262:1 by the l of years,

large
131:2 too l for creeds;
132:2 too l for creeds;
226:3 In love's l liberty.

larger
218:3 l thought of God;—
219:3 l thought of God;—
220:3 l thought of God;—

largess
3:4 l of a grateful heart

last
186:1 God, the First, the L,
187:1 God, the First, the L,
213:4 guard while ages l,
290:3 True to the l, press
312:2 stand complete at l.

lasting
196:2 More sweet and l prove,

late
141:4 summon, soon or l,

laud
264:4 Glory, l and honor
282:2 L and magnify His

law
134:3 Held in Thy l,
178:1 the l of kindness,
2 the l fulfilleth,
179:2 l does love fulfill.
182:3 Such is the l of Love.
216:1 ye God's l can
229:2 Love beyond all l,
297:3 Love's l divine
329:2 His l man's pathway
371:2 within Thy perfect l
394:3 Thy l revere.
395:3 Thy l revere.

laws
102:1 Thy l so pure and
103:1 Thy l so pure and
180:1 l fulfillment find.
282:1 L that never shall be
391:3 lives in eternal l,

lay
11:1 babe in meekness l,
30:4 swelled creation's l:
31:4 swelled creation's l:
32:4 swelled creation's l:
59:1 L hold on Life,
60:1 L hold on Life,
61:1 L hold on Life,
108:2 l aside each earthly
158:1 in solemn stillness l
159:1 in solemn stillness l
228:1 l our hand upon our
329:3 L hold of Thee aright.
391:2 ancient prophets' l,

laying
365:1 L hold upon His Word:
366:1 L hold upon His Word:

lead
39:3 L us, O Christ, thou
3 L us to God, our
104:4 L us to heaven's
169:1 L, kindly Light,
1, 2 L Thou me on.
2 Shouldst l me on;
3 l me on O'er moor
203:2 l us safely home
226:3 l forth this age
245:1 safely l us home.
304:3 L Thy lambkins to
305:3 L Thy lambkins to
306:3 L Thy lambkins to
307:3 L Thy lambkins to
308:3 L Thy lambkins to
309:3 L Thy lambkins to
311:2 l them safely, surely
420:2 l them safely, surely

leadest
134:3 l me by unsought ways,
245:1 follow where thou l,

leadeth
95:1 He l me, O blessed
1 God's hand that l
Ref. He l me, He l me,
By His own hand He l
2 His hand that l me.
253:7 whereto God l me.
254:7 whereto God l me.
255:7 whereto God l me.
256:7 whereto God l me.
257:7 whereto God l me.
330:2 ransomed soul He l,

leading
84:2 where His love is l.

leads
64:3 The way l upward
65:1 Love that l us on;
90:2 L me all my journey
216:2 He l you after His
245:2 L ever out of darkness
264:1 l against the foe;
281:1 He l His chosen
2 dawn l us on,
288:1 l to that eternal
289:1 l to that eternal
288:2 way that l to God.
289:2 way that l to God.
339:1 l from the shade,
354:1 God the Spirit l
376:1 l us home to God.
377:1 l us home to God.
383:3 l to cloudless day.
396:1 follow where he l,
397:1 follow where he l,

lean
53:1 the arm we l upon.
2 His arm to l upon.
108:1 weariness upon Thee l.
195:3 I l on Thee, in

leaning
57:3 on Thy goodness l;

leaps
271:3 prisoner l to loose
272:3 prisoner l to loose

learn
30:3 L, too, that wisdom's
31:3 L, too, that wisdom's
32:3 L, too, that wisdom's
46:1 l this lesson well.
47:1 l this lesson well.
57:3 l life's deeper
65:2 more we l to know
69:1 l to know myself in
423:1 l to know myself in
69:2 l to quell all selfish
423:2 l to quell all selfish
69:3 l to be more tender,
423:3 l to be more tender,
84:2 L the power of Love
2 L obedience,—and
181:3 We would l, O gracious
266:4 L how true Christians
343:4 that Life to l,
344:4 that Life to l,
429:4 that Life to l,
345:3 l how God Himself

learned
337:2 L scoffers may abuse
338:2 L scoffers may abuse

learning
85:3 courage, meekness l.

least
86:1 l like What men agree
87:1 l like What men agree

leave
76:1 mother l her children?
202:1 l thy dreams for
412:1 l thy dreams for
249:1 l unsung one blessing,
250:1 l unsung one blessing,
291:2 to Thy wisdom l;
357:2 Lord, our gladness l,
358:2 Lord, our gladness l,
407:2 Lord, our gladness l,

leaves
44:3 l no saddening trace;
141:3 L be gathered from
197:1 fair the l unfold,
198:1 fair the l unfold,

leav'st
229:1 Nor l us though we

led
81:1 pilgrim feet be l.
128:2 l his followers' way.
129:2 l his followers' way.
388:3 of loving-kindness l,

left
360:2 a well l empty?

legion
265:1 set a guardian l

legions
33:2 charge His angel l
200:2 scattered their l

length
119:3 all our fears at l;
245:3 With joy at l we come,
314:2 full corn comes at l.
326:4 and wins at l,
330:4 all the l of days

lengthen
77:2 day shall mercy l:
78:2 day shall mercy l:

less
230:3 words are l than deeds;
231:3 words are l than deeds;

lesson
46:1 learn this l well.
47:1 learn this l well.

lest
304:1 L my footsteps stray;
305:1 L my footsteps stray;
306:1 L my footsteps stray;
307:1 L my footsteps stray;
308:1 L my footsteps stray;
309:1 L my footsteps stray;
364:1 watch, l foes alarm;

let
1:1 So l it be on earth
5:1 l not fear enthrall.
10:3 l us know no fear,
411:3 l us know no fear,
12:2 l your works confirm
13:2 l your works confirm
14:4 l thy living light
16:1 l me sing my way
21:1-4 Beloved, l us love:
22:1-4 Beloved, l us love:
30:4 "L there be light,
31:4 "L there be light,
32:4 "L there be light,
39:3 Nor l us from thy
42:1 L each heart Thy
2 L us all, Thy love
49:2 L us, like them,
50:2 L us, like them,
49:3 L sense be dumb, l
50:3 L sense be dumb, l
49:4 l our ordered lives
50:4 l our ordered lives
51:3 L gladness ring from
52:3 L gladness ring from
62:1 L the Creator's praise
63:1 L the Creator's praise
62:1 L the Redeemer's name
63:1 L the Redeemer's name
72:1 L Thy light, Thy
405:1 L Thy light, Thy
88:2 L Thy life in mine
89:2 L Thy life in mine
91:2 l Thy light shine
422:2 l Thy light shine
97:2 L not fear thy
98:2 L not fear thy
105:1 L each his friendly aid
106:1 L each his friendly aid
107:1 L each his friendly aid
105:3 L us in all things
106:3 L us in all things
107:3 L us in all things
112:1 l song be soaring,
119:2 L the Love, that knows
120:2 L songs instead of
126:3 L love, in one
127:3 L love, in one

let
403:3 L love, in one
139:3 L childlike trust be
427:3 L childlike trust be
163:3 l us win our brother
164:1 L earth receive her
165:1 L earth receive her
417:1 L earth receive her
164:1 L every heart prepare
165:1 L every heart prepare
417:1 L every heart prepare
164:2 No more l sin and
165:2 No more l sin and
417:2 No more l sin and
168:1 L all the earth
1 L heaven return the
1 L every man His
170:1 L every creature
171:1 L us sing of Easter
413:1 L us sing of Easter
176:2,3 L there be light,
177:2 L Thy people see
2 L the gospel be
192:3 l the way appear,
193:3 l the way appear,
196:2 L all that now divides
2 L all that now unites
201:1 wide, l in the Word,
404:1 wide, l in the Word,
226:2 l the darkling past
234:1 Master, l me walk
235:1 Master, l me walk
234:4 Master, l me live.
235:4 Master, l me live.
236:2 No more l dire hate
2 L Truth be proclaimed,
2 l God's love be
4 L nations be one
271:4 L every creature rise,
272:4 L every creature rise,
271:4 L angel songs be
272:4 L angel songs be
273:1 l us bear the strife,
274:1 l us bear the strife,
275:1 l us praise with joy
283:1 L us extol Him
1 Come l us sing,
287:3 L there be light.
408:3 L there be light.
291:2 L me as a child
3 L me thus with Thee
311:3 praises l us sing
420:3 praises l us sing
315:1 l no harsh word mar
316:1 l no harsh word mar

let
324:1 my life, and l· it be
 1 days, L· them flow
 1 hands, and l· them move
 2 feet, and l· them be
 2 voice, and l· me sing
 2 lips, and l· them be
325:2 L· not thy foolish
329:3 O, l· my meditation
332:1 L· all the earth
334:3 L· everlasting thanks
346:1-3 L· there be light.
401:1-3 L· there be light.
352:4 L· it illume my way
353:4 L· it illume my way
355:1 l· us all unite,
368:3 l· thy wanderings
369:3 l· thy wanderings
386:2 l· our lips and lives
387:2 l· our lips and lives
386:2 l· our works and virtues
387:2 l· our works and virtues
394:3 l· there be Joy and
395:3 l· there be Joy and
398:2 L· all your lamps

letter
142:4 l· fails, the systems

liberation
179:1 thrall,—Love is l·.

liberty
 83:1 Life itself is l·;
201:2 the light of l·
404:2 the light of l·
226:3 In love's large l·.
340:1 is more than l·.
371:2 perfect law Our l·.

lie
 86:3 right doth really l·,
 87:3 right doth really l·,
123:3 thy pathway shall l·,
130:2 when we l· asleep,
222:1 still we see thee l·;
223:1 still we see thee l·;
242:2 selfish ease we l·,

lies
 59:2 way before us l·,
 60:2 way before us l·,
 61:2 way before us l·,
 64:1 pathway l· before me,
 67:1 Ambushed l· the evil
 68:1 Ambushed l· the evil
356:2 l· our active rest.
379:4 all our fullness l·.
380:4 all our fullness l·.

Life
 16:2 Love is L· eternally,

Life
 19:2 of Love and L·,
 23:4 Love, And deathless L·!
 24:4 Love, And deathless L·!
 25:4 Love, And deathless L·!
 26:4 Love, And deathless L·!
 27:4 Love, And deathless L·!
 28:4 Love, And deathless L·!
 30:5 Love alone is L·;
 31:5 Love alone is L·;
 32:5 Love alone is L·;
 40:1 L·, Truth, and Love;
 3 see the Bread of L·,
 48:2 not death who L· obeys,
 3 L· and Truth and Love,
 51:2 L·, Truth and Love
 52:2 L·, Truth and Love
 58:1 Thou art L· and Thou
 3 Love and L· forever
 59:1 Lay hold on L·,
 60:1 Lay hold on L·,
 61:1 Lay hold on L·,
 66:2 O perfect L·, in Thy
421:2 O perfect L·, in Thy
 83:2 God is L· and Soul.
 93:2 One L·, forevermore
101:3 rise to L· again;
112:3 lives in L· eternal
157:2 L· of all things,
160:4 There L· is light,
161:4 There L· is light,
162:4 There L· is light,
175:2 L· divine, Thy Word
188:3 I am L·, come unto Me.
206:3 our Father-Mother, L·,
428:3 our Father-Mother, L·,
207:1 L· divine, that owns
208:1 L· divine, that owns
209:1 L· divine, that owns
210:1 L· divine, that owns
211:1 L· divine, that owns
212:1 L· divine, that owns
218:1,4 L· that maketh all
219:1,4 L· that maketh all
220:1,4 L· that maketh all
218:4 L· that knows no
219:4 L· that knows no
220:4 L· that knows no
228:2 for L· Thou art.
229:2 L· o'ercoming death
230:1 O Love, O L·, our
231:1 O Love, O L·, our
237:2 L· that never sleeps.
267:3 Principle, the L·;
268:3 Principle, the L·;
288:1 Way, the Truth, the L·.
289:1 Way, the Truth, the L·.
288:2 He is the L·, the

Life
289:2 He is the L·, the
298:4 L· of all being divine:
299:4 L· of all being divine:
300:4 L· of all being divine:
301:4 L· of all being divine:
302:4 L· of all being divine:
325:3 L· Giveth thee victory
332:2 Him L· shall find,
342:3 For L· and Love
343:3 Thou art the L·:
344:3 Thou art the L·:
429:3 Thou art the L·:
343:4 Way, the Truth, the L·:
344:4 Way, the Truth, the L·:
429:4 Way, the Truth, the L·:
343:4 that L· to learn,
344:4 that L· to learn,
429:4 that L· to learn,
349:1 art L· and Truth
355:2 L·, Truth and Love
371:1 O God of L·, to Thee,
378:2 Thou art L·.
392:3 door of L· unseals
393:3 door of L· unseals
394:1 Word of L·, most pure,
395:1 Word of L·, most pure,

life
 4:3 by the l· of Jesus
 6:2 claims no l· is free,
 7:2 and l· no wretchedness;
 10:3 l· to all is giving;
411:3 l· to all is giving;
 30:5 l· most sweet, as heart
 31:5 l· most sweet, as heart
 32:5 l· most sweet, as heart
 43:2 I will give you l·.
 56:1 Thou Fount of l·,
 59:2 L· with its way before
 60:2 L· with its way before
 61:2 L· with its way before
 83:1 L· itself is liberty;
 88:1 Thy l· in mine reveal;
 89:1 Thy l· in mine reveal;
 88:2 Thy l· in mine appear;
 89:2 Thy l· in mine appear;
 92:1 l· of love and labor
111:3 L·, like a fountain
131:1 way, the truth, the l·,
132:1 way, the truth, the l·,
131:2 l·, indwelling, deep and
132:2 l·, indwelling, deep and
131:3 quick'ning l· from heaven,
132:3 quick'ning l· from heaven,
134:2 flows Thy quickening l·

life
135:1 know no $l\cdot$ divided, O
   Lord of $l\cdot$, from Thee;
   In Thee is $l\cdot$ provided
  1 Thy $l\cdot$ it is that frees
148:3 path in $l\cdot$ is free;
150:3 we thank Thee for $l\cdot$,
  3 the $l\cdot$ of our Lord.
154:1 my $l\cdot$ as God's own
155:1 my $l\cdot$ as God's own
156:1 my $l\cdot$ as God's own
172:1 storms of $l\cdot$ assail;
174:2 $L\cdot$ is of God, whose
190:1 tasks of $l\cdot$ seem hard
191:1 tasks of $l\cdot$ seem hard
199:2 Through all our $l\cdot$
201:4 $l\cdot$ is hid With Christ
404:4 $l\cdot$ is hid With Christ
217:3 loving $l\cdot$ a psalm
226:1 Lord of $l\cdot$, to Thee
228:1 Whose light of $l\cdot$
  2 In Thee our $l\cdot$,
238:2 Our common, daily $l\cdot$
239:2 Our common, daily $l\cdot$
249:2 $l\cdot$ from joy is minted,
250:2 $l\cdot$ from joy is minted,
273:1 the holiness of $l\cdot$.
274:1 the holiness of $l\cdot$.
275:3 $L\cdot$ is our heritage;
293:3 our $l\cdot$ to fill,
294:3 our $l\cdot$ to fill,
295:3 our $l\cdot$ to fill,
298:1 $l\cdot$ and the love of our
299:1 $l\cdot$ and the love of our
300:1 $l\cdot$ and the love of our
301:1 $l\cdot$ and the love of our
302:1 $l\cdot$ and the love of our
303:3 call it back to $l\cdot$;
319:1 Sun of our $l\cdot$, thy
  2 Lord of all $l\cdot$, below,
320:4 path of $l\cdot$ divine;
321:4 path of $l\cdot$ divine;
409:4 path of $l\cdot$ divine;
324:1 Take my $l\cdot$, and let
341:1 live a $l\cdot$ of prayer,
349:2 $l\cdot$ we know from Thee
359:3 thine immortal $l\cdot$ shall
381:1 Lord in $l\cdot$ arise.
418:3 $l\cdot$ that is to be,

Life-encrowned
23:3 Thou God-idea, $L\cdot$,
24:3 Thou God-idea, $L\cdot$,
25:3 Thou God-idea, $L\cdot$,
26:3 Thou God-idea, $L\cdot$,
27:3 Thou God-idea, $L\cdot$,
28:3 Thou God-idea, $L\cdot$,

life-giving
346:3 $L\cdot$, holy dove, Speed
401:3 $L\cdot$, holy dove, Speed

lifeless
333:3 rite, no $l\cdot$ creed,

Life's
171:2 behold $L\cdot$ purity,
413:2 behold $L\cdot$ purity,
253:5 rock, Upon $L\cdot$ shore,
254:5 rock, Upon $L\cdot$ shore,
255:5 rock, Upon $L\cdot$ shore,
256:5 rock, Upon $L\cdot$ shore,
257:5 rock, Upon $L\cdot$ shore,
391:1 $L\cdot$ pearl is cast.

life's
57:3 $l\cdot$ deeper meaning,
158:2 $l\cdot$ crushing load
159:2 $l\cdot$ crushing load
178:1 Love is $l\cdot$ true crown
253:3 show $L\cdot$ burdens light.
254:3 show $L\cdot$ burdens light.
255:3 show $L\cdot$ burdens light.
256:3 show $L\cdot$ burdens light.
257:3 show $L\cdot$ burdens light.
293:1 above $l\cdot$ raging sea.
294:1 above $l\cdot$ raging sea.
295:1 above $l\cdot$ raging sea.
333:1 Beneath $l\cdot$ weary load,
372:3 $l\cdot$ throng and press,
373:2 $l\cdot$ throng and press,

lift
  9:2 $l\cdot$ our thoughts above,
34:1 $l\cdot$ our blinded eyes
36:4 praise we $l\cdot$ on high,
45:3 We $l\cdot$ our hearts in
58:1 $L\cdot$ our hearts in joy
59:2 $L\cdot$ up thine eyes,
60:2 $L\cdot$ up thine eyes,
61:2 $L\cdot$ up thine eyes,
85:1 $L\cdot$ our hearts to
119:1 $L\cdot$ all burdens and all
172:1 $L\cdot$ up thy light,
204:2 $l\cdot$ up a light amid
226:1 $l\cdot$ Our hearts in praise
237:3 $L\cdot$ to Him the heart's
273:1 $L\cdot$ your hearts and
274:1 $L\cdot$ your hearts and
296:1 $l\cdot$ your banner high;
298:2 $l\cdot$ the shade of gloom,
299:2 $l\cdot$ the shade of gloom,
300:2 $l\cdot$ the shade of gloom,
301:2 $l\cdot$ the shade of gloom,
302:2 $l\cdot$ the shade of gloom,
314:3 $L\cdot$ up thine eyes,
322:3 $l\cdot$ her sacred wings,

lift
323:3 $l\cdot$ her sacred wings,
342:1, 3 $l\cdot$ up your voice.
351:3 lips of thousands $L\cdot$
371:1-3 We $l\cdot$ our hearts in
425:1 pilgrim, $l\cdot$ your head,

lifted
251:2 still thy light is $l\cdot$,
252:2 still thy light is $l\cdot$,
259:1 $l\cdot$ eye or bended knee.
331:1 $l\cdot$ eye and bended knee
370:2 risen Christ has $l\cdot$

lifteth
160:4 looseth thee, and $l\cdot$
161:4 looseth thee, and $l\cdot$
162:4 looseth thee, and $l\cdot$

lifting
141:4 $L\cdot$ hope above the sod,
378:1 $L\cdot$ our lives to Thee,

lifts
109:1 $L\cdot$ our thoughts from
110:1 $L\cdot$ our thoughts from
153:1 Him who $l\cdot$ the lowly,
179:2 $l\cdot$ the heart to gladness.
181:2 power that $l\cdot$ us To Thy
194:2 heart's own longing $l\cdot$
410:2 heart's own longing $l\cdot$

Light
35:1 true, the perfect $L\cdot$,
56:1 Thou $L\cdot$ of men,
84:1 Into $L\cdot$, O hear it
118:1 Holy Spirit, $L\cdot$ divine,
169:1 Lead, kindly $L\cdot$, amid
172:1 great $L\cdot$ divine,
201:4 Truth and $L\cdot$ and Love;
404:4 Truth and $L\cdot$ and Love;
218:2 seekers of the $L\cdot$ are
219:2 seekers of the $L\cdot$ are
220:2 seekers of the $L\cdot$ are
222:1 The everlasting $L\cdot$;
223:1 The everlasting $L\cdot$;
226:2 Shine forth, O $L\cdot$,
  3 O $L\cdot$ of light, within
230:2 $L\cdot$, the Truth, the Way.
231:2 $L\cdot$, the Truth, the Way.
232:2 O $L\cdot$, in Thy light
406:2 O $L\cdot$, in Thy light
233:3 toward Thee, the $L\cdot$.
419:3 toward Thee, the $L\cdot$.
367:4 God Himself is $L\cdot$.

light (noun)
  2:1 shines the blessed $l\cdot$;
  3 $l\cdot$ has broken forth,
  7:1 breaks the morning $l\cdot$;

light (noun)
9:2 All winged with $l\cdot$
11:2 still thy $l\cdot$ Shines
12:3 That $l\cdot$ whose glory,
13:3 That $l\cdot$ whose glory,
14:1 and Christ thy $l\cdot$,
2 Truth's clear $l\cdot$
3 wrong Obscure the $l\cdot$
4 living $l\cdot$ show forth
15:2 Revealed in radiant $l\cdot$.
19:1 the throne of $l\cdot$,
2 an ever clearer $l\cdot$,
21:3 for love is $l\cdot$,
22:3 for love is $l\cdot$,
23:1 Thy $l\cdot$ was born where
24:1 Thy $l\cdot$ was born where
25:1 Thy $l\cdot$ was born where
26:1 Thy $l\cdot$ was born where
27:1 Thy $l\cdot$ was born where
28:1 Thy $l\cdot$ was born where
30:4 "Let there be $l\cdot$, and there was $l\cdot$."
31:4 "Let there be $l\cdot$, and there was $l\cdot$."
32:4 "Let there be $l\cdot$, and there was $l\cdot$."
35:2 inward $l\cdot$ impart,
39:1 $l\cdot$ and comfort from
2 $l\cdot$ of Truth to us
40:2 $l\cdot$ of the straying,
43:2 I will give you $l\cdot$.
45:2 sunbeam, $l\cdot$ and flower
51:3 brought the $l\cdot$ again.
52:3 brought the $l\cdot$ again.
70:1 God giveth $l\cdot$ to all
2 A line of purest $l\cdot$.
3 God is thy $l\cdot$ and
71:2 $L\cdot$ by night, and
72:1 Let Thy $l\cdot$, Thy truth,
405:1 Let Thy $l\cdot$, Thy truth,
77:1 My $l\cdot$, my help is near:
78:1 My $l\cdot$, my help is near:
80:2 in eternity of $l\cdot$,
82:3 $l\cdot$ of the glorious
91:2 let Thy $l\cdot$ shine
422:2 let Thy $l\cdot$ shine
101:1 $l\cdot$ Man's heritage
104:3 Thou $l\cdot$ of men,
109:1 Fills with $l\cdot$ their
110:1 Fills with $l\cdot$ their
111:3 in Thy $l\cdot$ we all
112:3 the $l\cdot$ beholdeth.
113:1 dost dwell in $l\cdot$;
115:1 doubted, sent us $l\cdot$;
116:1 doubted, sent us $l\cdot$;
119:1 O'er . . . shed Thy $l\cdot$.
121:2 fullest $l\cdot$ of love;
122:2 fullest $l\cdot$ of love;

light (noun)
130:1 in Thy $l\cdot$ shall we see $l\cdot$.
136:1 Thy clear $l\cdot$ of Truth
138:3 Beneath whose $l\cdot$ I
142:3 Shine out, O $l\cdot$ divine,
143:1 shrinks from $l\cdot$,
144:2 would bring to $l\cdot$
145:2 would bring to $l\cdot$
146:2 Abide in heavenly $l\cdot$.
147:2 Abide in heavenly $l\cdot$.
149:1 pours forth her $l\cdot$;
426:1 pours forth her $l\cdot$;
149:3 radiant $l\cdot$ of adoration,
426:3 radiant $l\cdot$ of adoration,
154:1 Thy $l\cdot$ of glorious
155:1 Thy $l\cdot$ of glorious
156:1 Thy $l\cdot$ of glorious
160:4 There Life is $l\cdot$,
161:4 There Life is $l\cdot$,
162:4 There Life is $l\cdot$,
168:2 $l\cdot$ Of Gospel truth
2 work that $l\cdot$ impart,
171:1 $l\cdot$ that cannot fade.
413:1 $l\cdot$ that cannot fade.
172:1 Lift up thy $l\cdot$,
3 Send out its $l\cdot$
173:2 in the $l\cdot$ of day;
3 be fulfilled in $l\cdot$;
174:2 O, in that $l\cdot$, all
176:1 $l\cdot$, never failing;
2, 3 Let there be $l\cdot$,
2 and $l\cdot$ was there,
178:1 splendor of the $l\cdot$,
181:1 upward to the $l\cdot$.
185:1 secure in radiant $l\cdot$.
2 $L\cdot$ of the world,
199:2 our thoughts with $l\cdot$,
201:1 the $l\cdot$ of good;
404:1 the $l\cdot$ of good;
201:2 the $l\cdot$ of liberty
404:2 the $l\cdot$ of liberty
201:3 all . . . may $l\cdot$ receive
404:3 all . . . may $l\cdot$ receive
204:2 They lift up a $l\cdot$
206:2 Thy $l\cdot$ sublime,
428:2 Thy $l\cdot$ sublime,
226:1 $l\cdot$ that shineth more
2 Thine untroubled $l\cdot$.
3 O Light of $l\cdot$, within
228:1 $l\cdot$ of life has no
229:2 $l\cdot$ which glowed Upon
232:2 O Light, in Thy $l\cdot$
406:2 O Light, in Thy $l\cdot$
238:3 $l\cdot$ is breaking, calm
239:3 $l\cdot$ is breaking, calm
240:1 Spirit, source of $l\cdot$,
241:1 Spirit, source of $l\cdot$,
240:1 Reveal the $l\cdot$ of Mind.

light (noun)
241:1 Reveal the $l\cdot$ of Mind.
251:1 $l\cdot$ of earth's dark
252:1 $l\cdot$ of earth's dark
251:2 thy $l\cdot$ is lifted,
252:2 thy $l\cdot$ is lifted,
258:1 darkness and the $l\cdot$.
260:4 $l\cdot$ upon my way,
275:2 $L\cdot$ blesses opened
281:2 darkness into $l\cdot$.
2 $L\cdot$ of dawn leads
282:1 ye stars of $l\cdot$;
287:1 Great God of $l\cdot$,
408:1 Great God of $l\cdot$,
287:3 Let there be $l\cdot$.
408:3 Let there be $l\cdot$.
288:1 the darkness into $l\cdot$,
289:1 the darkness into $l\cdot$,
290:1 ye sons of $l\cdot$,
297:1 $L\cdot$ of the world,
1 whose $l\cdot$ we shall see
310:2 Be there $l\cdot$; And there was $l\cdot$.
311:1 constant shines its $l\cdot$,
420:1 constant shines its $l\cdot$,
313:1 Sometimes a $l\cdot$ surprises
2 God, in $l\cdot$ abiding,
314:3 Love's transforming $l\cdot$,
319:1 softened $l\cdot$ Cheers
2 Whose $l\cdot$ is truth,
3 claim One holy $l\cdot$,
334:1 A sanctifying $l\cdot$.
2 $l\cdot$ to every age,
335:1 morning $l\cdot$ is breaking,
337:2 cannot quench Her $l\cdot$.
338:2 cannot quench Her $l\cdot$.
339:1 up to $l\cdot$ they go.
345:1 $l\cdot$ of pentecostal
346:1-3 Let there be $l\cdot$.
401:1-3 Let there be $l\cdot$.
351:1 burns the guiding $l\cdot$;
2 $l\cdot$ of God's own
352:2 made to live in $l\cdot$?
353:2 made to live in $l\cdot$?
352:4 in thy $l\cdot$ be mine
353:4 in thy $l\cdot$ be mine
359:2 $L\cdot$ from His throne
363:2 $l\cdot$ Becomes effulgent
4 floods of $l\cdot$ and joy,
367:1-4 Walk in the $l\cdot$,
1 reigns in $l\cdot$ above.
2 in cloudless $l\cdot$ enshrined,
3 $l\cdot$ on thee hath shone
368:2 blessedness and $l\cdot$,
369:2 blessedness and $l\cdot$,
370:2 thoughts into the $l\cdot$,
$L\cdot$ of Truth wherein

light (noun)
371:3 glory in Thy l,
374:3 blessings, l and grace
375:3 blessings, l and grace
382:3 flee before the l.
385:3 and a shining l.
392:2 To l the Christ now
393:2 To l the Christ now
394:1 world awakes to l.
395:1 world awakes to l.
394:3 See Thy l, Thy law
395:3 See Thy l, Thy law
415:3 Redeemer, is its l.

light (adj.)
34:4 eventide it shall be l.
243:2 How hearts grow l,
244:2 How hearts grow l,
253:3 Life's burdens l.
254:3 Life's burdens l.
255:3 Life's burdens l.
256:3 Life's burdens l.
257:3 Life's burdens l.
383:1 l as breath of summer

light (verb)
226:3 L up Thy word;
  3 L up our way; lead

lighten
104:2 To l every woe.

lightens
79:1 and woe He l;

lightest
96:1 his l touch sufficed

lighting
29:1 L up each somber

light's
185:3 l triumphant glow

lights
361:3 God l the way

like
8:2 l Thyself my guide
19:2 L stars they shall
30:1 L brother birds,
31:1 L brother birds,
32:1 L brother birds,
49:2 trust l theirs who
50:2 trust l theirs who
49:2 Let us, l them,
50:2 Let us, l them,
71:3 l the Lord, the giver,
75:2 and hope, l flowers,
86:1 least l What men

like
87:1 least l What men
96:2 L him who went about
102:3 L the star of
103:3 L the star of
111:3 Life, l a fountain
120:1 L streams from living
133:3 a thought l this
424:3 a thought l this
137:1 tender voice l Thine
163:1 precept is l thine:
174:1 L as a mother,
192:2 l the wanderer,
193:2 l the wanderer,
196:2 L shadows of the
213:3 l an evening gone,
246:1 heaven l a tent,
264:2 L a mighty army,
265:3 cheering, l the sun,
275:2 Joys l the dawns
280:1 l us His praise
318:3 l the sparrows,
334:2 Majestic l the sun;
337:1 l clouds that sweep
338:1 l clouds that sweep
340:1 L the wideness of
352:2 l thee so calm,
353:2 l thee so calm,
352:2 l thee did ever go
353:2 l thee did ever go
352:3 l thee so humbly
353:3 l thee so humbly
359:1 seem so l a dream;
  1 pities l a father;
381:3 l exiles yearning
388:1 When l a stranger
414:3 hear it l the rest.

likeness
15:2 l clear and bright,
66:3 reveal Thy l true,
421:3 reveal Thy l true,
109:2 in Love's pure l
110:2 in Love's pure l
160:5 doth His will—His l
161:5 doth His will—His l
162:5 doth His will—His l

lilies
170:1 Christmas l bud and
318:3 l, how fair they
384:2 l grow And gladness

line
70:2 l of purest light.
418:3 a long, unresting l

lingering
363:4 the l mist away.

lips
66:1 l redeemed from woe,
421:1 l redeemed from woe,
128:1 From l of gentleness
129:1 From l of gentleness
142:2 Our outward l confess
163:2 l must only blessings
194:2 human l may never
410:2 human l may never
195:3 my l with song;
228:1 hand upon our l.
284:2 infant l can try;
285:2 infant l can try;
286:2 infant l can try;
324:2 Take my l, and let
331:1 l Thy praise prolong,
333:1 l baptized in humble
351:3 l of thousands Lift
386:2 l and lives express
387:2 l and lives express

list
20:1 l the voice within,
416:1 l the voice within,

listen
170:1 l, from no mortal
304:1 l for Thy voice,
305:1 l for Thy voice,
306:1 l for Thy voice,
307:1 l for Thy voice,
308:1 l for Thy voice,
309:1 l for Thy voice,

listening
128:1 l thousands gathered
129:1 l thousands gathered
136:1 l for Thy voice,
175:1 to every l ear.
237:1 L thus to hear

lit
311:1 l by Love divine
420:1 l by Love divine
352:1 l thy lonely pathway,
353:1 l thy lonely pathway,

little
74:2 the l open book
105:2 Our l stock improve;
106:2 Our l stock improve;
107:2 Our l stock improve;
222:1 l town of Bethlehem,
223:1 l town of Bethlehem,
291:1 as a l child,
  3 a l child relies
315:3 'tis a l thing,
316:3 'tis a l thing,

live
30:5 by Thy love ... we l,
31:5 by Thy love ... we l,
32:5 by Thy love ... we l,
42:2 praise and glory l.
46:4 to Thee I l;
47:4 to Thee I l;
55:1 L ... courageously.
58:3 children l to bless,
66:2 l and sing alway
421:2 l and sing alway
115:1 l to Thee alone;
116:1 l to Thee alone;
135:1 Because I l in Thee;
144:1 l, and move, and
145:1 l, and move, and
157:2 l in God alone;
206:3 we may l to Thee,
428:3 we may l to Thee,
234:4 Master, let me l.
235:4 Master, let me l.
266:2 Can l in enmity.
341:1 l a life of prayer,
352:1 made to l in light?
353:1 made to l in light?
356:1 we l and move;
360:2 only l in loving,

lived
386:1 He l the precepts
387:1 He l the precepts

lively
389:1 More l my hope

lives (noun)
49:1 In purer l Thy
50:1 In purer l Thy
49:4 our ordered l confess
50:4 our ordered l confess
55:1 our l courageously.
109:2 Reverent l unveil
110:2 Reverent l unveil
185:2 gently mold Our l
232:2 our l Thou dost
406:2 our l Thou dost
273:3 In our l our faith
274:3 In our l our faith
332:1 l with true content
 2 fill our daily l
340:3 our l would be all
345:3 purer l of men,
357:2 our l so bright.
358:2 our l so bright.
407:2 our l so bright.
371:1 our l enfold,
372:4 test our l by thine.
373:2 test our l by thine.

lives (noun)
378:1 Lifting our l to Thee,
386:2 lips and l express
387:2 lips and l express

lives (verb)
112:3 l in Life eternal
391:2 l and works to-day
 3 God l in eternal

liveth
96:2 Great Physician l yet

living
10:3 In Him we all are l.
411:3 In Him we all are l.
14:4 thy l light show
23:4 beam of l Love,
24:4 beam of l Love,
25:4 beam of l Love,
26:4 beam of l Love,
27:4 beam of l Love,
28:4 beam of l Love,
39:3 Christ, thou l Way,
55:3 smite the l fountains
58:1 In Thy Spirit l,
71:3 streams of l waters,
84:2 hear thy l voice,
105:3 Thee, our l Head,
106:3 Thee, our l Head,
107:3 Thee, our l Head,
114:3 show, by l faith,
120:1 streams from l fountains,
131:3 point that l way,
132:3 point that l way,
171:3 L meekly as the Master,
413:3 L meekly as the Master,
176:3 L stones we, each
178:2 Golden Rule of l,
197:3 His l presence we have
198:3 His l presence we have
203:1 l Truth that makes
251:2 Christ, the l Word.
252:2 Christ, the l Word.
259:2 l fount of joy
319:3 Thy l altars claim
330:2 streams of l water
345:1 l light of pentecostal
360:1 wealth is l grain;
 2 heart a l power?

load
108:2 aside each earthly l,
154:3 no l of care.
155:3 no l of care.
156:3 no l of care.
158:2 life's crushing l
159:2 life's crushing l
333:1 life's weary l,

loftier
94:1 presence of a l power?
363:2 wing, in l flight,

lone
265:1 seem drear and l;
304:2 Lab'ring long and l,
305:2 Lab'ring long and l,
306:2 Lab'ring long and l,
307:2 Lab'ring long and l,
308:2 Lab'ring long and l,
309:2 Lab'ring long and l,

lonely
34:2 the l heart is fed.
352:1 lit thy l pathway,
353:1 lit thy l pathway,

long
169:3 l Thy power hath
 3 have loved l since,
173:1 kind and suffers l,
176:1 L hast thou stood,
 1 L mid the tempest's
190:1 seem hard and l,
191:1 seem hard and l,
196:2 prophets l foretold,
201:2 l enslaved mind,
404:2 l enslaved mind,
229:2 L sought without,
245:1 l to follow thee,
271:4 repeat the l Amen.
272:4 repeat the l Amen.
276:2 so l have sought;
277:2 so l have sought;
296:3 l the conquest waits
304:2 Lab'ring l and lone,
305:2 Lab'ring l and lone,
306:2 Lab'ring l and lone,
307:2 Lab'ring l and lone,
308:2 Lab'ring l and lone,
309:2 Lab'ring l and lone,
319:1 Cheers the l watches
332:2 trust His promise l,
391:4 ages' l lament;
394:1 thee the nations l;
395:1 thee the nations l;
414:3 have loved so l.
415:2 I l have wandered
418:3 a l, unresting line

longing
9:3 l hearts that wait
51:3 The l to be good
52:3 The l to be good
194:2 heart's own l lifts
410:2 heart's own l lifts
269:2 With l unalloyed,
270:2 With l unalloyed,

longing
333:3 *l·* hearts which sought
414:1 satisfies my *l·*
415:2 *l·* heart, my *l·* heart

longings
56:2 *l·* turn to Thee,
93:3 homeless *l·* range,
237:3 find our earthly *l·*
360:2 ceaseless *l·* still.

long-suffering
385:3 *l·*, slow to wrath,

look
97:2 *L·* again, the fields
98:2 *L·* again, the fields
134:1 *l·* to Thee in every
  1 never *l·* in vain;
158:2 *L·* now, for glad
159:2 *L·* now, for glad
177:1 *L·*, ye saints, the day
181:1 Thy children *L·* to Thee
189:1 *l·* toward the mountains,
224:2 *l·* within the veil,
225:2 *l·* within the veil,
290:3 still *l·* in faith
303:3 *l·* of love bid
341:2 *l·* to God in prayer,
391:1 *l·* with tearful eyes

looking
171:3 *L·* ever to the radiance
413:3 *L·* ever to the radiance
351:2 earnest *l·* forward,

loose
271:3 leaps to *l·* his chains,
272:3 leaps to *l·* his chains,

loosener
297:4 *L·* of prison bands

looseth
160:4 Love *l·* thee, and
161:4 Love *l·* thee, and
162:4 Love *l·* thee, and

Lord
4:3 nearer Thee, O *L·*.
8:1 *L·*, with me abide.
10:1 given unto our *L·*,
411:1 given unto our *L·*,
10:2 *L·* is God alone,
411:2 *L·* is God alone,
12:3 glory, *L·*, is Thine.
13:3 glory, *L·*, is Thine.
33:1 Call the *L·* thy sure
35:2 Uncompanioned, *L·*, by

Lord
41:4 O *L·*, with Thee.
45:2 beauty, *L·*, from Thee
46:1 Give me, *L·*, my daily
47:1 Give me, *L·*, my daily
46:3 *L·*, my times are in
47:3 *L·*, my times are in
49:1 *L·* and Father of us
50:1 *L·* and Father of us
49:2 calling of the *L·*,
50:2 calling of the *L·*,
62:2 are Thy mercies, *L·*;
63:2 are Thy mercies, *L·*;
67:3 above all, hear thy *L·*;
68:3 above all, hear thy *L·*;
69:1-3 Give me, O *L·*,
423:1-3 Give me, O *L·*,
71:2 that the *L·* is near.
  3 like the *L·*, the giver,
73:1 God the *L·* belong;
77:2 on the *L·* reliance;
78:2 on the *L·* reliance;
77:2 *L·* will give thee peace.
78:2 *L·* will give thee peace.
83:3 Love alone, is *L·*.
100:1 Thus of the *L·* I now
101:1-3 we bless Thee, *L·*.
104:1 Help us, O *L·*,
105:1 help each other, *L·*,
106:1 help each other, *L·*,
107:1 help each other, *L·*,
108:1 *L·*, I'd see Thee
111:3 presence of my *L·*;
113:3 *L·*, praise to Thee
120:2 The *L·*, in strength
121:4 Christ the *L·* prepare;
122:4 Christ the *L·* prepare;
123:1 saints of the *L·*,
124:1 burdens on the *L·*,
402:1 burdens on the *L·*,
125:1 are Thy dwellings, *L·*,
  3 *L·*, both sun and
126:1 who love the *L·*
127:1 who love the *L·*
403:1 who love the *L·*
130:1 is Thy mercy, *L·*,
135:1 *L·* of life, from Thee;
  2 Between my *L·* and me:
136:1 way of freedom, *L·*,
137:1 Most gracious *L·*;
  3 Thy rich promise, *L·*,
138:1 I praise Thee, *L·*,
141:1 If the *L·* build not
150:3 the life of our *L·*.
151:1, 2 *L·*, I come to Thee;
152:1, 2 *L·*, I come to Thee;

Lord
153:1 magnify the *L·*,
  2 Thy power, O *L·*,
  2 I praise Thee, *L·*,
164:1 the *L·* is come,
165:1 the *L·* is come,
417:1 the *L·* is come,
170:2 the *L·* Christ born.
180:1 Love the *L·* thy God:
185:1 Master and *L·*,
189:1 My keeper is the *L·*,
195:1 *L·*, but what Thou
  3 Thee, my *L·* and God,
196:1 One common *L·* adore.
224:1 *L·*, I would delight
225:1 *L·*, I would delight
226:1 O *L·* of life, to Thee
227:1 *L·*, where'er Thy people
230:4 brother, and our *L·*,
231:4 brother, and our *L·*,
242:1 laborers for the *L·*.
246:Ref. He alone is *L·*.
251:2 guide us to our *L·*;
252:2 guide us to our *L·*;
259:1 grateful, *L·*, to Thee,
266:2 love each other, *L·*,
267:4 Thee *L·* of all.
268:4 Thee *L·* of all.
269:1 Ask not the *L·*
270:1 Ask not the *L·*
278:2 ask of thy *L·*,
279:2 ask of thy *L·*,
281:1 great and gracious *L·*,
282:1 Praise the *L·*, ye
  1, 2 Praise the *L·*, for
283:1-3 Praise we the *L·*,
291:1 Quiet, *L·*, my froward
297:1 glory of the risen *L·*;
298:1 the love of our *L·*.
299:1 the love of our *L·*.
300:1 the love of our *L·*.
301:1 the love of our *L·*.
302:1 the love of our *L·*.
313:1 *L·* who rises With
318:3 praise the *L·*, Publish
319:2 *L·* of all life, below,
320:3 wait upon the *L·*
321:1 wait upon the *L·*
409:3 wait upon the L.
322:2 *L·*, may Thy truth
323:2 *L·*, may Thy truth
324:1 Consecrated, *L·*, to
  3 *L·*, I pour At Thy
325:2 Thy *L·* for thee
329:3 strength, and *L·*.
331:1 homage, *L·*, to Thee;

Lord
332:1 L· is in His holy
335:2 The L· is come.
336:1 to Thy praise, O L·,
340:3 sweetness of our L·.
342:1, 3 the L· hath made;
   2 L· will hear before
   3 thank and bless the L·.
343:1 seek Him, L·, by thee.
344:1 seek Him, L·, by thee.
429:1 seek Him, L·, by thee.
347:4 servant of the L·.
348:4 servant of the L·.
357:2 L·, our gladness
358:2 L·, our gladness
407:2 L·, our gladness
361:2 unless the L· ordain.
362:2 great and mighty L·.
365:1 my soul, upon the L·,
366:1 my soul, upon the L·,
372:1 bring the L· Christ
373:1 bring the L· Christ
372:4 L· and Master of us
373:2 L· and Master of us
374:2 L· of all above,
375:2 L· of all above,
378:1 turn to Thee, O L·,
   3 L·, Thy salvation
381:1 saw her L· in life
385:1 of the L· beloved,
390:2 from our risen L·;
394:3 L· of harvest, let
395:3 L· of harvest, let
398:1 servants of the L·,
   3 L· with rapture see,

Lord God
117:1, 3 L· G· Almighty,
125:2 L· G· of Hosts, that

Lord's
  6:2 thy L· commands:

lose
137:2 l· their power
154:1 l· the earth-clouds
155:1 l· the earth-clouds
156:1 l· the earth-clouds
183:1 hast no time to l·
184:1 hast no time to l·

losing
 73:2 L· self, in Him we
 91:1 L· the mortal will
422:1 L· the mortal will
379:1 who, all things l·,
380:1 who, all things l·,

loss
 18:2 if hatred and l·,
168:3 our l· repair,
174:2 earthly l· is gain;
207:3 and l· is gain.
208:3 and l· is gain.
209:3 and l· is gain.
210:3 and l· is gain.
211:3 and l· is gain.
212:3 and l· is gain.

lost
144:2 sense is l· in sight.
145:2 sense is l· in sight.
169:3 and l· awhile.
181:2 gloom is l· in glory
183:2 toil that is not l·,—
184:2 toil that is not l·,—
217:1 Restores the l·, and

lot
160:1 what be thy l·,
161:1 what be thy l·,
162:1 what be thy l·,
186:3 Whatsoe'er our l·
187:3 Whatsoe'er our l·

loud
172:1 l· the storms of life
418:3 voices, l· and low,

Love
 7:3 L· divine, abiding
 9:2 whisper God is L·.
16:2 L· is Life eternally,
19:2 God's messengers of L·
20:3 whose name is L·,
416:3 whose name is L·,
21:1 for L· is God;
22:1 for L· is God;
23:4 beam of living L·,
24:4 beam of living L·,
25:4 beam of living L·,
26:4 beam of living L·,
27:4 beam of living L·,
28:4 beam of living L·,
30:3 that L·, divinely near,
31:3 that L·, divinely near,
32:3 that L·, divinely near,
30:4 L· whose finger traced
31:4 L· whose finger traced
32:4 L· whose finger traced
30:5 For L· alone is Life;
31:5 For L· alone is Life;
32:5 For L· alone is Life;
34:2 Who dwells with L·
39:1 Spirit, heavenly L·,

Love
40:1 Life, Truth, and L·;
 1, 3 but L· can remove.
  2 that L· cannot cure.
48:2 While merged in L·,
  3 Life and Truth and L·,
51:2 Love's work and L· must
52:2 Love's work and L· must
51:2 L· the pattern make,
52:2 L· the pattern make,
53:1 Everlasting arms of L·
54:1 L·, celestial L·,
58:1 Thou art L· and
  3 L· and Life forever
64:2 loveliness of L·
65:1 L· that leads us
  3 triumphs L· hath won.
66:2 Safe in Thy L·,
421:2 Safe in Thy L·,
66:3 love reflecting L·.
421:3 love reflecting L·.
69:3 Christly bands of L·
423:3 Christly bands of L·
71:3 from eternal L·,
75:3 changeless name of L·.
76:1 unchanging L· forget?
79:1-3 God is L·.
83:3 L·, and L· alone, is
84:1 Emblem of eternal L·;
  2 power of L· supernal,
91:1 O L· divine, Thee
422:1 O L· divine, Thee
91:2, 3 Thou L· divine,
422:2, 3 Thou L· divine,
93:2 L· His holiest name.
  3 Dwelling in L· that
102:3 L· will guide us
103:3 L· will guide us
104:2 Grant us, O L·,
119:2 the L· that knows no
133:1, 2 That God is L·.
424:1, 2 That God is L·.
133:3 Yes, God is L·:
424:3 Yes, God is L·:
133:3 For God is L·.
424:3 For God is L·.
134:1 Thy touch, eternal L·,
138:2 Truth and boundless L·?
139:1 I walk with L·
427:1 I walk with L·
139:2 Who walks with L·
427:2 Who walks with L·
139:2 Shall talk with L· and
     L· obey;
427:2 Shall talk with L· and
     L· obey;
139:2 all may walk with L·

Love
427:2 all may walk with L·
139:3 Come, walk with L·
427:3 Come, walk with L·
142:1 Immortal L·, forever
　　2 And comprehendeth L·.
　　4 Eternal L·, remains.
144:1 atmosphere of L· divine,
145:1 atmosphere of L· divine,
148:1 In heavenly L· abiding,
149:1 In L· divine all
426:1 In L· divine all
157:2 One the L· whose
　　2 Safe within this L·
160:1 So L· doth guide;
161:1 So L· doth guide;
162:1 So L· doth guide;
160:4 L· looseth thee,
161:4 L· looseth thee,
162:4 L· looseth thee,
171:1 L· has rolled the
413:1 L· has rolled the
171:2 find in L· the refuge
413:2 find in L· the refuge
175:2 L· divine, that
176:2 Steadfast the L·
179:1 L· frees from error's
　　1 L· is liberation.
　　2 L· knows no evil,
　　2 L· casts out every
　　2 L· heals our every
　　3 L· now is dawning over
　　3 L· bids all discord cease.
　　3 L·, L· alone is power.
180:2 seeds of L· are sown.
　　3 from L· is sought,
182:1 the streams of L·,
　　1 L· has overflowing
　　3 Such is the law of L·.
190:4 L· doth win;
191:4 L· doth win;
201:4 Truth and Light and L·;
404:4 Truth and Light and L·;
204:2 L· is Thy banner
206:1 our Father-Mother, L·,
428:1 our Father-Mother, L·,
207:1 Thou L· that guards
208:1 Thou L· that guards
209:1 Thou L· that guards
210:1 Thou L· that guards
211:1 Thou L· that guards
212:1 Thou L· that guards
207:2 L· is our refuge;
208:2 L· is our refuge;
209:2 L· is our refuge;
210:2 L· is our refuge;
211:2 L· is our refuge;

Love
212:2 L· is our refuge;
214:1 whose name is L·.
　　2 L· its holy influence
228:1 L· divine, that dwells
229:1 L· divine, whose
　　2 The rule of L·
230:1 O L·, O Life,
231:1 O L·, O Life,
232:1 L·, our Mother, ever
406:1 L·, our Mother, ever
232:3 Man is the loved of L·.
406:3 Man is the loved of L·.
233:1 L· whose perfect path
419:1 L· whose perfect path
237:2 L· divine its promise
243:2 When L· with touch of
244:2 When L· with touch of
243:3 grace of L· divine
244:3 grace of L· divine
245:1 L· will guide us,
253:7 offering pure of L·,
254:7 offering pure of L·,
255:7 offering pure of L·,
256:7 offering pure of L·,
257:7 offering pure of L·,
263:2 healing word of L·.
　　2 Feels the Father L·
　　2 L· outshines the night
　　3 L· is our at-one-ment,
266:1 Our God is L·, and
267:2 L· that never sleeps.
268:2 L· that never sleeps.
269:1 God is L·, unchanging L·,
270:1 God is L·, unchanging L·,
269:3 L· divine Forever waits
270:3 L· divine Forever waits
275:3 in L· confide.
288:2 Life, the Truth, the L·.
289:2 Life, the Truth, the L·.
298:2 L· wipes your tears
299:2 L· wipes your tears
300:2 L· wipes your tears
301:2 L· wipes your tears
302:2 L· wipes your tears
311:1 lit by L· divine
420:1 lit by L· divine
330:1 L· my Shepherd is,
339:3 ruled by L· alone.
342:3 For Life and L·
349:1 and Truth and L·,
350:1 L· that healed us,
355:2 all pervading L·,
　　2 Life, Truth and L·
356:1 L· divine, in whom
　　3 redeemed through L·,
371:3 O God of L·, to Thee,

Love
371:3 Father-Mother L·,
374:2 As everlasting L·.
375:2 As everlasting L·.
374:2 L· is not the author
375:2 L· is not the author
374:2 L· divine, we thank
375:2 L· divine, we thank
376:1 L· divine, that helps
377:1 L· divine, that helps
391:4 that event is L·.
392:3 L· its bound and
393:3 L· its bound and
love (noun)
　　2:3 peace and l·, united,
　　4:1 Be every action l·.
　　5:2 awake to l·:
　　6:3 And trust His l·
　　7:2 l· in all around I see
　　9:2 winged with light and l·;
　10:2 His l· to error's
411:2 His l· to error's
　12:2 l· and healing ministry
　13:2 l· and healing ministry
　17:3 God's messenger of l·,
　21:1 l· its true abode.
　22:1 l· its true abode.
　21:3 for l· is light,
　22:3 for l· is light,
　30:2 men one in l· remain.
　31:2 men one in l· remain.
　32:2 men one in l· remain.
　30:5 Fed by Thy l· divine
　31:5 Fed by Thy l· divine
　32:5 Fed by Thy l· divine
　40:3 to the feast of l·,
　42:2 Thy l· possessing,
　43:1 l· which cannot cease.
　44:2 pure repose and l·
　51:3 image of His l·.
　52:3 image of His l·.
　57:1 on Thy l· repose.
　65:2 fullness of His l·.
　66:3 l· reflecting Love.
421:3 l· reflecting Love.
　72:1 Father, in Thy l·,
405:1 Father, in Thy l·,
　77:2 l· thy joy increase;
　78:2 l· thy joy increase;
　84:2 His l· is leading.
　85:1 Thy l· we have for
　91:3 l· and perfect grace.
422:3 l· and perfect grace.
　92:1 life of l· and labor
　99:2 l· and watchful care
100:2 l· and watchful care
105:2 perfect us in l·.

love (noun)
106:2 perfect us in l.
107:2 perfect us in l.
108:3 not the l, is past
    4 feast of bliss and l.
109:1 Thy l is welcomed in.
110:1 Thy l is welcomed in.
113:2 Thy power and l,
    3 in the grace of l,
114:2 show a Saviour's l;
117:2 in power, in l and
121:2 fullest light of l;
122:2 fullest light of l;
126:2 show a brother's l.
127:2 show a brother's l.
403:2 show a brother's l.
126:3 Let l, in one
127:3 Let l, in one
403:3 Let l, in one
126:4 L is the golden
127:4 L is the golden
403:4 L is the golden
126:4 bosom glow with l.
127:4 bosom glow with l.
403:4 bosom glow with l.
130:2 Thy l doth every
134:3 deep in Thy dear l,
138:3 Thy l has always
140:2 gleam of l and prayer
142:2 l alone knows whence
144:3 perfect in His l,
145:3 perfect in His l,
149:2 Held by God's l
426:2 Held by God's l
150:3 For beauty and l
151:1 with l Thou fillest
152:1 with l Thou fillest
154:2 Within Thy l is safe
155:2 Within Thy l is safe
156:2 Within Thy l is safe
154:3 Thy l and truth are
155:3 Thy l and truth are
156:3 Thy l and truth are
163:2 ever flow A l
    3 wanderer back by l;
164:3 wonders of his l.
165:3 wonders of his l.
417:3 wonders of his l.
173:1 L is kind and
    1 L is meek and
    1 L than ... more strong;
    1-3 Therefore give us l.
    2 L will ever with us
    3 L will ever shine
    4 Faith and hope and l
    4 the best, is l.

love (noun)
174:1 Comfort is l,
    2 L is true solace
    3 O l of God,
178:1 L is life's true
    1 L the splendor of
    1 Holy works of l
    2 L, the Golden Rule
    2 L, our debt to God
179:1 L is the royal way.
    2 law does l fulfill.
    2 L is our answered
180:1 L is staff and rod
181:3 Thy healing l.
182:2 very founts of l
189:2 l doth e'er uphold
195:1 Thy l, not mine,
    2 Girt with the l of God
    2 I breathe that l
196:2 blest land of l.
199:1 countless gifts of l
    2 Enfolded in His l.
217:2 l dwells, the peace
221:1 l and brotherhood.
228:3 With l we meet
232:2 In l our lives
406:2 In l our lives
234:2 winning word of l;
235:2 winning word of l;
236:2 God's l be retold,
    4 His l doth outpour;
    4 one in a union of l,
238:4 God's l and blessing,
239:4 God's l and blessing,
240:3 mysteries of Thy l;
241:3 mysteries of Thy l;
253:2 With l perfumed.
254:2 With l perfumed.
255:2 With l perfumed.
256:2 With l perfumed.
257:2 With l perfumed.
259:3 deeds of peace and l
261:3 L, her communion cup.
262:3 L, her communion cup.
266:1 with l to God inspired,
    1 l to man will glow.
    3 In bonds of l
271:2 Dwell on His l
272:2 Dwell on His l
273:3 always works by l.
274:3 always works by l.
278:3 His l hath dissolved
279:3 His l hath dissolved
298:1 l of our Lord.
299:1 l of our Lord.
300:1 l of our Lord.
301:1 l of our Lord.

love (noun)
302:1 l of our Lord.
303:3 look of l bid
311:3 His gift of l
420:3 His gift of l
315:1 To rule by l
316:1 To rule by l
319:2 whose warmth is l,
322:1 revealed by His dear l.
323:1 revealed by His dear l.
324:1 impulse of Thy l.
    3 Take my l; O Lord,
327:3 His tender l All
328:3 His tender l All
330:3 in l He sought me,
339:3 healing l make known,
340:2 l of God is broader
    3 If our l were but
342:1 amplitude of God's ... l
    2 His l is shown.
346:3 Spirit of truth and l,
401:3 Spirit of truth and l,
349:2 sunshine of Thy l,
350:1 l of God our Saviour
    3 upon His l relying,
351:3 Father Reigns in l
352:1 wondrous l, O Son
353:1 wondrous l, O Son
360:2 serving, l will grow.
367:1 That fellowship of l
372:2 And l its Galilee.
373:1 And l its Galilee.
379:2 God, whose boundless l
380:2 God, whose boundless l
381:4 And works of l
390:1 in God's great l
392:1 l and peace and joy
393:1 l and peace and joy
414:1, Ref. Jesus and his l.

love (verb)
    4:2 To l not Thee
  18:2 those that l thee,
  21:1-4 Beloved, let us l:
  22:1-4 Beloved, let us l:
  21:2 for they who l,
  22:2 for they who l,
  30:1 who watch and l.
  31:1 who watch and l.
  32:1 who watch and l.
  91:1 Thee to obey and l
422:1 Thee to obey and l
126:1 who l the Lord
127:1 who l the Lord
403:1 who l the Lord
128:3 Obey them, l them,
129:3 Obey them, l them,

93

love (verb)
136:1 I l Thy way of
179:1 L one another,—
180:1 L the Lord thy God:
186:3 l Thee and be blest.
187:3 l Thee and be blest.
188:1 l and trust His plan.
207:3 l more for every hate,
208:3 l more for every hate,
209:3 l more for every hate,
210:3 l more for every hate,
211:3 l more for every hate,
212:3 l more for every hate,
217:2 to l each other;
224:3 l and praise Thee
225:3 l and praise Thee
253:6 I l to be.
254:6 I l to be.
255:6 I l to be.
256:6 I l to be.
257:6 I l to be.
266:2 Teach us to l
    4 true Christians l;
331:3 L God and man:
414:1-3, Ref. I l to tell the

loved
30:2 l and healed mankind:
31:2 l and healed mankind:
32:2 l and healed mankind:
169:2 I l to choose and see
    2 l the garish day,
    3 have l long since,
217:1 he whom Jesus l
232:3 Man is the l of Love.
406:3 Man is the l of Love.
266:2 we are l by Thee;
356:1 In Thy l Son, whom
381:3 For homelands l
414:3 I have l so long.

lovelier
140:2 old scenes, will l be,
317:1 l than the daylight,

loveliness
36:3 l That fills the morning
64:2 The l of Love is all
112:3 L and joy unfoldeth;

lovely
3:1 l, Godlike grace
125:1 l are Thy dwellings,

Love's
45:3 beauty of L holiness,
51:2 L work and Love must
52:2 L work and Love must

Love's
73:2 with L will blending;
109:2 in L pure likeness
110:2 in L pure likeness
112:1 to L dominion.
128:2 L immortal day.
129:2 L immortal day.
174:2 L giving is forever;
179:1 L way the Master
180:3 L presence gives
197:1 L immortal waking.
198:1 L immortal waking.
203:1 L sacred power
    2 Within L stronghold
221:3 L revelation Of Truth
    3 L sweet control.
237:3 by L pure fire.
269:1 prayer for L increase
270:1 prayer for L increase
297:3 L law divine
    4 through L all-power;
311:1 burns L holy glow,
420:1 burns L holy glow,
314:3 L transforming light,
381:4 safe in L protection,

love's
226:3 In l large liberty.

loves
3:4 l and blesses all.
179:1 He that l shall
180:2 his neighbor l,

lovest
67:3 thou l to obey;
68:3 thou l to obey;

loveth
21:3 he who l not
22:3 he who l not
21:4 God who l us.
22:4 God who l us.

loving
15:3 the l Master Saw
43:2 l words of Jesus,
56:1 joy of l hearts,
58:1 we Thy l children
69:3 gentle, l heart,
423:3 gentle, l heart,
85:1 we have for l,
143:3 And l Thee alone.
178:2 L hearts in friendship
181:1 L Father, we Thy
203:2 l Father-Mother,
217:3 l life a psalm
236:3 God's l children
245:1 tender, l Shepherd,

loving
267:4 hear Thy l call,
268:4 hear Thy l call,
269:3 O l Father, well we
270:3 O l Father, well we
283:1 joyous and l endeavor;
318:1 Gentle and l,
333:1 l friend to all
349:3 l servants of Thy
357:1 our l Father, God,
358:1 our l Father, God,
407:1 our l Father, God,
359:2 l from His face.
360:2 can only live in l,
376:2 Thy l care wilt show.
377:2 Thy l care wilt show.

loving-kindness
76:1 God is known in l,
216:1 sheltered by His l,
388:3 Through paths of l

low
57:3 L in the heart faith
94:3 In l, sweet accents
148:1 heart may l be laid;
158:2 forms are bending l,
159:2 forms are bending l,
228:3 meet the l despite
238:3 A l sweet prelude
239:3 A l sweet prelude
253:1 L, sad, and sweet,
254:1 L, sad, and sweet,
255:1 L, sad, and sweet,
256:1 L, sad, and sweet,
257:1 L, sad, and sweet,
360:2 strength sinks l;
418:3 voices, loud and l,

lowest
372:1 search the l deeps,
373:1 search the l deeps,

lowly
153:1 Him who lifts the l,
234:1 l paths of service
235:1 l paths of service
310:1 l Saviour's birth.
335:2 all the l Triumphant
388:1 l Jesus sojourned

loyal
58:3 L hearts can feel

loyalty
204:2 from their l move

luster
319:2 no l of our own.

M

made
54:2 m· the heart rejoice,
66:1 hearts m· whole,
421:1 hearts m· whole,
81:1 His way m· plain
83:1 m· all His creatures
99:1 God his guardian m·,
100:1 God his guardian m·
105:3 Thou hast m· us free
106:3 Thou hast m· us free
107:3 Thou hast m· us free
150:2 M· strong with Thy
153:2 hast m· me whole.
171:1 whom God hath m·,
413:1 whom God hath m·,
197:3 The Word m· flesh
198:3 The Word m· flesh
224:3 m· my heaven secure,
225:3 m· my heaven secure,
226:2 things that Thou hast m·:
237:3 longings All m· pure
258:1 can choice be m·
282:1 guidance hath He m·.
    2 hath m· His saints
298:1 Truth that m· us free,
299:1 Truth that m· us free,
300:1 Truth that m· us free,
301:1 Truth that m· us free,
302:1 Truth that m· us free,
315:2 unkindness m· them so ;
316:2 unkindness m· them so ;
327:1 God who m· both heaven
328:1 God who m· both heaven
329:1 Him who m· all things ;
339:3 all things m· new
342:1, 3 the Lord hath m· ;
352:2 m· to live in light ?
353:2 m· to live in light ?
367:2 heart m· truly His,

magnify
153:1 doth m· the Lord,
    1, 2 m· and bless Thee,
282:2 and m· His name.

maintain
113:3 M· Thy church To Thy

maintained
228:3 he m· the right ;

majestic
334:2 M· like the sun ;

majesty
113:1 Thou begirt with m·,
226:2 meaning and the m·

majesty
284:2 reach The M· on high.
285:2 reach The M· on high.
286:2 reach The M· on high.
292:2 m· shines in creation's

make
30:2 m· men one in love
31:2 m· men one in love
32:2 m· men one in love
51:2 could not m· imperfect
52:2 could not m· imperfect
51:2 Love the pattern m·,
52:2 Love the pattern m·,
57:3 dost m· us strong.
74:2 shall m· thee whole.
80:1 m· our heart afraid ?
    2 Whose streams m· glad
94:3 M· us Thy harmonies to
96:1 m· the weakest strong.
141:2 M· our planting timely,
181:4 M· us strong to
182:1 M· channels for the
183:1 M· haste, O man,
184:1 M· haste, O man,
190:1 Father, m· me strong,
191:1 Father, m· me strong,
207:3 O m· me glad for every
208:3 O m· me glad for every
209:3 O m· me glad for every
210:3 O m· me glad for every
211:3 O m· me glad for every
212:3 O m· me glad for every
214:2 and m· us free ;
238:2 m· our own time glad,
239:2 m· our own time glad,
240:2 teachings m· us know
241:3 teachings m· us know
291:1 M· me gentle, pure,
    1 M· me as a little
298:2 m· radiant room
299:2 m· radiant room
300:2 m· radiant room
301:2 m· radiant room
302:2 m· radiant room
304:2 M· self-righteousness be
305:2 M· self-righteousness be
306:2 M· self-righteousness be
307:2 M· self-righteousness be
308:2 M· self-righteousness be
309:2 M· self-righteousness be
319:3 truth to m· us free,
327:1 m· His promise vain.

make
328:1 m· His promise vain.
339:3 healing love m· known,
399:3 He will m· it plain.
400:3 He will m· it plain.

maker
275:1 M· of earth and heaven ;

makes
12:2 Truth that m· men free.
13:2 Truth that m· men free.
92:3 God's will he m· his
131:3 Truth that m· men free,
132:3 Truth that m· men free,
135:2 It m· no separation
164:3 m· the nations prove
165:3 m· the nations prove
417:3 m· the nations prove
203:1 Truth that m· men free.
215:1 celestial wisdom m·
221:1 healing power m· plain:
    3 Truth that m· us free.
258:2 m· ancient creeds uncouth ;
297:3 m· us priests and kings ;
298:3 Spirit that m· pure,
299:3 Spirit that m· pure,
300:3 Spirit that m· pure,
301:3 Spirit that m· pure,
302:3 Spirit that m· pure,
334:3 m· a world of darkness
363:1 m· its brightness more
379:2 M· the heart wherein
380:2 M· the heart wherein
383:2 temple m· with thee.
384:1 all creation m· anew,

maketh
7:1 Truth that m· free,
188:3 m· all men free.
218:1, 4 m· all things new.
219:1, 4 m· all things new.
220:1, 4 m· all things new.
230:1 Thy presence m· one ;
231:1 Thy presence m· one ;

mak'st
357:2 m· our lives so bright.
358:2 m· our lives so bright.
407:2 m· our lives so bright.

man
3:2 Girds m· with mighty
6:1 O m·, however fair
    1 call of God and m·.
11:2 God and m· fore'er

95

man
12:3 dominion unto m,
13:3 dominion unto m,
12:3 M pure and upright,
13:3 M pure and upright,
15:1 prove To m his native
20:2 m is seen as God's
416:2 m is seen as God's
51:1 M is the noblest
52:1 M is the noblest
51:2 not make imperfect m
52:2 not make imperfect m
51:3 m does stand as God's
52:3 m does stand as God's
72:1 Peace on earth to m
405:1 Peace on earth to m
72:1 M, the well-beloved
405:1 M, the well-beloved
73:2 M, His image, hears
88:3 unaided m must fail;
89:3 unaided m must fail;
92:1 Happy the m who knows
93:1 Happy the m whose
3 m finds release;
4 m can work what God
112:3 M who lives in Life
114:3 M can triumph over
119:2 treasure M can wish
130:2 alike on m and flower:
146:4 m is God's great heir.
147:4 m is God's great heir.
149:3 m beloved is in God's
426:3 m beloved is in God's
163:3 win our brother m,
168:1 every m His praise
171:1 m whom God hath made,
413:1 m whom God hath made,
172:1 m, arise and shine,
183:1 Make haste, O m,
184:1 Make haste, O m,
188:1 entered heart of m,
194:3 God and m commune.
410:3 God and m commune.
215:1 m who hears Instruction's
217:2 brother m, fold to
221:2 expressed By m, who
3 God's idea, m, rejoices,
232:1 M is the child of God.
406:1 M is the child of God.
232:2 m is ever one with Thee.
406:2 m is ever one with Thee.
232:2 m is God's own child.
406:2 m is God's own child.
232:3 M is the loved of Love.
406:3 M is the loved of Love.
238:1 steady gain of m.
239:1 steady gain of m.

man
258:1 every m and nation
266:1 love to m will glow.
269:2 mortal m ask Him
270:2 mortal m ask Him
331:3 Love God and m:
370:1 behold the perfect m;
382:1 thy birthright, m,

manhood
221:2 Christ, eternal m,

manifest
233:2 We m Thy tenderness:
419:2 We m Thy tenderness:

manifold
314:3 God's blessings m.

mankind
11:2 Truth, for all m,
30:2 loved and healed m:
31:2 loved and healed m:
32:2 loved and healed m:
73:2 hope, for all m.
82:2 brotherhood of all m,
135:1 all m and me:
141:3 the healing of m.
188:2 His Word to all m,
311:3 To us and all m:
420:3 To us and all m:
346:2 now to all m Let
401:2 now to all m Let
374:3 bid m to waken
375:3 bid m to waken

manna
46:1 Day by day the m
47:1 Day by day the m
46:2 Take the m of to-day.
47:2 Take the m of to-day.
71:2 feed upon the m,

man's
14:4 M unity with God.
15:3 m perfection shine,
101:1 M heritage revealed;
171:2 That is m security,
413:2 That is m security,
185:1 m perfect sonship
236:2 m spirit despoil,
329:2 His law m pathway

many
196:1 m a distant shore,
200:2 m thy foes, but

mar
315:1 no harsh word m
316:1 no harsh word m

march
82:3 M we forth in the
351:3 the m in God begun:

marching
264:1, Ref. M as to war,
351:1 M to the promised
418:3 are m to and fro;

mark
67:2 m each warrior's way;
68:2 m each warrior's way;
72:2 M the wonders of His
405:2 M the wonders of His
273:2 To the m unwearied
274:2 To the m unwearied

martyr's
260:3 m path who trod;

Mary's
381:1 M wondering eyes!

Master
15:3 the loving M Saw
41:1 does the M say,
92:1 His M to obey;
104:1 cross our M bore;
131:1 our blessed M said;
132:1 our blessed M said;
171:3 meekly as the M,
413:3 meekly as the M,
179:1 way the M trod;
185:1 M and Lord, 'tis good
203:2 our gentle M trod,
221:1 Jesus, our dear M,
234:1 M, let me walk with
235:1 M, let me walk with
234:4 With thee, O M,
235:4 With thee, O M,
264:1 Christ, the royal M,
372:4 Lord and M of us
373:2 Lord and M of us
386:1 Jesus our great M
387:1 Jesus our great M
396:2 M whom you serve
397:2 M whom you serve

Master's
228:3 such as hate our M
318:1 the M tender plea;
390:1 doth the M word

material
224:1 m streams are dried,
225:1 m streams are dried,

matters
160:1 It m not what be
161:1 It m not what be
162:1 It m not what be

meal
297:4 Christ's morning $m\cdot$

meaning
57:3 life's deeper $m\cdot$,
226:2 $m\cdot$ and the majesty

means
20:3 true $m\cdot$ true to God
416:3 true $m\cdot$ true to God
41:3 By $m\cdot$ the simplest

measure
119:2 Love, that knows no $m\cdot$,
148:3 hope I cannot $m\cdot$,
361:1 cares for thee past $m\cdot$,

measures
253:1 $m\cdot$ bind The power
254:1 $m\cdot$ bind The power
255:1 $m\cdot$ bind The power
256:1 $m\cdot$ bind The power
257:1 $m\cdot$ bind The power

meditation
329:3 $m\cdot$ Lay hold of Thee

meek
69:2 $m\cdot$ and contrite heart,
23:2 $m\cdot$ and contrite heart,
88:1 actions bold and $m\cdot$
89:1 actions bold and $m\cdot$
73:1 Love is $m\cdot$ and
14:2 To keep us $m\cdot$,
20:2 conquest to the $m\cdot$,
21:2 conquest to the $m\cdot$,
09:2 conquest to the $m\cdot$,
52:3 $m\cdot$, forgiving, Godlike,
53:3 $m\cdot$, forgiving, Godlike,
92:4 $m\cdot$ and bold defender
93:4 $m\cdot$ and bold defender

meekly
71:3 $m\cdot$ as the Master,
13:3 $m\cdot$ as the Master,

meekness
11:1 babe in $m\cdot$ lay,
29:2 a $m\cdot$ all divine,
57:3 in our $m\cdot$ Thou dost
85:3 patience, courage, $m\cdot$
22:3 $m\cdot$ will receive him,
23:3 $m\cdot$ will receive him,
52:1 That in true $m\cdot$ used
53:1 That in true $m\cdot$ used
59:3 and repent in $m\cdot$
70:2 $m\cdot$ and the might,

meet
30:5 when we $m\cdot$ and part.
31:5 when we $m\cdot$ and part.
32:5 when we $m\cdot$ and part.
37:3 $m\cdot$ the dawning day.
38:3 $m\cdot$ the dawning day.
227:1 where'er Thy people $m\cdot$,
228:3 $m\cdot$ the low despite
297:2 God and men do $m\cdot$,
326:2 a breastplate $m\cdot$,

meeting
196:1 Jew and Gentile, $m\cdot$

meets
6:3 $M\cdot$ all thy need
12:1 that $m\cdot$ your need.
13:1 that $m\cdot$ your need.
131:2 $m\cdot$ the heart's great
132:2 $m\cdot$ the heart's great
150:2 that $m\cdot$ every need,

melt
197:3 stone before him $m\cdot$,
198:3 stone before him $m\cdot$,

melting
173:2 $M\cdot$ in the light

men
12:2 that makes $m\cdot$ free.
13:2 that makes $m\cdot$ free.
30:2 $m\cdot$ one in love remain.
31:2 $m\cdot$ one in love remain.
32:2 $m\cdot$ one in love remain.
56:1 Thou Light of $m\cdot$,
86:1 $m\cdot$ agree to praise.
87:1 $m\cdot$ agree to praise.
101:2 sons of $m\cdot$ rejoice
104:3 Thou light of $m\cdot$,
117:2 eyes of sinful $m\cdot$
131:3 that makes $m\cdot$ free,
132:3 that makes $m\cdot$ free,
141:4 Cleansing $m\cdot$ of fear
157:3 all $m\cdot$ and nations
158:1 good will to $m\cdot$,
159:1 good will to $m\cdot$,
188:3 maketh all $m\cdot$ free.
203:1 that makes $m\cdot$ free.
204:3 Salvation to all $m\cdot$
218:1 the thoughts of $m\cdot$;
219:1 the thoughts of $m\cdot$;
220:1 the thoughts of $m\cdot$;
222:2 peace to $m\cdot$ on earth;
223:2 peace to $m\cdot$ on earth;
236:2 $m\cdot$ of good will may
258:1 made by all $m\cdot$
2 thought of $m\cdot$ incline

men
264:4 $M\cdot$ and angels sing.
297:2 God and $m\cdot$ do meet,
310:1 $M\cdot$ and angels, anthems
1, 2 good will to $m\cdot$.
345:3 purer lives of $m\cdot$,
352:3 the scoffs of $m\cdot$,
353:3 the scoffs of $m\cdot$,
381:3 $m\cdot$ are homeward turning
384:1 with $m\cdot$ to dwell,

mercies
62:2 Eternal are Thy $m\cdot$,
63:2 Eternal are Thy $m\cdot$,
140:3 New $m\cdot$, each returning
253:3 His unveiled, sweet $m\cdot$
254:3 His unveiled, sweet $m\cdot$
255:3 His unveiled, sweet $m\cdot$
256:3 His unveiled, sweet $m\cdot$
257:3 His unveiled, sweet $m\cdot$
283:2 Ever new $m\cdot$ providing.

merciful
117:1, 3 Holy, $m\cdot$ and mighty,
278:3 $m\cdot$, mercy shall find.
279:3 $m\cdot$, mercy shall find.

mercy
46:1 by constant $m\cdot$ fed,
47:1 by constant $m\cdot$ fed,
77:2 day shall $m\cdot$ lengthen:
78:2 day shall $m\cdot$ lengthen:
79:1 His $m\cdot$ brightens All
81:1 His wings of $m\cdot$
130:1 wondrous is Thy $m\cdot$,
150:1 In $m\cdot$, in goodness,
153:2 Remembrance of Thy $m\cdot$
192:3 In $m\cdot$ given;
193:3 In $m\cdot$ given;
249:1 God's $m\cdot$ Widespread
250:1 God's $m\cdot$ Widespread
275:3 $M\cdot$ and goodness forever
278:3 merciful, $m\cdot$ shall find.
279:3 merciful, $m\cdot$ shall find.
280:2 Widely as His $m\cdot$ flows.
283:1 His $m\cdot$ endureth forever.
326:4 at length, Through $m\cdot$,
340:1 wideness in God's $m\cdot$,
399:1 Are big with $m\cdot$,
400:1 Are big with $m\cdot$,

mercy's
35:2 thy $m\cdot$ beams I see;
259:1 laid on $m\cdot$ shrine,

mercy seat
227:1 they behold Thy $m\cdot s\cdot$;

mere
320:3 M· human energy
321:3 M· human energy
409:3 M· human energy

merged
48:2 While m· in Love,

message
73:2 understand His m·,
175:1 tender healing m·
181:4 strong to bear the m·
221:3 Science, God-sent m·
237:1 thus to hear the m·,
414:2 The m· of salvation

messages
324:2 with m· from Thee.

messenger
17:3 God's m· of love,

messengers
19:2 m· of Love and Life,
396:1 Ye m· of Christ,
397:1 Ye m· of Christ,

Messiah
258:1 cause, God's new M·,

met
222:1 m· in thee to-night.
223:1 m· in thee to-night.

metal
237:4 upon the precious m·

mid
95:2 m· scenes of deepest
176:1 m· the tempest's
178:2 M· the nations
263:1 M· the shade of

midnight
158:1 came upon the m·
159:1 came upon the m·
297:4 at m· hour,

midst
232:3 M· seeming sorrow,
406:3 M· seeming sorrow,
298:2 M· the glories of
299:2 M· the glories of
300:2 M· the glories of
301:2 M· the glories of
302:2 M· the glories of

might
5:2 requires unswerving m·:
16:2 boundless source of m·,

might
30:4 gave that word of m·
31:4 gave that word of m·
32:4 gave that word of m·
59:1 with all thy m·,
60:1 with all thy m·,
61:1 with all thy m·,
77:2 His m· thy heart
78:2 His m· thy heart
84:1 eternal m· the token,
113:1 with Thy great m·.
160:4 and wisdom m·,
161:4 and wisdom m·,
162:4 and wisdom m·,
206:3 Reveal in us Thy m·,
428:3 Reveal in us Thy m·,
246:1 for his m· on Thee
275:2 have seen His m·,
312:1 in His great m·,
370:2 meekness and the m·,

mightier
134:1 thought of Thee is m·
200:2 arm ... was m· far;
363:2 On m· wing, in loftier

mighty
2:2 swell the m· strain.
3:2 man with m· power.
36:1 m· is thy voice.
88:3 M· Spirit, dwell
89:3 M· Spirit, dwell
88:3 I myself would m·
89:3 I myself would m·
88:3 M· that I may prevail
89:3 M· that I may prevail
90:1 and Thou art m·,
111:2 judgments are a m·
112:2 Christ, our m· Counsel,
117:1, 3 merciful and m·,
130:2 judgments are a m·
153:2 who alone art m·
175:2 M· are to save
177:1 God, the m· God,
186:1 M· God, the First,
187:1 M· God, the First,
204:1 Thy m· salvation,
207:4 shadow of His m· wing;
208:4 shadow of His m· wing;
209:4 shadow of His m· wing;
210:4 shadow of His m· wing;
211:4 shadow of His m· wing;
212:4 shadow of His m· wing;
216:1 Delivered by His m·
243:1 m· power to heal
244:1 m· power to heal
264:2 Like a m· army,

mighty
281:1 All His m· acts
282:1 His m· voice obeyed;
292:1 is God's m· Word!
296:1 Servants of a m· cause,
329:1 m· power is known;
362:2 great and m· Lord,
371:2 bless Thy m· name
392:4 forth in m· splendor.
393:4 forth in m· splendor.
394:2 M· shall the harvest
395:2 M· shall the harvest
399:2 His m· purpose ripens
400:2 His m· purpose ripens

mild
291:1 gentle, pure, and m·,

mildew
197:2 blight and m· rested:
198:2 blight and m· rested:
360:1 Seeds which m· in

Mind
51:1 Eternal M· the Potter
52:1 Eternal M· the Potter
51:1 perfect as his M·
52:1 perfect as his M·
58:2 Thou our M· and Thou
66:3 O perfect M·, reveal
421:3 O perfect M·, reveal
73:2 God is M· and holy
83:2 in fellowship of M·,
104:4 our Spirit, M· divine,
136:3 the heights of M·,
141:3 work of perfect M·,
144:2 wonders of eternal M·,
145:2 wonders of eternal M·,
157:2 One the M· and Life
178:2 forth the perfect M·;
188:2 treasures of His M·.
236:4 M·, the M· we adore;
240:1 the light of M·.
241:1 the light of M·.
267:3 We see creative M·,
268:3 We see creative M·,
269:2 Our God is M·,
     the perfect M·,
270:2 Our God is M·,
     the perfect M·,
273:2 God, the only M·,
274:2 God, the only M·,
275:1 creative M·, Maker
370:2 beauteous things of M·.
381:2 Creative M·, all good
391:3 holds the M· and Cause;

mind
49:1 in our rightful m;
50:1 in our rightful m;
92:4 m, Which waits but Thy
140:1 m Be set to hallow
178:1 Healing m and heart
180:1 heart and soul and m.
190:2 confident and humble m,
191:2 confident and humble m,
201:1 do not bar your m
404:1 do not bar your m
201:2 long enslaved m,
404:2 long enslaved m,
227:2 them of humble m;
253:1 harpstrings of the m
254:1 harpstrings of the m
255:1 harpstrings of the m
256:1 harpstrings of the m
257:1 harpstrings of the m
311:3 glad and willing m
420:3 glad and willing m
331:2 humble, contrite m,
340:2 seen by human m,
346:2 to the sick in m,
401:2 to the sick in m,

mindful
168:1 m of our God's great

Mind's
64:2 reach M open door,
163:3 M most holy plan

minds
276:1 worldly m unknown;
277:1 worldly m unknown;

mingle
236:3 As bird-voices m

ministry
12:2 love and healing m
13:2 love and healing m
131:3 Is highest m.
132:3 Is highest m.

minted
249:2 life from joy is m,
250:2 life from joy is m,

mirror
15:2 as a m shows us
203:1 And m forth Love's

miss
230:3 m with chart of
231:3 m with chart of

mission
5:2 Your m is to heal.
166:4 fulfill thy holy m,
167:4 fulfill thy holy m,

mist
64:1 From m and shadow
79:2 Through the m His
359:2 illusive wreaths of m
363:4 sweeps the lingering m

mists
84:1 Piercing m, around,
142:3 m of earth away.
232:3 above the m of wrong:
406:3 above the m of wrong:
310:2 rolled the m away;

mite
303:4 bring thy m,

mocking
112:2 accuser's m voices

model
51:2 His m infinite;
52:2 His m infinite;

modes
194:3 With mortal m in tune,
410:3 With mortal m in tune,

mold
46:3 m my will to Thine.
47:3 m my will to Thine.
185:2 gently m Our lives

moment
258:1 the m to decide,

moments
324:1 m and my days,
418:2 our m onward flee,

moon
45:1 m and stars hast Thou
192:5 m, and stars forgot,
193:5 m, and stars forgot,
282:1 Sun and m, rejoice

moons
271:1 m shall wax and wane
272:1 m shall wax and wane

moor
169:3 O'er m and fen,

more
14:3 No m shall sin
34:2 Once m the lonely
35:3 M and m thyself
44:1 storms no m have
62:2 rise and set no m.
63:2 rise and set no m.
65:2 m and m we learn to
69:3 learn to be m tender,
423:3 learn to be m tender,
93:3 No m his homeless
112:2 fear no m enslaves
121:2 no m Than guidance
122:2 no m Than guidance
123:1 What m can He say
138:1 and thirst no m.
139:1 No m I suffer cruel
427:1 No m I suffer cruel
140:2 m of heaven in each
164:2 No m let sin
165:2 No m let sin
417:2 No m let sin
168:4 healing power once m
172:3 m and m shines to
173:1 than death ... m strong;
3 ever shine m bright;
181:4 no m dominion.
185:2 m closely to thine
196:2 M sweet and lasting
200:1 oppress thee no m;
205:2 m bright and clear
207:3 love m for every hate,
208:3 love m for every hate,
209:3 love m for every hate,
210:3 love m for every hate,
211:3 love m for every hate,
212:3 love m for every hate,
214:2 tender blessing m
215:2 rewards m precious
222:2 Christmas comes once m.
223:2 Christmas comes once m.
224:3 and praise Thee m.
225:3 and praise Thee m.
226:1 shineth m and m
230:3 is m than praise,
231:3 is m than praise,
236:2 No m let dire hate
238:4 heart shall sigh no m
239:4 heart shall sigh no m
242:1 M reapers for

more
242:1 M · laborers for
    2 no m · in dreams
253:3 A world m · bright.
254:3 A world m · bright.
255:3 A world m · bright.
256:3 A world m · bright.
257:3 A world m · bright.
259:1 thrice m · grateful,
269:1 can we ask for m ·?
270:1 can we ask for m ·?
269:1 m · than we accept;
270:1 m · than we accept;
271:1 wax and wane no m ·.
272:1 wax and wane no m ·.
326:3 m · than conqueror
340:1 is m · than liberty.
    3 were but m · simple,
359:2 No m · can move
363:1 brightness m · divine.
    2 effulgent m · and m ·.
    3 M · glorious still, as
389:1 M · lively my hope
414:2 M · wonderfully sweet.

morn
    2:2 the glorious m ·,
  23:1 Blest Christmas m ·,
  24:1 Blest Christmas m ·,
  25:1 Blest Christmas m ·,
  26:1 Blest Christmas m ·,
  27:1 Blest Christmas m ·,
  28:1 Blest Christmas m ·,
  35:2 cheerless is the m ·
169:3 And with the m · those
170:1 m · On which the holy
    2 every m · Feels in his
260:2 Each m · unfolds His
314:1 Sow in the m · thy
317:2 freshness of the m ·.
418:4 glorious m · shall break,

morning
    2:1 heralds of the m ·
    7:1 breaks the m · light;
  17:1 The m · star shines
  36:3 fills the m · sky.
117:1 in the m · our song
176:3 new m · whitens;
196:2 shadows of the m ·
222:2 m · stars, together
223:2 m · stars, together
297:4 Christ's m · meal

morning
317:1 purple m · breaketh,
    1 Fairer than m ·,
    3 m ·, When hearts awaking
335:1 m · light is breaking,
368:3 m · seems to dawn;
369:3 m · seems to dawn;
425:1, 2, Ref. joy . . . in the m ·.

morning's
287:2 Revealed in m · beam.
408:2 Revealed in m · beam.
304:3 Till the m · beam;
305:3 Till the m · beam;
306:3 Till the m · beam;
307:3 Till the m · beam;
308:3 Till the m · beam;
309:3 Till the m · beam;

morrow
  57:1 cometh with the m ·;
263:1 wait the brighter m ·;

mortal
  23:4 above All m · strife,
  24:4 above All m · strife,
  25:4 above All m · strife,
  26:4 above All m · strife,
  27:4 above All m · strife,
  28:4 above All m · strife,
  91:1 Losing the m · will
422:1 Losing the m · will
144:1 m · eyes may see
145:1 m · eyes may see
144:2 m · sense we must
145:2 m · sense we must
170:1 from no m · tongue,
194:1 No m · sense can
410:1 No m · sense can
194:3 With m · modes in tune,
410:3 With m · modes in tune,
269:2 Shall m · man ask Him
270:2 Shall m · man ask Him
293:2 from m · sense I flee,
294:2 from m · sense I flee,
295:2 from m · sense I flee,

mortals
376:1 The weapon m · sway,
377:1 The weapon m · sway,

mortals'
  86:3 To m · blindfold eye.
  87:3 To m · blindfold eye.

most
    9:1 glory be to God m · high,
  30:5 And life m · sweet,

most
  31:5 And life m · sweet,
  32:5 And life m · sweet,
  86:1 M · strange in all its
  87:1 M · strange in all its
  97:2 prospect seem m · dreary,
  98:2 prospect seem m · dreary,
  99:3 shall be God m · high;
100:3 shall be God m · high,
137:1 M · gracious Lord;
163:3 Mind's m · holy plan
201:3 this m · gracious hour.
404:3 this m · gracious hour.
251:1 Word of God, m · holy,
252:1 Word of God, m · holy,
340:2 m · wonderfully kind.
394:1 m · pure, m · strong,
395:1 m · pure, m · strong,

Mother
232:1 Love, our M ·, ever near,
406:1 Love, our M ·, ever near,

mother
  76:1 m · leave her children?
174:1 Like as a m ·, God
207:5 And m · finds her home
208:5 And m · finds her home
209:5 And m · finds her home
210:5 And m · finds her home
211:5 And m · finds her home
212:5 And m · finds her home

mother's
  23:2 natal hour and m · tear,
  24:2 natal hour and m · tear,
  25:2 natal hour and m · tear,
  26:2 natal hour and m · tear,
  27:2 natal hour and m · tear,
  28:2 natal hour and m · tear,

motion
284:1 m · of a hidden fire
285:1 m · of a hidden fire
286:1 m · of a hidden fire

motives
355:1 call With m · pure;

mount
  74:1 stand upon the m ·,
265:2 m · of vision won;

mountain
  16:1 sings the m · stream,
185:3 truth Shown on the m ·

mountain's
368:1 o'er yon m height
369:1 o'er yon m height

mountains
75:2 Before Him on the m
111:2 m their foundations
120:1 How beauteous on the m
189:1 look toward the m,
273:3 that m can remove,
274:3 that m can remove,
347:1 Though m may depart
348:1 Though m may depart
359:2 m from their base

mounteth
246:1 he, unwearied, m.

mounting
202:2 m footsteps of the
412:1 m footsteps of the

mourner
298:2 M, it calls you,—
299:2 M, it calls you,—
300:2 M, it calls you,—
301:2 M, it calls you,—
302:2 M, it calls you,—

mourning
134:3 turn'st my m into
150:1 for m, the garment of
275:2 m and sorrow end,

move
133:1 Almighty One, dost m;
424:1 Almighty One, dost m;
144:1 and m, and breathe;
145:1 and m, and breathe;
204:2 from their loyalty m
234:2 slow of heart to m
235:2 slow of heart to m
263:2 He doth m;
320:4 ardor onward m,
321:4 ardor onward m,
409:4 ardor onward m,
324:1 m At the impulse
346:3 M on the waters'
401:3 M on the waters'
356:1 in whom we live and m;
359:2 m the mountains from

moved
189:1 foot shall not be m,
385:1 God before her m,

moves
264:2 M the church of God;
326:3 omnipotence he m;

moving
58:1 In Thy Spirit ..., m,
281:2 m fire by night;

much
399:1 clouds ye so m dread
400:1 clouds ye so m dread

murky
23:1 though m clouds
24:1 though m clouds
25:1 though m clouds
26:1 though m clouds
27:1 though m clouds
28:1 though m clouds

music
11:1 Woke with m all
190:4 Heaven's m chimes
191:4 Heaven's m chimes

mute
194:3 m in that transcendent
410:3 m in that transcendent

mysteries
233:1 m are so clearly
419:1 m are so clearly
240:3 m of Thy love;
241:3 m of Thy love;

mystery
133:2 m clouds my darkened
424:2 m clouds my darkened

N

name
10:2 people, praise His n,
411:2 people, praise His n,
19:1 praise His holy n.
20:3 God whose n is Love,
416:3 God whose n is Love,
45:1 glorious is Thy n
62:1 Redeemer's n be sung
63:1 Redeemer's n be sung
66:1 gathered in Thy n,
421:1 gathered in Thy n,
75:3 His n shall stand
3 changeless n of Love.
76:2 In My hand thy n is
93:2 Love His holiest n.
96:1 use it in His n;
117:3 shall praise Thy n
142:2 lips confess the n
153:1 holy is Thy n.
168:1 our God's great n,

name
204:3 speak in Thy n,
214:1 Thy n we call,
1 whose n is Love.
221:2 Thy n we see
224:1 glory in Thy n.
225:1 glory in Thy n.
230:4 Nor n, nor form,
231:4 Nor n, nor form,
266:3 praise His holy n.
271:2 blessings on His n.
272:2 blessings on His n.
275:2 Father we call His n;
281:1 upon His holy n;
282:2 and magnify His n.
355:1 on Her n dare call
362:2 n shall be the Prince
371:2 bless Thy mighty n
372:4 Whate'er our n or
373:2 Whate'er our n or

name
378:3 we bless Thy n,
386:1 in his Father's n,
387:1 in his Father's n,

names
142:2 All other n above;

narrow
207:4 secret of the n way,
208:4 secret of the n way,
209:4 secret of the n way,
210:4 secret of the n way,
211:4 secret of the n way,
212:4 secret of the n way,
288:1 straight and n way
289:1 straight and n way
383:3 tread the n way:

natal
23:2 No n hour and mother's
24:2 No n hour and mother's

natal
25:2 No n hour and mother's
26:2 No n hour and mother's
27:2 No n hour and mother's
28:2 No n hour and mother's
303:1 waits its n hour.

nation
120:1 every tribe and n:
179:3 dawning over every n;
204:1 entreat every n,
258:1 every man and n
335:2 Flow thou to every n,

nations
73:1 all the power of n,
157:3 among all men and n
164:3 makes the n prove
165:3 makes the n prove
417:3 makes the n prove
178:2 Mid the n
236:4 Let n be one
335:1 Of n in commotion,
394:1 for thee the n long;
395:1 for thee the n long;
394:3 n far and near
395:3 n far and near

native
15:1 man his n worth.
284:3 Christian's n air:
285:3 Christian's n air:
286:3 Christian's n air:

nature
164:1 heaven and n sing.
165:1 heaven and n sing.
417:1 heaven and n sing.
317:2 Solemn the hush of n,

naught
57:3 N shall affright us,
136:3 space and fear are n
146:3 n against Infinity
147:3 n against Infinity
361:2 n unless the Lord
3 n His hand delays;
379:1 himself doth count as n,
380:1 himself doth count as n,

near
10:3 Our King is ever n;
411:3 Our King is ever n;
17:1 day of rest is n;
23:2 forever here and n,
24:2 forever here and n,
25:2 forever here and n,
26:2 forever here and n,
27:2 forever here and n,

near
28:2 forever here and n,
30:3 Love, divinely n,
31:3 Love, divinely n,
32:3 Love, divinely n,
35:1 from on high, be n,
58:3 and Life forever n.
59:3 His arms are n;
60:3 His arms are n;
61:3 His arms are n;
70:1 Truth is ever n.
71:2 that the Lord is n.
76:2 Blessedness and joy are n
77:1 light, my help is n:
78:1 light, my help is n:
82:1 time is **drawing** n;
94:3 of God, forever n,
113:2 Be Thou n to bless.
154:2 that Thou art n.
155:2 that Thou art n.
156:2 that Thou art n.
158:1 bending n the earth,
159:1 bending n the earth,
177:1 Joyful times are n
181:4 children far and n:
199:2 God . . . is n us,
232:1 our Mother, ever n,
406:1 our Mother, ever n,
237:4 with Him forever n.
265:1 legion Very n thee,
276:2 God of peace, be n
277:2 God of peace, be n
347:3 prosper nor come n.
348:3 prosper nor come n.
394:3 nations far and n
395:3 nations far and n
398:2 bridegroom draweth n.
418:1 shores are drawing n,

near-by
137:2 Stay Thou n;

nearer
4:3 Be n to each other
3 And n Thee, O Lord.
64:3 its goal draws n,
82:1 N and n draws
108:3 N than ever, still
192:1-5 N, my God, to Thee,
N to Thee.
193:1-5 N, my God, to Thee,
N to Thee.
253:6 grief afar, And n Thee,—
254:6 grief afar, And n Thee,—
255:6 grief afar, And n Thee,—
256:6 grief afar, And n Thee,—
257:6 grief afar, And n Thee,—

nearing
392:1 haven of rest is n.
393:1 haven of rest is n.

'neath
30:1 N which our spirits
31:1 N which our spirits
32:1 N which our spirits
69:2 And n Thy sheltering
423:2 And n Thy sheltering
371:3 triumph n Thy rod,

need (noun)
6:2 to-day hath n of thee.
6:3 Meets all thy n
12:1 that meets your n.
13:1 that meets your n.
42:1 supply Thy people's n.
91:2 warmth on all our n.
422:2 warmth on all our n.
134:1 to Thee in every n,
150:2 that meets every n,
189:2 Fulfilleth all my n;
229:1 Wide as our n
260:1 equal to my every n,—
327:3 All human n supplies.
328:3 All human n supplies.
342:2 And every n supply;
350:3 every n supplying,

need (verb)
7:3 I n not plead, Thou
8:2 I n Thy presence
9:3 angels that you n,
10:2 No other help we n;
411:2 No other help we n;
137:1-3 n Thee every hour,
Ref. n Thee, O, I n Thee;
Every hour I n Thee;
170:2 Keep while ye n it,
214:3 n no other rest.
332:1 n a sacred watchfulness,
2 n a perfect faith
357:2 We n not, Lord,
358:2 We n not, Lord,
407:2 We n not, Lord,

needed
151:2 give me n courage
152:2 give me n courage

needful
327:2 gives the hungry n
328:2 gives the hungry n
365:2 has promised n grace:
366:2 has promised n grace:
379:1 the one thing n

needful
380:1 the one thing n
396:2 n strength bestow;
397:2 n strength bestow;

needs
46:2 strength for daily n:
47:2 strength for daily n:
131:2 the heart's great n.
132:2 the heart's great n.
174:3 n but to be known!
280:2 daily n He knows;

needy
75:1 the poor and n,

ne'er
9:1 that n shall cease,
39:2 from Thee may n depart.
76:1 n will He forsake
93:1 goodness n will cease;
246:1 n is forspent,
269:2 n returneth void.
270:2 n returneth void.
318:3 glory kings n know;

neighbor
180:2 as himself his n

neighbor's
180:2 His n good his own.

neither
58:1 n faint nor fall.
179:2 n shade of sadness;
291:3 n strong nor wise,

nerve
134:2 n my faltering will:

nestling's
207:1 n faltering flight!
208:1 n faltering flight!
209:1 n faltering flight!
210:1 n faltering flight!
211:1 n faltering flight!
212:1 n faltering flight!

never (*see also* **ne'er**)
4:2 That we be n drawn
16:2 Whose blessings n cease.
18:2 but n the right.
19:1 joy shall n wane.
37:3 With n fainting ray;
38:3 With n fainting ray;
71:3 N fails from age to
75:3 n His covenant remove;
94:3 heavenly echoes n cease.
97:1 N tiring, n sleeping,
98:1 N tiring, n sleeping,
97:2 n weary, Let not fear

never (*see also* **ne'er**)
98:2 n weary, Let not fear
134:1 And n look in vain;
136:3 quest shall n cease,
142:1 A n ebbing sea,—
148:2 His sight is n dim;
175:2 divine, that faileth n,
176:1 thy light, n failing;
183:2 thing that n dies,
184:2 thing that n dies,
189:1 God who n slumbers,
 1 n shall forsake me;
194:2 words can n reach,
410:2 words can n reach,
194:2 human lips may n
410:2 human lips may n
199:2 We n shall remove,
224:2 word can n fail.
225:2 word can n fail.
236:3 As stars ... n contend,
237:2 Life that n sleeps.
259:3 stream has n wandered
263:1 divine shall n cease.
264:3 Gates of hell can n
267:2 Love that n sleeps.
268:2 Love that n sleeps.
267:3 n discord, strife.
268:3 n discord, strife.
282:1 n shall be broken
 2 N shall His promise
283:1 we be silent? Ah, n.
327:1 n quit His steadfast
328:1 n quit His steadfast
330:1, 4 goodness faileth n;
332:2 understanding n dim,
337:1 Truth ... can n die.
338:1 Truth ... can n die.
351:2 faith which n tires,
362:3 reign shall n cease;
370:1 sin can n Overthrow
414:2 some have n heard
418:1 and day they n cease;

nevermore
253:5 can shock, Oh, n!
254:5 can shock, Oh, n!
255:5 can shock, Oh, n!
256:5 can shock, Oh, n!
257:5 can shock, Oh, n!

new
19:2 Him in spirit n,
66:4 n heaven and earth
421:4 n heaven and earth
136:1 promise old and n,
140:1 N treasures still,
 3 N mercies, each
 3 N thoughts of God

new
158:3 n heaven and earth
159:3 n heaven and earth
171:3 with benedictions n.
413:3 with benedictions n.
176:3 n morning whitens;
218:1, 4 maketh all things n,
219:1, 4 maketh all things n,
220:1, 4 maketh all things n,
258:1 God's n Messiah,
 2 N occasions teach n
260:2 unfolds His blessings n,
283:2 n mercies providing.
313:2 find it ever n.
339:3 all things made n
363:3 N regions blest, n
  powers unfurled,
381:1 thrilled with n affection,
392:1 hail the n appearing;
393:1 hail the n appearing;
414:3 sing the n, n song

newborn
83:3 the n earth record

newly
317:2 of nature, n born;

news
11:1 gracious n to tell,
204:1 With n of Thy mighty

nigh
41:2 Harvest draws n.
99:3 His salvation ever n.
100:3 His salvation ever n.
137:2 When Thou art n.
189:1 Whose care is ever n.
207:2 high is here, and n,
208:2 high is here, and n,
209:2 high is here, and n,
210:2 high is here, and n,
211:2 high is here, and n,
212:2 high is here, and n,
281:2 retreat and refuge n.

night
2:1 darkness of the n.
3:3 watch by day or n.
7:1 banishing all n;
11:2 before us in the n,
18:1 the darker the n.
21:3 dwelleth in n.
22:3 dwelleth in n.
34:4 shades of coming n;
35:1 o'er the shades of n;
37:3 through the n,
38:3 through the n,

night
43:2 come to cheer the n.
57:1 Dark though the n,
67:1 ever n and day;
68:1 ever n and day;
71:2 Light by n, and
128:2 gloomy n he broke,
129:2 gloomy n he broke,
130:1 Thy presence is no n,
168:2 o'er darkest n,
169:1 The n is dark, and
   3 till The n is gone,
176:1 O'er n and chaos
181:1 in fear's dark n
186:1 watch within the n?
187:1 watch within the n?
200:1 n of thy sorrow
207:5 No n drops down
208:5 No n drops down
209:5 No n drops down
210:5 No n drops down
211:5 No n drops down
212:5 No n drops down
213:3 watch that ends the n
222:2 The dark n wakes,
223:2 The dark n wakes,
240:1 gloomy shades of n,
241:1 gloomy shades of n,
260:4 My rest by n, my
263:2 outshines the n of sin.
281:2 moving fire by n;
287:3 drear and gloomy n;
408:3 drear and gloomy n;
310:2 chaos, fear, and n;
311:1 pathway through the n,
420:1 pathway through the n,
319:1 watches of the n.
329:1 Each n its tribute
337:2 and call it n;
338:2 and call it n;
339:2 shall be no n.
351:1 n of doubt and sorrow
   1 fearless through the n.
368:1-3 tell us of the n,
369:1-3 tell us of the n,
385:3 storm the frequent n,
392:4 Has cleft the n
393:4 Has cleft the n
394:1 from its dreary n
395:1 from its dreary n
398:2 cometh through the n;
415:1, Ref. tarry but a n.
418:1 N and day they never
425: Ref. endure for a n,

nightfall
245:3 at n, Thou gently

night's
364:1 through n weary hours,

nights
275:2 N of our mourning

nobler
331:2 a n offering yields

noblest
51:1 the n work of God,
52:1 the n work of God,

nobly
273:1 N let us bear
274:1 N let us bear

noise
125:1 n and trouble free;

noiseless
36:2 How n and how pure;

noises
238:3 harsh n of our day,
239:3 harsh n of our day,

noisome
100:2 from the n pestilence

none
66:2 N can beyond Thy
421:2 N can beyond Thy
117:2 is n beside Thee,
139:1 n can take away
427:1 n can take away
143:2 Obeying n but Thee.
157:2 and injures n.
265:2 Christ road, and n other,
266:2 N who are truly born of
303:2 n can tell How vast
311:1 n can claim he doth
420:1 n can claim he doth
334:2 gives but borrows n.
339:1 n friendless, n afraid,
360:2 N but God its void can
361:1 Confide thou in n other,

noonday
230:1 trace the n sun.
231:1 trace the n sun.

notes
418:4 n will all be dumb,

nothing
92:3 n can him stay;
102:2 Knowing n but Thy
103:2 Knowing n but Thy
148:1 For n changes here.
   2 And n can I lack.

nothing
330:1 I n lack, for I am
360:2 N but a ceaseless
379:2 n knoweth But his God,
380:2 n knoweth But his God,
414:1 As n else can do.

nourish
141:2 N by a heavenly dew

now
1:1 here and n obeyed.
5:1 the sword n gird,
17:2 n Delay the Prince
42:1 N supply Thy people's
49:4 Take from us n
50:4 Take from us n
85:2 Open n our eyes
90:1 n and evermore.
100:1 of the Lord I n will
119:2 N in quickening showers
137: Ref. O bless me n,
138:1 n, my shallow cistern
158:2 Look n, for glad
159:2 Look n, for glad
158:3 n the angels sing.
159:3 n the angels sing.
168:4 n that healing power
169:2 n Lead Thou me on.
175:2 N and through eternity.
179:3 Love n is dawning
180:3 N may we all behold
186:2 before Thee n appears.
187:2 before Thee n appears.
196:1 N is the time
   1 N Jew and Gentile,
   2 all that n divides
   2 all that n unites
197:1 N sweeping down the
198:1 N sweeping down the
197:2 fruitage n are seen,
198:2 fruitage n are seen,
199:1 N thank we all our
221:1 Thy works, n understood,
232:1 n in this truth
406:1 n in this truth
232:2 n our waiting hopes
406:2 n our waiting hopes
238:4 Are n and here and
239:4 Are n and here and
240:2 N to our eyes display
241:2 N to our eyes display
275:1 Praise n creative Mind,
283:3 N will we raise
314:3 harvest n is white;
322:2 N fall and dwell

now
323:2 $N \cdot$ fall and dwell
322:3 prayer $n \cdot$ lift her
323:3 prayer $n \cdot$ lift her
346:2 $n \cdot$ to all mankind

now
401:2 $n \cdot$ to all mankind
356:3 $n \cdot$ redeemed through Love,
374:2 $n \cdot$ Thy children know
375:2 $n \cdot$ Thy children know

now
378:3 Thy salvation strong, $N \cdot$
391:4 divine event" Is $n \cdot$,
392:2 Christ $n \cdot$ guides us,
393:2 Christ $n \cdot$ guides us

O

obedience
48:1 this beacon here, $O \cdot$
84:2 Learn $o \cdot$,—and rejoice;
356:2 For in $o \cdot$ lies our

obey
5:1 $O \cdot$ the voice of Truth,
48:3 $o \cdot$ Thine every call,
67:3 Him thou lovest to $o \cdot$;
68:3 Him thou lovest to $o \cdot$;
91:1 Thee to $o \cdot$ and love
422:1 Thee to $o \cdot$ and love
92:1 His Master to $o \cdot$;
   3 And God alone $o \cdot$.
128:3 $O \cdot$ them, love them,
129:3 $O \cdot$ them, love them,
139:2 and Love $o \cdot$;
427:2 and Love $o \cdot$;
221:1 With joy may all $o \cdot$
362:1 tribes of earth $o \cdot$,
396:1 sovereign voice $o \cdot$;
397:1 sovereign voice $o \cdot$;

obeyed
1:1 here and now $o \cdot$.
282:1 His mighty voice $o \cdot$;

obeying
143:2 $O \cdot$ none but Thee.
203:1 $O \cdot$ gladly day by
278:2 $o \cdot$ the call of His
279:2 $o \cdot$ the call of His
390:1 Art thou $o \cdot$ this:

obeys
48:2 who Life $o \cdot$,

object
351:2 $o \cdot$ of our journey,

oblations
73:1 praise and pure $o \cdot$

obscure
14:3 $O \cdot$ the light divine,

observant
398:1 $O \cdot$ of His heavenly

occasions
258:2 New $o \cdot$ teach new

ocean
29:2 gone across the $o \cdot$,
335:1 that sweeps the $o \cdot$

o'er
2:1 $o \cdot$ the waking earth
30:1 Brood $o \cdot$ us with Thy
31:1 Brood $o \cdot$ us with Thy
32:1 Brood $o \cdot$ us with Thy
33:2 ward $o \cdot$ thee to keep,
35:1 Triumph $o \cdot$ the shades
39:1 $O \cdot$ every thought and
45:2 $o \cdot$ all the earth;
57:2 that Thou art $o \cdot$ us;
64:1 is breaking $o \cdot$ me,
81:1 $o \cdot$ me Are His wings
95:2 $o \cdot$ troubled sea,
99:3 angels charge $o \cdot$ thee,
100:3 angels charge $o \cdot$ thee,
104:2 victory won $O \cdot$ sense
119:1 $O \cdot$ Thy children shed
136:3 soar $o \cdot$ time and space;
148:3 will soon be $o \cdot$ me,
166:1 Rise $o \cdot$ sin and fear
167:1 Rise $o \cdot$ sin and fear
168:2 $o \cdot$ darkest night,
169:3 $O \cdot$ moor and fen, $o \cdot$
      crag and torrent,
176:1 $O \cdot$ night and chaos
197:3 peace is brooding $o \cdot$
198:3 peace is brooding $o \cdot$
200:1 bright $o \cdot$ thy hills
    1 thy sorrow is $o \cdot$.
229:1 $o \cdot$ the heads of all.
251:2 $O \cdot$ all the lands
252:2 $O \cdot$ all the lands
253:1 $O \cdot$ waiting harpstrings
254:1 $O \cdot$ waiting harpstrings
255:1 $O \cdot$ waiting harpstrings
256:1 $O \cdot$ waiting harpstrings
257:1 $O \cdot$ waiting harpstrings
253:4 $o \cdot$ earth's troubled,
254:4 $o \cdot$ earth's troubled,
255:4 $o \cdot$ earth's troubled,
256:4 $o \cdot$ earth's troubled,
257:4 $o \cdot$ earth's troubled,

o'er
304:1 $O \cdot$ the hillside steep,
305:1 $O \cdot$ the hillside steep,
306:1 $O \cdot$ the hillside steep,
307:1 $O \cdot$ the hillside steep,
308:1 $O \cdot$ the hillside steep,
309:1 $O \cdot$ the hillside steep,
314:1 Broadcast it $o \cdot$ the
325:3 victory $o \cdot$ the grave.
351:2 $O \cdot$ His ransomed people
368:1 $o \cdot$ yon mountain's
369:1 $o \cdot$ yon mountain's
368:2 $o \cdot$ all the earth.
369:2 $o \cdot$ all the earth.

o'ercame
67:2 the victors who $o \cdot$;
68:2 the victors who $o \cdot$;

o'ercome
312:2 $o \cdot$ through Christ alone,

o'ercoming
229:2 $o \cdot$ death and sin,

o'erflow
363:3 shall $o \cdot$ the world,—

o'erflowing
72:2 $o \cdot$ with His praise,
405:2 $o \cdot$ with His praise,

o'erwhelm
389:1 No cares can $o \cdot$ me,

off
391:1 far $o \cdot$ for paradise?

offer
55:1 the prayer we $o \cdot$;

offered
128:3 weary ones he $o \cdot$ rest;
129:3 weary ones he $o \cdot$ rest;

offering
253:7 An $o \cdot$ pure of Love,
254:7 An $o \cdot$ pure of Love,
255:7 An $o \cdot$ pure of Love,

offering
256:7 An $o\cdot$ pure of Love,
257:7 An $o\cdot$ pure of Love,
259:1 $o\cdot$ laid on mercy's
331:2 To Thee a nobler $o\cdot$

office
398:1 Each in his $o\cdot$ wait,

oft
115:1 dangers $o\cdot$ unknown.
116:1 dangers $o\cdot$ unknown.
258:1 $O\cdot$ to every man
330:3 foolish $o\cdot$ I strayed,
385:2 though $o\cdot$ unseen

oil
259:1 healing $o\cdot$ and wine,

old
96:1 He stood of $o\cdot$,
136:1 promise $o\cdot$ and new,
140:2 $O\cdot$ friends, $o\cdot$ scenes,
   3 $O\cdot$ fears are past,
    $o\cdot$ sins forgiven,
158:1 glorious song of $o\cdot$,
159:1 glorious song of $o\cdot$,
158:3 By prophets seen of $o\cdot$,
159:3 By prophets seen of $o\cdot$,
414:3, Ref. the $o\cdot$, $o\cdot$ story

olden
238:4 $o\cdot$ time and holier
239:4 $o\cdot$ time and holier

oldest
261:2 From $o\cdot$ time, on
262:2 From $o\cdot$ time, on

Olivet
372:1 faith has yet its $O\cdot$,
373:1 faith has yet its $O\cdot$,

omnipotence
  3:2 God's $o\cdot$, revealed,
80:1 Secure in His $o\cdot$,
326:3 With this $o\cdot$ he moves;
361:1 Thy helper is $o\cdot$.

omnipotent
37:2 One King $o\cdot$.
38:2 One King $o\cdot$.
123:2 gracious, $o\cdot$ hand;

omnipresence
66:2 beyond Thy $o\cdot$ stray;
421:2 beyond Thy $o\cdot$ stray;

once
34:2 $O\cdot$ more the lonely
168:2 $o\cdot$ bore the light
   4 healing power $o\cdot$ more

once
222:2 Christmas comes $o\cdot$ more.
223:2 Christmas comes $o\cdot$ more.
322:2 $o\cdot$ the weeds of error
323:2 $o\cdot$ the weeds of error

One
20:2 the only perfect $O\cdot$:
416:2 the only perfect $O\cdot$:
113:3 supreme and perfect $O\cdot$,
133:1 Thou, Almighty $O\cdot$, dost
424:1 Thou, Almighty $O\cdot$, dost
349:1 eternal, Holy $O\cdot$.
351:3 $O\cdot$ Almighty Father
382:1 Child of the perfect $O\cdot$;

one
11:2 and man fore'er at $o\cdot$.
20:2 self is $o\cdot$ with Him;
416:2 self is $o\cdot$ with Him;
29:2 united in $o\cdot$ band.
30:2 men $o\cdot$ in love remain.
31:2 men $o\cdot$ in love remain.
32:2 men $o\cdot$ in love remain.
37:2 $O\cdot$ holy church, $o\cdot$ army
38:2 $O\cdot$ holy church, $o\cdot$ army
37:2 $O\cdot$ steadfast high intent,
    $O\cdot$ working band, $o\cdot$
38:2 $O\cdot$ steadfast high intent,
    $O\cdot$ working band, $o\cdot$
37:2 $O\cdot$ King omnipotent.
38:2 $O\cdot$ King omnipotent.
67:1 lies the evil $o\cdot$:
68:1 lies the evil $o\cdot$:
72:2 $o\cdot$ eternal stream.
405:2 $o\cdot$ eternal stream.
83:2 $O\cdot$ in fellowship of
93:2 and God is $o\cdot$,
   2 $O\cdot$ Life, forevermore
   2 $O\cdot$ Truth unchanged
101:2 Of Truth, forever $o\cdot$,
126:1 In $o\cdot$ another's peace
127:1 In $o\cdot$ another's peace
403:1 In $o\cdot$ another's peace
126:3 $o\cdot$ delightful stream,
127:3 $o\cdot$ delightful stream,
403:3 $o\cdot$ delightful stream,
157:1 they may be $o\cdot$,
   2 $O\cdot$ the Mind and Life
   2 $O\cdot$ the Love whose
   2 find all being $o\cdot$.
169:1 $o\cdot$ step enough for me.
175:2 true being $o\cdot$ with Thee.
178:2 $O\cdot$ in Him, our heavenly
179:1 Love $o\cdot$ another,—
182:1 fill them every $o\cdot$.

one
196:1 $O\cdot$ Shepherd and $o\cdot$ fold.
   1 Around $o\cdot$ altar kneeling,
    $O\cdot$ common Lord adore.
218:2 of the Light are $o\cdot$:
219:2 of the Light are $o\cdot$:
220:2 of the Light are $o\cdot$:
218:3 $O\cdot$ in the freedom of
219:3 $O\cdot$ in the freedom of
220:3 $O\cdot$ in the freedom of
218:3 $O\cdot$ in the joy of paths
219:3 $O\cdot$ in the joy of paths
220:3 $O\cdot$ in the joy of paths
218:3 $O\cdot$ in the heart's
219:3 $O\cdot$ in the heart's
220:3 $O\cdot$ in the heart's
218:3 $O\cdot$ in the larger
219:3 $O\cdot$ in the larger
220:3 $O\cdot$ in the larger
230:1 Thy presence maketh $o\cdot$;
231:1 Thy presence maketh $o\cdot$;
232:2 ever $o\cdot$ with Thee.
406:2 ever $o\cdot$ with Thee.
236:4 Our God is $o\cdot$ Mind,
   4 Let nations be $o\cdot$
237:4 $O\cdot$ with Him forever
249:1 unsung $o\cdot$ blessing,
250:1 unsung $o\cdot$ blessing,
259:1 $O\cdot$ cup of healing oil
   1 $O\cdot$ offering laid on
260:1 $O\cdot$ thought I have,
261:1 $O\cdot$ holy church of God
262:1 $O\cdot$ holy church of God
261:2 $O\cdot$ unseen presence
262:2 $O\cdot$ unseen presence
264:2 All $o\cdot$ body we, $O\cdot$ in hope
    and doctrine, $O\cdot$ in
    charity.
266:4 all with $o\cdot$ accord
278:2 $o\cdot$ thing do thou ask
279:2 $o\cdot$ thing do thou ask
298:2 of $o\cdot$ endless day."
299:2 of $o\cdot$ endless day."
300:2 of $o\cdot$ endless day."
301:2 of $o\cdot$ endless day."
302:2 of $o\cdot$ endless day."
319:3 $O\cdot$ holy light, $o\cdot$ heavenly
351:2 $O\cdot$, the light of God's
   2 $O\cdot$, the object of
   2 $O\cdot$, the faith which
   2 $O\cdot$, the earnest looking
   2 $O\cdot$, the hope our God
   3 $O\cdot$, the strain the lips
   3 from the heart of $o\cdot$;
   3 $O\cdot$ the conflict, $o\cdot$ the peril,
    $O\cdot$, the march in
   3 $O\cdot$, the gladness of

one
379:1 the $o\cdot$ thing needful
380:1 the $o\cdot$ thing needful
391:4 "$o\cdot$ far-off divine event"
418:2 speaketh, aye, $o\cdot$ word,

oneness
157:3 understanding Of our $o\cdot$

ones
128:3 weary $o\cdot$ he offered rest;
129:3 weary $o\cdot$ he offered rest;
245:3 weary $o\cdot$, at nightfall,
261:3 her baptized $o\cdot$;
262:3 her baptized $o\cdot$;
315:2 gently to the erring $o\cdot$,
316:2 gently to the erring $o\cdot$,

only
5:2 $o\cdot$ know the real.
20:1 that is the $o\cdot$ real.
416:1 that is the $o\cdot$ real.
20:2 the $o\cdot$ perfect One:
416:2 the $o\cdot$ perfect One:
21:2 They $o\cdot$, are His sons,
22:2 They $o\cdot$, are His sons,
21:4 $o\cdot$ thus Shall we behold
22:4 $o\cdot$ thus Shall we behold
58:3 Seeing $o\cdot$ Thy creation,
115:2 Thou our $o\cdot$ guard
116:2 Thou our $o\cdot$ guard
123:3 I $o\cdot$ design
125:2 Thee $o\cdot$ will rely,
163:2 $o\cdot$ blessings know,
207:2 $o\cdot$ with mine eye
208:2 $o\cdot$ with mine eye
209:2 $o\cdot$ with mine eye
210:2 $o\cdot$ with mine eye
211:2 $o\cdot$ with mine eye
212:2 $o\cdot$ with mine eye
215:1 His early, $o\cdot$ choice.
263:1,3 $O\cdot$ God can bring
1,3 $O\cdot$ God can give
273:2 God, the $o\cdot$ Mind,
274:2 God, the $o\cdot$ Mind,
324:2 $o\cdot$, for my King.
3 $o\cdot$, all for Thee.
343:2 Thou $o\cdot$ canst unfold
344:2 Thou $o\cdot$ canst unfold
429:2 Thou $o\cdot$ canst unfold
360:2 $o\cdot$ live in loving,
367:1 His spirit $o\cdot$ can
390:3 we $o\cdot$ half believe

onward
81:1 Safely $o\cdot$ Shall my
102:2 may we press $o\cdot$,
103:2 may we press $o\cdot$,

onward
189:2 $o\cdot$ way doth trace,
258:2 upward still and $o\cdot$
264:1,Ref. $O\cdot$, Christian soldiers,
4 $O\cdot$, then, ye people,
265:1 $O\cdot$, Christian, though
320:4 With growing ardor $o\cdot$
321:4 With growing ardor $o\cdot$
409:4 With growing ardor $o\cdot$
335:2 Pursue thine $o\cdot$ way;
351:1 $O\cdot$ goes the pilgrim
355:1 $o\cdot$ in the right,
376:2 while pressing $o\cdot$,
377:2 while pressing $o\cdot$,
418:2 our moments $o\cdot$ flee,

open
58:2 $O\cdot$ hearts and willing
64:2 reach Mind's $o\cdot$ door,
74:1 earth to $o\cdot$ wide;
2 the little $o\cdot$ book
85:2 $O\cdot$ now our eyes
90:2 $O\cdot$ is the crystal
201:1 $o\cdot$ wide, let in
404:1 $o\cdot$ wide, let in
201:4 $o\cdot$ wide your heart
404:4 $o\cdot$ wide your heart
269:1 $o\cdot$ fount is free to
270:1 $o\cdot$ fount is free to
391:2 an $o\cdot$ eye to see.

opened
275:2 Light blesses $o\cdot$ eyes,

opening
243:3 breath of $o\cdot$ flower.
244:3 breath of $o\cdot$ flower.

opens
168:3 shuts and $o\cdot$ heaven,

oppose
396:3 hell in vain $o\cdot$;
397:3 hell in vain $o\cdot$;

oppress
200:1 foes shall $o\cdot$ thee

oppressed
43:1 come to hearts $o\cdot$.
327:2 all $o\cdot$ by wrong
328:2 all $o\cdot$ by wrong

oppression
75:1 comes to break $o\cdot$,

oppression's
2:2 It breaks $o\cdot$ chain.

oppressor
200:3 Th' $o\cdot$ is vanquished,

ordain
361:2 unless the Lord $o\cdot$.

ordained
45:1 stars hast Thou $o\cdot$.
83:1 God $o\cdot$ no other bands

order
213:2 hills in $o\cdot$ stood,
263:2 stars in $o\cdot$ going,
329:1 beauty, grandeur, $o\cdot$,

ordered
49:4 our $o\cdot$ lives confess
50:4 our $o\cdot$ lives confess

orders
92:2 $o\cdot$ come from heaven.

other
5:2 have no $o\cdot$ aim
8:1 When $o\cdot$ helpers fail,
10:2 No $o\cdot$ power we own;
No $o\cdot$ voice we heed,
No $o\cdot$ help we need;
411:2 No $o\cdot$ power we own;
No $o\cdot$ voice we heed,
No $o\cdot$ help we need;
58:2 hear no $o\cdot$ voices,
2 heed no $o\cdot$ call;
83:1 no $o\cdot$ bands Than
142:2 All $o\cdot$ names above;
214:3 know no $o\cdot$ guide,
3 need no $o\cdot$ rest.
265:2 Christ road, and none $o\cdot$,
361:1 Confide thou in none $o\cdot$,
(see also *each other*)

outpour
236:4 His love doth $o\cdot$;

outshines
263:2 $o\cdot$ the night of sin.

outspread
37:1 $O\cdot$ thy walls sublime;
38:1 $O\cdot$ thy walls sublime;

outward
142:2 Our $o\cdot$ lips confess
170:2 $o\cdot$ symbols disappear
259:2 of every $o\cdot$ grace;

outweigh
163:2 will all wrong $o\cdot$;

over (*see also* o'er)
48:3 Dominion $o\cdot$ all.
99:2 $o\cdot$ thee His wings
100:2 $o\cdot$ thee His wings

over (*see also* **o'er**)
114:3 can triumph $o \cdot$ death.
179:3 dawning $o \cdot$ every nation;
192:2 Darkness be $o \cdot$ me,
193:2 Darkness be $o \cdot$ me,
234:3 triumphs $o \cdot$ wrong.
235:3 triumphs $o \cdot$ wrong.
236:1 breaks $o \cdot$ the land,
278:1 Cared for, watched $o \cdot$,
279:1 Cared for, watched $o \cdot$,
290:2 Victorious $o \cdot$ every
292:2 as head $o \cdot$ all!
370:1 dominion $o \cdot$ evil:
381:2 triumphed $o \cdot$ cross
382:4 Dominion $o \cdot$ all.

overbrooding
142:4 The Spirit $o \cdot$ all,

overcometh
175:1 $o \cdot$ All the ills

overcoming
284:3 watchword, $o \cdot$ death:
285:3 watchword, $o \cdot$ death:
286:3 watchword, $o \cdot$ death:

overflow
139:3 your heart's rich $o \cdot$,
427:3 your heart's rich $o \cdot$,

overflowed
229:2 saw the darkness $o \cdot$

overflowing
182:1 Love has $o \cdot$ streams,

overthrow
370:1 $O \cdot$ the sacred rod

owed
260:3 secret strength they $o \cdot$,

own
10:2 No other power we $o \cdot$;
411:2 No other power we $o \cdot$;

own
12:3 Thine $o \cdot$ image we may
13:3 Thine $o \cdot$ image we may
20:2 seen as God's $o \cdot$ son,
416:2 seen as God's $o \cdot$ son,
46:4 Not my $o \cdot$, my Father's
47:4 Not my $o \cdot$, my Father's
51:3 as God's $o \cdot$ child,
52:3 as God's $o \cdot$ child,
71:1 for His $o \cdot$ abode:
88:1 Christ's $o \cdot$ gracious
89:1 Christ's $o \cdot$ gracious
92:3 God's will ... his $o \cdot$,
95:Ref. By His $o \cdot$ hand He
115:2 from our $o \cdot$ undoing,
116:2 from our $o \cdot$ undoing,
135:2 claim me as Thine $o \cdot$,
143:3 we with firmness $o \cdot$,
154:1 as God's $o \cdot$ child;
155:1 as God's $o \cdot$ child;
156:1 as God's $o \cdot$ child;
158:3 and earth shall $o \cdot$
159:3 and earth shall $o \cdot$
166:3 God's $o \cdot$ hand shall
167:3 God's $o \cdot$ hand shall
174:3 seeks and finds His $o \cdot$.
180:2 neighbor's good his $o \cdot$.
185:2 closely to thine $o \cdot$.
194:2 heart's $o \cdot$ longing
410:2 heart's $o \cdot$ longing
195:2 heaven's $o \cdot$ healing air;
216:2 after His $o \cdot$ counsel,
221:2 God's $o \cdot$ Son beloved,
230:2 $o \cdot$ in Thee The Light,
231:2 $o \cdot$ in Thee The Light,
232:2 man is God's $o \cdot$ child.
406:2 man is God's $o \cdot$ child.
237:4 God's $o \cdot$ image will
238:2 our $o \cdot$ time glad,
239:2 our $o \cdot$ time glad,
243:1 to all His $o \cdot$:

own
244:1 to all His $o \cdot$:
253:6 Thine $o \cdot$ children
254:6 Thine $o \cdot$ children
255:6 Thine $o \cdot$ children
256:6 Thine $o \cdot$ children
257:6 Thine $o \cdot$ children
258:3 watch above His $o \cdot$.
264:3 Christ's $o \cdot$ promise,
291:3 care beyond its $o \cdot$,
304:2 Thou know'st Thine $o \cdot$;
305:2 Thou know'st Thine $o \cdot$;
306:2 Thou know'st Thine $o \cdot$;
307:2 Thou know'st Thine $o \cdot$;
308:2 Thou know'st Thine $o \cdot$;
309:2 Thou know'st Thine $o \cdot$;
319:2 no lustre of our $o \cdot$.
325:3 in God's $o \cdot$ strength,
347:3 formed against His $o \cdot$
348:3 formed against His $o \cdot$
351:2 of God's $o \cdot$ presence,
354:1 strength is all His $o \cdot$.
367:3 $o \cdot$ Thy darkness passed
368:2 ages are its $o \cdot$;
369:2 ages are its $o \cdot$;
372:4 We $o \cdot$ thy sway,
373:2 We $o \cdot$ thy sway,
399:3 His $o \cdot$ interpreter,
400:3 His $o \cdot$ interpreter,
414:2 God's $o \cdot$ holy word.
425:1 in His $o \cdot$ Word

owns
130:2 creation $o \cdot$ Thy power.
207:1 $o \cdot$ each waiting hour,
208:1 $o \cdot$ each waiting hour,
209:1 $o \cdot$ each waiting hour,
210:1 $o \cdot$ each waiting hour,
211:1 $o \cdot$ each waiting hour,
212:1 $o \cdot$ each waiting hour,

P

page
176:3 $p \cdot$ beacons and brightens.
226:3 the fettered $p \cdot$
251:1 from the hallowed $p \cdot$,
252:1 from the hallowed $p \cdot$,
334:2 gilds the sacred $p \cdot$,
363:1 the Gospel's sacred $p \cdot$

pain
9:4 From $p \cdot$ and sorrow,
19:2 all $p \cdot$ and strife.

pain
34:4 is no $p \cdot$ or death
134:1 and $p \cdot$ and sorrow
154:3 have no $p \cdot$ or sorrow,
155:3 have no $p \cdot$ or sorrow,
156:3 have no $p \cdot$ or sorrow,
171:3 of $p \cdot$, and sorrow,
413:3 of $p \cdot$, and sorrow,
190:4 death, $p \cdot$ and sin,
191:4 death, $p \cdot$ and sin,

pain
202:2 banish $p \cdot$, and wipe
412:1 banish $p \cdot$, and wipe
207:5 pestilence or $p \cdot$;
208:5 pestilence or $p \cdot$;
209:5 pestilence or $p \cdot$;
210:5 pestilence or $p \cdot$;
211:5 pestilence or $p \cdot$;
212:5 pestilence or $p \cdot$;
221:1 cast out sin and $p \cdot$.

pain
232:3 sorrow, hate, and p,
406:3 sorrow, hate, and p,
253:1 bind The power of p,
254:1 bind The power of p,
255:1 bind The power of p,
256:1 bind The power of p,
257:1 bind The power of p,
263:3 prisoning p and
372:3 by our beds of p;
373:2 by our beds of p;
374:2 discord, p and fear;
375:2 discord, p and fear;
379:3 vale of tears and p.
380:3 vale of tears and p.

painful
158:2 p steps and slow;
159:2 p steps and slow;

pale
11:1 Saw a p star

Palestine
238:2 every land a P.
239:2 every land a P.

palm
261:2 the pine or p,
262:2 the pine or p,

panoply
312:1 The p of God.
326:2 p of truth complete,

paradise
391:1 far off for p?

parched
182:2 seem p and dried.
384:2 On p ground shall

pardon
43:1 p, grace, and peace,

part
30:5 when we meet and p.
31:5 when we meet and p.
32:5 when we meet and p.
69:1 choose the better p
423:1 choose the better p

partake
30:2 his spirit you p,
31:2 his spirit you p,
32:2 his spirit you p,

partners
273:1 P of a glorious hope,
274:1 P of a glorious hope,

pass
51:1 works p not away.
52:1 works p not away.
166:4 p thy pilgrim-days,
167:4 p thy pilgrim-days,
172:2 fear shall p, but Truth
196:2 Remove and p away,
297:3 p beneath His rod;
337:1 P like clouds that
338:1 P like clouds that
350:2 p through tribulation,

passes
108:4 comes and p by;

passeth
276:2 which p thought.
277:2 which p thought.

passing
7:3 every p hour,
8:2 every p hour;
11:1 pale star p by,
108:4 Yet p, points to

past
16:1 P rock and verdure
108:3 not the love, is p
130:2 wisdom p all seeking;
140:3 Old fears are p,
169:2 remember not p years.
186:1 as yesterday when p,
187:1 as yesterday when p,
213:1,4 help in ages p,
226:2 let the darkling p
238:2 good the p hath had
239:2 good the p hath had
297:2 till the storm be p;
312:2 all your conflicts p,
336:3 and earth have p
361:1 cares for thee p measure,
367:3 Thy darkness p away,
391:1 future and the p?

pastures
55:2 forever in green p
148:3 Green p are before
245:3 to Truth's green p
330:2 the verdant p grow,

path
59:2 Christ is the p,
60:2 Christ is the p,
61:2 Christ is the p,
75:2 Spring in His p
79:1 p in which we rove;
85:3 p that has no turning,
133:2 clouds my darkened p,
424:2 clouds my darkened p,

path
136:2 discord cross my p
148:3 My p in life is free;
169:2 choose and see my p;
233:1 Love whose perfect p
419:1 Love whose perfect p
245:1 rough the p may be;
2 p that thou hast trod
2 from that p we wander,
260:3 martyr's p who trod;
319:1 Sheds on our p
320:4 p of life divine;
321:4 p of life divine:
409:4 p of life divine;
339:1 shining p leads from
349:3 ever point the p
351:2 Brightening all the p
367:4 p, though thorny,
379:3 p of peace is taking
380:3 p of peace is taking
385:3 stoops on Judah's p

paths
115:1 our p were in Thy
116:1 our p were in Thy
146:2 all the p of earth,
147:2 all the p of earth,
215:3 all her p are peace.
218:3 joy of p untrod,
219:3 joy of p untrod,
220:3 joy of p untrod,
234:1 lowly p of service
235:1 lowly p of service
354:1 In p before unknown;
362:3 all his p are peace.
376:2 p are broad and wide.
377:2 p are broad and wide.
382:2 In Christly p apart.
388:3 p of loving-kindness

pathway
55:2 steep and rugged p
64:1 p lies before me,
70:2 p thou shalt see,
123:3 fiery trials thy p
131:1 Must in my p tread:
132:1 Must in my p tread:
311:1 p through the night,
420:1 p through the night,
329:2 His law man's p
352:1 thy lonely p, trod
353:1 thy lonely p, trod
376:2 may we tread the p,
377:2 may we tread the p,

patience
6:3 strength and p ask;
85:3 p, courage, meekness

patience
228:3 With p· he maintained
234:3 Teach me thy p·;
235:3 Teach me thy p·;
260:3 fountains of their p·

patient
91:3 P· of heart his way to
422:3 P· of heart his way to
263:1 P·, wait the brighter
352:2 p· through a world of
353:2 p· through a world of
381:3 through p· years,

pattern
51:2 and Love the p· make,
52:2 and Love the p· make,

peace
2:3 p· and love, united,
7:3 I know Thy p·,
9:1 on the earth be p·,
  1 the world knows p·.
  4 our hearts find p·.
40:1 Here health and p·
43:1 pardon, grace, and p·,
44:1 to the land of p·;
49:4 beauty of Thy p·.
50:4 beauty of Thy p·.
57:2 folded in Thy p·.
72:1 P· on earth to man
405:1 P· on earth to man
72:1 Thy truth, Thy p·
405:1 Thy truth, Thy p·
75:2 P·, the herald, go;
76:2 gentle P·, be still.
77:2 Lord will give thee p·.
78:2 Lord will give thee p·.
81:2 heart that p· inherit
83:3 children dwell in p·,
93:1, 3, 4 in perfect p·.
94:3 accents whispering p·,
102:2 sweet words: P·, be still.
103:2 sweet words: P·, be still.
118:2 Holy Spirit, P· divine,
  3 Thy p· my spirit fill.
120:1 reign of joy and p·.
126:1 In one another's p·
127:1 In one another s p·
403:1 In one another's p·
136:1 will give thee p·.
  2, 3 dost give me p·.
137:1 Thine Can p· afford.
139:3 p· shall crown your
427:3 p· shall crown your
157:3 dwell in joy and p·.
158:1 Of p· on earth,
159:1 Of p· on earth,

peace
160:1 pure p· is thine,
161:1 pure p· is thine,
162:1 pure p· is thine,
168:4 Our p· and health
171:2 know his promised p·.
413:2 know his promised p·.
174:1 home abides in p·.
176:2 p· to all it gave,
179:3 enthroning p·,
195:3 my soul with p·,
197:3 p· is brooding o'er
198:3 p· is brooding o'er
203:1 flag of hope and p·
207:1 p· and joy and power;
208:1 p· and joy and power;
209:1 p· and joy and power;
210:1 p· and joy and power;
211:1 p· and joy and power;
212:1 p· and joy and power;
215:3 all her paths are p·.
217:2 p· of God is there:
222:2 p· to men on earth;
223:2 p· to men on earth;
232:1 In perfect p· our
406:1 In perfect p· our
234:4 p· that God alone
235:4 p· that God alone
236:1 p· of the world,
  4 God's bountiful p·,
259:3 deeds of p· and love
263:1, 3 can give us p·.
276:1 P· be to this
277:1 P· be to this
276:1 P· to every heart
277:1 P· to every heart
276:1 P·, the earnest of
277:1 P·, the earnest of
276:1 P·, the fruit of
277:1 P·, the fruit of
276:1 P·, that speaks the
277:1 P·, that speaks the
276:1 P·, to worldly minds
277:1 P·, to worldly minds
276:1 P·, that floweth as
277:1 P·, that floweth as
276:2 O Thou God of p·,
277:2 O Thou God of p·,
276:2 P· of God which
277:2 P· of God which
293:3 P· is there our life
294:3 P· is there our life
295:3 P· is there our life
310:1, 2 P· on earth, good will
318:2 p· of sin forgiven,
322:1 Thy p· and calm
323:1 Thy p· and calm

peace
342:3 health and p· restored;
347:2 great shall be their p·.
348:2 great shall be their p·.
349:2 p· on earth from heaven
  3 freedom and in p·
362:3 all his paths are p·.
368:2 P· and truth its
369:2 P· and truth its
370:2 radiant p· we find,
379:3 path of p· is taking
380:3 path of p· is taking
381:4 Great p· have they,
392:1 love and p· and joy
393:1 love and p· and joy
396:1 p· attend your way.
397:1 p· attend your way.
418:1 do not bring us p·;
  4 joy and p· sublime,

peaceful
43:2 p· words of Jesus,
378:2 Blessings of p· hours,

peaks
287:2 Faith-lighted p·
408:2 Faith-lighted p·

pearl
345:3 priceless p· of gifts,
391:1 Life's p· is cast.

peculiar
271:4 bring P· honors to
272:4 bring P· honors to
365:2 Seem p· still to thee,
366:2 Seem p· still to thee,

penitent
40:2 Hope of the p·,

penitential
335:1 waking To p· tears.

pentecostal
345:1 light of p· glory,

people
10:2 Rejoice, ye p·, praise
411:2 Rejoice, ye p·, praise
12:1 Arise ye p·, take
13:1 Arise ye p·, take
72:2 p·, raise the song,
405:2 p·, raise the song,
177:2 p· see Thy power;
227:1 where'er Thy p· meet,
264:4 Onward, then, ye p·,
271:2 p· shall with joyful
272:2 p· shall with joyful
351:2 O'er His ransomed p·

people's
42:1 supply Thy $p\cdot$ need.

perennial
218:3 heart's $p\cdot$ youth,
219:3 heart's $p\cdot$ youth,
220:3 heart's $p\cdot$ youth,

perchance
315:2 $P\cdot$ unkindness made
316:2 $P\cdot$ unkindness made

Perfect
267:4 O, $P\cdot$ and Divine,
268:4 O, $P\cdot$ and Divine,
391:2 The $P\cdot$ lives and works

perfect
3:1 come to $p\cdot$ bloom.
20:1 Thy $p\cdot$ self, that
416:1 Thy $p\cdot$ self, that
20:2 God is the only $p\cdot$
416:2 God is the only $p\cdot$
20:2 $p\cdot$ self is one with
416:2 $p\cdot$ self is one with
34:2 with Love hath $p\cdot$ ease,
35:1 true, the $p\cdot$ Light,
   3 Shining to the $p\cdot$ day.
48:1 good and $p\cdot$ gifts
51:1 $p\cdot$ as his Mind
52:1 $p\cdot$ as his Mind
51:2 is the $p\cdot$ heir;
52:2 is the $p\cdot$ heir;
66:2 O $p\cdot$ Life, in Thy
421:2 O $p\cdot$ Life, in Thy
66:3 O $p\cdot$ Mind, reveal
421:3 O $p\cdot$ Mind, reveal
81:2 my $p\cdot$ guidance be,
85:2 seek Thy $p\cdot$ healing
   3 $p\cdot$, calm reflection;
91:3 love and $p\cdot$ grace.
422:3 love and $p\cdot$ grace.
93:1, 3, 4 in $p\cdot$ peace.
   4 The joy of $p\cdot$ work
105:2 And $p\cdot$ us in love.
106:2 And $p\cdot$ us in love.
107:2 And $p\cdot$ us in love.
113:3 supreme and $p\cdot$ One,
117:2 $P\cdot$ in power, in love
138:2 To $p\cdot$ Truth and
141:3 work of $p\cdot$ Mind,
144:3 $p\cdot$ in His love,
145:3 $p\cdot$ in His love,
154:2 truth a $p\cdot$ chiding,
155:2 truth a $p\cdot$ chiding,
156:2 truth a $p\cdot$ chiding,
172:3 shines to the $p\cdot$ day.
178:2 forth the $p\cdot$ Mind;
185:1 man's $p\cdot$ sonship

perfect
221:2 $p\cdot$, holy, blessed.
226:1 Unto Thy $p\cdot$ day.
232:1 In $p\cdot$ peace our
406:1 In $p\cdot$ peace our
233:1 Love whose $p\cdot$ path
419:1 Love whose $p\cdot$ path
258:2 side of $p\cdot$ justice
263:3 God the $p\cdot$ Friend;
269:2 Mind, the $p\cdot$ Mind,
270:2 Mind, the $p\cdot$ Mind,
297:1 Father and $p\cdot$ Son,
332:2 $p\cdot$ faith in Him,
342:1 All $p\cdot$ gifts are
345:2 $P\cdot$ and pure,
350:1 $P\cdot$ is the grace
356:1 our $p\cdot$ selfhood
363:3 reveals the $p\cdot$ whole,
367:3 In which is $p\cdot$ day.
370:1 behold the $p\cdot$ man;
371:2 within Thy $p\cdot$ law
382:1 Child of the $p\cdot$ One;

perfection
15:3 Saw man's $p\cdot$ shine,

performed
354:1 The work to be $p\cdot$

perfumed
253:2 With love $p\cdot$.
254:2 With love $p\cdot$.
255:2 With love $p\cdot$.
256:2 With love $p\cdot$.
257:2 With love $p\cdot$.

peril
351:3 conflict, one the $p\cdot$,

perish
177:2 shall every idol $p\cdot$,
264:3 thrones may $p\cdot$,
337:1 dogmas all may $p\cdot$;
338:1 dogmas all may $p\cdot$;

persuades
121:3 $P\cdot$, and they believe,—
122:3 $P\cdot$, and they believe,—
174:3 thy pure touch $p\cdot$ us,

persuasions
109:1 Thy tender sweet $p\cdot$
110:1 Thy tender sweet $p\cdot$

pervading
355:2 Come, all $p\cdot$ Love,

perverse
330:3 $P\cdot$ and foolish oft

pestilence
99:2 every harm and $p\cdot$.
100:2 from the noisome $p\cdot$
207:5 no fowler, $p\cdot$ or pain;
208:5 no fowler, $p\cdot$ or pain;
209:5 no fowler, $p\cdot$ or pain;
210:5 no fowler, $p\cdot$ or pain;
211:5 no fowler, $p\cdot$ or pain;
212:5 no fowler, $p\cdot$ or pain;

phantoms
382:3 The $p\cdot$ of thy fear

phrase
230:2 differing $p\cdot$ we pray;
231:2 differing $p\cdot$ we pray;

Physician
96:2 Great $P\cdot$ liveth yet

picture
251:2 the heaven-drawn $p\cdot$
252:2 the heaven-drawn $p\cdot$

pierce
35:3 $P\cdot$ the gloom of sin
172:3 $P\cdot$ thou the dark

piercing
84:1 $P\cdot$ mists, around,
143:1 dreads the $p\cdot$ eye;
333:3 His $p\cdot$ glance could

pilgrim
81:1 my $p\cdot$ feet be led.
90:1 $P\cdot$ through this barren
218:1 Our $p\cdot$ feet, wet with
219:1 Our $p\cdot$ feet, wet with
220:1 Our $p\cdot$ feet, wet with
260:4 $p\cdot$ staff and rod,
278:1 $P\cdot$ on earth, home
279:1 $P\cdot$ on earth, home
351:1 Onward goes the $p\cdot$
415:1, Ref. I'm a $p\cdot$, and I'm
425:1 O weary $p\cdot$, lift

pilgrim-days
166:4 shall pass thy $p\cdot$,
167:4 shall pass thy $p\cdot$,

pilgrims
233:1 $p\cdot$ with the gospel shod;
419:1 $p\cdot$ with the gospel shod;

pillar
90:2 fiery cloudy $p\cdot$

pillars
331:3 on eternal $p\cdot$ stand;

pine
261:2 the p or palm,
262:2 the p or palm,

pinion
112:1 faith's triumphant p;

pious
259:2 Within the p heart

pit
207:2 snare, the p, the fall:
208:2 snare, the p, the fall:
209:2 snare, the p, the fall:
210:2 snare, the p, the fall:
211:2 snare, the p, the fall:
212:2 snare, the p, the fall:

pities
359:1 p like a father;

place (noun)
99:3 within His secret p,
100:1 in His secret p abide.
3 within His secret p,
128:1 reverence filled the p.
129:1 reverence filled the p.
170:1 things of time and p.
176:3 each in his p,
181:2 Thy holy secret p,
227:1 every p is hallowed
249:1 Widespread in every p
250:1 Widespread in every p
261:1 Unchanged by changing p.
262:1 Unchanged by changing p
297:2 Sweet, secret p where
3 P of communion with
332:1 in His holy p,
341:1 throne in every p:
346:3 earth's darkest p
401:3 earth's darkest p

place (verb)
10:1 Him we p reliance;
411:1 Him we p reliance;
77:2 P on the Lord
78:2 P on the Lord
203:1 p our trust in Thee,

places
2:1 dark and hidden p
109:1 light their hidden p,
110:1 light their hidden p,

plain
41:1 idle on the harvest p?
51:3 Potter's work is p.
52:3 Potter's work is p.

plain
70:2 P shall His guidance
81:1 All His way made p
221:1 healing power makes p:
246:2 all is p before Him.
360:1 fill with gold the p.
399:3 will make it p.
400:3 will make it p.

plains
80:2 glad the heavenly p;

plan
12:3 God, whose p Hath given
13:3 God, whose p Hath given
20:3 fulfill our Father's p;
416:3 fulfill our Father's p;
51:2 He could not p,
52:2 He could not p,
163:3 Mind's most holy p
188:1 and trust His p.
370:1 the Father's holy p.
382:1 thy Father's p For

planned
46:3 my ... hopes have p,
47:3 my ... hopes have p,
216:2 for you His wisdom p;

plant
39:2 P holy joy in

planting
141:2 p timely, true,

plays
259:2 p, A living fount

plea
318:1 Master's tender p;

plead
7:3 I need not p,

pleasant
41:4 The toil is p,
414:2 'Tis p to repeat

pleasantness
215:3 are ways of p,

pleased
291:1 P with all that

pleaseth
291:1 all that p Thee.

pleasure
92:4 its highest p find

plenteous
97:1 p fruit be given,
98:1 p fruit be given,

point
2:3 P upward unto heaven.
131:3 p that living way,
132:3 p that living way,
349:3 ever p the path

points
54:1 Hope p the upward
92:1 God p out the way.
108:4 p to the glad feast

ponder
361:2 all His doings p,

poor
75:1 help the p and needy,
224:3 can I be p?
225:3 can I be p?
327:2 p and all oppressed
328:2 p and all oppressed

portal
64:2 and at its p I know

portends
368:2 truth its course p;
369:2 truth its course p;

portion
18:2 scorn be thy p,
258:3 p be the scaffold,

positive
365:3 Faithful, p, and
366:3 Faithful, p, and

possess
364:2 Every talent we p.

possessing
42:2 all, Thy love p,

Potter
51:1 Mind the P is,
52:1 Mind the P is,

Potter's
51:3 P work is plain.
52:3 P work is plain.

pour
109:1 P the fragrance
110:1 P the fragrance
214:2 its holy influence p
226:3 Thy radiance p,

pour	power	praise (noun)

pour
311:3 $P\cdot$ warmth and
420:3 $P\cdot$ warmth and
324:3 $p\cdot$ At Thy feet

pours
149:1 $p\cdot$ forth her light;
426:1 $p\cdot$ forth her light;
345:1 the splendor $p\cdot$.
363:4 day $P\cdot$ out its floods

poverty
249:2 Complaint is $p\cdot$,
250:2 Complaint is $p\cdot$,

power
3:2 man with mighty $p\cdot$.
7:2 Sin hath no $p\cdot$
3 Thou alone art $p\cdot$;
8:2 foil the tempter's $p\cdot$?
10:1 All $p\cdot$ is given unto
411:1 All $p\cdot$ is given unto
10:1 Almighty is His $p\cdot$;
411:1 Almighty is His $p\cdot$;
10:2 No other $p\cdot$ we own;
411:2 No other $p\cdot$ we own;
12:1 his $p\cdot$ receive.
13:1 his $p\cdot$ receive.
12:2 of God is $p\cdot$ divine.
13:2 of God is $p\cdot$ divine.
29:1 its holy $p\cdot$ feels,
30:5 whose $p\cdot$ our hope
31:5 whose $p\cdot$ our hope
32:5 whose $p\cdot$ our hope
34:1 again with holy $p\cdot$,
51:1 beauty, $p\cdot$ and grace,
52:1 beauty, $p\cdot$ and grace,
72:2 $P\cdot$ no empire can
405:2 $P\cdot$ no empire can
73:1 the $p\cdot$ of nations,
84:2 $p\cdot$ of Love supernal,
94:1 of a loftier $p\cdot$?
96:1 The $p\cdot$ that filled
2 be with $p\cdot$ endued
99:3 His $p\cdot$ and grace,
100:3 His $p\cdot$ and grace;
112:3 Word, whose $p\cdot$ supernal
113:2 Thy $p\cdot$ and love,
117:2 Perfect in $p\cdot$, in love
121:3 sign of heavenly $p\cdot$
122:3 sign of heavenly $p\cdot$
130:2 creation owns Thy $p\cdot$.
136:2 Thy $p\cdot$ is still my
137:2 Temptations lose their $p\cdot$
138:1 dream of human $p\cdot$;
141:2 Governed by a $p\cdot$ benign;
153:2 Thy $p\cdot$, O Lord, will I

power
163:1 O what $p\cdot$ divine
168:3 Reveal Thy $p\cdot$ through
4 healing $p\cdot$ once more
169:3 Thy $p\cdot$ hath blest
175:2 presence and Thy $p\cdot$
177:2 people see Thy $p\cdot$;
179:3 Love alone is $p\cdot$.
181:2 $p\cdot$ that lifts us
200:3 $p\cdot$ that hath saved
201:3 all who know its $p\cdot$;
404:3 all who know its $p\cdot$;
203:1 Love's sacred $p\cdot$
204:3 $p\cdot$ of Thy promise
207:1 peace and joy and $p\cdot$;
208:1 peace and joy and $p\cdot$;
209:1 peace and joy and $p\cdot$;
210:1 peace and joy and $p\cdot$;
211:1 peace and joy and $p\cdot$;
212:1 peace and joy and $p\cdot$;
221:1 healing $p\cdot$ makes plain:
227:3 the $p\cdot$ of prayer
243:1 mighty $p\cdot$ to heal
244:1 mighty $p\cdot$ to heal
243:3 tender, healing $p\cdot$.
244:3 tender, healing $p\cdot$.
253:1 bind The $p\cdot$ of pain,
254:1 bind The $p\cdot$ of pain,
255:1 bind The $p\cdot$ of pain,
256:1 bind The $p\cdot$ of pain,
257:1 bind The $p\cdot$ of pain,
275:1 $p\cdot$ to Him belong,
282:2 His $p\cdot$ proclaim;
292:2 $p\cdot$ and the glory,
298:1 $p\cdot$ of the Word?
299:1 $p\cdot$ of the Word?
300.1 $p\cdot$ of the Word?
301:1 $p\cdot$ of the Word?
302:1 $p\cdot$ of the Word?
303·1 deem it void of $p\cdot$;
2 vast its $p\cdot$ may be
320:1 in wisdom as in $p\cdot$,
321:1 in wisdom as in $p\cdot$,
409:1 in wisdom as in $p\cdot$,
329:1 mighty $p\cdot$ is known;
354:3 $p\cdot$ by which we act,
360:2 heart a living $p\cdot$?
362:3 His $p\cdot$, increasing,
371:2 Thy healing $p\cdot$.
378:3 Thy wondrous $p\cdot$

powerful
90:1 with Thy $p\cdot$ hand.

powers
312:2 $p\cdot$ of darkness down,
363:3 new $p\cdot$ unfurled,

praise (noun)
14:2 Sing $p\cdot$, O waking
16:2 $p\cdot$ must e'er increase,
36:4 Untiring $p\cdot$ we lift
42:2 To Thy $p\cdot$ and glory
49:1 deeper reverence, $p\cdot$.
50:1 deeper reverence, $p\cdot$.
54:1 The eloquence of $p\cdot$.
62:1 Creator's $p\cdot$ arise;
63.1 Creator's $p\cdot$ arise;
62:2 Thy $p\cdot$ shall sound
63:2 Thy $p\cdot$ shall sound
66:1 Thy $p\cdot$, O Father,
421.1 Thy $p\cdot$, O Father,
72:2 o'erflowing with His $p\cdot$,
405:2 o'erflowing with His $p\cdot$,
73:1 Glory, honor, $p\cdot$
1 gratitude and $p\cdot$
109·1 fragrance of Thy $p\cdot$.
110:1 fragrance of Thy $p\cdot$.
113:3 $p\cdot$ to Thee is due;
134:3 my mourning into $p\cdot$.
150:1 the garment of $p\cdot$.
166:4 and prayer to $p\cdot$.
167:4 and prayer to $p\cdot$.
168:1 man His $p\cdot$ proclaim.
170:2 fills them all with $p\cdot$.
192:4 Bright with Thy $p\cdot$,
193:4 Bright with Thy $p\cdot$,
206:2 thought attuned to $p\cdot$,
428:2 thought attuned to $p\cdot$,
226:1 lift Our hearts in $p\cdot$
230:3 is more than $p\cdot$,
231·3 is more than $p\cdot$,
249 1 this our hymn of $p\cdot$?
250·1 this our hymn of $p\cdot$?
259:2 fount of joy and $p\cdot$.
269.1 with breath of $p\cdot$
270:1 with breath of $p\cdot$
280.1 His $p\cdot$ should sing?
283:3 thanksgiving and $p\cdot$,
310:1 and shouts of $p\cdot$.
313.2 $p\cdot$ shall tune my voice,
324:1 flow in ceaseless $p\cdot$.
330:4 may I sing Thy $p\cdot$
331:1 lips Thy $p\cdot$ prolong,
336:1 shine not to Thy $p\cdot$,
342:1, 3 In $p\cdot$ lift up your
2 to bring Him $p\cdot$
356:3 deeply grateful $p\cdot$;
357:2 Our joyfulness for $p\cdot$
358:2 Our joyfulness for $p\cdot$
407:2 Our joyfulness for $p\cdot$
371:1-3 our hearts in $p\cdot$,

praise (verb)
10:2 people, $p \cdot$ His name,
411:2 people, $p \cdot$ His name,
19:1 $p \cdot$ His holy name.
86:1 What men agree to $p \cdot$.
87:1 What men agree to $p \cdot$.
117:3 shall $p \cdot$ Thy name
138:1 I $p \cdot$ Thee, Lord,
153:1 $P \cdot$ Him who lifts
　　2 I $p \cdot$ Thee, Lord,
181:3 awake to $p \cdot$ Thee
224:3 love and $p \cdot$ Thee
225:3 love and $p \cdot$ Thee
226:3 $p \cdot$ Thee evermore.
266:3 $p \cdot$ His holy name.
275:1 $P \cdot$ now creative Mind,
　　1 $p \cdot$ with joy and song.
280:1 $P \cdot$, my soul, the King
　1-3 $P \cdot$ Him, $p \cdot$ Him,
　　1 $P \cdot$ the everlasting King.
　　3 $P \cdot$ Him for His grace
　　3 $P \cdot$ Him still the same
281:1 $P \cdot$ our great and
282:1 $P \cdot$ the Lord, ye heavens
　　1 $P \cdot$ Him, angels, in the
　　1 $P \cdot$ Him, all ye stars
　1, 2 $P \cdot$ the Lord, for He
　　2 $P \cdot$ the God of our
283:1-3 $P \cdot$ we the Lord,
318:3 $p \cdot$ the Lord, Publish
374:1 $p \cdot$ Thee for Thy
375:1 $p \cdot$ Thee for Thy

praises
222:2 $p \cdot$ sing to God the King,
223:2 $p \cdot$ sing to God the King,
311:3 $p \cdot$ let us sing
420:3 $p \cdot$ let us sing

praising
45:3 be always $p \cdot$ Thee.
283:1 $P \cdot$ our God and our

pray
30:2 $P \cdot$ that his spirit you
31:2 $P \cdot$ that his spirit you
32:2 $P \cdot$ that his spirit you
67:1-3 Watch and $p \cdot$.
68:1-3 Watch and $p \cdot$.
71:2 them when they $p \cdot$.
125:1 those who $p \cdot$ to Thee.
140:3 hover while we $p \cdot$;
183:3 and work, and $p \cdot$.
184:3 and work, and $p \cdot$.
195:2 work and $p \cdot$, and follow
207:4 watch and $p \cdot$.
208:4 watch and $p \cdot$.
209:4 watch and $p \cdot$.

pray
210:4 watch and $p \cdot$.
211:4 watch and $p \cdot$.
212:4 watch and $p \cdot$.
230:2 differing phrase we $p \cdot$;
231:2 differing phrase we $p \cdot$;
237:3 $p \cdot$ to Him in secret
312:1 wrestle, fight, and $p \cdot$;
346:1 Hear us, we humbly $p \cdot$,
401:1 Hear us, we humbly $p \cdot$,
383:3 And $p \cdot$ of God, that

prayed
157:1 Nor $p \cdot$ he for these
169:2 $p \cdot$ that Thou Shouldst

prayer
54:3 And answer silent $p \cdot$.
55:1 hear the $p \cdot$ we offer;
　　Not for ease that $p \cdot$
70:1 ask with $p \cdot$ sincere;
75:3 shall $p \cdot$ unceasing,
76:2 $p \cdot$ to Him is answered,
　　2 $P \cdot$ confiding in His
102:1 Hear our $p \cdot$, O gracious
103:1 Hear our $p \cdot$, O gracious
140:2 gleam of love and $p \cdot$
146:4 silent, healing $p \cdot$,
147:4 silent, healing $p \cdot$,
149:1 And understanding $p \cdot$
426:1 And understanding $p \cdot$
151:1, 2 In speechless $p \cdot$ and
152:1, 2 In speechless $p \cdot$ and
157:1 Jesus' $p \cdot$ for all
166:3 and winged with $p \cdot$;
167:3 and winged with $p \cdot$;
166:4 and $p \cdot$ to praise.
167:4 and $p \cdot$ to praise.
168:3 through answered $p \cdot$.
179:2 is our answered $p \cdot$.
190:2 $p \cdot$ through every task
191:2 $p \cdot$ through every task
194:1 flight of silent $p \cdot$,
410:1 flight of silent $p \cdot$,
217:2 each kindly deed a $p \cdot$.
227:3 prove the power of $p \cdot$
253:7 My $p \cdot$, some daily good
254:7 My $p \cdot$, some daily good
255:7 My $p \cdot$, some daily good
256:7 My $p \cdot$, some daily good
257:7 My $p \cdot$, some daily good
269:1 $p \cdot$ for Love's increase
270:1 $p \cdot$ for Love's increase
269:2 $p \cdot$ That ne'er returneth
270:2 $p \cdot$ That ne'er returneth
284:1 $P \cdot$ is the heart's
285:1 $P \cdot$ is the heart's

prayer
286:1 $P \cdot$ is the heart's
284:2 $P \cdot$ is the simplest
285:2 $P \cdot$ is the simplest
286:2 $P \cdot$ is the simplest
284:3 $P \cdot$ is the Christian's
285:3 $P \cdot$ is the Christian's
286:3 $P \cdot$ is the Christian's
284:3 enters heaven with $p \cdot$.
285:3 enters heaven with $p \cdot$.
286:3 enters heaven with $p \cdot$.
287:1 $P \cdot$ with our waking
408:1 $P \cdot$ with our waking
322:1 holy, thoughtful $p \cdot$,
323:1 holy, thoughtful $p \cdot$,
322:3 May $p \cdot$ now lift her
323:3 May $p \cdot$ now lift her
333:1 baptized in humble $p \cdot$,
341:1 live a life of $p \cdot$,
　　2 look to God in $p \cdot$,
　　3 will answer every $p \cdot$,
374:1 hast heard our $p \cdot$.
375:1 hast heard our $p \cdot$.

prayer's
284:2 $p \cdot$ sublimest strain
285:2 $p \cdot$ sublimest strain
286:2 $p \cdot$ sublimest strain

prays
361:3 without ceasing $p \cdot$.

preach
12:2 as ye $p \cdot$ So let
13:2 as ye $p \cdot$ So let
331:3 Thy Well-Beloved $p \cdot$.

preached
168:4 at Thy will they $p \cdot$

precept
163:1 Jesus, what $p \cdot$ is
334:1 $P \cdot$ and promise still

precepts
39:3 from thy $p \cdot$ stray;
124:1 How kind His $p \cdot$ are;
402:1 How kind His $p \cdot$ are;
336:2 truth divine and $p \cdot$
386:1 $p \cdot$ which he taught.
387:1 $p \cdot$ which he taught.

precious
97:1 Bearing … the $p \cdot$ seed,
98:1 Bearing … the $p \cdot$ seed,
114:1 $P \cdot$ treasure, thou art
146:1 I find a $p \cdot$ gift
147:1 I find a $p \cdot$ gift

precious
215:2 her rewards more p·
221:1 Christ's p· Science
237:4 upon the p· metal
347:4 is thy p· heritage,
348:4 is thy p· heritage,
350:1 P· is the Love
390:2 O p· comfort breathing

prelude
238:3 A low sweet p· finds
239:3 A low sweet p· finds

prepare
121:4 Christ the Lord p·;
122:4 Christ the Lord p·;
164:1 heart p· him room,
165:1 heart p· him room,
417:1 heart p· him room,
190:3 shall the way p·;
191:3 shall the way p·;

prepared
176:2 Love that p· it.
188:1 God hath here p·
335:1 P· for Zion's war.

presence
3:3 angels of His p·
7:3 I know Thy p· every
8:2 I need Thy p· every
36:4 In p· of the King.
69:2 Thy sheltering p·
423:2 Thy sheltering p·
73:1 Come into His p·
80:3 With His unclouded p·
81:2 with me, and His p·
94:1 p· of a loftier power?
109:1 God, Thy healing p·
110:1 God, Thy healing p·
111:3 p· of my Lord;
130:1 in Thy p· is no night,
134:2 Thy p· fills my
136:1 My p· still shall go
2 Thy p· is with me,
3 Thy p· ever goes with
139:1 God's p· with me
427:1 God's p· with me
151:1 Thy p· healeth me.
152:1 Thy p· healeth me.
174:3 holy p·, that stills
175:2 Thy p· and Thy power
180:3 Love's p· gives
181:1 the angels of Thy p·
197:3 His living p· we have
198:3 His living p· we have
207:1 O gentle p·, peace and

presence
208:1 O gentle p·, peace and
209:1 O gentle p·, peace and
210:1 O gentle p·, peace and
211:1 O gentle p·, peace and
212:1 O gentle p·, peace and
214:1 God, whose p· glows
230:1 Thy p· maketh one;
231:1 Thy p· maketh one;
261:2 One unseen p· she
262:2 One unseen p· she
342:1 in His p·, unafraid,
351:2 light of God's own p·,

present
6:1 clear eye the p· scan,
3 The p· hour allots
3 For p· strength and
238:1 Through p· wrong,
239:1 Through p· wrong,
341:1-3 God is p· everywhere.
372:2 A p· help is he;
373:1 A p· help is he;
385:2 p· still, though oft
391:3 p· holds the Mind and

preserve
383:2 P· the tablet of

preside
39:1 O'er every ... step p·.

press
102:2 may we p· onward,
103:2 may we p· onward,
265:1-3 p· thou on.
273:2 To the mark ... p·,
274:2 To the mark ... p·,
288:1 P· on, dear traveler,
p· thou on,
289:1 P· on, dear traveler,
p· thou on,
288:2 P· on, and know
289:2 P· on, and know
290:1-3 P· on, p· on,
2 P· on to higher
355:1 P· onward in the
372:3 life's throng and p·,
373:2 life's throng and p·,

pressed
205:1 p· by every foe;

pressing
88:3 P· on and bearing up.
89:3 P· on and bearing up.
376:2 while p· onward,
377:2 while p· onward,

prevail
10:1 With Him we shall p·,
411:1 With Him we shall p·,
18:1 dare all and p·.
66:4 that shall p·.
421:4 that shall p·.
88:3 p· Where unaided man
89:3 p· Where unaided man
172:1 no tempest shall p·.
264:3 'Gainst that Church p·;
282:2 death shall not p·.
396:3 The cause ... will p·,
397:3 The cause ... will p·,

prevailing
176:1 O'er night and ... p·.

price
140:1 of countless p·,

priceless
188:2 p· treasures of His
345:3 p· pearl of gifts,

pride
30:3 p· and earth-born fear,
31:3 p· and earth-born fear,
32:3 p· and earth-born fear,
69:2 quell all selfish p·,
423:2 quell all selfish p·,
126:2 envy, scorn, and p·,
127:2 envy, scorn, and p·,
403:2 envy, scorn, and p·,
169:2 P· ruled my will:
325:2 thy foolish p· rebel;
359:3 that heart's p· which

priests
261:3 Her p· are all God's
262:3 Her p· are all God's
297:3 makes us p· and kings;

prince
17:2 p· of this world

Prince of Peace
17:2 Delay the P· of P·?
82:2 reign of the P· of P·?
158:3 P· of P· their King,
159:3 P· of P· their King,
362:2 shall be the P· of P·,
368:3 lo, the P· of P·,
369:3 lo, the P· of P·,

Principle
144:3 God, immortal P·,
145:3 God, immortal P·,
267:3 The P·, the Life;
268:3 The P·, the Life;

prison
18:2 If stripes or a p,
297:4 Loosener of p bands
345:1 the sunless p doors;

prisoner
271:3 p leaps to loose
272:3 p leaps to loose

prisoning
263:3 p pain and sorrow

prize
5:1 claims our p,
59:2 and Christ the p.
60:2 and Christ the p.
61:2 and Christ the p.
93:4 perfect work his p.
354:2 shall reach the p,

proclaim
120:2 Thy jubilee p;
168:1 man His praise p.
222:2 P the holy birth,
223:2 P the holy birth,
271:2 infant voices shall p
272:2 infant voices shall p
281:1 His mighty acts p.
282:2 His power p;
335:2 P, The Lord is come.
371:2 p Thy healing power.
386:3 we best p abroad,
387:3 we best p abroad,

proclaimed
236:2 Let Truth be p,

proclaimeth
175:2 Word p All true

proclaims
343:3 P thy conquering arm;
344:3 P thy conquering arm;
429:3 P thy conquering arm;

profess
386:2 holy gospel we p;
387:2 holy gospel we p;

prolong
331:1 lips Thy praise p,

promise
12:1 Christ's p stands:
13:1 Christ's p stands:
30:4 A bow of p on the
31:4 A bow of p on the
32:4 A bow of p on the
34:4 p of our God
46:2 Day by day the p
47:2 Day by day the p

promise
65:2 fullness of His p
136:1 Thy p old and new,
137:3 Thy rich p, Lord,
138:3 That Truth gives p
171:1 p and fulfillment,
413:1 p and fulfillment,
204:3 power of Thy p
236:1 day of fresh p
237:2 Love divine its p
264:3 Christ's own p,
278:3 Full is the p,
279:3 Full is the p,
282:2 Never shall His p
327:1 make His p vain.
328:1 make His p vain.
332:2 trust His p long,
334:1 Precept and p
365:1 His gracious p
366:1 His gracious p
365:3 Thy p full and free,
366:3 Thy p full and free,
368:1 signs of p are;
369:1 signs of p are;
390:2 How great the p,

promised
111:3 glories p in Thy
171:2 know his p peace.
413:2 know his p peace.
237:2 He hath p we shall
281:1 Canaan's p land,
351:1 Marching to the p
365:2 God has p needful
366:2 God has p needful
368:1 P day of Israel.
369:1 P day of Israel.
396:2 Depending on his p aid,
397:2 Depending on his p aid,

promises
269:1 God's p are kept.
270:1 God's p are kept.

prophecy
173:2 P will fade away,
297:4 dost fulfill all p.

prophet
229:2 sage and p saw,

prophets
158:3 By p seen of old,
159:3 By p seen of old,
196:1 By p long foretold,
226:1 p, who have shown
331:3 Thine ancient p teach,

prophets'
391:2 ancient p lay,

prospect
97:2 p seem most dreary,
98:2 p seem most dreary,

prosper
82:2 To p and increase
258:3 cause of evil p,
347:3 p nor come near.
348:3 p nor come near.

prosperous
385:2 shines the p day,

protected
278:1 beloved and p,
279:1 beloved and p,

protecting
115:2 trust in Thy p,
116:2 trust in Thy p,
283:2 p and guiding;
364:1 God's p arm.

protection
216:1 trusts in God's p
381:4 safe in Love's p,

prove
12:2 And p to all with
13:2 And p to all with
15:1 fires of Truth may p
17:3 Science yours to p.
66:3 we all must p,
421:3 we all must p,
79:2 changeless goodness p;
126:4 hearts that faithful p;
127:4 hearts that faithful p;
403:4 hearts that faithful p;
164:3 makes the nations p
165:3 makes the nations p
417:3 makes the nations p
185:3 we can p.
196:2 sweet and lasting p,
227:3 p the power of prayer
247:2 p His glory there.
248:2 p His glory there.
266:4 that grace to p.
356:1 Jesus came to p.
371:3 p That Thou art
379:2 pure and faithful p.
380:2 pure and faithful p.
386:2 To p the doctrine
387:2 To p the doctrine
391:4 p Unreal the ages'

proved
221:2 Within each heart is p.
347:1 His covenant be p.
348:1 His covenant be p.

proves
180:2 constant purpose p
326:3 more than conqueror p,

provide
140:1 will p for sacrifice.
182:2 Such channels to p,
224:3 here all good p;
225:3 here all good p;
291:2 Thou shalt to-day p

provided
135:1 life p For all

providence
134:2 Thy p turns all to

providing
283:2 new mercies p.
361:3 trusts in His p,

proving
85:1 truth is ours for p.

psalm
217:3 a p of gratitude.
249:1 a p to raise,
250:1 a p to raise,
261:2 silence or with p.
262:2 silence or with p.

psalms
73:1 P of gratitude

publish
318:3 P my call with

publishes
120:1 That p salvation;

publishing
179:3 p salvation,

pulses
49:3 the p of desire
50:3 the p of desire

pure
3:3 shrine so p and white,
12:3 Man p and upright,
13:3 Man p and upright,
15:3 God's child forever p
16:1 Thy p and happy
19:1 whose hearts are p,

pure
36:2 noiseless and how p;
40:2 fadeless and p;
3 p from above;
44:2 p repose and love
73:1 and p oblations
80:2 river p and bright,
91:3 Whose p affections
422:3 Whose p affections
102:1 laws so p and holy
103:1 laws so p and holy
109:2 in Love's p likeness
110:2 in Love's p likeness
118:1 in Thy p fire.
121:1 whose hearts are p;
122:1 whose hearts are p;
146:1 still, serene and p:
147:1 still, serene and p:
160:1 p peace is thine,
161:1 p peace is thine,
162:1 p peace is thine,
174:3 p touch persuades
206:2 p and cleansing rays
428:2 p and cleansing rays
233:2 Thy radiance is so p,
419:2 Thy radiance is so p,
237:3 p by Love's p fire.
253:7 offering p of Love,
254:7 offering p of Love,
255:7 offering p of Love,
256:7 offering p of Love,
257:7 offering p of Love,
261:3 The p in heart her
262:3 The p in heart her
269:3 p desire For growth
270:3 p desire For growth
291:1 gentle, p, and mild,
292:1 of p consecration,
298:3 Spirit that makes p,
299:3 Spirit that makes p,
300:3 Spirit that makes p,
301:3 Spirit that makes p,
302:3 Spirit that makes p,
329:2 judgments all are p,
331:2 The p, the humble,
345:2 Perfect and p,
352:2 so bright, So p,
353:2 so bright, So p,
355:1 call With motives p;
357:3 The p in heart are
358:3 The p in heart are
407:3 The p in heart are
370:1 p eternal union
379:2 and p and faithful
380:2 and p and faithful

pure
382:2 p and sinless heart;
394:1 most p, most strong,
395:1 most p, most strong,

purer
49:1 p lives Thy service
50:1 p lives Thy service
345:3 p lives of men,

purest
70:2 line of p light.

purge
206:1 P Thou our hearts
428:1 P Thou our hearts
345:1 p and hallow us,

purified
14:2 p thy thought.

purify
343:2 And p the heart.
344:2 And p the heart.
429:2 And p the heart.

purity
15:1 p shown forth,
117:2 in love and p.
171:2 behold Life's p,
413:2 behold Life's p,
371:1 all our ways Thy p.
383:1 Or stains thy p,

purple
317:1 p morning breaketh,

purpose
82:1 working His p out
180:2 By constant p proves
349:3 holy p to fulfill,
399:2 His mighty p ripens
400:2 His mighty p ripens

pursue
23:1 clouds P thy way,
24:1 clouds P thy way,
25:1 clouds P thy way,
26:1 clouds P thy way,
27:1 clouds P thy way,
28:1 clouds P thy way,
313:2 p The theme of God's
335:2 P thine onward way;
354:2 still p our way;

pursued
200:2 scourge that p them,

pursuing
18:1 Thy duty p, dare all
put
5:1 P armor on, the sword

put
292:1 P on the whole armor
296:1 P sloth and slumber
312:1 p your armor on,

put
343:3 p their trust in thee
344:3 p their trust in thee
429:3 p their trust in thee

Q

quell
69:2 q all selfish pride,
423:2 q all selfish pride,

quench
337:2 cannot q Her light.
338:2 cannot q Her light.

quest
136:3 q shall never cease,

question
92:2 not wait nor q ask

quickening
119:2 q showers descend;
131:3 q life from heaven,
132:3 q life from heaven,
134:2 flows Thy q life
319:1 thy q ray Sheds

quickly
243:2 How q burdens fall
244:2 How q burdens fall

quiet
55:3 we idly q stay,

quiet
57:2 q, folded in Thy peace.
291:1 Q, Lord, my froward
368:3 to thy q home.
369:3 to thy q home.

quietness
49:4 Thy still dews of q,
50:4 Thy still dews of q,

quit
327:1 never q His steadfast
328:1 never q His steadfast

R

race
59:2 Run the straight r
60:2 Run the straight r
61:2 Run the straight r
261:1 every age and r,
262:1 every age and r,

radiance
15:3 In r all divine.
29:1 r soft and clear;
119:1 all Thy r bright;
171:3 r Of his wondrous
413:3 r Of his wondrous
174:2 whose r cannot wane.
226:3 Through us Thy r
233:2 Thy r is so pure,
419:2 Thy r is so pure,
251:1 bless Thee for the r
252:1 bless Thee for the r
287:3 in Thy r vanishes
408:3 in Thy r vanishes
311:3 warmth and r from
420:3 warmth and r from
345:2 Thy stainless r
363:3 Its r shall o'erflow

radiancy
35:3 Fill me, r divine,
109:2 We reflect Thy r.
110:2 We reflect Thy r.
206:1 in Thy r divine
428:1 in Thy r divine

radiant
11:2 By those r beams
15:2 Revealed in r light.
149:3 r light of adoration,
426:3 r light of adoration,
185:1 secure in r light.
298:2 for you make r room
299:2 for you make r room
300:2 for you make r room
301:2 for you make r room
302:2 for you make r room
370:2 r peace we find,

rage
205:2 tempests r without;

raging
293:1 above life's r sea.
294:1 above life's r sea.
295:1 above life's r sea.

rain
97:1 Showers of r will fall
98:1 Showers of r will fall
313:1 cheer us after r.

raise
42:1 R the weak,
48:1 r this beacon here,
72:2 people, r the song,
405:2 people, r the song,

raise
72:2 hymns your voices r.
405:2 hymns your voices r.
73:1 Unto God the Father r.
160:2 To r up seed—
161:2 To r up seed—
162:2 To r up seed—
192:4 Bethel I'll r;
193:4 Bethel I'll r;
249:1 a psalm to r,
250:1 a psalm to r,
283:3 Now will we r Songs
310:1 anthems r; Hymns of

raised
261:3 serve the world r up;
262:3 serve the world r up;
388:2 and r the dead.

raiseth
192:1 cross That r me;
193:1 cross That r me;

rally
2:2 thousand freemen r,

rancor
178:2 Mid the nations r

rang
310:2 Truth triumphant r:

range
93:3 homeless longings r,

ransomed
280:1 R, healed, restored,
330:2 My r soul He leadeth,
351:2 O'er His r people

rapture
398:3 Lord with r see,

raptured
253:2 breathed in r song,
254:2 breathed in r song,
255:2 breathed in r song,
256:2 breathed in r song,
257:2 breathed in r song,

rare
104:3 Thy benediction r,

rave
172:3 sorrow round thee r,

ray
14:1 thou a steadfast r.
37:3 never fainting r;
38:3 never fainting r;
172:1 r of that great Light
    3 Truth's undaunted r,
226:1 wisdom's widening r,
234:4 sends a shining r
235:4 sends a shining r
319:1 thy quickening r
346:1 its glorious r,
401:1 its glorious r,
368:1 its beauteous r
369:1 its beauteous r
385:2 temper the deceitful r.

rays
206:2 pure and cleansing r
428:2 pure and cleansing r

reach
64:2 r Mind's open door,
121:4 human heart can r,
122:4 human heart can r,
194:2 words can never r,
410:2 words can never r,
284:2 r The Majesty on high.
285:2 r The Majesty on high.
286:2 r The Majesty on high.
335:2 Triumphant r their
354:2 shall r the prize,

read
74:2 r and understand.

reads
46:2 the promise r,
47:2 the promise r,

ready
58:2 R for Thy right
318:2 r to choose my way,

real
5:2 only know the r.
20:1 that is the only r.
416:1 that is the only r.
64:1 of all things r

reality
85:2 We behold r,
206:1 Thy will, r.
428:1 Thy will, r.
206:2 Behold r.
428:2 Behold r.
206:3 And know r.
428:3 And know r.
287:1 glow Of Thy r.
408:1 glow Of Thy r.

really
86:3 right doth r lie,
87:3 right doth r lie,
390:3 we r shall receive.

realm
6:1 in the r of dreams,
287:2 r of Soul supreme,
408:2 r of Soul supreme,

reap
97:2 r the fruits of joy:
98:2 r the fruits of joy:

reapers
242:1 r for white harvest
394:2 r still are few,
395:2 r still are few,

rebel
325:2 foolish pride r;

rebuke
333:2 His just r was

receive
12:1 his power r.
13:1 his power r.
42:2 Thy truth r;
121:3 Th' engrafted word r,
122:3 Th' engrafted word r,
164:1 earth r her King;
165:1 earth r her King;
417:1 earth r her King;
201:3 all . . . may light r
404:3 all . . . may light r

receive
222:3 meekness will r him,
223:3 meekness will r him,
291:2 as a child r,
327:3 blind r their sight,
328:3 blind r their sight,
357:2 for praise r,
358:2 for praise r,
407:2 for praise r,
390:3 we really shall r.

received
213:2 earth r her frame,

receiveth
318:2 r the Word as they,

reclothe
49:1 R us in our rightful
50:1 R us in our rightful

record
83:3 the newborn earth r

redeem
41:2 R the time:

redeemed
66:1 lips r from woe,
421:1 lips r from woe,
153:2 hast r my soul;
356:3 now r through Love,
378:2 hearts r from strife,

Redeemer
329:3 R, strength, and Lord.
415:3 My R, my R, is its

Redeemer's
62:1 Let the R name
63:1 Let the R name
326:4 in his R strength,
383:2 our R holy faith

redeeming
346:2 On thy r wing
401:2 On thy r wing

reed
30:2 bending r wouldst break
31:2 bending r wouldst break
32:2 bending r wouldst break

refine
123:3 thy gold to r.

reflect
109:2 We r Thy radiancy.
110:2 We r Thy radiancy.
181:3 r Thy healing love.
371:1 r in all our ways

reflected
51:1 R face to face.
52:1 R face to face.
237:4 Faithfully to Him r,

reflecting
66:3 love r Love.
421:3 love r Love.
146:2 R Truth and right,
147:2 R Truth and right,
206:3 our ways r Thee,
428:3 our ways r Thee,
349:2 R truly all Thou

reflection
85:3 Thy perfect, calm r;
233:2 by r constantly
419:2 by r constantly
345:2 in r finding all

reform
2:2 watchword of r:

refrain
236:3 mingle in joyful r,

refreshed
34:3 and thirsty are r,

refuge
53:3 r, strength and stay.
80:1 God is our r and
99:3 Thy r shall be God
100:3 Thy r shall be God
123:1 to God for your r
171:2 find in Love the r
413:2 find in Love the r
207:2 Love is our r;
208:2 Love is our r;
209:2 Love is our r;
210:2 Love is our r;
211:2 Love is our r;
212:2 Love is our r;
281:2 retreat and r nigh.
293:2 r from all wrong,
294:2 r from all wrong,
295:2 r from all wrong,
297:2 Harbor of r till
389:2 r in sorrow and danger;

refuse
337:2 blindly may r Her,
338:2 blindly may r Her,

region
265:1 r Where thou art

regions
33:2 through hostile r,
363:3 New r blest,

reign
82:2 r of the Prince of Peace?
120:1 r of joy and peace.
221:3 knows the r of Soul.
271:1 Our God shall r
272:1 Our God shall r
362:3 r shall never cease;

reigns
125:2 that r on high,
271:3 where'er He r;
272:3 where'er He r;
351:3 Father R in love
367:1 r in light above.
386:3 salvation r within,
387:3 salvation r within,

reject
101:3 R the falsehood

rejoice
10:2 R, ye people,
411:2 R, ye people,
54:2 made the heart r,
73:2 In His kindness may r.
84:2 obedience,—and r;
101:2 men r to know
168:1 earth with songs r;
243:2 grow light, r,
244:2 grow light, r,
263:1 our hearts r;
282:1 r before Him,
304:1 will follow and r
305:1 will follow and r
306:1 will follow and r
307:1 will follow and r
308:1 will follow and r
309:1 will follow and r
313:2 I cannot but r.
342:1,3 give thanks, r;
374:3 hear Thee calling: R,
375:3 hear Thee calling: R,

rejoices
112:2 all the world r,
171:1 That r every day,
413:1 That r every day,
199:1 In whom the world r;
221:3 God's idea, man, r,

rejoicing
56:2 R when Thy smile
153:1 My spirit hath r,
175:2 fearless, whole, r,
265:2 Tread it with r,
330:3 home, r, brought me.
351:3 the gladness of r

rejoicingly
55:2 May we tread r.

release
9:4 brings us sweet r;
93:3 man finds r;
120:1 From error gives r
136:2 Thy angels bring r,
170:1 R from things of
171:2 from self have won r,
413:2 from self have won r,
263:3 we all a sure r,

released
151:2 earthly thought r,
152:2 earthly thought r,

reliance
10:1 On Him we place r;
411:1 On Him we place r;
77:2 Place on the Lord r;
78:2 Place on the Lord r;

relies
291:3 As a little child r
364:3 on human strength r;

rely
59:3 On Him r and thou
60:3 On Him r and thou
61:3 On Him r and thou
125:2 on Thee only will r,
342:2 on His word r.

relying
350:3 upon His love r,

remain
30:2 men one in love r.
31:2 men one in love r.
32:2 men one in love r.
232:3 joy that ever will r
406:3 joy that ever will r
236:3 children in concord r.
264:3 Constant will r;
347:1 His kindness shall r
348:1 His kindness shall r

remains
80:2 city of our God r.
142:4 Eternal Love, r.
238:2 R to make our own
239:2 R to make our own
356:3 His joy r in us

remember
18:2 r the cross.
169:2 r not past years.
390:3 but O, r this,

remembrance
153:2 R· of Thy mercy

remotest
329:1 To earth's r· border

remove
40:1, 3 but Love can r·.
71:3 fear of want r·.
75:3 His covenant r·;
108:3 bread and wine r·,
133:3 gloomy thought r·,
424:3 gloomy thought r·,
138:2 and doubts r·;
196:2 R· and pass away,
199:2 We never shall r·,
273:3 mountains can r·,
274:3 mountains can r·,

removed
347:1 hills be far r·,
348:1 hills be far r·,

render
389:1 r· More lively my hope

rending
343:3 the r· tomb Proclaims
344:3 the r· tomb Proclaims
429:3 the r· tomb Proclaims

renew
247:1 strength He will r·;
248:1 strength He will r·;

renewer
150:1 Thou art the R·,

renewing
115:2 strength in Thee r·,
116:2 strength in Thee r·,

repair
168:3 our loss r·,
247:2 Without your God r·,
248:2 Without your God r·,

repeat
271:4 r· the long Amen.
272:4 r· the long Amen.
414:2 'Tis pleasant to r·

repeats
329:1 day r· the story,
345:1 r· its ancient story

repent
359:3 and r· in meekness

repine
166:2 can'st thou r·?
167:2 can'st thou r·?

replete
23:3 Beloved, r·,
24:3 Beloved, r·,
25:3 Beloved, r·,
26:3 Beloved, r·,
27:3 Beloved, r·,
28:3 Beloved, r·,

repose
44:2 pure r· and love
57:1 on Thy love r·.
71:1 shake thy sure r·?

reprove
133:2 dread and doubts r·;
424:2 dread and doubts r·;

requires
5:2 cause r· unswerving

requite
18:2 and He will r·;

rescues
280:2 R· us from all

resign
46:3 To Thy wisdom I r·,
47:3 To Thy wisdom I r·,

resigned
331:2 to Thy will r·,

resolve
290:2 With calm r· to

rest (noun)
17:1 God's day of r·
39:3 our heavenly r·,
41:4 sweet their r· shall be,
43:1 I will give you r·.
80:3 home, our hope, our r·.
128:3 weary ones he offered r·;
129:3 weary ones he offered r·;
192:2 My r· a stone;
193:2 My r· a stone;
195:1 my soul's true r·;
207:5 home and heav'nly r·.
208:5 home and heav'nly r·.
209:5 home and heav'nly r·.
210:5 home and heav'nly r·.
211:5 home and heav'nly r·.
212:5 home and heav'nly r·.
214:3 need no other r·.
260:4 My r· by night,

rest (noun)
271:3 weary find eternal r·,
272:3 weary find eternal r·,
304:2 earth's stupid r·.
305:2 earth's stupid r·.
306:2 earth's stupid r·.
307:2 earth's stupid r·.
308:2 earth's stupid r·.
309:2 earth's stupid r·.
355:2 shall see Eternal r·.
356:2 lies our active r·.
381:3 giveth r· from fears.
392:1 haven of r· is nearing.
393:1 haven of r· is nearing.
414:3 hear it like the r·.

rest (verb)
33:1 R· beneath th' Almighty's
57:1 Safely they r· who
93:1 whose heart can r·,
115:2 r· upon Thine arm,
116:2 r· upon Thine arm,
119:3 R· upon this congregation.
121:2 r· upon His word
122:2 r· upon His word
125:2 In Thee alone will r·.
143:2 God, on Thee we r·,
158:2 r· beside the weary
159:2 r· beside the weary
180:2 Here we r· content:
186:3 in this thought we r·:
187:3 in this thought we r·:
293:1 r· secure on Thee,
294:1 r· secure on Thee,
295:1 r· secure on Thee,
296:3 r· not, do the deeds

rested
197:2 blight and mildew r·:
198:2 blight and mildew r·:

resting-place
44:3 thy God, Thy holy r·.

restless
36:3 r· eyes of earth
118:2 r· heart of mine;
172:2 earth's r· tides,

restlessness
134:2 My r· to still;

restore
168:4 health to us r·.

restored
280:1 healed, r·, forgiven,
342:3 health and peace r·;

restores
217:1 R· the lost, and

rests
130:2 r· alike on man and
322:3 And r· her at His
323:3 And r· her at His

results
303:2 Nor what r· enfolded

resurrection
381:1 brightness dawned in r·
    4 rise from sin in r·,

retire
49:3 let flesh r·;
50:3 let flesh r·;
74:1 still small voice r·.

retold
236:2 God's love be r·,

retreat
281:2 Sure r· and refuge

return
35:2 Joyless is the day's r·,
168:1 r· the joyful voice;
356:3 r· to Zion, Singing

returneth
269:2 That ne'er r· void.
270:2 That ne'er r· void.

returning
140:3 mercies, each r· day,

reveal
66:3 r· Thy likeness true,
421:3 r· Thy likeness true,
88:1 Thy life in mine r·;
89:1 Thy life in mine r·;
121:1 shall God r· Himself,
122:1 shall God r· Himself,
140:3 of God r· our heaven.
168:3 R· Thy power through
206:3 R· in us Thy might,
428:3 R· in us Thy might,
221:1 R· their full effulgence
240:1 R· the light of
241:1 R· the light of
240:2 truth Thy words r·;
241:2 truth Thy words r·;
357:3 blameless hearts r·.
358:3 blameless hearts r·.
407:3 blameless hearts r·.

revealed
3:2 God's omnipotence, r·,
15:2 R· in radiant light.
65:1 wisdom is r· to us,
101:1 Man's heritage r·;
104:4 r· the Son;
246:2 glory of God be r·,
287:2 R· in morning's beam.
408:2 R· in morning's beam.
322:1 truths r· by His
323:1 truths r· by His
342:3 Love by Truth r·,
359:3 life shall be r·.

revealing
85:2 Truth of Thy r·.
202:2 to humble hearts r·
412:1 to humble hearts r·

reveals
201:3 Hid treasures it r·
404:3 Hid treasures it r·
363:3 r· the perfect whole,
392:3 heaven of heavens r·
393:3 heaven of heavens r·

revelation
85:1 Lift our hearts to r·,
179:1 Love . . . ,—word of r·;
221:3 Love's r· Of Truth

revelations
276:2 with all Thy r·,
277:2 with all Thy r·,

revere
394:3 Thy law r·.
395:3 Thy law r·.

reverence
49:1 In deeper r·, praise.
50:1 In deeper r·, praise.
128:1 r· filled the place.
129:1 r· filled the place.
151:1, 2 speechless prayer and r·,
152:1, 2 speechless prayer and r·,

reverent
109:2 R· lives unveil Thy
110:2 R· lives unveil Thy
217:3 Follow with r· steps

reward
41:4 the r· is sure;
114:2 give a rich r·;
150:3 and giving's r·,

rewards
215:2 r· more precious
    3 So her r· increase;

rich
111:3 fountain r· and free,
114:2 give a r· reward;
137:3 Thy r· promise, Lord,
139:3 heart's r· overflow,
427:3 heart's r· overflow,
224:3 While Christ is r·,
225:3 While Christ is r·,
259:3 spring not r· and fair,
360:1 grows r· in giving;

riches
249:2 gratitude is r·,
250:2 gratitude is r·,

richest
119:2 r· treasure Man

richly
135:2 r· shall inherit

richness
335:2 Nor in thy r· stay:

right
5:2 other aim than r·;
18:1 desert not the r·;
    2 but never the r·.
58:2 Thy r· commands.
59:1 and Christ thy r·;
60:1 and Christ thy r·;
61:1 and Christ thy r·;
70:2 but seek the r·;
77:1 God at my r· hand?
78:1 God at my r· hand?
86:3 r· doth really lie,
87:3 r· doth really lie,
86:4 For r· is r·, since
87:4 For r· is r·, since
86:4 r· the day must win;
87:4 r· the day must win;
125:3 ways are just and r·.
146:2 Truth and r·,
147:2 Truth and r·,
228:3 maintained the r·;
238:1 wrong, th' eternal r·;
239:1 wrong, th' eternal r·;
288:1 wrong and honors r·.
289:1 wrong and honors r·.
303:4 that serve the r·,
355:1 onward in the r·,

righteous
41:3 fulfill His r· will.

righteousness
35:1 Sun of r·, arise,
75:2 fountains Of r·
164:3 glories of his r·

righteousness
165:3 glories of his r
417:3 glories of his r
269:2 that yearns for r,
270:2 that yearns for r,
273:2 the crown of r.
274:2 the crown of r.
292:1 breastplate of r
326:2 r, a breastplate meet,
347:3 Established in His r,
348:3 Established in His r,

rightful
49:1 in our r mind;
50:1 in our r mind;

rightly
217:2 worship r is to love

ring
51:3 r from every tongue,
52:3 r from every tongue,
384:3 And joy . . . shall r.

rings
2:2 It r from hill and

ripening
394:2 r fields we see,
395:2 r fields we see,

ripens
150:2 For gladness that r
399:2 His mighty purpose r
400:2 His mighty purpose r

rise
5:1 The call to r
37:3 How r thy towers,
38:3 How r thy towers,
49:2 R up and follow
50:2 R up and follow
62:2 Till suns shall r
63:2 Till suns shall r
101:3 r to Life again;
108:3 as we r, the symbols
117:1 song shall r to Thee.
136:1 light of Truth I r
166:1 R o'er sin and fear
167:1 R o'er sin and fear
202:1 captive, r and sing,
412:1 captive, r and sing,
202:4 O captive, r, thy
412:2 O captive, r, thy
215:3 as her labors r,
227:3 faint desires to r,
264:3 Kingdoms r and
271:4 Let every creature r,
272:4 Let every creature r,

rise
296:Ref. R to conquer death
327:3 By Him the fallen r;
328:3 By Him the fallen r;
347:4 All tongues that r
348:4 All tongues that r
381:3 They r from sin
391:4 Then r and greet
418:2 changes r and fall,

risen
171:2 see the r Saviour;
413:2 see the r Saviour;
275:3 Ours is the r Christ,
297:1 glory of the r Lord;
370:2 r Christ has lifted
390:1 from our r Lord;

rises
7:1 Our day-star r,
150:3 courage that r
176:1 R thy light,
313:1 the Lord who r
317:3 R the glorious thought,

rising
65:1 r splendors glow,
92:2 R to every task,
97:2 r grain appear;
98:2 r grain appear;
213:3 Before the r sun.
260:2 r freshly to my view,

rite
333:3 No hollow r, no

ritual
230:4 nor form, nor r
231:4 nor form, nor r

riven
85:2 clouds of sense are r,

river
71:3 while such a r
80:2 r pure and bright,
276:1 floweth as a r
277:1 floweth as a r
335:2 Blest r of salvation,

road
158:2 beside the weary r,
159:2 beside the weary r,
247:1 with God along the r,
248:1 with God along the r,
260:2 take in trust my r;
265:2 By the Christ r,
352:4 ever on the r
353:4 ever on the r

roam
245:2 far astray we r,
311:2 to all who r,
420:2 to all who r,

roar
148:1 The storm may r

robes
19:1 stand in r of white
342:3 shining r of joy

rock
16:1 r and verdure wild,
37:4 upon th' eternal R,
38:4 upon th' eternal R,
85:1 R of our salvation;
104:1 the r Of Christ,
176:1 secure on timeless r
253:5 r, Upon Life's shore,
254:5 r, Upon Life's shore,
255:5 r, Upon Life's shore,
256:5 r, Upon Life's shore,
257:5 r, Upon Life's shore,
293:2 R of Truth, our
294:2 R of Truth, our
295:2 R of Truth, our
293:3 r we are secure;
294:3 r we are secure;
295:3 r we are secure;

Rock of Ages
71:1 On the R of A
293:1-3 R of A, Truth
294:1-3 R of A, Truth
295:1-3 R of A, Truth
320:1 The R of A stands;
321:1 The R of A stands;
409:1 The R of A stands;
365:3 R of A, I'm secure
366:3 R of A, I'm secure

rocks
55:3 r along our way.
74:1 The very r may seem

rod
30:3 wisdom's r is given
31:3 wisdom's r is given
32:3 wisdom's r is given
180:1 Love is staff and r
195:3 my staff, my r;
260:4 pilgrim staff and r,
297:3 pass beneath His r;
370:1 sacred r Of dominion
371:3 triumph 'neath Thy r,
376:1 Thy correcting r,
377:1 Thy correcting r,
382:4 Take then the sacred r;

123

roll
51:2 clouds of sense r back,
52:2 clouds of sense r back,
74:2 seven thunders r?
363:3 as centuries r,

rolled
171:1 r the stone away.
413:1 r the stone away.
310:2 r the mists away;

room
3:1 there is always r
164:1 heart prepare him r,
165:1 heart prepare him r,
417:1 heart prepare him r,
298:2 for you make radiant r
299:2 for you make radiant r
300:2 for you make radiant r
301:2 for you make radiant r
302:2 for you make radiant r

rough
245:1 r the path may be;

round
4:1 holy air is . . . r,
71:2 R each habitation
81:1 His glory r me
128:1 thousands gathered r
129:1 thousands gathered r
148:1 God is r about me,

round
172:3 sorrow r thee rave,
214:2 R each with all,
418:3 doth wrap us r,

rounds
96:2 walk the r with thee.

rouse
296:1 R ye, soldiers of
Ref. R ye, r ye,
3 R ye: long the
3 R ye, rest not,

rout
296:2 R the cringing host

rove
79:1 path in which we r;
114:2 chide me when I r,

royal
108:2 r wine of heaven;
179:1 Love is the r way.
264:1 Christ, the r Master,

rugged
3:2 stanch and r tower,
55:2 steep and r pathway
304:1 All the r way.
305:1 All the r way.
306:1 All the r way.
307:1 All the r way.

rugged
308:1 All the r way.
309:1 All the r way.

rule
75:1 And r in equity.
229:2 The r of Love
315:1 To r by love
316:1 To r by love

ruled
169:2 Pride r my will:
339:3 r by Love alone.

rules
164:3 He r the world with
165:3 He r the world with
417:3 He r the world with

rulest
204:1 r in all Thy creation;

run
59:2 R the straight race
60:2 R the straight race
61:2 R the straight race
93:2 unchanged while ages r;
182:1 they may broadly r;
218:2 to eye the signals r,
219:2 to eye the signals r,
220:2 to eye the signals r,
240:2 r the heavenly way,
241:2 r the heavenly way,
271:1 successive journeys r;
272:1 successive journeys r;

S

sacred
10:1 from out His s word
411:1 from out His s word
143:1 s truths the test
203:1 Love's s power
233:3 And every s shrine
419:3 And every s shrine
322:3 lift her s wings,
323:3 lift her s wings,
332:1 need a s watchfulness,
334:2 gilds the s page,
336:1 as Thy s Word.
363:1 Gospel's s page
370:1 Overthrow the s rod
382:4 Take then the s rod;
396:2 With s courage go.
397:2 With s courage go.

sacrifice
140:1 provide for s.
151:2 greater Than s
152:2 greater Than s

sad
188:3 s with dreams of death.
243:2 sinning and the s.
244:2 sinning and the s.
253:1 Low, s, and sweet,
254:1 Low, s, and sweet,
255:1 Low, s, and sweet,
256:1 Low, s, and sweet,
257:1 Low, s, and sweet,

saddening
44:3 leaves no s trace;

sadness
119:1 burdens and all s;
120:2 songs instead of s,
179:2 neither shade of s;
200:1 awake from thy s;
263:1 vain that end in s,
370:2 Truth wherein no s

safe
53:3 S in His encircling

safe
66:2 S in Thy Love, we
421:2 S in Thy Love, we
71:2 S they feed upon
148:1 s is such confiding,
154:2 s abiding From every
155:2 s abiding From every
156:2 s abiding From every
157:2 S within this Love
185:1 S and secure in
293:1 S above life's raging
294:1 S above life's raging
295:1 S above life's raging
381:4 s in Love's protection,

safeguard
33:3 In eternal s there.

safely
57:1 S they rest who on
69:2 'neath Thy . . . s hide.
423:2 'neath Thy . . . s hide.

safely
81:1 S· onward Shall my
203:2 lead us s· home
245:1 s· lead us home.
  2 bring us s· home.
311:2 lead them s·, surely
420:2 lead them s·, surely

sage
229:2 s· and prophet saw,

said
123:1 to you He hath s·,
131:1 Our blessed Master s·;
132:1 Our blessed Master s·;
425:1 His own Word hath s·

saint
23:5 thou our s·, Our stay,
24:5 thou our s·, Our stay,.
25:5 thou our s·, Our stay,
26:5 thou our s·, Our stay,
27:5 thou our s·, Our stay,
28:5 thou our s·, Our stay,

saints
123:1 s· of the Lord,
124:2 s· securely dwell;
402:2 s· securely dwell;
177:1 Look, ye s·, the day
  2 faithful s· adore.
264:2 the s· have trod;
282:2 His s· victorious,
399:1 Ye timid s·, fresh
400:1 Ye timid s·, fresh

saith
19:2 God s·, These are Mine.
188:3 find, the Spirit s·,
224:2 what my Saviour s·,
225:2 what my Saviour s·,

sake
265:3 for their s·, press

salvation
33:1 Lord thy sure s·,
77:1 God is my strong s·;
78:1 God is my strong s·;
85:1 Rock of our s·;
99:3 His s· ever nigh.
100:3 His s· ever nigh.
120:1 That publishes s·;
  2 glorious S· of our God.
166:1 child, thy full s·;
167:1 child, thy full s·;
179:3 publishing s·,
202:4 glorious tidings of s·
412:2 glorious tidings of s·

salvation
204:1 of Thy mighty s·.
  3 S· to all men
276:1 the earnest of s·;
277:1 the earnest of s·;
282:2 God of our s·;
283:3 is become our s·.
292:1 the helmet of s·—
313:2 theme of God's s·,
335:2 Blest river of s·,
350:2 such a full s·,
378:3 Lord, Thy s· strong,
386:3 His s· reigns within,
387:3 His s· reigns within,
414:2 The message of s·

salvation's
71:1 s· walls surrounded
326:2 S· helmet on his head,

same
30:1 on the s· branch
31:1 on the s· branch
32:1 on the s· branch
93:2 forevermore the s·,
96:1 Is evermore the s·.
153:1 Forevermore the s·,
154:3 s· to-day, to-morrow;
155:3 s· to-day, to-morrow;
156:3 s· to-day, to-morrow;
213:2 endless years the s·.
224:1 fullness is the s·;
225:1 fullness is the s·;
266:3 s· immortal bliss,
  3 hopes and aims the s·,
280:3 still the s· forever,

sanctifying
334:1 afford A s· light.

sand
216:1 builded on the s·.

sands
37:4 vain the drifting s·;
38:4 vain the drifting s·;

sang
9:1 angels s·, in days of
310:2 stars together s·,

sanguine
46:3 All my s· hopes
47:3 All my s· hopes

satisfied
149:3 But s·, complete,
426:3 But s·, complete,
160:5 likeness still—Is s·.
161:5 likeness still—Is s·.

satisfied
162:5 likeness still—Is s·.
224:1 with this be s·,
225:1 with this be s·,

satisfies
414:1 It s· my longing

save
76:2 s· both thine and thee.
172:3 joy to help and s·,
175:2 to s· and heal us,
381:2 forevermore to s·;

saved
200:3 power that hath s·
327:2 s· by His decree;
328:2 s· by His decree;

saves
112:2 mighty Counsel, s· us.

savest
56:3 Thou s· those that

saving
339:1 s· Truth who know,

Saviour
137:Ref. bless me now, my S·
150:3 Dear Father and S·,
153:1 my God and S·,
171:2 see the risen S·;
413:2 see the risen S·;
202:4 S· comes to thee.
412:2 S· comes to thee.
224:2 what my S· saith,
225:2 what my S· saith,
275:3 S· from death is He;
288:2 way the S· trod,
289:2 way the S· trod,
298:1 Saw ye my S·?
299:1 Saw ye my S·?
300:1 Saw ye my S·?
301:1 Saw ye my S·?
302:1 Saw ye my S·?
325:1 cross, the S· said,
350:1 love of God our S·
386:3 honors of our S·,
387:3 honors of our S·,

Saviour's
11:1 at the S· birth
114:2 to show a S· love;
  3 a S· tenderness;
310:1 the lowly S· birth.

saw
11:1 S· a pale star
15:3 S· man's perfection

125

saw
229:2 sage and prophet s,
   2 s the darkness overflowed
298:1 S ye my Saviour?
299:1 S ye my Saviour?
300:1 S ye my Saviour?
301:1 S ye my Saviour?
302:1 S ye my Saviour?
381:1 s her Lord in life

say
  41:1 does the Master s,
  99:1 of Him I'll s,
100:1 I now will s,
123:1 What more can He s
133:1 can always, always s
424:1 can always, always s

saying
  40:2 Comforter, tenderly s,

scaffold
258:3 portion be the s,
   3 s sways the future,

scalding
207:3 for every s tear,
208:3 for every s tear,
209:3 for every s tear,
210:3 for every s tear,
211:3 for every s tear,
212:3 for every s tear,

scan
   6:1 the present s,
399:3 s His work in vain;
400:3 s His work in vain;

scatter
  35:3 S all my unbelief;

scattered
200:2 And s their legions
360:1 S, fill with gold

scene
  97:2 the s of verdure
  98:2 the s of verdure
169:1 see The distant s;

scenes
  95:2 s of deepest gloom,
140:2 Old friends, old s,

Science
  17:3 S yours to prove.
221:1 Christ's precious S
   2 in Thy S Is perfect,
   3 S, God-sent message
297:1 S, the angel with
   4 S, thou dost fulfill

scoffers
337:2 Learned s may abuse
338:2 Learned s may abuse

scoffs
352:3 Scorn and the s of men,
353:3 Scorn and the s of men,

scorn
  18:2 If s be thy portion,
126:2 free from envy, s,
127:2 free from envy, s,
403:2 free from envy, s,
303:1 S not the slightest
352:3 S and the scoffs
353:3 S and the scoffs

scourge
200:2 s that pursued them,

scowling
  17:1 s shapes of darkness

screen
385:2 cloudy s To temper

sea
  45:1 earth and s and sky.
  49:2 Beside the Syrian s,
  50:2 Beside the Syrian s,
  82:1-3 waters cover the s.
  95:2 o'er troubled s,
117:3 earth, and sky and s;
118:2 calm the tossing s,
142:1 A never ebbing s,—
253:4 troubled, angry s
254:4 troubled, angry s
255:4 troubled, angry s
256:4 troubled, angry s
257:4 troubled, angry s
293:1 above life's raging s.
294:1 above life's raging s.
295:1 above life's raging s.
340:1 wideness of the s;

sealed
350:1 grace that s us,

seamless
146:4 In s gratitude
147:4 In s gratitude
372:3 healing of the s dress
373:2 healing of the s dress

search
143:1 bid us s and try.
320:1 s His word, and trace
321:1 s His word, and trace
409:1 s His word, and trace
372:1 s the lowest deeps,
373:1 s the lowest deeps,
391:1 Why s the future

searcheth
188:2 whose Spirit s deep

season
313:1 s of clear shining,

secret
  33:1 His s habitation
  99:3 within His s place,
100:1 in His s place abide.
   3 within His s place,
181:2 Thy holy s place,
207:4 s of the narrow way,
208:4 s of the narrow way,
209:4 s of the narrow way,
210:4 s of the narrow way,
211:4 s of the narrow way,
212:4 s of the narrow way,
234:1 Tell me thy s; help
235:1 Tell me thy s; help
237:3 pray to Him in s,
260:3 s strength they owed,
297:2 Sweet, s place
357:3 the s of His joy
358:3 the s of His joy
407:3 the s of His joy

secure
  80:1 S in His omnipotence,
104:1 s upon the rock
176:1 s on timeless rock
185:1 s in radiant light.
224:3 made my heaven s,
225:3 made my heaven s,
293:1 rest s on Thee,
294:1 rest s on Thee,
295:1 rest s on Thee,
293:3 rock we are s;
294:3 rock we are s;
295:3 rock we are s;
354:2 S in endless day.
365:3 Rock of Ages, I'm s
366:3 Rock of Ages, I'm s

securely
  58:3 house s dwelling,
124:2 saints s dwell;
402:2 saints s dwell;

security
171:2 That is man's s,
413:2 That is man's s,

see
   7:2 in all around I s
  12:3 s Man pure and
  13:3 s Man pure and
  34:1 blinded eyes to s;
  35:2 mercy's beams I s;

see
40:3 s· the Bread of Life,
        s· waters flowing
56:2 Thy smile we s·,
59:3 s· That Christ is all
60:3 s· That Christ is all
61:3 s· That Christ is all
69:2 s· Thee as Thou art
423:2 s· Thee as Thou art
70:2 pathway thou shalt s·,
71:2 S· the cloud and fire
    3 S·, the streams of
85:2 now our eyes to s·,
97:1 s· his toil succeed;
98:1 s· his toil succeed;
97:2 S· the rising grain
98:2 S· the rising grain
99:3 No evil . . . shalt thou s·;
    3 S· His salvation ever
100:3 No evil . . . shalt thou s·.
    3 S· His salvation ever
108:1 s· Thee face to face;
111:3 we all shall s·
117:2 Thy glory cannot s·.
121:1 shall His glory s·.
122:1 shall His glory s·.
130:1 shall we s· light.
136:3 s· Thee face to face.
138:3 light I am to s·,
140:2 in each we s·;
144:1 mortal eyes may s·
145:1 mortal eyes may s·
169:1 s· The distant scene;
    2 choose and s· my path;
171:2 s· the risen Saviour;
413:2 s· the risen Saviour;
173:4 hope and love we s·
177:2 people s· Thy power;
181:2 s· Thee face to face.
185:1 perfect sonship s·
186:3 s· as Thou dost s·,
187:3 s· as Thou dost s·,
202:4 blinded eyes to s·;
412:2 blinded eyes to s·;
221:2 s· expressed By man,
222:1 still we s· thee lie;
223:1 still we s· thee lie;
226:2 that we may s·,
229:1 eyes that will not s·,
230:2 we dimly s·,
231:2 we dimly s·,
232:2 Thy light we can s·
406:2 Thy light we can s·
238:1 s· the steady gain
239:1 s· the steady gain
246:2 All flesh shall s·

see
249:1 we s· God's mercy
250:1 we s· God's mercy
253:4 I s· Christ walk,
254:4 I s· Christ walk,
255:4 I s· Christ walk,
256:4 I s· Christ walk,
257:4 I s· Christ walk,
258:2 S· the thought of men
264:1 S·, his banners go.
267:1 S· baseless evil fall,
268:1 S· baseless evil fall,
267:2 s· Truth's glowing
268:2 s· Truth's glowing
267:3 We s· creative Mind,
268:3 We s· creative Mind,
275:2 s· Him our God
297:1 whose light we shall s·
311:1 s·, 'tis lit by Love
420:1 s·, 'tis lit by Love
317:3 s· the shadows flee,
318:1 ye who s· this sign
    3 S· ye the lilies,
326:1 warrior, s· him stand
336:2 heavenly beam I s·,
339:3 s· by faith all things
345:2 s· the glory shine
    3 all shall s· where Thine
355:2 shall s· Eternal rest.
367:4 thou shalt s· Thy path,
368:1 S· that glory-beaming
369:1 S· that glory-beaming
368:2 S·, it bursts o'er all
369:2 S·, it bursts o'er all
374:3 s· Thee face to face.
375:3 s· Thee face to face.
378:1 would Thy beauty s·,
391:2 an open eye to s·.
394:2 ripening fields we s·,
395:2 ripening fields we s·,
394:3 S· Thy light, Thy law
395:3 S· Thy light, Thy law
398:3 Lord with rapture s·,
418:1 strain our eyes to s·
    4 eyes the King will s·,

seed
42:1 the sower and the s·;
97:1 still the precious s·,
98:1 still the precious s·,
97:2 Sow thy s·, be never
98:2 Sow thy s·, be never
150:2 Sower's good s·.
160:2 To raise up s·—
161:2 To raise up s·—
162:2 To raise up s·—
303:1 each wind-wafted s·
314:1 in the morn thy s·,

seeds
180:2 s· of Love are sown.
360:1 S· which mildew in

seeing
58:3 S· only Thy creation,

seek
30:2 S· holy thoughts
31:2 S· holy thoughts
32:2 S· holy thoughts
56:3 To them that s· Thee
59:2 and s· His face;
60:2 and s· His face;
61:2 and s· His face;
70:2 but s· the right;
85:2 we s· Thy perfect
227:1 Where'er they s· Thee,
237:1 be still and s· Him,
        S· with consecration
266:4 s· that grace to prove.
267:4 s· no earthly shrine
268:4 s· no earthly shrine
269:3 s· Thy will to do,
270:3 s· Thy will to do,
332:2 they who s· Him
341:1 s· the throne of grace,
343:1 would the Father s·,
        Must s· Him, Lord,
344:1 would the Father s·,
        Must s· Him, Lord,
429:1 would the Father s·,
        Must s· Him, Lord,
361:1 S· Him who has thy
391:1 s· far off for paradise?

seekers
218:2 s· of the Light are
219:2 s· of the Light are
220:2 s· of the Light are

seeking
130:2 wisdom past all s·;
207:4 S· and finding,
208:4 S· and finding,
209:4 S· and finding,
210:4 S· and finding,
211:4 S· and finding,
212:4 S· and finding,

seeks
174:3 s· and finds His own.
194:1 s· God everywhere.
410:1 s· God everywhere.

seem
57:2 and skies s· dark
74:1 rocks may s· to break,
97:2 prospect s· most dreary,
98:2 prospect s· most dreary,
175:1 ills that s· to be,

seem
182:2 s parched and dried.
190:1 tasks of life s hard
191:1 tasks of life s hard
217:3 s our Father's temple,
265:1 s drear and lone;
359:1 s so like a dream;
365:2 S peculiar still to
366:2 S peculiar still to
383:3 dark soever it may s,
414:3 S hungering and

seemeth
79:2 hour that darkest s,

seeming
232:3 Midst s sorrow,
406:3 Midst s sorrow,

seems
6:1 however fair it s;
86:2 He s invisible.
87:2 He s invisible.
86:3 with what s wrong
87:3 with what s wrong
313:1 comfort s declining,
368:3 morning s to dawn;
369:3 morning s to dawn;
414:2 s, each time I tell

seen
20:2 s as God's own son,
416:2 s as God's own son,
45:2 goodness may be s.
148:3 yet I have not s;
158:3 By prophets s of old,
159:3 By prophets s of old,
171:1 S in glory of
413:1 S in glory of
188:1 No eye hath s,
197:2 fruitage now are s,
198:2 fruitage now are s,
275:2 have s His might,
340:2 s by human mind,
384:1 s with men to dwell,

sees
15:2 forever s His child

seize
273:2 S the crown of

self
20:1 perfect s, that knows
416:1 perfect s, that knows
20:1 s that is the only
416:1 s that is the only
20:2 perfect s is one with
416:2 perfect s is one with
20:3 to God above, To s,
416:3 to God above, To s,
73:2 Losing s, in Him we

self
104:4 O'er sense and s;
109:1 from s and sin,
110:1 from s and sin,
171:2 And from s have won
413:2 And from s have won
183:3 ease and s away;
184:3 ease and s away;

self-entwined
360:2 S its strength sinks

self-forged
297:4 s chains that fall

selfhood
66:3 That higher s which
421:3 That higher s which
356:1 perfect s In Thy

selfish
69:2 quell all s pride,
423:2 quell all s pride,
242:2 dreams And s ease

self-love
243:3 S and harshness
244:3 S and harshness

self-righteousness
304:2 Make s be still,
305:2 Make s be still,
306:2 Make s be still,
307:2 Make s be still,
308:2 Make s be still,
309:2 Make s be still,

self-surrender
109:2 through joyful s
110:2 through joyful s

send
72:1 S Thy blessings
405:1 S Thy blessings
113:2 S Thou forth Thy
119:2 or God can s.
3 S us Thine
158:3 s back the song
159:3 s back the song
172:3 S out its light
206:2 S forth Thy light
428:2 S forth Thy light
214:3 s its angel to our

sendest
192:3 All that Thou s
193:3 All that Thou s
204:1 s Thy witnesses,

sending
73:2 holy thought is s;

sends
9:3 s them to your side,
234:4 s a shining ray
235:4 s a shining ray
269:2 s up a prayer
270:2 s up a prayer

sense
4:1 every thought from s
49:3 Let s be dumb,
50:3 Let s be dumb,
51:2 clouds of s roll back,
52:2 clouds of s roll back,
64:1 From s to Soul my
85:2 Clouds of s are
104:4 O'er s and self;
144:1 s that would deceive.
145:1 s that would deceive.
144:2 mortal s we must
145:2 mortal s we must
144:2 s is lost in sight.
145:2 s is lost in sight.
160:3 darkling s, arise,
161:3 darkling s, arise,
162:3 darkling s, arise,
194:1 No mortal s can
410:1 No mortal s can
218:4 s of Life that
219:4 s of Life that
220:4 s of Life that
237:1 Far from s and
293:2 mortal s I flee,
294:2 mortal s I flee,
295:2 mortal s I flee,
374:3 turn from s to Soul,
375:3 turn from s to Soul,
383:1 dims thy s of truth

senses
298:3 the foul s within;
299:3 the foul s within;
300:3 the foul s within;
301:3 the foul s within;
302:3 the foul s within;

senses'
104:1 the s angry shock,

sent
101:1-3 He s His Word,
115:1 doubted, s us light;
116:1 doubted, s us light;
138:1 blessings s To break
175:1 Lo, He s His Word
180:2 Good from God is s
188:2 s His Word to all

sentinels
17:1 ye s of Truth,

128

separation
135:2 no s· Between my Lord

serene
37:3 towers, s· and bright,
38:3 towers, s· and bright,
104:2 The hope s· that
134:2 Thy calmness bends s·
146:1 still, s· and pure:
147:1 still, s· and pure:
228:1 divine, that dwells s·,

serenely
258:2 s· down the future

servant
41:1 each s· does the Master
347:4 Thou s· of the Lord.
348:4 Thou s· of the Lord.
398:3 O, happy s· he,

servants
168:2 Ye s· who once
296:1 S· of a mighty cause,
349:3 loving s· of Thy will.
398:1 Ye s· of the Lord,

serve
136:1 s· Thee is my choice,
261:3 To s· the world
262:3 To s· the world
303:4 all that s· the right,
396:2 Master whom you s·
397:2 Master whom you s·

service
41:3 but may do s· here;
49:1 purer lives Thy s·
50:1 purer lives Thy s·
113:3 To Thy s· true.
190:2 My joy in s·
191:2 My joy in s·
230:4 What may thy s· be?
231:4 What may thy s· be?
234:1 lowly paths of s·
235:1 lowly paths of s·
322:1 in God's healing s·
323:1 in God's healing s·
398:3 In watchful s· found;

serving
360:2 s·, love will grow.

set
62:2 suns shall rise and s·
63:2 suns shall rise and s·
69:1 bondage be s· free.
423:1 bondage be s· free.
75:1 s· the captive free,
82:3 s· their captives free,
40:1 Be s· to hallow

set
183:2 S· these before thine
184:2 S· these before thine
265:1 s· a guardian legion
370:2 s· our whole affection

sets
81:2 heals, and s· me free.
327:2 s· the captive free.
328:2 s· the captive free.
337:3 bondage s· them free.
338:3 bondage s· them free.

setteth
339:2 s· free from thought

seven
74:2 s· thunders roll?

sever
379:4 our hearts might s·
380:4 our hearts might s·

shade
23:3 Was but thy s·!
24:3 Was but thy s·!
25:3 Was but thy s·!
26:3 Was but thy s·!
27:3 Was but thy s·!
28:3 Was but thy s·!
33:1 th' Almighty's s·;
71:2 and s· by day,
99:1 th' Almighty's s·
100:1 th' Almighty's s·
179:2 neither s· of sadness;
203:2 wander through earth's s·,
263:1 s· of want and sorrow
298:2 lift the s· of gloom,
299:2 lift the s· of gloom,
300:2 lift the s· of gloom,
301:2 lift the s· of gloom,
302:2 lift the s· of gloom,
339:1 leads from the s·,
385:3 In s· and storm

shades
34:4 s· of coming night;
35:1 o'er the s· of night;
240:1 gloomy s· of night,
241:1 gloomy s· of night,

shadow
29:1 each somber s·,
64:1 From mist and s· into
207:4 s· of His mighty wing;
208:4 s· of His mighty wing;
209:4 s· of His mighty wing;
210:4 s· of His mighty wing;
211:4 s· of His mighty wing;
212:4 s· of His mighty wing;
258:3 God within the s·
263:2 dawn the s· cleareth,

shadows
20:2 dispels the s· dim.
416:2 dispels the s· dim.
44:1 From s· come away;
149:2 above the s· dim,
426:2 above the s· dim,
196:2 s· of the morning
204:2 amid s· of fear,
245:1 dark and heavy s·
317:1 and the s· flee,
  2 amid the changing s·,
  3 see the s· flee,
359:1 when the s· gather,
379:3 Walketh not in s·
380:3 Walketh not in s·

shake
71:1 s· thy sure repose?

shallow
138:1 s· cistern spent,

shame
325:2 nor heed the s·;

shape
236:2 s· tillers of soil,

shapes
17:1 scowling s· of darkness

share
41:2 that we all may s·;
58:3 s· Thy happiness,
  3 S· Thy joy and
70:3 all His glory s·.
182:3 For we must s·, if
322:1 s· The truths revealed
323:1 s· The truths revealed

shared
142:1 Forever s·, forever
176:2 in humility s· it.

Sharon's
331:2 or S· fields.

Sheba's
331:2 Than S· groves or

shed
45:2 s· abroad o'er all
81:1 glory round me s·.
119:1 s· Thy light.
351:2 O'er His . . . people s·,

sheds
319:1 S· on our path
346:1 S· not its glorious
401:1 S· not its glorious

sheep
297:3 s must pass beneath
304:1 How to feed Thy s;
305:1 How to feed Thy s;
306:1 How to feed Thy s;
307:1 How to feed Thy s;
308:1 How to feed Thy s;
309:1 How to feed Thy s;

Shekinah
297:2 Calm of S where hope

shelter
213:1 s from the stormy

sheltered
216:1 Is s by His

sheltering
30:1 with Thy s wing,
31:1 with Thy s wing,
32:1 with Thy s wing,
69:2 'neath Thy s presence
423:2 'neath Thy s presence
322:3 at His s throne.
323:3 at His s throne.

Shepherd
148:2 My S is beside
196:1 One S and one fold.
245:1 tender, loving S,
    2 We know, beloved S,
    2 call us, faithful S,
    3 S, Thy strong hand
    3 we find, O S,
304:1 S, show me how to
305:1 S, show me how to
306:1 S, show me how to
307:1 S, show me how to
308:1 S, show me how to
309:1 S, show me how to
304:3 S, wash them clean.
305:3 S, wash them clean.
306:3 S, wash them clean.
307:3 S, wash them clean.
308:3 S, wash them clean.
309:3 S, wash them clean.
330:1 King of Love my S
    4 Good S, may I

shepherds
11:1 S in the eastern

shepherds'
229:2 waiting s way,

shield
10:1 our s and tower,
411:1 our s and tower,
90:2 my strength and s.

shield
99:1 fortress, s and stay,
100:1 fortress, s and stay,
108:3 still my s and sun.
125:3 both sun and s,
292:1 s of true faith,
326:2 faith's broad s
350:1 stretched forth to s

shine
12:3 shall s That light
13:3 shall s That light
14:1, 4 arise and s,
15:3 man's perfection s,
19:2 shall forever s;
82:3 Gospel of truth May s
91:2 let Thy light s
422:2 let Thy light s
97:1 cheering sun will s;
98:1 cheering sun will s;
109:2 pure likeness s.
110:2 pure likeness s.
118:1 S upon this heart
142:3 S out, O light
160:1 For storm or s,
161:1 For storm or s,
162:1 For storm or s,
172:1 man, arise and s,
173:3 ever s more bright;
226:2 S forth, O Light,
    2 S forth, and let
    2 S forth, and touch
229:2 s on us with light
251:2 O'er . . . lands to s.
252:2 O'er . . . lands to s.
320:4 growing brightness s.
321:4 growing brightness s.
409:4 growing brightness s.
334:3 s With beams of
336:1 s not to Thy praise,
    3 s in cloudless day,
345:2 s from heart to heart.
352:1 meekness used to s,
353:1 meekness used to s,
363:1 beams of ages s;
386:2 works and virtues s,
387:2 works and virtues s,

shines
2:1 s the blessed light;
    3 s the blessed token
11:2 S before us in
17:1 morning star s clear.
111:1 in full glory s;
172:3 s to the perfect day.
176:3 the Word s forth,
205:2 faith that s more
229:1 whose constant beam S

shines
251:1 S on from age to
252:1 S on from age to
260:2 S forth the thought
292:2 His majesty s in
311:1 constant s its light,
420:1 constant s its light,
385:2 s the prosperous day,

shineth
79:3 His glory s;
222:1 in thy dark streets s
223:1 in thy dark streets s
226:1 s more and more

shining
35:3 S to the perfect
65:2 Is s from above,
101:2 s Word Of Truth,
102:3 star of Bethlehem s,
103:3 star of Bethlehem s,
146:4 s threads of ceaseless
147:4 s threads of ceaseless
176:1 S that all may
234:4 sends a s ray
235:4 sends a s ray
313:1 season of clear s,
339:1 s path leads from
342:3 s robes of joy
385:3 and a s light.
415:2 glory is ever s;

shock
37:4 surge's angry s,
38:4 surge's angry s,
104:1 senses' angry s,
253:5 winds and waves can s,
254:5 winds and waves can s,
255:5 winds and waves can s,
256:5 winds and waves can s,
257:5 winds and waves can s,

shod
92:3 feet are s for God
233:1 with the gospel s;
419:1 with the gospel s;
326:1 with the gospel s:

shone
14:2 on thee hath s,
367:3 on thee hath s
381:1 s in Mary's wondering

shore
62:2 sound from s to s,
63:2 sound from s to s,
196:1 many a distant s,
226:1 spreads from s to s,
238:4 time and holier s:
239:4 time and holier s:

shore
253:5 rock, Upon Life's s·,
254:5 rock, Upon Life's s·,
255:5 rock, Upon Life's s·,
256:5 rock, Upon Life's s·,
257:5 rock, Upon Life's s·,
271:1 stretch from s· to s·,
272:1 stretch from s· to s·,
304:2 on a barren s·,
305:2 on a barren s·,
306:2 on a barren s·,
307:2 on a barren s·,
308:2 on a barren s·,
309:2 on a barren s·,
351:3 the far eternal s·

shores
261:2 on farthest s·,
262:2 on farthest s·,
418:1 If thy s· are drawing

short
213:3 S· as the watch

shoulder
330:3 on His s· gently

shout
200:3 s·, for the foe is

shouts
310:1 and s· of praise.

show
12:2 S· forth the Truth
13:2 S· forth the Truth
14:4 living light s· forth
19:2 s· an ever clearer
51:2 roll back, and s·
52:2 roll back, and s·
66:4 S· the new heaven and
421:4 S· the new heaven and
109:2 consecration S· Thee
110:2 consecration S· Thee
114:2 s· a Saviour's love;
   3 s·, by living faith,
126:2 s· a brother's love.
127:2 s· a brother's love.
403:2 s· a brother's love.
142:3 s· How wide and far
186:2 All eternity can s·,
187:2 All eternity can s·,
253:3 s· Life's burdens light.
254:3 s· Life's burdens light.
255:3 s· Life's burdens light.
256:3 s· Life's burdens light.
257:3 s· Life's burdens light.
304:1 Shepherd, s· me how to
305:1 Shepherd, s· me how to
306:1 Shepherd, s· me how to

show
307:1 Shepherd, s· me how to
308:1 Shepherd, s· me how to
309:1 Shepherd, s· me how to
342:1 s· The amplitude of
376:2 loving care wilt s·.
377:2 loving care wilt s·.

shower
130:2 doth every blessing s·;

showers
75:2 s· Upon the thirsty
97:1 S· of rain will fall
98:1 S· of rain will fall
119:2 quickening s· descend;

showeth
178:2 S· forth the perfect

showing
71:2 S· that the Lord is
179:3 S· true brotherhood,
263:2 calm and comfort s·,

shown
15:1 Its purity s· forth,
65:3 wonders He hath s·
185:2 vision thou hast s·;
   3 S· on the mountain
226:1 have s· Thy gift
233:1 are so clearly s·
419:1 are so clearly s·
273:3 by holy actions s·;
274:3 by holy actions s·;
329:1 His handiwork is s·.
342:2 His love is s·.
356:1 Thou hast s· to us

shows
15:2 as a mirror s· us
221:3 S· forth Love's sweet
258:1 S· to each the bloom

shrine
3:3 s· so pure and white,
233:3 every sacred s·
419:3 every sacred s·
259:1 laid on mercy's s·,
267:4 seek no earthly s·
268:4 seek no earthly s·

shrink
205:1 faith that will not s·,
390:1 thy heart s· back

shrinking
2:2 hear in s· terror,

shrinks
143:1 Imposture s· from light,

shuts
168:3 key that s· and opens

sick
34:1 The s· are healed,
346:2 Health to the s·
401:2 Health to the s·
388:1 The s· were healed,

sickles
242:3 Thrust in our s·

sickness
298:3 sorrow and s· and
299:3 sorrow and s· and
300:3 sorrow and s· and
301:3 sorrow and s· and
302:3 sorrow and s· and
341:2 s·, in our health,

side
9:3 sends them to your s·,
74:1 Truth is at thy s·;
86:3 And dares to s· with
87:3 And dares to s· with
115:2 us ever at Thy s·.
116:2 us ever at Thy s·.
195:2 God, on every s·,
214:3 its angel to our s·,
258:1 good or evil s·.
   2 s· of perfect justice
296:Ref. O s· with God,

sigh
238:4 heart shall s· no more
239:4 heart shall s· no more

sighing
415:3 sorrow, nor any s·,
425:2 Sorrow and s· flee

sight
115:1 paths were in Thy s·.
116:1 paths were in Thy s·.
126:1 heavenly is the s·,
127:1 heavenly is the s·,
403:1 heavenly is the s·,
130:1 all things in Thy s·,
144:2 sense is lost in s·.
145:2 sense is lost in s·.
148:2 His s· is never dim;
166:4 Faith to s· and
167:4 Faith to s· and
170:2 inward s· is clear,
173:3 will vanish into s·;
186:1 ages in Thy s·
187:1 ages in Thy s·
213:3 ages in Thy s·
230:1 our faith and s·

sight
231:1 our faith and s
238:1 gleams upon our s,
239:1 gleams upon our s,
327:3 blind receive their s,
328:3 blind receive their s,
334:1 brings the truth to s;
346:2 Healing and s,
401:2 Healing and s,
346:2 S to the inly blind;
401:2 S to the inly blind;
355:1 freedom's star in s,
382:3 Truth dawns on the s;
418:3 for s or sound

sign
12:2 with following s
13:2 with following s
109:2 in healing's s,
110:2 in healing's s,
121:3 s of heavenly power
122:3 s of heavenly power
170:2 your Christmas s,
318:1 ye who see this s
372:4 our name or s,
373:2 our name or s,

signal
398:2 The s cometh

signals
218:2 eye to eye the s
219:2 eye to eye the s
220:2 eye to eye the s

signs
368:1 its s of promise
369:1 its s of promise
391:4 s that prove Unreal

silence
94:2 spake In s to thy
180:1 s thoughts of wrong
261:2 s or with psalm.
262:2 s or with psalm.
418:4 feel the s come;

silenced
347:4 s by His word;
348:4 s by His word;

silent
36:3 the s loveliness
54:3 answer s prayer.
94:2 to thy s heart,
146:4 s, healing prayer,
147:4 s, healing prayer,
183:2 The s toil that is
184:2 The s toil that is
194:1 flight of s prayer,

silent
410:1 flight of s prayer,
216:2 Be s in humility;
222:1 The s stars go by;
223:1 The s stars go by;
283:1 we be s? Ah, never.

silently
222:3 How s, how s,
223:3 How s, how s,
303:2 dwell Within it s.

simple
49:2 In s trust like
50:2 In s trust like
230:3 s trust can find
231:3 s trust can find
291:1 s, free from art;
340:3 love were but more s,

simplest
41:3 By means the s
284:2 s form of speech
285:2 s form of speech
286:2 s form of speech

simply
230:4 But s following thee.
231:4 But s following thee.

sin
5:2 Depart from s, awake
7:2 S hath no power
14:3 No more shall s
19:1 free from s or any
20:1 that knows no s,
416:1 that knows no s,
29:1 S it kills and
35:3 gloom of s and grief;
82:3 with sorrow and s,
86:4 falter would be s.
87:4 falter would be s.
108:2 calm of s forgiven.
109:1 from self and s,
110:1 from self and s,
112:1 Free from s, our
134:1 mightier far Than s
163:2 s shall die away.
164:2 No more let s and
165:2 No more let s and
417:2 No more let s and
166:1 s and fear and care;
167:1 s and fear and care;
172:3 world's s and sorrow
190:4 death, pain and s,
191:4 death, pain and s,
206:1 our hearts from s,
428:1 our hearts from s,
221:1 cast out s and pain.

sin
222:3 this world of s,
223:3 this world of s,
229:2 death and s,
263:2 the night of s.
276:1 of conquered s;
277:1 of conquered s;
282:2 S and death shall
290:3 conquers s and death;
296:Ref. conquer death and s;
298:3 and sickness and s."
299:3 and sickness and s."
300:3 and sickness and s."
301:3 and sickness and s."
302:3 and sickness and s."
303:3 love bid s depart
318:2 peace of s forgiven,
325:2 He conquered s,
326:4 S, death and hell
339:2 from thought of s,
342:3 For s destroyed,
343:1 From s and death
344:1 From s and death
429:1 From s and death
370:1 s can never Overthrow
381:4 They rise from s
383:1 count it s to thee.
386:3 the claim of s.
387:3 the claim of s.

since
135:2 S, whatsoe'er it be,
169:3 have loved long s,
207:3 s God is good,
208:3 s God is good,
209:3 s God is good,
210:3 s God is good,
211:3 s God is good,
212:3 s God is good,
238:1 s time began,
239:1 s time began,

sincere
70:2 ask with prayer s;
284:1 heart's s desire,
285:1 heart's s desire,
286:1 heart's s desire,
331:2 contrite mind, S and

sincerity
88:2 Follow Christ's s.
89:2 Follow Christ's s.
151:2 Sweet with s.
152:2 Sweet with s.

sinful
69:1 thus from s bondage
423:1 thus from s bondage
117:2 eyes of s men

sing
14:2 *S·* praise, O waking
16:1 let me *s·* my way
   3 *s·* my way to-day,
30:1 that soar and *s·*,
31:1 that soar and *s·*,
32:1 that soar and *s·*,
36:4 Unfaltering songs we *s·*,
66:2 live and *s·* alway
421:2 live and *s·* alway
73:1 *s·* to Him, ye joyous
112:2 *S·*, till all the
   2 *S·*! for fear no more
   3 *S·* the Word, whose
153:1 *S·* all in glad
158:1, 2 hear the angels *s·*.
159:1, 2 hear the angels *s·*.
158:3 now the angels *s·*.
159:3 now the angels *s·*.
164:1 heaven and nature *s·*.
165:1 heaven and nature *s·*.
417:1 heaven and nature *s·*.
171:1 *s·* of Easter gladness
413:1 *s·* of Easter gladness
171:1 *S·* of hope and faith
413:1 *S·* of hope and faith
202:1 captive, rise and *s·*,
412:1 captive, rise and *s·*,
207:4 with the angels *s·*:
208:4 with the angels *s·*:
209:4 with the angels *s·*:
210:4 with the angels *s·*:
211:4 with the angels *s·*:
212:4 with the angels *s·*:
222:2 praises *s·* to God
223:2 praises *s·* to God
264:4 Men and angels *s·*.
280:1 His praise should *s·*?
283:1 Come let us *s·*,
310:1, Ref. *S·*, ye joyous . . . , *s·*,
311:3 praises let us *s·*
420:3 praises let us *s·*
324:2 and let me *s·* Always,
330:4 I *s·* Thy praise
350:3 Faith can *s·* through
378:1 *s·* in sweet accord;
384:3 the dumb shall *s·*,
414:3 *s·* the new, new song

singeth
57:3 faith *s·* still her

singing
64:1 My heart is *s·*:
202:4 dumb to joyful *s·*;
412:2 dumb to joyful *s·*;
351:1 *S·* songs of expectation,
356:3 *S·* to Thee our deeply

sings
16:1 *s·* the mountain stream,
190:4 Faith *s·* in triumph,
191:4 Faith *s·* in triumph,
313:1 Christian while he *s·*;
392:2 heart . . . burns and *s·*,
393:2 heart . . . burns and *s·*,

sinks
360:2 strength *s·* low;

sinless
175:2 *S·*, fearless, whole,
382:2 pure and *s·* heart;

sinner
34:1 healed, the *s·* blest,
298:3 *S·*, it calls you,—
299:3 *S·*, it calls you,—
300:3 *S·*, it calls you,—
301:3 *S·*, it calls you,—
302:3 *S·*, it calls you,—

sinning
243:2 the *s·* and the sad.
244:2 the *s·* and the sad.

sin's
359:2 *s·* illusive wreaths

sins
140:3 old *s·* forgiven,

sisters
29:2 *s·* and our brothers

skies
35:1 glory fills the *s·*,
57:2 *s·* seem dark before
62:1 dwell below the *s·*
63:1 dwell below the *s·*
148:3 Bright *s·* will soon
275:1 Joy of the sun and *s·*,

sky
1:1 glory fills the *s·*,
11:1 in the eastern *s·*
36:3 fills the morning *s·*.
45:1 earth and sea and *s·*.
72:1 glory fills the *s·*;
405:1 glory fills the *s·*;
117:3 earth, and *s·* and sea;
192:5 Cleaving the *s·*,
193:5 Cleaving the *s·*,
242:2 forth beneath His *s·*.
251:1 earth's dark *s·*,
252:1 earth's dark *s·*,
336:1 glories of the *s·*,
337:1 that sweep the *s·*;
338:1 that sweep the *s·*;

slake
418:4 their thirst will *s·*,

slavery
83:3 all our *s·* cease,

sleep
6:2 not in *s·* to fold
33:2 desert wilds thou *s·*.
183:3 no time for thee to *s·*;
184:3 no time for thee to *s·*;
222:1 deep and dreamless *s·*
223:1 deep and dreamless *s·*
283:2 E'en while we *s·*

sleeping
97:1 Never tiring, never *s·*,
98:1 Never tiring, never *s·*,

sleeps
237:2 Life that never *s·*.
267:2 Love that never *s·*.
268:2 Love that never *s·*.

sliding
283:2 still holdeth from *s·*;

slightest
303:1 *s·* word or deed,

sloth
183:1 to lose in *s·*,
184:1 to lose in *s·*,
296:1 Put *s·* and slumber

slow
158:2 painful steps and *s·*;
159:2 painful steps and *s·*;
234:2 *s·* of heart to move
235:2 *s·* of heart to move
280:3 *S·* to chide, and
385:3 long-suffering, *s·* to

slumber
296:1 Put sloth and *s·*

slumbers
189:1 God who never *s·*,

small
49:3 still *s·* voice of calm.
50:3 still *s·* voice of calm.
54:2 the still *s·* voice
74:1, 2 that still *s·* voice
170:2 *s·* must be the choice
303:4 Nor care how *s·*
390:1 thy faith . . . so *s·*?

smart
69:3 each wound and *s·*
423:3 each wound and *s·*

smile
56:2 when Thy $s\cdot$ we see,
71:1 $s\cdot$ at all thy foes.
169:3 angel faces $s\cdot$,
217:2 Each $s\cdot$ a hymn,
357:1 $s\cdot$ is on the world
358:1 $s\cdot$ is on the world
407:1 $s\cdot$ is on the world
357:3 $s\cdot$ of God they feel;
358:3 $s\cdot$ of God they feel;
407:3 $s\cdot$ of God they feel;

smiles
166:2 Father's $s\cdot$ are thine;
167:2 Father's $s\cdot$ are thine;

smite
55:3 would $s\cdot$ the living

smoke
385:1 in $s\cdot$ and flame.

snare
33:3 dread no hidden $s\cdot$;
99:2 from the fowler's $s\cdot$,
100:2 from the fowler's $s\cdot$.
195:2 escaping every $s\cdot$.
207:2 $s\cdot$, the pit, the fall:
208:2 $s\cdot$, the pit, the fall:
209:2 $s\cdot$, the pit, the fall:
210:2 $s\cdot$, the pit, the fall:
211:2 $s\cdot$, the pit, the fall:
212:2 $s\cdot$, the pit, the fall:
207:5 No $s\cdot$, no fowler,
208:5 No $s\cdot$, no fowler,
209:5 No $s\cdot$, no fowler,
210:5 No $s\cdot$, no fowler,
211:5 No $s\cdot$, no fowler,
212:5 No $s\cdot$, no fowler,

snares
389:1 wiles and the $s\cdot$

soar
30:1 that $s\cdot$ and sing,
31:1 that $s\cdot$ and sing,
32:1 that $s\cdot$ and sing,
136:3 $s\cdot$ o'er time and space;
149:2 we $s\cdot$ and worship,
426:2 we $s\cdot$ and worship,
363:2 does knowledge $s\cdot$;

soaring
112:1 let song be $s\cdot$,

soars
64:3 Thought $s\cdot$ enraptured,
190:4 $s\cdot$ beyond death, pain
191:4 $s\cdot$ beyond death, pain
232:3 song That $s\cdot$ above
406:3 song That $s\cdot$ above
363:2 $s\cdot$, the Gospel light

sod
14:4 Uplift . . . from the $s\cdot$,
141:4 hope above the $s\cdot$,

soever
383:3 How dark $s\cdot$ it may

soft
29:1 radiance $s\cdot$ and clear;

softened
319:1 thy $s\cdot$ light Cheers

softening
140:2 $s\cdot$ gleam of love

soil
236:2 shape tillers of $s\cdot$,

sojourned
388:1 lowly Jesus $s\cdot$ here,

solace
174:2 Love is true $s\cdot$ and

soldiers
264:1, Ref. Onward, Christian $s\cdot$,
296:1 $s\cdot$ of the cross,
312:1 $S\cdot$ of Christ, arise,

sole
361:1 He is thy $s\cdot$ defense;

solemn
158:1 in $s\cdot$ stillness lay
159:1 in $s\cdot$ stillness lay
317:2 $S\cdot$ the hush of nature,

solitude
134:2 Thy presence fills my $s\cdot$;

somber
29:1 each $s\cdot$ shadow,

some
140:2 $S\cdot$ softening gleam
234:2 $s\cdot$ clear winning word
235:2 $s\cdot$ clear winning word
253:7 $s\cdot$ daily good to do
254:7 $s\cdot$ daily good to do
255:7 $s\cdot$ daily good to do
256:7 $s\cdot$ daily good to do
257:7 $s\cdot$ daily good to do
414:2 $s\cdot$ have never heard

something
166:1 $S\cdot$ still to do,
167:1 $S\cdot$ still to do,

sometimes
95:2 $S\cdot$ mid scenes of
2 $S\cdot$ where Eden's bowers

sometimes
238:1 $s\cdot$ gleams upon our
239:1 $s\cdot$ gleams upon our
313:1 $S\cdot$ a light surprises

Son
14:3 given thee His $S\cdot$,
104:4 revealed the $S\cdot$;
221:2 God's own $S\cdot$ beloved,
297:1 Father and perfect $S\cdot$,
312:1 His eternal $S\cdot$.
352:1 O $S\cdot$ of God.
353:1 O $S\cdot$ of God.
352:4 footsteps, $S\cdot$ of God.
353:4 footsteps, $S\cdot$ of God.
356:1 Thy loved $S\cdot$,
362:1 To us a $S\cdot$ is given;
368:3 $S\cdot$ of God is come.
369:3 $S\cdot$ of God is come.

son
20:2 as God's own $s\cdot$,
416:2 as God's own $s\cdot$,
382:1 For His beloved $s\cdot$?

song
9:1 $s\cdot$ that ne'er shall cease,
10:3 our hope, our $s\cdot$;
411:3 our hope, our $s\cdot$;
23:2 No cradle $s\cdot$, No natal
24:2 No cradle $s\cdot$, No natal
25:2 No cradle $s\cdot$, No natal
26:2 No cradle $s\cdot$, No natal
27:2 No cradle $s\cdot$, No natal
28:2 No cradle $s\cdot$, No natal
37:2 one harvest $s\cdot$,
38:2 one harvest $s\cdot$,
45:3 hearts in grateful $s\cdot$
57:3 singeth still her $s\cdot$;
65:1 this our joyous $s\cdot$;
72:2 people, raise the $s\cdot$,
405:2 people, raise the $s\cdot$,
73:1 before Him with a $s\cdot$.
112:1 let $s\cdot$ be soaring,
117:1 $s\cdot$ shall rise to Thee.
124:3 bear a $s\cdot$ away.
402:3 bear a $s\cdot$ away.
158:1 glorious $s\cdot$ of old,
159:1 glorious $s\cdot$ of old,
158:3 send back the $s\cdot$
159:3 send back the $s\cdot$
170:1 $s\cdot$ the angels sung,
190:1 with this triumph $s\cdot$,
191:1 with this triumph $s\cdot$,
192:1, 5 all my $s\cdot$ shall be,
193:1, 5 all my $s\cdot$ shall be,
195:3 my lips with $s\cdot$;
232:3 with this glad $s\cdot$
406:3 with this glad $s\cdot$

song
247:3 blend it with a s.
248:3 blend it with a s.
253:2 breathed in raptured s,
254:2 breathed in raptured s,
255:2 breathed in raptured s,
256:2 breathed in raptured s,
257:2 breathed in raptured s,
271:2 with sweetest s,
272:2 with sweetest s,
275:1 with joy and s.
310:1, 2 Hear th' angelic s
331:1 stranger to the s.
332:2 daily lives with s.
357:1 gladsome s begin,
358:1 gladsome s begin,
407:1 gladsome s begin,
378:3 is become our s,
414:3 the new, new s

songs
19:1 s of joy upon
36:4 Unfaltering s we
120:2 s instead of sadness,
168:1 earth with s rejoice;
271:4 angel s be heard
272:4 angel s be heard
283:3 S of thanksgiving
351:1 s of expectation,

sons
21:2 They only, are His s,
22:2 They only, are His s,
71:3 thy s and daughters,
101:2 s of men rejoice
261:3 all God's faithful s,
262:3 all God's faithful s,
266:1 His s His image bear,
271:3 s of want are blest.
272:3 s of want are blest.
290:1 on, ye s of light,
335:1 s of earth are waking

sonship
185:1 man's perfect s

soon
92:2 S as the word is
97:1 S shall see his toil
98:1 S shall see his toil
141:4 summon, s or late,
148:3 will s be o'er me,
418:4 S their notes will

sore
288:2 Though tasks are s,
289:2 Though tasks are s,

sorrow
9:4 From pain and s,
40:1, 3 no s but Love can
2 no s that Love cannot
57:1 turn away from s,
82:3 fight with s and sin,
101:2 dream of s done;
134:1 sin and pain and s
149:1 earth-born fear and s
426:1 earth-born fear and s
150:2 when s is healed;
154:3 have no pain or s,
155:3 have no pain or s,
156:3 have no pain or s,
164:2 let sin and s
165:2 let sin and s
417:2 let sin and s
171:3 Freed . . . of pain, and s,
413:3 Freed . . . of pain, and s,
172:3 world's sin and s
174:2 giveth joy for s,—
200:1 the night of thy s
232:3 Midst seeming s,
406:3 Midst seeming s,
263:1 shade of want and s
3 prisoning pain and s
275:2 mourning and s end,
298:3 s and sickness and
299:3 s and sickness and
300:3 s and sickness and
301:3 s and sickness and
302:3 s and sickness and
342:3 for s healed,
350:3 through days of s,
351:1 night of doubt and s
389:2 refuge in s and danger;
415:3 s, nor any sighing,
425:2 S and sighing flee

sorrow's
339:2 healeth s blight,

sorrows
365:2 the s of thy case
366:2 the s of thy case

sought
180:3 from Love is s,
229:2 Long s without,
276:2 so long have s;
277:2 so long have s;
330:3 in love He s me,
333:3 hearts which s him

Soul
64:1 From sense to S my
66:4 Thou, S, inspiring—
421:4 Thou, S, inspiring—

Soul
83:2 God is Life and S.
180:3 In S, not flesh,
221:3 knows the reign of S.
237:1 and hid in S.
267:3 S and substance find,
268:3 S and substance find,
287:2 realm of S supreme,
408:2 realm of S supreme,
374:3 turn from sense to S,
375:3 turn from sense to S,

soul
35:3 this s of mine,
153:1 My s doth magnify
2 hast redeemed my s;
180:1 heart and s and mind.
195:3 fills my s with peace,
280:1 Praise, my s, the King
330:2 My ransomed s He
365:1 Wait, my s, upon
366:1 Wait, my s, upon

soul's
195:1 my s true rest;

souls
418:4 our s their thirst

sound
17:3 s the trumpet call,
62:2 Thy praise shall s
63:2 Thy praise shall s
128:1 flowed the gospel s
129:1 flowed the gospel s
298:1 Heard ye the glad s?
299:1 Heard ye the glad s?
300:1 Heard ye the glad s?
301:1 Heard ye the glad s?
302:1 Heard ye the glad s?
418:3 yearn for sight or s

sounding
418:2 S clearly through

sounds
44:1 s of weeping cease,
242:1 S forth the ancient

source
16:2 boundless s of might,
119:1 Spirit, s of gladness,
224:2 s doth find in Thee;
225:2 s doth find in Thee;
240:1 Spirit, s of light,
241:1 Spirit, s of light,
259:2 s of every outward
276:1 th' eternal s alone.
277:1 th' eternal s alone.

sovereign
396:1 His s voice obey;
397:1 His s voice obey;

sow
97:2 S thy seed, be
98:2 S thy seed, be
304:1 gather, how to s,—
305:1 gather, how to s,—
306:1 gather, how to s,—
307:1 gather, how to s,—
308:1 gather, how to s,—
309:1 gather, how to s,—
314:1 S in the morn thy

sower
42:1 s and the seed;

sower's
150:2 the S good seed.

sown
180:2 seeds of Love are s.

space
136:3 o'er time and s;
  3 time and s and
267:2 in s No subtle error
268:2 in s No subtle error

spake
94:2 voice Of God that s

spares
280:2 He tends and s us,

sparrows
318:3 like the s, praise

speak
19:2 they s His Word,
49:3 S through the
50:3 S through the
88:1 gracious spirit s.
89:1 gracious spirit s.
118:2 S to calm the tossing
131:3 s The truth that makes
132:3 s The truth that makes
204:3 s in Thy name,
315:1 S gently, it is better
316:1 S gently, it is better
315:1 S gently, let no
316:1 S gently, let no
315:2 S gently to the
316:2 S gently to the
315:3 S gently, 'tis a
316:3 S gently, 'tis a

speaketh
418:2 s, aye, one word,

speaking
177:1 mighty God, is s

speaks
30:5 S kindly when we
31:5 S kindly when we
32:5 S kindly when we
40:2 Here s the Comforter,
73:2 Lo, He s, all
175:1 healing message S
276:1 s the heavenly Giver;
277:1 s the heavenly Giver;

speech
12:2 works confirm your s,
13:2 works confirm your s,
194:2 That glory into s.
410:2 That glory into s.
284:2 simplest form of s
285:2 simplest form of s
286:2 simplest form of s

speechless
151:1, 2 In s prayer and
152:1, 2 In s prayer and

speed
346:3 S forth thy flight;
401:3 S forth thy flight;

speedy
75:1 comes, with succor s,

spend
58:3 and s it freely.

spent
138:1 shallow cistern s,

sphere
388:1 stranger on our s

spheres
336:3 amid dissolving s,

Spirit
39:1 gracious S, heavenly
42:1 all-transforming S,
58:1 In Thy S living,
88:1 Gracious S, dwell
89:1 Gracious S, dwell
88:2 Truthful S, dwell
89:2 Truthful S, dwell
88:3 Mighty S, dwell
89:3 Mighty S, dwell
104:4 our S, Mind divine,
118:1 Holy S, Light divine,
  2 Holy S, Peace divine,
  3 Holy S, all divine,
119:1 Holy S, source of
  3 S of unfailing
142:4 S overbrooding all,

Spirit
154:1 S true and tender,
155:1 S true and tender,
156:1 S true and tender,
171:2 turn from earth to S,
413:2 turn from earth to S,
180:3 S and the bride.
188:2 He whose S searcheth
  3 find, the S saith,
240:1 S, source of light,
241:1 S, source of light,
247:3 In S ye are strong;
248:3 In S ye are strong;
287:2 peaks of S stand
408:2 peaks of S stand
292:1 sword of the S
298:3 S that makes pure,
299:3 S that makes pure,
300:3 S that makes pure,
301:3 S that makes pure,
302:3 S that makes pure,
354:1 God the S leads
355:2 O S blest.

spirit
19:2 worship Him in s
30:2 his s you partake,
31:2 his s you partake,
32:2 his s you partake,
44:2 s of the dove.
88:1 Christ's own gracious s
89:1 Christ's own gracious s
118:3 Thy peace my s fill.
153:1 My s hath rejoicing,
166:2 what s dwells within
167:2 what s dwells within
217:1 heals the s broken,
236:2 man's s despoil,
334:1 The s breathes upon
346:3 S of truth and love,
401:3 S of truth and love,
367:1 His s only can
391:2 deathless as His s

Spirit's
326:1 The S sword is in
350:2 through the S guiding;

spirits
30:1 'Neath which our s blend
31:1 'Neath which our s blend
32:1 'Neath which our s blend

spite
169:2 and, s of fears,
396:3 s of all His foes.
397:3 s of all His foes.

splendor
154:1 light of glorious s·
155:1 light of glorious s·
156:1 light of glorious s·
172:2 s· of her . . . star.
178:1 s· of the light,
345:1 the s· pours.
392:4 forth in mighty s·.
393:1 forth in mighty s·.

splendors
65:1 rising s· glow,

spoke
128:2 of heaven he s·,
129:2 of heaven he s·,
388:2 He s· the word

spoken
  2:3 watchword has been s·,
 71:1 things of thee are s·,
 84:1 eternal Word is s·,
217:1 he . . . has truly s·,
282:1 for He hath s·,

spot
368:2 s· that gave them birth?
369:2 s· that gave them birth?

spotless
105:3 And s· here below.
106:3 And s· here below.
107:3 And s· here below.

spread
 81:1 wings of mercy s·;
 99:2 His wings shall s·
100:2 His wings shall s·,
326:2 shield before him s·.
362:3 increasing, still shall s·;
394:1 S·, till from its
395:1 S·, till from its

spreadest
246:1 s· the heaven like

spreads
226:1 s· from shore to shore,

spring
 75:2 S· in His path to
259:3 where these s· not
384:2 gladness s· on every

springing
  2:1 Are s· into birth.
 71:3 S· from eternal Love,

springs
104:2 that from it s·
111:3 S· from the presence

spurn
 69:1 To s· the wrong and
423:1 To s· the wrong and

staff
180:1 Love is s· and rod
195:3 joy, my s·, my rod;
260:4 pilgrim s· and rod,

stain
 19:1 from sin or any s·,
141:1 without a s·.

stainless
345:2 Thy s· radiance

stains
383:1 Or s· thy purity,

stalk
314:2 blade, the s·, the ear;

stanch
  3:2 s· and rugged tower,

stand
 12:1 people, take your s·,
 13:1 people, take your s·,
 19:1 s· in robes of white
    1 s· before the throne
 41:1 dares s· idle on the
 51:3 man does s· as God's
 52:3 man does s· as God's
 64:2 where I s· is holy
 74:1 s· upon the mount,
 75:3 His name shall s·
 77:1 in the fight I s·;
 78:1 in the fight I s·;
 80:3 Firm . . . bulwarks s·;
 92:4 Thy great work to s·.
123:2 cause thee to s·,
134:3 in Thy law, I s·:
141:1 S· foursquare,
281:1 still shall s·.
287:2 peaks of Spirit s·
408:2 peaks of Spirit s·
312:1 S· then in His
    2 s· complete at last.
326:1 s· In all the armor
331:3 on eternal pillars s·;
342:1 S· in His presence,

standeth
258:3 S· God within the

stands
 12:1 Christ's promise s·:
 13:1 Christ's promise s·:
 34:4 of our God still s·:

stands
 37:4 The heavenly city s·.
 38:4 The heavenly city s·.
111:2 firm Thy justice s·,
124:3 goodness s· approved,
402:3 goodness s· approved,
222:2 charity s· watching
223:2 charity s· watching
320:1 The Rock of Ages s·;
321:1 The Rock of Ages s·;
409:1 The Rock of Ages s·;

star
 11:1 pale s· passing by,
    2 S· of being, still thy
 17:1 The morning s· shines
102:3 the s· of Bethlehem
103:3 the s· of Bethlehem
172:2 of her deathless s·.
236:1 O Bethlehem s· that
319:1 Blest s· of hope,
355:1 freedom's s· in sight,
368:1 that glory-beaming s·;
369:1 that glory-beaming s·;
368:2 yet that s· ascends;
369:2 yet that s· ascends;

starry
336:1 The s· firmament on

stars
 19:2 Like s· they shall
 45:1 moon and s· hast Thou
192:5 moon, and s· forgot,
193:5 moon, and s· forgot,
222:1 silent s· go by;
223:1 silent s· go by;
222:2 morning s·, together
223:2 morning s·, together
236:3 s· in their courses
263:2 s· in order going,
282:1 all ye s· of light;
310:2 s· together sang,

start
322:2 in freshness s·
323:2 in freshness s·

startled
  2:3 Upon the s· earth.

station
166:1 find, in every s·,
167:1 find, in every s·,

stay
  8:2 guide and s· can be?
 10:3 s· and fortress strong,
411:3 s· and fortress strong,

stay
23:5 saint, Our s, alway.
24:5 saint, Our s, alway.
25:5 saint, Our s, alway.
26:5 saint, Our s, alway.
27:5 saint, Our s, alway.
28:5 saint, Our s, alway.
53:3 refuge, strength and s.
55:3 we idly quiet s,
92:3 nothing can him s;
99:1 fortress, shield and s,
100:1 fortress, shield and s,
136:2 power is still my s,
137:2 S Thou near-by;
173:2 will ever with us s;
194:1 can still or s
410:1 can still or s
234:2 wayward feet to s,
235:2 wayward feet to s,
335:2 Nor in thy richness s:
     S not till all

stayed
118:2 S in Thy tranquillity.

steadfast
14:1 Be thou a s ray.
36:3 How s is thine eye,
37:2 One s high intent,
38:2 One s high intent,
172:1 arise and shine, S
176:2 S their trust in God's
   2 S the Love that
278:2 s though trials betide
279:2 s though trials betide
327:1 never quit His s truth
328:1 never quit His s truth

steadfastly
146:2 gratitude doth s Abide
147:2 gratitude doth s Abide

steady
238:1 the s gain of man.
239:1 the s gain of man.

steeds
200:2 vain were their s

steep
55:2 s and rugged pathway
304:1 O'er the hillside s,
305:1 O'er the hillside s,
306:1 O'er the hillside s,
307:1 O'er the hillside s,
308:1 O'er the hillside s,
309:1 O'er the hillside s,

steeps
372:1 climb the heavenly s
373:1 climb the heavenly s

step
36:2 Thy s how calm and
39:1 every thought and s
169:1 one s enough for me.
218:4 freer s, the fuller
219:4 freer s, the fuller
220:4 freer s, the fuller
238:1 s by s, since time
239:1 s by s, since time
278:1 with courage each s
279:1 with courage each s
291:3 take a s alone,
320:4 with unwearied s,
321:4 with unwearied s,
409:4 with unwearied s,

stepping
351:1 S fearless through

steps
158:2 painful s and slow;
159:2 painful s and slow;
192:3 S unto heaven;
193:3 S unto heaven;
217:3 with reverent s
360:1 s drag wearily?
388:2 With bounding s

still (adj.)
49:3 s small voice of calm.
50:3 s small voice of calm.
49:4 s dews of quietness,
50:4 s dews of quietness,
54:2 the s small voice
55:3 forever by s waters
74:1, 2 that s small voice
76:2 gentle Peace, be s.
102:2 words: Peace, be s.
103:2 words: Peace, be s.
118:3 troubled thoughts be s;
138:2 and fears grow s;
146:1 s, serene and pure:
147:1 s, serene and pure:
222:1 s we see thee lie;
223:1 s we see thee lie;
237:1 be s and seek Him,
304:2 self-righteousness be s,
305:2 self-righteousness be s,
306:2 self-righteousness be s,
307:2 self-righteousness be s,
308:2 self-righteousness be s,
309:2 self-righteousness be s,
332:1 all the earth be s,
   1 Be s and know that

still (verb)
118:2 S this restless heart
134:2 My restlessness to s;
194:1 s or stay The flight
410:1 s or stay The flight
303:3 And s unholy strife.
360:2 ceaseless longings s.

still (adv.)
8:3 I triumph s, if
11:2 s thy light Shines
  .2 S the tidings angels
34:4 of our God s stands:
46:1 S by constant mercy
47:1 S by constant mercy
57:3 singeth s her song;
67:2 S they mark each
68:2 S they mark each
75:3 kingdom s increasing,
90:2 S Thou art my strength
95:1 S 'tis God's hand
  .2 S 'tis His hand
97:1 Bearing s the precious
98:1 Bearing s the precious
108:3 s my shield and sun.
115:1 S Thine arm has been
116:1 S Thine arm has been
115:2 S our strength in
116:2 S our strength in
123:2 s give thee aid;
136:1 s shall go with thee
  .2 power is s my stay,
  .2 s Thy presence is
140:1 New treasures s,
160:5 His likeness s—
161:5 His likeness s—
162:5 His likeness s—
166:1 s to do, or bear.
167:1 s to do, or bear.
168:2 S may our work
169:3 s Will lead me on
175:1 S that Word of God
  .1 S its tender healing
  .2 S Thy presence and
180:3 S from Love is sought,
185:3 S in thy light's
186:2 On, s on, through
187:2 On, s on, through
192:1, 5 S all my song shall
193:1, 5 S all my song shall
195:2 follow s my guide,
199:1 s is ours to-day.
216:2 and s shall be;
222:3 s The dear Christ
223:3 s The dear Christ
234:3 s with thee In closer,
235:3 s with thee In closer,
242:1 s in accents sweet

still (adv.)
246:1 S' for his might
247:3 ye s' shall hail,
248:3 ye s' shall hail,
251:2 s' thy light is
252:2 s' thy light is
258:2 upward s' and onward
260:4 s' the light upon
273:2 S' forget the things
274:2 S' forget the things
280:3 s' the same forever,
281:1 Firm and changeless s'
283:2 footsteps s' holdeth
290:1 S' . . . each temptation
    2 to higher glory s'.
    3 s' look in faith
317:1 S', s' with Thee
320:3 In strength shall s'
321:2 In strength shall s'
409:3 In strength shall s'
334:1 and promise s' afford
350:2 Happy s', in God
354:2 s' pursue our way;
362:3 His power, increasing, s'
363:3 More glorious s',
364:3 Vainer s' the hope
365:2 peculiar s' to thee,
366:2 peculiar s' to thee,
379:1 S' the one thing
380:1 S' the one thing
385:2 present s', though oft
394:2 reapers s' are few,
395:2 reapers s' are few,

stilled
34:3 storms of earth are s'.
93:4 with tumult s',
371:1 All strife is s',

stilleth
178:2 nations rancor s';

stillness
158:1 in solemn s' lay
159:1 in solemn s' lay

stills
19:2 s' all pain and strife.
174:3 s' all our demanding,
195:1 s' the tumult of my

sting
8:3 Where is death's s'?

stirred
242:3 our hearts hath s',

stock
105:2 Our little s' improve;
106:2 Our little s' improve;
107:2 Our little s' improve;

stone
171:1 rolled the s' away.
413:1 rolled the s' away.
192:2 My rest a s';
193:2 My rest a s';
197:3 hearts of s' before him
198:3 hearts of s' before him

stones
160:2 s', or tyrants' thrones,
161:2 s', or tyrants' thrones,
162:2 s', or tyrants' thrones,
176:3 Living s' we, each in

stony
192:4 Out of my s' griefs
193:4 Out of my s' griefs

stood
56:3 unchanged hath ever s';
96:1 He s' of old, the holy
176:1 Long hast thou s',
213:2 hills in order s',

stoop
229:1 S' unseen o'er the

stoops
385:3 s' on Judah's path

store
324:3 Thy feet its treasure s'.

stores
215:2 all their s' of gold.

storm
23:1 s' enshrouds Nor dawn
24:1 s' enshrouds Nor dawn
25:1 s' enshrouds Nor dawn
26:1 s' enshrouds Nor dawn
27:1 s' enshrouds Nor dawn
28:1 s' enshrouds Nor dawn
102:2 every s' of error
103:2 every s' of error
136:2 Though s' or discord
148:1 s' may roar without
160:1 For s' or shine,
161:1 For s' or shine,
162:1 For s' or shine,
297:2 till the s' be past;
347:2 bids the s' to cease;
348:2 bids the s' to cease;
385:3 In shade and s'

storms
34:3 all the s' of earth
44:1 s' no more have sway.
93:4 where no s' arise,
172:1 s' of life assail;

stormy
213:1 shelter from the s'

story
158:1 wondrous s' told
159:1 wondrous s' told
292:2 creation's wondrous s',
329:1 day repeats the s',
345:1 repeats its ancient s'
414:1-3, Ref. to tell the s',
    Ref. old, old s' Of Jesus
    3 is the old, old s'

straight
59:2 Run the s' race
60:2 Run the s' race
61:2 Run the s' race
288:1 s' and narrow way
289:1 s' and narrow way

strain
2:2 swell the mighty s'.
30:2 and heavenly s',
31:2 and heavenly s',
32:2 and heavenly s',
49:4 the s' and stress,
50:4 the s' and stress,
234:1 bear The s' of toil,
235:1 bear The s' of toil,
253:1 There sweeps a s',
254:1 There sweeps a s',
255:1 There sweeps a s',
256:1 There sweeps a s',
257:1 There sweeps a s',
284:2 prayer's sublimest s'
285:2 prayer's sublimest s'
286:2 prayer's sublimest s'
351:3 One, the s' the lips
418:1 s' our eyes to see

strains
281:1 S' of joy tune every

strait
341:3 heart, in every s',

strange
86:1 Most s' in all its
87:1 Most s' in all its

stranger
331:1 a s' to the song.
388:1 When like a s' on
389:2 land of the s';
415:1, Ref. and I'm a s';

strangers
304:2 S' on a barren shore,
305:2 S' on a barren shore,
306:2 S' on a barren shore,

strangers
307:2 S· on a barren shore,
308:2 S· on a barren shore,
309:2 S· on a barren shore,

stray
39:3 from thy precepts s·;
66:2 None can beyond ... s·;
421:2 None can beyond ... s·;
142:3 wide and far we s·.
304:1 Lest my footsteps s·;
305:1 Lest my footsteps s·;
306:1 Lest my footsteps s·;
307:1 Lest my footsteps s·;
308:1 Lest my footsteps s·;
309:1 Lest my footsteps s·;
311:2 darkness they did s·
420:2 darkness they did s·

strayed
330:3 foolish oft I s·,

straying
40:2 light of the s·,

stream
16:1 the mountain s·,
72:2 Goodness one eternal s·.
405:2 Goodness one eternal s·.
126:3 in one delightful s·,
127:3 in one delightful s·,
403:3 in one delightful s·,
259:3 s· has found its way;
3 s· has never wandered

streameth
79:2 His brightness s·;

streams
71:3 s· of living waters,
80:2 Whose s· make glad
120:1 Like s· from living
182:1 for the s· of Love,
1 Love has overflowing s·,
224:1 material s· are dried,
225:1 material s· are dried,
330:2 s· of living water
384:2 Celestial s· shall

streets
222:1 thy dark s· shineth
223:1 thy dark s· shineth

strength
6:3 present s· and patience
7:1 Thou art our s·,
10:3 Our s·, our hope,
411:3 Our s·, our hope,
29:2 Godlike in its s·

strength
46:2 Daily s· for daily
47:2 Daily s· for daily
53:3 refuge, s· and stay.
55:1 for s·, that we may
59:1 Christ is thy s·,
60:1 Christ is thy s·,
61:1 Christ is thy s·,
65:3 s· to s· we go,
82:3 in the s· of God
90:2 my s· and shield.
104:2 the s· to drink
115:2 Still our s· in Thee
116:2 Still our s· in Thee
119:3 Spirit of unfailing s·.
120:2 Lord, in s· victorious,
204:3 They go in Thy s·,
247:1 s· He will renew;
248:1 s· He will renew;
260:3 secret s· they owed,
4 my s· by day,
275:1 S· where the hills
293:1-3 Thy s· forever mine.
294:1-3 Thy s· forever mine.
295:1-3 Thy s· forever mine.
312:1 s· which God supplies
1 With all His s· endued,
2 From s· to s· go on;
314:2 verdure, beauty, s·,
320:3 s· shall still increase.
321:3 s· shall still increase.
409:3 s· shall still increase.
325:3 in God's own s·,
326:4 in his Redeemer's s·,
329:3 Redeemer, s·, and Lord.
354:1 s· is all His own.
359:3 come s· in weakness,
360:2 its s· sinks low;
364:3 on human s· relies;
365:1-3 As thy days thy s·
366:1-3 As thy days thy s·
389:2 s·, should I suffer;
394:3 s· to work for Thee,
395:3 s· to work for Thee,
396:2 needful s· bestow;
397:2 needful s· bestow;

strengthen
77:2 thy heart shall s·,
78:2 thy heart shall s·,
123:2 I'll s· thee, help
199:2 To s· us and cheer us;
227:3 s· faith and sweeten

stress
49:4 the strain and s·,
50:4 the strain and s·,

stretch
271:1 s· from shore to shore,
272:1 s· from shore to shore,

stretched
350:1 s· forth to shield

strife
19:2 stills all pain and s·.
23:4 above All mortal s·,
24:4 above All mortal s·,
25:4 above All mortal s·,
26:4 above All mortal s·,
27:4 above All mortal s·,
28:4 above All mortal s·,
30:5 Free us from human s·.
31:5 Free us from human s·.
32:5 Free us from human s·.
43:2 come to end all s·.
72:1 s· and tumult cease.
405:1 s· and tumult cease.
150:3 rises undaunted by s·,
258:1 the s· of Truth with
267:3 But never discord, s·.
268:3 But never discord, s·.
273:1 let us bear the s·,
274:1 let us bear the s·,
303:3 And still unholy s·.
371:1 All s· is stilled,
378:2 hearts redeemed from s·,

stripes
18:2 s· or a prison,

strive
396:3 vain shall evil s·,
397:3 vain shall evil s·,

striving
361:2 taking thought and s·

strivings
49:4 all our s· cease;
50:4 all our s· cease;

strong
10:3 stay and fortress s·,
411:3 stay and fortress s·,
37:2 one army s·,
38:2 one army s·,
57:3 dost make us s·.
75:1 bid the weak be s·;
77:1 God is my s· salvation;
78:1 God is my s· salvation;
90:2 S· Deliverer!
96:1 make the weakest s·.
99:2 shall be thy s· defense.
100:2 shall be thy s· defense.
150:2 s· with Thy goodness

strong
173:1 than death ... more s;
180:1 this command forever s,
181:4 Make us s to bear
190:1 Father, make me s,
191:1 Father, make me s,
195:3 in weakness I am s.
234:1 faith sweet and s,
235:3 faith sweet and s,
242:1 accents sweet and s
245:3 s hand doth uphold;
247:3 In Spirit ye are s;
248:3 In Spirit ye are s;
258:3 Truth alone is s;
291:3 Being neither s nor
293:2 Truth, our fortress s,
294:2 Truth, our fortress s,
295:2 Truth, our fortress s,
312:1 S in the strength
326:4 s in his Redeemer's
332:2 shall in Him be s;
350:1 S the hand stretched
378:3 Thy salvation s,
384:3 The weak be s,
394:1 most pure, most s,
395:1 most pure, most s,

stronger
224:2 I had a s faith,
225:2 I had a s faith,

strongest
298:4 S deliverer, friend
299:4 S deliverer, friend
300:4 S deliverer, friend
301:4 S deliverer, friend
302:4 S deliverer, friend

stronghold
203:2 Within Love's s

stubborn
304:2 bind the s will,
305:2 bind the s will,
306:2 bind the s will,
307:2 bind the s will,
308:2 bind the s will,
309:2 bind the s will,

stupid
304:2 Break earth's s rest.
305:2 Break earth's s rest.
306:2 Break earth's s rest.
307:2 Break earth's s rest.
308:2 Break earth's s rest.
309:2 Break earth's s rest.

subdued
200:2 arm that s them

subdues
386:3 s the claim of sin.
387:3 s the claim of sin.

sublime
29:2 in its strength s;
37:1 thy walls s;
38:1 thy walls s;
206:2 forth Thy light s,
428:2 forth Thy light s,
418:2 in undertone s,
  4 joy and peace s,

sublimest
284:2 prayer's s strain
285:2 prayer's s strain
286:2 prayer's s strain

substance
267:3 Soul and s find,
268:3 Soul and s find,

subtle
29:2 every s error,
267:2 No s error creeps;
268:2 No s error creeps;

succeed
97:1 see his toil s;
98:1 see his toil s;

succeeds
82:1 year s to year,

successive
271:1 s journeys run;
272:1 s journeys run;

succor
75:1 comes, with s speedy,
292:2 when for s we call;

such
34:2 companions s as these.
45:2 S tender beauty, Lord,
71:3 while s a river
148:1 safe is s confiding,
176:3 worthy s a grace,
182:2 S channels to provide,
  3 S is the law of Love.
205:3 s a faith as this,
227:2 S ever bring Thee
228:3 s as hate our Master's
269:2 In s desire sends
270:2 In s desire sends
334:3 s a bright display
342:2 for s gifts alone,
350:2 s a full salvation,

suffer
75:1 those who s wrong;
139:1 No more I s cruel
427:1 No more I s cruel
318:1 S the children to
389:2 strength, should I s;

suffering
96:1 Amid the s throng,

suffers
173:1 kind and s long,

sufficed
96:1 his lightest touch s

sufficient
123:3 My grace, all s,

summer
383:1 breath of s air,

summon
141:4 Truth will s, soon

sun
14:1 God is thy s,
35:1 S of righteousness,
97:1 cheering s will shine;
98:1 cheering s will shine;
108:3 still my shield and s.
125:3 both s and shield,
192:2 The s gone down,
193:2 The s gone down,
192:5 S, moon, and stars
193:5 S, moon, and stars
213:3 Before the rising s.
230:1 trace the noonday s.
231:1 trace the noonday s.
265:3 cheering, like the s,
271:1 s Does his successive
272:1 s Does his successive
275:1 Joy of the s and
282:1 S and moon, rejoice
319:1 S of our life,
334:2 Majestic like the s;

sunbeam
45:2 s, light and flower

sung
62:1 Redeemer's name be s
63:1 Redeemer's name be s
170:1 song the angels s,

sunless
345:1 the s prison doors;

suns
62:2 Till s shall rise
63:2 Till s shall rise

sunshine
8:2 Thro' cloud and s,
340:3 lives would be all s
349:2 the s of Thy love,

supernal
30:3 Whence joys s flow,
31:3 Whence joys s flow,
32:3 Whence joys s flow,
84:2 power of Love s,
112:3 Word, whose power s

supplies
312:1 strength which God s
327:3 All human need s.
328:3 All human need s.
336:2 Thy holy Word s,

supply
6:3 love whose sure s
42:1 s Thy people's need.
71:3 Well s thy sons and
123:3 shall be thy s;
342:2 And every need s;

supplying
350:3 is every need s,
381:2 Mind, all good s,

supported
354:2 S by His grace,

supports
320:2 S the fainting heart;
321:2 S the fainting heart;
409:2 S the fainting heart;

suppression
329:3 O, aid me in s

supreme
113:3 s and perfect One,
258:2 to God's s design.
287:2 realm of Soul s,
408:2 realm of Soul s,
296:3 For valor's act s;
320:1 S in wisdom as in
321:1 S in wisdom as in
409:1 S in wisdom as in
392:1 peace and joy s
393:1 peace and joy s

sure
6:3 love whose s supply
33:1 Lord thy s salvation,
36:2 step how calm and s.
41:4 the reward is s;
71:1 shake thy s repose?
153:2 S help to Israel

sure
169:3 s it still Will lead
263:3 we all a s release,
281:2 S retreat and refuge
293:3 Truth, foundation s,
294:3 Truth, foundation s,
295:3 Truth, foundation s,
365:3 Faithful, positive, and s:
366:3 Faithful, positive, and s:
399:3 unbelief is s to err,
400:3 unbelief is s to err,

surely
82:1, 2 that shall s be,
97:2 Harvest time is s
98:2 Harvest time is s
311:2 lead them safely, s
420:2 lead them safely, s

surge's
37:4 the s angry shock,
38:4 the s angry shock,

surprises
313:1 Sometimes a light s

surround
10:2 care doth e'er s us.
411:2 care doth e'er s us.

surrounded
71:1 salvation's walls s

sustain
104:3 courage may s our way

sway
44:1 storms no more have s.
372:4 We own thy s,
373:2 We own thy s,
376:1 weapon mortals s,
377:1 weapon mortals s,

sways
258:3 scaffold s the future,

sweep
66:4 s away the veil,
421:4 s away the veil,
337:1 clouds that s the sky;
338:1 clouds that s the sky;

sweeping
197:1 s down the years
198:1 s down the years

sweeps
253:1 There s a strain,
254:1 There s a strain,
255:1 There s a strain,
256:1 There s a strain,

sweeps
257:1 There s a strain,
335:1 that s the ocean
363:1 s the lingering mist

sweet
9:4 brings us s release;
30:5 life most s, as heart
31:5 life most s, as heart
32:5 life most s, as heart
41:4 s their rest shall be,
94:3 In low, s accents
102:2 the s words: Peace,
103:2 the s words: Peace,
108:4 Giving s foretaste of
109:1 tender s persuasions
110:1 tender s persuasions
125:1 beautiful the s accord
126:1 How s, how heavenly
127:1 How s, how heavenly
403:1 How s, how heavenly
126:3 union s, and dear
127:3 union s, and dear
403:3 union s, and dear
133:2 my heart s comfort
424:2 my heart s comfort
151:2 S with sincerity.
152:2 S with sincerity.
196:2 More s and lasting
197:1 s and fair the leaves
198:1 s and fair the leaves
207:4 s secret of the narrow
208:4 s secret of the narrow
209:4 s secret of the narrow
210:4 s secret of the narrow
211:4 s secret of the narrow
212:4 s secret of the narrow
221:3 Love's s control.
234:3 faith s and strong,
235:3 faith s and strong,
238:3 A low s prelude
239:3 A low s prelude
242:1 accents s and strong
243:1 s and tender as
244:1 s and tender as
243:3 Is s as breath of
244:3 Is s as breath of
253:1 Low, sad, and s,
254:1 Low, sad, and s,
255:1 Low, sad, and s,
256:1 Low, sad, and s,
257:1 Low, sad, and s,
253:3 unveiled, s mercies
254:3 unveiled, s mercies
255:3 unveiled, s mercies
256:3 unveiled, s mercies
257:3 unveiled, s mercies
297:2 S, secret place

sweet
317:1 the $s\cdot$ consciousness,
322:1 $S\cdot$ hour of holy,
323:1 $S\cdot$ hour of holy,
372:2 warm, $s\cdot$, tender,
373:1 warm, $s\cdot$, tender,
378:1 sing in $s\cdot$ accord;
399:2 $s\cdot$ will be the flower.
400:2 $s\cdot$ will be the flower.
414:2 More wonderfully $s\cdot$.

sweeten
227:3 faith and $s\cdot$ care;

sweeter
54:2 $s\cdot$ far the still
329:2 $s\cdot$ far than honey,

sweetest
271:2 with $s\cdot$ song,
272:2 with $s\cdot$ song,

sweetly
128:1 $s\cdot$ flowed the gospel
129:1 $s\cdot$ flowed the gospel
313:2 We $s\cdot$ then pursue

sweetness
340:3 the $s\cdot$ of our Lord.

swell
2:2 $s\cdot$ the mighty strain.

swelled
30:4 $s\cdot$ creation's lay:
31:4 $s\cdot$ creation's lay:
32:4 $s\cdot$ creation's lay:

swift
166:4 $S\cdot$ shall pass thy
167:4 $S\cdot$ shall pass thy
233:2 and $s\cdot$ to bless,
419:2 and $s\cdot$ to bless,
280:3 and $s\cdot$ to bless.
324:2 $S\cdot$ and beautiful

swiftly
41:2 hours too $s\cdot$ fly,
158:2 Come $s\cdot$ on the wing;
159:2 Come $s\cdot$ on the wing;

sword
5:1 the $s\cdot$ now gird,
236:2 From cannon and $s\cdot$
292:1 $s\cdot$ of the Spirit
297:1 with the flaming $s\cdot$,
326:1 The Spirit's $s\cdot$

symbol
142:4 And every $s\cdot$ wanes:

symbols
108:3 the $s\cdot$ disappear;
170:2 outward $s\cdot$ disappear

sympathy
4:2 In $s\cdot$ divine, That we

Syrian
49:2 Beside the $S\cdot$ sea,
50:2 Beside the $S\cdot$ sea,
96:2 about The $S\cdot$ hillsides

systems
142:4 fails, the $s\cdot$ fall,

T

tablet
383:2 $t\cdot$ of thy thoughts

taint
23:5 or earth-born $t\cdot$:
24:5 or earth-born $t\cdot$:
25:5 or earth-born $t\cdot$:
26:5 or earth-born $t\cdot$:
27:5 or earth-born $t\cdot$:
28:5 or earth-born $t\cdot$:

take
12:1 people, $t\cdot$ your stand,
13:1 people, $t\cdot$ your stand,
46:2 $T\cdot$ the manna of
47:2 $T\cdot$ the manna of
49:4 $T\cdot$ from us now the
50:4 $T\cdot$ from us now the
74:2 Go, $t\cdot$ the little
75:1 $t\cdot$ away transgression,
85:3 $t\cdot$ at Thy direction,
138:2 I $t\cdot$ Thy hand and
139:1 joy that none can $t\cdot$
427:1 joy that none can $t\cdot$
260:2 I $t\cdot$ in trust my road;
291:3 not $t\cdot$ a step alone,
304:3 $T\cdot$ them in Thine arms;
305:3 $T\cdot$ them in Thine arms;
306:3 $T\cdot$ them in Thine arms;

take
307:3 $T\cdot$ them in Thine arms;
308:3 $T\cdot$ them in Thine arms;
309:3 $T\cdot$ them in Thine arms;
312:1 And $t\cdot$, to arm you
324:1 $T\cdot$ my life, and let it
 1 $T\cdot$ my moments and my
 1 $T\cdot$ my hands, and.let
 2 $T\cdot$ my feet, and let
 2 $T\cdot$ my voice, and let
 2 $T\cdot$ my lips, and let
 3 $T\cdot$ my every thought,
 3 $T\cdot$ my love; O Lord,
325:1-3 $T\cdot$ up thy cross,
329:3 Thee, I $t\cdot$ delight;
340:3 $t\cdot$ Him at His word;
382:4 $T\cdot$ then the sacred
399:1 fresh courage $t\cdot$,
400:1 fresh courage $t\cdot$,

takes
368:3 darkness $t\cdot$ its flight,
369:3 darkness $t\cdot$ its flight,

taketh
148:2 knows the way He $t\cdot$,
311:2 He $t\cdot$ in His arm;
420:2 He $t\cdot$ in His arm;

taking
361:2 $t\cdot$ thought and striving
379:3 path of peace is $t\cdot$
380:3 path of peace is $t\cdot$

talent
364:2 Every $t\cdot$ we possess.

talk
139:2 Shall $t\cdot$ with Love
427:2 Shall $t\cdot$ with Love
253:4 tenderly, Divinely $t\cdot$.
254:4 tenderly, Divinely $t\cdot$.
255:4 tenderly, Divinely $t\cdot$.
256:4 tenderly, Divinely $t\cdot$.
257:4 tenderly, Divinely $t\cdot$.

tarry
415:1, Ref. $t\cdot$, I can $t\cdot$ but a

task
6:3 hour allots thy $t\cdot$,
46:4 daily $t\cdot$ shalt give;
47:4 daily $t\cdot$ shalt give;
92:2 Rising to every $t\cdot$,
146:3 it hails each $t\cdot$,
147:3 it hails each $t\cdot$,
183:3 Up, face the $t\cdot$
184:3 Up, face the $t\cdot$

task
190:2 every $t\cdot$ assigned,
191:2 every $t\cdot$ assigned,
247:2 to your daily $t\cdot$
248:2 to your daily $t\cdot$
247:3 Each $t\cdot$ divine
248:3 Each $t\cdot$ divine

tasks
190:1 $t\cdot$ of life seem hard
191:1 $t\cdot$ of life seem hard
288:2 Though $t\cdot$ are sore,
289:2 Though $t\cdot$ are sore,

taste
108:2 $t\cdot$ afresh the calm
205:3 We $t\cdot$ e'en here
399:2 have a bitter $t\cdot$,
400:2 have a bitter $t\cdot$,

tatters
160:3 foes—truth $t\cdot$ those,
161:3 foes—truth $t\cdot$ those,
162:3 foes—truth $t\cdot$ those,

taught
4:3 life of Jesus $t\cdot$,
101:3 falsehood ages $t\cdot$
115:1 Thou hast $t\cdot$ us
116:1 Thou hast $t\cdot$ us
178:1 heavenly wisdom $t\cdot$
347:2 shall be $t\cdot$ of Him
348:2 shall be $t\cdot$ of Him
386:1 precepts which he $t\cdot$.
387:1 precepts which he $t\cdot$.

teach
137:3 $T\cdot$ me Thy will;
203:2 $T\cdot$ us to follow
227:3 $t\cdot$ our faint desires
234:2 $T\cdot$ me the wayward
235:2 $T\cdot$ me the wayward
234:3 $T\cdot$ me thy patience;
235:3 $T\cdot$ me thy patience;
258:2 occasions $t\cdot$ new duties,
266:2 $T\cdot$ us to love
278:3 tenderness $t\cdot$ thee
279:3 tenderness $t\cdot$ thee
331:3 ancient prophets $t\cdot$,
386:1 Master came To $t\cdot$
387:1 Master came To $t\cdot$

teachable
318:2 $T\cdot$, ready to choose

teachings
128:3 his $t\cdot$ all may come,
129:3 his $t\cdot$ all may come,
240:3 Thy $t\cdot$ make us know
241:3 Thy $t\cdot$ make us know

tear
23:2 No ... and mother's $t\cdot$,
24:2 No ... and mother's $t\cdot$,
25:2 No ... and mother's $t\cdot$,
26:2 No ... and mother's $t\cdot$,
27:2 No ... and mother's $t\cdot$,
28:2 No ... and mother's $t\cdot$,
54:2 dried the bitter $t\cdot$.
202:3 For every $t\cdot$ to bring
412:2 For every $t\cdot$ to bring
207:3 for every scalding $t\cdot$,
208:3 for every scalding $t\cdot$,
209:3 for every scalding $t\cdot$,
210:3 for every scalding $t\cdot$,
211:3 for every scalding $t\cdot$,
212:3 for every scalding $t\cdot$,
304:3 $T\cdot$ or triumph harms,
305:3 $T\cdot$ or triumph harms,
306:3 $T\cdot$ or triumph harms,
307:3 $T\cdot$ or triumph harms,
308:3 $T\cdot$ or triumph harms,
309:3 $T\cdot$ or triumph harms,

tear-drops
207:5 earth's $t\cdot$ gain,
208:5 earth's $t\cdot$ gain,
209:5 earth's $t\cdot$ gain,
210:5 earth's $t\cdot$ gain,
211:5 earth's $t\cdot$ gain,
212:5 earth's $t\cdot$ gain,

tearful
391:1 look with $t\cdot$ eyes

tears
8:3 and $t\cdot$ no bitterness;
133:3 $t\cdot$, all woes, to bliss,
424:3 $t\cdot$, all woes, to bliss,
202:2 wipe all $t\cdot$ away;
412:1 wipe all $t\cdot$ away;
298:2 Love wipes your $t\cdot$
299:2 Love wipes your $t\cdot$
300:2 Love wipes your $t\cdot$
301:2 Love wipes your $t\cdot$
302:2 Love wipes your $t\cdot$
335:1 To penitential $t\cdot$.
379:3 vale of $t\cdot$ and pain.
380:3 vale of $t\cdot$ and pain.
415:3 Nor any $t\cdot$ there,
425:2 wipe all $t\cdot$ away,

tell
11:1 gracious news to $t\cdot$,
40:1 here $t\cdot$ your anguish;
43:1 $t\cdot$ of benediction,
86:2 instinct that can $t\cdot$
87:2 instinct that can $t\cdot$
114:1 $t\cdot$ me whence I came;
1 $t\cdot$ me what I am;

tell
226:3 Thy truths may $t\cdot$,
228:2 hidden joy can $t\cdot$,
234:1 $T\cdot$ me thy secret;
235:1 $T\cdot$ me thy secret;
303:2 none can $t\cdot$ How vast
315:3 Eternity shall $t\cdot$.
316:3 Eternity shall $t\cdot$.
368:1-3 Watchman, $t\cdot$ us of
369:1-3 Watchman, $t\cdot$ us of
384:1 half the wonders $t\cdot$,
414:1-3, Ref. to $t\cdot$ the story,
Ref. $t\cdot$ the old, old story
2 each time I $t\cdot$ it,

telling
11:2 $T\cdot$ that the dawn
204:1 witnesses, $t\cdot$ Thy

tells
376:1 $t\cdot$ us not of anger,
377:1 $t\cdot$ us not of anger,

temper
385:2 $t\cdot$ the deceitful ray.

tempest
74:1 error's $t\cdot$ and its fire
76:2 voice above the $t\cdot$:
172:1 no $t\cdot$ shall prevail.

tempest's
176:1 mid the $t\cdot$ assailing,

tempests
205:2 When $t\cdot$ rage without;

temple
3:3 grateful heart a $t\cdot$
217:3 seem our Father's $t\cdot$,
383:2 Its $t\cdot$ makes with thee.

temptation
77:1 In darkness and $t\cdot$,
78:1 In darkness and $t\cdot$,
290:1 treading each $t\cdot$ down,

temptations
137:2 $T\cdot$ lose their power

tempter's
8:2 foil the $t\cdot$ power?

tempting
379:4 earth's $t\cdot$ vanities,
380:4 earth's $t\cdot$ vanities,

tender
34:3 The $t\cdot$ Christ is here
43:1 $t\cdot$ words of Jesus,
45:2 Such $t\cdot$ beauty, Lord,
69:3 be more $t\cdot$, kind,

tender
423:3 be more t, kind,
 91:2 shine With t warmth
422:2 shine With t warmth
 91:3 t love and perfect
422:3 t love and perfect
 99:2 His t love and
100:2 His t love and
109:1 t sweet persuasions
110:1 t sweet persuasions
137:1 t voice like Thine
154:1 Spirit true and t,
155:1 Spirit true and t,
156:1 Spirit true and t,
175:1 t healing message
214:2 bind its t blessing
221:2 A t ever-presence
243:1 sweet and t as
244:1 sweet and t as
243:3 t, healing power.
244:3 t, healing power.
245:1 t, loving Shepherd,
314:2 t blade, the stalk,
318:1 the Master's t plea;
327:3 care, His t love
328:3 care, His t love
372:2 But warm, sweet, t,
373:1 But warm, sweet, t,
374:1 t, constant care,
375:1 t, constant care,

tenderly
 40:2 Comforter, t saying,
253:4 and t, Divinely talk.
254:4 and t, Divinely talk.
255:4 and t, Divinely talk.
256:4 and t, Divinely talk.
257:4 and t, Divinely talk.
283:2 Watch doth He t keep;

tenderness
114:3 With a Saviour's t;
233:2 We manifest Thy t:
419:2 We manifest Thy t:
278:3 His t teach thee
279:3 His t teach thee

tends
280:2 He t and spares us,

tent
246:1 heaven like a t,

terror
 2:2 hear in shrinking t,
 77:1 What t can confound
 78:1 What t can confound
351:2 far the gloom and t,
368:3 and t are withdrawn;
369:3 and t are withdrawn;

terrors
389:1 no t appall;

test
143:1 truths the t invite,
249:2 They t our constancy.
250:2 They t our constancy.
372:4 We t our lives by
373:2 We t our lives by

tested
 15:1 gold by fire is t,

testimony
329:2 To heed His t,

thank
150:2 We t Thee for work
 3 we t Thee for life,
199:1 t we all our God
342:3 t and bless the Lord.
374:1, 2 t Thee and we bless
375:1, 2 t Thee and we bless
374:1, 3 t Thee, Father-Mother,
375:1, 3 t Thee, Father-Mother,
374:2 t Thee That good
375:2 t Thee That good
374:3 t Thee, when in
375:3 t Thee, when in
376:1 t Thee, heavenly
377:1 t Thee, heavenly

thanks
 10:3 give t to God
411:3 give t to God
 72:2 t to God belong;
405:2 t to God belong;
334:3 Let everlasting t
342:1, 3 give t, rejoice.

thanksgiving
 73:1 His presence with t,
150:1 Our tribute, t,
283:3 Songs of t and praise,

theme
 72:2 angels' glorious t;
405:2 angels' glorious t;
313:2 t of God's salvation,
414:Ref. my t in glory

theories
337:1 T, which thousands
338:1 T, which thousands

therefore
 99:3 No evil t shalt thou
100:3 No evil t shalt thou
173:1-3 T give us love.

therein
276:1 to every heart t;
277:1 to every heart t;
339:2 joy is found t,

thing
 86:1 is a wondrous t,
 87:1 is a wondrous t,
183:2 t that never dies,
184:2 t that never dies,
278:2 one t do thou ask
279:2 one t do thou ask
315:3 'tis a little t,
316:3 'tis a little t,
379:1 the one t needful
380:1 the one t needful

things
 14:3 all t are thine.
 64:1 dawn of all t real
 2 joy of t immortal,
 65:3 great t He hath done,
 71:1 Glorious t of thee
 86:1 of all t on earth,
 87:1 of all t on earth,
105:3 in all t grow;
106:3 in all t grow;
107:3 in all t grow;
108:1 handle t unseen;
120:1 tidings of good t;
121:4 far greater t than
122:4 far greater t than
130:1 all t in Thy sight,
134:3 Thy hand in all t
 3 all t in Thy hand.
153:2 done to me great t,
157:2 Life of all t,
170:1 t of time and place.
190:3 T deemed impossible
191:3 T deemed impossible
199:1 wondrous t hath done,
218:1, 4 maketh all t new,
219:1, 4 maketh all t new,
220:1, 4 maketh all t new,
224:2 have all t and abound,
225:2 have all t and abound,
226:2 t that Thou hast made:
240:3 vanity of t below,
 The joy of t above.
241:3 vanity of t below,
 The joy of t above.
273:2 forget the t behind,
274:2 forget the t behind,
312:2 having all t done,
329:1 Him who made all t;
339:3 all t made new
342:2 Good t are freely
370:2 beauteous t of Mind.

things	**thought**	**thoughts**
379:1 who, all $t\cdot$ losing,	134:1 $t\cdot$ of Thee is mightier	109:1 Lifts our $t\cdot$ from self
380:1 who, all $t\cdot$ losing,	139:3 Uplift your $t\cdot$, with	110:1 Lifts our $t\cdot$ from self
414:1 of unseen $t\cdot$ above,	427:3 Uplift your $t\cdot$, with	118:3 troubled $t\cdot$ be still;
think	151:2 earthly $t\cdot$ released,	121:1 guile their $t\cdot$ are free,
6:2 $T\cdot$ not in sleep to	152:2 earthly $t\cdot$ released,	122:1 guile their $t\cdot$ are free,
166:2 $T\cdot$ what spirit dwells	154:2 $t\cdot$ that giveth fear;	140:3 New $t\cdot$ of God reveal
167:2 $T\cdot$ what spirit dwells	155:2 $t\cdot$ that giveth fear;	180:1 silence $t\cdot$ of wrong
166:2 $T\cdot$ what Father's smiles	156:2 $t\cdot$ that giveth fear;	192:4 my waking $t\cdot$ Bright
167:2 $T\cdot$ what Father's smiles	154:3 No anxious $t\cdot$, no	193:4 my waking $t\cdot$ Bright
166:2 $T\cdot$ what Jesus did	155:3 No anxious $t\cdot$, no	199:2 fill our $t\cdot$ with light,
167:2 $T\cdot$ what Jesus did	156:3 No anxious $t\cdot$, no	218:1 the $t\cdot$ of men;
288:2 $T\cdot$ of the words:	160:2 in $t\cdot$ and deed—	219:1 the $t\cdot$ of men;
289:2 $T\cdot$ of the words:	161:2 in $t\cdot$ and deed—	220:1 the $t\cdot$ of men;
thinks	162:2 in $t\cdot$ and deed—	232:1 peace our $t\cdot$ abide;
173:1 meek and $t\cdot$ no wrong,	180:3 They whose every $t\cdot$	406:1 peace our $t\cdot$ abide;
	186:3 in this $t\cdot$ we rest:	253:2 angel throng Of $t\cdot$,
thirst	187:3 in this $t\cdot$ we rest:	254:2 angel throng Of $t\cdot$,
71:3 their $t\cdot$ assuage,—	206:2 $t\cdot$ attuned to praise,	255:2 angel throng Of $t\cdot$,
138:1 Thy font and $t\cdot$ no more.	428:2 $t\cdot$ attuned to praise,	256:2 angel throng Of $t\cdot$,
418:4 their $t\cdot$ will slake,	218:3 the larger $t\cdot$ of God;—	257:2 angel throng Of $t\cdot$,
thirsting	219:3 the larger $t\cdot$ of God;—	370:2 lifted All our $t\cdot$
414:3 Seem hungering and $t\cdot$	220:3 the larger $t\cdot$ of God;—	371:1 Thy $t\cdot$ our lives
	258:2 $t\cdot$ of men incline	383:2 tablet of thy $t\cdot$
thirsty	260:1 One $t\cdot$ I have, my ample	385:2 $t\cdot$ of Thee a . . . screen
34:3 and $t\cdot$ are refreshed,	1 It is the $t\cdot$ of God.	**thousand**
75:2 Upon the $t\cdot$ earth;	2 forth the $t\cdot$ of God.	2:2 A $t\cdot$ freemen rally,
thorns	3 their $t\cdot$ of God.	213:3 $t\cdot$ ages in Thy sight
164:2 $t\cdot$ infest the ground;	4 blessed $t\cdot$ of God.	**thousands**
165:2 $t\cdot$ infest the ground;	276:2 which passeth $t\cdot$.	128:1 listening $t\cdot$ gathered
417:2 $t\cdot$ infest the ground;	277:2 which passeth $t\cdot$.	129:1 listening $t\cdot$ gathered
thorny	287:1 our waking $t\cdot$ ascends,	337:1 which $t\cdot$ cherish,
367:4 path, though $t\cdot$, bright;	408:1 our waking $t\cdot$ ascends,	338:1 which $t\cdot$ cherish,
	298:4 Truth in $t\cdot$ and deed;	351:3 strain the lips of $t\cdot$
thought	299:4 Truth in $t\cdot$ and deed;	**thraldom**
4:1 $t\cdot$ from sense unbound,	300:4 Truth in $t\cdot$ and deed;	10:2 to error's $t\cdot$ came,
14:2 And purified thy $t\cdot$.	301:4 Truth in $t\cdot$ and deed;	411:2 to error's $t\cdot$ came,
30:2 By $t\cdot$ or word unkind,	302:4 Truth in $t\cdot$ and deed;	**thrall**
31:2 By $t\cdot$ or word unkind,	317:3 Rises the glorious $t\cdot$,	160:4 Ayont hate's $t\cdot$:
32:2 By $t\cdot$ or word unkind,	324:3 Take my every $t\cdot$,	161:4 Ayont hate's $t\cdot$:
39:1 O'er every $t\cdot$ and step	329:2 Word the $t\cdot$ enlightens,	162:4 Ayont hate's $t\cdot$:
51:1 $t\cdot$ th' eternal clay:	3 idle $t\cdot$ or word;	179:1 frees from error's $t\cdot$,—
52:1 $t\cdot$ th' eternal clay:	339:2 free from $t\cdot$ of sin,	382:4 art not error's $t\cdot$;
51:2 Unhallowed $t\cdot$ He could	361:2 taking $t\cdot$ and striving	**threads**
52:2 Unhallowed $t\cdot$ He could	386:1 every act, in every $t\cdot$,	146:4 shining $t\cdot$ of ceaseless
57:2 the $t\cdot$ that Thou art	387:1 every act, in every $t\cdot$,	147:4 shining $t\cdot$ of ceaseless
64:3 $T\cdot$ soars enraptured,	**thoughtful**	**three**
73:2 holy $t\cdot$ is sending;	322:1 of holy, $t\cdot$ prayer,	173:4 greatest of the $t\cdot$,
94:2 worthier $t\cdot$ awake,	323:1 of holy, $t\cdot$ prayer,	**thrice**
95:1 O blessed $t\cdot$, O words	**thoughts**	259:1 Is $t\cdot$ more grateful,
118:1 Cleanse my $t\cdot$ in Thy	9:2 lift our $t\cdot$ above,	**thrilled**
133:3 God is Love: a $t\cdot$	30:2 holy $t\cdot$ and heavenly	381:1 $t\cdot$ with new affection,
424:3 God is Love: a $t\cdot$	31:2 holy $t\cdot$ and heavenly	
133:3 gloomy $t\cdot$ remove,	32:2 holy $t\cdot$ and heavenly	
424:3 gloomy $t\cdot$ remove,	48:2 Upon his $t\cdot$ or deeds?	
	97:2 not fear thy $t\cdot$ employ;	
	98:2 not fear thy $t\cdot$ employ;	

throne
19:1 stand before the $t\cdot$
40:3 from the $t\cdot$ of God,
80:3 Firm as His $t\cdot$
258:3 upon the $t\cdot$ be wrong,
319:2 Thy ever blazing $t\cdot$
322:3 at His sheltering $t\cdot$.
323:3 at His sheltering $t\cdot$.
341:1 seek the $t\cdot$ of grace,
　　　Find that $t\cdot$ in
359:2 Light from His $t\cdot$
362:3 ever guards his $t\cdot$,
391:3 to-day upholds His $t\cdot$.

thrones
160:2 stones, or tyrants' $t\cdot$,
161:2 stones, or tyrants' $t\cdot$,
162:2 stones, or tyrants' $t\cdot$,
264:3 Crowns and $t\cdot$ may
337:3 $T\cdot$ may totter, empires
338:3 $T\cdot$ may totter, empires

throng
96:1 Amid the suffering $t\cdot$,
253:2 angel $t\cdot$ Of thoughts,
254:2 angel $t\cdot$ Of thoughts,
255:2 angel $t\cdot$ Of thoughts,
256:2 angel $t\cdot$ Of thoughts,
257:2 angel $t\cdot$ Of thoughts,
264:4 Join our happy $t\cdot$;
372:3 life's $t\cdot$ and press,
373:2 life's $t\cdot$ and press,

throughout
82:3 shine $t\cdot$ the world;
245:3 $T\cdot$ the way, dear
376:2 Thou $t\cdot$ the journey
377:2 Thou $t\cdot$ the journey

thrust
242:3 $T\cdot$ in our sickles

thunders
74:2 the seven $t\cdot$ roll?

tide
75:3 The $t\cdot$ of time shall

tides
172:2 earth's restless $t\cdot$,
229:2 $t\cdot$ of everlasting day.

tidings
11:2 the $t\cdot$ angels bring
41:2 the joyful $t\cdot$ bear;
120:1 Good $t\cdot$ of good things;
202:4 glorious $t\cdot$ of salvation
412:2 glorious $t\cdot$ of salvation
335:1 Brings $t\cdot$ from afar,

till
1:1 $T\cdot$ Thou art here and
9:1 $T\cdot$ all the world
35:2 $T\cdot$ Thy mercy's beams
2 $T\cdot$ they inward light
49:4 $T\cdot$ all our strivings
50:4 $T\cdot$ all our strivings
62:2 $T\cdot$ suns shall rise
63:2 $T\cdot$ suns shall rise
81:2 $T\cdot$ my heart that
105:3 $T\cdot$ Thou hast made us
106:3 $T\cdot$ Thou hast made us
107:3 $T\cdot$ Thou hast made us
109:2 $T\cdot$ through joyful
110:2 $T\cdot$ through joyful
112:2 $t\cdot$ all the world
136:3 $T\cdot$ time and space
149:2 $t\cdot$ found in Him.
426:2 $t\cdot$ found in Him.
157:3 $T\cdot$ among all men
169:1 $t\cdot$ The night is gone,
271:1 $T\cdot$ moons shall wax
272:1 $T\cdot$ moons shall wax
297:2 $t\cdot$ the storm be past;
304:3 $T\cdot$ the morning's beam;
305:3 $T\cdot$ the morning's beam;
306:3 $T\cdot$ the morning's beam;
307:3 $T\cdot$ the morning's beam;
308:3 $T\cdot$ the morning's beam;
309:3 $T\cdot$ the morning's beam;
335:2 $t\cdot$ all the lowly
2 $t\cdot$ all the holy
345:2 $T\cdot$ in reflection
394:1 $t\cdot$, from its dreary
395:1 $t\cdot$, from its dreary
394:3 $T\cdot$ the nations far
395:3 $T\cdot$ the nations far

tillage
141:3 fruitful shall our $t\cdot$

tillers
236:2 shape $t\cdot$ of soil,

timbrel
200:3 harp and the $t\cdot$

time
36:2 hurrying crowds of $t\cdot$
41:2 Redeem the $t\cdot$: its hours
75:3 tide of $t\cdot$ shall never
82:1 the $t\cdot$ is drawing near;
1 nearer draws the $t\cdot$,
1, 2 $t\cdot$ that shall surely be,
2 we do to hasten the $t\cdot$,
97:2 Harvest $t\cdot$ is surely
98:2 Harvest $t\cdot$ is surely
136:3 o'er $t\cdot$ and space;
3 $t\cdot$ and space and fear

time
157:1 through all $t\cdot$ God's
158:3 come the $t\cdot$ foretold;
159:3 come the $t\cdot$ foretold;
170:1 things of $t\cdot$ and place.
182:2 But if at any $t\cdot$ we
183:1 no $t\cdot$ to lose in sloth,
184:1 no $t\cdot$ to lose in sloth,
183:3 no $t\cdot$ for thee to sleep;
184:3 no $t\cdot$ for thee to sleep;
196:1 is the $t\cdot$ approaching,
213:1, 4 hope for $t\cdot$ to come,
238:1 since $t\cdot$ began, We
239:1 since $t\cdot$ began, We
238:2 our own $t\cdot$ glad,
239:2 our own $t\cdot$ glad,
238:4 olden $t\cdot$ and holier
239:4 olden $t\cdot$ and holier
258:2 $T\cdot$ makes ancient
261:2 From oldest $t\cdot$, on
262:2 From oldest $t\cdot$, on
414:2 each $t\cdot$ I tell it,
418:1-4 clanging bells of $t\cdot$,

timeless
176:1 secure on $t\cdot$ rock

timely
141:2 our planting $t\cdot$, true,

times
46:3 my $t\cdot$ are in Thy
47:3 my $t\cdot$ are in Thy
177:1 Joyful $t\cdot$ are near

timid
399:1 Ye $t\cdot$ saints, fresh
400:1 Ye $t\cdot$ saints, fresh

tired
149:3 bowed with $t\cdot$ labor,
426:3 bowed with $t\cdot$ labor,
221:3 To $t\cdot$ humanity,
253:6 $t\cdot$ joy and grief afar,
254:6 $t\cdot$ joy and grief afar,
255:6 $t\cdot$ joy and grief afar,
256:6 $t\cdot$ joy and grief afar,
257:6 $t\cdot$ joy and grief afar,

tires
351:2 faith which never $t\cdot$,

tiring
97:1 Never $t\cdot$, never
98:1 Never $t\cdot$, never

to and fro
418:3 marching $t\cdot$ and $f\cdot$;

to-day
6:2 $t\cdot$ hath need of thee.
16:3 sing my way $t\cdot$,
23:5 Fill us $t\cdot$ With all
24:5 Fill us $t\cdot$ With all
25:5 Fill us $t\cdot$ With all
26:5 Fill us $t\cdot$ With all
27:5 Fill us $t\cdot$ With all
28:5 Fill us $t\cdot$ With all
41:1 Master say, Go work $t\cdot$.
46:2 Take the manna of $t\cdot$.
47:2 Take the manna of $t\cdot$.
58:1 our hearts in joy $t\cdot$,
91:1-3 Grace for $t\cdot$,
422:1-3 Grace for $t\cdot$,
139:1, 2 walk with Love $t\cdot$.
427:1, 2 walk with Love $t\cdot$.
139:3 trust be yours $t\cdot$;
427:3 trust be yours $t\cdot$;
154:3 same $t\cdot$, to-morrow;
155:3 same $t\cdot$, to-morrow;
156:3 same $t\cdot$, to-morrow;
197:2 Christ $t\cdot$ to us
198:2 Christ $t\cdot$ to us
199:1 still is ours $t\cdot$.
221:1 $T\cdot$ Christ's precious
291:2 Thou shalt $t\cdot$ provide
342:2 come $t\cdot$ to bring
391:2 lives and works $t\cdot$
    3 $t\cdot$ upholds His throne.

together
196:1 all shall dwell $t\cdot$,
222:2 O morning stars, $t\cdot$
223:2 O morning stars, $t\cdot$
310:2 the stars $t\cdot$ sang,

toil
41:4 The $t\cdot$ is pleasant,
97:1 see his $t\cdot$ succeed;
98:1 see his $t\cdot$ succeed;
101:3 hosts who $t\cdot$ in vain
158:2 $t\cdot$ along the climbing
159:2 $t\cdot$ along the climbing
183:2 $t\cdot$ that is not lost,—
184:2 $t\cdot$ that is not lost,—
234:1 The strain of $t\cdot$,
235:1 The strain of $t\cdot$,
361:2 is thy $t\cdot$ in vain;
364:2 all our $t\cdot$ and labor,

toiled
315:2 have $t\cdot$ in vain;
316:2 have $t\cdot$ in vain;

token
2:3 shines the blessed $t\cdot$
84:1 $t\cdot$, Emblem of eternal

told
158:1 wondrous story $t\cdot$
159:1 wondrous story $t\cdot$

tomb
343:3 rending $t\cdot$ Proclaims
344:3 rending $t\cdot$ Proclaims
429:3 rending $t\cdot$ Proclaims

to-morrow
154:3 the same to-day, $t\cdot$;
155:3 the same to-day, $t\cdot$;
156:3 the same to-day, $t\cdot$;
291:2 What $t\cdot$ may betide
350:3 expect a bright $t\cdot$,

tongue
51:3 ring from every $t\cdot$,
52:3 ring from every $t\cdot$,
62:1 every land, by every $t\cdot$.
63:1 every land, by every $t\cdot$.
170:1 from no mortal $t\cdot$,
188:1 nor $t\cdot$ declared,
271:2 with joyful $t\cdot$ Dwell
272:2 with joyful $t\cdot$ Dwell
384:1 What $t\cdot$ can half

tongues
347:4 $t\cdot$ that rise condemning
348:4 $t\cdot$ that rise condemning

to-night
207:1 on upward wing $t\cdot$.
208:1 on upward wing $t\cdot$.
209:1 on upward wing $t\cdot$.
210:1 on upward wing $t\cdot$.
211:1 on upward wing $t\cdot$.
212:1 on upward wing $t\cdot$.
222:1 Are met in thee $t\cdot$.
223:1 Are met in thee $t\cdot$.

took
346:1 And $t\cdot$ their flight;
401:1 And $t\cdot$ their flight;

torrent
169:3 o'er crag and $t\cdot$,

tossed
347:2 afflicted, $t\cdot$ with doubt,
348:2 afflicted, $t\cdot$ with doubt,

tossing
118:2 calm the $t\cdot$ sea,

totter
337:3 Thrones may $t\cdot$, empires
338:3 Thrones may $t\cdot$, empires

touch
64:3 $t\cdot$ the fringes of
69:3 with Thy healing $t\cdot$,
423:3 with Thy healing $t\cdot$,
96:1 lightest $t\cdot$ sufficed
108:1 Here would I $t\cdot$ and
134:1 Thy $t\cdot$, eternal Love,
171:2 $t\cdot$ Truth's healing
413:2 $t\cdot$ Truth's healing
174:3 thy pure $t\cdot$ persuades
204:2 No trouble shall $t\cdot$
226:2 $t\cdot$ the future vast
243:2 with $t\cdot$ of gentleness
244:2 with $t\cdot$ of gentleness
303:2 word may $t\cdot$ the heart
372:3 We $t\cdot$ him in life's
373:2 We $t\cdot$ him in life's
392:3 His $t\cdot$ the door of
393:3 His $t\cdot$ the door of

toward
189:1 look $t\cdot$ the mountains,
376:2 $T\cdot$ Thee, while
377:2 $T\cdot$ Thee, while

tower
3:2 stanch and rugged $t\cdot$,
10:1 He is our shield and $t\cdot$,
411:1 He is our shield and $t\cdot$,

towers
37:3 How rise thy $t\cdot$,
38:3 How rise thy $t\cdot$,
364:1 bulwarks and our $t\cdot$,

town
222:1 little $t\cdot$ of Bethlehem,
223:1 little $t\cdot$ of Bethlehem,

trace
44:3 leaves no saddening $t\cdot$;
91:3 his way to $t\cdot$ Whose pure
422:3 his way to $t\cdot$ Whose pure
133:1 $t\cdot$ the way Where Thou,
424:1 $t\cdot$ the way Where Thou,
189:2 onward way doth $t\cdot$,
230:1 $t\cdot$ the noonday sun.
231:1 $t\cdot$ the noonday sun.
259:2 $t\cdot$ The source of every
311:1 $t\cdot$ for us His wise
420:1 $t\cdot$ for us His wise
320:1 $t\cdot$ The working of
321:1 $t\cdot$ The working of
409:1 $t\cdot$ The working of
352:4 $t\cdot$ thy footsteps, Son
353:4 $t\cdot$ thy footsteps, Son

traced
30:4 Love whose finger $t\cdot$
31:4 Love whose finger $t\cdot$
32:4 Love whose finger $t\cdot$

tramples
326:4 hell he $t\cdot$ down,

tranquillity
118:2 Stayed in Thy $t\cdot$.

transcendent
194:3 in that $t\cdot$ hour
410:3 in that $t\cdot$ hour

transfigured
230:1 $t\cdot$ clouds of white,
231:1 $t\cdot$ clouds of white,

transform
163:1 $t\cdot$ our earth to heaven.

transforming
314:3 Love's $t\cdot$ light,

transgression
75:1 To take away $t\cdot$,
329:3 keep me from $t\cdot$,

traveler
288:1 Press on, dear $t\cdot$,
289:1 Press on, dear $t\cdot$,
368:1 $T\cdot$, o'er yon mountain's
369:1 $T\cdot$, o'er yon mountain's
368:1 $T\cdot$, yes; it brings
369:1 $T\cdot$, yes; it brings
368:2 $T\cdot$, blessedness and
369:2 $T\cdot$, blessedness and
368:2 $T\cdot$, ages are its own;
369:2 $T\cdot$, ages are its own;
368:3 $T\cdot$, darkness takes
369:3 $T\cdot$, darkness takes
368:3 $T\cdot$, lo, the Prince of
369:3 $T\cdot$, lo, the Prince of

tread
55:2 we $t\cdot$ rejoicingly.
131:1 in my pathway $t\cdot$:
132:1 in my pathway $t\cdot$:
265:2 $T\cdot$ it with rejoicing,
312:2 $T\cdot$ all the powers
320:4 $t\cdot$ The path of life
321:4 $t\cdot$ The path of life
409:4 $t\cdot$ The path of life
351:2 all the path we $t\cdot$:
376:2 we $t\cdot$ the pathway,
377:2 we $t\cdot$ the pathway,
383:3 $t\cdot$ the narrow way:
388:3 triumphed we would $t\cdot$;

treadest
382:2 Thou $t\cdot$ undefiled

treading
264:2 $t\cdot$ Where the saints
290:1 $t\cdot$ each temptation

treasure
114:1 Precious $t\cdot$, thou art
119:2 richest $t\cdot$ Man can
130:1 the $t\cdot$ of Thy Word;
148:3 My Father has my $t\cdot$,
249:2 gladness is the $t\cdot$
250:2 gladness is the $t\cdot$
324:3 At Thy feet its $t\cdot$
361:1 Him who has thy $t\cdot$,
389:2 My $t\cdot$, my glory,

treasures
140:1 New $t\cdot$ still, of
188:2 priceless $t\cdot$ of His
201:3 Hid $t\cdot$ it reveals
404:3 Hid $t\cdot$ it reveals
215:2 has $t\cdot$ greater far
236:4 all earth's $t\cdot$ above.

tree
141:3 gathered from the $t\cdot$
384:2 spring on every $t\cdot$;

tremble
205:1 $t\cdot$ on the brink

trembles
284:1 $t\cdot$ in the breast.
285:1 $t\cdot$ in the breast.
286:1 $t\cdot$ in the breast.

trials
123:3 When through fiery $t\cdot$
249:2 $t\cdot$ bloom in blessings,
250:2 $t\cdot$ bloom in blessings,
278:2 steadfast though $t\cdot$
279:2 steadfast though $t\cdot$

tribe
120:1 every $t\cdot$ and nation:

tribes
362:1 $t\cdot$ of earth obey,

tribulation
19:1 out of $t\cdot$ came,
135:2 I fear no $t\cdot$, Since,
350:2 we pass through $t\cdot$

tribute
150:1 Our $t\cdot$, thanksgiving,
249:1 Can we withhold a $t\cdot$,

tribute
250:1 Can we withhold a $t\cdot$,
280:1 To His feet thy $t\cdot$
329:1 night its $t\cdot$ brings.

tried
115:2 turn to Thee when $t\cdot$,
116:2 turn to Thee when $t\cdot$,

trinity
355:2 be Our glorious $t\cdot$,

triumph
8:3 $t\cdot$ still, if Thou abide
35:1 $T\cdot$ o'er the shades of
114:3 can $t\cdot$ over death.
190:1 with this $t\cdot$ song,
191:1 with this $t\cdot$ song,
190:4 Faith sings in $t\cdot$,
191:4 Faith sings in $t\cdot$,
224:3 I $t\cdot$ and adore;
225:3 I $t\cdot$ and adore;
228:3 So may we $t\cdot$
290:2 to $t\cdot$ go; Victorious
304:3 Tear or $t\cdot$ harms,
305:3 Tear or $t\cdot$ harms,
306:3 Tear or $t\cdot$ harms,
307:3 Tear or $t\cdot$ harms,
308:3 Tear or $t\cdot$ harms,
309:3 Tear or $t\cdot$ harms,
371:3 $t\cdot$ 'neath Thy rod,

triumphant
88:3 Ever by $t\cdot$ hope
89:3 Ever by $t\cdot$ hope
112:1 on faith's $t\cdot$ pinion;
185:3 thy light's $t\cdot$ glow
310:2 the Truth $t\cdot$ rang:
335:2 $T\cdot$ reach their home:

triumphed
381:2 Had $t\cdot$ over cross
388:3 Where Jesus $t\cdot$ we

triumphs
65:3 $t\cdot$ Love hath won.
234:3 trust that $t\cdot$ over wrong.
235:3 trust that $t\cdot$ over wrong.

triumph-song
264:4 voices In the $t\cdot$;

trod
120:2 Upon thy foes has $t\cdot$;
179:1 way the Master $t\cdot$;
203:2 our gentle Master $t\cdot$,
245:2 path that thou hast $t\cdot$
260:3 martyr's path who $t\cdot$;
264:2 the saints have $t\cdot$;

trod
265:2 Jesus $t\cdot$ it, press thou
288:2 way the Saviour $t\cdot$,
289:2 way the Saviour $t\cdot$,
296:2 follow where he $t\cdot$;
352:1 $t\cdot$ In wondrous love,
353:1 $t\cdot$ In wondrous love,

trouble
80:1 In $t\cdot$ our unfailing
85:3 floods of $t\cdot$ flow
125:1 noise and $t\cdot$ free;
204:2 No $t\cdot$ shall touch
224:1 To Thee in every $t\cdot$
225:1 To Thee in every $t\cdot$

troubled
95:2 calm, o'er $t\cdot$ sea,
118:3 $t\cdot$ thoughts be still;
195:1 tumult of my $t\cdot$ breast.
207:5 upon the $t\cdot$ breast,
208:5 upon the $t\cdot$ breast,
209:5 upon the $t\cdot$ breast,
210:5 upon the $t\cdot$ breast,
211:5 upon the $t\cdot$ breast,
212:5 upon the $t\cdot$ breast,
253:4 earth's $t\cdot$, angry sea
254:4 earth's $t\cdot$, angry sea
255:4 earth's $t\cdot$, angry sea
256:4 earth's $t\cdot$, angry sea
257:4 earth's $t\cdot$, angry sea

true
20:1 Be $t\cdot$ and list the
416:1 Be $t\cdot$ and list the
20:1 Be $t\cdot$ unto thy high
416:1 Be $t\cdot$ unto thy high
20:3 $T\cdot$ to our God whose
416:3 $T\cdot$ to our God whose
20:3 $t\cdot$ means $t\cdot$ to God
416:3 $t\cdot$ means $t\cdot$ to God
21:1 love its $t\cdot$ abode.
22:1 love its $t\cdot$ abode.
35:1 Christ, the $t\cdot$, the
37:1 The $t\cdot$ thy chartered
38:1 The $t\cdot$ thy chartered
51:3 to be good and $t\cdot$
52:3 to be good and $t\cdot$
66:3 reveal Thy likeness $t\cdot$,
421:3 reveal Thy likeness $t\cdot$,
73:2 Every $t\cdot$ desire with
76:1 God, the $t\cdot$, eternal
113:3 To Thy service $t\cdot$.
141:2 planting timely, $t\cdot$,
154:1 Spirit $t\cdot$ and tender,
155:1 Spirit $t\cdot$ and tender,
156:1 Spirit $t\cdot$ and tender,
174:2 Love is $t\cdot$ solace

true
175:2 $t\cdot$ being one with Thee.
178:1 $t\cdot$ crown and glory,
179:3 Showing $t\cdot$ brotherhood,
195:1 my soul's $t\cdot$ rest;
249:2 $T\cdot$ gladness is the
250:2 $T\cdot$ gladness is the
259:2 $t\cdot$ and inward faith
263:3 find the $t\cdot$ atonement,
266:4 how $t\cdot$ Christians love;
269:3 The $t\cdot$ communion gain.
270:3 The $t\cdot$ communion gain.
290:3 $T\cdot$ to the last, press
292:1 shield of $t\cdot$ faith,
303:4 holy, $t\cdot$, and free.
313:2 $T\cdot$ praise shall tune
332:1 with $t\cdot$ content to fill.
339:3 we, God's children $t\cdot$,
343:2 $T\cdot$ wisdom doth impart;
344:2 $T\cdot$ wisdom doth impart;
429:2 $T\cdot$ wisdom doth impart;
352:1 That in $t\cdot$ meekness
353:1 That in $t\cdot$ meekness
360:1 $T\cdot$, the heart grows
379:1 with all $t\cdot$ bliss
380:1 with all $t\cdot$ bliss
414:1 I know 'tis $t\cdot$,

truly
19:2 witness $t\cdot$ to His Word,
121:2 $t\cdot$ rest upon His word
122:2 $t\cdot$ rest upon His word
125:2 $t\cdot$ blest Who on Thee
178:1 $T\cdot$ is God's counsel
1 $T\cdot$ all His ways
217:1 has $t\cdot$ spoken, That
266:2 are $t\cdot$ born of God
349:2 Reflecting $t\cdot$ all
367:2 heart made $t\cdot$ His,

trumpet
17:3 sound the $t\cdot$ call,

trust
6:3 And $t\cdot$ His love
49:2 simple $t\cdot$ like theirs
50:2 simple $t\cdot$ like theirs
76:1 $T\cdot$ His Father-
Motherhood.
115:2 $t\cdot$ in Thy protecting,
116:2 $t\cdot$ in Thy protecting,
121:2 In this their $t\cdot$,
122:2 In this their $t\cdot$,
124:1 $t\cdot$ His constant care.
402:1 $t\cdot$ His constant care.
130:2 $t\cdot$ us to Thy keeping.
139:3 childlike $t\cdot$ be yours
427:3 childlike $t\cdot$ be yours

trust
176:2 $t\cdot$ in God's great Word,
188:1 love and $t\cdot$ His plan.
189:1 $t\cdot$ me to His Word.
203:1 place our $t\cdot$ in Thee,
204:3 $t\cdot$ in Thy truth
216:2 O $t\cdot$ in God
230:3 simple $t\cdot$ can find
231:3 simple $t\cdot$ can find
234:3 In $t\cdot$ that triumphs
235:3 In $t\cdot$ that triumphs
260:2 take in $t\cdot$ my road;
332:2 $t\cdot$ His promise long,
343:3 their $t\cdot$ in thee
344:3 their $t\cdot$ in thee
429:3 their $t\cdot$ in thee
343:4 That Truth to $t\cdot$,
344:4 That Truth to $t\cdot$,
429:4 That Truth to $t\cdot$,
359:1-3 $T\cdot$ the Eternal
1 $T\cdot$ on and wait,
361:1 $T\cdot$ all to God,

trustful
265:3 $t\cdot$, calm endeavor,

trusting
44:3 Come, $t\cdot$ heart,

trustingly
7:2 who $t\cdot$ abide in Thee.
149:1 $t\cdot$ we turn to God
426:1 $t\cdot$ we turn to God

trusts
216:1 $t\cdot$ in God's protection
361:3 $t\cdot$ in His providing,

Truth
2:1 beam of $T\cdot$ displaces
3 blessed $T\cdot$ is given,
5:1 Obey the voice of $T\cdot$,
2 all of $T\cdot$ you must
7:1 $T\cdot$ that maketh free,
11:2 Christ, the $T\cdot$, for all
12:1 $T\cdot$ that meets your
13:1 $T\cdot$ that meets your
12:2 $T\cdot$ that makes men free.
13:2 $T\cdot$ that makes men free.
15:1 cleansing fires of $T\cdot$
17:1 ye sentinels of $T\cdot$,
20:2 $T\cdot$ dispels the shadows
416:2 $T\cdot$ dispels the shadows
23:4 $T\cdot$ infinite,—so far
24:4 $T\cdot$ infinite,—so far
25:4 $T\cdot$ infinite,—so far
26:4 $T\cdot$ infinite,—so far
27:4 $T\cdot$ infinite,—so far
28:4 $T\cdot$ infinite,—so far

Truth

34:4 In T there is no pain
39:2 light of T to us
40:1 Life, T, and Love;
48:2 when T he heeds;
   3 Life and T and Love,
51:2 Life, T and Love
52:2 Life, T and Love
69:3 bands of Love and T
423:3 bands of Love and T
70:1 His T is ever near.
74:1 T is at thy side;
   2 word of T is there
85:1 God of T, eternal
   2 T of Thy revealing.
93:2 One T unchanged
101:2 shining Word Of T,
104:3 Give us, O T,
113:1 Gird us with T,
136:1 clear light of T
138:2 perfect T and boundless
   3 That T gives promise
141:4 T will summon, soon
146:2 Reflecting T and right,
147:2 Reflecting T and right,
172:2 but T abides;
175:1 T divine, that
176:3 T the wide earth
183:1 all to T must come.
184:1 all to T must come.
188:3 T that maketh all
197:1 day of T is breaking;
198:1 day of T is breaking;
201:1 T will be your food.
404:1 T will be your food.
201:2 T will from error
404:2 T will from error
201:4 T and Light and Love;
404:4 T and Light and Love;
203:1 T that makes men
206:2 our Father-Mother, T,
428:2 our Father-Mother, T,
214:1 Whose Word is T,
221:3 T that makes us free.
229:2 T which sage and
230:2 Light, the T, the Way.
231:2 Light, the T, the Way.
233:3 With flames of T
419:3 With flames of T
236:2 Let T be proclaimed,
251:1 O T, unchanged,
252:1 O T, unchanged,
253:5 Thus T engrounds me
254:5 Thus T engrounds me
255:5 Thus T engrounds me
256:5 Thus T engrounds me
257:5 Thus T engrounds me

Truth

258:1 of T with falsehood,
   2 keep abreast of T,
   3 T alone is strong;
276:2 T which we so long
277:2 T which we so long
288:1 Way, the T, the Life.
289:1 Way, the T, the Life.
288:2 Life, the T, the Love.
289:2 Life, the T, the Love.
293:1-3 Rock of Ages, T
294:1-3 Rock of Ages, T
295:1-3 Rock of Ages, T
293:2 T, our fortress strong,
294:2 T, our fortress strong,
295:2 T, our fortress strong,
293:3 Christ, the T,
294:3 Christ, the T,
295:3 Christ, the T,
298:1 T that made us free,
299:1 T that made us free,
300:1 T that made us free,
301:1 T that made us free,
302:1 T that made us free,
298:4 T in thought and deed;
299:4 T in thought and deed;
300:4 T in thought and deed;
301:4 T in thought and deed;
302:4 T in thought and deed;
310:1 T has come again
   2 T triumphant rang:
   2 T hath rolled the
337:1 T Herself can never
338:1 T Herself can never
339:1 saving T who know,
342:3 Love by T revealed,
343:2 Thou art the T:
344:2 Thou art the T:
429:2 Thou art the T:
343:2 canst unfold that T,
344:2 canst unfold that T,
429:2 canst unfold that T,
343:4 Way, the T, the Life:
344:4 Way, the T, the Life:
429:4 Way, the T, the Life:
343:4 That T to trust,
344:4 That T to trust,
429:4 That T to trust,
349:1 and T and Love,
355:1 T comes alike to all
   2 Life, T and Love
363:3 T reveals the perfect
370:2 Light of T wherein
371:2 O God of T,
382:3 T dawns on the sight;

truth

10:1 t from out His
411:1 t from out His
42:2 Thy t receive;
56:3 Thy t unchanged
62:2 Eternal t attends
63:2 Eternal t attends
72:1 Thy light, Thy t,
405:1 Thy light, Thy t,
77:2 t be thine affiance,
78:2 t be thine affiance,
82:3 glorious Gospel of t
85:1 Thy t is ours for
99:2 His t shall be thy
100:2 His t shall be thy
111:1 Thy t shall break
131:1 way, the t, the life,
132:1 way, the t, the life,
131:2 A t, too large for
132:2 A t, too large for
131:3 t that makes men free,
132:3 t that makes men free,
139:2 God's healing t
427:2 God's healing t
143:3 t Thou dost impart
154:2 Within Thy t
155:2 Within Thy t
156:2 Within Thy t
154:3 Thy love and t
155:3 Thy love and t
156:3 Thy love and t
160:3 t tatters those,
161:3 t tatters those,
162:3 t tatters those,
164:3 with t and grace,
165:3 with t and grace,
417:3 with t and grace,
168:2 light Of Gospel t
185:3 we know that the t
204:3 trust in Thy t is
218:3 freedom of the t,
219:3 freedom of the t,
220:3 freedom of the t,
226:1 Of t that spreads
232:1 in this t confide:
406:1 in this t confide:
240:2 t Thy words reveal;
241:2 t Thy words reveal;
319:2 Whose light is t,
   3 t to make us free,
322:2 Lord, may Thy t
323:2 Lord, may Thy t
326:2 panoply of t complete,
327:1 quit His steadfast t
328:1 quit His steadfast t
333:2 witness to the t,
334:1 brings the t to sight;

truth
336:2 $t\cdot$ divine and precepts
346:3 Spirit of $t\cdot$ and love,
401:3 Spirit of $t\cdot$ and love,
350:3 $t\cdot$ we are applying,
368:2 Peace and $t\cdot$ its course
369:2 Peace and $t\cdot$ its course
383:1 dims thy sense of $t\cdot$

truthful
88:2 $T\cdot$ Spirit, dwell
89:2 $T\cdot$ Spirit, dwell
88:2 I myself would $t\cdot$ be,
89:2 I myself would $t\cdot$ be,
278:2 $T\cdot$ and steadfast
279:2 $T\cdot$ and steadfast

Truth's
14:2 $T\cdot$ clear light on thee
64:1 into $T\cdot$ clear day;
102:3 Into $T\cdot$ eternal day.
103:3 Into $T\cdot$ eternal day.
171:2 $T\cdot$ healing garment
413:2 $T\cdot$ healing garment
172:3 $T\cdot$ undaunted ray,
245:3 to $T\cdot$ green pastures
267:2 see $T\cdot$ glowing face,
268:2 see $T\cdot$ glowing face,
287:3 $T\cdot$ call, Let there
408:3 $T\cdot$ call, Let there
382:2 art $T\cdot$ honest child,

truths
143:1 $t\cdot$ the test invite,
226:3 Thy $t\cdot$ may tell,
322:1 $t\cdot$ revealed by His
323:1 $t\cdot$ revealed by His

try
143:1 bid us search and $t\cdot$.
284:2 infant lips can $t\cdot$;
285:2 infant lips can $t\cdot$;
286:2 infant lips can $t\cdot$;

tryst
275:3 we keep our $t\cdot$,

tumult
33:3 no $t\cdot$ can alarm thee,
72:1 strife and $t\cdot$ cease.
405:1 strife and $t\cdot$ cease.
93:4 peace, with $t\cdot$ stilled,
174:1 bids all $t\cdot$ cease;
195:1 And stills the $t\cdot$ of

tune
194:3 mortal modes in $t\cdot$,
410:3 mortal modes in $t\cdot$,
281:1 Strains of joy $t\cdot$
313:2 True praise shall $t\cdot$

turn
56:1 $t\cdot$ unfilled to Thee
  2 longings $t\cdot$ to Thee,
57:1 $t\cdot$ away from sorrow,
70:3 $T\cdot$ but to Him,
109:1 $T\cdot$ us home to heavenly
110:1 $T\cdot$ us home to heavenly
115:2 Help us $t\cdot$ to Thee
116:2 Help us $t\cdot$ to Thee
133:3 $t\cdot$ all tears, all
424:3 $t\cdot$ all tears, all
148:2 No want shall $t\cdot$ me
149:1 we $t\cdot$ to God aright.

turn
426:1 we $t\cdot$ to God aright.
171:2 When we $t\cdot$ from earth
413:2 When we $t\cdot$ from earth
218:1 In gladness hither $t\cdot$
219:1 In gladness hither $t\cdot$
220:1 In gladness hither $t\cdot$
229:1 though we $t\cdot$ from Thee.
232:1 To Thee we $t\cdot$ from
406:1 To Thee we $t\cdot$ from
233:3 weary child shall $t\cdot$
419:3 weary child shall $t\cdot$
374:3 $t\cdot$ from sense to Soul,
375:3 $t\cdot$ from sense to Soul,
376:2 Nor ever $t\cdot$ aside,
377:2 Nor ever $t\cdot$ aside,
378:1 We $t\cdot$ to Thee,

turning
85:3 path that has no $t\cdot$,
381:3 homeward $t\cdot$ To God

turns
134:2 Thy providence $t\cdot$ all
288:1 $t\cdot$ the darkness into
289:1 $t\cdot$ the darkness into

turn'st
134:3 Thou $t\cdot$ my mourning

twixt
258:1 $T\cdot$ the darkness and

tyrants'
160:2 stones, or $t\cdot$ thrones,
161:2 stones, or $t\cdot$ thrones,
162:2 stones, or $t\cdot$ thrones,

U

unafraid
136:2 All $u\cdot$ I wait,
203:2 Love's stronghold $u\cdot$.
226:2 hearts all $u\cdot$,
342:1 in His presence, $u\cdot$,

unaided
88:3 $u\cdot$ man must fail;
89:3 $u\cdot$ man must fail;

unalloyed
269:2 With longing $u\cdot$,
270:2 With longing $u\cdot$,

unbelief
35:3 Scatter all my $u\cdot$;
399:3 $u\cdot$ is sure to err,
400:3 $u\cdot$ is sure to err,

unbind
168:3 Our chains $u\cdot$,

unbound
4:1 thought from sense $u\cdot$,
10:2 from its chains $u\cdot$ us.
411:2 from its chains $u\cdot$ us.

unbounded
249:1 Of His $u\cdot$ grace,
250:1 Of His $u\cdot$ grace,

unceasing
75:3 Him shall prayer $u\cdot$,
194:1 prayer, $U\cdot$, voiceless,
410:1 prayer, $U\cdot$, voiceless,

unchanged
56:3 truth $u\cdot$ hath ever
93:2 $u\cdot$ while ages run;
124:3 $U\cdot$ from day to day:
402:3 $U\cdot$ from day to day:
251:1 Truth, $u\cdot$, unchanging,
252:1 Truth, $u\cdot$, unchanging,
261:1 $U\cdot$ by changing place.
262:1 $U\cdot$ by changing place.

unchanging
76:1 Can $u\cdot$ Love forget?
251:1 Truth, unchanged, $u\cdot$,
252:1 Truth, unchanged, $u\cdot$,
269:1 God is Love, $u\cdot$ Love,
270:1 God is Love, $u\cdot$ Love,
359:1 God the $u\cdot$ pities

unclouded
80:3 His u· presence

uncompanioned
35:2 U·, Lord, by thee;

unconfined
240:1 Thy grace is u·;
241:1 Thy grace is u·;

unconscious
311:2 U· of their harm:
420:2 U· of their harm:

uncouth
258:2 makes ancient creeds u·;

undaunted
150:3 rises u· by strife,
172:3 Truth's u· ray,

undefiled
382:2 u· In Christly paths

underneath
99:1 u· th' Almighty's shade

understand
73:2 may u· His message,
74:2 all To read and u·.
176:1 that all may u·
216:1 God's law can u·,
      2 trust in God and u·.
356:2 u· Thy holy counsel,

understanding
69:1 Lord, an u· heart,
423:1 Lord, an u· heart,
143:2 With u· blest, Created
149:1 And u· prayer is fully
426:1 And u· prayer is fully
157:3 u· Of our oneness
332:2 With u· never dim,

understood
85:1 Thou mayst be u·,
102:1 May be better u·.
103:1 May be better u·.
160:3 truth tatters . . ., When u·.
161:3 truth tatters . . ., When u·.
162:3 truth tatters . . ., When u·.
221:1 Thy works, now u·,

undertone
418:2 But in u· sublime,

undimmed
206:1 with eyes u· define
428:1 with eyes u· define
381:2 Christ, u· by dying,

undismayed
146:3 With courage u·,
147:3 With courage u·,

undisturbed
99:1 Fearless and u· abide;
263:1 U·, our hearts rejoice;

undoing
115:2 from our own u·,
116:2 from our own u·,

unending
36:4 U· festival we keep

unexpressed
284:1 Uttered or u·;
285:1 Uttered or u·;
286:1 Uttered or u·;

unfailing
80:1 In trouble our u·
119:3 Spirit of u· strength.

unfailingly
7:1 u· abide in Thee.

unfaltering
36:4 U· songs we sing,

unfilled
56:1 turn u· to Thee

unfold
197:1 fair the leaves u·,
198:1 fair the leaves u·,
215:2 east or west u·;
343:2 canst u· that Truth,
344:2 canst u· that Truth,
429:2 canst u· that Truth,

unfoldeth
112:3 Loveliness and joy u·;

unfolding
399:2 U· every hour;
400:2 U· every hour;

unfolds
149:2 U· a joy unknown
426:2 U· a joy unknown
260:2 u· His blessings new,

unfurled
82:3 banner of Christ u·,
203:1 flag of hope . . . u·,
363:3 new powers u·,

unguarded
99:2 cover thy u· head.
100:2 cover thy u· head,

unhallowed
51:2 U· thought He could not
52:2 U· thought He could not

unharmed
37:4 U· upon th' eternal
38:4 U· upon th' eternal

unheard
54:2 U· by human ear,

unholy
303:3 And still u· strife.

union
126:3 u· sweet, and dear
127:3 u· sweet, and dear
403:3 u· sweet, and dear
196:2 closer bond of u·,
236:4 one in a u· of love,
370:1 this pure eternal u·

unite
4:2 O God, u· us
266:3 love our hearts u·,
355:1 let us all u·,

united
2:3 peace and love, u·,
29:2 u· in one band.
83:1 u· hearts and hands.

unites
196:2 all that now u· us

unity
14:4 Man's u· with God.
297:1 and . . . Son, blest u·;

unkind
30:2 thought or word u·,
31:2 thought or word u·,
32:2 thought or word u·,

unkindness
315:2 u· made them so;
316:2 u· made them so;

unknown
91:1 a joy before u·.
422:1 a joy before u·.
115:1 through dangers oft u·.
116:1 through dangers oft u·.
149:2 u· till found in Him.

unknown
426:2 u· till found in Him.
258:3 behind the dim u·
276:1 to worldly minds u·;
277:1 to worldly minds u·;
354:1 In paths before u·;

unless
361:2 u· the Lord ordain.

unloosing
202:1 U· bonds of all
412:1 U· bonds of all

unmixed
121:3 faith u· with doubt
122:3 faith u· with doubt

unmoved
336:3 U·, amid dissolving

unreal
391:4 U· the ages' long

unresting
418:3 In a long, u· line

unsealed
109:1 our hearts, u·, adoring,
110:1 our hearts, u·, adoring,
176:3 with Book u·,

unseals
392:3 the door of Life u·
393:3 the door of Life u·

unseen
108:1 and handle things u·;
228:1 Thy comfort, though u·,
229:1 u· o'er the heads of
261:2 One u· presence
262:2 One u· presence
385:2 present ... though oft u·
414:1 Of u· things above,

unshod
297:2 walk with u· feet;

unsought
134:3 leadest me by u· ways,
381:4 peace ... and u· joy;

unspeakable
45:3 this Thy gift u·,

unsung
249:1 leave u· one blessing,
250:1 leave u· one blessing,

unswerving
5:2 requires u· might:

until
326:3 U· he more than

untiring
36:4 U· praise we lift
290:1 U· in your holy fight,

untold
180:3 gives a joy u·:
197:1 down the years u·,
198:1 down the years u·,

untrod
218:3 joy of paths u·,
219:3 joy of paths u·,
220:3 joy of paths u·,

untroubled
226:2 With Thine u· light.

unveil
109:2 Reverent lives u· Thy
110:2 Reverent lives u· Thy

unveiled
253:3 His u·, sweet mercies
254:3 His u·, sweet mercies
255:3 His u·, sweet mercies
256:3 His u·, sweet mercies
257:3 His u·, sweet mercies

unveiling
128:2 U· Love's immortal day.
129:2 U· Love's immortal day.

unwasted
261:1 U· by the lapse of
262:1 U· by the lapse of

unwearied
246:1 he, u·, mounteth.
273:2 To the mark u· press,
274:2 To the mark u· press,
320:4 They, with u· step,
321:4 They, with u· step,
409:4 They, with u· step,

upheld
123:2 U· by My gracious,

uphold
189:2 His love doth e'er u·
204:2 dost u· and approve
236:2 may their brethren u·.
245:3 strong hand doth u·;

upholds
391:3 to-day u· His throne.

uplift
14:4 U· thee from the sod,
139:3 U· your thought,
427:3 U· your thought,

uplifted
101:1 U· they beheld in
171:1 hope and faith u·;
413:1 hope and faith u·;

uplifts
243:2 U· the sinning and
244:2 U· the sinning and

upright
12:3 Man pure and u·,
13:3 Man pure and u·,
291:1 U·, simple, free

upward
2:3 Point u· unto heaven.
54:1 points the u· gaze;
64:3 way leads u· and its
181:1 u· to the light.
192:5 U· I fly,
193:5 U· I fly,
202:2 footsteps of the u· way.
412:1 footsteps of the u· way.
207:1 on u· wing tonight.
208:1 on u· wing tonight.
209:1 on u· wing tonight.
210:1 on u· wing tonight.
211:1 on u· wing tonight.
212:1 on u· wing tonight.
258:2 u· still and onward

upward-soaring
136:2 would check My u· way;

use
96:1 u· it in His name;
324:3 my every thought, to u·

used
352:1 meekness u· to shine,
353:1 meekness u· to shine,

useful
183:2 u· and the great,
184:2 u· and the great,

utterance
54:3 All u· faileth there;

uttered
284:1 desire, U· or unexpressed;
285:1 desire, U· or unexpressed;
286:1 desire, U· or unexpressed;

V

vain
37:4 In $v\cdot$ the surge's
38:4 In $v\cdot$ the surge's
37:4 In $v\cdot$ the drifting
38:4 In $v\cdot$ the drifting
53:3 fears and $v\cdot$ alarms
57:2 the $v\cdot$ cares that vex
101:3 hosts who toil in $v\cdot$
134:1 And never look in $v\cdot$;
141:1 labor build in $v\cdot$;
200:2 $v\cdot$ were their steeds
263:1 Joys are $v\cdot$ that
269:1 prayer for . . . is $v\cdot$;
270:1 prayer for . . . is $v\cdot$;
269:3 words alone are $v\cdot$,
270:3 words alone are $v\cdot$,
315:2 have toiled in $v\cdot$;
316:2 have toiled in $v\cdot$;
327:1 make His promise $v\cdot$.
328:1 make His promise $v\cdot$.
331:1 but $v\cdot$ homage, Lord,
1 In $v\cdot$ our lips
361:2 is thy toil in $v\cdot$;
364:1 $V\cdot$ our bulwarks and
2 $V\cdot$ were all our toil
2 $V\cdot$, without His grace
372:1 In $v\cdot$ we search the
373:1 In $v\cdot$ we search the
379:3 not in shadows $v\cdot$,
380:3 not in shadows $v\cdot$,
382:3 $V\cdot$ dreams shall
396:3 In $v\cdot$ shall evil
397:3 In $v\cdot$ shall evil
396:3 hell in $v\cdot$ oppose;
397:3 hell in $v\cdot$ oppose;
399:3 scan His work in $v\cdot$;
400:3 scan His work in $v\cdot$;

vainer
364:3 $V\cdot$ still the hope

vainly
364:1 $V\cdot$, through night's

vale
75:2 From hill to $v\cdot$
379:3 $v\cdot$ of tears and pain.
380:3 $v\cdot$ of tears and pain.

valiantly
292:1 righteousness $v\cdot$ gird,

valley
2:2 rings from hill and $v\cdot$,

valleys
185:3 Through all earth's $v\cdot$

valor's
296:3 For $v\cdot$ act supreme;

vanish
173:3 will $v\cdot$ into sight;
359:2 the clouds that $v\cdot$

vanished
202:3 ashes of the $v\cdot$ years;
412:2 ashes of the $v\cdot$ years;

vanishes
287:3 $v\cdot$ Death's drear and
408:3 $v\cdot$ Death's drear and

vanities
379:4 earth's tempting $v\cdot$,
380:4 earth's tempting $v\cdot$,

vanity
240:3 $v\cdot$ of things below,
241:3 $v\cdot$ of things below,

vanquished
200:3 Th' oppressor is $v\cdot$,

vast
226:2 touch the future $v\cdot$
303:2 $v\cdot$ its power may be

veil
66:4 sweep away the $v\cdot$,
421:4 sweep away the $v\cdot$,
224:2 look within the $v\cdot$,
225:2 look within the $v\cdot$,

veils
111:1 $v\cdot$ and darkens Thy
138:3 blinding $v\cdot$ are drawn,

veneration
216:2 wait on Him with $v\cdot$,

verdant
330:2 the $v\cdot$ pastures grow,

verdure
16:1 rock and $v\cdot$ wild,
97:2 scene of $v\cdot$ brightening,
98:2 scene of $v\cdot$ brightening,
314:2 In $v\cdot$, beauty, strength,

very
74:1 $v\cdot$ rocks may seem
182:2 $v\cdot$ founts of love
265:1 legion $V\cdot$ near thee,

vex
57:2 cares that $v\cdot$ our days

victorious
120:2 Lord, in strength $v\cdot$,
177:2 Let the gospel be $v\cdot$
282:2 made His saints $v\cdot$,
290:2 $V\cdot$ over every ill,

victors
67:2 $v\cdot$ who o'ercame;
68:2 $v\cdot$ who o'ercame;

victory
8:3 where, grave, thy $v\cdot$?
104:4 $v\cdot$ won O'er sense
204:3 battle the $v\cdot$ claim,—
292:2 The $v\cdot$ His, when
296:Ref. with Christ to $v\cdot$
325:3 $v\cdot$ o'er the grave.
326:3 who gives him $v\cdot$.

view
218:4 horizon's grander $v\cdot$;
219:4 horizon's grander $v\cdot$;
220:4 horizon's grander $v\cdot$;
260:2 rising . . . to my $v\cdot$,
384:1 dazzling glories $v\cdot$?

vigor
320:3 youthful $v\cdot$ cease;
321:3 youthful $v\cdot$ cease;
409:3 youthful $v\cdot$ cease;

vine
141:2 branches and the $v\cdot$.

violence
33:3 nor $v\cdot$ shall harm

virtues
386:2 works and $v\cdot$ shine,
387:2 works and $v\cdot$ shine,

vision
64:3 The $v\cdot$ infinite
66:4 give us $v\cdot$ clear,
421:4 give us $v\cdot$ clear,
185:2 clear $v\cdot$ thou hast
2 this $v\cdot$ gently mold
265:2 mount of $v\cdot$ won;
287:2 to our widening $v\cdot$
408:2 to our widening $v\cdot$

visit
35:3 $V\cdot$ then this soul

vital
284:3 Christian's $v\cdot$ breath,
285:3 Christian's $v\cdot$ breath,
286:3 Christian's $v\cdot$ breath,

155

voice
5:1 A v· from heaven
1 the v· of Truth,
10:2 No other v· we heed,
411:2 No other v· we heed,
20:1 list the v· within,
416:1 list the v· within,
36:1 mighty is thy v·.
49:3 still small v· of calm.
50:3 still small v· of calm.
54:2 small v· Unheard by
67:2 warning v· exclaim,
68:2 warning v· exclaim,
73:2 Man, ..., hears His v·.
74:1, 2 that still small v·
76:2 Hear His v· above the
84:2 hear thy living v·,
94:2 v· of God that spake
    3 v· of God, forever near,
121:4 No human v· declare.
122:4 No human v· declare.
136:1 listening for Thy v·,
137:1 tender v· like Thine

voice
168:1 return the joyful v·;
215:1 Instruction's warning v·;
263:1 heed the Father's v·.
282:1 His mighty v· obeyed;
304:1 listen for Thy v·,
305:1 listen for Thy v·,
306:1 listen for Thy v·,
307:1 listen for Thy v·,
308:1 listen for Thy v·,
309:1 listen for Thy v·,
313:2 shall tune my v·,
324:2 Take my v·, and let
342:1, 3 lift up your v·.
396:1 sovereign v· obey;
397:1 sovereign v· obey;
418:2 v· that must be heard,

voiceless
194:1 Unceasing, v·,
410:1 Unceasing, v·,

voices
36:1 v· of this earth

voices
58:2 hear no other v·,
72:2 hymns your v· raise.
405:2 hymns your v· raise.
112:2 accuser's mocking v·
194:3 v· that are worldly
410:3 v· that are worldly
199:1 grateful hearts and v·,
264:4 with ours your v·
271:2 infant v· shall proclaim
272:2 infant v· shall proclaim
273:1 hearts and v· up;
274:1 hearts and v· up;
418:3 v·, loud and low,

void
269:2 ne'er returneth v·.
270:2 ne'er returneth v·.
303:1 deem it v· of power;
360:2 God its v· can fill;

vows
75:3 daily v·, ascend;

W

wait
9:3 hearts that w· on God
77:2 heart, with courage w·;
78:2 heart, with courage w·;
92:2 not w· nor question
136:2 All unafraid I w·,
170:1 And w· within myself
207:3 W·, and love more
208:3 W·, and love more
209:3 W·, and love more
210:3 W·, and love more
211:3 W·, and love more
212:3 W·, and love more
216:2 O w· on Him with
247:1 W· on the everlasting
248:1 W· on the everlasting
263:1 w· the brighter morrow;
320:3 who w· upon the Lord
321:3 who w· upon the Lord
409:3 who w· upon the Lord
332:1 w· to do His will.
341:3 Father come, and w·;
359:1 Trust on and w·,
365:1 W·, my soul, upon
366:1 W·, my soul, upon
398:1 Each in his office w·,

waiting
207:1 owns each w· hour,
208:1 owns each w· hour,

waiting
209:1 owns each w· hour,
210:1 owns each w· hour,
211:1 owns each w· hour,
212:1 owns each w· hour,
229:2 w· shepherds' way,
232:2 our w· hopes behold
406:2 our w· hopes behold
253:1 O'er w· harpstrings of
254:1 O'er w· harpstrings of
255:1 O'er w· harpstrings of
256:1 O'er w· harpstrings of
257:1 O'er w· harpstrings of

waits
92:4 w· but Thy command,
229:1 And w· to bless us
269:3 Forever w· to bless.
270:2 Forever w· to bless.
296:3 long the conquest w·
303:1 w· its natal hour.

wake
9:4 O w· and hear the
160:5 earth-bound w·, God's
161:5 earth-bound w·, God's
162:5 earth-bound w·, God's
253:2 w· a white-winged angel
254:2 w· a white-winged angel
255:2 w· a white-winged angel

wake
256:2 w· a white-winged angel
257:2 w· a white-winged angel
253:3 w· to know A world
254:3 w· to know A world
255:3 w· to know A world
256:3 w· to know A world
257:3 w· to know A world

waken
296:2 W·, hear your Captain's
374:3 bid mankind to w·
375:3 bid mankind to w·

wakes
79:1 Bliss He w· and
222:2 The dark night w·,
223:2 The dark night w·,

waketh
148:2 His wisdom ever w·,
317:1 When the bird w·,

waking
2:1 o'er the w· earth
14:2 praise, O w· heart,
192:4 w· thoughts Bright
193:4 w· thoughts Bright
197:1 Love's immortal w·.
198:1 Love's immortal w·.

waking
202:1 dreams for joyful w',
412:1 dreams for joyful w',
287:1 our w' thought ascends,
408:1 our w' thought ascends,
335:1 sons of earth are w'

walk
33:2 thou w' through hostile
96:2 Shall w' the rounds
139:1 I w' with Love
427:1 I w' with Love
139:2 all may w' with Love
427:2 all may w' with Love
139:3 Come, w' with Love
427:3 Come, w' with Love
148:2 I will w' with Him.
   3 He will w' with me.
179:1 shall w' with God.
233:1 w' the ways of God,
419:1 w' the ways of God,
234:1 let me w' with thee
235:1 let me w' with thee
247:1 w' with God along
248:1 w' with God along
247:1 He will w' with you.
248:1 He will w' with you.
253:4 I see Christ w',
254:4 I see Christ w',
255:4 I see Christ w',
256:4 I see Christ w',
257:4 I see Christ w',
278:1 W' thou with courage
279:1 W' thou with courage
297:2 Horeb whereon we w'
349:3 We w' in freedom
367:1-4 W' in the light,
384:3 The lame shall w',

walketh
379:3 W' not in shadows
380:3 W' not in shadows

walks
139:2 Who w' with Love
427:2 Who w' with Love
296:2 faith that w' with God.

walls
37:1 Outspread thy w'
38:1 Outspread thy w'
71:1 By salvation's w'
227:2 within no w' confined,

wander
203:2 w' through earth's
245:2 from that path we w',
311:2 The lambs who w' by
420:2 The lambs who w' by

wandered
115:1 When we w', Thou
116:1 When we w', Thou
259:3 stream has never w'
415:2 w' forlorn and weary'

wanderer
163:3 bring the w' back
192:2 Though like the w',
193:2 Though like the w',

wanderers
43:2 Come unto me, ye w',
128:3 w' from the Father's
129:3 w' from the Father's

wanderings
368:3 let thy w' cease,
369:3 let thy w' cease,

wane
19:1 joy shall never w'.
174:2 radiance cannot w'.
264:3 Kingdoms rise and w',
271:1 moons shall wax and w'
272:1 moons shall wax and w'

wanes
142:4 And every symbol w':

want
71:3 fear of w' remove.
148:2 No w' shall turn me
224:3 What can I w' beside?
225:3 What can I w' beside?
263:1 Mid the shade of w'
271:3 sons of w' are blest.
272:3 sons of w' are blest.
341:2 w', or in our wealth,

war
200:2 their chariots of w'.
264:1, Ref. Marching as to w',
335:1 Prepared for Zion's w'.

ward
33:2 Watch and w' o'er thee

warfare
157:3 W' shall forever cease,
236:1 Gaunt w' is doomed,

warm
35:2 and w' my heart.
372:2 w', sweet, tender,
373:1 w', sweet, tender,

warmth
91:2 shine With tender w'
422:2 shine With tender w'

warmth
311:3 Pour w' and radiance
420:3 Pour w' and radiance
319:2 whose w' is love,

warning
67:2 with w' voice exclaim,
68:2 with w' voice exclaim,
215:1 Instruction's w' voice;

warrior
326:1 Christian w', see him

warrior's
67:2 mark each w' way;
68:2 mark each w' way;

wash
304:3 Shepherd, w' them clean.
305:3 Shepherd, w' them clean.
306:3 Shepherd, w' them clean.
307:3 Shepherd, w' them clean.
308:3 Shepherd, w' them clean.
309:3 Shepherd, w' them clean.

waste
120:2 O w' Jerusalem;

watch
3:3 w' by day or night.
30:1 those who w' and love.
31:1 those who w' and love.
32:1 those who w' and love.
33:2 W' and ward o'er thee
67:1-3 W' and pray.
68:1-3 W' and pray.
172:2 those who w' afar.
183:3 w', and work, and pray.
184:3 w', and work, and pray.
186:1 w' within the night?
187:1 w' within the night?
207:4 w' and pray.
208:4 w' and pray.
209:4 w' and pray.
210:4 w' and pray.
211:4 w' and pray.
212:4 w' and pray.
213:3 w' that ends the night
258:3 w' above His own.
283:2 W' doth He tenderly
364:1 w', lest foes alarm;

watched
278:1 Cared for, w' over,
279:1 Cared for, w' over,

watches
18:2 God w' above thee,
319:1 w' of the night.

watchest
130:2 Thou w when we lie

watch fires
37:3 How gleam thy w f
38:3 How gleam thy w f

watchful
99:2 tender love and w care
100:2 tender love and w care
124:2 Beneath His w eye
402:2 Beneath His w eye
237:2 watching with the w,
398:1 And w at His gate.
     3 In w service found;

watchfulness
332:1 We need a sacred w,

watching
222:2 charity stands w
223:2 charity stands w
237:2 God is w with the

watchman
368:1-3 W, tell us of the
369:1-3 W, tell us of the
368:1 W, does its beauteous
369:1 W, does its beauteous
368:2 W, will its beams
369:2 W, will its beams
368:3 W, let thy wanderings
369:3 W, let thy wanderings

watchword
2:2 The w of reform:
   3 w has been spoken,
284:3 w, overcoming death:
285:3 w, overcoming death:
286:3 w, overcoming death:

water
298:4 Thou the w, the bread,
299:4 Thou the w, the bread,
300:4 Thou the w, the bread,
301:4 Thou the w, the bread,
302:4 Thou the w, the bread,
330:2 streams of living w

waters
40:3 see w flowing Forth
55:3 forever by still w
71:3 streams of living w,
82:1-3 w cover the sea.
90:2 the healing w flow;
95:2 By w calm, o'er

waters'
346:3 Move on the w face,
401:3 Move on the w face,

wavering
138:2 yield his w will

waves
41:1 w the golden grain,
253:5 the winds and w can
254:5 the winds and w can
255:5 the winds and w can
256:5 the winds and w can
257:5 the winds and w can

wax
271:1 moons shall w and wane
272:1 moons shall w and wane

Way
39:3 Christ, thou living W,
185:3 Thou art the W,
230:2 Light, the Truth, the W.
231:2 Light, the Truth, the W.
288:1 I am the W, the Truth,
289:1 I am the W, the Truth,
343:1 Thou art the W: to thee
344:1 Thou art the W: to thee
429:1 Thou art the W: to thee
343:4 W, the Truth, the Life:
344:4 W, the Truth, the Life:
429:4 W, the Truth, the Life:
343:4 that W to know,
344:4 that W to know,
429:4 that W to know,

way
16:1 sing my w to Thee,
   3 sing my w to-day,
23:1 clouds Pursue thy w,
24:1 clouds Pursue thy w,
25:1 clouds Pursue thy w,
26:1 clouds Pursue thy w,
27:1 clouds Pursue thy w,
28:1 clouds Pursue thy w,
39:2 and choose Thy w;
53:3 keep us all the w,
55:2 ask our w to be,
   3 rocks along our w.
58:1 in Thy blessed w.
59:2 Life with its w before
60:2 Life with its w before
61:2 Life with its w before
64:1 I have found the w.
   3 w leads upward and
65:2 Encompasseth our w;
67:2 mark each warrior's w;
68:2 mark each warrior's w;
81:1 All His w made plain
85:3 All the w that
91:3 his w to trace Whose
422:3 his w to trace Whose
92:1 God points out the w.

way
102:3 guide us all the w,
103:3 guide us all the w,
104:3 w Out of the darkness
128:2 led his followers' w.
129:2 led his followers' w.
131:1 w, the truth, the life,
132:1 w, the truth, the life,
131:2 w that is not hedged
132:2 w that is not hedged
131:3 point that living w,
132:3 point that living w,
133:1 trace the w Where Thou,
424:1 trace the w Where Thou,
136:1 Thy w of freedom,
   2 My upward-soaring w;
139:1-3 with Love along the w,
427:1-3 with Love along the w,
148:2 the w He taketh,
158:2 along the climbing w
159:2 along the climbing w
179:1 w the Master trod;
   1 Love is the royal w.
189:2 onward w doth trace,
190:3 shall the w prepare;
191:3 shall the w prepare;
192:3 let the w appear,
193:3 let the w appear,
199:1 blessed us on our w
202:2 footsteps of the upward w.
412:1 footsteps of the upward w.
203:1 falter by the w
   2 w our gentle Master
207:4 secret of the narrow w,
208:4 secret of the narrow w,
209:4 secret of the narrow w,
210:4 secret of the narrow w,
211:4 secret of the narrow w,
212:4 secret of the narrow w,
226:2 Light up our w;
228:3 as hate our Master's w.
229:2 waiting shepherds' w,
234:2 in the homeward w.
235:2 in the homeward w.
234:4 future's broadening w;
235:4 future's broadening w;
238:3 prelude finds its w;
239:3 prelude finds its w;
240:2 run the heavenly w,
241:2 run the heavenly w,
245:1 Enshroud the w with
   3 Throughout the w,
259:3 has found its w;
260:4 light upon my w,
278:1 each step of the w.
279:1 each step of the w.
281:2 Israel on their w
288:1 straight and narrow w

way
289:1 straight and narrow $w\cdot$
288:2 $w\cdot$ the Saviour trod,
289:2 $w\cdot$ the Saviour trod,
288:2 $w\cdot$ that leads to God.
289:2 $w\cdot$ that leads to God.
304:1 All the rugged $w\cdot$.
305:1 All the rugged $w\cdot$.
306:1 All the rugged $w\cdot$.
307:1 All the rugged $w\cdot$.
308:1 All the rugged $w\cdot$.
309:1 All the rugged $w\cdot$.
311:2 wander by the $w\cdot$,
420:2 wander by the $w\cdot$,
318:2 ready to choose my $w\cdot$,
324:3 In the $w\cdot$ that Thou
329:2 Wisdom's $w\cdot$ to hold,
335:2 Pursue thine onward $w\cdot$;
352:4 illume my $w\cdot$ of woe
353:4 illume my $w\cdot$ of woe
354:2 still pursue our $w\cdot$;
361:3 lights the $w\cdot$ of duty,
376:1 keep the better $w\cdot$.
377:1 keep the better $w\cdot$.
376:2 $w\cdot$ will brighter grow,
377:2 $w\cdot$ will brighter grow,
383:3 tread the narrow $w\cdot$:
392:4 and Christ the $w\cdot$;
393:4 and Christ the $w\cdot$;
396:1 peace attend your $w\cdot$.
397:1 peace attend your $w\cdot$.

ways
49:1 Forgive our foolish $w\cdot$;
50:1 Forgive our foolish $w\cdot$;
86:1 strange in all its $w\cdot$,
87:1 strange in all its $w\cdot$,
109:1 home to heavenly $w\cdot$,
110:1 home to heavenly $w\cdot$,
125:3 $w\cdot$ are just and right.
134:3 by unsought $w\cdot$,
178:1 His $w\cdot$ are bright;
206:3 our $w\cdot$ reflecting Thee,
428:3 our $w\cdot$ reflecting Thee,
215:3 Her $w\cdot$ are $w\cdot$ of
230:3 can find Thy $w\cdot$
231:3 can find Thy $w\cdot$
233:1 walk the $w\cdot$ of God,
419:1 walk the $w\cdot$ of God,
342:2 the higher, deeper $w\cdot$
371:1 reflect in all our $w\cdot$
376:2 Allured by $w\cdot$ of error,
377:2 Allured by $w\cdot$ of error,

wayward
234:2 $w\cdot$ feet to stay,
235:2 $w\cdot$ feet to stay,

weak
34:3 The $w\cdot$ and thirsty
41:3 No arm so $w\cdot$ but may
42:1 Raise the $w\cdot$, the
75:1 bid the $w\cdot$ be strong;
384:3 The $w\cdot$ be strong,
390:3 If $w\cdot$ in faith, we

weakest
96:1 make the $w\cdot$ strong.

weakness
195:3 in $w\cdot$ I am strong.
359:3 come strength in $w\cdot$,

wealth
70:3 to Him, accept His $w\cdot$,
341:2 want, or in our $w\cdot$,
360:1 $w\cdot$ is living grain;

weapon
347:3 No $w\cdot$ formed against
348:3 No $w\cdot$ formed against
376:1 The $w\cdot$ mortals sway,
377:1 The $w\cdot$ mortals sway,

wear
67:1 $W\cdot$ it ever night and
68:1 $W\cdot$ it ever night and

wearied
418:1 $w\cdot$ with their chime,

wearily
360:1 steps drag $w\cdot$?

weariness
108:1 $w\cdot$ upon Thee lean.

weary
43:1 Come unto me, ye $w\cdot$,
97:2 Sow ..., be never $w\cdot$,
98:2 Sow ..., be never $w\cdot$,
128:3 $w\cdot$ ones he offered rest;
129:3 $w\cdot$ ones he offered rest;
158:2 beside the $w\cdot$ road,
159:2 beside the $w\cdot$ road,
233:3 And every $w\cdot$ child
419:3 And every $w\cdot$ child
245:3 $w\cdot$ ones, at nightfall,
271:3 $w\cdot$ find eternal rest,
272:3 $w\cdot$ find eternal rest,
333:1 Beneath life's $w\cdot$ load,
364:1 night's $w\cdot$ hours,
415:2 forlorn and $w\cdot$:
425:1 O $w\cdot$ pilgrim, lift

weave
146:4 $w\cdot$ A silent, healing
147:4 $w\cdot$ A silent, healing

weeds
322:2 $w\cdot$ of error grew.
323:2 $w\cdot$ of error grew.

weeping
44:1 sounds of $w\cdot$ cease,
97:1 goeth forth with $w\cdot$,
98:1 goeth forth with $w\cdot$,
425:Ref. $W\cdot$ may endure for

weight
8:3 Ills have no $w\cdot$,

welcomed
109:1 Thy love is $w\cdot$ in.
110:1 Thy love is $w\cdot$ in.

well
46:1 learn this lesson $w\cdot$.
47:1 learn this lesson $w\cdot$.
58:1 Knowing $w\cdot$ that Thou
71:3 $W\cdot$ supply thy sons and
124:2 guard His children $w\cdot$.
402:2 guard His children $w\cdot$.
134:1 all is $w\cdot$ again:
203:2 know that all is $w\cdot$
269:3 Father, $w\cdot$ we know
270:3 Father, $w\cdot$ we know
280:2 $W\cdot$ ... needs He knows;
290:3 His word, $W\cdot$ done!
315:3 the heart's deep $w\cdot$;
316:3 the heart's deep $w\cdot$;
350:1-3 All will be $w\cdot$;
  1-3 All must be $w\cdot$;
  1-3 All, all is $w\cdot$.
360:2 heart a $w\cdot$ left empty?
379:1-3 $W\cdot$ for him who,
380.1-3 $W\cdot$ for him who,

Well-Beloved
331:3 this Thy $W\cdot$ preach.

well-beloved
72:2 Man, the $w\cdot$ of heaven.
405:2 Man, the $w\cdot$ of heaven.

well-fought
312:2 win the $w\cdot$ day.

welling
228:2 $w\cdot$ fount, it fills

went
96:2 Like him who $w\cdot$ about
388:1 Where'er he $w\cdot$

west
215:2 east or $w\cdot$ unfold;

wet
218:1 w˙ with Thy dew,
219:1 w˙ with Thy dew,
220:1 w˙ with Thy dew,

whate'er
53:2 Faithful is, w˙ betide;
95:1 W˙ I do, where'er
160:1 peace is thine, W˙ betide.
161:1 peace is thine, W˙ betide.
162:1 peace is thine, W˙ betide.
205:3 then, w˙ may come,
372:4 W˙ our name or sign,
373:2 W˙ our name or sign,

whatever (see also whate'er)
3:4 W˙ else befall,
10:1 W˙ may assail;
411:1 W˙ may assail;
183:1 W˙ must be done;
184:1 W˙ must be done;
383:1 W˙ dims thy sense of

whatsoe'er
135:2 tribulation, . . . , w˙ it be,
186:3 W˙ our lot may be,
187:3 W˙ our lot may be,

whence
30:3 W˙ joys supernal flow,
31:3 W˙ joys supernal flow,
32:3 W˙ joys supernal flow,
57:1 w˙ our healing flows;
90:2 W˙ the healing waters
114:1 tell me w˙ I came;
142:1 knows w˙ it came,

where'er
40:1 w˙ ye languish,
95:1 w˙ I be, Still 'tis God's
164:2 W˙ he comes, his
165:2 W˙ he comes, his
417:2 W˙ he comes, his
224:2 All good, w˙ it may
225:2 All good, w˙ it may
227:1 w˙ Thy people meet,
   1 W˙ they seek Thee,
259:3 W˙ the stream has
271:1 reign w˙ the sun
272:1 reign w˙ the sun
271:3 blessings flow w˙ He
272:3 blessings flow w˙ He
388:1 W˙ he went

wherein
370:2 Truth w˙ no sadness
379:2 heart w˙ it gloweth
380:2 heart w˙ it gloweth

whereon
297:2 Horeb w˙ we walk

whereto
253:7 w˙ God leadeth me.
254:7 w˙ God leadeth me.
255:7 w˙ God leadeth me.
256:7 w˙ God leadeth me.
257:7 w˙ God leadeth me.

wherever (see also where'er)
148:2 W˙ He may guide
278:2 w˙ He guide thee,
279:2 w˙ He guide thee,

whisper
9:2 w˙ God is Love.

whispered
303:3 w˙ word may touch

whispering
94:3 low, sweet accents w˙

white
3:3 shrine so pure and w˙,
19:1 stand in robes of w˙
229:1 The w˙ wings of the
230:1 transfigured clouds of w˙,
231:1 transfigured clouds of w˙,
242:1 for w˙ harvest fields,
304:3 W˙ as wool, ere they
305:3 W˙ as wool, ere they
306:3 W˙ as wool, ere they
307:3 W˙ as wool, ere they
308:3 W˙ as wool, ere they
309:3 W˙ as wool, ere they
314:3 harvest now is w˙:

whitening
97:2 the fields are w˙,
98:2 the fields are w˙

whitens
176:3 the new morning w˙;

white-winged
253:2 a w˙ angel throng
254:2 a w˙ angel throng
255:2 a w˙ angel throng
256:2 a w˙ angel throng
257:2 a w˙ angel throng

whole
12:3 upright, w˙ and free.
13:3 upright, w˙ and free.
66:1 From hearts made w˙,
421:1 From hearts made w˙,
74:2 shall make thee w˙.
83:2 that endless happy w˙,

whole
130:2 w˙ creation owns Thy
142:1 shared, forever w˙,
153:2 hast made me w˙.
175:2 fearless, w˙, rejoicing,
237:1 with consecration w˙,
292:1 Put on the w˙ armor
363:3 reveals the perfect w˙,
370:2 set our w˙ affection
372:3 we are w˙ again.
373:2 we are w˙ again.
374:3 Rejoice, for thou art w˙.
375:3 Rejoice, for thou art w˙.

wholly
115:2 W˙ rest upon Thine
116:2 W˙ rest upon Thine
115:2 Follow w˙ Thy
116:2 Follow w˙ Thy

whoso
131:1 w˙ to the Father comes,
132:1 w˙ to the Father comes,

wide
9:3 all the world so w˙;
74:1 earth to open w˙;
142:3 w˙ and far we stray.
150:2 the w˙ harvest field,
176:3 w˙ earth enlightens.
201:1 But open w˙, let in
404:1 But open w˙, let in
201:4 open w˙ your heart
404:4 open w˙ your heart
217:3 the w˙ earth seem
218:4 w˙ horizon's grander
219:4 w˙ horizon's grander
220:4 w˙ horizon's grander
222:2 holds w˙ the door,
223:2 holds w˙ the door,
229:1 W˙ as our need Thy favors
345:1 w˙ we fling the . . . doors;
376:2 paths are broad and w˙.
377:2 paths are broad and w˙.

widely
280:2 W˙ as His mercy flows.

wideness
340:1 w˙ in God's mercy,
   1 the w˙ of the sea;

widening
226:1 Of wisdom's w˙ ray,
287:2 our w˙ vision dawns
408:2 our w˙ vision dawns

wider
65:1 As w˙ yet and w˙,

widespread
49:1 W in every place
50:1 W in every place

widow
17:1 w and the fatherless.

wild
16:1 rock and verdure w,
54:1 earth-clouds drear and w.
55:1 earth-clouds drear and w.
56:1 earth-clouds drear and w.

wilderness
84:2 w shall joyful be;

wilds
33:2 Though in desert w

wiles
89:1 w and the snares

will
19:2 They do His w,
41:3 His righteous w.
46:3 mold my w to Thine.
47:3 mold my w to Thine.
46:4 own, my Father's w.
47:4 own, my Father's w.
51:3 God's w is done;
52:3 God's w is done;
73:2 with Love's w blending;
76:2 confiding in His w;
91:1 Losing the mortal w
22:1 Losing the mortal w
92:3 God's w he makes his
02:2 nothing but Thy w;
03:2 nothing but Thy w;
84:2 nerve my faltering w:
86:2 human w and woe
87:3 Teach me Thy w;
88:2 yield his wavering w
51:2 To do Thy w is
52:2 To do Thy w is
57:1 God's w be done.
00:5 Who doth His w—
01:5 Who doth His w—
02:5 Who doth His w—
08:4 For at Thy w they
59:2 Pride ruled my w:
90:1-3 Thy w be done.
91:1-3 Thy w be done.
90:4 Thy w is done.
91:4 Thy w is done.
01:3 all who w may
04:3 all who w may
76:1 define Thy w, reality.
78:1 define Thy w, reality.
76:2 His w is done and

will
230:3 To do Thy w is
231:3 To do Thy w is
240:2 Delighting in Thy w.
241:2 Delighting in Thy w.
242:3 To do Thy w we
246:2 God's w is done,
269:3 seek Thy w to do,
270:3 seek Thy w to do,
304:2 bind the stubborn w,
305:2 bind the stubborn w,
306:2 bind the stubborn w,
307:2 bind the stubborn w,
308:2 bind the stubborn w,
309:2 bind the stubborn w,
331:2 to Thy w resigned,
332:1 wait to do His w.
349:1 Thy w, almighty Father,
    3 servants of Thy w.
354:3 works in us to w,
    (see also *good will*)

willed
93:4 what God hath w;

willing
58:2 hearts and w hands,
311:3 glad and w mind
420:3 glad and w mind
388:3 with w hands dispense

win
86:4 right the day must w;
87:4 right the day must w;
163:3 w our brother man,
166:2 what Jesus did to w
167:2 what Jesus did to w
190:4 Love doth w;
191:4 Love doth w;
296:Ref. with God, and w!
312:2 w the well-fought day.
315:2 w them back again.
316:2 w them back again.

wind
49:3 earthquake, w and fire,
50:3 earthquake, w and fire,

winds
142:3 Blow, w of God, awake
253:5 the w and waves can
254:5 the w and waves can
255:5 the w and waves can
256:5 the w and waves can
257:5 the w and waves can

wind-wafted
303:1 fruit in each w seed

wine
108:2 royal w of heaven;
    3 bread and w remove,
151:1 bread and w Thou art,
152:1 bread and w Thou art,
259:1 healing oil and w,
298:4 the bread, and the w.
299:4 the bread, and the w.
300:4 the bread, and the w.
301:4 the bread, and the w.
302:4 the bread, and the w.

wing
30:1 Thy shelt'ring w,
31:1 Thy shelt'ring w,
32:1 Thy shelt'ring w,
158:2 swiftly on the w;
159:2 swiftly on the w;
192:5 if on joyful w
193:5 if on joyful w
207:1 on upward w tonight.
208:1 on upward w tonight.
209:1 on upward w tonight.
210:1 on upward w tonight.
211:1 on upward w tonight.
212:1 on upward w tonight.
207:4 shadow of His mighty w;
208:4 shadow of His mighty w;
209:4 shadow of His mighty w;
210:4 shadow of His mighty w;
211:4 shadow of His mighty w;
212:4 shadow of His mighty w;
346:2 On thy redeeming w
401:2 On thy redeeming w
363:2 On mightier w,

winged
9:2 w with light and love;
166:3 and w with prayer;
167:3 and w with prayer;

wings
17:3 With healing in his w
81:1 Are His w of mercy
99:2 He over thee His w
100:2 He over thee His w
149:2 w of faith we soar
426:2 w of faith we soar
202:2 on his w of healing;
412:1 on his w of healing;
229:1 w of the Holy Ghost
246:1 On w of eagles he,
297:3 close her faltering w,
313:1 With healing in his w.
322:3 lift her sacred w,
323:3 lift her sacred w,
392:2 healing in his w
393:2 healing in his w

winning
234:2 w· word of love;
235:2 w· word of love;

wins
326:4 and w· at length,

wipe
202:2 w· all tears away;
412:1 w· all tears away;
425:2 w· all tears away,

wipes
298:2 Love w· your tears
299:2 Love w· your tears
300:2 Love w· your tears
301:2 Love w· your tears
302:2 Love w· your tears

wisdom
46:3 To Thy w· I resign,
47:3 To Thy w· I resign,
58:1 and Thou art w·,
65:1 w· is revealed to us,
72:2 W·, angels' glorious
405:2 W·, angels' glorious
79:1-3 God is w·, God is
88:2 w· kind and clear
89:2 w· kind and clear
130:2 w· past all seeking;
148:2 His w· ever waketh,
160:4 is light, and w· might,
161:4 is light, and w· might,
162:4 is light, and w· might,
178:1 in heavenly w· taught
190:3 Thy w· shall the way
191:3 Thy w· shall the way
215:1 who celestial w· makes
216:2 for you His w· planned;
251:1 w· from on high,
252:1 w· from on high,
263:2 word of w· heareth
291:2 to Thy w· leave;
320:1 Supreme in w· as in
321:1 Supreme in w· as in
409:1 Supreme in w· as in
343:2 True w· doth impart;
344:2 True w· doth impart;
429:2 True w· doth impart;

wisdom's
30:3 w· rod is given
31:3 w· rod is given
32:3 w· rod is given
226:1 w· widening ray,
329:2 W· way to hold,

wise
111:2 How w· the wonders
194:3 that are worldly w·,
410:3 that are worldly w·,
291:3 neither strong nor w·,
311:1 for us His w· design.
420:1 for us His w· design.
318:2 shall in this w· enter
336:2 divine and precepts w·,

wish
119:2 Man can w· or God can

wishes
126:2 Our w· all above,
127:2 Our w· all above,
403:2 Our w· all above,

withdrawn
368:3 and terror are w·;
369:3 and terror are w·;

withheld
125:3 No good ... shall be w·

withhold
249:1 we w· a tribute,
250:1 we w· a tribute,

within
20:1 list the voice w·,
416:1 list the voice w·,
67:3 Hide w· thy heart
68:3 Hide w· thy heart
94:1 thy heart w· thee
99:3 w· His secret place,
100:3 w· His secret place,
118:3 w· this heart of mine;
154:1 W· Thy light of
155:1 W· Thy light of
156:1 W· Thy light of
154:2 W· Thy love is safe
155:2 W· Thy love is safe
156:2 W· Thy love is safe
154:2 W· Thy truth a
155:2 W· Thy truth a
156:2 W· Thy truth a
157:2 Safe w· this Love
166:2 what spirit dwells w·
167:2 what spirit dwells w·
170:1 w· myself to know
186:1 watch w· the night?
187:1 watch w· the night?
203:2 W· Love's stronghold
214:1 W·, around us, and
221:2 W· each heart is
3 Thy kingdom, God, w·
224:2 look w· the veil,
225:2 look w· the veil,

within
226:3 light, w· us dwell,
227:2 w· no walls confined,
229:2 without, but found w·,
258:3 God w· the shadow
259:2 W· the pious heart
263:2 Father Love w·,
276:2 w· our hearts Thy
277:2 w· our hearts Thy
278:1 home and heaven are w·
279:1 home and heaven are w·
298:3 the foul senses w·;
299:3 the foul senses w·;
300:3 the foul senses w·;
301:3 the foul senses w·;
302:3 the foul senses w·;
303:2 dwell W· it silently.
330:4 W· Thy house forever.
357:1 joy our hearts w·.
358:1 joy our hearts w·.
407:1 joy our hearts w·.
371:2 w· Thy perfect law
386:3 salvation reigns w·,
387:3 salvation reigns w·,

without
49:2 like them, w· a word
50:2 like them, w· a word
75:3 A kingdom w· end.
141:1 w· a stain.
148:1 storm may roar w· me,
205:2 tempests rage w·;
229:2 home sought w·, but
247:2 W· your God repair,
248:2 W· your God repair,
361:3 who w· ceasing prays.
364:2 Vain, w· His grace

withstand
72:2 no empire can w·;
405:2 no empire can w·;

witness
19:2 w· truly to His Word,
109:2 Faithful w· bear of
110:2 Faithful w· bear of
333:2 w· to the truth,

witnesses
204:1 Thou sendest Thy w·,

woe
66:1 lips redeemed from w·,
421:1 lips redeemed from w·,
79:1 and w· He lightens;
104:2 To lighten every w·.
136:2 human will and w·
205:1 Of any earthly w·;

woe
352:2 through a world of w·?
353:2 through a world of w·?
352:4 illume my way of w·
353:4 illume my way of w·

woes
133:3 all w·, to bliss,
424:3 all w·, to bliss,
192:4 by my w· to be
193:4 by my w· to be

woke
11:1 W· with music all

won
65:3 triumphs Love hath w·.
104:4 victory w· O'er sense
171:2 self have w· release,
413:2 self have w· release,
265:2 mount of vision w·;

wonder
361:2 His works of w·,

Wonderful
362:2 W·, the Counsellor,

wonderfully
340:2 most w· kind.
414:2 More w· sweet.

wondering
381:1 Mary's w· eyes!

wonders
65:3 w· He hath shown us,
72:2 the w· of His hand:
405:2 the w· of His hand:
111:2 the w· of Thy hands;
144:2 w· of eternal Mind,
145:2 w· of eternal Mind,
164:3 And w· of his love.
165:3 And w· of his love.
417:3 And w· of his love.
384:1 half the w· tell,

wondrous
45:1 The w· heavens, Thy
86:1 God's glory is a w·
87:1 God's glory is a w·
130:1 w· is Thy mercy, Lord,
158:1 Their w· story told
159:1 Their w· story told
171:3 his w· Eastertide;
413:3 his w· Eastertide;
199:1 w· things hath done,
222:3 The w· gift is given;
223:3 The w· gift is given;

wondrous
292:2 creation's w· story,
352:1 w· love, O Son of God.
353:1 w· love, O Son of God.
378:3 Thy w· power acclaim,

wool
304:3 White as w·, ere they
305:3 White as w·, ere they
306:3 White as w·, ere they
307:3 White as w·, ere they
308:3 White as w·, ere they
309:3 White as w·, ere they

Word
12:2 W· of God is power
13:2 W· of God is power
19:2 they speak His W·,
2 witness ... to His W·,
84:1 eternal W· is spoken,
2 W· of God, O W·
101:1-3 He sent His W·,
1 His holy W·,
2 His shining W·
3 His faithful W·,
111:3 promised in Thy W·.
112:3 Sing the W·, whose
123:1 in His excellent W·.
130:1 treasure of Thy W·;
1 W· dispels all blindness.
168:4 W· Which cured disease,
175:1 Lo, He sent His W·
1 that W· of God is here.
1 In our hearts Thy W·
2 Thy W· proclaimeth
176:2 Clear as the W· that
2 in God's great W·,
3 the W· shines forth,
177:1 speaking By His W·
188:2 W· to all mankind,
The W· that bids
189:1 trust me to His W·.
197:3 The W· made flesh
198:3 The W· made flesh
201:1 let in the W·,
404:1 let in the W·,
214:1 Thy W· we bless,
1 Whose W· is Truth,
251:1 O W· of God, most
252:1 O W· of God, most
251:2 W· of God the Father,
252:2 W· of God the Father,
251:2 Christ, the living W·.
252:2 Christ, the living W·.
281:1 W· we have heard
292:1 is God's mighty W·!
298:1 the power of the W·?
299:1 the power of the W·?

Word
300:1 the power of the W·?
301:1 the power of the W·?
302:1 the power of the W·?
318:2 receiveth the W· as they,
329:2 W· the thought enlightens,
332:2 heed His faithful W·,
334:1 breathes upon the W·
336:1 as Thy sacred W·.
2 Thy holy W· supplies,
3 Thy W· shall shine
346:1 Thou whose almighty W·
401:1 Thou whose almighty W·
365:1 hold upon His W·:
366:1 hold upon His W·:
390:2 breathing from the W·.
425:1 God in His own W·

word
4:3 all his gracious w·,
10:1 out His sacred w·
411:1 out His sacred w·
30:2 thought or w· unkind,
31:2 thought or w· unkind,
32:2 thought or w· unkind,
30:4 gave that w· of might
31:4 gave that w· of might
32:4 gave that w· of might
42:2 Thy holy w· doth give;
49:2 without a w· Rise up
50:2 without a w· Rise up
62:2 truth attends Thy w·;
63:2 truth attends Thy w·;
67:3 within thy heart His w·,
68:3 within thy heart His w·,
71:1 w· cannot be broken,
74:2 w· of Truth is there
80:3 w· of His command,
92:2 as the w· is given,
121:2 rest upon His w·
122:2 rest upon His w·
121:3 Th'engrafted w· receive,
122:3 Th'engrafted w· receive,
126:1 so fulfill His w·;
127:1 so fulfill His w·;
403:1 so fulfill His w·;
153:1 faithful is His w·.
1 faithful is Thy w·.
179:1 w· of revelation;
189:2 faithful w· and deed.
197:2 w· and deed attested.
198:2 w· and deed attested.
224:2 w· can never fail.
225:2 w· can never fail.
226:3 Light up Thy w·;
3 That w· and deed
230:4 form, nor ritual w·,
231:4 form, nor ritual w·,

word	**work (noun)**	**works**
234:2 winning w of love;	12:3 ever through our w	274:3 always w by love.
235:2 winning w of love;	13:3 ever through our w	352:1 Thy w, how beauteous,
242:1 forth the ancient w:	51:1 noblest w of God,	353:1 Thy w, how beauteous,
3 Thrust . . . at Thy w,	52:1 noblest w of God,	354:3 w in us to will,
246:2 w and deed declare	51:2 Love's w and Love	3 w in us to do;
263:2 healing w of Love.	52:2 Love's w and Love	361:2 His w of wonder,
2 w of wisdom heareth	51:3 Potter's w is plain.	381:4 And w of love
278:2 the call of His w.	52:3 Potter's w is plain.	386:2 our w and virtues
279:2 the call of His w.	82:2 to work God's w,	387:2 our w and virtues
290:3 His w, Well done!	92:4 In Thy great w to	391:2 lives and w to-day
303:1 slightest w or deed,	93:4 The joy of perfect w	
3 whispered w may touch	141:3 w of perfect Mind,	**world**
315:1 no harsh w mar	150:2 We thank Thee for w	9:1 all the w knows peace.
316:1 no harsh w mar	168:2 Still may our w	3 all the w so wide;
320:1 search His w, and trace	217:3 holy w was doing good;	17:2 prince of this w
321:1 search His w, and trace	234:3 w that keeps faith	41:2 To all the w the
409:1 search His w, and trace	235:3 w that keeps faith	82:3 shine throughout the w;
329:3 idle thought or w;	242:2 for our Father's w,	112:2 all the w rejoices,
340:3 take Him at His w;	247:2 on your w His blessing	158:1 w in solemn stillness
342:2 Who on His w rely.	248:2 on your w His blessing	159:1 w in solemn stillness
343:2 Truth: thy w alone	354:1 w to be performed	158:3 all the w send back
344:2 Truth: thy w alone	394:2 Great the w they have	159:3 all the w send back
429:2 Truth: thy w alone	395:2 Great the w they have	164:1 Joy to the w,
347:4 silenced by His w;	399:3 And scan His w	165:1 Joy to the w,
348:4 silenced by His w;	400:3 And scan His w	417:1 Joy to the w,
388:2 He spoke the w		164:3 He rules the w
390:1 doth the Master's w	**work (verb)**	165:3 He rules the w
392:3 His w the heaven of	41:1 Go w to-day.	417:3 He rules the w
393:3 His w the heaven of	82:2 to w God's work,	177:2 Through the w
394:1 W of Life, most pure,	93:4 man can w what God	185:2 Light of the w,
395:1 W of Life, most pure,	183:3 face the task and w;	188:3 w is sad with dreams
398:1 of His heavenly w,	184:3 face the task and w;	199:1 whom the w rejoices;
414:2 God's own holy w.	183:3 and w, and pray.	203:1 bless a hungry w.
418:2 speaketh, aye, one w,	184:3 and w, and pray.	222:3 in this w of sin,
words	195:2 I w and pray, and	223:3 in this w of sin,
17:2 idle w must cease.	303:4 W and despair not;	236:1 O peace of the w,
36:2 Thy w, amid the w of	394:3 strength to w for Thee,	253:3 A w more bright.
43:1 tender w of Jesus,	395:3 strength to w for Thee,	254:3 A w more bright.
2 loving w of Jesus,		255:3 A w more bright.
2 peaceful w of Jesus,	**working**	256:3 A w more bright.
54:3 No accents flow, no w	37:2 One w band, one	257:3 A w more bright.
88:1 w that help and heal	38:2 One w band, one	261:3 To serve the w
89:1 w that help and heal	82:1 w His purpose out	262:3 To serve the w
95:1 w with heavenly	320:1 The w of His hands?	297:1 Light of the w,
102:2 sweet w: Peace, be still.	321:1 The w of His hands?	325:1 the w forsake,
103:2 sweet w: Peace, be still.	409:1 The w of His hands?	333:2 fetters of the w.
194:2 w can never reach,		334:3 w of darkness shine
410:2 w can never reach,	**works**	352:2 through a w of woe?
228:2 w our . . . joy can tell,	12:1 His w shall do,	353:2 through a w of woe?
230:3 w are less than deeds;	13:1 His w shall do,	357:1 on the w abroad,
231:3 w are less than deeds;	12:2 let your w confirm	358:1 on the w abroad,
240:2 truth Thy w reveal;	13:2 let your w confirm	407:1 on the w abroad,
241:2 truth Thy w reveal;	51:1 His w pass not away.	363:3 shall o'erflow the w,—
269:3 w alone are vain,	52:1 His w pass not away.	371:2 to the w . . . proclaim
270:3 w alone are vain,	117:3 Thy w shall praise	389:1 snares of this w
288:2 Think of the w:	178:1 Holy w of love	394:1 All the w awakes
289:2 Think of the w:	221:3 Thy w, now understood,	395:1 All the w awakes
	273:3 always w by love.	

world-enthralling
84:1 Out of darkness, $w\cdot$,

worldlings
337:2 $W\cdot$ blindly may refuse
338:2 $W\cdot$ blindly may refuse

worldly
194:3 that are $w\cdot$ wise,
410:3 that are $w\cdot$ wise,
276:1 to $w\cdot$ minds unknown;
277:1 to $w\cdot$ minds unknown;

world's
172:3 $w\cdot$ sin and sorrow

worlds
282:1 $W\cdot$ His mighty voice

worship
19:2 $w\cdot$ Him in spirit
141:4 the earth to $w\cdot$ God.
149:2 faith we soar and $w\cdot$,
426:2 faith we soar and $w\cdot$,
217:1 holier $w\cdot$, which God
    2 $w\cdot$ rightly is to love
357:2 To $w\cdot$ Thee aright;
358:2 To $w\cdot$ Thee aright;
407:2 To $w\cdot$ Thee aright;

worth
15:1 man his native $w\cdot$.
204:1 telling Thy $w\cdot$,

worthier
94:2 each $w\cdot$ thought awake,

worthy
176:3 $w\cdot$ such a grace,

wound
30:1 arrow that doth $w\cdot$
31:1 arrow that doth $w\cdot$
32:1 arrow that doth $w\cdot$
69:3 each $w\cdot$ and smart
423:3 each $w\cdot$ and smart
304:2 $W\cdot$ the callous breast,
305:2 $W\cdot$ the callous breast,
306:2 $W\cdot$ the callous breast,
307:2 $W\cdot$ the callous breast,
308:2 $W\cdot$ the callous breast,
309:2 $W\cdot$ the callous breast,

wounded
40:1 bring your $w\cdot$ hearts,

wrap
418:3 doth $w\cdot$ us round,

wrapt
149:3 Not $w\cdot$ in fear
426:3 Not $w\cdot$ in fear

wrath
163:2 $w\cdot$ and sin shall die
385:3 Thou, ..., slow to $w\cdot$,

wreaths
359:2 illusive $w\cdot$ of mist

wrestle
312:2 $w\cdot$, fight, and pray;

wretchedness
7:2 and life no $w\cdot$;

wrong
14:3 sin and $w\cdot$ Obscure
69:1 To spurn the $w\cdot$
423:1 To spurn the $w\cdot$
75:1 those who suffer $w\cdot$;
86:3 with what seems $w\cdot$
87:3 with what seems $w\cdot$
163:2 will all $w\cdot$ outweigh;
173:1 and thinks no $w\cdot$,
180:1 silence thoughts of $w\cdot$
232:3 above the mists of $w\cdot$:
406:3 above the mists of $w\cdot$:
234:3 triumphs over $w\cdot$.
235:3 triumphs over $w\cdot$.
238:1 Through present $w\cdot$,
239:1 Through present $w\cdot$,
258:3 upon the throne be $w\cdot$,
288:1 That buries $w\cdot$ and
289:1 That buries $w\cdot$ and
293:2 refuge from all $w\cdot$,
294:2 refuge from all $w\cdot$,
295:2 refuge from all $w\cdot$,
327:2 all oppressed by $w\cdot$
328:2 all oppressed by $w\cdot$

wrought
14:2 all thy God hath $w\cdot$;
176:1 $w\cdot$ by God's command,
178:1 works of love he $w\cdot$.

Y

year
82:1 $y\cdot$ succeeds to $y\cdot$,
115:1 $Y\cdot$ by $y\cdot$, Thy hand
116:1 $Y\cdot$ by $y\cdot$, Thy hand
363:2 From $y\cdot$ to $y\cdot$ does

yearn
418:3 $y\cdot$ for sight or sound

yearning
381:3 $y\cdot$ For homelands

yearns
269:2 $y\cdot$ for righteousness,
270:2 $y\cdot$ for righteousness,

years
46:4 shall added $y\cdot$ fulfill
47:4 shall added $y\cdot$ fulfill
158:3 the ever-circling $y\cdot$
159:3 the ever-circling $y\cdot$

years
169:2 remember not past $y\cdot$.
186:2 through farthest $y\cdot$,
187:2 through farthest $y\cdot$,
197:1 down the $y\cdot$ untold,
198:1 down the $y\cdot$ untold,
202:3 of the vanished $y\cdot$;
412:2 of the vanished $y\cdot$;
213:2 endless $y\cdot$ the same.
222:1 fears of all the $y\cdot$
223:1 fears of all the $y\cdot$
261:1 by the lapse of $y\cdot$,
262:1 by the lapse of $y\cdot$,
336:3 for everlasting $y\cdot$,
381:3 through patient $y\cdot$,

yesterday
186:1 as $y\cdot$ when past,
187:1 as $y\cdot$ when past,

yet
65:1 wider $y\cdot$ and wider,
74:1 $Y\cdot$ error's tempest
76:1 arm enfolds thee $y\cdot$.
96:2 Great Physician liveth $y\cdot$
108:4 $Y\cdot$ passing, points to
136:3 I $y\cdot$ shall know as I
148:3 $y\cdot$ I have not seen;
192:2 $Y\cdot$ in my dreams
193:2 $Y\cdot$ in my dreams
222:1 $Y\cdot$ in thy dark
223:1 $Y\cdot$ in thy dark
258:3 $Y\cdot$ 'tis Truth alone
    3 $Y\cdot$ that scaffold
330:3 But $y\cdot$ in love He
359:1 the day-star $y\cdot$ shall
368:2 Higher $y\cdot$ that star
369:2 Higher $y\cdot$ that star

yet
372:2 even y A present help
373:1 even y A present help
372:2 And faith has y its
373:1 And faith has y its

yield
112:1 our hearts adoring Y
138:2 y his wavering will
359:3 and will not y,

yields
331:2 a nobler offering y

yon
368:1 y mountain's height
369:1 y mountain's height

yore
9:1 sang, in days of y,
199:1 from the days of y

youth
218:3 heart's perennial y,
219:3 heart's perennial y,
220:3 heart's perennial y,

youthful
320:3 And y vigor cease;
321:3 And y vigor cease;
409:3 And y vigor cease;

Z

zeal
170:2 With honest z

Zion
71:1 Z, city of our God;

Zion
76:1 Z, ne'er will He
200:1, 3 O daughter of Z,
3 and Z is free.
356:3 We, . . ., return to Z,

Zion's
335:1 Prepared for Z war.

HYMNAL NOTES

BEING BRIEF STUDIES OF THE HYMNS AND HYMN
TUNES, THE POETS AND COMPOSERS
REPRESENTED IN THE

CHRISTIAN SCIENCE HYMNAL

BIBLIOGRAPHY

JOHN JULIAN: *Dictionary of Hymnology,* London, 1925

Grove's Dictionary of Music and Musicians, London and New York, 1928

JOHANN ZAHN: *Die Melodien der deutschen evangelischen Kirchenlieder. Sechs Bände,* Gütersloh, 1889–1893

C. HUBERT H. PARRY: *Johann Sebastian Bach*

ALBERT SCHWEITZER: *J. S. Bach*

CHARLES SANFORD TERRY: *Bach's Chorales*

DANIEL GREGORY MASON: { *Beethoven and His Forerunners* / *The Romantic Composers*

ROMAIN ROLLAND: *Beethoven: Les Grandes Époques Créatrices*

FREDERIK W. HORNE: *Literature of the Scandinavian North*

ÉMILE JEAN ALBERT SOUBIES: *États Scandinaves: Histoire de la Musique*

WALTER RUDOLF NIEMANN: *Die Musik Skandinaviens*

JAMES D. BROWN: *Biographical Dictionary of Musicians*

JAMES T. LIGHTWOOD: *Hymn Tunes and Their Story*

FRANK J. METCALF: { *American Writers and Compilers of Sacred Music* / *Stories of Hymn Tunes*

EDMUND S. LORENZ: *Church Music*

Handbook of The Church Hymnary: James Moffatt, Editor

Harvard University Hymn Book, edited by Edward Caldwell Moore and Archibald Thompson Davison

Hymns Ancient and Modern, Historical Edition

Yattendon Hymnal: Robert Bridges, Editor

And the usual biographies and encyclopædias.

FOREWORD TO NOTES

THE Hymnal Notes, as brief studies of the Christian Science Hymnal in its edition of 1932, were begun in *The Christian Science Monitor* for October 17, 1932. Incidentally, this was the date when the corner stone of the new Publishing House was laid.

The Notes would speak not so much from the standpoint of poetry and music, history and biography, as from that of service to humanity. Hymnody bears indeed an intimate relation to human life. The singing voice belongs to every man. Voices that sing nothing else, sing hymns. It is a sign of love and loyalty to be "instructed in the songs of the Lord" (I Chronicles 25:6, 7).

When men first began to know themselves free to find God, apart from priestly and political interference, they began to sing! And today, as groups of freemen meeting for prayer and praise to God, the churches may share each the other's worship, in their songs. Barriers of creed, culture, nationality, melt before the fluent power of sacred poetry and music. Hymnody is called a "mirror of Christian history." Mrs. Eddy wrote: "The law of Sinai lifted thought into the song of David" (*Science and Health with Key to the Scriptures,* page 200). What she elsewhere names "the chain of scientific being reappearing in all ages" (*ibid.,* page 271) may be traced as by a starry splendor, throughout the pages of hymnody.

Every great teacher of religion has been a maker of great hymns, as we perceive when we chant the Beatitudes. In 1897, Mrs. Eddy said in a letter touching the music used with her hymns:

"I wish somebody in the wide world would find some glorious music, such as our great masters, Haydn, Mozart and others, left as legacies to the world, and put the Mother's Evening Prayer with it" (*Historical Files of The Mother Church*).

Accordingly, two of Mrs. Eddy's hymns have been set to music of the rank called classic, that of Bach and of Orlando Gibbons. Fifty other tunes by the great masters give further support to this standard. Music from fifteen different countries is found in the Hymnal, much of it chosen by members of The Mother Church in those lands. The book is indeed the work of many hands, and of all the loving hearts that wish it well.

To an increased list of the best poets of hymnody have been added two hymns by Mrs. Eddy, Love and Satisfied. These are the crowning gift of the revised Hymnal.

A hundred of the hymns, or about one-third, are written from the standpoint of Christian Science. The new ones must await the judgment of time.

The writer of the Notes would gratefully acknowledge her obligation to Mrs. Florence M. Pray for collaboration in the Notes on the great masters, to the Hon. Mrs. Violet Hay, for most of the Notes on contemporary English composers, and to Mr. Richard G. Appel, in charge of the Division of Music at the Boston Public Library, for aid in research.

MARIA LOUISE BAUM

Hymns used more than once are discussed under their first number, with a few exceptions, which are indicated in the text.

The use of italic type, quotation marks, etc., is planned to stress the source books. Foreign titles are translated here. Many of these books have their original title in the Hymnal Index. Names of poems and tunes, and of works mentioned incidentally, are not given quotation marks. Cross references are chiefly to biography. A small c. in a date means "about" (Latin, *circa*).

The word "hymn" is used for words only. The new arrangement of the Hymnal page puts the name of the composer under the title of the tune, by the logical modern usage.

To have treated each hymn with equal fullness would have made the book too large. The Notes may open a door to study for which the table of Dates in Hymnody offers an outline.

The *Hymn and Tune Book* of Boston, which was the first Hymnal used in Christian Science services, says, in a Preface:

"Choirs do not expect to sing well without careful practice; why should a congregation? Some regularly organized plan to secure general musical culture, and stated rehearsals, should be a part of the working apparatus of each church. It will conduce much to its success also, if the book is made a familiar companion in the home circle."

THE HYMNS OF MARY BAKER EDDY

(Adapted from *The Christian Science Journal*, February, 1914)

MRS. EDDY'S achievement in hymnody stands alone, because in every line of hers is seen not only the spirituality, love and aspiration that mark a devout Christianity, but also the statement of a demonstrable Science.

In religious poetry, for the most part, what may be termed the heart element has predominated, and when hymns have sought to be theological or metaphysical, they have usually ceased to be poetry. Mrs. Eddy's hymns speak straight to the heart with the simple directness of pure lyric art, or they arouse fainting hope with a lofty clarion, yet they match her most careful prose in their fidelity to divine Principle.

To tell the beauty of these hymns is beyond the power of mere criticism. They are their own praise, their own proof of a supreme and unique literary achievement. Yet they were written in the midst of an amazing activity, during the years when their writer was declaring, proving, and teaching Christian Science, and establishing its world-wide organization. Her poems and hymns were interludes, as it were, in these arduous labors. They are known and loved wherever the English language prevails; yet internal evidence hints that most of them were written under stress, to give comfort, warning, inspiration. It is indeed this expression of the actual need of the hour, either on her own part or that of her church, which gives Mrs. Eddy's hymns their marvelous vitality. They express herself, her aspiration, abnegation, struggle, victory, unselfish love; the sorrowing and triumphing Leader, the friend of humanity, the mother of her flock. They are such deep self-revealings as have rarely been trusted to a printed page. Touching what may be read between these lines, the most reverent and tender words must fall silent.

Science and Health with Key to the Scriptures is of course Mrs. Eddy's greatest book. Of her mere literary power, her command of the grand style, as critics love to name truly noble writing, her brilliant sententiousness, clean and clear, one could speak at length. But there is one peculiar element of her style which may be touched on here, as a key to her poetry. Every word of hers is used for its exact and full value. No one can understand her writings who does not give to her simplest word or her most stately phrase its definite meaning and its whole content.

Even her poetry has no flowery hyperbole, no vaguely impassioned or cloudily metaphysical line. Direct, simple, with hardly a word of more than two syllables, her poems take the reader back to days when words meant what they said, and yea was yea. The spiritual realities made clear by English words in their best estate, not reduced to rags by heedless use,—these things are what the reader of Mrs. Eddy's hymns and poems must seek, as well as readers of her prose.

These hymns, then, written to say something that must be said, are before the world today. They are on the tongue and in the ears perhaps of more people more constantly than any other hymns in the language. The congregations of the Church of Christ, Scientist, the world over, could sing these without book, few voices faltering at any line.

The place held by these hymns in the lives of the people is proof that Mrs. Eddy has given voice to things that are *real*. She wrote what was present reality to her, not a distant ideal. By the light of her great revelation, she set forth in her hymns alike her own and the whole human plea for unity with divine, infinite Love, and her awareness of that unity. The self-restraint of her speech is like that of one looking directly upon that of which he speaks. This apparently stern sparing of words characterizes all Mrs. Eddy's writing. This "well of English undefiled" is unstained by heady wines of poetic fervor. Like the directness of the English Bible, so her clear speaking follows from a knowledge that what she says is true.

Her Mother's Evening Prayer (Hymnal, No. 207) is perhaps the most complete poetic expression of Mrs. Eddy's religious ideal and also of her own human experience and hope. We find her asking protection for her fledgling idea, and in affirming her assurance of this protection, she says: "His arm encircles me, and mine, and all."

Here is no David calling for vengeance on foes. She includes all the world in the mantle of tenderness. And in the "me, and mine" she defines, too, the right of each to individual place. "All" is not for her a vague generalization, but a unity of definite ideas, "sons and daughters of God" (*Science and Health*, p. 503).

For all its simple, prayer-like feeling, this poem really sounds the whole gamut of human aspiration after God, with the triumphant assurance of Him as all power. He "owns each waiting hour." He possesses us and all, even while His coming seems delayed. Pelion on Ossa piled, of mere verbal splendor, has never yet lifted such a beacon as sentences like the following:

> O make me glad for every scalding tear,
> For hope deferred, ingratitude, disdain!
> Wait, and love more for every hate, and fear
> No ill,—since God is good, and loss is gain.

These lines have power because they are filled with what Mrs. Eddy actually was, in aspiration and in deed. She lived these things before she wrote them.

In the next stanza she writes:

> Seeking and finding, with the angels sing:
> "Lo, I am with you alway,"—watch and pray.

After the triumphant assurance of God's presence comes the warning word. This also is characteristic of her writing everywhere. In the loftiest flight of her inspiration, she never forgets one least waymark that shall chart the course for those who would follow.

The poem Love (Hymnal, No. 30), first used as a hymn in the 1932 edition of the Hymnal, is one of the most poetic of the collected *Poems*. It opens with the Biblical image of brooding wings, a favorite with Mrs. Eddy, as seen in *Miscellaneous Writings*, page 263, and elsewhere. Its reference to the dove is illuminating, when this symbol of peace is followed in the Concordances to her books. In the affirmation that "Love alone is Life," this hymn speaks from the very heart of her teachings.

A vigorous phrase is:

> 'Twas Love whose finger traced aloud
> A bow of promise on the cloud.

She never hesitates to use the striking word when it serves her purpose. The word "aloud" recalls the imagery in the first chapter of Ezekiel, when the brightness was like the bow in the cloud and out of the brightness a voice spoke.

In Satisfied (Hymnal, No. 160), first used as a hymn in the 1932 edition, again her daring use of the effective word is seen, as in "Truth tatters those." The word "ayont," used for beyond, gives a touch of quaintness and also arrests attention at the significant line, "Ayont hate's thrall." This whole poem is nevertheless quite in the written style of today, in which succinctness, the short-cut of thought, expects of a reader quick and keen perceptions.

The passage, "And of these stones, or tyrants' thrones," touches perhaps both the words of John the Baptist and those in Jeremiah 43:9, 10, where a tyrant's throne serves the divine will. The last stanza speaks the deep conviction which lived in Mrs. Eddy that her message was the solution of human history:

> The centuries break, the earth-bound wake,
> God's glorified!

The Dark Ages, as they are called for their blindness to spiritual ideas, by no means closed with the discovery of printing. But that they ended with the great Discovery granted to Mary Baker Eddy was her unshakable faith,—a faith justified today as the vision brightens over all the earth. "The Lord gave the word; great was the company of those that published it" (Psalms 68:11).

Sometimes Mrs. Eddy's words are searched for faults, as in the line "How to gather, how to sow," the much-loved words of "Feed My Sheep" (Hymnal, No. 304). Does not the sowing come first? Yet the line says just what Mrs. Eddy means. We cannot sow till we have gathered. The quotation marks in this title are noteworthy, giving the words of Jesus as the theme.

The line "Tear or triumph harms" is another example of how much meaning the writer packs into a few words. Triumph harms as often as defeat, yet of those who strive, and ask for consolation, few remember to ask for protection in their victorious hour.

The Communion Hymn (Hymnal, No. 298) begins:

Saw ye my Saviour? Heard ye the glad sound?
Felt ye the power of the Word?

What more trenchant words could be spoken at this hour? What can be added or taken away? Later its "friend of the friendless" is a characteristic touch of Mrs. Eddy's universal human tenderness. This hymn, in the lofty reach of its Christian faith and love, as in its direct simplicity, rises above denominational barriers. It speaks for all Christendom.

In Christmas Morn (Hymnal, No. 23) again we note that use of concrete images which always marks the lyric gift. To the Christ belong

No cradle song,
No natal hour and mother's tear.

More of this clear-cut imagery is seen in Christ My Refuge (Hymnal, No. 253). This begins with the "waiting harpstrings," which, swept as by music, "wake a white-winged angel throng" of thoughts whose "song" is "perfumed" with love. The Christ who walks the troubled sea, and the rock, the shore, the winds and waves, make a vivid picture that seems to illustrate Mrs. Eddy's saying, "Spiritual teaching must always be by symbols" (*Science and Health,* page 575).

A significant change was made by Mrs. Eddy in this hymn when the collection of her poems was published in 1910. The hymn was long printed, "Wait to know a world more bright." In the *Poems* the phrase reads, "Wake to know a world more bright." This is in keeping with the change in the last line of Mother's Evening Prayer. Here the words "finds her home and far-off rest" were changed to "finds her home and heavenly rest." That the great love of God, the Love that is God, is ever present, not merely to be awaited in some far-off hereafter, is a triumphant message which she gave to the world, "with signs following."

MARIA LOUISE BAUM

174

HYMNAL NOTES

1 Old Hundredth. *Be Thou, O God, exalted high*

Make a joyful noise unto the Lord, all ye lands. . . .
Come before his presence with singing.

This is the trumpet call of the Psalm that has given its name to the noble tune so long known, so widely sung, as Old Hundredth. Here the Psalm becomes the significant keynote of a Hymnal prepared for use in all the lands.

The service of song in the worship of God is made illustrious by the work of David. He did much for his people in music and poetry. He wrote many of the Psalms and inspired others to write and to sing these songs of Zion's praise and prayer. It is David's influence that most persists in Christian hymnody to this hour. Certain groups of the early Protestants would use nothing but Psalms for church singing, and this is why there exist so many versions of the Psalms in meter, in so many languages. Even original Christian hymns draw from the Bible not only their inspiration, but their very language.

The words of the Doxology (praise-speaking) are from Psalm 57 in Tate and Brady's new version of the Psalter, which succeeded the old version, named for Sternhold (Note 99). The tune was used with Psalm 134 in the Genevan Psalter and became Old Hundredth through its application in 1561 to William Kethe's version of Psalm 100:

> Al people yt on earth do dwel,
>   sing to ye lord with chereful voice
> Him serve wt fear, his praise forth tel,
>   come ye before him and reioyce.

As Ein' feste Burg (Note 10) was first heard with the protest that made us Protestants, so the Genevan Psalter dates the Huguenot church. Everybody sang the inspiring music of Louis Bourgeois—in the homes, on the streets, in the very face of official edicts that tried in vain to stem the rising tide of praise to God. If anyone would account for the influence held over the people by the stern John Calvin, let him compute the power of song and the enthusiasm roused by the Psalms of Marot and Beza, sung to the music of Bourgeois and his fellows.

The germ of the Genevan Psalter lay in Clement Marot's Psalm 6, attached to the *Mirror of the Most Christian Princess Marguerite of France, Queen of Navarre* (1533). The French poet and his Psalms, which were sung at first to ballad tunes, were in high favor with Francis I and his redoubtable daughter-in-law, Catherine de' Medici. Even the Emperor Charles V accepted a gift of Psalms from Marot, and Henry II used one of Beza's Psalms as a hunting song.

The severe Huguenot, Theodore Beza (or de Bèze), took up Marot's unfinished work, at the demand of Calvin, even as Louis Bourgeois had left Paris with Calvin, to act as precentor and music editor for him at Geneva. The Genevan Psalter (1551) was surely Calvin's greatest gift to the church (Notes 62, 63).

2 Missionary Hymn. *A glorious day is dawning*

Psalms put into verse to be sung may be dated in England from about 700, when Bishop Aldhelm used to stand on the bridge in the dress of a gleeman and mingle his own versions of the Psalms with secular songs, to win the people. The English were always singers, and we read how six thousand people "of all sexes" gathered at Paul's Cross, in London, after service, and to the dismay of their clerical censors sang Sternhold's Psalms to the music supplied by John Crespin of Geneva (Note 107). And thus the English founders of New England brought a love of song into the wilderness. Winslow, one of the Pilgrim fathers, has borne witness to the sweetness of the Pilgrim Psalm-singing. The severer of the Boston Puritans held that music in church should be made in the heart, not audibly. Some were willing that professing Christians should sing hymns, the others joining in the Amen. The Rev. John Cotton, Boston's preacher, came to the rescue in 1647 with a tract named *Singing of Psalms a Gospel Ordinance,* and gave music its rightful place in church and home.

The first Psalter printed in New England was the *Bay Psalm Book,* 1640. Then tunes from English Psalters were included. From the beginning, hearts across the sea were bound by indissoluble ties of song. The first American composer was William Billings of Boston (1746–1800), a little man with a stupendous voice, a tanner, much esteemed by Samuel Adams. His *New England Psalm Singing* of 1770 had for motto: "Out of the mouths of babes and sucklings Thou hast perfected praise," which at least hints his modesty and may also have held a promise of things to come.

He loved fugues, and praised them, saying: "Now here, now there, now here again! O, ecstatic! Rush on, ye sons of Harmony!" American music was, like Nonconformist music of England, democratic, not ecclesiastical; fitting the words, varied in style, with many three-pulse meters; and having measures with notes of different lengths and even slurred notes.

All this prepared the way for Lowell Mason (1792–1872), represented in the Hymnal by nine tunes and arrangements. Born in Massachusetts, he spent fourteen years in a bank in Savannah, Georgia, incidentally leading choirs and making a collection of music, which he gave in 1822 to the Handel and Haydn Society of Boston. The book had really an amazing circulation. Mason afterward was a president of this Society, was head of the Boston Academy of Music, and was the first supervisor of public school music. He made many collections for the singing schools that had early been organized all over the country. These were both musical and social centers, where people did their own singing instead of listening to others. Josef Hofmann has warned us that those who are "hearers only" of music, by radio, etc., and never its makers, may lose their sense of music. Groups that gather for hymn practice do much to restore this happy old-time association.

The Missionary Hymn is perhaps best known of Mason's tunes. It is used here with words that are especially appropriate for the first American tune in the Hymnal. They appeared in the first edition, 1892, with this tune.

3 Epsom. *A grateful heart a garden is*

John Arnold (1720–1792), of Essex, England, compiled an *Essex Harmony* which he described as a "choice collection of the most celebrated songs and catches, for 2, 3, 4, and 5 voices, from the most eminent masters." From his *Complete Psalter* of 1756 is taken the tune Epsom. The words, by Ethel Wasgatt Dennis, a Christian Scientist, are suited to this singable melody that helps to make "a grateful heart."

4 Pater Noster. *A holy air is breathing round*

Pater Noster (Our Father) offers an example of the changed time signature, common enough in all music. Sometimes the change is marked by placing both signatures at the beginning, as here, 4/2 and 6/2. The rhythmical variation in the music is intended to leave unhampered the normal utterance of the words.

The composer, Dr. Percy C. Buck, was for twenty-six years identified with Harrow, one of the most ancient and famous of English schools. Founded in 1571, it is traditionally musical. The boys hold "sing-songs" every fortnight, and by long tradition, this singing, as also the chapel service, is always in unison. Dr. Buck believed that here was opportunity to advance the music beyond the square-cut form of the conventional hymn tune. So he wrote tunes for unison singing with a freer rhythm, of which his music in the *Christian Science Hymnal* gives typical examples. These beginnings were so successful that thirty of his free-rhythm melodies were used in various ways. After he left Harrow Dr. Buck found that many of his old boys remembered these tunes and even asked to include them in other hymn books. The appointment of Dr. Buck as King Edward professor of music in the University of London and as

177

professor of the Royal College of Music, bears witness to the importance of his work for musical education in England. (See Note 271.)

The writer of these words, Dr. Abiel Abbot Livermore (1811–1892), was a Unitarian minister of Keene, New Hampshire, who later became president of the Theological School at Meadville, Pennsylvania.

5 Forest Green. *A voice from heaven we have heard*

This is a Traditional melody with the rhythm of English folk music which has so much brightness and energy. This vigorous hymn, with its "call to rise from earth," is well sustained by the melody. It was written for the Hymnal by Irving C. Tomlinson, a Christian Scientist.

6 Melcombe. *Abide not in the realm of dreams*

Samuel Webbe (1740–1816) began life as apprentice of a cabinetmaker in London, and became one of the most loved musicians there, for his kindly disposition, as well as for his good music. The present tune is one of his best and appeared in his *Motets or Antiphons,* set to O Salutaris Hostia. His essay on plain chant gave the first known printing of a very great hymn tune, Adeste Fideles. His famous glee, Glorious Apollo, was written for a London glee club, and he acted as secretary for the Noblemen's and Gentlemen's Catch Club. His study began with a teacher who was organist at the Portuguese and Bavarian embassies in London, and he himself was later organist at the Sardinian embassy.

Of the poet William Burleigh (1812–1871), Julian finds that his hymns are more valued in England than in his own country. He was born in Woodstock, Connecticut, and was a Unitarian, a strong abolitionist, and a zealot for temperance. In Pittsburgh, Pennsylvania, he published journals for these causes and then was editor of *The Freeman,* Hartford, Connecticut.

7 Eventide. *Abide with me; fast breaks the morning light*

William H. Monk (1823–1889) is recorded as a purist in musical style, with a leaning to Gregorian music; but he evidently realized that modern forms and rhythms are good for congregational singing. He was organist at King's College, London, and at Stoke Newington, where he developed congregational singing. It is said that he wrote the tune Eventide in a time of deep personal sorrow, after watching a golden sunset. It was written for *Hymns Ancient and Modern,* of which he was the first music editor.

The poem here is a worthy companion of Lyte's famous hymn, from which it was drawn, as a spiritual interpretation of the original. Here Lyte's faith is turned to sight, where things hoped for are known as present reality. This poem, by Mrs. Bertha H. Woods, appeared in the *Christian Science Sentinel* for March 28, 1901. Its use with this music recalls the promise, "At evening time it shall be light" (Zechariah 14:7).

8 Eventide. *Abide with me; fast falls the eventide*

Of this great hymn of Henry Francis Lyte (1793–1847), his daughter has told the following story: During his last illness, the beloved preacher insisted on speaking once more to his people, who crowded the church at Lower Brixham and heard him with breathless attention. In the evening he gave his daughter a paper with the words of "the little hymn" and a tune he had written for it. It was not intended as literally an evening hymn, though often so classed. It was the voice of his own living, loving faith, at an hour of supreme testing.

Lyte, born in Ednam, near Kelso, Scotland, was educated at Portora (the Royal School of Enniskillen), and at Trinity, Dublin. In 1823 he became perpetual curate at Brixham, Devon. He wrote *Tales in Verse* illustrative of the Lord's Prayer, and it was his estimate of the poetry of Henry Vaughan, in his edition of Vaughan's *Sacred Poems and Private Ejaculations,* that lifted Vaughan to notice as one of England's great metaphysical poets, with Donne and Herbert. Many of the poets and musicians are thus twice famous, for their own work and for their generous appreciation of the work of others.

9 Carol. *All glory be to God most high*

David Gregor Corner (1587–1648) was born in Silesia. Having served as a pastor there, at forty he joined the Benedictines and became rector of the University of Vienna. His *Song Book* (1625) was collected from many sources. The carol used here has been widely sung in schools in the United States with the words, "A babe lies in a manger." The hymn written for it by Violet Hay, a Christian Scientist, reflects the "peace on earth" of the Nativity.

10 Ein' feste Burg. *All power is given unto our Lord*

The century of the Reformation saw the rise of that mighty stream of hymnody of which Ein' feste Burg is perhaps the greatest example. Called the "battle hymn of the Reformation," it has come ringing down the years with its sturdy challenge to whatever might question the power and the goodness of God. Opponents said that Martin Luther accomplished more by his hymns than by his preaching.

The century of Martin Luther (1483–1546) was perhaps the most picturesque, contradictory, and significant of them all. It saw the high tide of the Renaissance, that new birth of Greek and Roman learning, which nearly carried men back to the pagan ideal of life. It saw a new birth of the very globe itself, doubled in extent by the continents and seas unfolding in the West. It saw kings meeting in fields bright with cloth of gold, to strengthen their hold of the scepter. It saw the pen of a Montaigne, a Shakespeare, a Bacon, a Cervantes, winning a more enduring kingship over men; and it saw Martin Luther, a humble man of the people—who shocked the scholarly Erasmus—facing the tyrannies of his time and saying, "Here I stand. I can do no otherwise; so help me God! Amen!" (Quoted by Mrs. Eddy on page 268 of *Science and Health with Key to the Scriptures.*)

Luther's work for human liberty was threefold: first, his stand for a purer religion, humbler before God; second, the gift of the Bible to the people, by which the one God, the God of Israel, was exalted above the so-called gods many of pagan culture. Through the Bible, as Luther said, "God might speak directly to the people," and so came his third gift to them. In order that they might answer the Word directly, he gave them German songs to sing.

The contradictions of his times were in Luther. Son of a poor miner, he rose to fame by brilliant lectures in philosophy. A mighty wrestler with "the tempter," whom he assailed with his inkwell, he was a friend of little children. A "divine" pledged to "expound and defend the Holy Scriptures," he used the music of popular songs for hymns, so that "the devil might not have all the good tunes."

"Ein' feste Burg ist unser Gott" (A mighty fortress is our God) was written for the Diet (council) of Spires, 1529, when the German princes, stirred by Luther's reveille, made that protest, against the invasion of their rights, from which came the name Protestant. The hymn was used throughout Germany during the long struggle for religious liberty. Melanchthon was heartened, hearing it on the lips of a child. Gustavus Adolphus, the Swedish hero of Protestantism, had it sung by his whole army before the battle near Leipzig, which he won for liberty, in 1631. (See Note 168.)

The splendid balanced tune is the only one of the Reformation chorales which we can attribute with certainty to Luther. It appeared first in his *Spiritual Songs,* Wittenberg, 1529, with the words, which are also certainly his.

The paraphrase used here was made for the 1910 edition of the Hymnal by Frederic W. Root, a Christian Scientist. His last line, "His kingdom is forever," coincides with Hedge's version of Luther's "Das Reich muss uns doch bleiben"; but its use to close each stanza is a stroke of Mr. Root's own genius. At least seventy translations of Luther's hymn have been made into English.

11 Salzburg. *Angels at the Saviour's birth*

Of the sixteen harmonizations that are chosen for the *Christian Science Hymnal* from the great Bach (Notes 14 and 252) Salzburg is a very simple one. The first two phrases are repeated, then brightened by modulation or a change of key. The melody was written for a memorial poem by the German poet Albinus, but joyful yet tender words are given it by Marion Susan Campbell, a Christian Scientist. For his chorales Bach often used a familiar tune, as even those in his longer works were sung by the congregation.

Jakob Hintze (1622–1702) was a Prussian musician at the court of Berlin. The tune appeared in Crüger's *Praxis* (Note 199) of which Hintze was later an editor.

12 Melita. *Arise ye people, take your stand*

This name is used in Acts 28:1 for Malta, where Paul was shipwrecked. The words here, by Violet Hay, have much of the spirit of Paul's mission. For the composer, John B. Dykes, see Note 169.

13 Ermuntre dich. *Arise ye people, take your stand*

Johann Schop (?–1664) is recorded as a skillful player on the lute, violin, and trombone for the court band of Wolfenbüttel. We find him next at the Danish court and then as director of town music at Hamburg, and also town organist. "Incomparable as an instrumentalist," he is still known by his chorales. He contributed many tunes to Johann Rist's collections of hymns. Ermuntre dich (Rejoice) are the first words of Rist's poem to which this tune is set in Crüger's *Praxis* (Note 199). Bach used this chorale in his Christmas Oratorio, as No. 12: "Break forth, O beauteous, heavenly light."

14 Potsdam. *Arise, arise and shine*

The name given to Bach's melody here is a reminder of the promise in Proverbs 22:29, "Seest thou a man diligent in his business? he shall stand before kings." For Bach—who said that his glorious achievement was for any man who would work as hard—not only stood, but sat, before Frederick the Great. Invited to Potsdam in 1747, Bach interrupted the king in an evening practice of the flute among his court musicians. With some excitement Frederick turned to them: "Gentlemen, old Bach is here!" And Bach had to go over the castle, with king and court in admiring attendance, improvising from time to time upon the organ and several Silbermann "forte-pianos."

The work of Johann Sebastian Bach (1685–1750) is often summed, in awe-inspiring phrase, as "contrapuntal polyphony"; but even plain Martin Luther knew that this merely meant "a heavenly dance," for he said (of vocal counterpoint): "One man sings a simple tune . . . together with which three, four, or five voices also sing, and play and skip delightedly round this simple tune, and wonderfully grace and adorn it with manifold devices and sounds, performing as it were a heavenly dance."

Bach's own comment goes deeper: "Like all music [it] should have no other end and aim than the glory of God, and the recreation of the soul; where this is not kept in mind, there is no true music." He marked his scores: S. D. G. (Soli Deo Gloria: to God alone be praise). The words, by Mary I. Mesechre, are from *The Christian Science Journal,* February, 1908, and are worthy of this splendid tune.

It is simple, with a repetition of the E major "figure," a fifth above, in B major. Then the figure is a little unfolded, and again repeated. This is the subject of a fugue in Part II of the *Well-Tempered Clavichord* (or Forty-eight Preludes and Fugues), the work that still makes Bach the great master for piano students. The word "tempered" refers to the slight changes in pitch made in tuning the strings of clavichord or piano, so that all major and minor keys can be played upon the twelve half-tones.

Bach was known as the "king of organ and prince of clavier players," but his surpassing genius as a composer was not understood. In 1723, when he asked for the post of cantor at the Thomas School, Leipzig, he had to agree to teach Latin, besides teaching boys music and singing, and preparing the music for two churches where there must be a cantata and a motet every Sunday! Thus two hundred cantatas and three hundred and seventy chorales, with all his other mighty works, attest that this great man was indeed "diligent in his business" (Note 252).

15 Fulfillment. *As gold by fire is tested*

The Danish words given on the Hymnal page mean "The great Master comes" and they introduce the vivid imagery of the original hymn, which was put into English prose, then into English verse, for use here. The poet Bernhard S. Ingemann (1789–1862) was born in Torkildskrup in Falster, Denmark, and entered college at Copenhagen. He became a professor of Danish literature, and his historical romances have long been the delight of Danish youth, while his stories for children rank next to Grimm's. For his seventieth anniversary, the Danish children gave a halfpenny each toward a gift for their favorite story-teller.

When, in 1855, the church synod decided to revise the *Psalm Book* of Kingo, the task was entrusted to Ingemann. Kingo, Bishop of Fyen, was the famous hymnist who gave his name to the book that had appeared in 1699, after nearly twenty-five years of preparation.

Caspar Christian Hoffmann (1839–1893), the composer, was born in Vindinge, Denmark, and in 1867 was appointed organist at Naestved. Here he taught music and then was made professor of music and organist at Herlufsholm, a boarding school near Naestved.

16 Aynhoe. *As sings the mountain stream*

In St. James's Palace, London, which dates from the time of Henry VIII, is still held, twice a Sunday, a full choral service, sung by the Gentlemen and the Children of the Chapel Royal. The children still wear the brilliant dress that dates from Tudor times. The Chapel music is mentioned in 1135, and the Children of the Chapel are heard of in the time of Henry V. The royal chapels in Europe had each its own staff of composers, organists, and singers, and, especially in England, to serve among these was a distinction so marked that most of the famous names in English music are found in the Chapel rolls.

The composer, James Nares (1715–1783), began his musical career as a child of the Chapel Royal. Then he became organist at St. George's Chapel, Windsor, which, like Westminster Abbey and the Chapel Royal, was named a Royal Peculiar, exempt from episcopal control.

Nares was organist of York Cathedral for twenty years, and then composer, organist, and master of the children, at the Chapel Royal during thirty years. He published books on music, and wrote catches and canons and glees, fifty anthems, and his Royal Pastoral. The words here, by Violet Ker Seymer, a Christian Scientist, reflect the brightness and charm of the music.

17 Walsall. *Be firm, ye sentinels of Truth*

A brilliant and beautiful youth with thick locks curling round his head—this is the picture which Sir Godfrey Kneller, court painter to Charles II, gives us of Henry Purcell (1658–1695), to whom this tune is attributed.

The story of Purcell is the story of his times, with Charles Stuart restored to the throne, and bringing to England French fashions, including the charming music of Lully. The master of the Chapel Royal, Humphrey, developed his chorister Purcell in this new style, and when the young man became himself master, his chapel anthems are said to have "provided a discreet entertainment" for the men and women of fashion who made up Charles's court. While not deeply religious, Purcell's church pieces had high musical worth, for they showed his "capacity for happiness," and also his gift of a sudden thrust of feeling, secured by unexpected turns of harmony.

If Purcell ranks as the "greatest and most original of English composers," this distinction is due largely to his grasp of song, for his music, in anthem, ode, or opera, gave to the English language the normal accent of speech. This may be seen in his operatic recitatives, to which Purcell gave melody so natural to the language that they could be sung in almost normal "time." He wrote music for many plays, and his opera, Dido and Æneas, is "one of the masterpieces of music drama, the only English one."

Handel, coming to England, learned to simplify his own chorus effects after the clearer manner of Purcell. The Purcell Society has brought out more than twenty volumes of his works, about half of them sacred. His purely instrumental music is unique because of its approach to modern ideas.

The tune Walsall is typical of its time, with its expressive minor quality, which is not a sadness, but rather a mood of meditation, or what Germans call "inwardness." The impressive words are by Edmund Beale Sargant, a Christian Scientist, whose book, *Songs of Deliverance,* was published in London in 1923.

18 Lyons. *Be firm and be faithful*

In a copy of the *Christian Science Hymnal* which Mrs. Eddy used in her home, appears a note written by her own hand: "Sing often in The Mother Church the hymn 173" (present No. 18). She never gave any formal expression of this wish; but her thought of these words has significance for all who use the Hymnal.

Michael Haydn (1737–1806) is the younger brother of the famous Joseph. He was too devoted to his home in Salzburg, Austria, to leave it for Vienna, when Prince Esterhazy, Joseph's patron, offered him the place of assistant chapelmaster.

Self-taught in composition, Michael rates as an eminent composer, and Joseph said that Michael's work was superior to his own, "in earnestness, severity of style, and sustained power." Like Bach, he used to sign his scores, "To the glory of God." When the French entered Salzburg, Michael's work stopped, and the Empress of Austria befriended him, "commanding" a Mass, in which she herself sang the soprano solos. Franz Schubert told of his reverence for the "clear and calm spirit of Michael Haydn."

The name of the tune is a reminder of Peter Waldo of Lyons (c. 1170), who dared to stand against ecclesiastical tyrannies, and whose ideas lived on in the thoughts of French liberals until, transmitted to the courage and enterprise of the Pilgrims, they had their first full experiment at Plymouth in America.

19 Purity. *Behold, they stand in robes of white*

In the land of the Northmen, poetic inspiration is worthily honored: this is attested in the experience of Hans Adolph Brorson (1694–1764), the poet here, who was actually made a bishop for the beauty of his poetry.

The inspiring quality of Brorson's poetry came at a time when Danish hymnody had become rather dryly argumentative; and so the people rejoiced in the refreshment of his verse. To honor the poet equally with the preacher was to hark back to the very days of David, the Psalmist, when a shepherd boy, his harpstrings hung with blue lilies (so Robert Browning sees him), came to dispel with singing the black moods of King Saul.

The quiet pastoral music here is fit companion for Brorson's words, and is named for his first line, "The white-robed multitude." The lovely line and serene grace of the melody have the charm of Norwegian folk music. The tune is given an English name, here, from the prevailing idea of the words. It is from the Norwegian *Chorale Book*.

Brorson's hymn uses the passage from Revelation which is the foundation of the English version; but he stresses the great tribulation out of which men have come. Indeed, all his poetry has a rather melancholy tone, flowing from his personal griefs.

20 Pixham. *Be true and list the voice within*

Horatio W. Parker (1863–1919) grew up like many a young man of Boston origins, in the atmosphere of books and music. His father was an architect, his mother a poet and musician. She gave the boy his first music lessons and was delighted when he brought her fifty of Kate Greenaway's poems set to his own music. Next he studied with Boston teachers, among them the composer, George W. Chadwick, afterward director of the New England Conservatory. In 1881, he went to Munich, where Rheinberger, much interested in his promise, taught him for three years. Later Parker taught at the National Conservatory in New York, under Anton Dvořák, and in 1893 was called back to Boston, as organist and choirmaster at Trinity Church. This was the year of his oratorio, Hora Novissima (the last hour), its words from Bernard's Latin hymn, A Rhythm of the Celestial Country. It begins: "This is the last hour, these the most evil times, let us be watching." The music is very beautiful, though rather ecclesiastical in tone. It was first sung by the New York Choral Society, and then at the Cincinnati and Worcester (Massachusetts) festivals. In 1899, at the Three Choirs Festival in Worcester, England, it was the first American composition admitted to those historic programs.

Later Professor Parker won two prizes for American opera, by his Mona and Fairyland. In 1894, he was called to the chair of music at Yale University, where he advanced the department rapidly. His works number eighty-four; not a large output, but carefully wrought. The words by Kate L. Colby are from *The Christian Science Journal*, July, 1890. They were used in the first edition of the Hymnal, 1892.

21 Grandpont. *Beloved, let us love*

The addition to the Hymnal of two more hymns by Horatius Bonar (1808–1889) is a reminder that Mrs. Eddy must have felt a kinship of thought with this poet-preacher of the Scots, whom she twice quoted in *Miscellaneous Writings*.

A Scot is one who always knows that "Maxwellton's braes are bonnie," and who loves to hear "a melody that's sweetly played in tune," and so, reading Bonar, we know very well where was his native heath. All his poetry breathes the love of music, and of nature seen as a promise of something fairer than herself; and its dominating thought is the assurance of the "second coming." In his long autobiographical poem, *My Old Letters,* finished in the year 1876, that closed a significant decade, he wrote:

Sorely and long has this sick world of ours
Needed a healer, for her wounds are deep . . .
Thou unborn light, descending from above,
Making the dead alive, the prisoner free,
We bid thee welcome. . . .
Hell cannot stay Thee in Thy radiant march
Nor the deep grave bar Thy victorious way . . .
Creation waiteth for the healing breath
Of Him from whom all sickness flees.

And he speaks of the bread of God, that "maketh sick men whole." In 1866, he wrote:

No joy is true, save that which has no end,
No life is true, save that which liveth ever.
No health is sound save that which God doth send,
No love is real save that which changeth never.

In 1843, at what is called the "Disruption," when more than four hundred clergymen of the Established Church joined Dr. Chalmers in forming the Free Kirk of Scotland, Bonar was one of them. Born and educated in Edinburgh, he worked for liberty there in yet another form, by aiding the Total Abstinence Society. A little yellow-covered tract survives, dated 1854, named *Christian Witness-bearing to the Sin of Intemperance,* wherein Bonar answers a question of our own times— whether the Bible requires of men more than temperance. Bonar's uncompromising reply is that "total abstinence is the only unmistakable protest" against the growing evil.

The vigor of his prose is seen in such phrases as these:

Do something! If you cannot do what we advise, do something!
O, be on the side of God, out and out. Don't trifle with religion!
Health is with God. Health came not from man, but from the love
and power of God.

Poet, prophet, philanthropist, reformer, lover of God and of men, Bonar illustrated, in his own, the life which he has defined as "a great and noble creed."

For Stainer, the composer, see Note 160. Grandpont is a place near Oxford.

22 Dennis. *Beloved, let us love*

For G. Thalben-Ball, the composer, see Note 26.

23 Serenity. *Blest Christmas morn*

This gentle tune by Wallace has long been familiar with Mrs. Eddy's beautiful Christmas song. William Vincent Wallace (1814–1865) was a true minstrel of Ireland, that home of minstrelsy. He led a roving life, so that he is traced from his childhood in Waterford to London, where he was loved for his violin playing, and then he is found plunging into the bush, the wild places, west of Sydney, Australia. Someone hearing him play was astonished to find real music in the wilderness. This led to some years of musical success in Sydney. Then back he came to London, to compose and produce his opera Maritana. Next he was off to South America on a concert tour, and then for fourteen years he found musical satisfactions in Germany.

He had a commission to write for the Opéra in Paris, but his search for health, not to say his love of new places, sent him to the Pyrenees, on his last journey.

24 Christmas Morn. *Blest Christmas morn*

The music of Christmas Morn was written for Mrs. Eddy's hymn of that name in 1903, by Albert F. Conant, long the organist of The Mother Church.

25 Kington. *Blest Christmas morn*

This tune, through which we seem to hear an echo of bells, is excellently suited to Mrs. Eddy's hymn of Christmas. It is the only hymn tune yet published by Rev. F. Llewellyn Edwards, Rector of Kington Magna, Dorset, whose musical interests include the long-honored art of bell ringing. He belongs to the Ancient Society of College Youths, established in 1637 as an order of Change Ringers. He is Secretary of the Salisbury Diocesan Guild of Ringers, and member of the Central Council of Church Bell Ringers. When King George V was crowned in 1911, the bells of Kington Magna, sounding just before half past three in the morning, were the first to "ring in" the new monarch. The Rector often plays the bells, and also the church organ, which was built entirely by local craftsmanship.

Born at Kington Magna, educated at Bath, Oxford, and Cambridge, he was ordained at Liverpool. He went as chaplain to the English Church at Seville, Spain, and then to Cyprus, returning to his home parish as its Rector in 1908. This tune was given a prize by the Dorset Choral Association, Dr. Fuller Maitland acting as judge. The tune has been used in several hymnals.

26 Dransfield. *Blest Christmas morn*

This melody is one of three tunes composed by G. Thalben-Ball for the hymns of Mrs. Eddy. This setting has much of the strength of the words and of their tenderness. The composer was born in New South Wales, Australia, and began his career in London as an exhibitioner and scholar at the Royal College of Music. He became acting organist at the famous Temple Church, with Sir Walford Davies, whom he succeeded as organist in 1923. He was added to the staff of the Royal College and made an examiner for the Royal College of Organists.

Several of the musicians represented in the Hymnal have been connected with the Temple Church, which still maintains its long reputation for upholding all that is fine in its musical services. The church is of unique historical interest, as dating from the Crusades. Through these musicians the *Christian Science Hymnal* touches those centuries of endeavor to place a Christian banner over Jerusalem, a hope which was fulfilled in 1917.

The Knights Templar, the Red Cross knights, were one of the three great military orders founded in the twelfth century for the defense of the Latin kingdom of Jerusalem. The Templars were named for the Temple of Solomon, on the site of which they had their quarters. The order spread over Europe, filled with the flower of knighthood, and had a headquarters in Paris. In 1185, the Templars living in London held land on the banks of the Thames, which they divided as the Inner, the Middle and the Outer Temple. The Templars' churches were built round in shape, like the Temple at Jerusalem, and the London Temple is the finest of the four ancient round churches still remaining in England.

By grant of King James I, the whole of the Temple was put into the hands of the two Societies of Lawyers. Here stand the two Inns of Court, the Inner Temple, and the Middle Temple, which Ben Jonson called "the noblest nurseries of humanity and liberty in the kingdom," and within whose precincts have lived and toiled so many famous lawyers, poets, dramatists, and novelists.

The stately beauty of the ancient buildings, mostly designed by Wren; the quiet courts, the green lawns and flower gardens stretching down to the Thames, have a remarkable atmosphere of peace and dignity, maintained in the very heart of the busy city. These Inns of Court are rightly counted among the most prized possessions of London. Spenser wrote of them in his Prothalamion:

> . . . Those bricky towers
> The which on Thames' broad aged back do ride,
> Where now the studious lawyers have their bowers,
> There whilome wont the Templar Knights to bide
> Till they decayed through pride. . . .
> Sweet Thames, run softly, till I end my song.

27   Infinitas.   *Blest Christmas morn*

Percy Whitlock's fine setting of Mrs. Eddy's hymn shows variations of rhythm that yield to the natural sway of the words. He has other delightful settings for Mrs. Eddy's words at Nos. 162, 211, 257.

28 Selworthy. *Blest Christmas morn*

E. Norman Greenwood composed this beautiful music for Mrs. Eddy's words, with special cadences to fit the rhythm of the poem, as where it carries the thought over from the fourth stanza to the fifth, at "All mortal strife." He is a Christian Scientist who composed seven Hymnal tunes.

Mr. Greenwood studied organ, piano, and composition at the Royal College of Music, in London. He held the Kent scholarship, and was awarded the medal which is presented triennially to the most distinguished student at the College, by the Worshipful Company of Musicians, a society founded in 1604. Later he was made Honorary Associate of the College.

Beginning as a chorister, he has had close association with the music of the Temple Church (Note 26), where he has frequently acted as organist and choir-trainer. He has filled various posts as organist, giving many recitals, and also stands high as a concert pianist.

29 Everton. *Breaking through the clouds of darkness*

For Henry Smart, composer here, see Note 42. These words are by Florence L. Heywood, and appeared in *The Christian Science Journal,* July, 1886. They were used in the first edition of the Hymnal, 1892.

30 Love. *Brood o'er us with Thy shelt'ring wing*

This music, specially composed for Mrs. Eddy's great poem by Walter E. Young (Note 161), has a spontaneous charm that shows it to have been inspired by the words.

31 Vita. *Brood o'er us with Thy shelt'ring wing*

Eaton Faning (1850–1927) was born in Cornwall and learned music first from his father. After more study in London he was engaged at the Royal Academy to teach harmony and piano, and in 1885 was made director of music at Harrow, a post he filled for fifteen years. He composed two operettas, a symphony, two quartets, an overture, and a vocal work with full orchestra performed at St. Paul's. His Song of the Viking won popular favor. This tune Vita (Life) makes a sympathetic accompaniment for this poem by Mrs. Eddy.

32 Gottlob. *Brood o'er us with Thy shelt'ring wing*

This music, Praise God, by Johann Sebastian Bach, was adapted to these words of Mrs. Eddy's by the omission of one or two repeated notes. Matching the words in loveliness, it makes this a hymn of great beauty.

33 St. Oswald. *Call the Lord thy sure salvation*

St. Oswald is named for Dr. Dykes' own church (Note 169) and has Montgomery's words (Note 83). His original line was, "Call Jehovah thy salvation."

189

34 Home. *Christ comes again with holy power*

Home is an example of the symmetry and poise of Mozart's melody. (See Notes 93, 109.) The beautiful poem, of the second coming, is by Marion Susan Campbell.

An interesting fact of Mozart's life is recorded in his cantata Maurer-freude (Mason's Joy) composed from his interest in the Masonic order to which he belonged. His friend Haydn, we know, referred music to a divine inspiration. What we know of Mozart hints that he, too, conceived of music as a gift of God. This joy in music sustained him under neglect in his later years. For Mozart might have sung with one whose victory outstripped his own:

> O make me glad for every scalding tear,
> For hope deferred, ingratitude, disdain.

Mary Baker Eddy, writer of the quoted lines (Hymnal No. 207), was indeed an understanding hearer of Mozart. Out of her own necessity to express a supreme vision, she recognized that the musician, too, "experienced more than he expressed" (*Science and Health with Key to the Scriptures*, p. 213). Comparing him with Beethoven, she said that Mozart "measures himself against deeper grief" (*Message to The Mother Church for 1900*, p. 11).

Mozart said that before he put pen to paper he beheld his symphony as a perfect whole, which he could survey all at once, like a great building. Musicians place his three greatest symphonies (those of 1788, including the Jupiter) as the crown of his work. His string quartets were "the first really great and perfect examples" of this form of music, and those dedicated to Haydn, his teacher, in 1782, are "among the select few of the highest value in existence."

But it was for his opera The Marriage of Figaro, based on the play by Beaumarchais (friend of American liberty), that Prague received him with shouts of *Viva*. There, as he wrote home, he heard everywhere, sung and whistled, "nothing but Figaro." His Don Juan shows a power of broader, more intense, if not actually tragic beauty. The libretto of this opera, as well as that of his Magic Flute (with its talking animals and other magical amazements—promising Wagner's), proved that the music, not the play, is the thing.

One song, The Violet (Goethe), shows what Mozart might have done with the Lieder (songs) that made so large a part of the fame of Schubert, Schumann, and Mendelssohn.

35 Dix. *Christ, whose glory fills the skies*

Treuer Heiland (Faithful Saviour) are the first words of the hymn with which this music was used in Kocher's *Voices from God's Kingdom*, Stuttgart, 1838. Conrad Kocher (1786–1872) of Wüttemberg studied church music in Italy and founded a church choral society in Stuttgart, where he was organist of the Cathedral. His *Harp of Zion* was a large collection of chorales published 1854–55. The poem Faithful Saviour was by Christian H. Zeller (1779–1860), a teacher in Switzerland. The melody had seven lines, but when used in England for a poem by W. C. Dix (Note 43) the fifth line was omitted, as here. The words here are by Charles Wesley (Note 105).

36   Falmouth. *Church of the ever-living God*

These words by Bonar (Note 21) are from a long poem called The Little Flock. Three new stanzas have been chosen for the present Hymnal. The melodious tune Falmouth, composed for these words by Walter E. Young (see Note 161), was named for the street where stands The Mother Church.

37   St. Agnes. *City of God, how broad and far*

This hymn is particularly interesting because it is perhaps the highest inspiration in poetry that came to the beloved poet-preacher, Samuel Johnson (1822–1882), during his work in Lynn, Massachusetts, where he preached from 1853 to 1870. He was striving to build up what was then called a Free church, one with no creed. He conceived of God as transcending all formulas of the past; and he was unwilling to be classed with any denomination of the time, even the Free Religionists. This was, of course, the period when the Christian Science textbook was being prepared and written by another resident of Lynn, Mary Baker Eddy.

Born in Salem, educated at Harvard, Johnson entered his ministry without ordination. But Samuel Longfellow, his friend and collaborator in hymnody (Note 134), spoke of Johnson as having "absolute faith in the divine." His life was so marked by brotherhood that at his passing he was called "the universal friend."

The Rev. Samuel B. Stewart, who appears also in the story of Mrs. Eddy, preached a sermon eulogizing Johnson. Thomas W. Higginson said that Johnson's so-called unbelief was more devout than other men's creeds. The third stanza of his hymn, omitted from the Hymnal, reads:

> How purely hath thy speech come down
> From man's primeval youth!
> How grandly hath thine empire grown
> Of freedom, love and truth.

One likes to think that this poet would have been glad to know that this "speech" of the holy city was even then being made plain for all men to understand, through the great book which Mrs. Eddy named *Science and Health with Key to the Scriptures.*

This serene music by Dr. Dykes (Note 169) is an excellent setting for this noble hymn.

38 Richmond (Chesterfield). *City of God, how broad and far*

The story of Thomas Haweis brings into the Hymnal's interesting circle a striking figure, in the composer's patron, Lady Selina, Countess of Huntingdon (1707–1791). Beginning as a follower of John Wesley, she separated from him, with George Whitefield, to whom she afterward gave a scarf as her private chaplain. He preached often at her house to groups that included such men as the Earl of Chesterfield (of the Letters), Horace Walpole, Henry St. John Bolingbroke.

She held that if she had the right to appoint one chaplain, she could appoint as many as she had chapels to fill. She built and supported about sixty, and founded in Wales a college to train her chaplains. Her ideas were called a Calvinistic Methodism, tending to Congregationalism. But she remained a member of the Established Church of England until her chaplains were forbidden to preach in a hall she hired in London.

Thomas Haweis (1734–1820) held the curacy of St. Mary Magdalen's at Oxford, then was rector elsewhere, after which he became chaplain and manager for Lady Huntingdon. Perhaps ten collections of hymns were published for the use of her followers, including Haweis' *Carmina Christo* (Songs to the Saviour) of 1792. The tune Richmond appeared in this book. Another of her hymns celebrates the departure of missionaries from her college for America, 1772. Through Whitefield, she also helped to establish a boys' orphanage at Bethesda, near Savannah, Georgia.

This music was arranged by Samuel Webbe, Jr. (1770–1843), who studied with his father and with Clementi. He was organist in Liverpool and London and published a *Collection of Psalm Tunes,* 1808, and also four volumes of madrigals, glees, canons, catches, etc.

39 Frainsby. *Come, gracious Spirit, heavenly Love*

The composer here is Dr. George Dyson, who, besides serving as professor of composition at the Royal College of Music, London, has been connected with several of the great boys' schools of England, and has been in sympathetic touch with young people all his days. His tunes for the *Christian Science Hymnal* were all taken from the *Marlborough College Hymn Book,* edited by Dr. Dyson when he was director of music there. He afterward became director at Winchester College, for which he also edited a new hymn book. His hymn melodies have rare charm and vocal ease.

Music has long been the handmaid of poetry. The famous epics, as the Lay of Beowulf, or the Song of Roland, were chanted or sung. The folk singer, over his work, or the bard at the court, fell naturally into a "sing-song" of words. As the voice flowed freely the tones became more musical, more varied in pitch, until, at last, there was melody!

Dr. Dyson, known as both lecturer and writer, in his *Progress of Music* (1932) shows the development of church music onward from the early chanting of the Psalms and plain-song. He says: "Repeat a significant word, and it becomes a cadence. A sentence becomes a chant, a chant a melody. . . . Speech gradually changes into song." He finds the origin of some of the most ancient church melodies in the old Hebrew music used with the Psalms. His book *The New Music* examines the technic of modern composition. Among Dr. Dyson's works are Three Rhapsodies for String Quartet, piano pieces, songs, and church music.

The words here are by Simon Browne (1680–1732), a contemporary of Isaac Watts, and like him an Independent. His hymns were "designed as a Supplement to Dr. Watts." Of these, the hymn given here, "Come, gracious Spirit," has been widely used, and Julian tells us that few hymns have been subjected to so many alterations and changes as this. The title was, The Soul giving itself up to the Conduct and Influence of the Holy Spirit. The first two lines of the original are interesting:

> Come, Holy Spirit, heavenly Dove,
> My sinful maladies remove.

40 Consolator. *Come, ye disconsolate*

The biographer of Thomas Moore (1779–1852) sees in Moore's industry—as witness his research for his oriental romance, *Lalla Rookh*— a proof of sounder character than is always credited to this charming young Irish gentleman, who, Orpheus-like, drew all London society after him, by his songs.

The son of a small tradesman in Dublin, he went to London to read law, and actually shared with Lord Byron the honors of popularity as a poet. His "Oft in the stilly night," "The harp that once through Tara's halls," " 'Tis the last rose of summer," won all hearts—and made him the welcome guest of the highest in the land. In 1816 he published his *Sacred Songs,* all set to popular airs of various nations, among them "Come, ye disconsolate."

This poem was supplied with its present third stanza by the American Thomas Hastings (Note 97) to replace Moore's stanza, "Go ask the infidel."

Moore is especially interesting to Christian Scientists for the passage from *Lalla Rookh* (1817) which is cited by Mrs. Eddy (*Miscellaneous Writings,* p. 51):

> When from the lips of Truth one mighty breath
> Shall, like a whirlwind, scatter in its breeze
> The whole dark pile of human mockeries;
> Then shall the reign of Mind commence on earth,
> And starting fresh, as from a second birth,
> Man in the sunshine of the world's new spring,
> Shall walk transparent like some holy thing.

This occurs in the story of the Veiled Prophet. The capitalization as above is Moore's own.

The sympathy of "Come, ye disconsolate," further speaks the deeper nature of Moore, and its second line, "Come to the mercy seat, fervently kneel," altered here, shows a humble heart. (For the composer, Samuel Webbe, see Note 6.)

41 Qui laborat orat. *Come, labor on*

England ranks Sir Hugh P. Allen as one of the foremost authorities in matters musical, who brought to his high service the rare combination of great musicianship and great scholarship. On his appointment to the important posts of Professor of Music to the University of Oxford, and Director of the Royal College of Music, London, his administrative ability and untiring energy won for him immediately the respect and admiration of the musical world.

The three tunes by him found in the *Christian Science Hymnal* are likely to become especially popular, because of their admirable expression of the spirit of the words—for which they were composed.

His hymns here are from *Cheltenham Ladies College Hymnal,* 1922.

The music of Qui laborat orat (Who labors, prays) gives the summons to labor as if by a trumpet, and the three long lines of the verse are uttered in the natural word-tune of the poetry.

The words are from *Thoughts for Thoughtful Hours* by Jane Borthwick of Edinburgh (1813–1897), who is widely remembered for her translations from German, named *Hymns from the Land of Luther.*

42 Regent Square. *Come, Thou all-transforming Spirit*

In this hymn are met together a lawyer's clerk, who left his dusty papers for the fresher world of song, and a ribbon-factory hand, who became a lay preacher.

Henry Smart (1813–1879), the lawyer's clerk, had "extraordinary natural faculties for music" and though largely self-taught won success both as organist and composer. His anthem for the tercentenary of the Reformation, in 1835, so impressed S. S. Wesley that he headed a subscription to have it published. Smart was for eight years organist at St. Philip's, Regent Street, for twenty years at St. Luke's, and was finally chosen for St. Pancras. His best work was a cantata, The Bride of Dunkerron, composed for the Birmingham Festival. His cantatas, anthems, and an opera were performed, but he is remembered today for part songs and organ pieces. This tune is from *Psalms and Tunes,* 1867.

These words, by Jonathan Evans (1748?–1809), appeared in Burder's collection of 1789. At thirty, Evans joined the Congregationalists of Coventry, and when their preacher George Burder went to London, Evans took his place.

43 Abendlied. *Come unto me, ye weary*

The perfect ease of a Schubert melody is in this tune, with modulations as natural and right as the blooming of a flower. With its persuasive eighth notes and restful half tones it is well named Evensong. The plaintive words suit the melody, too.

Schubert spent his brief life in Vienna (1797–1828). His work ended when he was thirty-one, the age at which Beethoven was but beginning his mightiest music. That Schubert could have advanced far beyond his youthful self is shown especially by his Unfinished Symphony. His piano music is loved, but it is by his songs that Schubert sways the hearts of humanity. The composing of Hark, hark, the lark—on the back of a menu in a noisy restaurant—is typical of the spontaneity of his songs, that almost seem to have flowed to the paper of themselves. Of no other composer have we so few letters or biographical details. He has left us only his music, to tell us what he was, under that awkward, shy exterior.

He was the first to make his accompaniments an interpretation of the poem and he played these accompaniments like a master, with his stubby fingers. Lovely as his melodies are, they sing with deeper effect against this background of beauty. Here the brook is flowing through the piano part, under the Questioner's entreaty; there, as in The Wanderer, mountain and valley shine, or ring with echoes of home. The imitation of galloping hoofs in The Erl King is especially familiar.

Schumann's tribute to Schubert really tells his life-story: "Everything that he touched turned to music."

William Chatterton Dix (1837–1898) was born in Bristol and became manager of a merchant marine insurance company in Glasgow. But he had a marked gift for poetry and his many hymns were much in demand for their expressive beauty. This one appeared in *The People's Hymnal*, 1867.

44 Franconia. *Come to the land of peace*

This tuneful melody comes from the *Harmonious Song Treasury* of Johann König (1691–1758), choirmaster of Frankfort, Germany, in old Franconia, home of the Franks, who gave their name to the "sweet France" of Charlemagne. König's is a monumental collection of 1,940 tunes. This tune was set to the song, "What is it that troubles me?" The form here is an adaptation made by W. H. Havergal (1793–1870) for his *Old Church Psalmody*, 1847.

Canon Havergal devoted himself to the betterment of church music. He wrote hymns, but is best remembered for his music and as the father of Frances Ridley Havergal. He was long Honorary Canon of Worcester Cathedral.

The hymn is by Felicia Dorothea Hemans, née Browne (1793–1835), whose name is much beloved in the United States for her great hymn, The Landing of the Pilgrim Fathers. She draws an authentic picture of many a "wild New England shore," though it hardly fits the quiet Plymouth Bayside. Its spirit, however, is truly in keeping with her theme. The words here, from her *Works*, 1839, show how a hymn may be improved by an unknown editor. The original meter runs thus:

> Fear hath no dwelling there,
> Come to the mingling of repose and love,
> Breathed by the silent spirit of the dove,
> Through the celestial air.

The revised version is credited to *Briggs' Collection,* in a Boston hymnal of 1848.

Mrs. Hemans was born in Liverpool, but spent years in Wales and in Dublin.

45 Herongate. *Dear God, how glorious is Thy name*

Pleasant trails are opened for exploration by many of the place names given to the tunes. For example, two American girls, driving in Essex, England, passed a quaint old signpost with the name Herongate, and turning, came to a delightful village, with thatched cottages, black barns, and an air of immemorial peace. When they afterward opened their new Hymnal and found this very name, they cried, "Our village!" As the name hints, the tune is used in Essex with a ballad. The name is for an Essex family named Heron, one member of which was the sixteenth-century schoolboy who is pictured on a memorial brass in a local church. The words used here are by J. Palmer Snelling, a Christian Scientist, and are so melodious that they dispense with rhyme.

46 Manna. *Day by day the manna fell*

Louis Moreau Gottschalk (1829–1869) spent his life wandering on three continents. He was born in New Orleans, son of an English father and a French mother. Gottschalk studied in Paris and toured Europe as a pianist, having special success in rhythm-loving Spain. Then he traveled in his native land, conducting music festivals, and presently composed a symphony, Tropic Night. His two operas, one with Charles IX as subject, were never performed, but few young ladies of those days who played the piano failed to try Gottschalk's Last Hope. Strakosch, manager for Adelina Patti, arranged Gottschalk's American concert tour. He was last heard in Rio de Janeiro.

These words are by Josiah Conder (1789–1855), an editor and bookseller in London. He edited the *Congregational Hymn Book,* 1844, which had this poem. It was the fourth of six hymns on the Lord's Prayer, in his *Choir and Oratory,* 1837.

47 Nottingham. *Day by day the manna fell*

Nottingham is the picturesque county in England where Robin Hood led his merry men, and where stood the manor house of Scrooby. Here, sheltered behind a lifted drawbridge, on an estate great enough to have been coveted by Queen Elizabeth, the friends of William Brewster formed a church for free worship (1607) that now in Plymouth, Massachusetts, is named "the Church of Scrooby, Leyden, and Plymouth." The tune is from the Twelfth Mass, long attributed to Mozart, but now counted only a patchwork of his themes and other fragments, put together perhaps by Müller or by Zulehner. (See Notes 34, 93, 109.)

48 Saffron Walden. *Dear Father-Mother, Thou dost grant*

This tune name touches harpstrings of memory, as one of the many town names in the United States that repeat those in England. It speaks, too, of Henry Thoreau, who made the name of his Walden solitudes so well remembered in Concord, Massachusetts.

We are especially happy that such echoes are found in the world of hymnody. This one connects the music of Christian Science with the historic church in Saffron Walden, Essex. Arthur H. Brown (1830–1926) spent most of his life in the neighboring town of Brentwood, Essex, where for forty years he was organist of the parish church.

The Walden church dates from the reign of Henry VII, and is an excellent example of the "perpendicular" style of architecture. The town existed before the Norman conquest and was early named Walden. This was changed to Saffron Walden, because of its saffron culture in the fifteenth century. We can imagine the ancient town, dominated by its stately church and surrounded by the purple blooms of the *crocus sativus,* whose stigmas make saffron. Its many uses are hinted in a phrase from Winter's Tale, as "saffron to color the warden pies." (See Note 337.)

The tune is from *The Hymnal Companion,* 1890. The poem is by Edmund Beale Sargant, whose book, *Songs of Deliverance,* was published in London in 1923.

49 Rest. *Dear Lord and Father of us all*

Whittier is the poet here, a reference to whom as "grandest of mystic poets" is cited in Mrs. Eddy's *Pulpit and Press* (pp. 53, 54). Two of his stanzas are quoted, including "The healing of the seamless dress" (372); and in a footnote Mrs. Eddy tells of healing Mr. Whittier at his home in Amesbury, while one of her early poems comments on his famous Snow Bound. His poem, A Legacy, speaks of

> The knowledge that from thine,
> As from the garments of the Master, stole
> Calmness and strength, the virtue which makes whole
> And heals without a sign.

This shows his thought in his advanced years.

John Greenleaf Whittier (1807–1892) grew up on a farm near Haverhill, Massachusetts, a gentle-valiant defender of the weak. Coming in from the spring plowing or the little shoe shop in winter, he wrote poems for the *Haverhill Gazette*. These grew to be a fiery demand for justice to men enslaved. Heartbreaking tales of African bondage filled the poems that duly brought him fame—and blame, as when a mob burned the Philadelphia building where he was editing an anti-slavery paper. His poem, Pennsylvania Pilgrim, tells the story of the Friends of God, German Pietists, who came at the call of William Penn, and perhaps fixed for the Quakers their sweeter name of Friends. The pure spiritual beauty of his hymns, their love and tenderness, are evidence of the "inner light" by which he lived. (For the present words, see Note 50.)

His compassion covered all humanity. He ranges from Toussaint, hero of Haiti, to Sophia Sturge, of the British Complete Suffrage Association; from his Ichabod, reproachful of Daniel Webster, to a song of Shoemakers, or a demand for the liberty of Finland, or a campaign song, "For Lincoln goes in when the Quakers are out"—to vote! His triumphant Laus Deo, beginning, "It is done," rang in the Anti-slavery Amendment, and was apparently the model of Mrs. Eddy's Laus Deo for a different victory. Her poem, one may say, has more of the rhythm and clear insistence of the bells. Whittier's poems are all as autobiographic as his Snow Bound, for they show us the man.

Mrs. Eddy spent some time in Amesbury, just before the writing of *Science and Health with Key to the Scriptures*. She was long remembered there as writing, writing, absorbed in Bible study, while her notes drifted over the floor. (See *The Christian Science Monitor* for February 21, 1914.) The town name is for old Ambresbury, one of the earliest religious centers of Britain, and means "anointed stones" (Whittier's note). Surely these two great people whose lives touched at Amesbury were both "anointed stones," and "lively," in Bible phrase, fitted to sustain the spiritual building of the Hymnal.

The composer of Rest is Frederick C. Maker (1844–1927), who spent his days in Bristol, England, where he was born. He began as chorister in the old Cathedral (founded 1142), and then was organist in several non-conformist churches. Bristol is the port from which sailed Sebastian Cabot, the first Englishman to see the North American continent. An old Bristol chronicle remarks casually: "This year (1497), on St. John the Baptist's day, the land of America was found by the merchants of Bristowe in a ship . . . called St. Matthew."

50 Repton. *Dear Lord and Father of us all*

Sir Hubert Parry (1848–1918), one of the most eminent of English composers, was writing hymn tunes at the age of eight. Unlike many English composers, he excelled, not as an organist, but as a singer, and in piano playing and song composition. Even before he left Eton he had earned his degree of Bachelor of Music at Oxford, where he later took his Bachelor of Arts degree, thereafter to devote himself wholly to music. Professor of Music at Oxford, he became in 1894 director of the Royal College of Music in London, a post which he long filled, with energy and distinction.

His numerous musical compositions have strong individuality, reaching at times rare beauty and grandeur, while the soundness and purity of his artistic ideals have deeply influenced English music, partly through his various books on music.

Repton is from a contralto aria in Parry's cantata Judith. It was adapted to these words of Whittier, for use at Repton School, and in 1924 the hymn was included in the new Repton Hymn Book. It appeared in Novello's *Choir Book*, with the Whittier words, and also in the Harrow Hymn Book.

The words are from a rather strange poem, The Brewing of Soma, in which Whittier (Note 49) tells of the brew made from the East Indian plant, soma, and used in religious ceremonials. Then begins, "Dear Lord and Father of mankind [us all]." The Quaker poet prays again for

> That deep hush subduing all
> Our words and works that drown
> The tender whisper of Thy call.

Rarely has a better mating been made of music with words than of this serene and tender melody with these words of tenderness and calm. This is an excellent example of Parry's music in its purity of form, where not a phrase breaks out of the lovely balance of his line.

51 Spohr. *Eternal Mind the Potter is*

A poem called The Potter and the Clay appeared anonymously in *The Christian Science Journal* for September, 1890, with this foreword: "The following grew out of a suggestion that Science should by this time bring forth words for its own Hymnal. It is offered without any attempt at self-justification or maternal pride." The words were prompted by Jeremiah 18:1–6.

The poem thus modestly introduced by the author, Mary Alice Dayton, was indeed a pioneer of the revised Hymnal of 1932. It was included in the first edition of the *Christian Science Hymnal*, which appeared in 1892.

This music was taken from Calvary by Louis Spohr (1784–1859), an oratorio in which this air is set to the words, "Though all thy friends forsake thee." Dr. Gauntlett arranged it as a hymn tune in 1851.

Louis Spohr was born in Brunswick, Germany, and studied music there, specializing in the violin. He conducted orchestral concerts in Europe, introducing his wife, who was a harpist, and then he became director of the Court Theatre orchestra at Cassel. The swinging 6/8 measure makes his tune easy to sing with these inspiring words.

52 St. Matthew. *Eternal Mind the Potter is*

This tune appeared in the 1708 edition of the Tate and Brady Psalter (Note 99), which had thirty new tunes, "ten composed by the best masters."

William Croft (1678–1727) was a child of the Chapel Royal (Note 16), under the great Dr. Blow. Organist of St. Anne's, in 1700, he was made a "gentleman extraordinary" of the Chapel Royal, and finally was organist there. He taught the "children" reading, writing, and arithmetic, as well as music. When he became organist at Westminster Abbey, he was still composer for the Chapel Royal. He produced many noble anthems used at public thanksgiving for victories, as for that at Blenheim, and two odes for the Peace of Utrecht, 1713. Croft also wrote sonatas for flute and violin, and was a founder of the Academy of Vocal Musick. There is a monument to him in Westminster Abbey. (See Notes 213, 236.)

53 Galliard. *Everlasting arms of Love*

John Dowland (1563–1626) was a "rare lutist," and we can imagine him in some nonchalant strummer who saunters across on Shakespeare's stage. He was for a time "lutenist" to the King of Denmark, which warrants the Shakespearean association, especially when we recall Hamlet the Dane handling the flute-like recorders.

Dowland is called the Schubert of England for the charm of his melody, and his "ayres" are among the first English art songs. His playing helped to popularize this charming music that was in the style of the Italian madrigal. He is mentioned by the poet Barnfield in a song to his lady. He sings: "Dowland to thee is dear," and goes on to praise his "heavenly touch upon the lute"—an instrument like the guitar, with a pear-shaped body. The galliard was a gay dance, and its music here adds brightness and confidence to these simple and confident words.

John Macduff (1818–1895) came from Bonhard, Perth, and was parish minister in various places, including the parish of Sandyford, Glasgow. The University of New York, as well as that of Edinburgh, gave him honorary degrees. His religious writings were widely read, and this hymn appeared in his *Altar Stones,* 1853.

54 Westminster. *Faith grasps the blessing she desires*

Of James Turle (1802–1882) are recorded sixty-five years given to one most august service, that of Westminster Abbey. At fifteen years of age he was engaged there as assistant to the organist, meanwhile also playing elsewhere. In 1831 he was himself made organist, and so he remained—at the last, *emeritus*—till his passing.

200

He sang as a boy at Wells Cathedral, then went to London for study. He played at music festivals under Mendelssohn and Spohr, but Westminster was ever the home of his heart; and so the name is now given to this melody, perhaps his best, which appeared in 1836 in Novello's *Psalmist*.

Turle excelled in improvisation, and liked deep rolling chords on the organ, which had amazing effect in the resounding spaces of the great Abbey. A memorial window with his portrait was placed in the Abbey, including the portrait of his well-beloved wife.

The poet here is Harriet Martineau (1802–1876), who, like her American friend, Mrs. Stowe, was the sister of a famous preacher. James Martineau used some of her hymns in his collection. She said that the hymns belonged to "her Unitarian period." She gave her incisive pen to forward good causes, and became a distinguished figure in London society. Returning from a visit in America she wrote frankly of the faults she found here. Her tales and one novel, her books on history, education, and philosophy, show extraordinary powers of application.

55 Gott will's machen. *Father, hear the prayer we offer*

This fine tune, by J. Ludwig Steiner (1688–1761), is named for a hymn, beginning "God will bring it to pass," by John Herrnschmidt. He was a poet of the Pietistic movement, or "Revival," in Germany, among the supporters of which were this poet and Freylinghausen, in whose Hymnal this poem appeared. Julian remarks that the great religious revivals have all been "sung, as well as preached and written, into the hearts of the people," and that the leaders have been always themselves writers of noble hymns. Steiner was a trumpeter in Zurich. There is the ringing precision of the trumpet in this simple melody.

In this connection, then, it is interesting to turn again to New Hampshire, as a source of helpful words. For this poem is by Mrs. Love Maria Willis (1824–1908) of Hancock, New Hampshire, and appeared first in *Tiffany's Monthly* (1859), where it was written in the first person, singular.

56 Crispinian. *Father, Thou joy of loving hearts*

This beautiful tune was taken from the Hymn Book of Marlborough College, England, with the permission of the composer, John W. Ivimey, for some time director of music there. The original of these words is among the most famous of the old Latin hymns, long attributed to St. Bernard, but recently found in an earlier manuscript. The hymn has been called "the sweetest and most evangelical hymn of the Middle Ages."

In an old printing in the British Museum, dated Douay, 1580, it is headed, "Certaine sweetest prayers of the glorious name of Jesus, commonly called Jesus Mattens . . . from a Latin verse written above two hundred years ago." This version begins, "O Jesu meeke, ye sweetest thought."

Dr. Ray Palmer (1808–1887) made one of the best versions, which is used here with certain adaptations. Dr. Palmer was born in Connecticut, and was pastor of a Congregational church in Bath, Maine. He is described as "cheerful, buoyant, loved by all who knew him." He was at first a clerk in a Boston shop, then studied at Phillips Andover and at Yale. He published his *Poetical Works* in 1876. They include, "My faith looks up to Thee," and many other familiar hymns.

57 Welwyn. *Father, to Thee we turn away from sorrow*

Sir Alfred Scott-Gatty (1847–1918), born in Ecclesfield, Yorkshire, delighted to work for young folk. His early interest was in *Aunt Judy's Magazine*, edited by his mother, and later he wrote and directed musical plays for children. His Tattercoats was given at the Savoy, London. He founded the Magpie Madrigal society, and his songs had vogue for their natural charm of melody, though he rates as an amateur musician. This tune is from the *Arundel Hymns*, 1902.

Frederick Lucian Hosmer (1840–1929), born at Framingham, Massachusetts, also had a care for the children, and prepared a book of services for Sunday Schools. After he left Harvard, his work as a Unitarian minister led him from a pastorate in New England to California, by way of Cleveland, Quincy (Illinois), and St. Louis. His hymns are judged by Julian the most powerful and original among Unitarian hymnists of his time. (See Note 260.) His poems speak a clear sense of immediate dependence upon God. A friendly critic of the *Christian Science Hymnal* selected this hymn, with its editorial changes, to illustrate Christian Science thought, noting that where Hosmer wrote, "Father, to Thee we turn in all our sorrow," Christian Scientists sing, "Father, to Thee we turn away from sorrow." (See Note 260.)

58 Joy. *Father, we Thy loving children*

The work of Beethoven (1770–1827) expresses for many people the fullness of music, its glory, joy, beauty, tenderness, sorrow, mirth, struggle, and victory. Bach has sometimes been called "the musician's musician"; Mozart for many is the acme of pure loveliness; but no other music expresses for so many so wide a range of thought and feeling, such depths of experience, such heights of exaltation, as Beethoven's. Mrs. Eddy touches on this when she says: "The deaf Beethoven besieges you with tones intricate, profound, commanding" (*Message to The Mother Church for 1900*, p. 11).

A New York critic once said that his music records "the words he has had with God." It is as if he had searched out the whole of human experience, and had found beyond the turmoil, everywhere beauty, everywhere God.

This mighty conviction of ever-present good is declared especially in his Ninth Symphony (1824), which crowns the orchestra with the life and conscious joy of human voices. The melody used for this hymn is the joy song of these voices. The words Beethoven gave to it are Schiller's Ode to Joy, and words of joy were written for this hymn by Elizabeth C. Adams, a Christian Scientist.

Beethoven had here reached a point where gratitude—the key to joy for all men—must become articulate. So he set a great choir of people singing the joy of brotherhood, under a heavenly Father's love.

This splendid work comforts those who most regret Beethoven's long deafness; for this music shows his genius so lifting him above limitation that he must move others to rejoice. Music opened to his silence vistas of harmony and beauty that are fitly called heavenly, for they promise the ultimate perfection.

The tune is simplicity itself, but those who recall how it is used in the great unity of orchestra and voices, hear in it always the morning stars singing together, and all the sons of God shouting for joy. It must be sung joyfully, then, with plenty of movement, not slowly.

Research has never found the tune elsewhere. It is Beethoven's own conception of pure folk melody. In an English version of the Ode, the chorus sings:

> Joy, thou spark of heavenly brightness,
> Daughter of Elysium! . . .
> All mankind are friend and brother,
> When thy soft wing fans the heart.

Now all men are called to join in the jubilee, and the song goes on, the sopranos climbing and standing on high A, in a German poet's behest to humanity:

> O embrace now, all ye millions,
> Here's a kiss to all the world! . . .
> Brothers, o'er yon azure fold
> Is a loving Father dwelling—

This was the voice of the man who sat in eternal silence, amid the beauty of sound which he had recorded for others, while his heart sang with them, Joy! Joy! (See Notes 181, 422.)

59 Park Street. *Fight the good fight with all thy might*

Neither Beacon Street nor Massachusetts Avenue is a name more familiar to Boston ears than Park Street. Its one short block climbs Beacon Hill from the old Park Street Church to the State House, under its gilded dome. At No. 2 was Hawthorne Hall, facing Boston Common. Here in the eighties, services of Christian Science were held, and here Mrs. Eddy used to preach. Park Street Church and the Stone (or King's) Chapel were centers of the town's musical life in early days, and later the vast old Music Hall stood near. But in 1900 music moved into the Back Bay, and Symphony Hall is now the neighbor of The Mother Church.

Lowell Mason probably found this tune in Gardiner's *Sacred Melodies,* put it into his Handel and Haydn collection, and named it for the church in whose choir the oratorio society had started. The composer was Frederic Marc Antoine Venua (1788–1872). Born in Paris, of an Italian family, he entered the Paris Conservatory, and when the family moved to London, he learned composition there, and was made chief of the orchestra for ballets at the King's Theatre, also composing for them. He became a member of the Royal Society of Musicians, and the story goes that he retired to Exeter, a wealthy man.

John S. B. Monsell (1811–1875) is chiefly remembered for this stirring hymn, which has been widely sung ever since it was given, in 1838, to Ferguson's *Selection of Hymns for British Seamen.* Montgomery named it Valiant for the Truth, in his collection. Monsell was born at St. Columb's, Londonderry, and educated at Trinity, Dublin. He was chaplain for Bishop Mant, and finally rector of St. Nicholas, Guildford, England. Of his home here it is said that it was "quite an ideal household, full of the beauty of holiness, with genial brightness and gaiety playing like sunshine over all the troubles of life."

60 Pentecost. *Fight the good fight with all thy might*

William Boyd (1847–1927), born of a Scottish family, in the island of Jamaica, began to compose when he was ten. Baring-Gould was his tutor in London, and when the teacher went to Iceland to prepare his book, *Iceland, its Songs and Sagas,* he sent to Boyd Icelandic tunes to harmonize for the book. This energetic tune Pentecost was composed when Baring-Gould needed a tune to be sung by Yorkshire miners to the hymn Come, Holy Ghost, which explains the name of the tune. It appeared in *Thirty-two Hymn Tunes,* composed by members of the University of Oxford, 1868. It was Sullivan who first applied it to Monsell's words. Boyd was Vicar of All Saints Church, Hyde Park.

61 Valour. *Fight the good fight with all thy might*

For Monsell's hymn, Sir Hugh Allen (Note 41) gives music as stirring and buoyant as the words.

62 Old Hundredth. *From all that dwell below the skies*

Someone has remarked that Watts made David a Christian. For his book has the title, *The Psalms of David Imitated in the Language of the New Testament, And apply'd to the Christian State and Worship.* For the music, see Note 1.

The work of Isaac Watts (1674–1748), whose multitudinous verse came chiefly when he was twenty-two years old, is the quarry from which hymnists have long drawn. He of course drew on the Bible, and his words here are from Psalm 117. He was the son of an English Nonconformist,

204

who was twice imprisoned for his religious opinions. Isaac was ordained in 1702 as pastor over the distinguished congregation of Independents of Mark Lane, London. His health seeming to fail, he became a lifelong guest at the beautiful country estate of Sir Thomas Abney. He received honorary degrees from the universities of Edinburgh and Aberdeen, and at his passing a monument was erected to him in Westminster Abbey. His gentleness, piety, and cheerfulness in distress earned for him the name of the Melanchthon of his day. Up to the middle of the last century Watts' *Catechisms,* his *Scripture History,* and *The Divine and Moral Songs* were still the books most in use for the religious education of children.

The Earl of Selborne ranked Watts as the father of English hymnody, though Watts had the example of psalmodists who preceded him; but to what someone calls Watts' "healthy strength of thought and a habit of broad jubilant praise," later writers owe much. Watts had also a way of breaking into sudden beauty amid a wilderness of dry lines—as in "Run up with joy the shining way to meet my blessed Lord," or "Let me within thy courts be seen, like a young cedar fresh and green." Watts' hymns were the first to show what Montgomery was later to define as necessary to a right hymn: that is, "a beginning, a middle and an end."

63 Old Hundredth. *From all that dwell below the skies*

The original version of this great tune (Note 1), as written by Louis Bourgeois himself, with measures of half and of whole notes (minims and semi-breves), is a form which many musicians prefer to the modern version.

64 Elgin. *From sense to Soul my pathway lies before me*

Of the older tune that was named Elgin, Burns wrote what might also be applied to this music by Dr. Dyson (Note 39):

> Noble Elgin beats the heavenward flame,
> The sweetest far of Scotia's holy lays.

These words, by Violet Hay, were written for the music, in a particularly perfect unity.

65 Alford. *From glory unto glory*

This tune by Dykes (Note 169) gives joyous support to Miss Havergal's vivid words. The tune was composed for "Ten thousand times ten thousand," by Dean Alford, for whom it is named (Note 324).

66 Sine nomine. *From these Thy children gathered in Thy name*

Dr. R. Vaughan Williams, composer of Sine nomine (without a name), has a place of great distinction among the composers of the time. From his earliest years he chose musical composition as his definite object.

After wide studies in England and Germany, he discovered that from English folk songs flowed his greatest inspiration. From their modal and rhythmic influences, he evolved his own essentially individual style.

His music is well known in the United States, where, a welcome guest, he came to conduct his own works. Most of the large cities, from Boston and Philadelphia to San Francisco, have heard orchestral works of his, including the London Symphony (with its Westminster chimes and the cry of the lavender seller), his Pastoral Symphony (with its misty vales and its magical singing voice), his First Norfolk Rhapsody, the Fantasia, on a theme by Tallis, his Shepherds of the Delectable Mountains, on a passage from *Pilgrim's Progress,* and the Antiphon.

This tune was composed for *The English Hymnal* when Mr. Williams was its editor. It is held to be one of the noblest melodies of English Hymnody, and stands as a classic. No Hymnal of the time seems complete without it.

The words are by Violet Hay, and have a similar strength and significance.

67   Capetown. *Gird thy heavenly armor on*

Charlotte Elliott (1789–1871), the poet here, spent her early years in Clapham, England, then went to live in Brighton. Her acquaintance with the French poet and evangelist, César Malan, of Geneva (Note 186), had, it is said, a strong influence on her writing. This hymn begins "Christian, seek not yet repose," and comes from her *Morning and Evening Hymns for a Week.*

The composer, Friedrich Filitz (1804–1876), was a collector of sixteenth and seventeenth century chorales. Born in Thuringia, he lived long in Munich. This tune is from his *Four-part Chorale Book,* published in 1845.

68   Vigilate. *Gird thy heavenly armor on*

For the composer, W. H. Monk, see Note 7. The tune was composed for these words, hence its name,—*Watch!*

69   Song 24. *Give me, O Lord, an understanding heart*

Hallelujah: Britain's Second Remembrancer is the breezy title given by George Wither to the second edition of his *Hymns and Songs of the Church* (1623). In Palgrave's *Golden Treasury,* Wither is still asking his petulant question, "If she be not so to me, what care I how fair she be?" and it seems strange to meet him here as responsible for the very first hymn book published in England. Ignored at the time, his book is famous today, because it contains sixteen tunes by Orlando Gibbons (1583–1625). Wither's facility, and perhaps his sense of humor, appear in this second edition, with hymns for all men's doings, as: When Washing; On a Boat;

206

Sheep-shearing; For Tailors, Jailer, Prisoner, Member of Parliament, etc. In his later life, having become a thoroughly persuaded and valiant Puritan, Wither wished men to make a joyful noise unto the Lord all day long. His *Hallelujah*, however, did not include the tunes.

Orlando Gibbons was the youngest and most gifted of three gifted brothers, who all held important posts as organists, the two elder at Bristol, at Exeter, and at Salisbury Cathedral. Orlando, when only twenty-one, was made organist at the Chapel Royal, and became one of His Majesty's "musicians for the virginalles" (instruments of the spinet type), his playing of which was second only to his mastery of the organ. *Parthenia*, collected by Gibbons, Bull, and Byrd, had six pieces by Gibbons for the virginals. After Oxford gave him the degree of Doctor of Music, 1622, he was made organist of Westminster Abbey.

He was in attendance upon the new King, Charles I, at Canterbury, where Queen Henrietta Maria was arriving on her way from Paris. Here Gibbons suddenly passed on, and the burial was in the historic Cathedral.

His works suffered long neglect, though in 1850 Dr. Dykes was placing the exquisite choral song, The Silver Swan, on programs at Durham. Gibbons' first published work was some Fantasias for viols in 1610; and forty anthems remain, many of great beauty. The work which perhaps shows him at his best is Madrigals and Motets, for viols and voices, where the words also attest his fine, austere taste. His music, understood, makes an impression of cool, yet shining beauty. (See Note 397.)

As the tunes in Wither's hymnal were identified by number only, Gibbons' music is given here with these old numbers. This Song 24 is a noble minor, breaking into major brightness in the middle line. The prayerful words, by James J. Rome, appeared in the *Christian Science Sentinel*, January 11, 1913.

70 Mornington. *God giveth light to all*

This is a long familiar hymn tune in the United States, and so its origin is learned with the more surprise; for its composer was the father of the Duke of Wellington. As plain Garrett Wellesley (1735–1781), the first Earl of Mornington was also the first professor of music at Dublin University. Born at Dangan, Ireland, he was largely self-taught in music, and when he applied for lessons was told that he knew as much as the teachers. He wrote mainly for the voice, and his glees and madrigals were collected by Henry R. Bishop.

This tune was composed for a chant and was so used in the Dublin cathedrals throughout the last century. But it had early been shaped into a hymn tune for Miller's *David's Harp*, 1805, where Lowell Mason (Note 2) found it and added it to his Handel and Haydn collection, at Boston. The plain, clear words here, that sing of light, were written for the Hymnal by Elizabeth C. Adams.

71 Austria. *Glorious things of thee are spoken*

As this fine poem by John Newton, once an unknown sailor, ranks with the world's great hymns, so this tune of Haydn's, though written to order for the Emperor's birthday celebration, is one of the world's great tunes. An ordinary folk song, it was developed by Haydn into his strong and inspiring music. Later, he used the melody in his Kaiser Quartet for his "four magical strings," as he called the quartet instruments.

This is probably the most familiar of Haydn's song tunes, though his lovely "My mother bids me bind my hair" is a delight of singers. The two mark the range of strength and grace in Haydn's works, which are said to be "more consistently refreshing than those of any other great composer" (Notes 170, 185).

The story of John Newton (1725–1807) tells what a mother's faith and the memory of another good woman did to reclaim a young man from wrong, and give him to the needy of the world as a saving influence.

Newton's mother passed on when he was seven years old, but not before she had stored his memory with Scripture, and inclined his heart to spiritual loyalties. Then the boy went to sea, and among the rough companions he too turned to reckless ways, till he had to leave the British navy, in disgrace. He took service under a slave dealer, and lived in wretchedness. His star of hope was now the thought of a young girl, who later became his wife. It was the reading of Thomas à Kempis that turned him towards home. In due time he found himself at work with Whitefield and Wesley, until he went to the humble parish at Olney, and to his friendship with Cowper. This hymn appeared in the *Olney Hymns* (Note 334). Newton had a vigorous, sailor-like directness of expression that reached those who needed courageous handling. This vigor is in his hymns. One of his friends was the "pious and vivacious" Hannah More.

72 Benevento. *Glory be to God on high*

John Taylor (1750–1826), writer here of all but the first four lines, which are Wesley's, belonged to a musical family of English Unitarians. His grandfather, a Hebrew scholar, minister of the Octagonal Chapel in Norwich, published an early collection of *Tunes in various Airs*. John Taylor was for fifty years a deacon in the Chapel. In 1802, he made a hymn book "for social worship," and his own hymns were collected in 1863, by his son Edward, a professor of music. The stanzas of his hymn here were rearranged to avoid closing with the idea of strife.

This music, by Webbe (Note 6), has another version at No. 405.

73 Gratitude. *Glory, honor, praise and pure oblations*

Hymn singing in the Netherlands seems to have begun with translations from German, used among the Dutch Lutherans. Though a synod at Utrecht, in 1612, had permitted the Gospel story to be put into hymns, the Synod of Dort, in 1619, forbade public use of anything but Datheen's *Psalms* (1566), taken from those of Marot (Note 1). By 1713, however, the Anabaptist Psalter had an appendix of twelve hymns. A Separatist congregation used a collection by Groenewegen of 1750, when a book of Mennonite hymns also appeared. In 1783, the poet, Van Alphen, urged the use of hymns in which music and poetry would be abreast of the taste of that day, and in 1796 the aid of Engelbert, Minister of Hoorn, and of Abraham Rutgers, Minister of Haarlem, was invited. Thus, in 1803, a commission met at The Hague, and two years later produced a hymn book for public use, recording obligations to the work of Sluiter (1661) and Van Lodensteyn, and to the moderns, Van Alphen, Van den Berg, Feith, etc. Abraham Rutgers adapted hymns from his cantata, The Hope of Blessedness, and made translations from German, on one of which the present hymn is based. This music is from *Spiritual Songs*, Celerina, 1765. Celerina is a village in the Upper Engadine, Switzerland. The Dutch words on the Hymnal page, "Endless thanks and honor," are the first of Rutger's words. With German words, translated, the Dutch have also used many German chorales.

74 Auch jetzt macht Gott. *Go forth and stand upon the mount*

"Even now God makes it plain" was the German hymn used with this tune in Koch's *Chorale Book*, Magdeburg, 1816. It is an especially clear and simple melody.

The words are by Edmund Beale Sargant, whose book, *Songs of Deliverance*, was published in London in 1923.

75 Aurelia. *God comes, with succor speedy*

It is pleasant to think of the grandson of the inspired and inspiring Charles Wesley as rising to high honors in the musical world of England. Samuel Sebastian Wesley (1810–1876) was accounted not only the greatest English organist of his day, but the leading composer of church music. He began at ten years old as chorister in the Chapel Royal. Later his post as organist at Hereford Cathedral meant also the honor of conducting the Three Choirs Festival. Six years at Exeter Cathedral established his fame, and in 1839 Oxford gave him degrees. He was called to Leeds Parish church; then 1849 found him at Winchester Cathedral, and 1864 at the Cathedral at Gloucester. His last words are expressive of his lifelong aspiration, for he said, "Let me see the sky."

Aurelia, sometimes called Golden, for its use with Jerusalem the Golden, is his best known hymn tune, because it was sung in 1872 for the Thanksgiving at St. Paul's, for the recovery of the Prince of Wales. It appeared in Kemble's *Psalms and Hymns*, which Wesley edited, 1864.

Wesley's *European Psalmist,* of 1872, was the fruit of long labors, but was not popular. His fame rests, probably, on his twelve anthems of 1853.

Montgomery's hymn is from his Psalm 72, beginning, "Hail to the Lord's Anointed." (See Note 83.) This is one of the Messianic Psalms.

76 Grace. *God is known in loving-kindness*

The Swedish words on the Hymnal page mean "The Lord reveals Himself in grace," and are from the Swedish translation of the German poem of Johannes Heermann (1585–1647). He was born in Silesia, and was Vicar of Köben. The town saw much of the Thirty Years' War, and Heermann's courage and devotion placed him among the noblest of the Lutheran clergy. In poetical powers he was a forerunner of Gerhardt, an honor indeed, in a literature of a hundred thousand German hymns!

Jakob Boëthius (1647–1718) is another name of conviction and courage. A preacher in Dalecarlia, Sweden, he sent to the King and the Archbishop a letter that criticized some of their doings, and for this letter he was arrested and sentenced to death. His writings were publicly burned by a mob. The sentence was changed to imprisonment for life, but he was eventually released. He looked upon the Bible as the standard for monarchy and government. He lectured in Greek and on theology, and shared in the revision of the Swedish Hymn Book. Wallin (see Note 263), much later, revised Boëthius' version of Heermann's words.

Per Ulrick Stenhammar (1829–1875) was not only a composer and peacher, but an architect and a naturalist, as well. Born in Tornevalla, Sweden, he studied at the Stockholm Institute of Technology and at the Academy of Art where he became a teacher. He was appointed architect in the Board of Public Works and Buildings, for which he designed many churches. Self-taught in music, he won popularity by songs and other vocal works. His oratorio, David and Saul, is Old Testament-like in vigor, simplicity, and faith.

77 Munich. *God is my strong salvation*

This tune is named for one of the greatest centers of art and music in Germany. Mendelssohn used the music in his Elijah (Note 118), having harmonized it from the *Meinigen Hymn Book,* of 1693. This collection was anonymous, but many of its lines are found among the tunes of Hieronymus Kradenthaller, an organist of Regensburg. The words are from Montgomery's Psalm 27 (Note 83).

78 King's Lynn. *God is my strong salvation*

King's Lynn is a traditional melody, with a name that is a landmark in the history of Christian Science. For this is the old Lynn Regis (King's Lynn), for which Lynn, Massachusetts, was named, to honor the first pastor at this wilderness foothold of faith. Old Lynn had been a possession of the bishops of Norwich, and when Henry VIII took it over, the name was changed to Lynn Regis. The new Lynn was settled in 1629, the year before Boston, and was named, we see, for a city of the King. Here Johnson wrote his hymn, "City of God," about 1865, and here Mrs. Eddy wrote the book that tells wonderful things of the "city of the great King" (*Science and Health*, p. 575).

An article in *The Christian Science Monitor* for May 29, 1914, records Mrs. Eddy's work for temperance in Lynn, and quotes the hymn she wrote for the dedication of a temperance hall there, August 4, 1866. This was sung on that occasion, and thus is the first hymn by Mary Baker Eddy known to have been publicly used as such (*Poems,* pages 39 and vi). The lines:

> A temple, whose high dome
> Rose from a water-cup

seem to thoughtful hearts almost as if prophetic of the dome which was thereafter to rise in testimony to the work of the woman who later wrote, speaking of the people's need: "Give them a cup of cold water in Christ's name, and never fear the consequences" (*Science and Health,* p. 570).

Another stanza of this hymn is significant:

> And she—last at the cross,
> First at the tomb, who waits—
> Woman—will watch to cleanse from dross
> The cause she elevates.

On January 31, 1866, three days before her fall on the icy streets of Lynn, which opened the door to a new understanding of Life, Mrs. Eddy, then Mrs. Patterson, wrote from Swampscott to *The Lynn Reporter,* about the "memories" of the Good Templar's Union: "A memory, too, that needs no headstone of marble to preserve, but will continue legible and strong as sculptured stone."

On March 19, of that year, in what is probably her first published writing after her healing, she wrote: "The skies at Swampscott are unveiled . . . Ay, they are spiritually bright . . ." and, "to catch an occasional glimpse . . . of one's spiritual self . . . is to see what shadows we are and what shadows we pursue" (*The Lynn Reporter*).

79 Merton. *God is Love*

The poem is by Sir John Bowring (1792–1872), twice a member of Parliament, a man of political consequence, and distinguished in literature. He edited the *Westminster Review* until he was sent as a commissioner to France. His next port of call was Hongkong, where he went as British consul, in 1849, to be made its governor after five years, when he was also knighted. His published works show him acquainted with such languages as Russian, Serbian, Polish, Magyar, and others. He wrote several books of sacred poetry and his hymns have been much used by Unitarians. For the composer, W. H. Monk, see Note 7.

211

80 Eisenach. *God is our refuge and defense*

Eisenach, with its memories of both Luther and Bach, offers an excellent name for a hymn tune. Johann H. Schein (1586–1630) made the melody, which was harmonized by Bach. Schein wrote his own words for it (1628). It was called, A Little Song of Comfort, written after the passing of Margarita, wife of the town-councilor, Werner, at Leipzig, who was warden of the famous St. Thomas Church, where Schein was cantor. It was at the Thomas School here that Bach spent his long fruitful years. This melody, with a version of the Comfort song, was in the English *Lyra Davidica* (Note 413). Montgomery's words are appropriate for this memorial tune.

81 Kingly Vale. *God is with me, gently o'er me*

This music, by Sir Hugh Allen (Note 41), is well adapted to these words. Kingly Vale, for which it is named, is a beautiful valley of the South Downs, in Sussex, that land of romance and history. Kingly Vale begins in a great cleft in the hills beyond Chichester Harbor. It has an avenue of yew trees so large and spreading that they are believed to be at least a thousand years old. In the autumn thousands of missel thrushes feed on the scarlet yew berries. Overlooking the valley from the high Down are grassy tumuli or mounds, whose origin is not known. The avenue of yews perhaps led up to this place of "barrows," as a center of Druid religious ceremonies. Legends say that in 900 A. D. the Danes landed here and, after a great battle, these mounds marked the burial place of those who fell. But the lovers of Kingly Vale prefer the more ancient tradition and like to imagine the train of white-robed Druid priests marching up the noble avenue of trees, to the ceremonials that are a fascinating and baffling subject of modern research.

The Saxon church, at the little village of Bosham, near Chichester, is pictured in the Bayeux tapestry, and is the place where Harold Godwin, son of the great Earl of Wessex, worshiped before he set sail to be wrecked on the coast of France—there to be coerced by William, the future Conqueror, into forswearing his realm of England.

The poet here is Theodore Chickering Williams (1855–1915), a Unitarian minister, whose middle name is a reminder of the instruments that have long added to the musical fame of Boston, in a suburb of which he was born. He was pastor of All-Souls, New York, and then headmaster of a school in Tarrytown.

82 Purpose. *God is working His purpose out*

This melody illustrates the gift of Sir Walford Davies (Note 159) for reaching the hearts of all people, in an animated tune suited to inspiriting words. The poet, Arthur C. Ainger (1841–1919), was an assistant master at Eton when the hymn was written.

83 Innocents. *God made all His creatures free*

This is an old French melody, named perhaps for a church festival. It was printed in *The Parish Choir*, 1850, in England, as an ancient litany. Joseph Smith was an amateur musician of Halesowen, near Birmingham, among whose papers the tune was found, and some of his friends believed he had originated it. It was often played on the church chimes.

The words are by James Montgomery (1771–1854), from whom more hymns were selected for the Hymnal than from any other poet but Whittier. Montgomery had, with inspiration, both facility and charm of expression, that lend themselves readily to music. He was the son of a Moravian minister, of Ayrshire, Scotland, and of his four hundred hymns, one hundred are still in common use. He was much loved as a hymnist, and a Wesleyan chapel in England is named for him. He edited a liberal paper, *The Sheffield Iris*, for thirty years, and was twice imprisoned in York Castle for his political opinions; yet in 1833, he received a royal pension.

This poem is an arrangement from a collection called *Songs on the Abolition of Slavery* (published 1850), all characteristic of the generous thought of this truly great maker of hymns.

84 Repentance. *God's eternal Word is spoken*

These words are by Theodore V. Oldenburg (1805–1842), a Danish pastor, in Sorterup, Sorö. The English version was made for the Hymnal. The words under the title mean, "Lord, I have done wrong," and are from a Norwegian version of a German poem by Johann Franck, to which the tune was originally sung.

Ludvig M. Lindeman (1812–1887) was born in Trondhjem, Norway, of a family of musicians. As a boy of ten, he appeared as a pianist at one of his father's concerts. He studied theology, but soon turned wholly to music. After playing the 'cello in the Oslo theater, he succeeded his brother as organist at the Church of our Saviour, a post which he held lifelong.

He went to London, invited with four or five of the great organists of Europe, to test and dedicate the new giant organ of Albert Hall. Lindeman played for the King of Belgium, among others, and had great success.

He stands as one of the most learned musicians of Norway; and to a marvelous technique he added rare ability in improvisation. He insisted that the inspiration of Norwegian music must flow from the national character and background. His greatest musical work is his collection of Norwegian folk tunes. He traveled throughout Norway, in remote and quiet places, where, with endless patience, he persuaded the reticent people to fiddle or sing for him the priceless treasures of their traditional melodies. His first volume is now very rare. The edition of 1853 is of three volumes, with six hundred and fifty pieces.

213

Not second to this is his influence on Norwegian church music. His chorale book, authorized in 1877, held nearly two hundred tunes, sixty of which were his own. Several cantatas bear his name and some piano music. Mathematics was the amusement for his spare time, doubtless a byplay of his contrapuntal powers. (See Note 176.)

85 Liebster Jesu. *God of Truth, eternal good*

In a book named *New Spiritual Devotions for Sunday throughout the Year* Johann R. Ahle (1625–1673) used this tune with German words, Dearest Jesus, a hymn by Tobias Clausnitzer. Ahle's life passed in Erfurt, his birthplace, and in Mülhausen, where he served on the town council, and became burgomaster. He worked for the advancement of church music, and published a book on singing. He avoided the old polyphony in his writing, and sought simplicity. This arrangement of the tune was made by Bach for his own *Chorale Hymns*. The words here, in their depth of thought, worthily reflect this noble music. They are by Edith Gaddis Brewer, a Christian Scientist.

86 Coronation. *God's glory is a wondrous thing*

The experience of Oliver Holden (1765–1844) is typical of the pioneer days in American music. Born in Shirley, Massachusetts, he removed to Charlestown to carry on his trade of carpentry. The rebuilding of the town, after the burning in the Revolution, brought him prosperity, with success in real estate ventures, so that he was able to advance from building houses to building tunes. He gave the land for a Baptist church; and the Puritan church, a new organization, chose him for its preacher. He represented Charlestown in the Massachusetts Legislature, or General Court, as it is still called from Colonial days, and was a leading Mason.

His collections of music were of more value than his original pieces, but the tune Coronation, which appeared in his *Union Harmony*, 1793, has been widely used. The name comes from Perronet's hymn, "All hail the power of Jesus' name." (See Note 341.)

With Holden, the American Puritan, is associated in this hymn Frederick Faber (1814–1863), Englishman, who, a student at Oxford, was won over by Newman, whom he followed into the church of Rome. The name of this hymn is, The Right must Win. Faber said that he always wrote especially for the needs of the people, and so his hymns have marked vitality.

87 Mendip. *God's glory is a wondrous thing*

This English traditional melody is named for the historic range of hills in Somerset, where the tune is sung to the ballad of the Miller's Apprentice.

214

88 Halle. *Gracious Spirit, dwell with me*

This tune, compared with Hursley, No. 227, shows how the old melodies were changed, often to adjust them to different hymns. The form of the tune used here is found in a Viennese Catholic collection, dedicated to the Empress Maria Theresa, and so must have existed before 1780. It is sometimes named Pascal, and has also been called Huguenot Melody, attributed to Peter Ritter (1760–1846), Chapelmaster to the Duke of Baden. Having crossed the Atlantic, it became Framingham, for a town near Boston, in Mason's Handel and Haydn collection. Then in Hastings and Mason's *Sacred Songs for Family and Social Worship*, 1842, it is called Halle, perhaps because this is the name of the German university that from the first stood strongest for Protestant theology. In Ireland the tune was called Stillorgan, for a town near Dublin, and a Hymnal of 1880 names it Te Deum.

Thomas Toke Lynch (1818–1871), the poet, was minister for small groups here and there in London, and seems to have been one of those free natures who, during the nineteenth century, questioned the limitations of creed. After he opened his new Mornington Church in Hampstead Road, London, his influence spread among young theological students, who came to hear his fresh and inspiring message. His book of hymns, *The Rivulet* (1855), roused much discussion in the Congregational body with which he was allied, but time has declared in favor of these hymns, for their depth of understanding.

89 Jesu, Jesu, du mein Hirt. *Gracious Spirit, dwell with me*

Paul Heinlein (1626–1686) is another of the many Germans who have provided chorale melodies for others to harmonize. Gifted and industrious, he learned from a town musician in Nuremberg, his birthplace, to play the keyboard, and all the wind instruments. After study in Italy, he was made musician to the Council in his own city, and was organist in three of its churches. The tune still is named for the words with which it was first sung, as above: Jesus, thou my shepherd, in the *Nuremberg Hymn Book*, 1676.

George Herbert Palmer, who harmonized the melody, was an Oxford graduate, curate of St. Margaret's, in Toxteth Park, Liverpool, and then of St. Barnabas, Pimlico. He edited *The Hymner* (1904), with versions of most of the Latin hymns of the *Sarum Breviary*, half of them Dr. Neale's translations.

90 Corinth. *Guide me, O Thou great Jehovah*

This is one of the hymns which have special interest because of associations with Mrs. Eddy. Dr. Powell's biography records how, on her first visit to the original edifice of The Mother Church, April 1, 1895, she stood at the desk to repeat first the Ninety-first Psalm, and then this hymn. It was sung at the hymn singings in her own home, of which a member of her former household has written (*Christian Science Sentinel*, May 3, 1930); and it was for these occasions that she made the two changes in the words which now appear in the revised Hymnal of 1932. First, instead of "I am weak," she gave the words, "I am Thine, and Thou art mighty"; and at the end of the first stanza she restored an old reading, found in the *Wesleyan Hymnal*, "Feed me now and evermore."

These words were originally written in Welsh, by William Williams (1717–1792), known as "Williams of Pantecelyn." Thirty years later, they were put into English by Peter Williams and the author. To be named "the sweet singer of Wales" is high praise for any man in that land which is music's home—but so Williams was named. He began as a representative of the English Church, but kindling to the enthusiasms of Lady Huntingdon and Whitefield, he became an itinerant preacher. He traveled throughout Wales, and the people flocked to him. Many even learned to read, from their delight in his hymns. Collected in 1758, they numbered more than eight hundred. He did for Wales what Watts and Wesley did for England. This hymn was named: Strength to pass through the Wilderness. Williams, with Peter Williams, became the founder of the Welsh Calvinistic Methodists, or Presbyterians.

The music is from Webbe's *Motets or Antiphons* (Note 6), but it appeared first in his essay on plain chant, where it was named The Hymn at Benediction, and had Latin words.

91 Birling. *Grace for today, O Love divine*

This tune is from an anonymous manuscript of the early nineteenth century. The words, by Nemi Robertson, are adapted to it from the *Christian Science Sentinel* of June 29, 1912. The last stanza was altered to include a reference to Mrs. Eddy's words, of Jesus, "Out of the amplitude of his pure affection, he defined Love" (*Science and Health with Key to the Scriptures*, p. 54).

92 Dominica. *Happy the man who knows*

The poet, Thomas Cogswell Upham (1799–1872), was born in Connecticut and educated at Dartmouth and Andover. As a Congregational minister, he taught philosophy at Bowdoin College, in Brunswick, Maine, for more than forty years. The hymn used here was named Obedience (1872). For the composer of Dominica (Sunday), Herbert Oakeley, see Note 133.

93 Peace. *Happy the man whose heart can rest*

This music is from the slow movement of Mozart's G-major Trio, and is an example of his gracious rhythm, which has here a hymn of like serenity and tenderness, called The Peace of God, written by William P.

216

McKenzie. (*The Christian Science Journal,* August, 1902, reprinted in the author's *Heartsease Hymns,* published in Cambridge, Massachusetts, in 1928.)

The story of Mozart's boyhood is much like a fairy tale. There is happiness in recalling that early series of triumphs in which he took a childlike and modest pleasure, and also in remembering that he could always escape from the trouble of his later days into that place of beauty and peace to which his music gave the key.

The names given him at birth, in Salzburg, 1756, hint that much was expected of him. They were Joannes Chrysostomus Wolfgangus Theophilus Sigismundus. The Biblical Theophilus, meaning in Greek, "loved of God," was written in German Gottlieb, and put into Latin as Amadeus. He chose to sign "Wolfgang Amadeus."

Mozart's father draws the boy's picture as so intent when at work that interruption, especially of jokes and laughter, was a distress. He lived in visions of peace and perfectness that were altogether lovely. Yet when work was laid by, none was merrier nor more boyish than young "Wolferl," as friends called him, and this boyish simplicity endured to his passing, at thirty-five.

The father lived for the musical success of his son. In the most brilliant cities of Europe, from Vienna to Paris, from Rome to London, the boy's genius was acclaimed by royal courts and learned academies. It is rather touching to know that this child, always on exhibition among grown people, made a close friendship in Florence with a lad of his own age, also gifted in music, from whom he parted with tears.

Incidents of these tours are many, as the full transcription he made from memory after a single hearing at the Sistine Chapel of a work forbidden even to be read. He was received by the stately Vatican guard like a young prince, because the Pope had given him the Order of the Golden Spur, and so he could sign himself "Signor Cavaliere Amadeo." The academy of Bologna gave him its title of "composer" at thirteen. Again, his opera, Mithridate, written for Milan, when he was fifteen, drew shouts of *Viva* for "the little master." In the next year he composed seven symphonies and six other pieces. His works total six hundred. (See also Notes 34, 47, 109.)

In expressing her desire in respect to a musical setting for one of her hymns, Mrs. Eddy wrote, "God give you the inspiration of a Mozart to sing, and the vision of a revelator to utter my thoughts in harmony" (Historical files of The Mother Church).

94   Uffingham. *Hath not thy heart within thee burned*

Robert Bridges, poet laureate of England from 1913 to 1930, gave high praise to the music of Jeremiah Clark (1670–1707), the neglect of which he deplored. Clark is the inventor of the modern English hymn

217

tune. His tunes have clear beauty, with the plaintive grace that characterized him. Six of them appear in the *Christian Science Hymnal.*

Clark was almoner and master of the choristers at St. Paul's Cathedral, and then organist. In 1704, he was made joint organist with Dr. Croft (Note 236) at the Chapel Royal. Uffingham is used in the *Yattendon Hymnal* (Note 225), with Bridges' words, "Come gentle peace, when shadows fall." In Playford's *Divine Companion*, of 1701, the tune was set to "Sleep, downy sleep, come close my eyes." It is a very beautiful example of minor music, expressive of the reverence and awe in these words of Bulfinch.

Stephen Greenleaf Bulfinch (1809–1870) was the son of Charles Bulfinch, the architect of the beautiful "Bulfinch front" of the State House in Boston. Stephen was born in Boston, but removed to Washington when his father became architect of the new Capitol. There he went to Columbian College, and then prepared for the Unitarian ministry at Cambridge.

This hymn is from his *Contemplations of the Saviour*, and his work includes significant hymns on the miracles of Jesus. The present hymn followed the poet's "Remarks on the Walk to Emmaus." His attitude is a reminder of the position taken by James Freeman Clarke, another famous Unitarian, who stated his opinion, in 1866, in *Orthodoxy: Its Truths and Its Errors*, that the miracles of Jesus pointed to a power which other men would some day comprehend and use.

It is fitting that the family of this famous Boston builder should be represented in the Hymnal of an organization that has added so worthily to the architecture of the city.

95 Aughton. *He leadeth me, O blessed thought*

"By the deep sea, and music in its roar" was the early home of William B. Bradbury (1816–1868), who went from York, Maine, to Boston, to work in music of another kind. He helped Mason and Webb in their collections, and played the organ for the Brookline Baptist Church. When he was called to the Tabernacle in New York, he worked with the busy Thomas Hastings in singing classes for children and other doings that made music popular. He went to England to study educational methods, and to Germany for work with Moscheles and Hauptman. Returning, he was just in time to stem the tide of street music which was invading American Sunday Schools. He made many collections for Sunday Schools, his *Jubilee* having reached a fabulous circulation. His cantata, Esther, was long popular. He was also associated with the making of the Bradbury piano.

"Pure religion and undefiled" ever dwells with humility. This song, He leadeth me, a hymn which a child can sing, was written by a professor of Logic and of Hebrew! This author, Joseph H. Gilmore (1834–1918), was born in Boston, educated at Brown University, Providence, Rhode

Island, and the Newton Theological Seminary. After a Baptist ministry he went to Rochester, New York, where he preached, and taught in the University. The hymn was written after a sermon in the First Baptist Church of Philadelphia, in 1859. A fifteen-story business building now occupies the site of the church. The building bears a memorial tablet, with the first stanza of the hymn, and a tribute to the Rev. Dr. Gilmore, "son of a former Governor of New Hampshire."

96 Soll's sein. *He stood of old, the holy Christ*

The words that name this tune (Shall it be) are from a hymn inspired by a thunderstorm that swept Thuringia long ago. (See Note 393.) The tune is one of *Three beautiful, new, spiritual Songs,* Munich, 1637, possibly a later edition of Caspar Fuger's work of that name, 1592.

The words are from Whittier's poem, The Healer, dedicated "To a Young Physician, with Doré's Picture of Christ Healing the Sick." Here again is seen the poet's reverent thought of healing (Note 49).

97 Ilsley. *He that goeth forth with weeping*

Thomas Hastings (1784–1872) was one of those men with vision, who undoubtedly prepared the way for the advanced American musical taste of today. Hastings said that he worked for the greater glory of God.

His father was one of the pioneers of central New York state, and came from Connecticut, in 1786. The son worked for nine years in Utica, as editor of *The Western Record,* a religious weekly. He then accepted a call from twelve churches in New York city, that combined to secure him as choir leader. Hastings was called "a Bible Concordance in himself," and New York University gave him the degree of Doctor of Music. He wrote six hundred hymns, composed a thousand hymn tunes, and edited fifty volumes of music.

This music, by Frank G. Ilsley (1831–1887), might have been made for these words, as it varies with their mood. Ilsley was of a musical family of Portland, Maine, and is heard of later in Newark, New Jersey.

98 In Babilone. *He that goeth forth with weeping*

As this is one of the Dutch traditional tunes, it may serve to commemorate New Netherland, especially as applied to a hymn by a poet and musician (see Note 97) of the great city that was once New Amsterdam, when eighteen languages might be heard in the overgrown village that offered refuge for fugitives from persecuted Europe. (See Note 246.)

99 Bera. *He that hath God his guardian made*

The first music printed in an English version of the Psalms was a single tune of four lines, in Common Meter; and to this one tune all the Psalms had been more or less awkwardly fitted. This was the Psalter of

Robert Crowley, in 1549. It was preceded by Coverdale's, of 1539, named *Goostly psalmes and spirituall songes,* translated from Luther's hymn book, and printed with thirteen German tunes. Other attempts at versifying the Psalms had been made, as by Wyatt and Surrey, or even by the Princess who was to be Queen Elizabeth.

But it was Sternhold's Psalter, of 1549, which, with additions and revisions, was found in the churches until after the *New Version* was made by Tate and Brady, in 1696. Theirs was "fitted to the tunes used in the churches." (See Note 107.) The old Psalter was so loved that as late as 1710 a bit of satire was flung at the new one as "fine and modish" and "flourished with wit and fancy."

The words here are Psalm 91, adapted from Tate and Brady. They were both Irishmen. Nahum Tate (1652–1715), who helped Dryden with the second part of his *Absalom and Achitophel,* succeeded Shadwell as Poet Laureate. Nicholas Brady (1659–1726) was an adherent of King William, to whom he was made chaplain, later becoming the incumbent of Stratford-on-Avon.

The tune Bera appears in other hymnals as four lines only, without repetitions. John E. Gould (1822–1875) was born in Bangor, Maine, and began early to compose. He went to New York to start a music store and later moved it to Philadelphia. He published two books, a *Harmonia Sacra,* and the tune Bera was written for his *Songs of Gladness,* for Sunday Schools.

100 David's Harp. *He that hath God his guardian made*

The musician, Robert King, was at work composing from 1684 to 1711. He was a player in the band of William and Mary and also of Queen Anne. In 1689, he was given a license to establish a "concert," as a band of players was then called. He published *Choice Ayres,* the *Banquet of Music,* etc. This tune was used in Playford's *The Divine Companion, or David's Harp New Tuned.*

The words from No. 99 are rearranged here to suit what may be called the "logic" of the music. At No. 99, the music falls into two groups of three lines each. At No. 100, the plan of the tune is in couplets, or three groups of two lines each, as is shown by the rhymes. No. 99 is rhymed as A A B. C C B.; No. 100, as AA. BB. CC.

101 Lobt Gott. *He sent His Word, His holy Word*

It was the French critic Taine who sought to show how geography, in its relation to climate, society, history, has affected the arts. There might indeed seem to be some such explanation of the fact that Luther, Bach, and Handel all spent their childhood within fifty miles of the Weimar of Goethe's manhood.

220

Over the mountains from this ancient, master-making Saxony lies the Bohemian Joachimsthal, a place that grew up in a night, almost like an American mining town of early days, from a mere hamlet. For silver began to be mined there in 1516 and, almost at once, to it came—no one knows whence, but he must have come from Saxe-Something—the excellent musician, poet, and scholar, Nicholas Herman, to teach Latin and music to the children, to play the organ, lead the choir, and to cap the preacher's best sermons with a better hymn. The silver mined here was so famous that the German word thaler (dollar) is taken from the name Joachimsthal (vale). The *thaler* may have left the *thal* behind in the race for notoriety, but at least two of the melodies in our Hymnal lead us back to this interesting town.

The melody of 101 is by Herman (1485?–1561), who set it to the Christmas song he wrote for the children, Lobt Gott (Praise God), in his *Sunday Evangel for the whole Year,* 1560. He published it first in a tract of seven leaves, with his words, "Come here, you dear little sister." His verses are said to have the naïveté of Hans Sachs, Wagner's singing cobbler. Hans Hassler (Note 252), whose tune also attracted the busy Bach, was of a Joachimsthal family.

The words for 101, by Maude de Verse Newton, appeared in the *Christian Science Sentinel* for March 22, 1930. They are well matched with this music for their nobility of form as well as of thought.

102 Cross of Jesus. *Hear our prayer, O gracious Father*

When John Stainer (Note 160) once heard some children singing his music, he said that he would rather be sung by children than win the highest worldly honors. This tune is from The Crucifixion, 1887, which like a Bach cantata has several hymns to be sung by the congregation. His words for this tune begin, "Cross of Jesus." The words are by Florence L. Heywood and appeared in *The Christian Science Journal* for May, 1887. They were used in the first edition of the Hymnal, 1892.

103 Glück zu Kreuz. *Hear our prayer, O gracious Father*

This tune name is the first phrase of a hymn by J. W. Petersen, and means "Welcome cross." (See Romans 5:3.) The hymn and tune appeared in the *Darmstadt Hymn Book* of 1698. Charles Wood (1866–1926), who harmonized the melody, wrote chiefly for voices and orchestra. Perhaps his most important work was the incidental music for the Ion and the Iphigenia in Tauris, of Euripides. These performances of Greek drama in the original roused so much interest at the English universities that leading musicians prepared music for them. Wood was professor at the Cambridge University and at the Royal College of Music. He came from Armagh, Ireland, where his father was lay vicar at the Cathedral.

104 Campfields. *Help us, O Lord, to bear the cross*

The composer, Mark J. Monk, was born in 1858, in Yorkshire, and was educated at York Minster. He was organist in various places, and then, in 1890, at Truro Cathedral, and conductor of the Truro Philharmonic. He also became a fellow of the Royal College of Organists. The tune appeared in *The Church Hymnary* for 1898. The deeply prayerful words are by Duncan Sinclair, a Christian Scientist.

105 Dedham. *Help us to help each other, Lord*

There is something very beautiful in the story of the Wesley family. Divided in religious opinion though they were, they stated their ideas frankly, and continued faithfully to love one another. The eldest brother, Samuel, was of High Church associations and remonstrated with John and Charles when, through their Oxford experience, about 1730, they joined the group that was already known as Oxford Methodists, of whom John Wesley was to be the renowned leader.

Charles agreed with John in desire for a simpler form of worship and in his missionary zeal. But when John began to ordain his own clergymen, Charles disapproved. To the last he claimed membership in the Established Church of England. But he rendered to his brother's work an immense service, in the hymns which came singing from his heart, straight to the hearts of the people. He found occasion for a hymn in every event of private or public life—his own conversion, his marriage, the earthquake panic, the defeat at Culloden, the Gordon riots, every festival and every doctrine of the church, countless Bible passages, and the experiences of all his friends!

Critics say that if we consider both the high quality of his work and its astonishing amount, Wesley is the most amazing hymn writer of them all. For he published four thousand hymns and left two thousand more in manuscript. For spontaneity and simplicity of feeling, a free outpouring of love to God and man, few hymnists equal him. He was also a great preacher, second only to his brother John.

The Wesley family claimed descent from the de Wellesleys, one of whom was made a thane (or baron) by Athelstan, grandson of Alfred the Great. Perhaps it was this sense of long homemaking in England which brought the brothers back from Georgia, in America, where they went in 1735, Charles as secretary to General Oglethorpe, the founder of that colony, and John to represent the missionary society. (See Note 336.)

The words here are from a hymn beginning, "Try us, O God, and search the ground of every sinful heart."

The tune Dedham appeared anonymously in Gardiner's *Sacred Melodies from Haydn, Mozart, and Beethoven.* William Gardiner (1770–1853), born in Leicester, England, traveled much on the Continent to seek out music and music makers. He was at Bonn for the unveiling of the Beethoven statue. Queen Victoria and Prince Albert were there, and the young Englishman was asked to sign his name next to theirs on the parchment put into the base of the statue. Gardiner, indeed, claimed to have been the first to introduce the music of Beethoven into England.

106 Bromsgrove. *Help us to help each other, Lord*

Bromsgrove, from the *Psalmodia Evangelica,* 1789, is a tune with more freedom of movement than the two others here applied to these words. This collection was made by Thomas Williams, who arranged the music "in three parts for public worship." Nothing is known of him, except that he worked in England.

107 Windsor. *Help us to help each other, Lord*

This is one of the famous old church tunes that appeared in Damon's Psalter of 1591. The story of this collection gives a glimpse of the musical status of that day, in a general love of music, and general skill in reading and writing it.

William Damon, "one of her Majesty's Musitions"—this Majesty being Queen Elizabeth—used to visit his friend John Bull, "citizen and goldsmith of London," to make music, and left with him many new four-part settings of the popular "church tunes." John Bull, without Damon's knowledge, published these, "by peece meale gotten . . . from the fertile soyle of his honest frend Guilielmo Damon," who had "never meant them to the use of any learned and cunnyng Musition, but altogether respected the pleasuryng of his private frend." Then Damon, to save his reputation, made two other far better collections of the tunes, arranged in motet style.

These "church tunes," some of them still sung in English churches, first appeared in an edition of Sternhold's Psalter (Note 99), which was printed for Protestant exiles in Geneva, in 1556, by John Crespin. The melodies were described in Ravenscroft's Psalter (1621) as "English tunes imitating the High Dutch, Italian, French and Netherlandish tunes." When Elizabeth came to the throne, this Psalter found its way to England, and the Queen gave formal permission for the use of the "church tunes" in the churches. An old record tells how, when psalm singing started in London, other towns began to vie with each other in practice.

This tune has also been called Eton and Suffolk, and in Scotland was known as Dundee. Burns speaks of "Dundie's wild music," in his Cotter's Saturday Night. In the Scottish Psalter of 1615 (see Note 215) there were given for the first time a number of "Common" tunes, as distinguished from the "Proper" tunes, which were used with particular Psalms. The Common tunes were: Olde Common Tune, Kinges Tune, Dukes, English, French, London tunes; The Stilt; Dumfermeling, Dundie Tune, Abbay, Glasgow, and Martyrs.

223

108 Toulon (Old 124th). *Here, O my Lord, I'd see Thee face to face*

Old One Hundred and Twenty-fourth of the Genevan Psalter (Note 1) has been especially dear to the city of Geneva, that has so long been a rallying point for lovers of justice and liberty. In 1602, when the Duke of Savoy attacked the town in what was called the Escalade, he was repulsed by the citizens. The white-haired Theodore Beza led their thanksgiving in this lofty Psalm 124. Since then it has been sung in Geneva on the anniversary of this great deliverance.

Scotland, too, has its story of the tune. When Durie, a free-speaking minister of Edinburgh, was banished, he came back amid popular rejoicing, and as the people thronged round him, marching to the kirk, they sang this Psalm.

The tune has been credited to Claude Goudimel, a French editor and composer for the Psalter. It was used with Psalm 124, in the French version of Beza, and then, for the Scottish *Psalm Book*, Beza's words were translated into English, so that this Psalm is the one example of tune and words that have been used together onward from the Reformation.

The words used here are the great Communion hymn of Horatius Bonar (Note 21), one of the greatest poems of English hymnody. Bonar wrote, "Too soon we rise"; the slight change here gives a deep metaphysical value to his phrase.

109 Ellesdie. *Here, O God, Thy healing presence*

Of Mozart's music used in the Hymnal, this is specially characteristic of his clear form and exquisite melody. It was arranged by Hubert Platt Main (1839–1928). Born in Connecticut, he studied under Thomas Hastings, and composed music for Sunday Schools. He was connected with the firm of Biglow and Main, music publishers in New York, from 1868. The words were written specially for the music by Maria Louise Baum, a Christian Scientist.

110 Zum Frieden. *Here, O God, Thy healing presence*

This tune, For Peace, is one of sixteen tunes listed from Bach in the Hymnal, and is one of four wholly composed by him. It appeared in *The Musical Hymn Book*, of Christian Schemelli, Leipzig, 1736. Bach delighted to take his theme from the music of others, and work it out to new beauty by the harmony.

111 Eschol. *High in the heavens, eternal God*

"And they came unto the brook of Eshcol, and cut down from thence a branch with one cluster of grapes, and they bare it between two upon a staff" (Numbers 13:23). It may be noted that the Bible spelling was altered by the composer; but it is more than probable that he was thinking of this Bible passage. It is also recorded of the first Europeans to visit the American continent that Leif Ericson's men were amazed at the profusion of the wild grapes.

The name of this tune is a pleasant reminder of those grapes of Eshcol, that were the first fruits of the Promised Land. The composer, George M. Garrett (1834–1897), was son of the choir master at Winchester Cathedral, and became assistant to Samuel Wesley there. He was organist at Madras Cathedral, and then at Cambridge University, where he lectured on music. The words are another great hymn by Isaac Watts, from his Psalm 36 (Note 62).

112   Security. *High to heaven let song be soaring*

The Swedish words here mean "Safer can no one be," the first line used with the tune in the Swedish *Psalm Book*. The English words were written by Maria Louise Baum for the music, and refer to a passage in *Science and Health with Key to the Scriptures* by Mary Baker Eddy (p. 568): "A louder song, sweeter than has ever before reached high heaven, now rises clearer and nearer to the great heart of Christ; for the accuser is not there, and Love sends forth her primal and everlasting strain."

The composer, Carl Ivar Widéen, was born in Jönköping county, Sweden, and studied at the Stockholm Conservatory, 1889–1891. He became organist at Laholm, and in 1900 was appointed to the organ in the cathedral at Skara, where he also taught school and led the local Music Society. He is known especially for his four-part songs, which are marked by melodic charm and pure diatonic harmony, as in his fine quartet, Sunday Morning, and his Dala March. He has composed fifty-four hymns, a requiem, cantatas, and one hundred and fifty choral preludes for organ. In 1915, he was made conductor of the Småland Singing Association and member of the Swedish Psalm Book Committee.

113   Armenian Hymn. *Holiness becomes Thy house*

"And they escaped into the land of Armenia" (II Kings 19:37). This meant Ararat, a name given of old to part of Armenia. The Armenians claim to have had a Christian church as early as 34 A. D., tracing it to a letter written to the ruler by Christ Jesus. The historic foundation of the church was by St. Gregory, the Illuminator, who was consecrated Bishop of Armenia in 302 A. D. He had won the king to Christianity by healing him.

This music was published in *The Divine Liturgy of the Armenian Apostolic Church,* at the Mekhitarian Order, Vienna, 1896. The words are from *The Handbook of Divine Liturgy, etc.,* by Leon Tourian, Armenian Bishop of Manchester and the North of England, 1926.

225

114 Orientis partibus. *Holy Bible, book divine*

The use of these words with this tune is a striking illustration of how the lofty and the lowly come together in praise to God. Here an Archbishop of Sens, France (?–1222), is joined with John Burton, a man of the handicrafts in Nottingham, England, who passed on about six hundred years after the Archbishop, Pierre de Corbeil.

The name of the tune is from the first line of the Latin words to which it was sung, "From Eastern parts the Ass comes striding," etc. (In the French there is a refrain for each stanza, "Hey, sir Ass!")

The song is an example of what were called mystery plays,—very simple performances of Biblical scenes or church traditions. They were meant to impress upon the people lessons which they could not have read, even had the Bible then been in their hands.

This play was called "The Sequence or Prose of the Ass," and commemorated the Flight into Egypt. (See Note 242.) The English words here, singing of the Bible, today the treasure that all men may own, are a happy choice for this Bible-story music. Found in the Library of Sens, it was not until 1853 that the melody was used as a hymn tune, adopted by Richard Redhead (Note 367). It appears five times in the Harvard University Hymn Book.

John Burton (1773–1822) was a Baptist, much interested in Sunday Schools. His hymn, one of the best known in all English-speaking countries, appeared in 1803, in Burton's *Youth Monitor in Verse*, and in 1806, in his *Hymns for Sunday Schools: or Incentives to Early Piety.*

In the Preface of *The Book of Praise* Selborne says that writers who do not in general rise above mediocrity sometimes produce beautiful hymns. And then a good hymn is defined: "A good hymn should have simplicity, freshness, and reality of feeling; a consistent elevation of tone, and a rhythm easy and harmonious, but not jingling or trivial. Its language may be homely; but it should not be slovenly or mean."

Hymns like Burton's show that simplicity, which is sincerity, may send its message far.

115 Lux Eoi. *Holy Father, Thou hast taught us*

The name of Sullivan's *Lux Eoi* means "Light of the morning star." The word *Eoi* is from a Latinized Greek form, as found in Virgil: *Postera jamque dies primo surgebat Eoo:* "Already the coming day was rising at the first appearing of the morning star," a happy association of ideas for a hymn tune. It appeared in *Church Hymns with Tunes*, 1874, set to a hymn from the tenth century, singing that Christ "shines upon the morning skies" (Note 264).

Dr. John Mason Neale, of England, was a famous translator of Latin hymns, though the words used here are original. They are from his collection for children,—"intended chiefly for village schools." When one knows of his long service to the welfare of children, in connection with the famous Sisterhood of St. Margaret's, the simple words of this hymn are even more significant. The original words were in the first person, singular, and begin: "Blessed Saviour, who hast taught me."

Dr. Neale's "Jerusalem the golden" and "For thee, O dear, dear country" are as well known and much loved as any original hymns, though they are translated from the Latin. Strangely misunderstood in his life (1818–1866), he is now worthily honored.

116 Llansannan. *Holy Father, Thou hast taught us*

Here is a Welsh melody, of 1873, apparently a product of the revival of psalmody in Wales during the last century. (See Note 345.)

117 Nicaea. *Holy, Holy, Holy, Lord God Almighty*

The life of Reginald Heber (1783–1826) is as full of beauty as the familiar portrait of him in the vestments of his high office. Born at Malpas, Cheshire, he was of an old Yorkshire family in which the eldest son must be the "squire," or the country gentleman, while the younger ones were expected to enter the church. Thus the gentle and studious Reginald was at five years of age "a little Bible Concordance," so his father said, and at ten was often found deep in Spenser's *Faërie Queene*, so preparing for his double mission as preacher and poet.

Heber was always interested in India, and always dreaming over its old routes which he traced in maps; but his hymn "From Greenland's icy mountains to India's coral strands" was written long before he dreamed of what was to be, for himself. The hymn, in fact, was written in about twenty minutes, on a sudden demand for one to be used at a service in support of foreign missions.

At Hodnet, where he was vicar, he was quite as much the neighborly squire, and his serene candor and gentle playfulness bound to him many friends. Here his hymns were written. In 1823, he went as Bishop to Calcutta, to follow those old, old trails, to Bengal, to Bombay, to Ceylon, and Delhi. It is said that nothing in Indian annals is nobler than the three years of travel, administration, and "saintly enthusiasm" which Heber gave there. He made his last address at a confirmation in Trichinopoly, in the Madras Presidency, passing on there, at only forty-four years of age.

Heber's poetry brought freedom to the hymnody of England, with much of the lyric mood of Scott and Byron. His "Brightest and best of the sons of the morning" is an example of this, and so is the present hymn, perhaps the most purely lyrical of them all. Tennyson called this the finest hymn in the language. It is based on Revelation 4:8–11.

Dykes's tune has the name of the city of Asia Minor where, in 325 A. D., a council framed the Nicene creed (Note 169).

118 Elijah. *Holy Spirit, Light divine*

Felix Mendelssohn-Bartholdy (1809–1847) is the shining example of musical genius unattended by struggle and disappointment. His music never touched that rapture of beauty reached by many less fortunate, otherwise, than he; but it has clear structure, melodic grace and charm, with a delicacy that is wholly his own. He was so much admired, wherever he went, that it was said, "Felix cannot put his head out of a window anywhere, but someone shouts 'Hurrah!' "

The poet Shelley has been named Ariel, for the elusive sprite in Shakespeare's Tempest; but the name applies even better to Mendelssohn, joyously awing above earth's toil. His On Wings of Song, to Heine's words, is in itself a kind of commentary on his own poise and charm, seen in all his music. He excelled in the painting of water scenes, as in his Hebrides music, the Isles of Fingal, or Meeresstille (sea calm). He succeeded notably in every line of composition, and fuller maturity might have done much for him. At sixteen, he was busy with his overture for Midsummer Night's Dream, which at once stamped him a genius. His later music for this play included the hard-worked wedding march.

His oratorio, St. Paul, appeared in 1836, and was sung the same year in England. His Song of Praise and the music of Racine's Athalie followed. His marriage, in 1837, was very happy, and he and his beautiful wife were fêted in England, where he was greatly honored and beloved. It was his organ playing that turned the English organists to their recognized mastery of this instrument.

His friendship with Jenny Lind, "the Swedish nightingale," is memorable for the noble air, "Hear ye, Israel," in Elijah. The repeated upper F-sharp was used because her voice had special beauty at that point. Elijah was first sung at the Birmingham festival of 1846, under Mendelssohn's baton. This was the year before his passing, at only thirty-seven years of age.

The music here is the prayer from Elijah, with words of the same prayerful feeling, which were adapted by Samuel Longfellow from Andrew Reed's "Holy Ghost! with light divine." Reed was an English Congregationalist, pastor of the Wycliffe Chapel, built by his efforts in 1830. He was the founder of five asylums for the unfortunate in London, in which work his wife was active. His hymns were collected in *The Wyckliffe Supplement*, in 1872. He said, "I have lived for the people, the most for the most unhappy."

119 Sicily. *Holy Spirit, source of gladness*

This melody has survived long vicissitude at the hands of verse makers. It began as a song of Sicilian fishermen, and then, with Latin words, was more proudly named Hymn of Sicilian Mariners.

In 1816 the tune was taken over by Johannes D. Falk, of Danzig, a friend of Herder and of Goethe, and also a very good friend of neglected children. Falk set to it his much-loved words, "O thou joyful Christmastide." Falk's care for children was seen in the institute he founded, so that neglected boys and girls could be trained to the industries.

The words here are chosen from Gerhardt, as words that have the joyous spirit of the music. They are Longfellow's adaptation of Jacobi's translation. Paul Gerhardt (1607–1676) was one more of the poet-preachers who sacrificed worldly advantage to religious conviction. He, the gentle-hearted and gentle-voiced, who knew no contentions, gave up his happy Lutheran pastorate in Berlin, rather than promise to ignore the differences between the Lutheran and the "Reformed" or Calvinistic ideas. He stands next to Luther as a hymnist. Superior to him in poetic power, he is like Luther in his manner, "unconstrainedly pious, naïve and hearty."

The translator, Jacobi, was a native German, who went to England about the same time as Handel. He was appointed keeper of the Royal German Chapel at St. James's Palace, London, and served under Georges I and II. He published collections of hymns translated from German into English.

120 Greenland. *How beauteous on the mountains*

Benjamin Gough (1805–1877) was a merchant in Kent, who, retiring from business, became a lay preacher for the Wesleyan "Connexion" (or following). These words appeared in his *Lyra Sabbatica,* 1865. A significant story may be read between the lines of this brief statement. A clear sign of human advance in the walk with God is seen in the work done by laymen, for the spiritual encouragement of their fellows. They bring good tidings of great things, and what Gough's quaint phrasing named "Jubilee release": because the consciousness of God, and the jubilation of love for Him, mean release from error.

The tune here is by J. Michael Haydn (Note 18).

121 Manoah. *How blest are they whose hearts are pure*

When Gioacchino A. Rossini (1792–1868) left the Lyceum in Bologna, he could not hope, his master said, ever to write church music. "Do I know enough to write operas?" Rossini asked; and rejoiced in the affirmative answer.

He was in due time acclaimed as the greatest master of Italian opera, though his familiar success, The Barber of Seville, was hissed at its first performance. This opera is based on the story of Beaumarchais' famous Figaro, whom Mozart also celebrated. It is difficult today to realize that Figaro was regarded as a revolutionist, by the censorship of Beaumarchais' day, so that the two plays about him were first banned. Today he is rated as a dramatic figure almost equal with Molière's Tartuffe.

Rossini's last opera was also concerned, but more seriously, with an idea of human liberty, for it was William Tell, which he produced in Paris in 1829, while director of the Italian opera there. That he succeeded also in church music is proved by his widely known Stabat Mater (the mother was standing).

The very simple melody used here has Rossini's tunefulness. The name Manoah means "Rest." The poet is William Goode (1762–1816), who, educated by a Dissenting minister, preferred the Established Church. After graduating at Oxford, he eventually became rector at St. Anne's, Blackfriars, and was a founder of the Foreign Missionary Society. These words are from his Psalm 119.

122 Winchester Old. *How blest are they whose hearts are pure*

This tune has for generations sounded over the December fields of England in the Christmas caroling of the "waits." It is used with Tate's "While shepherds watched their flocks by night." Its beginnings are traced to Dr. Tye (Note 225), and its finished form is from the famous book of Thomas Este, or East (1540–1608), *The Whole Booke of Psalmes with their wonted Tunes. . . . compiled by sondry Authors. 1592.* East was the publisher of Damon's Psalter (Note 107) and he brought out Byrd's *Sonnettes and Songs,* and also the *Musica Transalpina,* founded on the fine work of the English madrigalists. John Dowland (Note 53) was one of the harmonists of Este's Psalter.

123 Adeste fideles. *How firm a foundation*

This tune is named for the first line of a Latin hymn of French or German origin, not earlier than the eighteenth century. It began:

O come, all ye faithful,
Joyful and triumphant,
O come ye, O come ye, to Bethlehem. (Tr.)

It has been much used for Christmas. The tune probably belongs to the same century. At one time it was called the Portuguese Hymn, because in 1797 it was sung in the Chapel of the Portuguese Embassy in London, where Vincent Novello was organist. He ascribed the music to John Reading, an organist of Winchester Cathedral. It was also attributed to Marcus Portugal, chapelmaster to the King of Portugal. The earliest manuscript in which it is found is *Cantus Diversi* (Divers Songs), by John Francis Wade, Stoneyhurst, 1751.

The words used were found in *Rippon's Selection,* 1787, and have been attributed to three persons, whose names all begin with K—Kirkham,

Keen, and George Keith. Julian gives reasons for deciding on the name Keen. The words have a joyful confidence, that makes them fit companions for this triumphant tune.

124 Camberwell. *How gentle God's commands*

The tune is from S. S. Wesley's *European Psalmist,* of 1872 (Note 75), set to a favorite hymn by Doddridge (Note 398).

125 St. Peter. *How lovely are Thy dwellings, Lord*

John Milton (1608–1674), born the year of the Pilgrim exodus from Scrooby to Leyden, grew up into the Puritan struggle for religious liberty. His years at Cambridge University, where for his personal beauty and refinement he was dubbed "the Lady," foretold his intellectual mastery, and founded those long friendships, one of which was later to prompt his great poem, Lycidas, but those years did not promise the mighty epic that was to be judged by Dryden as greater than those of the ancients.

Milton was developed by the struggle with misfortune, lifted to heights of vision beyond the common lot; and his last statement of faith showed him relying for truth wholly on the Bible. He saw it as a revelation from God, of what men could not have learned for themselves.

Unlike Cromwell, he opposed the union of state and church, wishing the latter to be left to private support. At the last, he held no creed, no church associations. The persecuted young Quaker, Thomas Ellwood, befriending him in his obscurity, found fellowship in Milton, who, rejecting Calvin, "denied the co-equality of Christ with absolute Deity, but regarded him as clothed with a certain derivative divinity" (Masson). It was Ellwood who gave Milton the idea of writing a *Paradise Regained.*

In old New England, it is said, the center table in the best room always held a huge family Bible and a copy of *Paradise Lost.* Mrs. Eddy's writings refer to Milton once, where in *Science and Health with Key to the Scriptures* (p. 372), she speaks of "elementary mortal mind,—likened by Milton to 'chaos and old night.' "

Milton himself said that his real work was poetry, yet he was drawn into Cromwell's struggle, and for having been "Secretary for foreign tongues" to the Commonwealth—even after his blindness—he was listed by the Parliament of Charles II for punishment. He escaped, perhaps by the influence of Monk, but lived in obscurity and loneliness. His picture of Samson fitted himself:

> Now blind, disheartened, shamed, dishonored, quelled,
> To what can I be useful? wherein serve
> My nation and the work from heaven imposed?

His biographer, David Masson, was wise enough to add: "That might be the appearance, but it was not the reality. All the while of his

seeming degradation . . . he had been building up his *Paradise Lost.*"
The idea had come to him in 1640, twenty-seven years before its publication, in 1667. Milton knew, as he said, that "they also serve who only stand and wait."

Music was always a chief delight to him, and the splendid upbuilding of phrase in his poetry may in part be due to early association with the work of his father, who was an organist.

Milton made metrical versions of the Psalms, too literal to show his poetic power. This hymn illustrates what good editing may do, for no one knows who said:

> How beautiful the sweet accord
> Of those who pray to Thee.

These lines generally replace Milton's, which read (Psalm 84):

> How lovely are Thy dwellings fair,
> O Lord of Hosts, how dear
> The pleasant tabernacles are
> Where Thou dost dwell so near.

The composer, Alexander R. Reinagle (1799–1877), was son of a famous 'cellist, Joseph Reinagle. Alexander was organist for thirty years at St. Peter's-in-the-East, Oxford, whence the tune's name. The Domesday survey of Oxford, in 1086, names this church, so our tune name, at least, goes back to the Conquest! The tune was printed in Reinagle's *Psalm Tunes for Voice and Pianoforte,* 1830. His uncle Alexander came to Philadelphia, c. 1786, and was concerned in the New Theatre, Chestnut Street. Sonatas of his are in the Library of Congress.

126 Ballerma. *How sweet, how heavenly is the sight*

This tune is almost as romantic in its quality as the story that goes with it. It is traditionally a Spanish air from the tenth century, but is doubtless more modern than that. This tradition would place it near the days of the *Song of Roland* and the Knights of Charlemagne, with whom the tune is now associated. It was set to a ballad of French chivalry, named Belerma and Durandarte, from an old romance, *The Monk,* by M. G. Lewis. The song was published by Barthélémon, and then included by Turnbull in his *Selection of Original Sacred Music,* Glasgow, 1833. He probably meant that the idea of using it for a hymn was "original."

Roncesvalles is that pass in the Pyrenees where Roland raised his gauntlet skyward in final token of fealty to God. Durandarte was another of the knights who fell there, leaving a message for his lovely Belerma. The story appears in the "Cave of Montesinos" chapters in *Don Quixote.* Again a hymn tune takes us into famous company.

The poet, Joseph Swain (1761–1796), was apprenticed to an engraver, of Birmingham, England, and spent his leisure carelessly, as youth sometimes does, until one day he opened the Bible and, reading alone, was converted. He soon entered the Baptist ministry, preaching at Walworth, for which his *Walworth Hymns* are named. This one holds the affection of those who enjoy the naïve and direct expression of the older Christian fellowship.

127 Liverpool. *How sweet, how heavenly is the sight*

Robert Wainwright (1748–1782) was an organist and composer, whose father and brother were also musicians of repute. Robert succeeded his father at the Collegiate Church of Manchester, and in 1775 became organist at St. Peter's, Liverpool. His oratorio, The Fall of Egypt, was sung at Liverpool in 1780.

128 Ward. *How sweetly flowed the gospel sound*

This Scottish melody was arranged by the American, Lowell Mason (Note 2). The words are from Bowring's *Matins and Vespers* (Note 79).

129 Illsley. *How sweetly flowed the gospel sound*

John Bishop (1665–1737) has been called a composer of the Purcellian school, and the clearness of this graceful melody may hint why. It seems rather too graceful, indeed, for Kethe's Psalm 100, with which it was used in Bishop's *Sett of New Psalm Tunes*, though it certainly permits men to "sing to the Lord with cheerful voice." Bishop, a "lay vicar" of King's College, Cambridge, England, was organist of Winchester College and also of Winchester Cathedral. An inscription to him in the cloister of Winchester College honors his integrity and his musicianship, during his forty-two years of service there.

130 Congregation. *How wondrous is Thy mercy, Lord*

Harnack O. C. Zinck (1746–1832) was a Danish organist, born near Copenhagen. He was singing master at the Royal Theatre there, and organist at the Church of Our Saviour. In 1801, he published his well-known chorale book. The Danish words on the page, "We meet before Thy presence here," are the first line of the original words.

131 Beulah. *I am the way, the truth, the life*

Beulah is a reminder of Isaiah 62:4, with the promise that Jerusalem shall no more be termed Forsaken nor its land Desolate. It is curious that the Hymnal's two tunes by Garrett (Note 111) are named for the promise of Eshcol, and for the promise of Beulah, as if the composer knew that God does not leave Himself without witnesses in the life of the church. The words, by Miss L. T. Caswell, appeared in *Prayers and Hymns for Church and Home*, New England Universalist Publishing House, Boston, 1867.

132   Etherington. *I am the way, the truth, the life*

The question is sometimes asked why certain hymns are marked, "To be sung in unison," and others, "May be sung in unison." Where the former direction appears, the music will be found to lack notes, in one or more of the voices, to use with all the syllables, as here, at the end of the second brace. Some composers recommend unison singing as more effective than most part singing, while others feel that even a scattered filling in of the parts adds color to the singing. Then the choice is left to the congregation. This tune is from Davies' *Students' Hymnal* (Note 159).

133   Abends. *I cannot always trace the way*

We first hear of Sir Herbert Oakeley (1830–1903) as reporting music festivals for *The Manchester Guardian.* From this he was advanced to a knighthood for his service to music. He was composer to Queen Victoria; and nine universities, also the Archbishop of Canterbury, gave him the degree of Doctor of Music. In 1865, he was appointed to the Reid chair of music at the University of Edinburgh, and was conductor of the Reid concerts. The choice of a nonprofessional musician roused opposition, but Oakeley was sustained, and did much to develop in Scotland a taste for orchestral and choral music, and also to reconcile the people to the use of the organ in churches. This tune, Abends (At Evening), was written for Keble's "Sun of my Soul." The poem used here is from *Hymns for the Poor of the Flock,* by Bowring (Note 79).

134   Wessex. *I look to Thee in every need*

Wessex, by Dr. Hopkins (Note 208), is named for the historic region in England whose later aspects Thomas Hardy made so familiar. The words are by Samuel Longfellow, brother of the poet, Henry Wadsworth Longfellow, whose family home in Portland, Maine, is preserved as a museum, with memorials of both the brothers. Their mother was daughter of Peleg Wadsworth, of the old Duxbury family that traces itself to John Alden and Priscilla, whose story the elder poet told in his poem "The Courtship of Miles Standish."

Samuel Longfellow (1819–1892) was educated at Harvard as a Unitarian minister, and with his friend, Samuel Johnson, did a great work for New England hymnody in two collections of songs for the liberal faith. Their *Hymns of the Spirit* was published in Boston, in 1864. Many of its poems appear in the *Christian Science Hymnal.* Mr. Longfellow was pastor in Fall River, in Brooklyn, and in Germantown, Philadelphia. His biography of his brother was published in 1886. Both were men of generous culture, and of a wide humanity which was the high secret of their poetic appeal.

234

135 Wordsworth. *I know no life divided*

It is told of both Burns and Kipling that they were often heard singing, when they were working out a poem, because words seem to shape themselves so easily to the rhythmical outline of a good tune. Of Carl J. Spitta (1801–1859), the poet here, it is said that his verse flowed to him while he sat playing harp or piano. His poetry so appealed to the general heart that his great collection, *Psaltery and Harp*, 1833, had to be reprinted every year, reaching its fiftieth edition in 1884. One secret of the singing quality in the *Christian Science Hymnal* is that many of the hymns were specially written and adapted to the music.

Spitta was early apprenticed to a watchmaker in Hanover, his home, and then his family discovered that he was secretly longing to be ordained for the ministry. He made up for lost time by hard study, and at twenty was ready for the theological course at Göttingen. His hymns did much for the revival of Evangelical religion in Germany. His son, J. A. P. Spitta, was the author of the famous life of Bach. The family name was from a French Huguenot family, L'Hôpital, which is Spital (hospital) in German, whence Spitta.

This hymn, that begins "O Jesus, my sun," is given here in the version of Richard Massie, of Chester, England, whose *Lyra Domestica*, 1860, was a translation of Spitta's book. Massie also translated Luther's hymns. He was a man of independent fortune, devoted to literature, and is remembered as wearing a red wig and a tall beaver hat, and interesting himself in gardening. This tune is named for Bishop Wordsworth (Note 173), whose *Holy Year* was set to music by W. H. Monk (Note 7). This music was set to "O day of rest and gladness."

136 Heavenward. *I love Thy way of freedom, Lord*

The story of this tune opens vistas of Irish history and legend. The tune antedates musical history, going back to those unrecorded days of folk music—here always so rich in melody, with the unmistakable Irish lilt—that accompanied the everyday occupations of the people. We can easily imagine this tune sung to the whir of the spinning wheel. Even so the Hymnal words, with the allusion to one who soars "o'er time and space," speak the air pilot behind his whirling blades, as he takes his upward way alone. Many of the most beautiful tunes have these homely associations that link duty with beauty, and both with the thought of God.

This melody is found in Petrie's *Ancient Music of Ireland*, London, 1902, without words or even a name. This is a standard work in three volumes, published under the auspices of the "Society for the Preservation and Publication of the Ancient Music of Ireland," founded in 1851. Villiers Stanford is the editor. Petrie classified his tunes carefully as those without words, those with English words, and those with Irish words. It is therefore clear that this one had no association with ballad words, though it is possible that it was one of the tunes of the ancient Irish church, like St. Columba, No. 339. The tune was published in 1892, with pensive words of longing for Ireland, by the modern poet, Alfred Perceval Graves, and arranged by Villiers Stanford.

Like another beautiful Irish tune, the Londonderry Air, No. 412, Heavenward may be applied to merely secular words; but as is the case with so many of the great German chorales or the English traditional tunes, the sacred words gradually cause the secular to be forgotten.

Ireland was in the early days the seat of a remarkable artistic and Christian civilization. Her music was held in high repute, and was continually praised by early writers, including Dante. John of Salisbury (twelfth century) writes: "The attention of this people to musical instruments I find worthy of commendation, in which their skill is . . . superior to that of any other nation I have seen." According to Dr. Fleischer, "Irish tunes have been found in eleventh century MSS" and hymns were composed in the sixth century that are counted in Irish hymnody as St. Columba's.

This tune has qualities that have caused it to survive its varied experience, and for this beauty and vitality it surely deserves at last to have found in the *Christian Science Hymnal* an abiding place and a new name —"Heavenward."

The words are by Violet Hay. They voice that upward-soaring aspiration, of which the conquest of the air is in our day so significant a symbol. We may think of this as of the hymns "for those in peril on the sea," invoking divine protection for the adventurer.

137   Need. *I need Thee every hour*

The names of collections by Robert Lowry (1826–1899) are a commentary on the work of this lover of childhood and of Sunday Schools. His books were *Bright Jewels, Pure Gold, Royal Diadem, Tidal Wave,* etc. For all these, Mrs. Annie Sherwood Hawks (1835–1918) wrote many verses. She was born in Hoosick, New York, and lived long in Brooklyn. Dr. Lowry was born in Pennsylvania, and when ordained to the Baptist ministry, preached in Pennsylvania, then in New York and neighboring cities. His song, "Shall we gather at the river," was improvised in 1865, and used widely in Great Britain, as at home. "Where is my wandering boy tonight?" was published in his *Fountain of Song,* 1877. Many of his hymns appeared later in the Moody and Sankey books.

138   Festus. *I praise Thee, Lord, for blessings sent*

The name Festus (joyful) was vital in Paul's experience. It was before Festus that he told the story of his conversion so eloquently that King Agrippa said, "Almost thou persuadest me to be a Christian," and it was Festus who sent Paul to Rome, because he had appealed to Cæsar. The tune is from Freylinghausen's *Hymn Book,* and the words are by Samuel Johnson (Note 37). They long appeared as anonymous, perhaps because of the change in his first line, which reads, "I bless thee, Lord, for sorrows sent."

139 Surrey. *I walk with Love along the way*

Henry Carey (1692?–1743) was an Englishman of varied occupation and talent. He was a teacher and tutor in families, and a writer of ballad operas, farces, and songs. His charming ballad, Sally in Our Alley, is alone a hold on both musical and poetic fame. In such songs, as in this hymn tune, he is almost Mozartean in grace. In 1740, he published a collection of one hundred ballads. This tune, from Church's *Introduction to Psalmody,* was set to Joseph Addison's version of Psalm 23, "The Lord my pasture shall prepare." Here it is applied to a hymn by Minny M. H. Ayers, a Christian Scientist, that also tells of the walk with Love, the shepherd.

140 St. Olave. *If on our daily course, our mind*

John Keble (1792–1866) is widely loved as the poet of *The Christian Year.* His work is poetry, rather than hymnody only, and it is difficult to select stanzas for a hymn without losing something. The poems have a certain obscurity, as of the poet absorbed in his own vision, and show everywhere his deep love of nature. This hymn is from the first poem of *The Christian Year,* beginning, "Hues of the rich unfolding morn." We may note that the word "hallow," in the first stanza, anticipates the last word of that stanza, since to "sacrifice" is from the Latin to "make sacred," or to hallow. This use of the word is rare, but is significant here.

The regret of Keble's life was the secession of John Henry Newman, his friend, to Rome. He wrote at this time his *Lyra Innocentium,* poems about children, rather than for them, and so found relief from controversy. He was associated with the Lake Poets, and this influence, with his intelligent Bible study, developed his poetic gifts. He was Poetry Professor at Oxford when his famous sermon there, in 1833, started the Oxford Movement, so Newman declared, as a call for a more consecrated Christianity. He even wrote some of the *Tracts for the Times,* that gave it the name Tractarianism. In 1836, he went as vicar to Hursley, where he spent the remainder of his years.

Lovers of singing are glad to encounter a singer among the makers of hymn tunes. Robert Hudson (1732–1815) was a popular tenor at the gardens of Marylebone and Ranelagh, but his real joy was in his church singing. He became assistant organist at St. Mildred's, London, and then vicar choral of St. Paul's Cathedral, before he was made a gentleman of the Chapel Royal. Here he was also almoner, and master to the children. St. Olave appeared in Wesley's *European Psalmist,* 1872. It is named for an old London church.

237

141 Cheerfulness. *If the Lord build not the house*

The Danish words here come first in the hymn which was sung to this music, and is a favorite with the Norwegian people. It begins, "Always cheerful when you tread ways that God may know." The English words were written by Maria Louise Baum to fit the tune, and to meet the need of a "building song."

The composer, Christopher E. F. Weyse (1774–1842), was born in Altona, Germany, but lived in Copenhagen from the age of ten, and became naturalized as a Dane. He was organist at the Reformert Church and at the Church of Our Lady. He wrote light operas, but also much sacred music, a symphony, and piano pieces. He was founder of a musical society in Copenhagen, and his chorale book was published in 1839.

142 Bishopthorpe. *Immortal Love, forever full*

This fluent, graceful tune, by Clark (Note 94), is found in Miller's *Psalms of David,* 1790. Whittier's words are from his poem, Our Master, using the first three stanzas and the ninth (Note 49).

143 Windermere. *Imposture shrinks from light*

Sir Arthur Somervell early gave great promise as a composer. His songs and choral works are settings of English lyrics, from Shakespeare to Tennyson and Browning, and in these his art illustrates delightfully the unity of feeling between poetry and music. His cycle, Maud, is a classic of English song. Gradually, however, he devoted his time mainly to education, and became Principal Inspector of Music to the Board of Education and Scottish Education Department (Whitehall). He was successful in raising the standard of musical education in the schools and teachers' colleges. He helped compile songs suitable for school use, and to make known to the children of England their own country's beautiful old folk songs. He produced various orchestral works, including his symphony, Thalassa, a violin concerto, a Mass, etc. The style of his music is unusually direct and unaffected.

To an inquiry as to the tune Windermere, Sir Arthur replied: "I wrote the tune for *The English Hymnal,* and, knowing that tunes were supposed to have place names, I chose the name I love best in the world."

It is not surprising that such a simple, delightful confession came from one who could look back to a childhood's home set in an atmosphere of such poetic and romantic beauty as surrounds Lake Windermere. This "River-lake," as it is called, winds its ten miles of blue waters (which never exceed one mile in width) through a valley in the mountainous country known as the Lake District of England, world famous for its remarkable and individual beauty. The mountains dominate the landscape, and with the many lakes, widely varied in character, produce scenery of intense interest and haunting loveliness.

This beautiful countryside is intimately connected with the story of English literature, as the name "Lake Poets" reminds us. Many poets and writers—Wordsworth, Coleridge, Southey, De Quincey, Ruskin—were born or resided there, while Shelley, Keats, Carlyle, Tennyson, Sir Walter Scott, Matthew Arnold, Nathaniel Hawthorne, Clough, Mrs. Hemans, loved and visited it. During the sixty years of his life in the Lake District, Wordsworth made it a Mecca for poets and lovers of English poetry, whose influence "was wholly for good, wholly for an upward trend of thought."

Thomas Scott (1705–1775), the hymnist here, was pastor of the Presbyterian chapel in Ipswich, England, and his hymns appeared in 1772. This one is named Private Judgment, its Rights and its Duties. One of his works was to translate the Book of Job into English verse.

144 Mount Calvary. *In atmosphere of Love divine*

For the composer, Robert P. Stewart, see Note 172. The words appeared in the *Christian Science Series,* August 15, 1890, signed H.

145 Irish. *In atmosphere of Love divine*

Irish is called by this endearing name in Ashworth's collection of 1760. It is traced to 1749, in *A Collection of Hymns and Sacred Poems,* by Powell. The dotted quarter and eighth (crotchet and quaver) seem characteristic of the free tunefulness of Irish melody.

146 Newbury. *In God I find a precious gift*

This is a traditional melody, with the traditional English cheerfulness in the dancing "quavers," as the English call the arithmetical "eighth notes" of America. It is an old carol, which began, "There is six good days set in a week." The confident and happy words used here were specially written for the music by Violet Ker Seymer. The tune appears in *The English Hymnal.*

147 Holy Trinity. *In God I find a precious gift*

Perhaps no name in the English hymnody of the last century carried further, outside of England, than that of Joseph Barnby (1838–1896). His melody everywhere touched the popular heart by its sweetness. Chorister at York Minster, he began his career with song, and to song he was enduringly loyal. He played the organ at St. Andrew's, London, and then at St. Anne's, Soho, where he produced a Bach work yearly—one of his most important services to musical England. Then he was organist and precentor for Eton College, where he did much for musical education.

239

The Barnby Choir, started in 1867 by Novello, for oratorio, became the Royal Choral Society, which Barnby conducted. He was principal of the Guildhall School of Music, and was knighted in 1892. His list of hymn tunes counts up to two hundred and forty-six, with other works. This tune is from a fine collection named *The Hymnary*. Barnby was its editor, in 1872. The nature of the harmony here is explained in the fact that the music was intended for unison singing.

148 Ewing. *In heavenly Love abiding*

This is one of the most loved and also one of the best written hymns in popular use. Anna Laetitia Waring (1820–1910) was born at Neath, Glamorganshire, Wales. Her modesty is shown in the publication, in 1850, of nineteen hymns, only, and with her initials only, as *Hymns and Meditations by A. W. L.*

Alexander Ewing (1830–1895) was a soldier who, ranking as an amateur musician, in a life devoted to his profession, has given the world a melody that lives, and, as Dr. Neale said, passes the sure test of a hymn tune, in being popular with children. Colonel Ewing at first studied for the law, but in 1855 entered the British Army and served in Crimea, in South Australia, and in China. Returning to England, he married Miss Gatty, known as writer of "Jackanapes" and other children's stories.

Ewing was "a good performer," and sang with the Haydn Society of Aberdeen and with the Harmonic Choir, specializing in old English music. One night at rehearsal he confessed to having tried to write a tune! It was taken up eagerly by the choir, and approved. He had written it in triple time, and when they altered it to its present meter, he said, "It now seems to me a good deal like a polka." It was his first and only tune, and an excellent one. It is an almost perfect setting for Miss Waring's words, though it was originally set to Dr. Neale's "For thee, O dear, dear country." The change of words may be seen as a reminder that "In heavenly Love abiding" we find our country, here and now!

149 St. Barnabas. *In Love divine all earth-born fear and sorrow*

The story of Barnabas is found in Acts. His name means "consolation," and this calmly flowing tune is well suited to these luminous and reassuring words, written by Susan F. Campbell, a Christian Scientist. For Dr. Buck's music, see Note 4.

150 St. Denio. *In mercy, in goodness, how great is our King*

This Welsh melody has characteristic swing and stress. The strong, inspiring words, that move so perfectly with the rhythm of the tune, were specially composed for it by William P. McKenzie.

151 Rutherford. *In speechless prayer and reverence*

In Chrétien Urhan (1790–1845) we have a French lad who taught himself to play the piano and other instruments, and wrote waltzes before he was in his teens. Born at Montjoie, at fifteen he was playing in Aix-la-Chapelle, when the Empress Josephine heard him, and carried him off to Paris for study. He became a brilliant violinist and was known for his success on the viol d'amour, so that Meyerbeer wrote a solo for him into his opera, The Huguenots. Urhan was for thirty years first violinist in the orchestra of the Opéra Française and the story is told that he never once looked at the stage, on account of his religious devoutness. He lived an ascetic, dressing like a clergyman, but was most kindly disposed toward the needs of others. He was organist at the Church of St. Vincent de Paul, Paris.

His composition was clear and expressive, as in this tune. It appeared as a hymn tune in a French collection, *Christian Songs,* 1834, and was adopted in England by Dr. Rimbault for *Psalms and Hymns for Divine Worship,* 1867. The English name comes from the use of the tune with a curious hymn, that was made up by Mrs. Anne Cousin, from sayings of Samuel Rutherford. He was a Royalist, named by Milton in a sonnet called New Forcers of Conscience under the Long Parliament. Thus the hymn leads thought back, on one hand, to Milton, on the other, to the brilliant court of Napoleon. Hymnody thus traced is an interesting record of history. Of all the arts, it is nearest to the life of the people, enjoyed by everybody, not merely by the instructed few. For the words here, see Note 152.

152 Es ist ein' Ros' entsprungen. *In speechless prayer and reverence*

This music has the sweetness and reverence of pure melody, drawn perhaps from the words with which it has so long been sung. They speak love and praise for the gentle mother of the child Jesus. Beginning, as above, "There has a rose come forth,"* the poem uses the image of a rose sprung from the "stem of Jesse," and applies it to Mary as mother of the child. The song has had wide use in many lands, in slightly different forms. This is one of the Swedish contributions to the Hymnal.

It is found in the *Cologne Hymn Book,* 1599, but is believed to have come down from the fifteenth or sixteenth century as a Christmas or Twelfth Night carol, used in the diocese of Trier. This was ancient Treves, in Rhenish Prussia, that claims to be the oldest town in Germany.

---

* Opinion is divided as to the meaning of the word Ros' in this title. It might be a provincialism for Reis, which means rod or scion. Zahn's *Psalter und Harfe* retains the apostrophe, for the German *Rose.*

241

The town was certainly one where Cæsar came, saw, and conquered; and the place grew in importance till, in the fourth century, it was referred to as "Rome beyond the Alps."

These tender words are by Ellen J. Glover, a Christian Scientist, and were written especially for the 1932 edition of the Hymnal. As adapted to this melody, they seem pervaded by the rose's fragrance, and by the love and humility of the Mary to whom the old song paid tribute.

153   St. Theodulph. *In Thee, my God and Saviour*

The story of this tune is one more record of the courage and faith shown by early groups of Protestants. Valerius Herberger was pastor of an Evangelical church in Poland, but in 1604 he and his followers were put out of the church for their convictions. They secured a meeting place of their own, at the town gates, and because their first service was held on Christmas Eve, the place was called *Kripplein Christi* (little crib of Christ). Melchior Teschner, composer of this tune, was precentor of this little group.

During a pestilence that began in 1613, Herberger devoted himself to his people, and one of his few hymns is The Farewell, which he set to Teschner's music. The hymn appeared first in Leipzig, as a "broadside," and was named "The Farewell of Valerius Herberger, that he gave to the world in the autumn of the year 1613, when he every hour saw death before his eyes, but mercifully and also as wonderfully as the three men in the furnace at Babylon, was nevertheless spared."

The words, by Maria Louise Baum, are an arrangement of the Magnificat, or Mary's rejoicing (Luke 1:46), one of the earliest passages chosen for Protestant hymns.

The broadside, used in early days of printing for the spread of songs and other material, was a forerunner of the newspaper. In Winter's Tale, the sale of ballad sheets by the singing peddler, Autolycus, illustrates their use. The girls crowd round him to buy, and say that they love a ballad in print, for then they know it is true!

Teschner's tune was used by Bach in his St. John Passion Music, and in Cantata 95. In England it was applied to Dr. Neale's version of a Latin hymn attributed to St. Theodulph. Thus the tune was named for him. Theodulph was an Italian, brought to France by Charlemagne, and made Bishop of Orleans. So we have here William Shakespeare, Johann Sebastian Bach, Charlemagne, and St. Luke, gathered round the "Kripplein Christi."

NOTE: The plan of this ten-line tune repeats the first two quiet lines, making four. Then the fifth and sixth lines bring variety and intensity, with a new key (G). The seventh and eight modulate back to the original key (C), the eighth repeating the sixth in the key of C. The ninth and tenth lines are the first and second repeated, like a refrain.

154 Alma. *In Thee, O Spirit true and tender*

These words, much loved by the people, appeared in *The Christian Science Journal* for October, 1888. They are by Frances A. Fox. An omitted stanza reads:

Thy grace is all sufficient for me,
Thy precious Life a perfect light,
No evil thought can come before Thee;
Thy Mind is pure, Thy home is bright.

The music, by Lyman Brackett, was composed for the words for the first edition of the Hymnal, 1892. Alma is an Italian word for spirit, soul.

The work of Mr. Brackett, as music editor of the first *Christian Science Hymnal,* of 1892, is gratefully remembered. When the church membership was small, Mrs. Eddy relied upon him to help the committee appointed to that important task. The hymns had three tunes each, one set above the words, two on the opposite page. The third tune was specially written to fit the words and to make them easily singable. The good congregational singing found in Christian Science churches may in part be due to the use of these easy and vocal tunes.

155 St. Vincent. *In Thee, O Spirit true and tender*

The story of Sigismund Neukomm (1778–1858) is one of an amazing popularity, which his talent did not long sustain. According to Grove, he was called the King of Brummagem (Birmingham) for the success of his David, an oratorio composed for the Festival of 1834. In Paris he had had similar success under the restored Bourbons. In 1815, he went to the Congress of Vienna with Talleyrand, his intimate friend, and there he composed a requiem for Louis XVI, the royal sacrifice of the French Revolution. This was performed with acclaim, and for it Louis XVIII later made him chevalier of the Legion of Honor.

Neukomm was born in Salzburg and studied with both the Haydns, Joseph treating him almost as a son. He was chapelmaster and director of the German theater at old St. Petersburg, and then went to Paris. He also sought out Rio de Janeiro, where he was chapelmaster to Dom Pedro. Finally it is told that he was "the most popular person in England," for two songs, Napoleon's Midnight Review and Barry Cornwall's The Sea. He was so steady a worker that one thousand pieces of music are listed to his composing. He loved Palestrina, the great Italian master, and tried to revive his style.

James Uglow (1814–1898) began his work in music as choirmaster at Gloucester Cathedral, and later was a pupil of Sigismund Neukomm, from whose work he arranged the tune St. Vincent. It was first published in Kemble's *New Church Hymn Book,* London, 1875.

243

156 Evensong. *In Thee, O Spirit true and tender*

This lovely music is owned by Marlborough College, in England, where the composer, Arthur C. Heberden, was musical director. The tune was written for the college Hymn Book.

157 Atkey. *Jesus' prayer for all his brethren*

The words of this hymn, by Violet Hay, were written with special recognition of the mission of *The Christian Science Monitor*. The music by Dr. Dyson (Note 39) has three changes of time signature, but the rhythm of the words is so matched to the music that the normal speech-accents easily lead the singer through the melody.

158 St. Asaph. *It came upon the midnight clear*

Giovanni Marie Giornovichi (1745–1804) was a restless Italian artist, who ended his years in Russia. A distinguished violinist, he was received in Paris, in 1770, with acclaim that lasted ten years. Personal difficulties compelled departure, and he wandered from Warsaw to London, and after a time to Hamburg, where he lived obscurely, and then reached Russia. The world is grateful for this singable melody, whatever its background.

The writer of this favorite hymn was a Unitarian minister, of Massachusetts, Edmund H. Sears (1810–1876). The words appeared in *The Christian Register* in 1850.

159 Pentatone. *It came upon the midnight clear*

Of the extensive work carried on by Sir H. Walford Davies, whose compositions have yielded nine melodies for the Hymnal, a few lines can hardly give an adequate idea. He has accomplished great things for music in England, through his power of putting himself into sympathy with every kind of musical audience.

He was for five years organist at St. George's Chapel, Windsor, where he had started his career as chorister, under Sir Walter Parratt; from 1898 to 1923 he was organist and choir director of the famous Temple Church, where he succeeded Dr. Hopkins (Note 208) ; in 1919 he was made chairman of the Council of Music in the University of Wales, for which, in 1923, he edited *A Students' Hymnal,* as a "coöperative enterprise in composition." Finally came the radio, with the opportunity by broadcasting lectures and courses in music to extend still further his long educational influence.

The opportunities offered by the Temple Church gave Sir Walford conditions that exactly suited his liberal sense of music. He was thus able to develop church music free from purely ecclesiastical traditions. Organist there for twenty-five years, he established a widely eclectic repertoire, to which he himself contributed music of great value and beauty. His works include an oratorio, named The Temple. (See also Notes 26, 210.)

In 1909 he supervised the rebuilding of the organ, which recalls, in the story of the Temple Church, an episode which in its day (1684) excited great interest. It was known as the Battle of the Organs. The Benchers, or governing members of the Inns of Court, in the grounds of which the Temple Church stands, were set upon having the best organ in London. The competition lay between two organ builders, Smith and Harris. The debate lasted for nearly a year. Drs. Blow and Purcell exploited Father Smith's organ, and Draghi, organist to Queen Catherine, played on the Harris organ. No decision was reached, and so the formidable Lord Chief Justice Jeffreys took this matter, like so many others, into his own hands and decided on Smith's organ. This shows how deeply interested the members of the Inns of Court have long been in their music.

The melody, Pentatone, is so named because it uses the old five tone scale, 1, 2, 3, 5, 6. The black keys of the piano give this scale, when the group of three black keys is played first. The seventh appears in the music only as a passing note.

160 Gloaming. *It matters not what be thy lot*

In this music has been found, for Mrs. Eddy's Satisfied, a tune that admirably suits the mood and rhythm of the words. It has their vigor, directness, and bright clarity, with an onward rush to the final solving verb.

Sir John Stainer (1840–1901) is one of the English musicians who have served in many places in many ways to advance the cause of music. He was an organist at the age of fifteen, and his work at Oxford raised the Magdalen choir to a high level. He was on the examining board for musical degrees there, and at the same time was a member of the board for musical studies at Cambridge (also examiner there and later at London University). He received the decoration of the Legion of Honor at Paris, and succeeded Sullivan as principal of the National Training School for Music, in 1888. He was organist at St. Paul's Cathedral for sixteen years, and on resigning was knighted, and then appointed professor of music at Oxford. His music is simple, not chromatic or venturesome, and his hymn tunes have a clear outline for the benefit of congregations.

Questions have been asked as to the slurs at the top and bottom of the second page. They are arranged to suit the words. "Faith" has two notes, the less important syllable "un-" only one, in the soprano.

161 Fortitude. *It matters not what be thy lot*

The music here is a beautiful setting, with a beautiful name for Mrs. Eddy's Satisfied. It was composed by Walter E. Young, who was long organist of The Mother Church.

162 Satis. *It matters not what be thy lot*

Satis (Enough), for Mrs. Eddy's hymn, Satisfied, has a changed time signature in one measure, so that the music may linger a little, with the words. For Mr. Whitlock's work, see Note 211.

163 Warrington. *Jesus, what precept is like thine*

Mrs. Mary A. Livermore, née Rice (1820–1905), was an American reformer, especially interested in improving the conditions of prisons, a cause for which this hymn was written. The original reads, "'Twas mind that formed that holy plan." The line, as altered, puts the word Mind on a music accent.

Ralph Harrison (1748–1810), born in Derbyshire, England, was the Presbyterian preacher at Cross Street Chapel, Manchester, and professor at the Academy there. The tune was in his *Sacred Harmony,* 1784.

164 Nativity. *Joy to the world, the Lord is come*

Henry Lahee (1826–1912), born in Chelsea, London, studied with Sterndale Bennett and Sir John Goss, and at twenty-one became organist at Holy Trinity, Brompton, where he stayed for nearly thirty years.

An English critic once ranked him with the "Purcellians," for his love of vocal music. He took prizes for glees and madrigals at Bristol, Manchester, Glasgow, and London, and one of the family heirlooms is the silver goblet given him by the Nottingham Glee Club, for a setting of The Bells by Edgar Allen Poe. He set Longfellow's Building of the Ship for chorus, and Tennyson's Sleeping Beauty for women's voices.

His daughter was a pupil of Garcia, and his son, Henry C. Lahee, has been, since 1879, a well-known figure in the musical life of Boston. He recalls that The Bells was inspired by the bells of St. Luke's, in Chelsea, on an evening when his father stood to listen, and to speak with his son of the beauty of the hour and scene.

Nativity was among Mr. Lahee's *One Hundred Hymn Tunes,* prepared for Dr. W. J. Irons, Vicar of Brompton.

The son recalls an incident of his own boyhood, typical of a lad from a musical family. Asked at school to sing a song to amuse the boys, young Lahee replied, "I don't know any funny song, but I can sing Gibbons in F."

The poem is from Watts' Psalm 98, the second part, named The Messiah's Coming and Kingdom (Note 62).

165 Plenitude. *Joy to the world, the Lord is come*

The variations in meter found in this music by Sir Walford Davies (Note 159) aid in singing the words with their natural stress and rhythm. The music is from *A Student's Hymnal*, 1923.

166 Gott des Himmels. *Know, O child, thy full salvation*

Heinrich Albert (1604–1651) is one of the German students who had adventures in their wanderings. On his way to study at Königsburg, in 1626, he was taken prisoner by the Swedes, and did not reach the city till 1628. He was a nephew of the famous Schütz, and stands next to him as a founder of German opera, exampled by his Comedy Music, for the centenary of the Königsburg University. He became organist at the Cathedral there, but is also remembered for his poetry. He joined the Poetical Union, and his verse, of a "loving and artistic" quality, appeared with his *Airs, Sacred and Secular*. He is poet and composer of the Morning Hymn, from which comes this tune, God of Heaven. It is said that for more than two hundred years no day has dawned when there has not somewhere in German lands been lifted to God, Albert's Morning Hymn. His works were published under the patronage of the Emperor of Germany, the King of Poland, and the Elector of Brandenburg.

The words are by Lyte (Note 8), from his hymn, "Jesus, I my cross have taken," which was in use for some time signed merely G, before published in Lyte's first collection, 1833.

167 Gott des Himmels. *Know, O child, thy full salvation*

Here is Albert's melody from No. 166 as harmonized by Bach.

168 Vom Himmel hoch. *Let all the earth with songs rejoice*

The name was given to this tune because it has long been used with a hymn of Luther's which begins, "Vom Himmel hoch da komm ich her" (From the high heaven hither I come), written for the Christmas festival of his own children. The first seven verses were sung by a man dressed as an angel, and in eight other stanzas the children sang their reply. Luther's words were translated in *Gude and Godlie Ballates*, 1539–1556, begun by John Wedderburn during his German exile from Dundee.

The beautiful melody first appeared in Luther's *Geistliche Lieder* of 1539, and may have been composed by him. Nearly two hundred years later, Bach used it in his Christmas Oratorio. The setting here is his.

The first German Protestant hymn book was dated 1524 and was called the Achtliederbuch (Eight-song book). Four of the eight were by Luther. The book was taught in schools, and was carried over the country by traveling scholars. Six other collections of his hymns, original and selected, followed.

The simplicity, even homeliness, of his hymns favored their use by the people. The words from the Latin which are used here have a similar directness of expression, though less naïve. These are from the tenth or eleventh century, and are remarkable for their simple acceptance of the healing mission of Jesus and his followers. This translation was made by Richard Mant, an English bishop (1776–1848), who is known for his translations of Latin hymns.

The reference to the key of heaven is perhaps from Matthew 16:19. To think of heaven, not as a place, but as a state of consciousness, makes it clear that the key of understanding both opens and closes (protects) this mental state of harmony.

Of Luther's manner of writing, a contemporary said, "The rimes are easy and good, the words choice and proper, the meaning clear and intelligible, the melodies lovely and hearty, and all so rare and majestic, so full of pith and power, so cheering and comforting, that you will not find his equal, much less his master."

Luther's Bible (published complete 1534) was the first important book in what is called High German, and it earned for him the name of "father" of the German language and literature.

Luther played both the flute and the lute, and had a fine singing voice. Johann Walther, the composer who aided him, said that Luther invented tunes on his flute, which Walther wrote down. Luther made music for both Gospels and Epistles. He wished the Word of God to "dwell among the people by means of song also." He knew that the hope of the race lies in the salvation of the common man. Perhaps he would have liked the name given to a Psalter of 1609 in Germany, *The Pharmacy of David: a powerful-to-heal and well-equipped Art of Medicine from the spiritually rich and holy* (literally healing) *Psalter* (Pharmaceutica Davidica: das ist eine heilwertige und bewehrte Arzneykunst aus dem geistreichen heiligen Psalter). (See Note 10.)

169   Lux benigna. *Lead, kindly Light*

This is one of the best known and loved of English hymns, and one in which much discussion has centered. John Henry Newman (1801–1890) tells the story of its writing in his *Apologia* or Justification of my Life. He says that, in 1832, European religion and politics seemed to him in a state of hopeless confusion. To regain his poise, he went to Europe to travel, and reaching Palermo in 1833, was eager to return to England, but must wait for a boat. He embarked, however, in an orange boat, bound for Marseilles, in which he was becalmed for a week. The famous hymn was written then. It expresses his longing for guidance, but he says that at the time he had no thought of leaving the English church. Many interpretations have been given for the "angel faces" in the third stanza— as those of faith and assurance, hidden for a while; or of friends he longed to see at home. Newman's reply to a letter, in 1879, indicated that he could not recall what were this thoughts as he lay "homesick and seasick" in that little boat on the Mediterranean. Perhaps his word "homesick" is the real clue.

Newman, involved in the so-called Oxford Movement with Keble and Pusey, turned to Rome in 1845, and was made a cardinal in 1879.

In St. Oswald's Church, Durham, a window is dedicated to John B. Dykes (1823–1876) as its former vicar; and the organ is a gift from an American who loved his music—another sign of how one strain of music makes the Christian world kin. E. V. Lucas, writing of Dykes in the *London Times*, has said that he has not yet had the honor due for his remarkable offering to the church of one hundred and eighty-four good hymn tunes. Many of these are known throughout the English-speaking world. At his passing, a large memorial fund was contributed for the benefit of his family.

It was upon hearing Jenny Lind sing in Mendelssohn's Elijah that Dykes determined thereafter to devote his musical talents to making music for the church. He stands first in what is sometimes called the "Hymns Ancient and Modern" school of music, referring to the new hymnal that gained such favor with church people of 1860. Mr. Lucas counts these words and music, Lux benigna (Kindly Light), the most beautiful hymn in the language.

170 Creation. *Let every creature hail the morn*

This tune is "The heavens are telling the glory of God," one of the noblest of the choruses in Haydn's Creation. The words used here are from Whittier's poem, The Mystic's Christmas, and were specially arranged for the Hymnal. This is one of three poems by Whittier (Notes 49, 50, 96) which were added to the Hymnal of 1932. It is of marked interest, as recording the ideas which helped to prepare thought for Mrs. Eddy's great statement of Christian Science.

This music has the supple vigor and never-failing grace of Haydn. Its singing must not be allowed to drag. The groups with three notes to the syllable need vigor and steadiness. Haydn uses three solo voices with this chorus, the angels Raphael, Gabriel, and Uriel, who are narrators of the story.

When The Creation was sung in Paris with a French text, Napoleon went to hear it and approved. So when the French troops occupied Vienna, after Austerlitz, they surrounded the unpretentious house of Haydn, and the brilliant French band swung into the graceful soprano aria, "With Verdure Clad," from The Creation. By Napoleon's orders, troops were left to guard the house.

The Creation and The Seasons were Haydn's last great works. The libretto of the former was one that had been refused by Handel. It was drawn from the Bible and from Milton's *Paradise Lost,* but had to be translated into German for Haydn's use. Translated from German back into English, it has not much of Milton left.

Haydn's last public appearance (1808) was a triumph. The Creation was being sung when he entered the hall, and he was greeted with a flourish of trumpets and shouts, "Long live Haydn." At the passage "Let there be light" again they cheered him, while he lifted his hand heavenward, crying, "It all came from there."

The simple devoutness of Franz Joseph Haydn is shown in the headings of his manuscript: "In the name of Lord." Of The Creation he said, "I prayed God every day to strengthen me for my work." (See Notes 71, 185.)

171 Alleluia. *Let us sing of Easter gladness*

For the composer, S. S. Wesley, see Note 75; for the hymn, see Note 413.

172 Eucharistica. *Lift up thy light*

Celia Laighton Thaxter (1836–1894) was the daughter of a New England public man who, wearying of political life, retired to the Isles of Shoals, off the short coast of New Hampshire, where he lived as keeper of the light on White Island. Here the young girl learned to know the ocean, the sea birds, winds, and tides, and the light, on whose faithful tending so much depended.

She won a large circle of friends by the poems that reflect her life there. Famous writers and artists visited her on Appledore, the rocky island that was her home after her marriage to Mr. Thaxter. Her garden here was so beautiful that artists often came to paint it.

The poem was named My Lighthouse, and was printed, with several others, in 1890, as a Christmas card or booklet, by Prang, with illustrations painted by Mrs. Thaxter, one of them the lighthouse which had long guarded the shore of New Hampshire.

The card was found in a neglected book in a Cambridge home, and was offered at once to the Hymnal. The poem is not included in Mrs. Thaxter's collected works, and special permission to use it as a hymn was given by her son, the late Professor Thaxter, of Harvard University. The words have a fine vigor and sweep, and their use here perpetuates a noble parable from the human life of our time.

The music is by Sir Robert P. Stewart, of Dublin (1825–1894), who was an organist of wide repute, a professor in Dublin University, and incidentally an authority on bagpipes. The tune name is from the Greek for thanksgiving and refers to the Lord's Supper.

173 Huddersfield. *Love is kind and suffers long*

The composer is Sir Walter Parratt (1841–1924), who, the son of an organist at Huddersfield, England, had so thorough a training from his father that at the age of seven the boy played a church service and at ten played from memory the forty-eight Preludes and Fugues of Bach.

At eleven years he was appointed organist at Armitage Bridge Church, and then held various organ posts, including that at Magdalen College, Oxford. Appointed to St. George's Chapel, Windsor, in 1882, he became "Master of the Queen's Musick" and private organist to Queen Victoria.

He did comparatively little in composition, but Grove's estimate of him as an organist reads: "The champion of a style founded on accurate part-playing, clean phrasing, and simple registration." By his example and forty years of teaching at the Royal College of Music, he revolutionized the playing of organists in England and elsewhere.

The words of this hymn are by Christopher Wordsworth, Bishop of Lincoln, and nephew of the great poet. Bishop Wordsworth's *The Holy Year* contains hymns to teach truth, among them this hymn, based on I Corinthians 13. He believed that there was danger to the church in accepting for the ancient interpretation of the Old Testament, the literalism of those who see in it nothing but "common history." He said that the Gospel history gave "only what Jesus *began* to do and to teach on earth." The Apocalypse was the Bishop's favorite book.

174 Consolation. *Like as a mother, God comforteth His children*

This music is from Mendelssohn's Songs without Words, Opus 30, No. 3. (See Note 118.) The words were written for it by Maria Louise Baum.

175 Hyfrydol. *Lo, He sent His Word and healed them*

The composer of Hyfrydol was Rowland. H. Prichard (1811–1887), who was born near Bala, Wales, where he spent most of his life. When nearly seventy years old, he removed to Holywell Mill, as a loom-tender's assistant in a flannel factory. He had a fine voice and was an excellent precentor.

Hyfrydol was written before he was twenty. Soon after he was thirty, he published *The Singer's Friend,* mostly his own music; also a booklet for children. The *Harvard University Hymn Book* uses Hyfrydol five times and says of it, "A national tune much sung during the Welsh revival of 1904–1905." It was used in *The English Hymnal,* 1906. It is elsewhere spoken of as a hymn that deserves wide recognition as illustrating modern Welsh music. The hymn of healing set to it here is by Violet Hay. Hyfrydol may be translated Delightful.

251

176 Church. *Long hast thou stood, O church of God*

A student in the United States, Norwegian by birth, writes of her delight at finding in the *Christian Science Hymnal,* music by the Norwegian Ludwig M. Lindeman, and words by Scandinavian poets. When from love of her native language this student takes out her old Lutheran Hymnal, our Numbers 19 and 176 are the hymns to which she most often turns.

The poet here was Nicolaj F. S. Grundtvig (1783–1872), a Danish preacher, who sought for a more spiritual Christianity, and so fearlessly that his first sermon bade fair to be his last! He took as text, "Why has the Word of God departed from His House?" and dared to chide the clergy of Copenhagen for their "lifeless religion." The clergy frowned but the people delighted in his "joyful Christianity" with its "living word," of the new inspiration that comes daily to men. He was the true "scald," in the old Scandinavian meaning—a poet wholly possessed by his lofty message.

Grundtvig also worked for people's high schools in the three countries, to secure Christian and Scandinavian culture, in contrast with the old Latin schools. That the church forgave his early zeal is shown by his consecration as Bishop about 1860.

The poem, here reproduced from an English prose version, begins with the Danish words on the page, "The church is an old house." The first stanza echoes Grundtvig's youthful reproaches, and therefore is modified here. The tune is a favorite with the Norwegians, and the composer is Lindeman (Note 84), who "taught the Norwegian people to sing." The tune proves what beauty and vigor may be expressed in the minor. We may note that the first part is exactly repeated, and that at the word "understand" (page two) a touch of the major gives color.

NOTE: A simple major triad, or three-tone chord, is made minor by lowering the middle tone half a step. A triad is made up of three alternate tones of the scale, as 1, 3, 5; or 4, 6, 8. It is called a major chord when the "interval" from the first to the middle tone is two full steps, as from C to E. Thus C E G is a major triad; C E-flat G is a minor triad, or chord. A minor melody uses the minor scale, in which the third tone is half a step lower than in the major.

177 Feniton Court. *Look, ye saints, the day is breaking*

The poet, Thomas Kelly (1769–1855), was born in Dublin, the son of an Irish judge. He was educated for the bar, but began clerical training in the Established Church and then went over to the Independents. His hymns rank high, and all are hymns of praise. His *Hymns on Various Passages of Scripture,* 1804, was extended until the edition of 1853 held 765. Kelly also wrote tunes for his hymns. For Dr. Hopkins, the composer, see Note 208.

178   Light. *Love is life's true crown and glory*

The Danish words here mean "Love is the source of light." For composer and poet, see Notes 84 and 176.

179   Integer vitae. *Love one another,—word of revelation*

Integer vitae, the ode of Horace, the Latin poet (65–8 B. C.), which gives its name to this music, has been sung perhaps more widely than any other song in the universities of Germany, England, and the United States. The first words have been translated:

> Unsullied honor, pure from sin,
> Roams the wide world, serene, secure.

The ode celebrates the man "blameless of life," who needs no weapons to defend himself. His "integrity" protects him, and wherever he goes he fails not to sing the praise of lovely Lalage.

The tune was specially set to the Latin words by Friedrich Ferdinand Flemming (1778–1813), a physician, born in Saxony, who was a composer of music for men's voices.

The words given it in the Hymnal are perfectly fitted in point of rhythmic form and melodic beauty; and they suit as well the generous animus of the Latin. They were written for the music by Margaret Morrison, a Christian Scientist.

180   Charity. *Love the Lord thy God*

Jens N. L. Schjørring (1825–1900) was born near Lemvig, Jutland, and became pastor in Ørslev, near Skelskør. The Danish words on the Hymnal page mean "Love from God," and are the first words of the poem, which was translated into literal English prose and then set to the music in English verse. The composer, Carl F. Jähnigen (1813–1887), was born on the island Langeland, and become choirmaster at Holmens Kirke in Copenhagen.

181   Sardis. *Loving Father, we Thy children*

Soon after the Hymnal appeared in 1932, a popular vote of women put Mary Baker Eddy at the head of the women leaders in the United States, during the past one hundred years. At a time that so recognizes woman's power of leadership, we are glad to remember that the one opera by Ludwig van Beethoven (1770–1827), which he named Leonora, celebrates the heroism of woman. His Leonora is no vociferous Brunnhilde, but she is strong in the achieving power of love. After a night of suffering, she rises, of her innate genius, to a clearer sky. Against Beethoven's protest, his friends changed the title of the work to Fidelio, the name under which Leonora, disguised as a boy, enters a revolutionary prison, to save her husband.

The third overture written for Leonora ranks as the finest work of its class. A New York critic has stated that at the triumphant close, this music rises to a rejoicing that lifts us above the personal victory of the story, to joy for the liberation of all humanity. Of this opera, that so honors womanhood, Beethoven said, "Among all my children, Leonora is the dearest," adding that he held her worthiest of them all to serve "the science of art."

In his grasp of the true dignity of humanity, then coming to light, Beethoven was a son of his times. A story is told of Goethe and Beethoven walking one day in Vienna, and noting the approach of the imperial family, also afoot, Goethe at once stood off the walk, hat in hand, bowing from the waist in Continental fashion. Beethoven walked steadily onward to exchange greetings with royalty, eye to eye.

Today Beethoven's figure stands in bronze in every great city, and his music flows on the air, and even overseas, to encourage and inspire men in troubled times. His name is familiar where the Hapsburgs are hardly known.

Beethoven's time was marked by an unfolding love of nature, in which he shared. Notebook in pocket, he roamed field and byway, intent on the working out of some musical theme, yet always responsive to the beauty around him.

Beethoven's grandfather had removed from Antwerp, in old Flanders, to Bonn, Germany, as court musician to the Elector of Cologne. Ludwig's mother was a German, a loving, sensitive woman whom he named his best friend. In his sturdy independence he was like his Flemish grandfather. In both men, moral earnestness was the foundation of character. (See Notes 58, 422.)

Of his melodies in the Hymnal, Sardis speaks the twofold quality of his music, in its power and tenderness. It is from his Romance for violin and orchestra, Opus 40. The words, by Rosemary B. Hackett, a Christian Scientist, speak also of power and love.

182   Colchester. *Make channels for the streams of Love*

This music is admirably suited to its words. The rhythmic motive, a dotted quarter and an eighth (crotchet and quaver), gives a flowing life to the tune. It illustrates the happiness of Purcell (Note 17) even as the words characterize the loving-kindness of their author, Archbishop Trench. The name of this favorite hymn tells us that he meant his poem to define "The Law of Love." He takes as text II Kings 4:1–6, unfolding it in his first two verses. The first runs:

> Pour forth the oil, pour boldly forth,
> It will not fail until
> Thou failest vessels to provide
> Which it may largely fill.

254

There is no biography of Richard Chenevix Trench (1807–1886), theologian, prelate, philologist, scholar, poet, and lover of men. He did not wish it. His daughter, therefore, merely published some of his letters, with explanatory pages. They show him, throughout his life, a true shepherd of his ever-increasing flock.

Archbishop of Dublin, he carried the Irish church through its period of disestablishment, with an unfailing charity, reconciling to him those who could not agree with his rather "high-church" position. Born in Dublin, but brought up in England, he was able to forward a better understanding between church people of the two nationalities.

His *Notes* on the Miracles and Parables show both spiritual and scholarly discernment. His *Study of Words* has endless charm, unfolding the history, reason, poetry, that are recorded in words, even considered singly.

His daughter saw that what characterized her father was "humility, love, and generosity." He either did not perceive the little flaws in others, or "they were so dim in the light of his loving gaze as to be insignificant to him." His mother wrote of his boyhood, "He is a clever, steady, *grave, gay,* little person . . . with a deep love of reading"; and a sense of humor that served him lifelong—as in his letter home after his installation at Dublin: "I think Thatcher's (his servant) notion of an archbishop must be a succession of ceremonials, shows, spectacles, and feasts, in a succession of different dresses." Some one has named him, in Arnold's phrase, "sweetness and light embodied"; and among his sayings he identifies himself: "To say that a person is perfectly simple is to my mind the highest praise that you can give." A familiar stanza of his reads:

> Wise it were to welcome and make ours
> Whate'er of good, though small, the present brings;
> Kind greetings, sunshine, song of birds, and flowers,
> With a child's pure delight in little things.

183   Heath. *Make haste, O man, to do*

These words are from Bonar's poem named Live, which begins, "Make haste, O man, to live" (Note 21). For Mason, see Note 2; for Webb, Note 335.

184   Sandys. *Make haste, O man, to do*

This is traditional music from Sandys' *Christmas Carols, ancient and modern,* 1833, which included the most popular carols from the west of England and the French provinces. William Sandys (1792–1874) made a hobby of carols, and his work revived interest in them, after long neglect. Both Byrd and Gibbons wrote carols. The best of them were lullaby carols of the Nativity, and the Wise Men were also a favorite theme, as were the Shepherds. A carol widely known is mentioned at Note 152. Carols were printed on broadsheets, or in "garlands," which was a pretty name for small collections, or "anthologies," a word that means to gather flowers (of literature). (See Note 237.)

185 Bowen. *Master and Lord, 'tis good to be here*

The name Haydn stands for sunshine and content, here and now, even as the name Mozart hints a joy that sees beyond here and now. The experience of the two great composers, who were such close friends, shows a like contrast. Joseph Haydn (1732–1809) was born in a peasant's cottage, amid the simple folk music of lower Austria. Mozart's childhood saw the royal drawing rooms where he was caressed and fêted for his wonderful harpsichord playing. Haydn's maturity was so sheltered that his genius could reach its full fruitage at a period when genius is supposed to have passed its glory—despite the various examples of a masterpiece put forth, as by Goethe or Verdi, at a riper age. But the year that saw Haydn's almost royal "progress" in England saw Mozart at thirty-four nearly penniless, working over the Requiem, which proved, as he said, to be really for himself.

For this freedom from care that enabled Haydn to compose his great work, The Creation, at the age of seventy-seven, we are grateful. As the "father of the symphony" he wrote more than one hundred symphonies, many of which are still delightful to modern ears. His attempts at opera were not successful, though one of them earned him a gold gift box from the King of Spain. His oratorio, The Creation, and his cantata, The Seasons, were inspired by the success of Handel's oratorios in England.

Haydn's long, happy years in service of the Esterhazy family, patrons of music in Vienna, gave him opportunity, at their great country estate, sometimes called a second Versailles, to experiment with his orchestra, and so to develop his pattern for the symphony and the string quartet. His symphony was in four movements, carefully diversified. The first, energetic and broad, unfolding its themes rather fully; next a songlike theme—the andante or slow movement; then the merry movement, with a minuet and trio; and then the gay, rushing finale. With modifications, this has been the general plan of the symphony ever since Haydn.

The tune Bowen is an excellent example of the gracious and tender music of Haydn, with its lovely melodic line, dipping here and there into graceful eighth notes. The significant words, by Benjamin S. Pray, a Christian Scientist, refer to the Transfiguration, Matthew 17. (See Notes 71, 170.)

186 Hendon. *Mighty God, the First, the Last*

Largely because of differences in meter, French hymns have not often been translated into English. But because the greatest of the French hymnwriters was also a composer, the Hymnal can include César H. A.

256

Malan in its list of names. This strong, clear tune is a link with the Huguenot body that sent so many excellent citizens to the Netherlands, to England, and to the New World. César's father went from Paris to Geneva, when the Edict of Nantes was revoked, so that César is of Genevan birth (1787–1864). A minister in the Genevan church, he became one of the leaders away from the growing Unitarianism back to Calvinism. In this he was influenced by the Scottish evangelist, Robert Haldane. In his own garden, Malan built a chapel of *Témoignage* (Witness) which was crowded with the followers of the *Réveil* (Awakening). His *Songs of Zion,* 1841, showed a wealth of resource, like that of Watts or Wesley.

In the name of William Gaskell (1805–1884), the poet here, the lovers of the older England, which is seen in so many delightful pages, are glad to discover that their surmise is true. Yes, he was Mrs. Gaskell's husband, and his experience makes her book *Cranford* even more real. For at the age of twenty-three, he went to preach at the Cross Street Unitarian Chapel in Manchester, and remained there as its minister for fifty-six years! He met Miss Stevens, who became Mrs. Gaskell, in a neighboring village, where lived the people whom we know so well from her bright and tender pages. Mr. Gaskell's hymns were among the Martineau Hymns of 1840, and he published a small collection of Temperance rhymes. This noble Unitarian hymn has excellent support in the music of Malan, who thought he opposed Unitarianism!

187 Tunbridge. *Mighty God, the First, the Last*

The words set to this tune of Jeremiah Clark's (see Note 94), in Playford's *Divine Companion,* 1701, were, "How uneasy are we here." The resounding tune has a better companion in William Gaskell's words. (See Note 186.)

188 Rockingham. *No eye hath seen, nor tongue declared*

Few of the tune names have more memorable associations than this one, given for Miller's friend and patron, Lord Rockingham, Prime Minister under George III. John Fiske, American historian, has written that "the advent of Lord Rockingham's ministry meant . . . the independence of the United States." George Washington and Cornwallis had met at Yorktown, Lord North had resigned his ministry, and so came into power the Rockingham group, "staunch friends of America, all of them" (*American Revolution* II, 289–90).

An interesting coincidence here is not alone in the inspiring hymn with its promise of freedom through the Word, but in the name of the poet, Elizabeth C. Adams, for we recall the influence an Adams had in shaping that generous treaty of 1782—namely, John Adams, later to become President of the United States. Burke, another friend of America, wrote of Rockingham, "A man worthy to be held in esteem because he did not live for himself."

Edward Miller (1731–1807) was for fifty-six years organist of the parish church at Doncaster. He had good literary attainments, as well as musical. The son of a stone mason, and brought up to that trade, he demanded music, and took himself off to London to become a student of Dr. Burney, and to play the flute in Handel's orchestra.

Miller worked for better music in the church and his *Psalms of David*, 1790, with tunes, was very popular. It was widely subscribed for, from King George down, and even in the Isle of Man, delighted Manxmen united to buy a barrel organ that played Miller's tunes.

Rockingham had unprecedented success. Miller found the idea for it in a tiny book, three inches long, drawn from Williams' *Universal Psalmodist*. The tune later became associated with Watts' lofty words:

> When I survey the wondrous cross
> On which the Prince of glory died,
> My richest gain I count but loss
> And pour contempt on all my pride.

189 Bohemian Hymn. *Mine eyes look toward the mountains*

This is one of the most familiar of the old tunes attributed to the Bohemian Brethren. It was sent to the Hymnal by the Swedish Christian Scientists, and is used in Sweden, as here, with Psalm 121.

At the museum in Prague is a worn copy of the first known hymn book, dated 1501. It was perhaps the work of the Bohemian Lucas. In 1467, certain Bohemian and Moravian reformers resolved together on separation from the Roman church. They all believed in the power of song, and at least three hymn books published in Prague antedated Luther's. In 1541, came John Horn's large collection, and in 1561, Bishop Blahoslav's great volume of 744 hymns. (See Note 378.)

190 Almsgiving. *My God, my Father, make me strong*

Frederic Mann, an English clergyman, made a most inspiring paraphrase of a familiar hymn by Charlotte Elliott (Note 67), in which her first stanza reads:

> My God, my Father, while I stray
> Far from my home on life's rough way,
> O, teach me from my heart to say,
> Thy will be done.

The poet's own account of his hymn is cited here through the kindness of A. W. Ridley and Company, London, owners of the copyright. He wrote:

"It has been remarked that this hymn 'My God, my Father, while I stray,' with the refrain 'Thy will be done,' contains no suggestion that

God could will other than our misery. We must admit that there is in that well-known composition a sacred tenderness of tone that may have brought to many sufferers an immense comfort in the thought of God as in some good way present in their sufferings. I have ventured . . . to adopt the general form of the hymn in order to present what appear to me truer views of the will of God as the direct source of the best and most joyous things in life. If these verses, though written for quiet thought, should be used for a hymn, the tune ought to contain no note of sadness, but rather a kind of marching, with the refrain 'Thy will be done,' recurring as a repeated cheer of victory."

Mr. Mann belonged to a family which originally came from the Isle of Man, whence the name. His father before him was a Wesleyan minister and missionary, and Frederic began as a Wesleyan preacher, but later joined the Church of England. After London University, he took the Archbishop of Canterbury's examination for his M. A. degree. Ordained at St. Albans, he became vicar of Temple Ewell, near Dover, where he remained till 1917. He was greatly beloved by the "shut-ins," to whom his visits meant sympathy and hope. He published *Poems of Hope and Vision.* This hymn was first used in *The Hymns We Sing at St. Martin's.* (For Dykes, see No. 169.)

191   Es ist kein Tag. *My God, my Father, make me strong*

This tune, "There is no day," is from *The Soul's Joy* of Johann Meyer, c. 1692. He was town councillor at Ulm.

192   Bethany. *Nearer, my God, to Thee*

This tune of Lowell Mason's (Note 2) deserves a place in the Hymnal that records the people's love and praise to God, if only because it has been the comfort of thousands whom loftier music might not have reached. It is doubtless the poem, more than the tune, that has had this mission to humanity. For the words of Sarah Flower Adams (1805–1848) are not likely to be outgrown until humanity has found itself indeed "nearer" to God. She was an English Unitarian, the daughter of Benjamin Flower, editor of *The Cambridge Intelligencer.* Robert Browning was a friend of the family, and spoke of Sarah as a wonderful woman.

The words were first published in Fox's *Hymns and Anthems,* 1841. They are based on Genesis 28:10–22.

193   Horbury. *Nearer, my God, to Thee*

Dykes's tune for this popular hymn is named for a church where he once held service during a visit to an old friend. He composed the tune then. (See Note 169.)

194 Contemplation (Consolation). *No mortal sense can still or stay*

This melody, by Beethoven, accompanying here the thought of silent prayer, is well named either Consolation or Contemplation. The words by Samuel Greenwood are from *The Christian Science Journal,* July, 1903. (See Notes 58, 422.)

Dr. Leo Rich Lewis, Professor of Music at Tufts College, Massachusetts, whose scholarly and sympathetic study of the revised Hymnal appeared in *The Christian Science Monitor* of August 29, 1932, was particularly impressed with this poem which he pronounced one of the book's very best, and added: "The term 'silent prayer' is a very familiar one to Christian Scientists; it will become more widely known to the public through this hymn, and in time they will come to love this wonderful embodiment of deep personal experience."

When on three occasions in presidential conventions a representative of this church was invited to act as chaplain in opening the session, the perfect silence followed by the repetition of the Lord's Prayer in unison was most impressive.

195 All Souls. *Not what I am, O Lord, but what Thou art*

Here is an excellent hymn tune, only one generation away from England, that stands as an American tune. For the composer was born in Portsmouth, Ohio, the son of an Englishman who belonged to that great order of English organists which has given so much to the treasures of hymnody. John Yoakley, the son, became a member of the American Guild of Organists, and was organist at the Church of the Advent and of Christ Church, Cincinnati, playing also for the A. A. Scottish Rite. His name appears on various pieces of church music. This tune is from *The English Hymnal,* 1906.

Like all Bonar's poetry, these words are said to have come out of actual spiritual experience, at a turn of the road. Here is a full outpouring of his deep-rooted faith. (See Note 21.)

196 Day of Rest. *Now is the time approaching*

Many of us, both sides of the sea, grew up with the old green Mother Goose book; her bright portrait on the cover, and within, fascinating pictures of the cat and the fiddle, or of Jumping Joan, or Simple Simon—all of them singing pretty songs we could sing, too. But the last place where we expected to be reminded of those joys was in the pages of a hymn book! Yet here they are, in the person of James W. Elliott, who wrote those tunes, for the sake of which that edition of Mother Goose was printed.

Mother Goose herself belonged to Boston, where her son-in-law, Thomas Fleet, printed her rhymes in 1719. Mr. Elliott (1833–1915) was for thirty-six years the organist of St. Mark's, Hamilton Terrace, London. Every visiting American might well make a pilgrimage to his church in gratitude for the happiness he has given to so many children.

The words used here, by Miss Borthwick, "When all shall dwell together," are well chosen for Elliott's music, Rest, in that children the world over have long been dwelling together in their common delight over Mr. Elliott's book. The old saying may be revised: "Let me make the songs of the *children,* and I care not who makes the laws." What promise of friendship there indeed is for the children all round this world, who are learning the songs of the *Christian Science Hymnal!*

197   Science. *Now sweeping down the years untold*

These words by Laura C. Nourse are from *The Christian Science Journal,* January, 1890. The poem, In Transitu, begins, "In vain I stretch my weary hope." This familiar melody is by Lyman Brackett (Note 154). Tune and words appeared in the first edition of the Hymnal, 1892, and have significance and beauty.

198   Wisdom. *Now sweeping down the years untold*

This setting by G. Thalben-Ball (Note 26) presents an interesting use of the downward scale.

199   Nun danket. *Now thank we all our God*

This tune is an excellent example of the Reformation chorale, although the arrangement is by Mendelssohn, and so of a later period. He arranged it for his *Song of Praise.*

The "chorale" was a form of the early Protestant hymn tunes, which were intended for congregational use. At first it was to be sung in unison. This explains its form. It had to be simple and strong, with a certain stately, resounding sweep so that the tune would flow broadly; and it had an even rhythm with few divided beats.

Gradually, as the people learned part-singing, the under parts were filled in, as simple harmony, that supported the treble melody or tune: unlike the old contrapuntal music, written for the choir, in which each of the voices (or parts) had its own melody or theme, all these weaving together.

Short songs in the people's speech were early used in German churches, and the Christmas mystery plays also used the people's songs. Sometimes folk tunes were adopted outright for the chorales; thus a chorale melody is seen to be essentially simple. It should not be sung too slowly.

After Luther and before Bach, the great composer of chorales was Johann Crüger (1598–1662), who made this music, which is named for its words. This tune with these words probably stands next to Ein' feste Burg in popularity, not only in Germany but elsewhere—as in the United States.

Crüger was cantor of the Cathedral Church, St. Nicholas, in Berlin, and founder of its famous choir. His *Praxis Pietatis Melica** (Lyric Practice of Piety), with fifty or sixty editions, was a great source of Lutheran hymnody.

Crüger's contemporary, Martin Rinkart (1586–1649), was author of the words, which begin like this English version. He was chorister and cantor before he became archdeacon at Eilenberg. This town was conspicuous during the war for religious liberty, and Rinkart gave unselfish devotion to his people. He was crowned as a poet as early as 1614; he was also a good musician.

The hymn appeared at first with the name Grace, or Little Prayer at Table. It is called the German *Te Deum* because of its constant use at national festivals. It has many English versions. The translator here is Miss Catherine Winkworth (1829–1878), who was first to bring German hymns into use in England. Her series of translations is known as the *Lyra Germanica*. She is also remembered for her interest in the advancement of women.

* This name goes back to the Greek word for "practice," defined in Liddell and Scott's *Lexicon,* as "opposed to *pathos,* suffering."

200   Swanage. *O daughter of Zion*

This is an old hymn, believed to be of American origin, which was especially loved by Mary Baker Eddy. It appeared anonymously in the Fitzgerald collection of 1830, and in Mason and Greene's *Church Psalmody,* in 1831 (Boston).

In *The First Church of Christ, Scientist, and Miscellany,* Mrs. Eddy devotes the whole of Chapter V to the Christian Science Hall, in Concord, New Hampshire, the pleasant city, on the borders of which she so long made her home. The story of the preparation of this hall for the use of Christian Scientists is told in *The Christian Science Journal* (Vol. XV, p. 589). It stood on the site of the present church edifice, at State and School Streets. A two-story dwelling was there, the upper story of which was thrown into a single room, or hall, that seated two hundred people. The reading room was on the lower floor.

In the windows of the hall were designs in glass, one a cross and crown, another the open Bible, others the star and the anchor. On the wall was the first stanza of this hymn:

> Daughter of Zion! awake from thy sadness,
>   Awake! for thy foes shall oppress thee no more;
> Bright o'er the hills dawns the day-star of gladness,
>   Arise! for the night of thy sorrow is o'er.

262

The hymn was sent for use in the revised *Christian Science Hymnal* by a member of Mrs. Eddy's former household, who said that she had requested the use of these words on the walls of the hall. In the reading room of the Concord Church hangs an illuminated quotation of the first two lines of this hymn, which was formerly in Mrs. Eddy's room in the church. For the Hymnal, slight changes were made to suit the music.

In the address read from Mrs. Eddy at the second Sunday service in the hall (*The First Church of Christ, Scientist, and Miscellany*, p. 147), she said: "Over a half century ago, between the morning and afternoon services of the First Congregational Church, the grand old elm on North State Street flung its foliage in kindly shelter over my childhood's Sunday noons. And now, at this distant day, I have provided for you a modest hall, in which to assemble as a sort of Christian Science kindergarten for teaching the 'new tongue' of the gospel with 'signs following,' of which St. Mark prophesies."

On page 126 of *Miscellaneous Writings* she writes: "God hath indeed smiled on my church,—this daughter of Zion."

This excellent melody was especially written for the hymn by E. N. Greenwood (Note 28).

201 St. George. *O do not bar your mind*

Talented boys probably like pocket money as well as the others do; but even under the spur of cates and comfits, only a very precocious boy could have done what is told of Henry Gauntlett (1805–1876). His father, Vicar at Olney, promised the boy a farthing for every Psalm tune he would copy out; and within ten days he brought in a thousand! Then the Vicar asked his people to buy an organ. "Who will play it?" they asked. He assured them that he would provide an organist. The organ installed, young Henry, nine years old, was presented, tested, and formally appointed. When he was only fifteen, he arranged and carried through a performance of the Messiah, to celebrate the accession of George IV. This boy advanced in musical scholarship until the Archbishop of Canterbury gave him the first degree of Doctor of Music conferred from that source in two hundred years. In 1851, Dr. Gauntlett even took out a patent for applying magnetic power to the organ.

In spite of his talent, he was educated as a lawyer and succeeded in that calling. But he worked with Canon Havergal (Note 44) as a pioneer in modern hymnody, in which few have had more influence than Dr. Gauntlett. They brought out their *Comprehensive Tune Book*, 1846, and soon their *Church Hymn and Tune Book*, which included this tune, St. George. The words are by Charles Parsons, and appeared in *The Christian Science Journal* for November, 1888, and in the first edition of the Hymnal, 1892.

202 Ancient of Days. *O dreamer, leave thy dreams for joyful waking*

This tune of Horatio Parker's (Note 20) shows how music may affect words. Here the assurance and bright promise of the words are most in evidence; as the music at No. 412 brings out, in the same words, their love and tenderness.

203 Firmament. *O Father, may we bear each hour*

Here is an example of the clean-cut form of Davies' melody (Note 159). After the repetition, on the first page, comes progression of tonal figures, in the first two lines of the second page, with the climax note immediately echoed an octave lower, to give varied interest and firm-knit unity. The clear, strong words are by Lewie Prittie Castellain, a Christian Scientist.

204 Thy Kingdom Come. *O Father, Thy kingdom is come upon earth*

That a poet and musician should find time to become also a highly honored political minister is indeed proof of power. Gunnar Wennerberg (1817–1901) was all of these, and, in addition, a teacher. He was a singer, and composed, for tenor, baritone, and bass, the Merry Trios, which were specially popular, but his Gluntarna (The Boys), thirty duets for baritone and bass, spread his fame. He received the Karl Johan prize from the Swedish Academy for "songs too well known to need further testimonials." Thus was a prophet honored in his own country.

He taught in the public school at Skara, and in 1860 was called to the Ministry of Public Worship and Education, in Stockholm; later, in his capacity as Minister for Education, he worked for the advancement of women. He was for thirteen years Lieutenant-Governor of Kronoberg, and also a member of Parliament.

His musical style differed from the music of his time. It was vivid, had sentiment and clear form, and captivated everybody. He wrote the words for his songs, which have brightness and charm. He set many of the Psalms; and these melodies, rather in the style of Handel, are used not only in Sweden but in Germany, Scotland, and America. He wrote four oratorios, and his works fill four volumes. He was a strong Lutheran, and in talk with a Swedish nobleman, who had been converted to an older faith, he cried: "What does it matter whether you are happy? Go home and know and confess your sin!" A statue to him by Karl Eldh was unveiled in Minneapolis, Minnesota, in 1915, a gift to the city from the American Association of Swedish Musicians. It stands in Minnehaha Park.

The poet here, Karolina Vilhelmina Berg, née Sandell (1832–1903), was born in the county of Jönköping, the daughter of a well-known preacher, Jonas Sandell. She became the wife of the Roumanian Consul-General in Sweden, who was a speaker on temperance and publisher of religious magazines, to which she contributed. She published *Tales for the Sunday School,* and two volumes of collected songs. The song here is used in the new Swedish Hymn Book with this melody. It is a missionary hymn, and was rewritten in English verse, modified for the sake of the music, and also with reference to the work of Christian Science lecturers. The Swedish words on the page are Mrs. Berg's, "Thy kingdom come."

205 Belmont. *O for a faith that will not shrink*

This would seem to be a tune with a various past. It has been charged to Mozart, to Samuel Webbe, to his son, to a popular song, and all the while Gardiner was claiming it as his own, in his *Music and Friends.* It is apparently an adaptation from a tune in his *Sacred Melodies,* and is found in several arrangements. Later Thalben-Ball (Note 26) joined the train and made a notable arrangement of a well-tested tune.

William H. Bathurst (1796–1877), the poet here, was born near Bristol, and was rector of a parish near Leeds. He retired because he could not fully accept the Book of Common Prayer. This hymn's deep consecration speaks his sincerity. In *Prayers and Hymns for Church and Home,* Boston, 1867, this is credited to "Bath Collection," a name that has been used in America, mistakenly, for it is only an abbreviation of Mr. Bathurst's name!

These words, entitled The Power of Faith, appeared in the poet's *Psalms and Hymns,* 1830, Leeds, England.

206 Newcastle. *O God, our Father-Mother, Love*

The composer, Henry L. Morley, has escaped the research of hymnodists, and is known only as an organist who resigned from St. Paul's Church, Herne Hill, London, in 1883, and came to America. The words, waking thought to clear consciousness of reality, were written specially for the Hymnal, by Duncan Sinclair.

207 Morecambe. *O gentle presence*

This melody so long published anonymously was composed by Frederick C. Atkinson (1841–1897), an organist at Norwich Cathedral, England. It was arranged for these words, in 1910, by Albert F. Conant, who, we are told, made the ascending phrase for the words "on upward wing to-night," at the request of Mrs. Eddy. (See Note 24.)

208 Benediction (Ellers). *O gentle presence*

Benediction is an excellent name for a tune used with these words of Mary Baker Eddy, that are indeed a blessing to those who sing them. The tune was much loved in the past century, when music of this type, by English composers, gave a new incentive to congregational singing. Dr. Edward J. Hopkins (1818–1901) was trained as a child of the Chapel Royal, and early played in services at Westminster Abbey. He was long the organist of the famous Temple Church in London, where he raised the music to so high an excellence that the church has ever since been a place of pilgrimage for music lovers, for the serious beauty and power of its musical services.

Dr. Hopkins was born at Westminster, and, except for a few early years, worked in London all his days. This tune was given by him in 1869 to the *Brown-Borthwick Tune Book for Unison Singing*. Dr. Hopkins was an editor of *Hymns Ancient and Modern*, of the 1877 Wesleyan Hymnal, and others. He published a *Temple Choral Service Book*. Dr. James Moffatt cites of him these words: "His music is hallowed with a devotional fervor which lifts it into a region not far removed from the perfection of sanctified art."

209 Expectation. *O gentle presence*

Next to the interest and delight in new hymns by Mary Baker Eddy, the friendly appreciations of the revised Hymnal seem most to stress the sense of Christian unity in the book. They say that it is as if the world had united to praise God. This follows not only from the use of traditional melodies chosen from fifteen different countries, but from the spirit of brotherhood and oneness that is everywhere expressed in the hymns.

This unity is seen in the use, with this great hymn by Mrs. Eddy, of a Danish melody, chosen from the Norwegian *Chorale Book*. The music is by Andreas P. Berggreen (1801–1880), a Danish composer whose music expresses the devotion and beauty of the words almost as if it had been written for them. The Danish words begin, "Think when once the mists of earth have vanished," and the first three words are used on the page to identify the music, after the European custom.

New interest in Scandinavian art awoke, early in the last century, and the heart of it was found in the work of Berggreen, in Denmark. He studied folk music constantly, and made the first large collection of Danish Folk Songs. He was a pupil of Weyse and of Gade, and worked especially to organize singing, in school and in church, with the use of native music. His own work is clearly marked by this folk quality, which is felt in the present melody, with its clear vocal beauty. Born in Copenhagen, he was organist at Trinitatis Church there, and in 1853 published a chorale book.

210 Limpsfield. *O gentle presence*

The name of this tune is given, like Ophelia's rosemary, "for remembrance," and the story is especially touching in connection with this great poem by Mary Baker Eddy, which sings that "loss is gain." The music

266

was composed for an English collection, named *Laus Deo,* made to celebrate the peace of 1918. Dr. Walford Davies (now Sir Walford: Note 159) was a major in the British Air Force, and was made editor of this book of thanksgiving. Andrew Freeman, a pupil of Davies, and then organist at Lambeth Church, was assistant editor.

Major Davies one day rejected a tune offered for the hymn, "O valiant hearts;" and so, riding home on the bus that night, the young organist composed this tune for the words, and offered it next day, anonymously. Major Davies accepted it, and it was named for the home of two brothers, musical friends of Dr. Freeman, who, he says, had "joined up in the first month or so of the war," and fell, most valiantly. Dr. Freeman is now resident at Standish Vicarage, Stonehouse, Gloucester.

211   Presence. *O gentle presence*

For this noble hymn by Mary Baker Eddy, we have here music printed without bars. It was written for the hymn by Percy Whitlock, who sought to express the beauty and meaning of these words, without imposing any technical barrier to their free and right utterance. Large congregations sing it easily, because they know the words so well.

It was a pianist who said, "For the first time, I got outside bars!" He meant that for the first time he had played the music as a continuous whole, not thinking of it as cut up into separate bits called measures. For the musical singer, bars do not exist. So, in the early days of spontaneous song, the notes were set down without bars or time signatures.

Sidney Lanier, famous poet of the southern states of the Union, was also a musician. His important book, *The Science of English Verse,* shows that the effort to govern English verse by the rules of Latin and French verse never succeeded. English poetry has long been "out of bars." This is one secret of its supreme beauty.

To show the relation of word-reading with the reading of music, we may observe that in books to teach the meter of verse, the words or syllables are separated by the same short vertical lines that appear in music as "bars." These show the "feet" in the word-lines, which correspond to measures in music. Efforts to make music-reading a little less mechanical are indicated in the Hymnal in a few instances and encourage a more musical sense of music.

The English composer, Percy Whitlock, began his musical work as chorister of Rochester Cathedral, where he was afterward assistant organist. He held the Kent scholarship at the Royal College of Music, London, for four years, and studied under Vaughan Williams, Gustav Holst, and other eminent composers, having a particularly brilliant college career. Later he became organist and choirmaster at St. Stephen's, Bournemouth. His published compositions include church music and pieces for organ.

212 Song 22. *O gentle presence*

Orlando Gibbons' Song 22 is named by many musicians the most beautiful of the settings for Mrs. Eddy's Mother's Evening Prayer. The words used with this music in Wither's Hymn Book (see Note 69) began, "O Lord of Hosts and God of Israel."

213 St. Anne. *O God, our help in ages past*

This noble old tune, with all the dignity of a chorale, appeared with Psalm 42 in the Supplement to Tate and Brady's new version of the Psalter, in 1708. Dr. Croft (Note 52) worked on the book when he was organist at St. Anne's, Soho, and in Hart's *Melodies Proper to be sung to the Psalms of David*, 1720, the tune is credited to him. The first section is note for note like a tune in George Sandys' Psalter, 1638, with music by Henry Lawes (Grove).

For Isaac Watts, see Note 62.

214 Angelus. *O God, whose presence glows in all*

The name of this tune links it with a far-off past; for Angelus Silesius was the pen name of Johann Scheffler (1624–1677), for whose hymns Georg Joseph used to compose music. Joseph was a court musician, in Breslau. The music in its present form appears in *Spiritual Songs*, Munich, 1847. Two sources are given for the music—Johann Angelo Silesio and Georgio Josepho's *Holy Delight of the Soul*, 1657, and Braun's *Echo of Celestial Hymnody*, 1675.

The poet, Nathaniel L. Frothingham (1793–1870), born in Boston and educated at Harvard, was pastor of First Church, Unitarian, from 1815 to 1850, and then for twenty years more an attendant there. His *Metrical Pieces* was published in 1855. This hymn was written for the ordination of W. B. Lunt, who was later pastor of the Quincy Unitarian Church. Frothingham's son, Octavius Brooks Frothingham, was known as a leader of the Free Religious movement.

215 Caithness. *O happy is the man who hears*

Caithness is from the Scottish Psalter of 1635, and is named for the northeastern county of Scotland. This Psalter was first printed in 1564, and based on Crespin's Anglo-Genevan Psalter (Note 107), enlarged and much improved. The "Paraphrase" of 1650, the version still used in Scotland, was praised as striking a golden mean between the homeliness of the old version and the "artificial modernism" of the new—that of Tate and Brady. One of the most famous Scottish Psalter versions is Old Hundredth by William Kethe (Note 1), which ends:

> His truth at all times firmly stood
> And shall from age to age endure.

Michael Bruce (1746–1767), the hymnist here, is a rather romantic figure, for the young poet of Kinrosshire, passing on before he was twenty-one, was a center of much literary discussion. John Logan, of Midlothian, had been interested in Michael's poetry, and offered to attend to having it published, so the papers left by the boy were put into Logan's hands. In time they reappeared in print, under the name of Logan—or so the friends of Michael declared. Julian compares various data, and is certain that the words used here are by Michael Bruce, though often attributed to Logan. This is a right Scottish hymn, with both words and music native to the land.

216 Neumark. *O he who trusts in God's protection*

We rarely find a hymn with both words and music by one writer, as here. Luther's is the only other example in the Hymnal. Georg Neumark's story illustrates the wanderings of students in old days, which song and story often describe. Neumark (1621–1681) was the son of a clothier, in Thuringia. Finishing school in Gotha, he went with a party of merchants to the Michaelmas Fair at Leipzig. Thence he started out for Königsberg University, but the party was attacked by highwaymen, who took all that Neumark had, except his prayer book and a little money sewed into his clothing. He wandered from town to town, looking for work, and almost despairing, found a friend at last in a pastor at Kiel, who recommended him to a post as tutor. This sudden end of his troubles prompted the writing of this hymn. He said: "This coming so suddenly as if from the skies, greatly rejoiced me, and on that very day I composed this hymn in honor of our beloved Lord." That these words and music have so long been valued is proof of their inherent beauty and the gratitude which inspired them.

After more adventures Neumark returned home, where the Duke of Saxe-Weimar was president of the "Fruit-bearing Society," the chief German literary union. The Duke made Neumark his court poet and secretary of the Ducal Archives.

Bach used both words and music of this hymn in a cantata, "If thou but suffer God to guide thee," and has made five arrangements of the music. When Neumark wrote the music for the poem he named it a hymn "of consolation, that God will care for His own in His own time, after the saying, Cast thy burden on the Lord, Psalms 55:22." Mendelssohn has the melody in his St. Paul with "To Thee, O Lord, I yield my spirit." The version here was specially made for the Hymnal.

217 Seccomb. *O, he whom Jesus loved has truly spoken*

This composer, Charles H. Morse (1853–1927), of Bradford, Massachusetts, was a thoroughgoing American. He was a graduate of the New England Conservatory of Music, a piano pupil of Perabo and of Carl

269

Baermann, the German pianist who did so much, so long, for Boston students; and a pupil in composition of Whiting, and of Paine, who later directed the music school at Harvard. Morse learned conducting with Carl Zerrahn, another famous German of Boston, who was so long conductor of the Handel and Haydn Society.

Morse began teaching in the Conservatory and went on with his studies at the Boston University till, in 1876, he won the first degree of Bachelor of Music ever given in the United States. He was long organist at Tremont Temple in Boston, and the first director of music at Wellesley, one of the largest American colleges for women. Then he was called to organize the new Northwestern Conservatory at Minneapolis, Minnesota, and returned to be organist at Plymouth Church, Brooklyn, New York. Not satisfied with these various "firsts," he now became the first professor of music at Dartmouth College. He was one of the first Americans to play the works of Guilmant, and to produce the choral works of Gounod. He was editor of the *Plymouth Hymnal*, 1893, with Lyman Abbot. In all this, we see an American musician at work, much in demand for scholarship, and also for the faculty of getting things done.

The words are from Whittier's poem, Worship (Note 49), which is headed by the passage defining "pure religion and undefiled," James 1:27.

218 Missionary Chant. *O Life that maketh all things new*

This is one of the famous tunes of American hymnody, used three times in the *Harvard University Hymn Book* of 1926. In its name of "Chant," it is clear that the repeated notes take on something of the nature of a chanted strain, without the loss of regular rhythm.

Its composer, Heinrich Christoph Zeuner (1795–1857), was a native of Saxony, who came to the United States early in the last century, and did much for American music. He tells this story: He was sitting on a bench on Boston Common on a most beautiful moonlight night, all alone, when suddenly this music flowed to his thought, and he literally ran home, to get it down on paper. He was at the time organist for Park Street Church and for the Handel and Haydn Society (Note 352), but later went to Philadelphia. Of his oratorio, The Feast of the Tabernacles, only one copy remains, which is in the Congressional Library, at Washington. This tune appeared in his collection, *The American Harp*, 1832.

This poem, perhaps the greatest hymn of a great American hymnist, Samuel Longfellow (Note 134), was written for the Festival of the Free Religious Association, held in Boston, in 1874. It appears in *The Unitarian Faith set forth in Fifty Unitarian Hymns* (Boston), under the heading, "Unitarians affirm the freedom of the truth, and the constant renewal and expansion of religious thought and life," with a reference to II Corinthians 3:17, "Where the Spirit of the Lord is, there is liberty."

219 Affection. *O Life that maketh all things new*

This melody is by John Greenwood, a musician and teacher in Leeds. His *Psalmody Harmonized in score, with accompaniment of organ and piano,* appeared in Halifax, England, in 1838.

220 Lansdowne. *O Life that maketh all things new*

This joyous music was composed by E. N. Greenwood for these favorite words. (See Note 28.)

221 St. Hilda. *O Jesus, our dear Master*

This long-popular tune has sometimes been attributed to E. Husband, an English composer, who only arranged Knecht's melody. Justin H. Knecht (1752–1817), born at Biberach, Württemberg, studied under Krämer and with Schmidt of Esslingen. He was music director at Biberach and at Stuttgart. In 1799, he edited, with J. F. Christmann, the *Württemberg Chorale Book,* with ninety-seven tunes of his own, including this. The earnest, loving words were written for the music by Margaret Glenn Matters, a Christian Scientist.

St. Hilda was founder of the old abbey of Whitby, 657, where were developed the poetic gifts of Caedmon, whose high praise is that he "began, first in time, and among the first in genius, the strain of English poetry" (Morley).

222 St. Louis. *O little town of Bethlehem*

This carol is especially welcome to the revised *Christian Science Hymnal,* as a link with the well beloved Phillips Brooks (1835–1893), who was the most celebrated contemporary of Mary Baker Eddy during her foundational work in Boston.

The biography by Bishop Lawrence, Brooks' successor, begins with the moment when Phillips Brooks, a young man of twenty, six feet four inches tall, rushed out of the President's House at Harvard, with a white face of despair. He saw himself a failure! After his Harvard Commencement he had tried teaching in the Boston Latin School, but, unable to control the boys, he had resigned. He who was to be an honored speaker in Westminster Abbey wrote, "I have failed myself most signally in teaching school, but I am not yet quite ready to acknowledge myself wholly unequal to all this wide world's work."

At his mother's wish, he now took his first communion, and we see her leading her "gigantic, bashful boy" up the aisle. Soon we find him at Commencement at the Alexandria Divinity School (1859), saying in his thesis, "This new Christian simplicity is not perfect until it recognizes the world's hope in its own."

He was called at once to the Church of the Advent, Philadelphia, and when, in 1865, the nation mourned Abraham Lincoln, Brooks' eloquent obituary sermon was published. He spent Christmas, 1865, at Bethlehem, in Palestine, and two years later Lewis H. Redner, organist of Trinity, Philadelphia, urged him to write a Christmas carol, saying, "We will call it St. Philip." But Brooks replied, "You must write the music, and we will call it St. Louis." And so we have this carol with its familiar music.

In 1869, Boston called Brooks home to Trinity Church, where he preached until 1891, when he was made Bishop of Massachusetts. Of his moving eloquence we read, "As the rush of words, thought and conviction gained increasing force, one could almost hear the walls of tradition and orthodoxy fall down." His concept of prayer is memorable. He said that prayer is not conquering God's reluctance, but availing ourselves of His willingness.

223   Christmas Carol.   *O little town of Bethlehem*

The exquisite melody given here was composed by Sir Walford Davies (Note 159) for these much-loved words, and appeared in Horder's *Worship Song*, 1905. William G. Horder was a Congregational minister of England, who compiled several collections of hymns, including *The Treasury of American Sacred Song*, 1896. He was the first to use part of Lowell's The Present Crisis as a hymn (Note 258).

224   St. Leonard.   *O Lord, I would delight in Thee*

John Ryland (1753–1825), the writer here, was ordained as co-pastor with his father at Northampton, England, then became president of the Baptist college at Broadmead, Bristol, and was pastor of the church there for thirty years. Some of his hymns were written when he was only sixteen years old. Of this one, dated 1777, he said, "I recollect deeper feelings of mind in composing this hymn than perhaps I ever felt in any other."

The music is by Henry Hiles (1826–1904), who was born at Shrewsbury, England, and was organist there and elsewhere until he went to St. Paul's, Manchester. Here he was also professor in certain schools and colleges. His works include The Crusaders and other vocal music, a *Grammar of Music* and similar books.

225   Yattendon 15.   *O Lord, I would delight in Thee*

In tracing the threads of fact and fancy with which the hymns of the people are woven into the fascinating fabric we call history, we find how the early hymnists depended on the Bible. The famous Christopher Tye, for example (1497–1572), perhaps striving for something more dramatic than Psalms, chose the Acts of the Apostles and put fourteen chapters into meter; he then set them to music, and had them "imprynted at London, by William Seres, dwellynge at the sygne of the Hedghogge, 1553." They were soon sung in the chapel of Edward VI, whose music master Dr. Tye had been.

Tye was so much valued by Henry VIII that in Rowley's play of that name, Dr. Tye has a place, and the Prince is made to say to him:

> Oft have I heard my father merrily speake
> In your hye praise and thus his Highnesse sayth:
> "England one God, one truth, one Doctor hath
> For music's art, and that is Doctor Tye."

After the dissolution of the monasteries, music owed its recovery largely to Dr. Tye. He was probably also music master to the two princesses who succeeded Edward on the throne, and was surely organist to Elizabeth. The venerable teacher was privileged, and when her Majesty sent him word that he had played out of tune, he retorted: "Tell her Majesty that her ear is out of tune."

To his Acts is traced a first crude form of two famous hymn tunes, found in our Hymnal: Windsor (107) and Winchester Old (122).

Even more incongruous than Tye's use of the Acts were other experiments of that time: as, a metrical version of the Genealogies, and *Hunnis's Hyve full of Hunny,* with the First Book of Moses, and Merbecke's *History of King David,* from Samuel. The songs of Moses, of Deborah, Hannah, and Habakkuk were versified and sung; also parts of Proverbs, Ecclesiastes, etc.

Tye's tune, with its abundance of grouped eighth notes, is a reminder of the grace and fluency of music in that Elizabethan age, which saw English music and poetry both at their height. This music was arranged by H. E. Wooldridge, professor of fine arts at Oxford, and author of two volumes of the *Oxford History of Music.* It is the fifteenth tune in *The Yattendon Hymnal* (1899), a collection which added to the fame of Robert Bridges, poet laureate from 1913 to 1930.

Dr. Bridges began his life work as a physician, and then settled down to literary work at Yattendon, Berkshire, where, deeply interested in congregational singing, he directed the singing in the parish church. He wanted better music—words adapted to the tunes, tunes arranged not for the organ, but for unaccompanied singing. Professor Wooldridge was his associate in preparing his hymnal, that uses specially beautiful type and paper, and has rescued much neglected music.

226   Ellacombe. *O Lord of life, to Thee we lift*

This excellent tune, from the *Mainz Hymn Book* of 1833, edited by L. Hartig, is an example of balance of phrases—as statement, repetition, then contrast and restatement. The divided beats (eighth notes, or quavers) insure variety and fluency. This hymn of gratitude is by the American, Washington Gladden, a Congregational minister and editor of the nineteenth century (Note 234).

227 Hursley. *O Lord, where'er Thy people meet*

These words are from Cowper's poem headed, Opening of a place of worship. They are interesting for their illustration of the unconscious citation of another writer's work, that often befalls close students and readers. The line, "And bring all heaven before our eyes," is borrowed from Milton's Il Penseroso, where, near the end, we read, "And bring all Heaven before mine eyes." (See Note 313.)

The tune name, for the parish where Keble was so long vicar, was probably given when the music was set to his hymn, "Sun of my soul." This form of the tune (see Note 88) is found in Schicht's *Chorale Book*, 1819, "for churches, schools, singing societies and piano and organ players." The first known chorale book, dated 1586, had only fifty tunes. Schicht's has twelve hundred of these fine old melodies; nearly three hundred are his own work.

John G. Schicht (1753–1832) stood high as cantor and church composer at the old Thomas School, in Leipzig, where Bach had reigned so long; and he edited the Motets of Bach. (For *motet,* see Note 272.)

228 Mendon. *O Love divine, that dwells serene*

This is one of the fine old melodies that come from unknown German sources. Its first appearance in the United States was as German Air, in Samuel Dyer's *Sacred Music*. In the next edition he dropped a note from each line, and said, "It is believed that this is the original form." This form is used here. The name Mendon was probably given by Lowell Mason (Note 2).

Samuel Dyer (1785–1835) was born in England, and came to New York in 1811, as choir leader and teacher, removing soon to Philadelphia, where he was made leader of the new oratorio society. In 1815, he visited London and brought back new music, now settling in Baltimore, where he published his *Sacred Music*. He traveled from Savannah, Georgia, to Salem, Massachusetts, to introduce his book, teaching singing schools, and striving to improve church music.

The poem, by William P. McKenzie, is named The Secret Joy, in *Heartsease Hymns,* published in Cambridge, Massachusetts. The loving consecration of the words finds expression in the lovely melody.

229 Constancy. *O Love divine, whose constant beam*

This melody is from the allegretto of Mendelssohn's fourth organ sonata (Note 118). The words are from Whittier's long poem, *The Shadow and the Light,* prefaced by words of St. Augustine: "Where is evil . . . since God, the Good, has created all things? . . . And I beheld that Thou madest all things good, and to Thee is nothing whatsoever evil . . . and Thou never departest from us." A slight change in the last line of each stanza, here, fits the words to the music, using stanzas 18, 20, 22, 23. (See Note 49.)

230 Simpson. *O Love, O Life, our faith and sight*

For Spohr's music, see Note 51. The words are from Whittier's poem, Our Master, stanzas 24, 26, 28, 34 (Note 49).

231 Radlett. *O Love, O Life, our faith and sight*

This inspiring music was composed by E. N. Greenwood for these words. (See Note 28.)

232 Hampstead. *O Love, our Mother, ever near*

This is a beautiful melody, which admirably suits the reverent words, written for it by Margaret Glenn Matters. They illustrate a definition in the Glossary of *Science and Health with Key to the Scriptures,* by Mary Baker Eddy: "MOTHER. God; divine and eternal Principle; Life, Truth, and Love" (p. 592). This is probably the first hymn that has directly addressed divine Love as Mother, though Waterston, long ago, sang of Truth with the feminine pronouns. (See Note 337.) The composer, Sir Walford Davies, gave special permission for the use of this music with these words.

233 Das walt' Gott. *O Love whose perfect path is known*

Daniel Vetter was Bach's predecessor at the St. Nicholas Church in Leipzig. Bach often used the tunes of his predecessors in Leipzig, as here, and in No. 80, Eisenach. Vetter was born in Breslau, Silesia. His collection, *Musical Delight of Church and Home,* appeared in 1713. The tune is named for a poem to which it was set by Vetter, beginning "May God grant," by Martin Behm. The beautiful poem used here is by Robert Ellis Key, a Christian Scientist.

234 Maryton. *O Master, let me walk with thee*

Concerning H. Percy Smith (1825–1898), one incident thrills the reader of *Water Babies* and of *Westward Ho.* For after graduating at Oxford, Smith was curate at Eversley, under Charles Kingsley. Then he became perpetual curate at York Town in Surrey, and at last was chaplain in Cannes, and Canon of Gibraltar. This tune was written for *Church Hymns with Tunes,* 1874.

Washington Gladden (1836–1918), author of these words, chose Maryton as the tune which should always be sung with this, his most popular hymn. He was born at Pottsgrove, Pennsylvania, was educated at

Williams College, and entered the Congregational ministry. He was long the editor of the New York *Independent* and of *Sunday Afternoon,* in which this hymn appeared, 1879. In 1882 he became pastor of the First Congregational Church in Columbus, Ohio.

235 Brockham. *O Master, let me walk with thee*

Jeremiah Clark (Note 94) has here a simple tune, with his usual melodic charm. It appeared in Playford's *Divine Companion,* 1709. It is also called Confidence, a name that suits the trustful words. Gladden elsewhere writes:

> When the anchors that faith had cast
> Are dragging in the gale,
> I am quietly holding fast
> To the things that cannot fail.

236 Hanover. *O peace of the world*

For a great tune of long traditions, no better theme could have been chosen than this noble song of peace, written by Irving C. Tomlinson. The music was attributed to Handel, because it became popular when Handel was in England. It was actually the work of Croft (Note 52), and named in honor of the newly enthroned House of Hanover. It appeared with St. Anne and St. Matthew in the Tate and Brady *Supplement,* of 1708. In 1742, *The Foundery Tune Book* published it as Bromswick, also in compliment to the reigning house. The Foundery was a building near Moorfield, which had been used for casting cannon. Wesley bought it, in 1739, and turned it into the first Methodist Meeting House, and this is another right association for this hymn of peace, that sings of shaping guns into "tillers of soil." In Wilkins' *Book of Psalmody,* 1699, the tune was credited to Dr. Croft. (See Wesleyan Hymnal, 1877, Dr. Hopkins, editor.)

237 Carol Melody. *O may we be still and seek Him*

The carols, so long typical of England, for all church festivals, seem to have harked back to the old ring-dance, from which the word carol derives: as Italian, *carola,* a ring-dance. (See also Webster.) Chaucer writes of the caroling, in his day, thus:

> What ladies fayrest ben, or best dancing
> Or which of 'hem can carole best or sing.

The "fayre ladies" may have danced and sung to tunes like this, which belongs to their fourteenth century. (See Notes 184, 242.) The happy words are by Fay Linn, a Christian Scientist. The tune was first printed in Triller's *Booklet,* Breslau, 1555.

238 Germany (Fulda). *O, sometimes gleams upon our sight*

Gardiner's *Sacred Melodies* included this tune, attributed to Beethoven, but not traced to him. Recalling how much the *Sacred Melodies* were used in America, it is interesting to know that among Beethoven's notebooks it is written: "Buhler notes the Oratorio for Boston. I cannot write what I should best like to write." The Handel and Haydn Society of Boston wrote to ask for a new work by the great master, which marks the town as even then keeping abreast of its times in music, as it does today. The words are from Whittier's long poem, The Chapel of the Hermits, using stanzas 11, 12, 18, and 94. The lines,

> Through the harsh noises of our day,
> A low sweet prelude finds its way;

are followed by this stanza, especially interesting to Christian Scientists,

> That song of Love, now low and far,
> Ere long shall swell from star to star!
> That light, the breaking day, which tips
> The golden-spired Apocalypse.

This poem presents Rousseau and Bernardin de St. Pierre as meeting to talk of their life experience (Note 49).

239 St. Gregory. *O, sometimes gleams upon our sight*

This tune is from König's *Harmonious Song Treasury* (Note 44), and set by Monk (Note 7). The *Church Hymnary Hand Book* gives the theme in a more florid form, and in ¾ time, as in the *New Helicon with its Nine Muses,* Nuremberg, 1684. There it was set to a hymn by Christian Knorr, editor of the book, who was created Baron von Rosenroth by Emperor Leopold for his oriental scholarship. He may have composed the tune.

240 Thatcher. *O Spirit, source of light*

The tune is paraphrased from the aria, "Rendi 'l sereno al ciglio" in the opera, "Sosarme," by Georg Friedrich Handel, first performed at King's Theatre, London, in 1732. The original tune is also used in a religious song entitled "Lord, remember David." The words are by Benjamin Beddome (1717–1795), who was born in Warwickshire, the son of a Baptist minister. At twenty-five, he began to preach at Bourton-on-the-water, Gloucestershire, where, despite calls to London or elsewhere, he remained for more than fifty years, the beloved pastor of his flock. Beddome's chief popularity as a hymnist has been in America, and in 1770 he was given an honorary degree by Rhode Island College, Providence, now Brown University. He wrote a hymn every week, with no idea of publishing. The poems were first in print in 1817, to the number of eight hundred and thirty. Some of them were gathered from among his faithful congregation.

241 St. Edmund. *O Spirit, source of light*

This composer, Edmund Gilding, passed on in London, in 1782. He was organist of St. Martin's and of St. Edmund-the-King, when he contributed to Riley's *Parochial Harmony*, 1762. The name lends added interest to this tune, for King Eadmund of East Anglia, bound to a tree and shot with arrows by the Northmen, in 868, became the St. Sebastian of England. The Abbey of St. Edmundsbury perpetuates his memory.

242 Capel. *O, still in accents sweet and strong*

This music is called an English Traditional Carol Melody, because it is a true folk song, found in use among the people. These simple dancing songs were often sung to celebrate Christmas or Easter, and so today the word usually means "a popular song or ballad of religious joy."

The music appears in *English Traditional Songs and Carols*, collected chiefly in Sussex and Surrey, by Lucy E. Broadwood. Perhaps the most interesting contributors were the gypsies who tramped in the neighborhood of Horsham and Dorking. A family named Goby gave the melody which appears here. They sang it to words of a very old and quaint Christmas Carol that tells the miracle of the "seedless harvest," which happened in the flight into Egypt. It begins, "King Pharaoh sat a-musing."

The gypsies used the name "King Pharaoh" instead of "Herod," because they believed themselves Egyptians, with Pharaoh for king. In an Arabic Gospel of the Infancy, we read: "Thence they (Joseph, Mary and Jesus) went down to Memphis and having seen Pharaoh they staid three years in Egypt; and the Lord Jesus wrought many miracles in Egypt."

The following words illustrate well the naïveté and charm of the true Christmas Carol, and the words used with all these old melodies:

> They traveled further and further
> The weather being so warm,
> Till they came unto a husbandman
> A-sowing of his corn.
>
> "Come, husbandman!" cried Jesus,
> "Throw all your seed away,
> And carry home as ripened corn
> That you have sowed this day;
>
> "For to keep your wife and family
> From sorrow, grief and pain
> And keep Christ in remembrance
> Till seed-time comes again."

This story of the Instantaneous Harvest appears in the Apocryphal Gospels.

278

The music is named Capel, from a village near Dorking, where gypsies gathered, and which was named in turn for the chapel—*capella*—maintained there by the parish of Dorking.

For Samuel Longfellow, the poet, see Note 134.

243   Ombersley.   *O sweet and tender as the dawn*

The composer of Ombersley was the son of the famous Prime Minister. The son, William H. Gladstone (1840–1891), was born at Hawarden, the estate which he was to inherit from his mother's family. He gave many years to the House of Commons. He was a fine Greek and Latin scholar, a good singer, and able musician. An excellent organist, he was especially interested in the music of the English church, and Sir Walter Parratt said of the hymnal compiled by Gladstone that it was the only one he knew that had no bad tunes.

The melodious words, "O sweet and tender as the dawn," are by Ella A. Stone, a Christian Scientist, and are suited to the melodious tune.

244   Hesperus.   *O sweet and tender as the dawn*

Henry Baker (1835–1910) was the son of Rev. James Baker, chancellor of the diocese of Durham, and so he came naturally by his interest in church music. He was a civil engineer by profession, in India. Then Dr. Dykes encouraged him to work for a degree in music at Oxford, 1867. He contributed this tune to *Gray's Hymnal,* 1866.

245   Homeland.   *O tender, loving Shepherd*

Homeland, the first hymn tune composed by Sir Arthur Sullivan, was set to words, The Homeland, in *Good Words,* 1867, when Sullivan was organist at St. Michael's, London.

The words were written by Frederic W. Root, for the 1910 Hymnal. They are among the most lovely of the many songs drawn from the Twenty-third Psalm, and are suited to the music, even to its very name.

246   Valerius.   *O Thou who spreadest the heaven like a tent*

This tune, named for himself, and Protection (Note 292), were chosen by Valerius, poet of patriotism, from the traditional folk songs of the Netherlands, for use with words of prayer and praise. This was during the long struggle, led by William of Orange, that liberated the Low Countries from the rule of Spain.

It was fitting that the American historian, Motley, should write a great book on this famous patriotic effort. Not alone the city of New York (once New Amsterdam), and the state (once New Netherland), but the whole of the United States owes much to the fact that the first fifty years of the colony (1614–1664) were under Dutch control. The roll of Dutch-American names deriving from those days ranges from

279

Schuyler of Saratoga, to Roosevelt, marking two Presidents. These, with the debt which all religious liberty owes for Dutch hospitality in Leyden to the English Pilgrims, are fitly commemorated by the use of these hymns in the *Christian Science Hymnal.*

This hymn was used by Valerius to celebrate an event of 1585. Elizabeth of England had sent Leicester to the Netherlands with an army, intending to help the Dutch. The modern editor of the song says that Valerius' joyful poem was a prophecy of the deliverance which was at last to be God-given, and not the gift of human help. Valerius used verses from Isaiah 40, beginning with the image of the tent in verse 22. The true name of Valerius was Adriaan Wouterssohn (Walter's son).

247   St. Leonard.   *O walk with God along the road*

Of Henry Smart (Note 42) it may be mentioned that he was a believer in good congregational singing and liked unison. His hymn tunes are clear and fine, and his best work, such as his Service in F, is of a high order. He was especially interested in organ building, and set up the organ in St. Andrews Hall, Glasgow, after he had lost his eyesight. This tune was contributed to *Psalms and Hymns for Divine Worship,* 1867.

Thomas Hornblower Gill (1819–1906) was born near Birmingham, of a Presbyterian family, that had become Unitarians. Perhaps through his studies with Dr. Jeune, afterward Bishop of Peterborough, Gill's hereditary Unitarianism had been discarded, yet he was unable to enter Oxford, because in those days students were required to subscribe to the Articles of the English church.

Gill thus came to live a solitary life of theological study, which gives the key to his hymns. He shows the religious devoutness of his Puritan ancestry, the ethical earnestness of the Unitarians, and his own poetic gift. His solitary habit may be seen in the unconventionality of his style. It was James Freeman Clarke, the great American Unitarian, who named Gill "a more intellectual Charles Wesley." His hymns have sweetness and a certain quaintness of phrase, and are mainly used by English Nonconformists. They first appeared in his *Golden Chain of Praise,* 1869, and another volume of hymns was named *Luther's Birthday.* So the glimpses we have of the experience of a poet like Gill again stress the wide scope of hymnody, which gathers thus into one volume the recorded faith, hope, and love of so many earnest men and women, each worthy, whatever the creed, to be called, with Abraham, a friend of God.

248   St. Hugh.   *O walk with God along the road*

St. Hugh is another old English melody, with divided beats to give movement to the tune. It is from an air sung to the ballad of St. Hugh of Lincoln.

The story is found in Chaucer's Prioress' Tale.

249   Berno.   *O, when we see God's mercy*

This composer, Arthur H. Mann (1850–1929), began as a chorister in Norwich Cathedral, sometimes helping at the organ. After work at Beverley Minster, he was organist for King's College, Cambridge, and then for the Univeristy. He edited the Tallis Motet, written for forty voices, was an authority on Handel, and music editor of *The Church of England Hymnal*, 1895. This excellent hymn was written by Vivian Burnett, a Christian Scientist.

250   Wolvercote.   *O, when we see God's mercy*

William Harold Ferguson, the composer here, was ordained in 1902, became assistant master at St. Edward's School, Oxford, and after working elsewhere, returned to St. Edward's as Warden. In 1925, he went as Warden to Radley College. With Geoffrey Shaw he was music editor of *The Public School Hymn Book*, for which this tune was composed. It is a well-planned tune, that finishes with a repetition of its delightful first phrases.

251   Bentley.   *O Word of God, most holy*

Singing classes in London, attended by thousands, were Hullah's chief claim to fame. He is described as a personality of great charm, much loved by his many students. He used the fixed *Doh*, an idea he had adopted during his study in Paris. John Pyke Hullah (1812–1884) is also remembered for having written the music for a libretto, The Village Coquettes, given him by a certain young Charles Dickens. Hullah published a history, and various "grammars," of music, and Edinburgh University gave him a degree, in 1876. He was also an honorary member of the St. Cecilia Academy at Rome.

The poet, Bishop William Walsham How (1823–1897), is recalled as a man of a "genial humanity" which attracted men high and low, and made him familiarly known in London as "the poor man's bishop." He had no worldly ambitions, and twice refused more important distinctions than those to which his work led him. Rector of Whittington, he was made honorary canon of St. Asaph, in 1860, and then suffragan bishop for East London, and, in 1888, Bishop of Wakefield. He was an unceasing worker, making every moment count, by a rigid system he imposed on himself. He had engraved on his pastoral staff the words of St. Bernard: "Feed with the word; feed with the life."

Bishop How is the author of various important works, and has about sixty hymns in common use. His poetic style is direct and clear, giving warmth to the sort of detail not often touched by poetry, as the present hymn illustrates. The original first line is, "O Word of God Incarnate." It was published in the Supplement to Morell and How's *Psalms and Hymns*, 1867.

252 Herzlich thut mich verlangen. *O Word of God, most holy*

The love and aspiration, the solace for human hearts, that gather round the old chorales, are nowhere more manifest than in the story of this tune. Its name, "My heart is filled with longing," is from a hymn by Christoph Knoll, written for the comfort of his neighbors during an epidemic of 1599. It was sung to the music of a popular madrigal by Hans Hassler (1564–1612), an organist in Augsburg and Nuremberg. The hymn prevailed in favor over the love song, until in Crüger's *Praxis* (Note 199) the poet Paul Gerhardt used the tune for his Passiontide Hymn from Latin words of about the year 1150, translated, "Hail, thou head ensanguined."

Bach used this hymn of Gerhardt's, both words and music, five times in his St. Matthew Passion (Acts 1:3), and put the melody into his Christmas Oratorio, first to foreshadow what was to come to the Child, and at the close to promise the victory of the Christ. This use, by the greatest master of sacred song, gives this music high authority. Bishop How's hymn offers a significant parallel with the Latin hymn, for those who see the Crucifixion as the proof of "Christ, the living Word."

If we knew of Bach only the words he chose for the Matthew Passion music, we should know him well. His librettos may sometimes seem crude, but they speak the simple devotion which finds God not far from any one of us. Here is the heart of the Protestant idea, to which Bach's mighty genius was consecrated. His music had been almost forgotten, however, when the young Felix Mendelssohn again brought the Matthew Passion to light in a performance of 1829, just one hundred years after its first hearing. Soon after this, Bach's works began to be collected by the Bach Society in the first complete edition, for which music lovers are profoundly grateful. (See Note 14.)

253 Pleasant Street. *O'er waiting harpstrings of the mind*

This music was set to Mrs. Eddy's Christ My Refuge, at her request, in 1905, by William Lyman Johnson, a Christian Scientist. The name is a reminder of the home which she loved so well, on Pleasant Street, Concord, New Hampshire.

254 Norton. *O'er waiting harpstrings of the mind*

This tune was written for Mrs. Eddy's hymn, which was used in the first edition of the *Christian Science Hymnal,* 1892.

255 Refuge. *O'er waiting harpstrings of the mind*

Percy Buck's music (Note 4) is chosen, because it may be used to follow closely the words, by Mrs. Eddy, so that they may be sung almost as they would be read. The phrase, "with free rhythm," and the double time signature, are aids to this free expression.

256 Oldown. *O'er waiting harpstrings of the mind*

The reserve and simplicity that mark the music of Dr. Basil Harwood may be seen in this music, which applies itself so well to the words of Mrs. Eddy. As organist and composer of church music, he served in Ely Cathedral, and at Christ Church Cathedral, Oxford, where he was conductor of the Oxford Bach Choir, choragus of the University, and editor of *The Oxford Hymn Book*, 1908. His works for organ are important, and his Pæon was played by Sir Walter Parratt at the reopening of the organ at York Minster. Oldown was composed for *The Public School Hymn Book*, 1919.

Because this hymn has seven stanzas, the second half of the melody is repeated for stanza five (5), as the numbers show.

257 Oblation. *O'er waiting harpstrings of the mind*

Though there are no time signatures in this setting of Mrs. Eddy's hymn by Mr. Whitlock (Note 211), the alternation of 4-pulse (or beat), with 3-pulse phrases is easily followed with the eye. This freedom of rhythm gives leisure to utter the words with their own expressive beauty.

By the arrangement of the stanzas here, the first three are sung from the first page, before the second page is begun.

258 Ton-y-Botel. *Oft to every man and nation*

James Russell Lowell (1819–1891) is one of the men of vision who have lifted a standard for the people, and he clearly has a place in the great company of those that publish the Word. Mrs. Eddy's appreciation is shown by the lines she cites (*Miscellaneous Writings*, p. 368) from his inspiring poem, The Present Crisis, from which this hymn comes. The "Crisis" was the question between the North and South, in 1844, as to the admission of Texas to the American Union as a slave state.

The first arrangement of Lowell's words for a hymn was made by an English Congregationalist, W. G. Horder, in 1876. In 1906, the words appeared in *The English Hymnal*, then in the English *Songs of Praise*, and more recently in the Episcopal Hymnal, published in Boston, in different arrangements. The tune Ton-y-Botel is used with the words in two of these books, and is a favorite hymn at Yale University.

In view of Lowell's work, as American Minister to England, to cement the enduring friendship between the two nations, this union of a favorite British tune with his words is a happy one.

Beside the far-famed Biglow Papers—with their New England dialect, and their keen yet kindly satire—his greatest poem, among many beautiful things, is the Ode recited at the Harvard Commemoration, July 21, 1865. This has the moving tribute to Abraham Lincoln and those final lines of love for his country "O Beautiful! my Country! ours once more."

Of Ton-y-Botel, tradition says that a Welsh sailor made the melody and, facing shipwreck, jotted it on a slip of paper, which he sealed in a bottle and tossed into the sea. The bottle came ashore in Wales, and the rescued tune was named Ton-y-Botel, "tune in a bottle." *The Church Hymnary Handbook,* however, names the tune Ebenezer, and credits it to T. J. Williams, born in 1869, in Glamorganshire, Wales.

The legend has a different guise in Alfred de Vigny's great poem, The Bottle from the Sea. Henning says of this, that "the bottle represents discovery . . . the sea, the world. Whatever else may perish, thought is imperishable." Vigny's own explanation is: "God is the God of ideas. . . . Gathering fruitage, in holy solitude, let us throw our work to the sea of the multitudes. God will convey it to port." This seems to speak Mrs. Eddy's own assurance concerning her "offering pure of Love" (No. 253).

The peculiarity of this tune is in the triplets. These are not difficult, when the slight stress on the first of each three notes is remembered. The tune should be sung with a marching steadiness, and not too slowly.

259   Galilee. *One cup of healing oil and wine*

The music here is by Philip Armes (1836–1908), who began as a chorister in Norwich, England, and then sang in Rochester Cathedral, so delightfully that the dean and chapter made him a gift of a grand piano! He was later installed as organist at Durham Cathedral, and was much honored and loved in that city. He composed oratorios, church services, and hymn tunes. Galilee was written for *Hymns Ancient and Modern,* 1875.

The poem is by William H. Drummond (1772–1856), who was born at Ballyclare, Antrim, Ireland, and educated at Glasgow for the ministry. He was pastor of the Second Presbyterian Church in Belfast, and of the Strand Chapel, Dublin. The hymn is from his book, *Who are the Happy?,* a poem on the Beatitudes, 1818.

260   Fingal. *One thought I have, my ample creed*

Fingal, with its breath of the sea, is a delightful name for a tune. This one appeared in *The Scottish Hymnal,* 1885. James S. Anderson, the composer, was born at Crail, Fifeshire, 1853, and after study in Edinburgh, worked with Dr. Peace at Glasgow. He was called to various posts as organist in Edinburgh, and contributed to many hymnals. This hymn, by Frederick Hosmer (Note 57), gave its title to his collection, *The Thought of God in Hymns and Poems.*

When fifty hymns were published by the Unitarian Association in Boston, as representative of that denomination, twenty-eight poets were included in the book. Nearly one-quarter of the poems, however, were

284

from a single poet. These were the twelve chosen from Dr. Hosmer. Samuel Longfellow and Dr. Holmes stood next, but with only four each (Note 218).

261 Nox praecessit. *One holy church of God appears*

The Latin name of this tune, "Night has gone before," refers to words for which it was composed in *The Christian Hymnal*, 1873—"Bride of the Lamb, awake!" John Baptiste Calkin (1827–1905), the composer, was born in London, and learned music from his father. He became organist at St. Columba's College, Ireland, and then played at various London churches, while he was professor at the Guildhall School and at Croydon Conservatory.

These words are one of the strongest hymns of Samuel Longfellow, expressing alike the breadth and depth of thought that distinguished him (Note 134).

262 Song 67. *One holy church of God appears*

This is a chorale-like melody, simple and strong, by Gibbons (Note 69). The long note at the start gives the proper importance to the word "one."

263 Gladness. *Only God can bring us gladness*

The name of this hymn, "Gladness without God is not found," is the first line of its Swedish words, by Johann Olof Wallin (1779–1839), Archbishop at Upsala. Tegnér, the great Swedish poet, named Wallin "the David's harp of the North." In the *Psalm Book* of 1819 a total of two hundred and sixty-five hymns have Wallin's name, one hundred and twenty-eight original, the rest translated or adapted. He was much interested in the music, too, and the finished work was in use for more than one hundred years.

Wallin was a man of the people, born in Dalecarlia, of poor parents. He rose step by step, vicar at Solna, rector in Stockholm, dean at Westerås, pastor primarius in Stockholm, dean of the Orders, chief court chaplain, Archbishop, and pro-chancellor. He was a member of most of the Academies, and was awarded the highest prize ever given by the Swedish Academy, for his tribute to Gustavus III. The people came to know him as their "greatly renowned preacher, orator and poet." His hymns were "unsurpassed in scope of their subjects and in their solemn elevation of tone." And yet there is a Swedish folk song quality in them that attests their simple sincerity. Of his other poems, one to George Washington deserves mention for its "glowing enthusiasm."

He was much concerned for education. A training home-school, the Hill school, and the Wallin school, were his work. Of his preaching it was said that he was a greater poet in prose than in verse. His poetry shows the dual nature of northern genius—melancholy, and a vivid enthusiasm. The version of his words used here was made from a literal translation into English, with certain necessary emendations.

The composer of the music, Gustav Düben (1624–1690), belonged to the famous Swedish family in which the post of master of the court chapel at Stockholm was hereditary for three generations. The library at the famous university at Upsala contains the Düben collection of music. The family kept up close relations with the composers of northern Germany, visiting them and copying the music that pleased them, as was the fashion in the days when Bach used to write out countless pages of other people's manuscript, as well as his own.

This music has an exceptionally lovely, flowing melody, with a naïve folk song quality suited to the words.

264 St. Gertrude. *Onward, Christian soldiers*

The first singing of Onward, Christian Soldiers was promise of its long use as a processional hymn by earnest youthful voices. Sabine Baring-Gould published the words in *The Church Times* (England), in 1865. A few years after, Arthur Sullivan was visiting friends in an old house that had its private chapel, where Sunday services were held for the household. Here Sullivan set these stirring words to music which he named, for his hostess, St. Gertrude. The hymn was practiced by the children of the family for the coming Sunday. They begged to sing one verse alone, and to make their own choice. On Sunday the composer sat at the little harmonium in the chapel, behind a curtain, and could hardly restrain his laughter when the childish voices piped up alone, singing valiantly, "Like a mighty army"!

No one who was growing up in the last years of the ninteenth century forgets the absorbed delight with which everybody heard Pinafore, Patience, The Mikado, and the rest, whose tunes and Gilbert's tripping verses are still as household words.

Arthur Seymour Sullivan (1842–1900) published his first anthem at the age of thirteen. At twenty, he composed music for Shakespeare's Tempest. The tune St. Gertrude was first published in 1872. His oratorio, The Golden Legend, uses the words of Longfellow. Others are his Prodigal Son and Light of the World. He was knighted in 1883.

Sabine Baring-Gould (1834–1924) was an English clergyman and writer, whose *Lives of the Saints* fill fifteen volumes. He was much interested in English and French folk lore and songs. (See Notes 60, 351.)

265 Stuttgart. *Onward, Christian, though the region*

The Sacred Psalmody, 1715, was compiled by Christian F. Witt (1660–1716), court organist at Gotha, who is sometimes credited with the authorship of this tune. The words are by the American, Samuel

Johnson (Note 37). His first line is, "Onward, onward, though the region." For the second stanza he wrote, "By the thorn road and no other," . . . "Tread it without shrinking, brother." These changes illustrate the trend of Christian Science thought.

Johnson, it has been said, was the most unfaltering and consistent of the group so deeply influenced by the teachings of Ralph Waldo Emerson. The last line of this hymn places him in close fellowship with those who know that love is of God.

266 Martyrdom (Avon). *Our God is Love, and all His sons*

Hugh Wilson (1766–1824) was born in Fenwick, Ayrshire, Scotland, where he learned the shoemaking trade, with his father. In his spare time, he studied mathematics and made sundials, besides leading the singing in the local church and teaching music to the villagers. He finally rose to a place of responsibility in the mills of William Dunn, at Duntochter, where he helped found the first Sabbath school. The tune Martrydom was printed on slips for the use of his music classes, but in 4/4 time. It appeared in Smith's hymnal for St. George's Church, Edinburgh, in the year 1825.

This example of the short and simple annals of the poor, hints the reward of plain fidelity. For this humble workingman, who did with all his heart whatever he had to do, is now printed here along with the scholars and divines and titled persons, who, as kings of the earth, do also bring their honors into the holy place of Christian hymnody.

The words "Our God is Love," appeared in *Selections of Psalms and Hymns*, 1819, made by Thomas Cotterill (1779–1823). He was son of a woolstapler in Staffordshire, and a graduate and Fellow of Cambridge. He held the incumbency of Lane End, Staffordshire, and then became perpetual curate of St. Paul's, Sheffield. His volume of *Family Prayers* reached six editions. Many of the edited changes, or "readings," found in popular hymns, are from Cotterill's *Selections*.

267 Moseley. *Our God is All-in-all*

This hymn was used in the first edition of the Hymnal, 1892. In *The Christian Science Journal*, March, 1890, this poem by Emily F. Seal appeared in eleven stanzas, signed Kathleen. For the composer, Henry Smart, see Note 42.

268 Quam dilecta. *Our God is All-in-all*

This music, named "How Beloved," is by Henry Lascelles Jenner (1820–1898), who was born at Chiselhurst, Kent, and educated at Harrow and Cambridge. Vicar of Preston-next-Wingham, near Sandwich, Kent, he was made the first bishop of Dunedin, New Zealand, but soon returned to Preston, resigning his bishopric. The tune was written for *Hymns Ancient and Modern,* 1861.

The words which gave the name to the tune were Dean Bullock's "We love the place, O God," written in 1827 for the dedication of a church at Trinity Bay, Newfoundland.

269   Haydn. *Our God is Love, unchanging Love*

Haydn's name refers us to Notes 71, 170, 185, for his story. Here may be recalled the amusing incident connected with William Gardiner (Note 105). Amateur of music, he was also a stocking manufacturer; so when Haydn visited England, Gardiner gave him a pair of hose, with the opening notes of the Austrian Hymn woven into them. The words here are one of the fine hymns written for the 1910 edition of the Hymnal, by Frederic W. Root, a Christian Scientist.

270   Kingsfold. *Our God is Love, unchanging Love*

This is a Traditional melody, with the earmarks of the English folk music, wherein a minor may express good cheer. It was popularly known as the Red Barn. It appeared in *The English Hymnal,* 1906.

271   Gonfalon Royal. *Our God shall reign where'er the sun*

This is one of the best examples of Watts' Psalms. The wide use of this hymn began with the growth of foreign missions. It was sung when certain South Sea islands exchanged a heathen form of government for one based on Christianity, in 1862, and dusky chiefs and warriors sat with their King George, amid a thousand natives of Tonga, Fiji, and Samoa.

The work of Dr. Buck is described in Note 4, but we may add here that earlier he was organist at Wells and then at Bristol Cathedral, and professor of music at Trinity College, Dublin, besides lecturing at Glasgow University. This tune was written for *The Public School Hymn Book,* 1919.

A gonfalon, a small flag hung horizontally, is sometimes used as an ecclesiastical banner.

272   Tallis' Canon. *Our God shall reign where'er the sun*

Thomas Tallis (1510–1585) is sometimes called the father of English cathedral music, though his associate Byrd was also very active in music of that time. Tallis appears to have been a gentleman of the Chapel Royal, under Henry VIII, Edward VI and Mary, and its master under Elizabeth.

This tune is a canon, that is, a strict "imitation," in which a second voice takes up the first melody and repeats it. Here, in the tenor, at the words "where'er the sun," this echo of the soprano melody begins, and continues to their uniting at the close. A popular "round," such as "Row, row, row your boat," illustrates the canon form, which may use two or several voices.

Of Tallis it is said that "the difficulties of music were to him as child's play." His greatest composition is a motet arranged for forty voices, in eight choirs of five parts each. Moffatt cites an opinion that this is "probably the noblest achievement of the English nation in sacred music." (A motet is unaccompanied vocal music, in which each voice-part has its own melody, set to sacred words.)

273   St. Bees. *Partners of a glorious hope*

These words of Wesley's (Note 105) were selected by an unknown editor, from a poem of one hundred and twenty-eight lines and four parts, in *A Collection of Hymns for the use of the People called Methodists,* as the Wesleyan Hymnal was still called, in 1877. This shows the composite nature of much good hymnody, where lines rearranged may make, as here, an excellent hymn. For Dykes, see Note 169. St. Bees appeared in Chope's *Congregational Hymn and Tune Book,* 1892. In 1816 St. Bees College was founded on the coast of Cumberland and named for a nunnery started there in 650. There is a reference to it in Scott's *Ivanhoe.*

274   Vienna. *Partners of a glorious hope*

For the composer of this tune, Justin Knecht, see Note 221. The music is found in his collection of Chorales, 1799.

275   Crusader's Hymn. *Praise now creative Mind*

Tradition clings round this hymn, with its splendid stride of pilgrims ranged for a long march. It was believed to have been sung by Germans on their way to the Holy Land, in the crusades of the twelfth century; but it was found among Silesian haymakers. The words used with this tune were Fairest Lord Jesus, which are found in the *Münster Hymn Book* of 1677. In *Silesian Folksongs,* Leipzig, 1842, both words and tune are said to have been taken down "from oral recitation," in the district of Glaz. Liszt used the melody in his oratorio, St. Elizabeth, and in a note he thanks Herr Cantor Gottschlag for "the old pilgrim song that probably dates from the time of crusades."

The newly discovered tune was adopted, in England, by Dr. Gauntlett, under the name Askelon (for a Crusaders' victory there), and in 1850 Richard S. Willis arranged it for his Church Chorals, in the form used here. Willis was a graduate of Yale University, who entered the field of American journalism. He wrote three books on music and contributed to R. G. White's *National Hymns,* 1861.

Whatever the source, the music has the "feel" of a group that goes forward, with a lofty purpose held steadily in view. The famous Bach Choir, of Bethlehem, Pennsylvania, one of the greatest choral bodies for the singing of Bach, uses the Crusader's Hymn in an impressive way. Before public performances, the people are summoned by the sound of this melody, as well as Bach chorales, played by sixteen trombones, placed high in the tower of the church where the Bach Festival is held.

As early as 1743, a "singing" was held in Bethlehem, a Moravian settlement, which thus linked the New World with the old Hussite hymn singing (Note 378). None who are concerned for the beauty of church music and of congregational singing can fail to value the work of this people's chorus, developed by Frederick Wolle, in that town, amid the woods of William Penn. So all strong hearts that have wrought for "pure religion and undefiled" are knit into the ever-widening circle of Christian worship.

The words here used for the Crusader's Hymn, specially written by William P. McKenzie, suit themselves to the melody in a true union of the type long ago called music "married to immortal verse."

276 Beecher. *Peace be to this congregation*

With a celebrated American name, this tune is by a German, who for thirty years played the organ in Beecher's Plymouth Church, in Brooklyn, New York. John Zundel (1815–1882) was born in Mecklenburg, and was trained both as violinst and organist. After seven years in Russia, he migrated to New York, where he rose to high repute as organist and musician. These words, by Charles Wesley, are an example of his generous use of his gifts. They originally began, "Peace be to this *habitation,*" and were written for friends whose house he had visited. (See Note 105.)

277 Bethany. *Peace be to this congregation*

This tune of Henry Smart's was composed for Lyte's "Jesus, I my cross have taken," and is thus sometimes called Crucifer. It appeared in *Psalms and Tunes for Divine Worship,* in 1867 (Note 42).

278 Wallog. *Pilgrim on earth, home and heaven are within thee*

Wallog is a small place near Aberystwyth, the university town, in Wales. For Sir Walford Davies, the composer, see Note 159. The words here are one of the mysteries of hymnody. They appeared in a collection by Bishop Ryle, *Songs for the Church on Earth* (about 1875), without other signature than P. M. The preface of the collection states that most of the hymns are "modern," i. e., of that period. Peter Maurice was writing in that decade, and is known to have signed always P. M., but no further trace of this particular hymn is found. The words have been largely adapted for the *Christian Science Hymnal*. For example, the first line originally read, "Pilgrim on earth that art journeying to heaven," and the last line of this stanza was, "Art thou discouraged because of the way?" Maurice was an English clergyman, editor of *The Choral Hymn Book*, 1861.

279 Lime Street. *Pilgrim on earth, home and heaven are within thee*

Geoffrey Shaw, the composer, was educated at St. Paul's Cathedral School and at Cambridge, and began early to work for better church music, and also to promote musical education for the people, reviving interest in good music, everywhere. He was an editor of *The Public School Hymn Book*, and came to be one of His Majesty's Inspectors of Music, for the Board of Education, London.

This music is interesting for its changes from minor to major, particularly in the unexpected major chord at the close.

280 Lauda anima. *Praise, my soul, the King of heaven*

Sir John Goss (1800–1880) began as a child of the Chapel Royal, then sang for a time in opera, and then succeeded his beloved teacher, Attwood, as organist of St. Paul's Cathedral. He was knighted in 1872. His anthem, O Saviour of the world, is praised as "the most natural, purely written, and expressive" of all anthems, and is compared with Mozart's last work, a sacred motet. Goss never began writing an anthem without asking a blessing on his work, and he meant each one to be "a sermon in music." St. Paul's has a cenotaph to his memory.

This tune, Praise, my soul, was composed for these words of Lyte's (Note 8). It appeared in the Brown-Borthwick *Hymn and Tune Book*, 1869. It is here reharmonized by G. Thalben-Ball (Note 26).

281 Mooz Zur. *Praise our great and gracious Lord*

To students of the Bible there are few things more interesting than to discover among the Hebrew people of today the customs that reflect what is found in the Book of books. For example, in John 10:22 we read, "And it was at Jerusalem the feast of the dedication, and it was winter." There is delight in learning that this feast of the dedication still comes to the synagogue and to the homes as the Chanuka ("Hanukka," Webster), or festival of lights. The feast celebrates the new kindling of sacred lamps at the altar set up by Judas Maccabæus, 165 B. C., when he triumphed over the hosts of the Syrians who had profaned the temple at Jerusalem with idolatry.

Mooz Zur (Rock of Ages) is the tune which for perhaps four hundred years has been used during this festival of lights. The tune is not

291

Hebraic in origin, yet, in his *Jewish Music,* Idelsohn says that the chorale, Now Rejoice, and the old German battle hymn, Benzenauer, undoubtedly entered the Ghetto and there were "fused in the mind of some Jewish singers as the joyous theme of the victory of the Maccabees." This tune, so derived, was given the name of the Hebrew words to which it was sung. The words are traced back to a Mordecai of the fourteenth century. Idelsohn's *Jewish Song Book* translates the German version, by Leopold Stein, in part as follows:

> Rock of Ages, let our song praise Thy saving power;
> Thou amid the raging foes wast our sheltering tower. . . .
> Kindling new the holy lamps, priests approved in suffering
> Purified the nation's shrine, brought to God their offering.

This music has surely an appropriate place among the songs of another people who today are striving to keep their lamps "trimmed and burning."

Again, when we read that both Mooz Zur and Leoni (Note 371) are listed among the "Ashkenazic" songs, we turn to Genesis 10:3, and read there the name "Ashkenaz" which medieval lore gave to ancient Germany. The name is still applied to the Jews of Germany and to other north European groups, and also to their descendants in America and elsewhere.

The chorale which is said to have furnished the first half and the close of Mooz Zur is in turn traced to a simple German folk song that charmingly begins, "I know what pleases me; the little flower on the wide heath."

We see here how popular songs could develop into good hymn tunes. Hardly a stronger, statelier tune appears in the Hymnal than this which began as a song about a little flower!

The words used here were chosen because their joyous, confident mood is like the Hebraic words. They were slightly altered to fit the music. The poet is Harriet Auber (1773–1862), granddaughter of Pierre Aubert, a French Huguenot, who fled to England at the revocation of the Edict of Nantes. She is best known for her rarely beautiful hymn, Our blest Redeemer, based on John 14:16–26. She is also remembered for a character of singular beauty and charm, and for her long friendship with Miss Mary McKenzie, a writer on the Parables and Miracles.

282   Sursum voces. *Praise the Lord, ye heavens, adore Him*

These words, long marked "Author Unknown," have an interesting history. Based on Psalm 148, their authorship "has been a matter of serious inquiry for some years," as Julian notes. They were found, unsigned, on a broadsheet pasted into the back of the 1796 and 1801 editions of the Foundling Hospital collection of hymns, made specially for children of this asylum. Their carefully trained singing attracted crowds, and Handel took great interest in them, giving annually a performance of The Messiah in their chapel. This hymn, as Julian indicates, is a traditional favorite in English-speaking countries.

Sursum Voces (Let us Lift our Voices) is by H. Elliott Button (1861–1925), who is remembered as having been an excellent singer. He was also a good violinist and is said to have read music before he could read words. His chief work was done for Novello, the London music publishing house in which he served for forty years. He was an editor of *The Bristol Tune Book.*

283 Praise. *Praise we the Lord*

When the revised Hymnal was in preparation, a letter was sent by The Christian Science Board of Directors to all the churches of the denomination in Europe, asking for words and music for the Hymnal. There were some duplications in the offerings, and one hymn was sent in from five countries. This is "Praise we the Lord," with the noble chorale named Praise the Lord.

The original words, by Joachim Neander, were taken from Psalms 103 and 150, and appeared in 1680 in *Alpha and Omega . . . Neander's Practice of Faith and Love.* Neander adapted to his words this music from the *Stralsund Hymn Book* of 1665. Bach used the music in a cantata for the Feast of St. Stephen in 1740. But the words of Neander have been associated with it since 1680. The translation here was specially made for the *Christian Science Hymnal.*

Neander (1650–1680), born in Bremen, was called the Psalmist of the New Covenant, from his overflowing sense of the goodness of God. Neander was the Greek form of his name Neuman. His sudden conversion and his later trend to Pietism made his brief career significant. He lived for a time, a recluse, in a cave that is still called by his name.

284 Beatitudo. *Prayer is the heart's sincere desire*

This much-loved tune by Dr. Dykes (Note 169) is especially suited to the Prayer of Montgomery (Note 83). It was composed for other words, *Hymns Ancient and Modern,* 1875.

285 Prayer. *Prayer is the heart's sincere desire*

Here is an excellent expression in modern music of these familiar words, by E. N. Greenwood (Note 28). The tune is melodious and simple.

286 Cheshire. *Prayer is the heart's sincere desire*

For the first time in the story of hymnody, we find in Este's Psalter of 1592 (Note 122), tunes with a name of their own. Cheshire was one of three thus honored. It gives an example of a changed time signature. The adapter is Charles Wood (Note 103).

287 Nun danket all. *Prayer with our waking thought ascends*

The tune (Let All Thank) is from Crüger's *Praxis* (Note 199). In the fourth and tenth measures it gains a crisp effect by starting the line on the second beat. The brave and confident words suit the clean-cut tune. They are by Edith Gaddis Brewer.

288 Valete. *Press on, dear traveler, press thou on*

Sir Arthur Sullivan (Note 264) used this tune in *Church Hymns with Tunes,* 1874, for the hymn "Sweet Saviour, bless us ere we go," whence its name, Farewell. The words, written by M. Bettie Bell, appeared in *The Christian Science Journal,* April, 1886, and were used in the first edition of the Hymnal, 1892.

289 Yattendon 12. *Press on, dear traveler, press thou on*

The name of this tune is explained in the fact that it is the twelfth song in *The Yattendon Hymnal* (Note 225). It is an old English melody found in Smith and Prelleur's *Harmonious Companion,* 1732. Pierre Prelleur was a French musician, who appeared in London early in the eighteenth century, as organist, accompanist, and composer.

290 Church Triumphant. *Press on, press on, ye sons of light*

For James W. Elliott, the composer, see Note 196, and for William Gaskell, Note 186. The words here are well represented by the title of this joyous tune.

291 Paschal. *Quiet, Lord, my froward heart*

Paschal is a word from the Hebrew *pesakh,* meaning passover, and is applied to Easter. The Norwegian words on the page mean "Easter Morning quenches sorrow," and are from the hymn used with the tune in Norway. The English words show in John Newton (Note 71) the humble and loving nature that made this sturdy sailor the friend and rescuer of desperate men. For Lindeman, the composer, see Note 84.

292 Protection. *Put on the whole armor of pure consecration*

This music, with the traditional words, is known as the Dutch Prayer of Thanksgiving. The English words, used widely in the United States, begin, "We gather together to ask the Lord's blessing." Later we find:

> So from the beginning the fight we were winning,
> Thou, Lord, wast at our side, let the glory be Thine.

The words by Maria Louise Baum repeat, as closely as may be, passages from Ephesians 6:11–17 and I Chronicles 29:11, which give the idea of Protection, the name used here for this splendid tune.

History knows no more valiant years than are commemorated in the original words of this patriotic song. They take us to 1597, when special days of prayer were set apart to celebrate the final assurance of liberty that followed upon the victory of Prince Maurice, younger son of William of Orange. (See also Notes 98 and 246.) This music must not be sung too slowly. As in many tunes that have folk song origins, the beat of a deliberate dance or march may be felt in this. The best congregational singing relies on rhythm that is well-marked, in order to hold the many voices together.

293 Toplady. *Rock of Ages, Truth divine*

This is one of the hymns that have a definite incident connected with their origin, as Augustus Toplady himself relates. He was one day caught in a heavy thunderstorm, when tramping through the Mendips of Somerset. He reached a rocky glen in the heart of these hills, and apparently in the heart of the storm. A crag one hundred feet high was there, with a deep fissure. Into this shelter he entered, and waiting for the storm to pass, he wrote the hymn which has been sung all round the world. The words first appeared in *The Gospel Magazine,* 1776. The critic, George Saintsbury, calls this a "really great poem."

Visitors to the Mendips are still taken to see the cleft in the rock where the hymn was written.

The son of a British officer who fell at Cartagena, Toplady (1740–1778) was for a time at Westminster School, London, then his mother removed to Ireland, and entered him at Trinity, Dublin. He tells the story of his own conversion as follows: "Strange that I, who had sat so long under the means of grace in England, should be brought right unto God in an obscure part of Ireland, midst a handful of people met together in a barn, and by the ministry of one who could hardly spell his name." (James Morris, the preacher of the barn meeting, was, however, an educated man.) Toplady was soon ordained in the Church of England, and preached for it till he became minister of the Chapel of French Calvinists, in Leicester Fields, London. He was a stern Calvinist, and could not be reconciled to John Wesley.

The tune used with the original words in the United States, called Toplady or popularly Rock of Ages, is by the American, Thomas Hastings (Note 97).

The paraphrase used here, by Frederic W. Root, was made for the 1910 edition of the Hymnal. It interprets the symbolism of the original in a most impressive way. It roused much discussion, at first, but in time it came to be so highly valued, on both sides of the Atlantic, that there was a general demand to retain it in the revised *Christian Science Hymnal.*

294 Houghton. *Rock of Ages, Truth divine*

This tune is said to have been named Houghton-le-Spring, by the composer, Samuel Wesley, in *A Selection of Psalms and Tunes,* by Kemble and Wesley, 1864, where it is marked "composed for Rock of Ages." Then in a collection of 1866, by J. Gray, rector of Houghton-le-Spring, the tune appeared with the name Sebastian, Wesley's middle name. This looks like a bit of friendly rivalry, each man trying to honor the other, in the name of the tune. The name Sebastian, it may be remarked, was given to Wesley for the great Bach. (See Note 75.)

295 Nicht so traurig. *Rock of Ages, Truth divine*

The tune name, meaning, "Not so sadly," repeats words of Paul Gerhardt (Note 119), to which the music was set, in Bach's *Four-part Chorale Songs,* 1769. The music is applied to Rock of Ages in *The Church Hymnary.* We have here, for Mr. Root's paraphrase, music by an American, an Englishman, and a German. (For the work of Bach, see Notes 14, 252, 361.)

296 Amsterdam. *Rouse ye, soldiers of the cross*

Amsterdam may well have been written by Dr. Nares for the sturdy boy singers whom he had in charge at the Chapel Royal (Note 16). The words were written by Maria Louise Baum to fit the music and to replace a similar hymn by M. H. Tipton. This music was first used in the *Foundery Collection,* 1742. Its name is an example of the usage that gives to hymn tunes names of places. The name may be applied because the tune is a Traditional melody found in that locality, or because the composer or the poet lived or sojourned at the place; or the name is for a church with which the composer had associations. So from Boston to Moscow, from Capetown to Westminster, from Londonderry to Stuttgart, from Caithness to Alpine Solothurn, thought may gather together the thousands who have lifted voices in these tunes, in loyal praise to God.

297 Dalkeith. *Science, the angel with the flaming sword*

Dalkeith was the residence of the Duke of Buccleuch, whom the composer, Thomas Hewlett (1845–1874), served as organist. Hewlett wrote this tune for Abide with Me. He played in several of the Edinburgh churches, and at his passing, the Edinburgh Choral Union set up a monument to commemorate him. The fine words of the hymn, written by Roberta B. Lynch, appeared in the *Christian Science Sentinel,* February 2, 1929.

298 Communion. *Saw ye my Saviour?*

This tune, by Lyman Brackett, appeared in the first edition of the Hymnal, 1892, for the Communion Hymn of Mrs. Eddy (Note 154).

299 Saviour. *Saw ye my Saviour?*

This is one of the best settings for Mrs. Eddy's Communion Hymn. It was composed by Walter E. Young (Note 161).

300 Laundon. *Saw ye my Saviour?*

Here is a thoughtful interpretation of Mrs. Eddy's Communion Hymn, by G. Thalben-Ball. (See Note 26.)

301 Faith. *Saw ye my Saviour?*

Mrs. Eddy's Communion Hymn has five settings, all specially composed for her words. Faith, by G. O'Connor Morris, is adapted with great care to the normal flow of the lines. The time signatures (3/2 and 2/2) are printed at the beginning to allow the words themselves to unfold the rhythm.

G. O'Connor Morris is from King's County, Ireland. His father was a barrister and author, but he himself, at the age of six, was set forth on a musical career, studying first piano and then the organ, in Dublin. At seventeen, he went to London, to the Royal College of Music, and was very soon appointed assistant organist at Carlisle Cathedral, and organist at the principal church there. Returning to London, as organist of a city church, he soon became known as a gifted accompanist, much in demand for concerts and recitals. He conducted opera with the Beecham and Carl Rosa opera companies, and became professor at the Guildhall School of Music, adjudicator at festivals, and examiner for Trinity College.

302 Freedom. *Saw ye my Saviour?*

This beautiful melody was written by E. Norman Greenwood specially for the Communion Hymn of Mrs. Eddy. (See Note 28.) The harmonization is extremely modern, and requires study.

303 St. Hugh. *Scorn not the slightest word or deed*

This tune is from *Chope's Congregational Tune Book*, 1862. For the work of Dr. Hopkins, see Note 208. The words are anonymous. They were used in Ticknor and Fields' Hymns, Boston, 1848.

304 Guidance. *Shepherd, show me how to go*

Copyright for this tune by Lyman Brackett was taken in the name of Mary Baker Eddy, in 1887. Of these words, it has often been said in the Christian Science Sunday Schools that no matter what hymn is given out the "littlest ones" always sing "Shepherd." The hymn was used in the first edition of the Hymnal, 1892, with this music.

305 Shepherd. *Shepherd, show me how to go*

This tune, by Albert F. Conant, a Christian Scientist, has been in use since 1909, with this dearly loved hymn by Mrs. Eddy.

306 Concord. *Shepherd, show me how to go*

This earnest, prayerful music, by William Lyman Johnson, was composed for the words of Mrs. Eddy, in 1905, at her request. It is named for the city in New Hampshire where she so long made her home.

307 Llanfair. *Shepherd, show me how to go*

The Island of Anglesey, on the north shore of Wales, is familiar to readers of George Borrow's *Wild Wales*, where he tells of his visit to Llanfair, the former home of the poet-preacher, Goronwy Owen. Robert Williams (1781–1821) was another singer of Anglesey, blind from birth, who learned basket-weaving to earn his living, and, singing at his task, made this melody, now sung with these beloved words by Mary Baker Eddy. He could repeat, and even write down, any tune on once hearing it.

308 Egerton. *Shepherd, show me how to go*

This is one of the two melodies specially set to these favorite words of Mrs. Eddy, for this revision of the Christian Science Hymnal. For the work of G. Thalben-Ball, see Note 26.

309 Benevolence. *Shepherd, show me how to go*

This lovely modern melody was specially set to Mrs. Eddy's words by E. N. Greenwood (Note 28).

310 Bethlehem. *Sing, ye joyous children, sing*

The tune name is a reminder that the music is much sung with "Hark, the herald angels sing." It was taken from the Festival Song which Mendelssohn composed for a printer's art anniversary. Here is another joyful version written by John Randall Dunn, a Christian Scientist. William H. Cummings (1831–1915), the adapter, was leading tenor at the Temple Church, also at Westminster Abbey, and at the Chapel Royal, appointments which he resigned when he began singing in concerts. He was "identified" with the tenor part in Bach's Passion Music, as sung in England. He was a founder of the Purcell Society, and succeeded Barnby at the head of the Guildhall School of Music.

311 O Jesu. *So brightly burns Love's holy glow*

This is a simple, cheerful tune, in which the first two phrases, ascending, are repeated, with two descending phrases that follow, to make a six-line stanza. It is from the *Hirschberg Hymn Book* of 1741. Hirschberg, a beautifully situated place in Lower Silesia, has one of the Evangelical churches which were guaranteed to Silesian Protestants by the treaty between Charles XII of Sweden and the Emperor of Austria. When that hymn book was published, the organist was Johann B. Reimann (1702–1749), and as he was known for his skill in writing tunes, he is believed to have edited the Hymn Book, perhaps to have composed this tune. The reverent and happy words used here are by Robert Ellis Key, and were written especially for the 1932 edition of the *Christian Science Hymnal*.

312   Diademata. *Soldiers of Christ, arise*

Sir George Elvey is one of the many musicians of England whose service to their art has earned a knighthood. He began as chorister in Canterbury Cathedral, which is today the seat of the Primate of All England, because it was here that St. Augustine came in 596. Chaucer's *Canterbury Tales* record the old town as a place of pilgrimage, and even the word "canter" is from the name, indicating the easy gait adopted by the mounted pilgrims.

Elvey was organist of St. George's Chapel, Windsor, for nearly thirty years, and conducted the Windsor and Eton choral society, and some of the great Festivals. He wrote a Festival Ode for the marriage of the Princess Louise, in 1871, and soon after that was knighted. He composed oratorios and odes, and his Diademata is a tune of strength and dignity, admirably suited to Wesley's words (Note 105). The tune was composed for *Hymns Ancient and Modern*, 1868, for "Crown him with many crowns," by Matthew Bridges (Note 388), from which comes the tune name.

313   Meirìonydd. *Sometimes a light surprises*

This interesting music is the work of a cattle-dealing farmer of Wales, who, traveling much in England, never failed to lend an ear to the singing of congregations. He was William Lloyd (1786–1852), born in Carnarvon, that famous region made splendid by the Snowdon range. He was sought out as a teacher, and finally did his traveling for the sake of the singing meetings he conducted.

His Meirìonydd is based on a traditional Welsh melody, The Lassies of County Merion, and was used in the United States in 1840, in Richard Mills' *Songs of Zion*, published in Welsh in Utica, New York. Utica has long had a large Welsh population, keeping up their eisteddfods (Note 350), and publishing a newspaper called *Drych*.

The words are from the *Olney Hymns* of William Cowper (1731–1800). Among them is one called, "I am the Lord that healeth thee," in which Cowper uses two incidents of healing from Mark's Gospel. Those who know something of the poet's long struggle with illness are touched by this evidence that he turned in thought to the healing of the Master.

The *Olney Hymns* were begun in 1771, while the poet was working with John Newton among the poor of Olney. Cowper ranks high among English poets, for his long poem, *The Task,* which won him praise as "the first poet of the age." His works, especially his translations of Mme. Guyon, the French Quietist, show that he sought, as one of his hymns sings, "a closer walk with God."

He is one of the few writers, noted for secular poetry, who have written beautiful hymns.

314   Selma. *Sow in the morn thy seed*

The sponsor for Selma was Robert Archibald Smith (1780–1829). His father was a Paisley silk weaver. Robert could play the violin when he was ten, and in 1807 was precentor of the Abbey church in Paisley. He published a collection of tunes, and then helped compile the *Sacred Psalmody* for St. George's Church, Edinburgh, 1820, in which this tune was used. There the Town Council gave him the post of precentor, and he lifted St. George's to a proud place among the churches. He was said to have a "vein of melody not equalled then in Scotland." He published *The Scottish Minstrel* of Lady Nairn, with Auld Robin Gray and several hundred of the best Scottish songs; also *The Irish Minstrel,* suppressed because he infringed Moore's copyright; and then *Selected Melodies of All Nations.*

Selma was marked by Smith as "Ancient Scottish melody, noted in the Island of Arran." The words used here are from Montgomery's The Field of the World. Our third stanza was written for the Hymnal.

315   Sawley. *Speak gently, it is better far*

This little poem had wide appeal, and bade fair to become truly "folk lore," in being known to everyone, and its author unknown. Even Julian could only say of it that it appeared in Sharpe's *London Magazine,* 1848, unsigned. It has been attributed to George Washington Hangford, misspelled Langford in the 1910 Hymnal. But it was written by an American poet, David Bates (1810–1871), whose collected poems, arranged by his son, were published in Philadelphia in 1870. The son tells the popular use of the poem, and states that it appeared in his father's first collection, *The Æolian,* 1849, but had been in circulation before that. Ticknor's *Book of Hymns,* Boston, 1848, prints it as anonymous. The tune, Sawley, is by an English composer, James Walch (1837–1901), and appeared in *The Congregational Church Hymnal,* 1887.

Walch was born at Bolton, England, and was organist there, also conductor of the Philharmonic Society. This, his best known hymn tune, was composed when he was twenty years old.

316 Fragment. *Speak gently, it is better far*

This melody, called Fragment, arranged by Sir Walford Davies (Note 159), is from the *Sarum Gradual,* of 1527. What was known as the Sarum Use was the form of liturgy arranged for the English church by Osmund, Bishop of Salisbury (New Sarum) in 1087, and used until the time of the Reformation. The Gradual was the book of music for the mass, a gradual being an antiphon, or response. The name Sarum goes back to Old Sarum, a fortress held probably by some of Cæsar's Belgæ, before it became a Roman fortress. Beside it, on Salisbury Plain, William the Conqueror reviewed his army and met his English landlords over the Domesday Book.

317 Strength and Stay. *Still, still with Thee when purple morning breaketh*

The writer of *Uncle Tom's Cabin* was probably more astonished even than her friends at the unprecedented success of her homely story. We read of the busy wife and mother writing away at her book in the midst of home duties, snatching an hour, when she could, for the task she had set herself, which was to show both the best and the worst of the institution of slavery.

Mrs. Harriet Beecher Stowe (1812–1896) was born in Litchfield, Connecticut, and was sister of Henry Ward Beecher, the famous preacher. She married Professor Stowe in Cincinnati, where she received her first impressions of the problem that then so agitated the country. Her husband was called to Bowdoin College, Maine, in 1850, and there she wrote the story which brought her world renown. It was published serially in *The National Era,* an anti-slavery journal of Washington, D. C.

When she visited England, in 1853, Mrs. Stowe was received with marked attention, partly through her friendship with Harriet Martineau (Note 54), but more for the heart-felt sympathy her book roused there.

Mrs. Stowe wrote a number of novels or tales, such as *Dred, The Minister's Wooing, The Pearl of Orr's Island,* etc. The famous book was translated into twenty languages, including Chinese and Japanese, and when dramatized was for years a stage favorite. This hymn appeared in Mr. Beecher's *Plymouth Collection,* 1855. One of the most vocal of Dr. Dykes' tunes (Note 169) is excellently adapted to this favorite hymn, which has here been restored in places to the original. The music was written for O Strength and Stay, from a Latin hymn attributed to St. Ambrose.

318 Bairn. *Suffer the children to come to me*

This Danish folk tune is one of the special favorites of the Scandinavian churches. The name Bairn, the Scottish word for child, was given for the Danish name, "God's Little Child." The English words para-

301

phrase the tender rebuke of Jesus to the disciples. The lines on the lilies and birds were included as expressing the same tenderness for what is simple, familiar, and dear.

The music has an unusual pattern, because it mounts early to the climax, on the first page, and then falls slowly back again to the quiet last line, with the repeated, "Come unto me." The poet is Grundtvig (Note 176).

319 Rivaulx. *Sun of our life, thy quickening ray*

Dr. Oliver Wendell Holmes (1809–1894) was a professor at Harvard, an essayist, and a poet of vivid and delicate touch. The reverence and tenderness that are in his hymns marked him also as one of the most loved of the literary fellowship that made Boston the "Athens" of America. Of his books of sketches, casual talk, verse, with a thread of a story, *The Autocrat of the Breakfast Table* was most famous. With the *Professor* and the *Poet* it was read everywhere.

This hymn appeared in the *Autocrat*, in 1859, and his best-known poem, The Chambered Nautilus, was also printed there, while the book was coming out in the *Atlantic Monthly*. This is the poem with the inspiring call:

> Build thee more stately mansions, O my soul,
> As the swift seasons roll!
> Leave thy low-vaulted past!
> Let each new temple, nobler than the last,
> Shut thee from heaven with a dome more vast,
> Till thou at length art free.

Here is also an echo of Shelley's line, "Life, like a dome of many colored glass," except that Holmes saw it as the dome, or house, of advancing thought, which we build of our own choice. His humor is seen especially in some of his verse, as where he says his wants are few, he only asks "a hut of stone"—"A very plain brown stone will do."

His house was on the river side of Beacon Street, Boston, and on the Esplanade behind it is now a memorial of the gentle and merry Autocrat. He was a Unitarian, attending King's Chapel, the little square stone church that keeps its colonial name, and even part of the Episcopal service. The first line of this hymn is, "Lord of all being, throned afar."

This tune has the name of an old Abbey of Norman days, founded in 1131, by Walter L'Espec, in Yorkshire, that land of interesting old buildings. For Dr. Dykes, see Note 169.

320 Azmon. *Supreme in wisdom as in power*

That William Cameron (1751–1811) was a poet in his own right, is proved by this arrangement of Watts' rather ragged version of Isaiah 40:27–30, where he begins, "Whence do our mournful thoughts arise?"

302

Watts' fourth stanza only is found in Cameron's version. He was the grandson of Cameron of Glen Nevis, and born at Ballater, Aberdeenshire. Graduating at Aberdeen, he became minister at Kirknewton, Midlothian, and was one of the chief workers on the revision of the Scottish *Translations and Paraphrases.*

Azmon was written by Carl G. Gläser (1784–1829), of Wessenfels, Germany. He studied under Hiller, at the St. Thomas School in Leipzig, and though he went there to study law, he finally gave it up and settled in Barman as a teacher of music. Hastings arranged this tune in waltz time, with a half note and a quarter (minim and crotchet) in each measure; Mason made the arrangement used in the 1910 Hymnal. (See also No. 409.) The arrangement for No. 320 was made for the revised Hymnal, retaining the original 4/4 form of the melody.

321   Burford. *Supreme in wisdom as in power*

Burford has been attributed to Purcell, but cannot be traced in his works. It appeared in Chetham's *Psalmody,* 1718, by Sir John Chetham (?–1763), who was schoolmaster and curate at Skipton, England. His book of tunes had current use for one hundred and fifty years. It was without tune names, but the name Burford was given by Gawthorn in *Harmonia Perfecta,* 1730.

322   Canonbury. *Sweet hour of holy, thoughtful prayer*

This, the only Schumann melody in the Hymnal, is an arrangement from a piano Nocturne (Opus 23, No. 4), which, like so much of Schumann's piano music, has the life and beauty of song.

Robert Schumann (1810–1856) is unique among composers for his work in criticism. His literary gifts aided him in writing his poetic studies of the work of other men. In this age of flippant or cynical criticism often by those who have no work of their own to stand on, it is most refreshing to recall, with Schumann's biographer, that the "foundation of his criticism lay in kindness."

He could write only of what was in some degree deserving. He was at his best when he could praise generously. He was not afraid of enthusiasm: an attitude rather out of fashion among today's reviewers. In him was no trace of jealousy. What he did for Chopin and for Brahms is well known, and his loyalty to Mendelssohn.

Through his work for the musical journal he owned, Schumann endured hardness—for example, in ridicule for having so far overestimated the young Brahms! His mythical Davidsbund wrote out his own musical theories, and demanded for music a wide wing, a freedom, forbidden by the conventions of his day.

His Davidsbündler were imaginary young men who, David-like,

dared, with their slight weapon, the pen, the formidable mass of the Philistine (or unmusical) majority.

Schumann did great things in most of the forms of music. In his songs we may easily trace his "music of the future." Never before had voice, piano, and poem formed so perfect and eloquent a unity. When the mood of a stanza changed, the music changed, instead of uttering every verse to the same tune.

The words here are by Caroline Gilman, née Howard (1794–1888), born in Boston. She became the wife of Dr. Samuel Gilman of Boston, Unitarian preacher in Charleston, South Carolina, from 1819 to 1856.

323 Puer nobis nascitur. *Sweet hour of holy, thoughtful prayer*

This melody (To us a Child is born) is used in Prætorius' *Muses of Zion* (Note 366), and is traced back by Zahn to a carol by Cyriakus Spangenberg (1528–1604), who, as a student at Wittenberg, lived in Luther's house. Then he became rector and preacher at Eisleben, where in 1568 he published a little book with this melody.

324 Theodora. *Take my life, and let it be*

This famous air is from Handel's oratorio, Theodora, where it is set to the words, "Angels ever bright and fair." It was specially arranged for the Hymnal, because of Mrs. Eddy's liking for it.

The story of Georg Friedrich Handel (1685–1759) is one of advancing success, in a foreign country, which heartily adopted him for its own. He went to London to compose Italian opera, but his success was made as a composer of oratorio.

Handel had been chapelmaster for the Elector of Hanover, but, in 1710, he "deserted" this post, so said the Elector, to try his fortunes in London. Soon the Elector appeared there, as King George I of England, ignoring the young musician, until Handel's Water Music, composed for a royal fête on the Thames, restored him to favor.

The world-famous oratorio, The Messiah, was composed in twenty-four days, and swept Dublin with enthusiasm on the first performance, in 1741. Thus Handel reached full recognition of his great gift at the age of fifty-six years.

The list of his vocal works, operas as well as oratorios, is very long. The *Encyclopædia Britannica* for 1901 declared that Handel's name was "absolutely paramount" in the history of English music, and that "never has a composer been more essentially national than the German Handel became in England." It was "under the influence of English poetry, and of English national and religious life," that Handel's concept of music "gained the dignity and grandeur which we see in his oratorios," as com-

304

pared with his Italian operas. Handel became "the interpreter of the sufferings and aspirations of a nation, or . . . of mankind." After this panegyric, the Britannica writer found that the public exaltation of Handel impeded the work of English composers, by driving them into narrower fields of composition.

Theodora, 1749, is spoken of as "a Christian oratorio." A biographer of Handel believes that it failed, not from lack of beautiful music, but because its appearance coincided with the London earthquake! The noble air, "Angels ever bright and fair," still appears on concert programs, and, in various arrangements, has long been used for hymns. The song is a prayer for deliverance, when Roman soldiers try to compel Theodora, one of the early Christians, to worship pagan gods. She sings:

> Angels ever bright and fair,
> Take, O take me to your care.

The words used here, by Frances Ridley Havergal (1836–1879), were chosen for their likeness to the original. Miss Havergal's whole life, we read, was consecrated to singing sweetly and simply the praise of God. She was the daughter of Canon W. H. Havergal (Note 44), and was a woman of high culture. Fifty of her hymns are in common use. (See Note 65.)

325 Duke Street. *Take up thy cross, the Saviour said*

John Hatton, born in Warrington, England, lived in Duke Street, St. Helens, and passed on in 1793. The tune first appeared in *A Select Collection*, by Henry Boyd, a teacher of Psalmody, Glasgow, 1793. In *Euphonia*, a tune book, Liverpool, 1895, it was named Duke Street.

Charles W. Everest (1814–1877), born in Windsor, Connecticut, planned to become a journalist, but instead took orders for the Episcopal Church at Trinity College, Hartford. He was long rector at Hampden, near New Haven. His poems were published in 1833, and his "Take up thy cross" is one of the best known American hymns, but has been much altered. Its form in Horder's *Hymnal for the Free Churches*, London, 1884, is nearest the original.

326 Truro. *The Christian warrior, see him stand*

Truro is a very popular tune, and is found in the 1790 edition of Thomas Williams' *Psalmodia Evangelica* (Note 106). The change in the first note agrees with the early record of the tune.

Julian might say that this hymn reflects the nature of its poet, who bequeathed to the church the wealth of a "true genius and a sanctified heart." Montgomery, "with the faith of a strong man united the beauty and simplicity of a child." (See Note 83.)

327   Coventry. *The God who made both heaven and earth*

This English folk tune was arranged for the Hymnal, edition of 1910, by Frederic W. Root. Its source, like that of the words, is not traced.

328   St. Magnus. *The God who made both heaven and earth*

This tune appeared in Playford's *Divine Companion*, 1709, without a name. In Riley's *Parochial Harmony*, 1762, it is named for a church, St. Magnus the Martyr, at London Bridge. The church was built by Wren in 1676, and has the monument of Miles Coverdale, whose version of the Bible, 1535, was the first one printed in English. For Clark, see Note 94.

329   St. Anselm. *The heavens declare the glory*

This melody has the smooth "step by step" movement of many Barnby tunes, and the words follow well its rise to the stress of the high notes. For Barnby, see Note 147. The noble paraphrase of Psalm 19 was made for the 1910 edition of the Hymnal, by Frederic W. Root.

St. Anselm was Archbishop of Canterbury, 1093–1109.

330   Dominus regit me. *The King of Love my Shepherd is*

This hymn has its famous Dykes melody (Note 169), with a Latin name that means "The Lord directs me *without deviation*" (Clédat). The last words on the lips of this poet, Sir Henry Baker (1821–1877), were lines from this, his admirable version of the Twenty-third Psalm. He is also remembered for his devoted work as editor of *Hymns Ancient and Modern*. Born in London, he became vicar at Monkland, and succeeded his father as baronet. (See Note 400.)

331   St. Sepulchre. *The lifted eye and bended knee*

George Cooper (1820–1876) showed his gifts early, and at a festival of the Sons of the Clergy the chief organist at St. Paul's Cathedral made George extemporize on the organ, to the interest and pleasure of Mendelssohn. Before he was fourteen he was organist in a small church and an assistant at St. Paul's. He succeeded his father as organist at St. Sepulchre. Then he was made organist at the Chapel Royal, and followed Gauntlett as editor of the Wesleyan Hymnal. The words here are by Thomas Scott (Note 143), a hymn named Devotion vain without Virtue.

332   Nestling. *The Lord is in His holy place*

The Danish words on the Hymnal page are the first line of the naïve old hymn with which this music has also been sung. They express the devout sincerity of early hymn writers, saying: "Like a hen clucking tenderly, so the church bells are ringing: O come, ye little ones, quickly to me; See how I spread my wings to guard you with strength and diligence, against hawk or fox forever, as the hen her tiny ones."

The composer, August Henrick Winding (1835-1899), was born in Taars, Lolland Island, Denmark. He was a pupil of Gade and Reinecke, and became associate director of the Copenhagen Conservatory. Famous as a pianist, his chief compositions were for the piano, including concertos, preludes, idyls; but he wrote also in the form of symphony, overture, chamber music. His music is marked by northern color and the genial humor of folk song.

The words here are from an English prose version of Grundtvig's Danish poem (Note 176), and were written for the music.

333 Abridge. *The loving friend to all who bowed*

This is a rather famous tune by a rather obscure man, and even the name is from an obscure village on the edge of Epping Forest. The most striking fact that is recorded of Isaac Smith (1725-1800) is that he advised all congregations to have a song practice every week! He was precentor in the Alie Street Meeting House, Goodman's Fields, London, where he received a salary of twenty pounds a year!—a second striking fact. About 1770, he published a collection of Psalm tunes set in three parts, of which Abridge was one. It is said that Smith's week days were spent in the service of a linendraper's shop. If this is true, his success in music deserves the more praise. The hymn is by Samuel Longfellow (Note 134).

334 St. Stephen. *The spirit breathes upon the Word*

William Jones (1726-1800) was educated at the historic Charterhouse School and at Oxford. He was made perpetual curate of Nayland, Suffolk, and was familiarly known as Jones of Nayland, a person of many accomplishments. He was knowledgeable in theology of the High Church type, in philosophy and in natural science, and was a musician of ability. His *Treatise on the Art of Music* was of value. In 1789, he published *Ten Church Pieces for the Organ,* which included this tune; and he established *The British Critic.* The poem is one of Cowper's *Olney Hymns* (Note 313).

335 Morning Light. *The morning light is breaking*

Morning Light is a characteristically American hymn, though the composer of the vigorous tune, George J. Webb (1803-1887), was born in Wiltshire, England. Intended for the ministry, he eventually gave himself to music. After acting as organist at Falmouth, England, he came to the United States, in 1830, and soon reached a position of marked influ-

307

ence. He was for forty years organist at the Old South Church, one of the most celebrated of the colonial foundations that are still maintained in Boston, dating from 1669. The church later removed into the Back Bay, and is now known as the New Old South, to distinguish it from the lowly building, with its slim, old-time steeple, which is one of the first objectives for visitors to historic Boston. For this was the church where, late one night, a silent, waiting crowd saw a group masquerading as Indians, stepping quietly out, and quietly down to the wharf, for a Gargantuan brewing of tea!

George Webb, Englishman, worked with Lowell Mason, New Englander, to build up the Boston Academy of Music. In 1870, Webb removed to Orange, New Jersey, as organist. He was a Swedenborgian in belief, and arranged the music service for the Church of the New Jerusalem. This tune appeared in *The Odeon*, a book of secular melodies "for adult singing schools and for social music parties," Mason and Webb, 1837. The words for this tune were, "'Tis dawn, the lark is singing." Its first use as a hymn tune was in the *Wesleyan Psalmist*, 1842.

The words are by Samuel Francis Smith (1808–1895). His name is one of reverent memory to Americans, for his familiar hymn that speaks patriotic love. "My country, 'tis of thee" was written in 1832, for a children's Fourth of July celebration at Park Street Church, Boston.

"The morning light is breaking" was written at the same time, as a missionary hymn, and appeared in Hastings' *Spiritual Songs*. Dr. Smith recorded that he had himself heard it sung in five or six different languages in Europe and Asia.

Dr. Smith, born in Boston, was a graduate of Harvard, and then of Andover, for he entered the Baptist ministry and became editor of the *Missionary Magazine*. He was pastor at Waterville, Maine, and professor of modern languages at the college. Then at Newton, Massachusetts, he edited and wrote for the *Baptist Psalmist*. In 1870, Smith published a collection called *Rock of Ages*.

336 Winchester New. *The starry firmament on high*

John Wesley's copy of the old German collection, from which he chose this tune for use in his hymn book, is still preserved in the Library of the Wesleyan College, Richmond, England. It was Freylinghausen's *Hymn Book*, in the 1704 edition of which this melody appeared, with words by Crasselius. The tune was in the *Musical Handbook*, Hamburg, 1690, with Neumark's hymn, No. 216.

In this connection, it is interesting to note that "the first hymn book compiled for use in the Church of England" (Julian) was the first edition of Wesley's hymn book, which he published in South Carolina, during his stay in America. The title reads: *A Collection of Psalms and Hymns*.

Charles-town. Printed by Lewis Timothy, 1737. It was reprinted in facsimile in 1882, by T. Woolmer, London. (See Note 105.)

The words used here are of exceptional beauty and interest. They were by Sir Robert Grant (1785–1838), who was born at Inverness, and educated at Cambridge University. In 1826, he was Member of Parliament for Inverness, then Privy Councillor, and, in 1834, was sent to Bombay as Governor. His poems were collected by his brother, Lord Glenelg, and this one had the following note: "This is intended as a sequel or counterpart to Addison's hymn, 'The spacious firmament.' It corresponds to the latter portion of the Nineteenth Psalm as Addison's does to the former."

337   St. Mabyn. *Theories, which thousands cherish*

The music here is by Arthur H. Brown (Note 48), who was chosen organist at Brentwood, Essex, when he was ten years old. He made several collections of hymns and wrote seven hundred hymn tunes.

The words are by a Unitarian minister, of Boston, Robert C. Waterston (1812–1893), whose work as preacher, writer, and educator, is described in Putnam's *Singers and Songs of the Liberal Faith* (1874). Whittier's poem, Naples, is inscribed to Waterston.

This hymn, "Theories, which thousands cherish," is notable for its use of feminine pronouns in referring to divine Truth. Another stanza from the original hymn reads:

> From the glorious heavens above Her
> She has shed Her light abroad,
> That the souls who trust and love Her
> May become the sons of God.

Because of the work of the Pilgrims, as founders of the Congregational Church, in which Mary Baker Eddy so long held her membership, two interesting facts may be touched on here. The first is that the Pilgrims' English pastor, John Robinson, bade them farewell with these words: "I am very confident that the Lord has more truth yet to break out of His holy word." Phillips Brooks (Note 222) cited this in an address at Cambridge University, England, and called it "the noblest utterance of hopeful tolerance in all that noble century."

The second fact is that the American Unitarian Church is affiliated with the Plymouth foundation. This is recorded on a tablet in the wall of the Unitarian Church which stands by that storied hill beyond Plymouth Rock. Like the Congregational Church, it claims to be "the Church of Scrooby, Leyden and Plymouth." Scrooby was the meeting place of the Separatists in England, before they found protection in liberal Holland, where they had closer association with the French idea of Congregationalism, which, by way of Plymouth, finally went into England as "the New England way."

So the steady advance of spiritual enlightenment is traced in history, and perhaps will be the single shining thread of such records that shall remain, as captains and kings depart, tumults and shoutings, creed and ritual, cease; and humanity is united in one worship of one God.

338 Sussex. *Theories, which thousands cherish*

This is an English Traditional melody, named, no doubt, for the region where it prevailed. It is found in *The English Hymnal,* 1906.

339 St. Columba (Erin). *There are none friendless, none afraid*

St. Columba appears in the Hymnal of the Irish Episcopal Church, 1874, with the following note: ". . . collected by Dr. George Petrie in the remote parts of Ireland and believed by him to be a hymn of the Ancient Irish Church." In that hymnal it is named Erin, but the name St. Columba is a tribute to the Irish saint who founded the religious houses of Derry and Darrow, and converted northern Scotland to Christianity, from his island fastness of Iona. He was born in Donegal, in 521, and it has been guessed that his name—the Dove—was given for his gentleness; but it was doubtless his own. Records of him are said to be rather more authentic than is the case with many legendary saints of such early times.

We know that he was a bard and the protector of bards, and that his last work was a transcription of the Psalms—the story reminding us of the passing of the holy Bede. Many of the events recorded of Columba are legendary, but the careful *Encyclopædia Britannica* finds "there can be no doubt as to the holiness of his life, his influence on his times, and the love he uniformly manifested to God and to his neighbor." His transcription ended with the line, "They that seek the Lord shall not want any good thing."

The words used with this Irish tune have a beautiful relation to the story of Columba. They are the poem, Truth, from *Heartsease Hymns,* by William P. McKenzie, published in Cambridge, Massachusetts. When this book of poems was sent as a gift to Mrs. Eddy, she chose this hymn, and another named The Present, as among the finest. The latter poem ends:

> The future and past are man's,
> The Present belongeth to God.

340 Slingsby. *There's a wideness in God's mercy*

Edmund Sardinson Carter (1845–1923) was a member of the Oxford University Eleven, famous for his athletic prowess, while he was also winning honors for scholarship. He belonged as well to the Oxford Eight, and, in 1869, to the Eleven of Victoria, Australia. Born in Malton,

Yorkshire, he became vicar choral of York Minster, in 1875, so he must have added singing to his accomplishments. Later he was rector of St. Martin-cum-Gregory, and then vicar of St. Michael-le-Belfrey, both in York. He is rated as a self-taught musician, but this favorite tune has carried his voice very far. It is well adapted to Faber's splendid words. Faber, too, was known for his fine voice, and was called "the preacher with the golden voice" (Note 86).

341 Peacefield. *They who seek the throne of grace*

When Canon Wilson offered this old Irish air to the editors of the Irish *Church Hymnal*, 1917, he introduced it as the first air he ever heard! For it is the lullaby that is sung over the cradle of all Irish children. It is preserved in Dr. George Petrie's *Collection of Ancient Irish Music*, which has 1580 of the old melodies.

Canon David F. R. Wilson was ordained in the Irish Episcopal Church, in 1895, and was master of the Choir School, St. Patrick's Cathedral, Dublin, and then canon and precentor there. He was general editor of the Irish *Church Hymnal*, and applied this tune to Miss Havergal's "Now the daylight goes away." His arrangement has been widely used. It· is named for the old homestead of Canon Wilson's mother, in County Armagh, where, under a tree still pointed out, John Wesley preached at Peacefield.

The words are by the American, Oliver Holden, composer of Coronation (Note 86). In a small book, published in Boston before 1808, are twenty-one hymns by him, signed only "H." Only one copy of this book remains. These words, like his courageous living, show the liberal faith that was already arising in Boston. The early associations of the tune have a lovely fitness with the words, "God is present everywhere."

342 Angels' Song. *This is the day the Lord hath made*

This melody is from Mendelssohn's Song without Words, Opus 19, No. 1 (Note 118). It is arranged by Dr. Hopkins (Note 208). The strong, joyous words are by Laura Lee Randall, a Christian Scientist.

343 Stracathro. *Thou art the Way*

This delightful melody, from Scottish hymnody, has for sponsor Charles Hutcheson (1792–1860), a merchant of Glasgow, a member of St. George's Church. He was an amateur composer, with a fine singing voice, and a special interest in church music. He was also a founder of the Glasgow Dilettante Society. This tune appeared in his book, *Christian Vespers*, 1832.

George Washington Doane (1799–1859) was born in Trenton, New Jersey, and educated at Union College, Schenectady, New York. In 1828, he was called as rector to Trinity Church, Boston, and afterward was

311

made Bishop of New Jersey. He was one of the great prelates of his time, and much beloved. This poem appeared in his *Songs by the Way*, 1824. Julian says that it ranks, both in America and in England, with the most popular of the great English hymns.

344 St. André. *Thou art the Way*

The composer here is Sir Walford Davies (Note 159). The strong minor tune is very interesting, leading on to the close in the major key.

345 Charterhouse. *Thou living light of pentecostal glory*

The name Charterhouse is a quaint illustration of how French words have been anglicized; for it is really Chartreuse—the little French town, site of the first Carthusian monastery. After the London Charterhouse (founded 1371) was taken over by Henry VIII, it was a residence of the Howards, until, in 1611, it was used for a boys' school. In 1872, the school was removed to Godalming, retaining the historic name. Frank Fletcher, one of the first laymen to have been made head master of such a school, became head of Charterhouse (1911), and this tune, composed for his hymn, "O Son of man, our hero strong and tender," was named in his honor. The words used for it here, written by Lucy M. Goodenough, appeared in the *Christian Science Sentinel,* June 22, 1929, as an interpretation of the Pentecostal glory, that shines for all men, not only for the chosen few.

The composer of the music is David Evans, born in 1874, in Glamorganshire, Wales. After graduation at Oxford, he was organist and choirmaster at a Welsh Presbyterian church, London, then was called back to Wales as professor of music at the University college in Cardiff, and finally became senior professor of the University of Wales. He organized a strong department of music at Cardiff, and widely influenced congregational singing, especially as leader of the great Psalmody Festival of Wales. He was also made chief adjudicator at the National Eisteddfod (Note 350). His collection of standard tunes was published in 1920. Of his many works for chorus and orchestra, his cantata, The Coming of Arthur, is best known—a reminder of the connection of the Arthurian legends with Wales. He was an editor of *The Church Hymnary,* for which this tune was written.

346 Moscow. *Thou whose almighty Word*

The Italian composer of this tune (*Lock Collection,* 1769) is reported by Dr. Burney, historian of English music, to have been received by London with greater applause than was ever accorded to anyone but Sheridan.

Felice de Giardini (1716–1796) was born in Turin, Italy, lived long in England, and closed his career in Moscow. Thus his familiar tune is called both Moscow and Italian Hymn (No. 401). He started as a singer in the Milan Cathedral choir. He then became first violin at the opera in Rome and in the San Carlo Theater at Naples. A brilliant executant, he improvised runs and cadenzas for the airs sung on the stage. Once the composer Jommelli sat by him in the orchestra, at an opera of his own. The young violinist improvised profusely, until Jommelli turned and boxed his ears! The story is worth recording, if only to emphasize the spontaneity of melody and its ornaments in Italy, the land of song.

In London, he played in concerts, then became manager at the Italian Opera, and was leader at the Three Choirs festivals.

John Marriott (1780–1825), the poet here, is another English clergyman who has given the world a great and truly popular hymn. It was first published in 1825, with the title, Missionary Hymn, unsigned. The fourth stanza (omitted) is interesting for the definition of the Trinity, as "Wisdom, Love, Might." The hymn has been widely translated.

Marriott is remembered for his modesty and charm. He refused to allow any of his hymns to be published till after his passing. Sir Walter Scott, a friend of his, dedicated the second canto of Marmion to him.

347 Bristol. *Though mountains may depart from thee*

Edward Hodges (1796–1867) was born in Bristol, England, and is probably the only musician of the Hymnal who is remembered for his inventiveness in the practical arts, as, for example, an invention that improved the organ bellows. When St. James's Church, London, installed a new organ, it was remodeled under Hodges' direction. In 1838, he came to America as organist for the Cathedral of Toronto, then went to New York as organist of Trinity, whose tiny spire still stands serene, among the topless towers of Manhattan. The Trinity organ was made over by Hodges' specifications. He stood high in this country for his organ playing, during twenty years. His son, John Sebastian Bach Hodges, was rector at St. Paul's, Baltimore, and an excellent organist. His daughter, Faustina Hasse Hodges, was also an organist. The fine Biblical hymn used here was drawn from Isaiah 54:10–17 by Una R. Lias, a Christian Scientist.

348 Bangor. *Though mountains may depart from thee*

Bangor Tune is famous. Carlyle has a reference to it in his *Cromwell,* when he cites one Hodgson: " 'The Lord General made a halt and sang the 117th' . . . at the foot of Doon Hill; there we uplift it to the tune of Bangor, and roll it strong against the sky." Carlyle (or Hodgson) was perhaps anticipating. But lines by Burns also celebrate the music, and show how singing went in the good old days. He wrote:

> Make haste and turn King David owre
> And lilt wi' holy clangor;
> O' double verse come gie us four,
> And skirl up the Bangor.

313

This tune was especially popular in Scotland, and a Scottish dame is remembered who could—or would—sing no other. Whatever the rest of the congregation might "skirl up," she always sang Bangor.

William Tans'ur—who insisted on the apostrophe in his name—has been referred to as an eccentric. But his fame carried far. For in a *Boston Gazette* of 1767 was this announcement:

"Tans'ur's Royal Melody Compleat . . . may be had at John Perkins's shop in Union Street, Boston, next door to Mr. Frederick William Geyer's. N. B. At the same place may be had a large assortment of Paper Hangings for Rooms."

In the *Compleat Melody* of 1734, Bangor Tune appeared, as "composed in three parts, W. T." The melody itself may have antedated this arrangement.

Tans'ur (1706–1783) was the son of a laborer in Warwickshire, whose name was spelled Tanzer. *A Compleat Melody or, The Harmony of Sion* was "the most curiosest Book that ever was published," and Tans'ur's other eight volumes include *A New Musical Grammar* and *Poetical Meditations.* He went from town to town, as a teacher of psalmody, and did much to improve the singing in churches.

349   Remembrance. *Thy will, almighty Father, Thine*

The tune here is by S. S. Wesley (Note 75). The words are from *The Christian Science Journal,* December, 1890.

350   Ar Hyd y Nos. *Through the love of God our Saviour*

This tune is known, from its Welsh name, as All through the Night, and much used as a hymn tune, a serenade, a lullaby; but it began in a simpler form, with nursery words:

> Look at me, my little dear, Un, dau, tri;
> Let me whisper in thine ear, Un, dau, tri;
> Bid thy playmates all retire,
> Sit thee down and draw thee nigher,
> See the bright inviting fire, Un, dau, tri!

Here the phrase which, in the present hymn, sings, "All will be well," had only three notes, rising stepwise, and separated by rests, for the "One, two, three" of the child's song. (From John Parry, cited in *The Minstrels of Wales,* Alfred Moffatt, London, 1906.)

Recalling that Wales was a land of harpists, we can hear the sweep of the harper's fingers, in this "One, two, three"; and in all Welsh music we are helped to sing by remembering the harp. George Borrow, visiting Wales in 1854, heard a harper playing, during his first meal, and said, "Of a surety, I am in Wales." As many hymn tunes show that they were composed for the organ, in the active motion of the under parts, so we

314

may listen for the harp strings in Welsh tunes. The marked rhythm is useful for congregational singing, or what the Welsh call "cymanfaoedd." The harping was prominent in the Eisteddfod, the music festival still held every summer, alternately in North and South Wales. It traces back to the twelfth century, to the "annual congress of bards and minstrels, and literati."

This tune has long been sung in England and America, with words by Heber, "God that madest earth and heaven." Mary Bowly Peters (1813–1856), whose words are used here, was not only a writer of hymns still used in England, but of a seven-volume history entitled, *The History of the World, from the Creation to the Accession of Queen Victoria.*

351   St. Asaph. *Through the night of doubt and sorrow*

St. Asaph is the cathedral of northern Wales, and dates back to 560. It was then called Llan-Elwy, the Church on the Elwy, and its first bishop was probably Asaph, whom Kentigern, the founder, left in charge, when he himself went back to Scotland. The third church built here was destroyed during the wars of Owen Glendower. The greater part of the present building, one of the smallest cathedrals in Great Britain, dates from about 1480.

For the poet, Ingemann, see Note 15, and for Baring-Gould, the translator, Note 264. The tune is by William S. Bambridge (1864–1911).

Bambridge, born in New Zealand, came to England when he was six. He sang as chorister at St. George's, Windsor, graduated at Oxford, and was music master at Marlborough College.

Baring-Gould had an "inexhaustible versatility," and we are told that more works in the British Museum were listed under his name than under that of any contemporary.

352   Federal Street. *Thy works, how beauteous, how divine*

This tune is named for a street in old Salem town, where Henry Oliver lived. Salem was once the rival of Boston, for its excellent port, that sent ships around Cape Horn and far over the Pacific. With its Hebrew name for "Peace," Salem was really the mother-town for Boston, as Endicott welcomed Winthrop and his people there, on their first landing in the strange new world. And later when the port of rebellious Boston was closed, all the ships must dock at Salem. Besides the sorry year of the witchcraft superstition, Salem has stories of a pleasanter kind, in the pages of Nathaniel Hawthorne, her best-known citizen.

Henry Kemble Oliver (1800–1885) was born in Beverly, and as a boy sang in the Park Street choir in Boston. He was a graduate of Dartmouth, and going to teach in Salem, played the organ there, and

315

started a choral society. He grew in popular favor, was Mayor of Lawrence, and then of Salem, also Adjutant General of Massachusetts, and its Treasurer.

The Handel and Haydn Society started in 1815, in a jubilee held to sing the Peace of Ghent. The Park Street choir, young Oliver among them, led the chorus, which had ninety men and ten women. They sang in the Stone Chapel, which today has its older name, King's Chapel, and after this, a meeting was called "for the cultivation and improvement of a correct taste in the performance of sacred music." The young Society at first practiced from the old *Lock Hospital Collection* (Note 396) and its first concert gave Haydn's Creation, also music by Handel. For the poet, Bishop Coxe, see Note 353.

353 Babylon's Streams. *Thy works, how beauteous, how divine*

Thomas Campion (1575?–1619) was a physician, a poet, and a composer of music. It is for his poetry that he is best remembered. He published some of it, with his own tunes, in his three books of "Ayres." This tune was set to a version of Psalm 137, "By the rivers of Babylon." He is an example of the outpouring of talent in that age of Elizabeth, which saw the great poetical and dramatic power of Shakespeare and his fellows, preparing the beauty of language that makes the King James Version of the Bible so glorious.

Samuel Pepys, of the following generation, tells in his assiduous diary how part-singing was a pastime of social evenings, when everybody was supposed to read music at sight, and to be ready to join in madrigal or glee, as all sat round some hospitable table.

The words used with Campion's tune are by the distinguished American, Bishop Arthur Cleveland Coxe (1818–1896), who was rector of Grace Church, in Baltimore, and then of Calvary Church, in New York. The words are from a volume curiously entitled, *A Halloween Romance, and Lays.* They are in a long poem (one of the "lays") named Hymn to the Redeemer, with the first line, "When o'er Judea's vales and hills." The poem was published in 1870. Bishop Coxe was a man of great sympathy, and much beloved.

354 St. Thomas. *'Tis God the Spirit leads*

The words used here, by Beddome (Note 240) are from a hymn beginning, "That we might walk with God," which appeared anonymously in Bickersteth's *Christian Psalmody*, 1833. It was probably written in 1795, and was mistakenly attributed to Montgomery in the 1910 edition of the Hymnal. Montgomery said of Beddome's hymns that each embodied a central thought, clearly developed.

The tune, St. Thomas, was printed in Aaron Williams' *Universal Psalmodist*, 1770, which was popular alike in England and in New England. Of Aaron Williams (1731–1776) it is recorded that he recommended the use of pipe organs in churches, because they were "very convenient to drown the hideous cries of the people," a rather too harsh judgment, one suspects. Williams was a publisher, and teacher of music, and clerk to the Scots Church, London Wall.

355 Serug. *Truth comes alike to all*

Serug (Genesis 11:20) was the great-grandfather of Abram, and the name belongs now to a town in Mesopotamia. The tune appeared in Wesley's *European Psalmist* (Note 75). The words by Samuel J. Avery are from *The Christian Science Journal*, January, 1886.

356 Belhaven. *To Thee, O God, we bring our adoration*

Thomas C. L. Pritchard was born in 1885, educated at Glasgow University, and went to Trinity College, Dublin, for music study. After serving in several churches as organist, he went, in 1913, to Belhaven United Free Church, and was also made professor at the Athenæum School of Music there. He was superintendent of music in the schools, and his organ recitals added to his reputation. He worked on the revision of *The Church Hymnary*, for which this tune was composed. The deeply prayerful words are by Nellie B. Mace, a Christian Scientist.

357 Evan. *To Thee, our loving Father, God*

As if it had suffered a sea change, the name of Havergal's tune became Eva, when Lowell Mason (Note 2) rearranged it for his *New Carmina Sacra* (Sacred Songs), 1850, where it was merely signed H. The original tune was set to Burns' poem, "O Thou dread power." Canon Havergal (Note 44) wrote, with mild satire, "As the American arrangement is a sad *estrangement*, I have reconstructed the tune." Mason was criticized, even at home, for the rhythmical changes he made in other people's tunes. Mr. Havergal's original rhythm was 6/4, and every measure began with an impressive half note (minim). His revision is in 4/4 time, with half notes only. Doubtless Mason hoped to let a little sunshine into the old world's dim religious light. Evan New, No. 407, also retains Mason's divided first beat in most of the measures. The source of these words is unknown.

358 St. Bernard. *To Thee, our loving Father, God*

This tune is from a collection published in Cologne, 1741, *Songs for Church and Home . . . of the Daughter of Zion*. It was used in England with words long attributed to St. Bernard (see Note 56), which gave the name.

359 Willingham. *Trust the Eternal when the shadows gather*

Prussian Saxony was the home of Franz Abt (1819–1885). His father was a clergyman there, and wished the boy to follow in his steps, but he allowed him a sound musical education, too, and so at Leipzig Franz entered the Thomas School for music, in addition to his courses at the University. Finally music demanded the whole of him, and he became chapelmaster at Zurich, where he worked especially for men's voices. He was then made director of the Court Theatre at Brunswick. His four hundred pieces are mostly Lieder (Songs), some of them known the world over. He had a gift of melody, that makes his tunes still pleasing. This tune is a good example of them, and is suited to the thoughtful unfolding of this deeply poetic hymn, The Eternal, which is from *Heartsease Hymns*, Cambridge, Massachusetts, 1928.

The collection, by William P. McKenzie, appeared first in 1895, in Toronto, with a tune name given for each hymn. This one was sung with Mason's Henley, found at No. 171 in the 1910 Hymnal.

360 Rustington. *True, the heart grows rich in giving*

This tune is named for a village near the home of the composer, Sir Hubert Parry (Note 50). The words are by an Englishwoman, Mrs. Elizabeth Charles (1828–1896), long known to young readers both sides of the Atlantic for her story of Luther's boyhood, *The Schönberg-Cotta Family*. Her hymn is called The Cruse of Oil, beginning, "Is thy cruse of comfort failing?"

361 Innsbruck. *Trust all to God, the Father*

The song that gives its name to this music, "Innsbruck, I must leave thee," was a Wanderlied, or song of a traveling artisan. Its popularity showed that it voiced a general affection for this beautiful old town in the Austrian Alps, where the Hapsburg emperors loved to live.

The Emperor, Charles V, stayed in Innsbruck when he was scheming to abolish Protestantism, by controlling the Council of Trent. News came that the Protestant Maurice of Saxony was advancing on the town to take Charles prisoner (1552). As Charles fled, rather ignominiously at midnight, through torrents of rain, over the mountain passes, perhaps someone in his suite was humming, "Innsbruck, ich muss dich lassen"!

Heinrich Isaac (c. 1450–1527) is called "the first of Germany's masters of music," though he was born in Flanders, which in his youth fell into the hands of the Hapsburgs. He was for ten years organist of the Medici Chapel in Florence, Italy, and teacher of the children of Lorenzo the Magnificent. His name as Arrigo Tedesco (Heinrich the German) appears on the musical settings of carnival songs, written and even sung in the streets by Il Magnifico himself. Working later in Innsbruck, as court composer to Emperor Maximilian, Isaac arranged this tune as a part song. Long afterward it was set to the hymn, "O world, I must leave thee," and then to Gerhardt's "Now all the woods are sleeping," which gave its name to the melody.

Bach has used this chorale five times, twice in the Matthew Passion, from which this arrangement is taken. The words used here are from another hymn of Gerhardt's (Note 119), Commit thy Way, which is regarded as the most comforting of all his hymns. The story goes that when Queen Louise of Prussia left Berlin—because Napoleon had taken control of Prussia—she reached a refuge, and went to the harpsichord to sing this hymn of Gerhardt's, for its strong, sustaining power. The English words are based on a Danish translation, by Stener J. Stenersen (1789–1835).

362 Christmas. *To us a Child of Hope is born*

This is a brilliant melody from Handel's opera, Siroe, where it is used with the words, "It does not please you" (Note 324). It was first used as a hymn tune in Arnold and Calcott's *The Psalms of David,* 1791.

The poet here, John Morison (1749–1798), was a parish minister of Canisbay, Caithness. He was one of those appointed to revise the *Translations and Paraphrases* of 1745, for the *Scottish Psalter.* The hymn used here is widely known, and well adapted to the music of Handel. A change in the last line avoids the thought of separation implied in Morison's words "above" and "below."

The words are drawn from Isaiah 9:6.

363 Philippine. *Upon the Gospel's sacred page*

The composer, Robert Edwin Roberts, born in Llangerniew, Wales, in 1878, was successively assistant master at the Choir School, Westminster Abbey, precentor of Peterborough Cathedral, vicar of St. Marks, a chaplain in France in 1915 and 1916, and vicar and precentor of Knighton, Leicester. These words are from Bowring's poem, Progress of Gospel Truth, in *A Memorial Volume of Sacred Poetry,* published by his wife (Note 79).

364 Marching. *Vainly, through night's weary hours*

The authorship of these words, usually given to Henry Francis Lyte, and sometimes, as in the Hymnal of the Century Company, New York, to Miss Harriet Auber, has long been a puzzle. The *Dictionary of Hymnology* resorts to a judgment of Solomon, and divides it between them. Each poet published a volume called *The Spirit of the Psalms,* and from this arose confusion. But the fact that this hymn appears in Miss Auber's *Psalms,* but not in Lyte's collected works, seems to decide the question in favor of Miss Auber (Note 281).

The tune, which Martin Shaw composed for Ingemann's "Through the night of doubt and sorrow" (No. 351), appeared in *Additional Tunes and Settings used at St. Mary's, Primrose Hill*, 1915, where Mr. Shaw became organist and director of music, as also at St. Martin's-in-the-Fields, London, and at the Guildhouse, master of music.

After his study at the Royal College of Music, Mr. Shaw was conductor for Ellen Terry, the English actress. He has composed songs and church music, and was, with Vaughan Williams, editor of *Songs of Praise*, a hymnal for all churches, published by Oxford University Press, in England. He also made a League of Nations Hymn Book. Like his brother, Geoffrey, he became known for his work to foster community singing. His music is marked by "dignity, massiveness and reserve." (See Note 279.)

365 Seymour. *Wait, my soul, upon the Lord*

The family ties that linked Carl Maria Friedrich Ernest von Weber (1786–1826) with the great Mozart are of interest in comparing their positions in the world of opera. Weber came from a very musical family that included three grown-up girl cousins, all charming singers, two of whom, Aloysia and Constance, played important parts in the life of Mozart before Carl was born. Thus Weber's father, Baron Franz von Weber, an army officer and a violinist, hoped to make Carl a boyish prodigy like Mozart, who had married Constance Weber.

We hear of Carl, not overstrong, wandering the land with his impecunious, but optimistic father, who gave performances with his children. This was like—yet how different from—the life of the boy Mozart, fêted by princes. After study with Michael Haydn at Salzburg, Carl was taken to Munich for concert playing. Before he was eighteen he was conducting opera at Breslau, and so it came about that he, like Mozart, is popularly remembered for his operas. Indeed, Weber ranks as the originator of "romantic opera," rather in the style of Mozart's Magic Flute, but making marvels appear veritable—such as a silver bullet, with magic powers, in Der Freischütz (free shooter). Its story shows the triumph of good over evil, and here is the serious touch that lifted Weber's romance above the "fairy operas" that preceded him.

Freischütz is Weber's greatest work. His Euryanthe has the same story as Cymbeline and might rank as a grand opera, as it has no spoken dialogue. His last work was an English opera, its text taken from Wieland's Oberon. This was produced in London, 1826, under Weber's direction. His works count more than two hundred and fifty pieces, symphonies, masses, songs, etc. The melody Seymour illustrates the grace and tenderness of his music. It is from the Fairy music, in Oberon. For the words here, see Note 366.

366 Carne (Schönheit). *Wait, my soul, upon the Lord*

The great work of Michael Prætorius (1571–1621) was his *Musical Treatise*, with a title in nine lines of Latin, showing that it covered most of what was known of the history of music and its ancient and (then) modern practice. The account of this monumental work has a certain reproof for readers of our time, many of whom can hardly be persuaded to use even a dictionary. Prætorius' works number forty printed volumes, including sixteen volumes of music oddly named *Muses of Zion,* where the tune Carne appeared. Its German name, Schönheit, means Beauty. The tune is out of the common run, in that it is in triple time and rises to its climax, not in the third phrase as in so many of the hymns, but at the end of the last phrase.

Prætorius was chapelmaster at Lüneburg, and later was in the service of the Duke of Brunswick, as chapelmaster and composer. His *Polyhymnia* included fifteen volumes of music set to Latin or to German words.

William F. Lloyd (1791–1853), the hymnist here, was especially interested in Sunday School work and in editing magazines for young people. He was made a secretary of the Sunday School Union in 1810. In 1853 he published his own hymns under the modest title, *Thoughts in Rhyme* (London).

367 Metzler. *Walk in the light, so thou shalt know*

Richard Redhead (1820–1901) began as chorister at Magdalen, Oxford, then was organist at All Saints' Church, London, and for thirty years at St. Mary Magdalene. This tune appeared in his *Ancient Hymn Melodies and other Church Tunes,* 1859. The tune appears as *Metzler's Redhead,* No. 66, in *The English Hymnal,* 1906. The name comes from that of a well-known music publishing firm in London. George Metzler, of this family, wrote verse, and his lyrics were set by Hatton and Smart. This firm introduced the Mason and Hamlin organ, of American make, to extensive use in England.

Bernard Barton (1784–1849) is called the Quaker poet. He was a merchant at Woolbridge, Suffolk, and later held a post in the bank there. He has ten volumes of poetical works. Many of his hymns appeared in the Scottish *Evangelical Union Hymnal,* 1878. The hymn is named The Children of the Light, and is one of his best known poems. He was much beloved, and among his distinguished friends were Charles Lamb, Byron, and Edward Fitzgerald.

368 Watchman. *Watchman, tell us of the night*

This poem, by Sir John Bowring, is perhaps his most familiar hymn, often used with this tune of Lowell Mason. (See Notes 2, 79.) The swinging rhythm of 6/8 meter is good for congregational singing.

369 St. George's Windsor. *Watchman, tell us of the night*

This tune is named for the chapel at Windsor Castle (Note 16), where the composer Elvey was organist (Note 312). It is from *A Selection of Psalms and Tunes,* edited by E. H. Thorne, for Morrell and How's *Psalms and Hymns,* 1858.

370 Deerhurst. *We are hid with Christ forever*

James Langran (1835–1909), composer of Deerhurst, was born in London, and studied music with Calkin and others. He was organist of Holy Trinity Church, Tottenham, and of its parish church. He was music editor of *The New Mitre-Hymnal,* named for the figure of a mitre on the cover. This tune was in the 1863 edition, and was composed for the Choral Festival in Peterborough Cathedral, 1862. The earnest words are by Nellie B. Mace.

371 Leoni. *We lift our hearts in praise*

This tune is interesting not only for its own story, but because its name—given for the singer, who was chorister, or *hazan,* of the Great Synagogue in London about 1770—leads us straight back to "the chief Musician" who is addressed at the head of about fifty Psalms in our King James Version.

This "chief Musician" in London, Meyer Lyon (or Meier Leon), drew a great attendance, "even of gentiles," we read, for his "sweet and wonderful singing." He used this tune for the Hebrew creed, or Yigdal, and when Thomas Olivers, a Welsh Wesleyan preacher, heard it, he determined to make a paraphrase of the Yigdal, giving it "a Christian character." This was the famous hymn, The God of Abraham Praise, which has had such wide use with this noble melody.

Lyon wrote out the tune for Olivers, who named it Leoni, for the singer; and a collection of 1791 (Aaron Beer) credits it to "Leon, Singer." But in *Jewish Music* A. Z. Idelsohn traces the tune further back, to a folk-song motive that appeared in various Spanish-Basque, Slavic, and Jewish songs. He gives eight records of the tune, bringing it down to the Moravian Symphony (1879) of the Czech composer, Smetana.

It is significant that the words, written by Margaret Morrison, for the tune, take the form of praise to God, the God who is Life, Truth, Love, though the writer did not know either the character of the Hebrew words or of Olivers' paraphrase. The music is still used in the synagogue with the Yigdal. (See *Jewish Song Book,* Idelsohn, p. 100.) The words begin, "Extolled be the living God, and praised be Him who lives beyond all time, eternally," and end, "Time comes when men shall all in Him rejoice."

In Genung's *Guidebook to Biblical Literature* (p. 445), the reference "to the chief Musician" is explained, with the Hebrew words that accompany it. "To the chief Musician on Neginoth upon Sheminith" (Psalm 6) means "on stringed instruments, on the octave," that is, with men's voices. To continue, "A song upon Alamoth" (Psalm 46) means "set to women's voices." "Upon Nehiloth" (Psalm 5) probably means "with wind instruments." Such phrases as "Aijeleth Shahar" (Psalm 22) or "Jonathelem-rechokim" (Psalm 56) are names of the familiar folk songs to which these Psalms were set, showing that, like many Christian hymn tunes, and like Leoni itself, the earlier religious melody of Israel had a popular origin.

372 Arlington. *We may not climb the heavenly steeps*

This music is by Dr. Thomas A. Arne (1710–1778), whose name stands for so much that is delightful in English music. He was the most notable composer of his day. He was educated at Eton, and then placed in a law office—to his chagrin, but not to his discouragement. He smuggled a spinet into his bedroom, and practiced on it at night, the strings muffled. He used to borrow a livery to be admitted to the servants' gallery at the opera.

Finding that the love of music was incorrigible in the boy, the father at last allowed him to study, and the family were soon proud of his violin playing. His reputation in composition was established by the graceful flowing melodies of his music for Milton's Comus. He composed the Masque of Alfred to celebrate the coming of the House of Hanover to the English throne. His setting for Thomson's Rule Britannia appeared in it. It was sung at Cliveden, the seat of the Prince of Wales. Then he set the songs of *As You Like It*. His opera Artaxerxes is his largest work. A melody from a minuet in the overture, used in Harrison's *Sacred Harmonies*, 1784, was this tune, Arlington. Arne also wrote many glees and catches for the aristocratic Catch Club, and Oxford gave him his degree of Doctor of Music in 1759.

Whittier's words are from his poem Our Master, stanzas 5, 13, 14, 16. Two other hymns, Nos. 142 and 230, are from this same poem.

373 Noel. *We may not climb the heavenly steeps*

This Traditional English melody, especially clear and smooth, has the French name for Christmas. It was arranged by Sir Arthur Sullivan for *Church Hymns with Tunes*, 1874. The word Noel comes from the word for birth.

374 All Saints New. *We thank Thee and we bless Thee*

Henry Stephen Cutler (1824–1902) was born in Boston, and went to Germany for music study. He returned as organist of the Church of the Advent, Boston, and was then organist at Trinity, New York. These joyous, vital words, by John Randall Dunn, are well suited to the vigorous tune.

375 Thornbury. *We thank Thee and we bless Thee*

This tune by Basil Harwood (Note 256) is an excellent support for the joyful reveille of these words. The music was composed for the 1916 edition of *Hymns Ancient and Modern*.

376 Reliance. *We thank Thee, heavenly Father*

Reliance is arranged from Mendelssohn, and was used with these same prayerful words, in the 1910 Hymnal. The story of the words is interesting. They were marked anonymous originally, but careful search discovered them in *The Christian Science Journal*, July, 1894, placed at the end of a prose article. When the writer of the prose, M. Fannie Whitney, was consulted, she admitted that the verses were hers, and that her friends had long urged her to claim them, but she had been content in knowing that they were useful.

377 Gosterwood. *We thank Thee, heavenly Father*

Again we have a Traditional melody with its unmistakable English swing. The tune was a folk song called "The brisk young lively lad."

378 Hussite Hymn. *We turn to Thee, O Lord*

One of the great forerunners of the Protestant Reformation was John Huss (1369–1415), whose persecuted followers were called Hussites, and groups of whom later formed the nucleus of the religious body known as Bohemian Brethren (Note 189).

The power of the Hussite Hymns is proved by an edict of 1418, three years after John Huss went to the stake. It orders the state to "repress the Hussite preaching and hymn-singing." Thus, one hundred years before Luther spoke, there were voices in Bohemia declaring "freedom to worship God."

This hymn is one of these early Protestant songs, and the music is still used in Czechoslovakia. Its words were rather martially national, and therefore other words, written by Frances Thompson Hill, have been set to it here.

379 Rathbun. *Well for him who, all things losing*

The words which are here translated from the German by Miss Winkworth are from a poem beginning, "O he who has lost all," which appeared in the Freylinghausen *Hymn Book*, in 1705. Miss Winkworth placed her version in her *Lyra Germanica*, 1855. The hymn was used, also, in a Moravian Hymnal of 1754, and credited to Gottfried Arnold, but this attribution is doubtful.

This tune is said to have been named for a little town in Pennsylvania. Its earliest known printing was in Greatorex's *Collection of Church Music* (New York), 1851. It was so much used with "In the cross of Christ I glory," by missionaries, that when a soldier rode into a village of Africa to ask for food and was denied, he began to sing this hymn and tune. It caught the ear of the chief, who gave the singer what he needed, because the missionaries had been kind.

Ithamar Conkey (1815–1867), born in Shutesbury, Massachusetts, worked mainly in New York, as bass singer and choir leader in Calvary Church, Grace Church, and the Madison Avenue Baptist Church.

380 Courage. *Well for him who, all things losing*

Here is a tune from the University of Wales collection, arranged by Sir Walford Davies (Note 159) for *A Students' Hymnal.*

381 St. Clement. *What brightness dawned in resurrection*

This music is by Clement Cotterill Scholefield (1839–1904), son of a Member of Parliament, who stood for Birmingham for twenty years. Graduating at Cambridge, the son was curate at Brighton and at Chelsea, then chaplain at Eton College, and finally vicar of Holy Trinity, Knightsbridge. The tune was composed for *Church Hymns with Tunes,* 1874.

The hymn is by William P. McKenzie, and was written specially for this music. These words, touching a faithful Mary's recognition of the risen Christ, have world-wide significance, and are a happy association with the music of Ellerton's hymn, of "the Church unsleeping," whose voice sounds round the world. The tenderness for "exiles yearning" is in harmony with Phillips Brooks' call for a Christianity that sees the world's hope in its own (Note 222).

382 St. Cecilia. *What is thy birthright, man*

The music of St. Cecilia is by Leighton G. Hayne (1836–1883), who, educated at Oxford, was appointed Coryphæus there (conductor of chorus), and public examiner in the school of music, then was made cantor and organist at Eton. Becoming rector of Mistley, he also succeeded his father at Bradfield rectory. A large five-manual organ he had built into the music room at Eton was rebuilt as two, for his two churches. This tune appeared in the *Merton Tune Book,* 1863, and in the *Christian Science Hymnal* of 1892.

The name of St. Cecilia, who "drew an angel down" to earth, and is everywhere the beloved of musicians, is a gracious one to associate with these words by Emily F. Seal, which were published in *The Christian Science Journal,* June, 1890, and in the first edition of the Hymnal, 1892. The poem is named The Seal of Love.

383 Horsley. *Whatever dims thy sense of truth*

The use of this music of William Horsley (1774–1858), with the words of Mary Hale, is one of the happy matings of the Hymnal. For she was a teacher of youth in New England, and Horsley was organist and teacher at the girls' Orphan Asylum in London. The tune was published in his collection of 1844, and was written for the children to sing. His son, J. C. Horsley, the painter, has left a word-picture from his own childish memories. He went with his father to hear a service at the Orphans' chapel, and when a hundred buxom girls, all dressed alike, rose up and sang at their little visitor, the child joined his voice with theirs in startled protest! In 1835 Horsley became organist at the Charterhouse School.

Mary Whitwell Hale (1810–1862) grew up in her father's house in Hollis Street, on the edge of the old South End, then a fashionable part of Boston. She became a successful teacher—long at Keene, New Hampshire, then at Taunton, Massachusetts, and at Bristol Academy. The hymn used here is named The Mother's Counsel, and is headed by the actual counsel of the mother of John Wesley: "Whatever obscures your sense of God, or takes out the relish of spiritual things . . . that is sin to you . . . however innocent it may be in itself."

384 Morning Hymn. *When God is seen with men to dwell*

This is a tuneful melody, and the story of its composer is also full of color. François Hippolite Barthélémon (1741–1808) was born at Bordeaux, France. His mother was an Irish lady, from a good family in Queen's county. Thus the young man found his place in Berwick's Regiment of the Irish Brigade, and so made friends with the Earl of Kelley, who, an amateur in music, encouraged the talents of the gay young Irish-French officer. Barthélémon therefore settled in England, where, with the help of his aristocratic friend, he reached high repute as a violinist, becoming leader of the band at Marylebone Gardens. Later he made a concert tour through Europe, and revisited Dublin. He married a niece of the popular Dr. Arne. He composed this melody for Bishop Ken's hymn, Awake my soul.

The story of Hosea Ballou (1771–1852), the poet here, is in striking contrast with the life of the composer. Hosea was a farm boy, who made Ballou one of the famous names of his native state. Born in Richmond, New Hampshire, he was so literally self-educated that he taught himself to make the letters of the alphabet, drawing them on birch bark with charcoal. He kindled to the ideas of John Murray, an English Methodist, who had organized an Independent Church at Gloucester, Massachusetts. When about twenty years old, the New Hampshire boy began to preach, and his *Treatise on Atonement,* 1808, unfolded the imperishable idea of universal salvation, out of which came the Universalist movement, of which he stands as the chief American founder.

He saw in this idea of the redemption of all men through Christ, the Second Advent, and gave this name to this hymn. Long before him, however, Jonathan Edwards, of Connecticut, had foreseen and actually dated the return of the Christ to earth in 1866.

385 Solothurn. *When Israel, of the Lord beloved*

The words of this hymn were written by Sir Walter Scott (1771–1832), for his novel, *Ivanhoe.* He says that he has ventured to make a translation of the Hebrew hymn, but it is not a close rendering of Psalm 105, on which it is based.

The use of two stanzas from it by Mrs. Eddy in *Science and Health with Key to the Scriptures* (p. 566) is significant, for they occur at the close of her interpretation of Revelation 12:6, "And the woman fled into the wilderness, where she hath a place prepared of God." The words are sung by Rebecca, the noble Hebrew maiden, who is waiting trial on a charge of sorcery, brought against her by the Knights Templar. In Rebecca's talk with her persecutor, Scott becomes special pleader for the greatness and glory of the Chosen People of old, to whom it was given, as his Rebecca says, to hear the Voice of God.

A friend once described to Scott the difficulties of the Jews in Europe, and asked him to use some Jewish characters in a novel. So Rebecca and her father found their place in the brilliant throng that moves across the stage in *Ivanhoe,* this drama of the time of Richard Lion-heart. When Washington Irving visited Scott, the great story teller was trying to find a model worthy of his heroine. Irving told him about a beautiful Jewish maiden in Philadelphia, who is still remembered by her descendants as Scott's Rebecca.

The use of these words with the famous old tune, Solothurn, is especially appropriate. We know how Scott sought out the popular legends of his people. Solothurn is the fruit of similar research for traditional melodies that had no other record than the loving memory of the Swiss. It is named for one of the Swiss Cantons. A number of tunes in the Hymnal have this popular origin.

This tune has the quality of the Swiss mountain music, and brings to thought the Alpine herdsman or hunter, as he sends his voice, or the resonant call of his horn, across the stern, snowy heights of the old Helvetian stronghold of liberty.

The music of three lines ends with long, slow chords that step downward to a place of rest (or "resolution"), and well convey the solemn image of the words.

386 Hamburg. *When Jesus our great Master came*

We are told, rather oracularly, that Hamburg was arranged "from the first Gregorian tone," in the Handel and Haydn collection edited by Lowell Mason, Boston, 1824 (Note 2). It is headed, also, Benedictus, there; and in the *Church Hymnary* of 1901, it is named Boston.

The second and third stanzas of the words are from Watts' hymn, based on Titus 2:10–13 and named, Holiness and Grace. The first stanza is not found in Watts, and may have been written by Montgomery. This form of the hymn was used in the first edition of the *Christian Science Hymnal,* 1892.

387 Ely. *When Jesus our great Master came*

Thomas Turton (1780–1864) was Lucasian Professor of Mathematics at Cambridge University, but, like so many learned Englishmen, he appears to have "kept up his music," with good effect. Later he was Regius Professor of Divinity, Prebendary of Lincoln Cathedral, Dean of Peterborough and of Westminster, and finally Bishop of Ely. The tune appeared in *The People's Music Book,* 1844, by Turle and Taylor. It was originally named St. Catherine.

388 Bromley. *When like a stranger on our sphere*

This is one of Clark's "melodious inventions" (Note 94), harmonized by Matthew M. Bridges (1800–1894), who was also a writer of hymns. Some of them were used in the *Plymouth Collection* of the American preacher, Henry Ward Beecher. Brought up in the English church, Bridges wrote a book that examined Roman beliefs, and twenty years later he entered that church. He lived for some time in Quebec. Dr. Robert Bridges believes that this tune of Clark's inspired the Rockingham of Miller (No. 188), and is superior to Miller.

The hymn here is from Montgomery's Volume V, page 245, a poem of ten stanzas. The first stanza is as given here except the fourth line, which there reads, "And sickness raised her drooping head." The second stanza here paraphrases his stanzas 4, 5, 6, and the present third is his seventh, altered. It is not known who made this clear-cut hymn out of a rather wandering poem; but the result is perhaps an answer to Montgomery's objections to editorial revision of his work—even when he was himself amending the work of others. This version appeared in the first edition of the *Christian Science Hymnal,* 1892.

389 O christliche Herzen. *While Thou, O my God, art my help and defender*

The *Portnersches Hymn Book* was apparently the work of Canon S. Portner, for use in the Diocese of Würzburg. The German words used with the tune begin, as above, O Christian Hearts. The hymn here is by William Young, probably rightly identified with the Rev. William Young of the London Missionary Society, a number of whose hymns were translated into the dialects of China. The line, "In this land of the stranger," speaks one living far from home.

390 Langran. *Why is thy faith in God's great love so small?*

Langran bears the name of its composer (Note 370). The words are by William F. Sherwin, a Baptist, of Massachusetts (1826–1888). He studied music in Boston under Lowell Mason (Note 2), and became a teacher and composer of vocal music. He was associated with the Rev. Robert Lowry (Note 137) in Sunday School work and composed songs for children. His hymns are few. This one is named, Safety in Jesus.

391 Wareham. *Why search the future and the past?*

Wareham was written by William Knapp (1698–1768), who was born in Wareham, England. He was parish clerk at St. James, Poole, Dorset. One of the duties of parish clerk was to announce the hymns, saying, "Let us all sing to the praise and glory of God." This is a well-made melody with only a single skip—in the first line. The words are by Charles H. Barlow and appeared in *The Christian Science Journal,* July, 1888. The first line is "Man longs through life's dark day of pain," with the title, Thy Word is Nigh.

392 Golden Sheaves. *With love and peace and joy supreme*

Sullivan's Golden Sheaves has a charming name, and is a capital tune for these significant words from the same long poem, In Transitu, which is used at No. 197. This hymn, written by Laura C. Nourse, appeared in the Hymnal of 1892. Two additional stanzas were adapted from the poem, to fit the hymn to this eight-line tune.

The music was composed for Dix's Harvest hymn, of singing valleys that stand thick with corn.

393 Ach Gott und Herr. *With love and peace and joy supreme*

A thunderstorm that burst over Weimar, more than three hundred years ago, is commemorated in the name of this tune, proving that music is indeed an efficient "remembrancer." Dr. Johann Major, too, is remembered, for he preached a sermon about the storm at Jena, and published his "sermon on the fierce storm and frightful floods" that had devastated Thuringia and driven all the inhabitants to shelter. At the end of the sermon the hymn appears, beginning, as above, O God and Lord. It has often been put into English, notably in the *Moravian Hymn Book,* with "As small birds use A hole to chuse"—indicating the refuge provided by divine care.

The hymn was set to music by Christoph Peter (1626–1669), and published in Leipzig in 1652. Then Peter altered it for his *Cymbals of Devotion,* 1658, and in this form it was adopted by Bach. Peter was born in Weide, Vogtland, and became singing master at Guben.

394   Pleyel's Hymn. *Word of Life, most pure, most strong*

The words of the Town Preacher at Oberstenfeld, Württemberg, sing for us in this noble hymn. He was Jonathan F. Bahnmeier (1774–1841), a worker in education and in Missionary and Bible societies, and also on the committee for revising the *Württemberg Hymn Book.* This fine version is by Miss Catherine Winkworth, in her *Lyra Germanica II* (Note 199).

The story of Ignace J. Pleyel (1757–1831) is specially interesting for the attempt to bring him into rivalry with his teacher, Joseph Haydn, which was foiled by the pupil's loyalty and the master's magnanimity. The Professional Concerts in London had been in charge of Haydn's manager, but in 1791, Pleyel, then chapelmaster at Strassburg Cathedral, was invited to direct this famous series. Pleyel, however, placed a symphony by Haydn on his first program, and afterward master and pupil agreed together that there was fame enough for them both. In France, Pleyel was charged with enmity to the Republic, but afterward was able to settle there as a music seller, and in 1807 founded in Paris the piano factory so long famous under his name. He also published the quartets of Haydn, dedicating the edition to Bonaparte, as First Consul. Pleyel wrote twenty-nine symphonies, and other instrumental works in proportion. Mozart expected great things of him, but, perhaps because he wrote so much, he became a mere imitator of his master Haydn, to the disadvantage of them both. He was born in Lower Austria, and studied at Vienna and in Italy.

395   Palms of Glory. *Word of Life, most pure, most strong*

The tune's name, no doubt, goes back to the Gospel scene where Jesus entered Jerusalem to shouts of Hosanna and the tribute of palm branches, as in John 12. It is a beautiful name for this poem of the Word of Life. The composer, William D. Maclagan (1826–1910), was a clergyman, who came to his ordination after having studied law, and served in the Indian army. He rose high in the church, from his early service as curate, and as secretary of the London Diocesan Church Building Society. In 1878, he was consecrated Bishop of Lichfield. Now he became honorary chaplain to the Queen, and finally Archbishop of York, the second highest ecclesiastical honor in England. It was he who crowned Queen Alexandra at the coronation of Edward VII. Maclagan's music seems to be confined to the hymn tunes that have been as popular as his few hymns.

396 Carlisle. *Ye messengers of Christ*

The name Lockhart (1745–1815) leads back to the Lock Hospital of London, that names the collection of hymns which was the practice book of the young Handel and Haydn Society of Boston, in 1815. Charles Lockhart was organist for this great philanthropy of Martin Madan, who, hearing Wesley preach, was suddenly converted, took orders, and then founded and became the chaplain of this famous place. Lockhart was noted for his success in training choirs of children. The words, "Ye messengers of Christ," have never been traced beyond the single sheet on which they appeared in 1791, with the signature, Mrs. Vokes. Others of her hymns appeared in Griffin's *Selection of Missionary and Devotional Hymns,* 1797.

397 Song 20. *Ye messengers of Christ*

Gibbons' music here has specially exquisite alternations of minor and major color, showing how strong and expressive a minor can be, with no hint of sadness. The clearness and purity of this music give it supreme beauty. Austere and tender, searching, it makes one feel of Gibbons that he. "nothing common did or mean." The inscription in Canterbury Cathedral says of him that his "manner of life and sweetness of temper vy'd with that of his art" (Note 69).

398 St. Ethelwald. *Ye servants of the Lord*

The grandson of one of the ministers in Cromwell's Commonwealth might have been expected to refuse even a university career, if it obliged him to "conform." So when the Duchess of Bedford told the poet here, Philip Doddridge (1702–1751) that she would send him to Oxford if he would be ordained in the Established Church, he refused. He was finally appointed at Castle Hill Meeting, Northampton, where many students gathered round him, mostly to be prepared for the ministry. He taught Hebrew, Greek, Trigonometry, Logic and Divinity, and the University of Aberdeen could do no less than give him a Master's degree. He was a friend of Watts and Whitefield. From this gentle friendly divine we have two hymns. (See Note 124.) For the composer, W. H. Monk, see Note 7. This tune was composed for *Hymns Ancient and Modern,* 1861.

399 Southwell. *Ye timid saints*

Cowper wrote, "Ye fearful saints," but editors have perhaps felt this was extreme reproach. The hymn begins, "God moves in a mysterious way," and is entitled, Light Shining out of Darkness (Note 313).

Southwell is by Herbert S. Irons (1834–1905), nephew of Sir George Elvey (Note 312). Born at Canterbury, he sang as a boy at the Cathedral, so famous in English history. Then he was cantor at St. Columba's

331

College, Ireland, a place with other famous associations, and then organist at Southwell Minster. Later he was organist at Chester Cathedral and at St. Andrew's, Nottingham.

400 Clearway. *Ye timid saints*

The name Clearway is given for the street on the north side of the Christian Science Publishing House of 1932. For the composer, see Note 330.

401 Italian Hymn. *Thou whose almighty Word*

For words and music, see Note 346. Here the soprano melody is retained, as in the 1910 edition of the Hymnal.

This, the first hymn in the Supplement of the *Christian Science Hymnal*, offers an example of tunes repeated from the main body of the book, usually in a simpler form. Other hymns and tunes were chosen, or were restored from the 1910 edition, too late to have their alphabetical place in the book.

402 Dennis. *How gentle God's commands*

Switzerland sent this tune to America a hundred years ago. Hans Georg Naegeli (1768–1836) was a music publisher in Zurich, who brought out classic works in especially fine editions. These included three of Beethoven's greatest sonatas, and the composer wrote most friendly letters to his publisher, that show him trying to help circulate the poetry of Naegeli, whose life was devoted to the musical progress of his home province. Naegeli became president of the Swiss Association for the Cultivation of Music. When Lowell Mason visited Europe to seek out new music for his music-hungry countrymen, this tune was among the manuscripts he bought. He gave it the name Dennis and printed it in *The Psaltery*, 1845, set to the same words as are used here. For Doddridge, see Note 398.

403 Balerma. *How sweet, how heavenly is the sight*

The tune and words from No. 126 are repeated here, the music in 3/4 measure. The name is spelled more nearly like the Spanish original, Belerma.

404 Olmutz. *O do not bar your mind*

The words are repeated here from No. 201, and the tune from the 1910 edition of the Hymnal. Mason perhaps named the tune for the town where an important conference between Austria and Prussia was held in 1850. In an old Wesleyan Hymnal it stands as Olmutz, in 4/4 time, with quarter notes (crotchets) throughout, except at the close of three phrases. It is marked Gregorian, but with Mason's name.

332

405 Benevento. *Glory be to God on high*

This hymn and tune are from No. 72, the music being given here with a much more active bass.

406 St. Margaret. *O Love, our Mother, ever near*

For more than thirty years, Albert L. Peace (1844–1912) played the organ for the people of Glasgow, and was so beloved that Dr. Boyd, the preacher, said he never dared give out the hymn, Peace, Perfect Peace, lest the organist should take it to himself! Peace was another child who read notes before he could read words, and at nine years of age was made organist at Holmfirth. At twenty-one, he went to Glasgow as organist of Trinity Congregational Church, and in 1879 became organist of Glasgow Cathedral. In 1897, he was made organist of St. George's Hall, in Liverpool, where he worked to popularize good music by organ recitals. He set Psalm 138 for voices and orchestra, and wrote a cantata, St. John the Baptist. It is interesting, in view of Dr. Boyd's bit of humor, to find here the words "perfect peace" used with this music. It was composed for *The Scottish Hymnal*, 1885. For the inspiring words, see Note 232.

407 Evan New. *To Thee, our loving Father, God*

This arrangement of Evan, No. 357, was made especially for the Hymnal.

408 Gerontius. *Prayer with our waking thought ascends*

These inspiring words are repeated from No. 287. Here they have the music composed by Dr. Dykes (Note 169) for Newman's hymn, from his Dream of Gerontius, a work set to music by Sir Edward Elgar.

409 Azmon New. *Supreme in wisdom as in power*

Here is an adaptation from Mason's arrangement of Gläser's tune at No. 320.

410 Dalehurst. *No mortal sense can still or stay*

The composer here was a studious member of the legal profession, who evidently tossed off a tune for relaxation. Arthur Cottman (1842–1874) published *Ten Original Tunes* in 1874, which seem to have been his last work. The words are from No. 194.

411 Ein' feste Burg. *All power is given unto our Lord*

This is No. 10, in a higher key and slightly simplified, as in the 1910 edition of the *Christian Science Hymnal*.

333

412 Londonderry. *O dreamer, leave thy dreams for joyful waking*

The Londonderry air is one of the world-famous tunes of the Hymnal. It is known not only to hymn books, especially those of Ireland, but to popular song, fragrant with memories of home. It has tender sentiment, not mere sentimentality, and so it is lovely alike to musicians and to those who "only know what they like." Sir Hubert Parry, discussing folk music in his *Evolution of the Art of Music,* describes this air as "one of the most perfect in existence."

Its name takes us back to the day of James I, when, in the scheme for colonizing Ireland, the old Derry of northern Ireland was allotted to the citizens of London, and named Londonderry. This name reappears in Londonderry, Vermont, the town that was the home of Asa Gilbert Eddy and of his family.

This tune is found in an old manuscript preserved in the British Museum, in London, England. Its origin is unknown, but it is admittedly Irish. It began, perhaps, as a violin or flute melody, extemporized and developed by some wandering minstrel. From time to time, such airs were given words, romantic, patriotic, or religious, for they were irresistibly singable.

The surprising beauty of this tune may be partly understood from its structure. It is built up in a series of rising motives, the "crisis" of which falls on a dotted quarter note. These rise and repeat, reëchoed, until the final climax comes in the seventh line. The music thus develops a broader sweep than is felt in tunes of four lines. This soaring climax on the upper F, an octave above the first dotted quarter, gives the voice its delighted escape into the blue sky.

The tune is exceptionally vocal, because it is properly adjusted to the nature of song. The human voice is made for, and needs, these occasional upliftings into purer air, above the earth. The daily round limits the voice to its speaking range. Song is more than this. Even those who think that a high note is hard to reach find in the long run that to keep the voice always at the speech level is tiresome and inexpressive. The voice is meant to vary and to soar.

The words by Rosa M. Turner, a Christian Scientist, seem to have been carefully molded to this melody, to express its lovely mood of meditation and tenderness—of yearning aspiration. It is altogether the song of those who know that they seek a country.

413 Easter. *Let us sing of Easter gladness*

The tune Easter first appeared in London, in 1708, in a little anonymous book named *Lyra Davidica, or a Collection of Divine Songs and Hymns, . . . set to easy and pleasant tunes.*

No one knows who was the editor—perhaps some Anglo-German. The words he gave to this one of his "easy and pleasant tunes" were from a Latin hymn:

> Jesus Christ is risen today, Halle-halle-lujah;
> Our triumphant Holyday, Halle-halle-lujah;
> Haste ye females from your fright, Halle-halle-lujah;
> Take to Galilee your flight, Halle-halle-lujah;
> To his sad disciples say, Halle-halle-lujah;
> Jesus Christ is risen today! Halle-halle-lujah.

The tune was an innovation, in using so many groups of two notes to a syllable. It became very popular, and Dr. Burney is responsible for the statement, in 1789, that only two new tunes had been introduced into the church service for one hundred years, and these were the stately Hanover and this "easy and pleasant tune" of Easter.

The words here begin

> Let us sing of Easter gladness
> That rejoices every day,

and were written, and especially adapted to this music, by Frances Thompson Hill, a Christian Scientist. They show that no limited Easter celebration belongs to the Christian Science churches, because the Resurrection may be discerned, and sung, on any and every day. A similar idea for Christmas appears in the words of Whittier, at No. 170.

414   I Love to Tell the Story. *I love to tell the story*

At Communion time, in 1904, Mrs. Eddy sent to The Mother Church a brief message, that included what she described as "Kate Hankey's excellent hymn" (*The First Church of Christ, Scientist, and Miscellany,* p. 15). This hymn appeared in Miss Hankey's *Heart to Heart,* 1870, where it was named, The Love of Jesus. It was used in Bliss's *Gospel Songs,* Cincinnati, 1874. Miss Hankey's "Tell me the old, old story" was a Life of Jesus, in two parts, called "The Story Wanted" and "The Story Told." It was written in 1866, and has been widely published, including versions in Welsh, German, Italian, Spanish, etc. Julian says that some of Miss Hankey's hymns are "of great beauty and simplicity," and her music also "may be consulted with advantage."

Arabella Katherine Hankey (1834–1911), always known as Kate Hankey, was one of a band of Evangelicals in England, known as the Clapham Sect. At eighteen, she started a Bible class in London for the girls who worked in the big shops, and she kept up a lifelong friendship with many of them. She published, besides her verse, a book of *Bible Class Teachings.*

William G. Fischer (1835–1912), whose tune has recently been called Hankey, was born in Baltimore, Maryland. He showed his aptitude for leading people in song so early that at eight years he was chosen to lead the singing in a Baltimore church. At twenty-three, he was a professor of music in Girard College, Philadelphia, and during the Moody and Sankey meetings there he directed a choir of one thousand singers.

415 Pilgrim. *I'm a pilgrim, and I'm a stranger*

These familiar words come to the Hymnal from Beaufort, South Carolina, where Mary Stanley Bunce was born, in 1810. When she married Charles E. Dana, of New York, they removed to Iowa, in 1838, and the following year, Mrs. Dana returned home, a widow. Afterward she married the Rev. Robert D. Shindler, a professor at Shelby College, Kentucky. In 1840–1841, she published the *Southern Harp* and the *Northern Harp,* from which her hymns are taken.

The tune that is always used with these words has here been slightly altered.

416 Linwood. *Be true and list the voice within*

Another setting of these words is at No. 20, and the composer, Rossini, is found in Note 121.

417 Antioch. *Joy to the world, the Lord is come*

Antioch, much sung with Isaac Watts' splendid "Joy to the world," has long been attributed to Handel, as arranged by Mason. Though the melody is not traced, the first line or two are Handelian enough, for he was fond of using the descending scale in melody. In Theodora (Note 324), the last line but one illustrates this characteristic. It is supposed that this tune, Antioch, was from Gardner's *Sacred Melodies,* into which Mason so often delved, but much altered by him.

A change has been made in Watts' words, for obvious reasons. To say that blessings flow "Far as the curse is found," would seem to make the reach of blessing depend on its opposite. The more affirmative statement shows blessing flowing everywhere. The words are from No. 164.

418 Eternity. *O, the clanging bells of time*

It is remembered of Philip Paul Bliss (1838–1876) that when he went into the work of an evangelist, he gave the whole of his income from his songs to support the cause. Born in Pennsylvania, he went to Chicago to work with George F. Root, in musical institutes, and making songs for Sunday Schools. Among his familiar hymns are "Only an armor bearer," and "Ho, my comrades, see the signal." He wrote words as well as music.

Ellen M. Gates, née Huntington, was born in Torrington, Connecticut, and wrote hymns for missions and Sunday Schools. The hymn here is named Yearning for Heaven. Her collected verses were published in 1895.

419 Holley. *O Love whose perfect path is known*

The composer of this familiar tune, George Hews (1806–1873), was born near Boston, where he became organist at Brattle Street Church and a manufacturer of pianos. The Harvard Musical Association used to meet at his rooms, and made him an honorary member. This tune appeared in the Boston Academy's collection, 1835, with Bishop Doane's "Softly now the light of day." The words are from No. 233.

420 Compassion. *So brightly burns Love's holy glow*

Compassion is a good name to go with these expressive words from No. 311. The music is by C. B. Rich, an American.

421 Sarum. *From these Thy children gathered in Thy name*

Barnby's Sarum bears the historic name of English church tradition, and with its "Alleluia" refrain, after the steady measure of the tune, has rather an atmosphere of a bygone day (Note 147). The words were written for the 1932 edition of the Hymnal by Violet Hay. They appear also in No. 66. Sarum was written for Dr. How's For all the Saints.

422 Alsace. *Grace for today, O Love divine*

The music of Alsace is from the slow movement of Beethoven's Second Symphony, a work that is the fullest expression possible to the older or "classic" style seen in Handel and Mozart. After that, Beethoven opened a new world of music, never before explored. His great Third Symphony shows music not as merely a formal beauty or art, or "frozen architecture," but as poetry, alive with human experience. The beautiful building now is a home of humanity.

The nine symphonies of Beethoven are a compendium of music, indicating even its modern freedom. In 1817 (before the Ninth Symphony), he ranked the Third (1804) above all the others. He wrote the name Bonaparte into its title, but afterward erased it, perhaps because of his hero's imperial ambitions. He sought to portray in music a whole man. Romain Rolland calls this symphony the "Lazarus arise" that followed the desolation of the "Testament," a farewell letter which Beethoven wrote to his brothers, when to him deafness first seemed inevitable (1802). Rolland says that the hero of this symphony, called the *Eroica* (heroic), was always and only Beethoven himself.

George Sand once wrote of the wings of courage that lifted her hero, a friendless little boy, above fear. Beethoven, stricken with deafness at about thirty, but rising to his most glorious music after that, truly put forth wings of courage. Of his deafness, he said, ". . . it shall not drag me down."

The notebooks of Beethoven show his tremendous working power. From the simple outlines of his first jottings, he worked out, by patient revision, the rich color and intricate forms that mark his mature work. Daniel Gregory Mason counts in Beethoven four leading traits: virile energy, tenderness or sentiment, irrepressible gayety, and that "mood of mystery," wherein the master reached out for "the illimitable, the transcendent." Humor is a mark of Beethoven's greatness, for it is a sign of courage. We owe to him the Scherzo (literally a "joke") which came with its "inspired rush," out of the more sedate minuet of Haydn's third movement, in his symphonies.

Speaking of Mozart as "a musician beyond what the world knew," Mrs. Eddy wrote in *Science and Health* (p. 213): "This was even more strikingly true of Beethoven, who was so long hopelessly deaf." Her incisive definition, "Music is the rhythm of head and heart" (*ibid.*) is very perfectly illustrated by Beethoven's music, in which, as Mason said, eloquence of expression [heart] and beauty of form [head] were always held in exact and controlled balance. (See Notes 58, 181.) The words are from No. 91.

423   Penitentia. *Give me, O Lord, an understanding heart*

This tune by Edward Dearle (1806–1891), with its regular alternations of measures all "white" notes, and those including "black" notes, is well balanced, and well fitted to the strong and earnest words. (See No. 69.) The composer was born in Cambridge, England, and was at first organist at St. Paul's, Deptford. At Newark, he was "song schoolmaster," 1835–1864. He became one of the founders of Trinity College, London, and a composer of songs and part songs. Among other teachers at Trinity have been Sir John Goss, Henry Smart, George Cooper, Dr. E. J. Hopkins, Sir George Elvey, Sir Herbert Oakeley, Sir Hubert Parry, Sir Joseph Barnby, and Sir Arthur Sullivan, all of them represented in the Hymnal.

424   Comfort. *I cannot always trace the way*

Two tunes by C. B. Rich, this and No. 420, have names of compassion, which perhaps may hint the nature of this unknown composer. The words are from No. 133.

425   Joy cometh in the Morning. *O weary pilgrim, lift your head*

This hymn is clear evidence of the reason why songs of this character have been a strength and stay to thousands, and have had an influence beyond the work of many more excellent poets and composers. The vitality of this song is in its repetition of the Bible promises. Its refrain is word for word from Psalms 30:5. The second stanza, again, is

Biblical. The music is by Edmund S. Lorenz, writer of two books on Church Music, and composer of many popular tunes. He is an American.

In the memoirs of a Christian Scientist, with whose family Mrs. Eddy was long in close association, is told the simple story of the hymn, "Joy cometh in the morning," which cheered the Leader of the Christian Science movement, after a night of waiting on God. Mrs. Eddy loved the Bible words from which it is drawn. She also loved the great music of the masters, as she recorded in the letter cited in our Foreword. She was able to take what was for her, wherever it might be spoken, even from the lips of a child. She never set musical or other "taste" above the direct statement of man's whole dependence upon God, a dependence which often places very simple hymnody truly "on the side of the angels."

426   Jehovah. *In Love divine all earth-born fear and sorrow*

These beautiful words are repeated from No. 149. For the work of Dr. Hopkins, see Note 208.

427   Rest. *I walk with Love along the way*

The sweet and appealing words are from No. 139. The tune is an interesting example of rising motives, repeated at higher intervals. For Stainer, see Note 160.

428   Hammersmith. *O God, our Father-Mother, Love*

The rhythm of the poem, Reality, so prayerful in its spirit, is well expressed by this music of Mr. Gladstone. (See Notes 206, 243.)

429   Boston. *Thou art the Way*

The association of ideas found in this tune name and its words, makes an inspiring and reassuring close for the *Christian Science Hymnal*. The words are by the beloved Bishop Doane, who once preached in Boston (Note 343). The tune, so well adapted to this devout hymn, for which it was specially composed, is named for the home of the composer.

Miss E. Elizabeth Siedhoff, a Christian Scientist, was born in Lockport, New York. She studied at the Longy School in Boston and with the composer Frederick Converse. During three years in Berlin, studying piano with Breithaupt and Schnabel, composition with Leichtentritt, and organ with Walter Fischer, she was the first woman organist at the American Church there. After studying with Godowsky, she had three seasons with Tobias Matthay in London. She has given successful concerts on both organ and piano in Europe and America.

Thus the Hymnal opens with the most widely known song of all Hymnody, and closes with a tune written for this Hymnal, and named for the city in which the *Christian Science Hymnal* was first published, just forty years before this edition of 1932.

DATES IN HYMNODY

Selected names of poets and musicians, from the *Christian Science Hymnal*, 1932, are grouped here in approximately fifty year periods of activity. This outline for study may be extended by use of the Hymnal Index, with its lists of Traditional melodies. Figures here refer to the Notes, except a few dates. The Index of the Notes gives full lists of the work of each poet or composer, as found in the Hymnal.

POETRY	MUSIC
David. The Psalms, from which the Psalters are taken.	Gregorian modes, named for Gregory the Great (540–604) who systema-
Armenian Liturgy, 113. Said to have been taken from that of the Church of Jerusalem.	tized the plain song, or chanting, of the early church. For modes, or scales, see Webster's Dictionary, *mode*. Notes 7, 386, 404; 159.
Aldhelm, c. 700, Note 2.	St. Columba (521–597), Note 339. Irish Traditional airs, possibly from
Metrical versions of the Psalms.	the ancient church. 136, 145, 412.

900–1200

Notes 56, 168; words from old Latin hymns. See Lyra Davidica, 413.	Pierre Corbeil, music for mystery play. 114.

1300–1600(?)

Old carol words, 242; modern example, 222.	Carols: 146, 152, 184, 237, 242. Modern examples, 222, 223.

1400–1450

(Bible words used in Hymnal.)	John Huss and his followers, 378. Bohemian Brethren, 189.

1450–1500

(Gerhardt's words, c. 1635, used in Hymnal.)	Heinrich Isaac, called the first German musician, 361.

1500–1550

Sarum Use, Note 316.	Sarum Gradual, 316.
Hebrew words tr. in Notes, 281, 371.	Mooz Zur, 281; Leoni, 371. (?)
Ein' feste Burg, Luther, 10.	Luther, 10, 168.
Christmas play, 168. Wedderburn, 168.	Nicolas Herman, 101.

Sternhold's Psalter, 99, 107.

"Let it be remembered for the honor of this parish, that from it sounded out the Psalms of David in English metre, by Thomas Sternhold and John Hopkins." (Old register of Awre, Gloucestershire.)

340

POETRY	MUSIC

1550–1600

Genevan Psalter, Marot and Beza, Notes 1, 108.

Acts of the Apostles, Tye, 225.

Anglo - Genevan Psalter, Sternhold. Used in Church of England, 107.

Many versions of Psalms in meter, as William Hunnis: *Seven Sobs of a Sorrowful Soul for Sinne.*

Genevan Psalter, Bourgeois, 1, 62–3; Goudimel, 108.
Christopher Tye, 225; Tallis, 272.
Anglo-Genevan Psalter, with "church tunes," imitating European music. Crespin, 2, 107, 215.
Damon's and Este's and the Scottish Psalters, 107; 122, 286; 215. (See Psalters, Index.)

1600–1650

Wither's Hymn Book, 69.
Heermann, 76; Rinkart, 199.
Bay Psalm Book, Note 2.
Published Cambridge, 1640, by Stephen Day. The first book ever printed in the Colonies. Seventy editions, Boston, London, Edinburgh.
Gerhardt, 119; Neumark, 216; Milton, 125.

Dowland, 53; Campion, 353; Orlando Gibbons, 69.
Corner, Carol, 9.
Reformation Chorale.
Hassler, 252; Praetorius, 366; Crüger, 199; Teschner, 153.
Albert, 166; Neumark, 216; Hintze, 11; Ahle, 85; Schop, 13; Heinlein, 89; Peter, 393; Joseph, 214.

1650–1700

The Psalms, Hymns, and Spiritual Songs of the Old and New Testament . . . for the comfort of the Saints . . . especially in New England. By President Dunster of Harvard.
Neander, 283.
A New Version of the Psalms of David, Fitted to the Tunes used in the Churches. By N. Tate and N. Brady, London, 1696. Note 99, see Index.

Playford's first collection, 1671.
These books (*Divine Companion*) continued for a century, by Playford of London or successors. See Index of Notes, Playford.
Düben, 263; Crusader's Hymn (?), 275.
Henry Purcell, 17; 182.
Clark, 94; Croft, 52.
J. Bishop, 129; Chetham, 321.

1700–1750

Watts, 62; Doddridge, 124.

S. Browne, 39.

John Wesley: First Hymn Book, used in Church of England, was his *Psalms and Hymns,* Charleston, S. C., 1737. Note 336.

Charles Wesley (1707–1788), 105. His first large collection of poems, 1749.

Brorson, 19.

Fitzgerald collection, 200.

Johann Sebastian Bach, 14, 252, etc.
Georg Friedrich Handel, 324.
Lyra Davidica, 413.
Steiner, 55; Vetter, 233; Konig's Choralbuch, 44, 239.
Tans'ur, 348; Arne, 372; Nares, 16; Giardini, 346; I. Smith, 333; Jones, 334.
Cotton Mather: *Psalterium Americanum.*
Psalms fitted to the Tunes . . . used in our Churches. Boston, in New England.

POETRY	MUSIC

1750–1800

Cowper, 313; Williams, W., 90; Newton, 71; Beddome, 240.
Morison, 362; Cameron, 320.
Rutgers, 73; Holden, 86, 341.

Haydn and Mozart, Notes 71, 170, 185; 34, 93.
Miller, 188; Haweis, 38; Webbe, 6; Barthélémon, 384; Giornovichi, 158.

1800–1850

Montgomery, 83; Scott, 385; Ballou, 384; Bahnmeier, 394; Moore, 40.

Auber, 281; Elliott, 67; Heber, 117; Keble, 140; Bowring, 79; Hemans, 44; Lyte, 8; Newman, 169.

Frothingham, 214; Doane, 343.

Trench, 182; Bonar, 21; Wordsworth, 173; Faber, 86; Gaskell, 186; Gill, 247; How, 251.

Whittier, 49; Mrs. Stowe, 317.

Wallin, 263; Grundtvig, 176; Ingemann, 351; Oldenburg, 84; Spitta, 135.

Beethoven, 58, 181, 422.
Flemming, 179.
Weber, 365; Schubert, 43; Schumann, 322; Mendelssohn, 118.
Malan, 186; Urhan, 151.
Rossini, 121.
Gardiner's *Sacred Melodies* used by Mason in Boston, 2; 105.
Handel and Haydn Society, 352; Zeuner, 218.
Reinagle, 125; Gauntlett, 201; Goss, 280; Turle, 54; S. S. Wesley, 75.
Berggreen, 209; Lindeman, 84; Wennerberg, 204; Stenhammar, 76; Winding, 332.

1850–1900

Holmes, 319; Lowell, 258; Longfellow, 134; Johnson, 37; Coxe, 353.
Neale, 115; Baker, 330; E. Charles, 360; Baring-Gould, 264; Dix, 43; Havergal, 65.
Gladden, 234; Brooks, 222; Hosmer, 57; T. C. Williams, 81.
First Christian Science Hymnal, 1892.

Redhead, 367; Smart, 42; Elvey, 312; Hopkins, 208; Baker, 400; Dykes, 169; Monk, 7; Stewart, 172.
Barnby, 147; Stainer, 160; Sullivan, 264; Parratt, 173; Parry, 50.
Morse, 217.
Horatio Parker, 20.

1900

Christian Science Hymnal, Revision of 1932.
With seven hymns by Mary Baker Eddy (see below) and ninety by other Christian Scientists.

Sir Walford Davies, 159; Vaughan Williams, 66; David Evans, 345; Sir Hugh Allen, 41; Dyson, 39; Ferguson, 250; G. Shaw, 279; M. Shaw, 364; Somervell, 143. (See below.)

MUSIC FOR MRS. EDDY'S HYMNS

COMPOSED	SELECTED	

Brackett, 254, 298, 304.
Conant, 24; 305; 207 (arranged by).
Greenwood, 28, 302, 309.
Johnson, 253, 306.
O'Connor-Morris, 301.
Thalben-Ball, 26, 300, 308.
Whitlock, 27, 162, 211, 257.
Young, 30, 161, 299.

Atkinson, 207.
Bach, 32.
Berggreen, 209.
Buck, 255.
Edwards, 25.
Faning, 31.
Freeman, 210.
Gibbons, 212.

Harwood, 256.
Hopkins, 208.
Stainer, 160.
Wallace, 23.
R. Williams, 307.

EDITIONS OF THE
CHRISTIAN SCIENCE HYMNAL

First Edition, 1892. Committee appointed in 1890. (See Note 154.) Hymns by Mary Baker Eddy: "Feed My Sheep," Communion Hymn, and Christ My Refuge. A dozen hymns were taken from *The Christian Science Journal*.

First Revision, 1898. Words printed under notes, syllable by syllable, as at present. Many tunes deleted.

Edition of 1901 included the Communion Doxology.

Edition of 1903 included Mrs. Eddy's Christmas Morn.

Second Revision, 1910. Committee appointed, 1909, by The Christian Science Board of Directors. Alternate new tunes were added, and new poems by a Christian Scientist, Frederick W. Root. Mrs. Eddy's Mother's Evening Prayer appeared as the most notable addition. (See Note 207.)

Third Revision, 1932. In June, 1928, a Committee appointed in Boston, as Advisory to The Christian Science Board of Directors, for research, and to examine and select from all the material contributed. Committee appointed by London branch churches, for research and to forward contributions from the British Isles. Many Continental branch churches also invited to send contributions to Boston. The entire Christian Science field was invited through the *Sentinel* to send contributions to Boston. In September, 1930, a Final Committee was appointed in Boston, with advisers of high musical standing. The manuscript was delivered to The Christian Science Publishing Society early in 1931. After a year and a half given to copyrights and to mechanical production, on September 4, 1932, appeared the Third Revision of the *Christian Science Hymnal*. In this book, almost doubled in size, the most welcome additions were the two hymns by Mrs. Eddy, Love and Satisfied.

USE OF THE METRICAL INDEX

The Metrical Index, page 606 of the Hymnal, is a reminder of days when words and music were not always printed together. Many collections of metrical psalms, and of more modern hymns, appeared with only the words. To indicate what tunes could be used with each hymn, the meter of the words was marked above the hymn. These meter marks are now seen after the name of each tune in the Hymnal.

Common Meter, marked C. M.; Short Meter, or S. M.; Long Meter, or L. M., were the usual measures found in words and music. Common Meter, as in No. 144, was at first the most used. It was called Chevy Chace Meter, from the ballad of that name, or ballad meter. It is a stanza of four lines. The first line has eight syllables and the first line of the tune has eight notes (or tune units). The second line of words and of tune has six syllables and six notes; the third line has eight, and the fourth, six. This is "8.6.8.6. meter." Short Meter, as in No. 14, has four lines, with 6.6.8.6. notes and syllables respectively. Long Meter, almost as common now as Common Meter, has eight syllables and eight notes for all the four lines; or, "8.8.8.8.," as in No. 218.

Where a "D" follows the meter mark, as in No. 52, the tune is "double"—having eight instead of four lines. Both halves of every double tune have the same meter. Other eight-line tunes may have an irregular number of syllables in a line, as line 6 in No. 350, 84.84.88.84.

Where slurs occur in the tune, as in No. 52, that special line of music has more than the regular number of notes. Then two notes must be sung together on one syllable, or "slurred." Occasionally even three notes are slurred, as in the second half of No. 170, Creation. Each slurred group counts as a single melodic unit. So the tune No. 170 is marked L. M. D. (or 8.8.8.8. D.) because only eight units (notes, or groups of notes) are counted for every line, to match the eight syllables of the words.

Other forms of meter are marked by figures to show the number of syllables and notes and lines. In No. 41 the stanza has five lines, with respectively 4 10 10 10 4 syllables. The points (periods) are used to group the musical phrases: as, 4.10 10.10 4. This might also have been marked 4.10 10 10.4 to show the peculiar structure of the stanza, in which the three middle lines make a three-line group.

The music set to these words matches them perfectly, with only one note for each syllable, and so no slurs are used. When the words are irregular in any line, a tie may be used, where the note is held, for a single syllable, instead of being divided for two. An example of "tying" appears in No. 253, "O'er waiting harpstrings," by Mrs. Eddy. At the words, "And nearer Thee," the word "Thee" is to be held to the end of the measure, which throws the first syllable of "Father" over to the strong (first) beat of the next measure. Otherwise it would be mispronounced *"Fa-ther'."* In No. 210, "O gentle presence," by Mrs. Eddy, tiny added notes appear for the words, "No ill, since," to place the chief music accent on the word "No." The half note (minim), D, had to be divided into two quarter notes (crotchets), to provide for the word "since."

In No. 82, ties and slurs adjust the music to the irregularities of the words. The tune is marked "C. M. D. (Irregular)." The word Iambic (light-heavy syllables, as *"pro-tect"*) and Dactylic (heavy-light, as *"beau'ti-ful"*) refer to the "feet," of verse. (See pp. 608, 609.)

To find a tune that fits every syllable of a hymn may be the work of long research. Sometimes beautiful poems are discarded because their meter is too irregular to fit any known tune.

In a hymnal like this, in which every syllable is printed under its proper note, the metrical marks are not essential to the singer. But they are useful to anyone who might like to apply other words to a given tune; and they help, in choosing a group of hymns, to secure variety in meter.

INDEX

Names of tunes and of poets and composers, including incidental references to famous names, are listed here. Full-face figures indicate the most important Notes in each group; figures after a semicolon, the least important. Figures as 222–3, or 139 (427), mean repeated hymns. The Hymnal Indexes supply lists of Traditional melodies, with a few special tune names and book titles not repeated here.

GENERAL INDEX
TO THE
CHRISTIAN SCIENCE HYMNAL

GENERAL INDEX

First lines are not repeated. Blank numbers guide to alternative tunes on opposite page.

NO.	FIRST LINE	AUTHOR OR SOURCE	NO.
1	COMMUNION DOXOLOGY	Nahum Tate *and* Nicholas Brady	1
2	A glorious day is dawning	*Author Unknown*	2
3	A grateful heart a garden is	Ethel Wasgatt Dennis	3
4	A holy air is breathing round	Abiel Abbot Livermore	4
5	A voice from heaven we have heard	Irving C. Tomlinson	5
6	Abide not in the realm of dreams	William H. Burleigh	6
7	Abide with me; fast breaks the morning light	Bertha H. Woods	7
		Based on a hymn by H. F. Lyte	
8	Abide with me; fast falls the eventide	Henry Francis Lyte	8
9	All glory be to God most high	Violet Hay	9
10	All power is given unto our Lord	Frederic W. Root	10
411			411
11	Angels at the Saviour's birth	Marion Susan Campbell	11
14	Arise, arise and shine	Mary I. Mesechre	14
12	Arise ye people, take your stand	Violet Hay	12
13			13
15	As gold by fire is tested	*Based on the Danish of*	15
		Bernhard S. Ingemann	
16	As sings the mountain stream	Violet Ker Seymer	16
17	Be firm, ye sentinels of Truth	Edmund Beale Sargant	17
18	Be firm and be faithful	Anonymous	18
1	Be Thou, O God, exalted high	Nahum Tate *and* Nicholas Brady	1
20	Be true and list the voice within	Kate L. Colby	20
416			416
19	Behold, they stand in robes of white	*Based on the Danish of*	19
		Hans A. Brorson	
21	Beloved, let us love	Horatius Bonar	21
22			22
23	Blest Christmas morn, though murky clouds	CHRISTMAS MORN	23
24		Mary Baker Eddy	24
25			25
26			26
27			27
28			28
29	Breaking through the clouds of darkness	Florence L. Heywood	29
30	Brood o'er us with Thy shelt'ring wing	LOVE	30
31		Mary Baker Eddy	31
32			32
33	Call the Lord thy sure salvation	James Montgomery	33
34	Christ comes again with holy power	Marion Susan Campbell	34
35	Christ, whose glory fills the skies	Charles Wesley	35
36	Church of the ever-living God	Horatius Bonar	36

356

GENERAL INDEX

Abbreviations: *arr.* = arranged; *fr.* = from; *har.* = harmonized; *tr.* = translated or translator.

NO.	TUNE	COMPOSER OR SOURCE	METER	NO.
1	Old Hundredth	*Genevan Psalter,* 1551	L. M.	1
2	Missionary Hymn	Lowell Mason	7. 6. 7. 6. D.	2
3	Epsom	*Arnold's Complete Psalter,* 1756	C. M.	3
4	Pater Noster	Percy C. Buck	C. M.	4
5	Forest Green	*English Traditional Melody*	C. M. D.	5
6	Melcombe	Samuel Webbe	L. M.	6
7	Eventide	William H. Monk	10. 10. 10. 10.	7
8	Eventide	William H. Monk	10. 10. 10. 10.	8
9	Carol	*Arr. fr.* David G. Corner *by* H. Walford Davies	86. 86. 6.	9
10	Ein' feste Burg (C)	Martin Luther	87. 87. 66. 667.	10
411	Ein' feste Burg (D)	Martin Luther	87. 87. 66. 667.	411
11	Salzburg	Jakob Hintze. *Har. by* Johann Sebastian Bach	7. 7. 7. 7. D.	11
14	Potsdam	*Arr. fr.* Johann Sebastian Bach	S. M.	14
12	Melita	John B. Dykes	88. 88. 88.	12
13	Ermuntre dich	Johann Schop	88. 88. 88.	13
15	Fulfillment (Den store Mester kommer)	C. Christian Hoffman	7. 6. 8. 6.	15
16	Aynhoe	James Nares	S. M.	16
17	Walsall	*Attributed to* Henry Purcell	C. M.	17
18	Lyons	J. Michael Haydn	11. 11. 11. 11.	18
1	Old Hundredth	*Genevan Psalter,* 1551	L. M.	1
20	Pixham	Horatio W. Parker	L. M.	20
416	Linwood	Gioacchino A. Rossini. *Arr.*	L. M.	416
19	Purity (Den store, hvite flokk)	*Norwegian Folk Melody*	8. 8. 8. 6. D.	19
21	Grandpont	John Stainer	6. 4. 6. 4. (10. 10.)	21
22	Dennis	G. Thalben-Ball	6. 4. 6. 4. (10. 10.)	22
23	Serenity	*Arr. fr.* William V. Wallace	8. 4. 8. 4.	23
24	Christmas Morn	Albert F. Conant	8. 4. 8. 4.	24
25	Kington	F. Llewellyn Edwards	8. 4. 8. 4.	25
26	Dransfield	G. Thalben-Ball	8. 4. 8. 4.	26
27	Infinitas	Percy Whitlock	8. 4. 8. 4.	27
28	Selworthy	E. Norman Greenwood	8. 4. 8. 4. D.	28
29	Everton	Henry Smart	8. 7. 8. 7. D.	29
30	Love	Walter E. Young	86. 86. 88.	30
31	Vita	Eaton Faning	86. 86. 88.	31
32	Gottlob	Johann Sebastian Bach. *Slightly altered*	86. 86. 88.	32
33	St. Oswald	John B. Dykes	8. 7. 8. 7.	33
34	Home	*Arr. fr.* Wolfgang Amadeus Mozart	L. M.	34
35	Dix	*Arr. fr. "Treuer Heiland."* Conrad Kocher	77. 77. 77.	35
36	Falmouth	Walter E. Young	C. M.	36

357

GENERAL INDEX

GENERAL INDEX

NO.	TUNE	COMPOSER OR SOURCE	METER	NO.
37	St. Agnes	John B. Dykes	C. M.	37
38	Richmond (Chesterf'ld)	Thomas Haweis. *Arr. by* S. Webbe, Jr.	C. M.	38
39	Frainsby	George Dyson	L. M.	39
41	Qui laborat orat	Hugh P. Allen	4. 10 10. 10 4.	41
42	Regent Square	Henry Smart	87. 87. 87.	42
44	Franconia	*König's Choralbuch. Arr. by* W. H. Havergal	S. M.	44
43	Abendlied	Franz Schubert	7. 6. 7. 6. D.	43
40	Consolator	Samuel Webbe	11. 10. 11. 10.	40
46	Manna	*Arr. fr.* Louis M. Gottschalk	7. 7. 7. 7.	46
47	Nottingham	*Attr. to* Wolfgang Amadeus Mozart. *Arr.*	7. 7. 7. 7.	47
48	Saffron Walden	Arthur H. Brown	8. 8. 8. 6.	48
45	Herongate	*English Traditional Melody*	L. M.	45
49	Rest	Frederick C. Maker	86. 886.	49
50	Repton	C. Hubert H. Parry	86. 886.	50
51	Spohr	Louis Spohr	C. M. D.	51
52	St. Matthew	William Croft. *Modern form of tune*	C. M. D.	52
53	Galliard	*Melody by* John Dowland	7. 7. 7. 7.	53
54	Westminster	James Turle	C. M.	54
55	Gott will's machen	J. Ludwig Steiner	8. 7. 8. 7.	55
56	Crispinian	John W. Ivimey	L. M.	56
57	Welwyn	Alfred Scott-Gatty	11. 10. 11. 10.	57
58	Joy	*Arr. fr.* Ludwig van Beethoven	8. 7. 8. 7. D.	58
59	Park Street	Frederick M. A. Venua. *Arr.*	L. M.	59
60	Pentecost	William Boyd	L. M.	60
61	Valour	Hugh P. Allen	L. M.	61
62	Old Hundredth	*Genevan Psalter,* 1551	L. M.	62
63	Old Hundredth	*Genevan Psalter,* 1551. *Original Version*	L. M.	63
65	Alford	John B. Dykes	76. 76. 76. 86.	65
64	Elgin	George Dyson	11. 10. 11. 10.	64
66	Sine nomine	R. Vaughan Williams	10. 10. 10. 4.	66
421	Sarum	Joseph Barnby	10. 10. 10. 4.	421
67	Capetown	Friedrich Filitz	7. 7. 7. 3.	67
68	Vigilate	William H. Monk. *Slightly revised*	7. 7. 7. 3.	68
69	Song 24	Orlando Gibbons	10. 10. 10. 10.	69
423	Penitentia	Edward Dearle	10. 10. 10. 10.	423
71	Austria	Franz Joseph Haydn	8. 7. 8. 7. D.	71
72	Benevento	Samuel Webbe	7. 7. 7. 7. D.	72
405	Benevento (Revised)	Samuel Webbe	7. 7. 7. 7. D.	405
73	Gratitude (Eeuwig dank en eere)	*Canzuns Spirituelas, Celerina,* 1765	10 7. 10 7. 10 10. 77.	73
74	Auch jetzt macht Gott	*Koch's Choralbuch,* 1816	86. 86. 88.	74
75	Aurelia	Samuel S. Wesley	7. 6. 7. 6. D.	75
70	Mornington	Garret Wellesley	S. M.	70
76	Grace (Herren sig i nåd förklarar)	Per U. Stenhammar	8. 7. 8. 7. D.	76
79	Merton	William H. Monk	8. 7. 8. 7.	79

GENERAL INDEX

GENERAL INDEX

NO.	TUNE	COMPOSER OR SOURCE	METER	NO.
77	Munich	*Meiningen Gesangbuch,* 1693 *Har. by* F. Mendelssohn-Bartholdy	7. 6. 7. 6. D.	77
78	King's Lynn	*English Traditional Melody*	7. 6. 7. 6. D.	78
80	Eisenach	*Melody by* Johann H. Schein *Harmony fr.* J. S. Bach	L. M.	80
81	Kingly Vale	Hugh P. Allen	87. 87. 47.	81
82	Purpose	H. Walford Davies	C. M. D. (Irreg.)	82
83	Innocents	*Old French Melody. Arr. by* J. Smith	7. 7. 7. 7.	83
85	Liebster Jesu	Johann R. Ahle. *Arr. by* J. S. Bach	78. 78. 88.	85
84	Repentance (Herre, jeg har handlet ille)	Ludvig M. Lindeman	87. 87. 88.	84
86	Coronation	Oliver Holden	C. M.	86
87	Mendip	*English Traditional Melody*	C. M.	87
91	Birling	*From an early* 19th *Century MS.*	L. M.	91
422	Alsace	Ludwig van Beethoven. *Arr.*	L. M.	422
88	Halle	*Schicht's Choralbuch,* 1819	77. 77. 77.	88
89	Jesu, Jesu du mein Hirt	*Melody by* Paul Heinlein *Har. by* G. H. Palmer	77. 77. 77.	89
90	Corinth (Tantum ergo)	Samuel Webbe's *Motetts or Antiphons,* 1792	87. 87. 87.	90
92	Dominica	Herbert S. Oakeley	S. M.	92
93	Peace	*Arr. fr.* Wolfgang Amadeus Mozart	L. M.	93
94	Uffingham	Jeremiah Clark	L. M.	94
95	Aughton	William B. Bradbury	L. M. and Refrain	95
101	Lobt Gott	Nicolas Herman. *Har. by* J. S. Bach	86. 86. 6.	101
96	Soll's sein	*Fr. Drei schöne neue geistliche Lieder,* 1637	C. M. D.	96
97	Ilsley	Frank G. Ilsley	8. 7. 8. 7. D.	97
98	In Babilone	*Dutch Traditional Melody*	8. 7. 8. 7. D.	98
99	Bera	John E. Gould. *Arr. by* Walter E. Young	88. 8. 88. 8.	99
100	David's Harp	Robert King *in "The Divine Companion,"* 1772	88. 88. 88.	100
102	Cross of Jesus	John Stainer	8. 7. 8. 7.	102
103	Glück zu Kreuz	*Darmstadt Gesangbuch,* 1698 *Har. by* Charles Wood	8. 7. 8. 7.	103
104	Campfields	Mark J. Monk	86. 886.	104
105	Dedham	William Gardiner	C. M.	105
106	Bromsgrove	*Psalmodia Evangelica,* 1789	C. M.	106
107	Windsor	*Melody from Damon's Psalter,* 1591	C. M.	107
109	Ellesdie	Wolfgang Amadeus Mozart *Arr. by* H. P. Main	8. 7. 8. 7. D.	109
110	Zum Frieden	Johann Sebastian Bach	8. 7. 8. 7. D.	110
108	Toulon (Old 124th)	*Arr. fr. the Genevan Psalter,* 1551	10. 10. 10. 10.	108
111	Eschol	George M. Garrett	L. M.	111
112	Security (Tryggare kan ingen vara)	Ivar Widéen	8. 8. 8. 8.	112
113	Armenian Hymn	*Hymnologh of the Armenian Apostolic Church*	77. 745.	113
114	Orientis partibus	*Old French Melody* Pierre de Corbeil(?). *Arr.*	7. 7. 7. 7.	114

GENERAL INDEX

GENERAL INDEX

GENERAL INDEX

GENERAL INDEX

365

GENERAL INDEX

GENERAL INDEX

GENERAL INDEX

GENERAL INDEX

NO.	TUNE	COMPOSER OR SOURCE	METER	NO.
224	St. Leonard	Henry Hiles	C. M. D.	224
225	Yattendon 15	Christopher Tye. *Arr. by* H. E. Wooldridge	C. M. D.	225
226	Ellacombe	*Mainz Gesangbuch,* 1833	C. M. D.	226
227	Hursley	*Schicht's Choralbuch,* 1819	L. M.	227
228	Mendon	*Old German Melody. Arr. by* Samuel Dyer	L. M.	228
229	Constancy	Felix Mendelssohn-Bartholdy. *Arr.*	L. M. D.	229
230	Simpson	Louis Spohr. *Arr.*	C. M.	230
231	Radlett	E. Norman Greenwood	C. M.	231
232	Hampstead	H. Walford Davies	88. 886.	232
406	St. Margaret	Albert L. Peace	88. 886.	406
233	Das walt' Gott	Daniel Vetter. *Harmony fr.* J. S. Bach	L. M.	233
419	Holley	George Hews	L. M.	419
234	Maryton	H. Percy Smith	L. M.	234
235	Brockham	Jeremiah Clark	L. M.	235
237	Carol Melody	*14th Century Carol*	8. 7. 8. 7.	237
236	Hanover	William Croft	10. 10. 11. 11.	236
238	Germany (Fulda)	*Gardiner's Sacred Melodies,* 1812 *Attributed to* Ludwig van Beethoven	L. M.	238
239	St. Gregory	*Harmonischer Liederschatz,* 1755 *Har. by* W. H. Monk	L. M.	239
240	Thatcher	*Arr. fr.* Georg Friedrich Händel	S. M.	240
241	St. Edmund	Edmund Gilding	S. M.	241
242	Capel	*English Traditional Carol Melody*	C. M.	242
243	Ombersley	William H. Gladstone	L. M.	243
244	Hesperus	Henry Baker	L. M.	244
245	Homeland	Arthur S. Sullivan	7. 6. 7. 6. D.	245
418	Eternity	Philip Paul Bliss	77. 77. 77. 744.	418
246	Valerius	*Old Dutch Hymn*	10. 10. 11. 11. and Refrain	246
247	St. Leonard	Henry Smart	C. M.	247
248	St. Hugh	*English Traditional Melody*	C. M.	248
425	Joy cometh in the morning	Edmund S. Lorenz	8. 8. 8. 8. and Refrain	425
249	Berno	Arthur H. Mann	7. 6. 7. 6. D.	249
250	Wolvercote	W. Harold Ferguson	7. 6. 7. 6. D.	250
251	Bentley	John P. Hullah	7. 6. 7. 6. D.	251
252	Herzlich thut mich verlangen	Hans L. Hassler. *Har. by* J. S. Bach	7. 6. 7. 6. D.	252
253	Pleasant Street	William Lyman Johnson	8. 4. 8. 4. D.	253
254	Norton	Lyman Brackett	8. 4. 8. 4.	254
255	Refuge	Percy C. Buck	8. 4. 8. 4.	255
256	Oldown	Basil Harwood	8. 4. 8. 4. D.	256
257	Oblation	Percy Whitlock	8. 4. 8. 4.	257
258	Ton-y-Botel	*Welsh Hymn Melody*	8. 7. 8. 7. D.	258
259	Galilee	Philip Armes	L. M.	259
261	Nox praecessit	John B. Calkin	C. M.	261
262	Song 67	Orlando Gibbons	C. M.	262
260	Fingal	James S. Anderson	C. M.	260

GENERAL INDEX

GENERAL INDEX

GENERAL INDEX

GENERAL INDEX

NO.	TUNE	COMPOSER OR SOURCE	METER	NO.
297	Dalkeith	Thomas Hewlett	10. 10. 10. 10.	297
303	St. Hugh	Edward J. Hopkins	C. M.	303
304	Guidance	Lyman Brackett	7. 5. 7. 5. D.	304
305	Shepherd	Albert F. Conant	7. 5. 7. 5. D.	305
306	Concord	William Lyman Johnson	7. 5. 7. 5. D.	306
307	Llanfair	*Arr. fr.* Robert Williams	7. 5. 7. 5. D.	307
308	Egerton	G. Thalben-Ball	7. 5. 7. 5. D.	308
309	Benevolence	E. Norman Greenwood	7. 5. 7. 5. D.	309
310	Bethlehem	*Arr. fr. Mendelssohn by* W. H. Cummings	7. 7. 7. 7. D. and Refrain	310
311	O Jesu	*Hirschberg Gesangbuch,* 1741	86. 86. 88.	311
420	Compassion	C. B. Rich	86. 86. 88.	420
312	Diademata	George J. Elvey	S. M. D.	312
313	Meirionydd	*Welsh Hymn Melody.* William Lloyd	7. 6. 7. 6. D.	313
314	Selma	*Traditional Melody, Isle of Arran Arr. by* R. A. Smith	S. M.	314
315	Sawley	James Walch. *Arr.*	C. M.	315
316	Fragment	*From The Sarum Gradual,* 1527 *Arr. by* H. Walford Davies	C. M.	316
317	Strength and Stay	John B. Dykes	11. 10. 11. 10.	317
318	Bairn (Lille Guds Barn)	*Danish Folk Melody*	98. 884.	318
319	Rivaulx	John B. Dykes	L. M.	319
320	Azmon	Carl G. Gläser. *Arr.*	C. M.	320
321	Burford	*Chetham's Psalmody,* 1718	C. M.	321
409	Azmon New	Carl G. Gläser. *Fr. adaptation by* L. Mason	C. M.	409
322	Canonbury	Robert Schumann. *Arr.*	L. M.	322
323	Puer nobis nascitur	Michael Praetorius	L. M.	323
324	Theodora	*Arr. fr.* Georg Friedrich Händel	77. 77. 77.	324
325	Duke Street	John Hatton	L. M.	325
326	Truro	*Psalmodia Evangelica,* 1790	L. M.	326
327	Coventry	*English Melody. Arr. by* Frederic W. Root	C. M.	327
328	St. Magnus	Jeremiah Clark	C. M.	328
329	St. Anselm	Joseph Barnby	7. 6. 7. 6. D.	329
330	Dominus regit me	John B. Dykes	8. 7. 8. 7.	330
331	St. Sepulchre	George Cooper	L. M.	331
332	Nestling (Som Hønen klukker mindelig)	August H. Winding	86. 86. 888.	332
333	Abridge	Isaac Smith	C. M.	333
335	Morning Light	George J. Webb	7. 6. 7. 6. D.	335
334	St. Stephen	William Jones	C. M.	334
336	Winchester New	*Musikalisches Handbuch,* 1690	L. M.	336
337	St. Mabyn	Arthur H. Brown	8. 7. 8. 7.	337
338	Sussex	*English Traditional Melody. Arr.*	8. 7. 8. 7.	338
339	St. Columba (Erin)	*Old Irish Hymn Melody*	C. M.	339
340	Slingsby	Edmund S. Carter	8. 7. 8. 7.	340
341	Peacefield	*Ancient Irish Melody Har. by* D. F. R. Wilson	7. 7. 7. 7.	341
342	Angels' Song	Felix Mendelssohn-Bartholdy *Arr. by* E. J. Hopkins	C. M. D.	342

GENERAL INDEX

GENERAL INDEX

GENERAL INDEX

GENERAL INDEX